THE ROUTLEDGE COMPANION TO WORLD CINEMA

The Routledge Companion to World Cinema explores and examines a global range of films and filmmakers, their movements and audiences, comparing their cultural, technological and political dynamics, identifying the impulses that constantly reshape the form and function of the cinemas of the world. Each of the forty chapters provides a survey of a topic, explaining why the issue or area is important, and critically discussing the leading views in the area. Designed as a dynamic forum for forty-three world-leading scholars, this companion contains significant expertise and insight and is dedicated to challenging complacent views of hegemonic film cultures and replacing outmoded ideas about production, distribution and reception. It offers both a survey and an investigation into the condition and activity of contemporary filmmaking worldwide, often challenging long-standing categories and weighted—often politically motivated—value judgements, thereby grounding and aligning the reader in an activity of remapping that is designed to prompt rethinking.

Contributors: James Chapman, Paolo Cherchi Usai, Anne Ciecko, Paul Cooke, David Craig, Virginia Crisp, Sean Cubitt, Stuart Cunningham, Stephanie Dennison, Marijke de Valck, Jonathan Driskell, Dunja Fehimović, Rosalind Galt, Felicity Gee, Jeffrey Geiger, Christopher E. Gittings, Mark Goodall, Olof Hedling, Mette Hjort, Kate Ince, Huw D. Jones, Geoff King, Alex Marlow-Mann, David Martin-Jones, Madhuja Mukherjee, Lúcia Nagib, Elżbieta Ostrowska, Lydia Papadimitriou, Jonathan Rayner, Ian-Malcolm Rijsdijk, Joanna Rydzewska, Viviane Saglier, Karl Schoonover, Deborah Shaw, Paul Julian Smith, Rob Stone, Niamh Thornton, Dolores Tierney, Belén Vidal, Ginette Vincendeau, James Walters, Vito Zagarrio, Yingjin Zhang.

Rob Stone is Chair of European Cinema and Professor of Film Studies at the University of Birmingham, where he co-directs B-Film: The Birmingham Centre for Film Studies.

Paul Cooke is Centenary Chair of World Cinemas at the University of Leeds and the Director of the Centre for World Cinemas and Digital Cultures.

Stephanie Dennison is Chair of Brazilian Studies and a founding member of the Centre for World Cinemas and Digital Cultures at the University of Leeds.

Alex Marlow-Mann is Lecturer in Italian at the University of Kent.

THE ROUTLEDGE COMPANION TO WORLD CINEMA

Edited by Rob Stone, Paul Cooke, Stephanie Dennison and Alex Marlow-Mann

LONDON AND NEW YORK

First published 2018
by Routledge
2 Park Square, Milton Park, Abingdon, Oxon OX14 4RN

and by Routledge
711 Third Avenue, New York, NY 10017

Routledge is an imprint of the Taylor & Francis Group, an informa business

British Library Cataloguing-in-Publication Data
A catalogue record for this book is available from the British Library

Library of Congress Cataloging-in-Publication Data
Names: Stone, Rob, 1965- editor. | Cooke, Paul, 1969- editor. | Dennison, Stephanie editor. | Marlow-Mann, Alex editor.
Title: The Routledge companion to world cinema / edited by Rob Stone, Paul Cooke, Stephanie Dennison and Alex Marlow-Mann.
Description: New York : Routledge, 2017. | Includes index.
Identifiers: LCCN 2017020062 | ISBN 9781138918801 (hardback)
Subjects: LCSH: Motion pictures—History. | Motion pictures.
Classification: LCC PN1993.5.A1 R75 2017 | DDC 791.4309—dc23
LC record available at https://lccn.loc.gov/2017020062

ISBN: 978-1-138-91880-1 (hbk)
ISBN: 978-1-315-68825-1 (ebk)

Typeset in Bembo Std
by Swales & Willis Ltd, Exeter, Devon, UK

Printed in the United Kingdom
by Henry Ling Limited

CONTENTS

ILLUSTRATIONS

CONTRIBUTORS

James Chapman is Professor of Film Studies at the University of Leicester, UK, and editor of the *Historical Journal of Film, Radio and Television*. He is the author of several books on British cinema including *The British at War: Cinema, State and Propaganda, 1939–1945* (1998), *Licence To Thrill: A Cultural History of the James Bond Films* (1999; 2nd edn 2007), *Past and Present: National Identity and the British Historical Film* (2005) and *A New History of British Documentary* (2015).

Paolo Cherchi Usai is Senior Curator of the Moving Image Department at the George Eastman Museum in Rochester, NY, Adjunct Professor of Film at the University of Rochester and Resident Curator at the Telluride Film Festival. He co-founded the Giornate del Cinema Muto in Pordenone and the L. Jeffrey Selznick School of Film Preservation, of which he is currently Director. His most recent publications include *Film Curatorship: Archives, Museums, and the Digital Marketplace* (2008), "The Lindgren Manifesto" (2010) and *La storia del cinema in 1000 parole* (2012). He is author of the experimental feature films *Passio* (2007), adapted from his book *The Death of Cinema* (2001), and *Picture* (2015), with live music by the Alloy Orchestra.

Anne Ciecko is an Associate Professor of International Cinema in the Department of Communication and a core faculty member in the Interdepartmental Program in Film Studies at the University of Massachusetts-Amherst, USA, where she coordinates the Graduate Certificate in Film Studies and curates the film series New Asia Cinema/Arab Cinema Panorama.

Paul Cooke is Centenary Chair of World Cinemas at the University of Leeds, UK. He has written on world cinema's engagement with Hollywood and on the legacy of both National Socialism and the GDR in contemporary German culture. He is one of the series editors of Routledge's *Remapping World Cinema* book series. He is currently running an AHRC community filmmaking project exploring the gap between the way the BRICS present their soft power "national narrative" to the outside world and how this is experienced by some marginalized communities internally.

David Craig is Clinical Assistant Professor, University of Southern California Annenberg School for Communication and Journalism, USA, where he teaches graduate courses in traditional, digital, and social media and entertainment industries, management, culture and practice. He is also a multiple Emmy-nominated television producer and programming executive.

Virginia Crisp is Lecturer in the Department of Culture, Media and Creative Industries at King's College London. She is the author of *Film Distribution in the Digital Age: Pirates and Professionals* (2015) and co-editor of *Besides the Screen: Moving Images through Distribution, Promotion and Curation* (2015). She is the co-founder, with Gabriel Menotti Gonring (UFES, Brazil), of the Besides the Screen Network, www.besidesthescreen.com.

Sean Cubitt is Professor of Film and Television at Goldsmiths, University of London and Honorary Professorial Fellow of the University of Melbourne. His publications include *Timeshift: On Video Culture* (1991), *Videography: Video Media as Art and Culture* (1993), *Digital Aesthetics* (1998), *Simulation and Social Theory* (2001), *The Cinema Effect* (2004), *EcoMedia* (2005), *The Practice of Light: A Genealogy of Visual Technology from Prints to Pixels* (2014) and *Finite Media: Environmental Implications of Digital Technologies* (2017). He has worked in Canada, New Zealand and Australia, has an interest in the film and media of these countries. He is on the editorial boards of a number of journals including *Screen, Cultural Politics, Animation, International MIRAJ* and *The New Review of Film and Television Studies*, and he is series editor for Leonardo Books, MIT Press. His research focuses on the history and philosophy of media, political aesthetics, media art history and eco-criticism.

Stuart Cunningham is Distinguished Professor of Media and Communications, Queensland University of Technology, Australia. His most recent books include *Digital Disruption: Cinema Moves Online* (2012) edited with Dina Iordanova, *Screen Distribution and the New King Kongs of the Online World* (2013) with Jon Silver, and *Media Economics* (2015) with Terry Flew and Adam Swift.

Stephanie Dennison is Chair of Brazilian Studies, and a founding member of the Centre for World Cinemas, at the University of Leeds, UK. She is co-author with Lisa Shaw of two monographs on Brazilian cinema (*Popular Cinema in Brazil*, 2004; *Brazilian National Cinema*, 2007), co-editor with Song Hwee Lim of *Remapping World Cinema* (2006) and editor of *World Cinema: As Novas Cartografias do Cinema Mundial* (2013). She is one of the series editors of Routledge's *Remapping World Cinema* book series. In 2015 she was a Leverhulme International Academic Fellow at the Film Department of Unicamp (the State University of Campinas, Brazil), where she carried out research for a project entitled "Brazilian Film Culture in the Context of World Cinema".

Marijke de Valck is Associate Professor in Media Studies at Utrecht University, Netherlands. She is the co-founder of the Film Festival Research Network, co-editor of Palgrave Macmillan's book series Framing Film Festivals, and co-editor of the NECSUS festival review section. She publishes regularly on film festivals, and her publications include *Film Festivals: From European Geopolitics to Global Cinephilia* (2007) and the co-edited text book *Film Festivals: History, Theory, Method, Praxis* (2016).

Jonathan Driskell is Senior Lecturer in Film and Television Studies at Monash University, Malaysia. He is the author of *Marcel Carné* (2012) and *The French Screen Goddess: Film Stardom and the Modern Woman in 1930s France* (2015).

Dunja Fehimović is Lecturer in Spanish at Newcastle University, UK. Her doctoral project at the University of Cambridge examined the reconfiguration and recycling of national identity in Cuban films made between 2000 and 2014. She has published in the *Journal of Latin American Cultural Studies* and the *Bulletin of Latin American Research*. She is co-editor with Rob Stone of the annual Screen Arts issue of the *Bulletin of Hispanic Research* and was co-convenor of the international conference Branding Latin America. Her reflections on branding and Cuban cinema are featured in *Nation Branding: Concepts, Issues, Practice* (2016) and her research interests include national identity, branding, soft power, consumption, ethics and cosmopolitanism.

Rosalind Galt is Professor of Film Studies at King's College London, UK. She is the author of *Pretty: Film and the Decorative Image* (2011) and *The New European Cinema: Redrawing the Map* (2006). Together with Karl Schoonover, she is the co-author of *Queer Cinema in the World* (2016) and co-editor of *Global Art Cinema: New Theories and Histories* (2010).

Felicity Gee is Lecturer in International Film, and Director of the Centre for Interdisciplinary Film Research at the University of Exeter, UK. She has published on Japanese avant-garde film, Surrealism, and affect theory, and is the author of *Magic Realism: The Avant-Garde in Exile* (2018), which explores the critical inception of magic realism and its place within film studies. Her research interests include the modernist avant-garde, affect theory, the history of emotions, and film-philosophy. Since returning to the UK from an extended period working in Osaka, Japan, she has continued to work on Japanese art, film and literature.

Jeffrey Geiger is Professor of Film Studies and Director of the Centre for Film and Screen Media at the University of Essex, UK. His books include *Facing the Pacific: Polynesia and the U.S. Imperial Imagination* (2007), *American Documentary Film: Projecting the Nation* (2011), the co-edited *Film Analysis: A Norton Reader* (2nd edition 2013) and *Cinematicity in Media History* (2013). His essays have appeared in many books, and journals such as *Film International, Third Text, African American Review, Cinema Journal, PMLA* and the *TLS*.

Christopher E. Gittings is Associate Professor of Film Studies at the University of Western Ontario, Canada. His work has appeared in *Cinema Journal, Canadian Journal of Communications, Canadian Journal of Film Studies, Great Canadian Film Directors* (2007), *Making Avonlea: L.M. Montgomery and Popular Culture* (2002) and *The Perils of Pedagogy: The Works of John Greyson* (2013). He is the author of *Canadian National Cinema: Ideology, Difference and Representation* (2002) and editor of and contributor to *Imperialism and Gender: Constructions of Masculinity* (1996).

Mark Goodall is Senior Lecturer in the School of Media, Design and Technology at the University of Bradford, UK. He specialises in the cult and experimental films of the 1960s and 1970s and is the author two monographs and numerous articles, including *Sweet and Savage: the World through the Shockumentary Film Lens* (2006), *Gathering of the Tribe: music and Heavy Conscious Creation* (2013) and *New Media Archaeologies* (2017) co-edited with Ben Roberts.

Olof Hedling is Associate Professor in Film Studies at Lund University, Sweden. His recent research activities have dealt with queries located at the intersection between several scholarly fields, including Swedish and Scandinavian film history, film production studies, economics, critical film policy review and regional development. He is co-author and co-editor of *Historical Dictionary of Scandinavian Cinema* (2012) and *Regional Aesthetics: Locating Swedish Media* (2010).

Mette Hjort is Professor of Film Studies at the University of Copenhagen, Denmark, Affiliate Professor of Scandinavian Studies at the University of Washington, Seattle, USA, and Honorary Professor of Visual Studies at Lingnan University in Hong Kong. Recent publications include *A Companion to Nordic Cinema* (2016), *The Education of the Filmmaker in Africa, the Middle East and the Americas* (2013) and *The Education of the Filmmaker in Europe, Australia and Asia* (2013). Her current research projects focus on film in the context of human rights, public values, and environmental aesthetics, and on transnational talent development initiatives linking the Nordic region to West Africa, East Africa and the Middle East.

Kate Ince is Reader in French Film and Gender Studies at the University of Birmingham. She is the author of *Georges Franju* (2005) and numerous essays on European filmmakers, as well as the editor of *Five Directors: Auteurism from Assayas to Ozon* (2008). Her work on women's cinema and feminist film philosophy since the mid-2000s recently culminated in *The Body and the Screen: Female Subjectivities in Contemporary Women's Cinema* (2017).

Huw D. Jones is Lecturer in Film Studies at the University of Southampton, UK. From 2014 to 2016 he worked as a Postdoctoral Research Associate on the Mediating Cultural Encounters through European Screens (MeCETES) project, funded by Humanities in the European Research Area (HERA): www.mecetes.co.uk/

Geoff King is Professor of Film and TV Studies at Brunel University London, UK. He is author of books including *American Independent Cinema* (2005), *Indiewood, USA: Where Hollywood Meets Independent Cinema* (2009), *Indie 2.0: Change and Continuity in Contemporary American Indie Film* (2014) and *Quality Hollywood: Markers of Distinction in Contemporary Studio Film* (2016).

Alex Marlow-Mann is Lecturer in Italian at the University of Kent, UK. He is the author of *The New Neapolitan Cinema* (2011), the editor of *Archival Film Festivals* (2013) and one of the series editors of Routledge's *Remapping World Cinema* book series. He is also one of the founding members of the British Association of Film, Television and Screen Studies and the managing editor of the Manchester University Press journal, *Film Studies*.

David Martin-Jones is Professor of Film Studies at the University of Glasgow, UK. His interests lie at the intersection of film-philosophy and world cinemas. He has published four books on Gilles Deleuze and cinema including *Deleuze, Cinema and National Identity: Narrative Time in National Contexts* (2006), *Deleuze and World Cinemas* (2011) and the co-editor of *Deleuze and Film* (2012) with William Brown. He serves on several editorial boards and is co-editor of the monograph series *Thinking Cinema* (Bloomsbury) and online resource deleuzecinema.com. His book *Transnational Histories on Film: Ethics Amidst a World of Cinemas* is forthcoming.

Madhuja Mukherjee is Associate Professor and teaches in the Department of Film Studies, Jadavpur University, Kolkata. She has published widely on the Indian film industry, technology and aesthetics, as well as on archiving and art projects and the soundscape of Indian films. She is the author of *New Theatres Ltd., The Emblem of Art, The Picture of Success* (2009) and has edited anthologies titled *Aural Films, Oral Cultures* (2012) and *Voices and Verses of the Talking Stars* (2017). Her feature film *Carnival* (2012) premiered at the International Film Festival Rotterdam in 2012 and she published her graphic-novel *Kangal Malsat* (in Bengali) in 2013.

Lúcia Nagib is Professor of Film and Director of the Centre for Film Aesthetics and Cultures at the University of Reading. Her single-authored books include *World Cinema and the Ethics of Realism* (2011) and *Brazil on Screen: Cinema Novo, New Cinema, Utopia* (2007). Her edited books include *Impure Cinema: Intermedial and Intercultural Approaches to Film* (2013) with Anne Jerslev, *Theorizing World Cinema* (2011) with Chris Perriam and Rajinder Dudrah, *Realism and the Audiovisual Media* (2009) with Cecília Mello, and *The New Brazilian Cinema* (2003).

Elżbieta Ostrowska teaches film at the University of Alberta, Canada. Her publications include *The Cinematic Bodies of Eastern Europe and Russia*, co-edited with Ewa Mazierska and Matilda Mroz (2015), *Women in Polish Cinema*, co-authored with Ewa Mazierska (2006), *The Cinema of Roman Polanski: Dark Spaces of the World*, co-edited with John Orr (2006), *The Cinema of Andrzej Wajda: The Art of Irony and Defiance*, co-edited with John Orr (2003), and *Gender in Film and the Media: East-West Dialogues*, co-edited with Elzbieta Oleksy and Michael Stevenson (2000). Her articles have appeared in *Slavic Review*, *Studies in European Cinema*, and *Holocaust and Genocide Studies*. She is a deputy editor of *Studies in Eastern European Cinema*.

Lydia Papadimitriou is Reader in Film Studies at Liverpool John Moores University, UK. She has published on Greek and Balkan cinema, documentary, film festivals and distribution. She is the author of *The Greek Film Musical* (2006) and the Principal Editor of the *Journal of Greek Media and Culture*.

Jonathan Rayner is Reader in Film Studies at the University of Sheffield, School of English, UK. His books include *The Cinema of Michael Mann* (2013), *The Naval War Film: Genre, History and National Cinema* (2007), *The Films of Peter Weir* (1998, 2nd edition 2003), *Contemporary Australian Cinema* (2000) and *The New Zealand and American Films of Geoff Murphy* (1999). He is also co-editor with Julia Dobson of *Mapping Cinematic Norths* (2016), of *Film Landscapes* (2013) and *Cinema and Landscape* (2010) with Graeme Harper, and of *Filmurbia: Screening the Suburbs* (2017) with Graeme Harper and David Forrest. His research interests span Australasian cinema (especially Australian Gothic), auteur and genre studies, cinema and landscape, and the representation of naval history in film, television and popular culture.

Ian-Malcolm Rijsdijk is Senior Lecturer in the Centre for Film and Media Studies and Environmental Humanities South at the University of Cape Town. He has published widely on Terrence Malick, as well as articles on South African film, wildlife documentary and literary fiction. He is currently working on early South African cinema and South Africa imagined in international films.

Joanna Rydzewska is Senior Lecturer in Film and TV Studies at Swansea University, UK. Her research interests lie in the field of European cinema, transnational cinema, migration, gender theory, and issues of identity in film. She has published on Polish émigré directors and the representation of Polish migration in both Polish and British film and television, and her articles have appeared in *Journal of British Cinema and Television*, *Studies in European Cinema*, *Journal of Contemporary European Studies* and *Critical Studies in Television*. She has co-edited *Representing Gender in Cultures* with E.H. Oleksy (2004), and her books include *Sculpting Stories: The Cinema of Paweł Pawlikowski* (2018) and *From Valiant Warriors to Bloody Immigrants: Poles in Cinema* (2019).

Viviane Saglier is a PhD candidate in Film and Moving Image Studies at Concordia University in Montreal, Canada. Her research examines the formation of a transnational Palestinian film economy in the Post-Oslo era. Her broader interests include media anthropology; the political economies of film festivals, media industries, and human rights, and the critical study of time under capitalism.

Karl Schoonover is an Associate Professor in the Department of Film and Television Studies at the University of Warwick, UK. He is the author of *Brutal Vision: The Neorealist Body in Postwar Italian Cinema* (2012) and, together with Rosalind Galt, is the co-author of *Queer Cinema in the World* (2016) and co-editor of *Global Art Cinema: New Theories and Histories* (2010).

Deborah Shaw is Reader in Film Studies at the University of Portsmouth, UK. Her research interests include transnational film theory, and Latin American cinema, and she has published widely in these areas. She is the founding co-editor of the Routledge journal *Transnational Cinemas*, and her books include *Contemporary Latin American Cinema: Ten Key Films* (2003), *The Three Amigos: The Transnational Filmmaking of Guillermo del Toro, Alejandro González Iñárritu, and Alfonso Cuarón* (2013), *The Transnational Fantasies of Guillermo del Toro*, co-edited with Ann Davies and Dolores Tierney (2014), and *Latin American Women Filmmakers: Production, Politics, Poetics* (2017) co-edited with Deborah Martin.

Rob Stone is Chair of European Cinema and Professor of Film Studies at the University of Birmingham, UK, where he co-directs B-Film: The Birmingham Centre for Film Studies. He has published widely on European, Spanish, Basque, Cuban and independent American cinema and is the author of *Spanish Cinema* (2001), *Flamenco in the Works of Federico García Lorca and Carlos Saura* (2004), *Julio Medem* (2007) and *Walk, Don't Run: The Cinema of Richard Linklater* (2013, 2nd edition 2017). He also co-authored *Basque Cinema: A Cultural and Political History* (2016) and *Cine Vasco* (2016) with Maria Pilar Rodriguez, and co-edited *The Unsilvered Screen: Surrealism on Film* (2007) with Graeme Harper, *Screening Songs in Hispanic and Lusophone Cinema* (2013) with Lisa Shaw, *A Companion to Luis Buñuel* (2013) with Julián Daniel Gutiérrez Albilla and *Screening European Heritage* (2016) with Paul Cooke. He is one of the series editors of Routledge's *Remapping World Cinema* book series and co-editor with Dunja Fehimović of the annual Screen Arts issue of the *Hispanic Research Journal.*

Paul Julian Smith is a specialist in film and television in Spain and Mexico. He is Distinguished Professor in the Hispanic and Luso-Brazilian Program in the Graduate Center, City University of New York, USA, and was for twenty years the Professor of Spanish in the University of Cambridge, UK. He was a regular contributor to *Sight & Sound* and is now a columnist for *Film Quarterly*. His seventeen authored books include *Desire Unlimited: The Cinema of Pedro Almodóvar* (2014) and *Amores Perros* (2003). They have been translated into Spanish, Chinese and Turkish. His most recent book is *Dramatized Societies: Quality Television in Spain and Mexico* (2016). He was a juror at the Morelia International Film Festival in 2008 and at the San Sebastián International Film Festival in 2013.

Niamh Thornton is Reader in Latin American Studies at the University of Liverpool, UK. She is a specialist in Mexican Film, Literature, and Digital Cultures with a particular focus on War Stories, Gendered Narratives, Star Studies, Cultures of Taste, and Distributed Content. She has published widely. Her books include *Revolution and Rebellion in Mexican Cinema* (2013),

International Perspectives on Chicana/o Studies: This World is My Place (2013), and *Memory and Trauma in Mexican Visual Culture* (2018).

Dolores Tierney is Senior Lecturer in Film Studies in the School of Media Film and Music at Sussex University, UK. She has published widely on Latin(o/a) American and Spanish media including articles in *Screen, Revista Canadiense de Estudios Hispánicos, New Cinemas* and *Studies in Hispanic Cinema*. She is the author of *Emilio Fernández* (2007) and *New Transnationalisms in Contemporary Latin American Cinemas* (2018) and the co-editor of two anthologies: *Latsploitation: Exploitation Cinemas and Latin America* (2009) with Victoria Ruétalo and *The Transnational Fantasies of Guillmero del Toro* (2014) with Ann Davies and Deborah Shaw.

Belén Vidal is Senior Lecturer in Film Studies at King's College London, UK. She is the author of *Figuring the Past: Period Film and the Mannerist Aesthetic* (2012) and *The Heritage Film* (2012) and co-editor of *The Biopic in Contemporary Film Culture* (2014). She has published articles on cinephilia in relation to Spanish cinema, including the work of filmmakers Isabel Coixet, Pablo Berger and Isaki Lacuesta.

Ginette Vincendeau is Professor of Film Studies at King's College London, UK, and a regular contributor to *Sight and Sound*. Among her books are *Pépé le Moko* (1998), *Stars and Stardom in French Cinema* (2000), *Jean-Pierre Melville: An American in Paris* (2003), *La Haine* (2005) and *Brigitte Bardot* (2013).

James Walters is Head of Film and Creative Writing at the University of Birmingham, UK. His books include *Alternative Worlds in Hollywood Cinema* (2008), *Film Moments: Criticism, History, Theory* (2010), *Fantasy Film* (2011), *The Thick of It* (2016) and *Television Performance* (2018).

Vito Zagarrio is Professor of Film, Television and Photography at the University of Rome 3, Italy. He received an MA and a PhD in Cinema Studies at NYU and a certificate in Film Direction at the Italian National Film School. He teaches Italian Film at NYU in Florence and has been senior research scholar at Oxford Brookes, visiting professor at IU Bloomington, and at Northwestern Evanston as a Fulbright scholar. He has published several monographs on Francis Ford Coppola, Frank Capra and John Waters, and has written several essays on Film and History.

Yingjin Zhang is Distinguished Professor and Chair of the Department of Literature at University of California, San Diego, USA. His English books include *Cinema and Urban Culture in Shanghai* (1999), *Screening China* (2002), *Chinese National Cinema* (2004), *From Underground to Independent* (2006), *Cinema, Space, and Polylocality in a Globalizing China* (2010), *Chinese Film Stars* (2010), *A Companion to Chinese Cinema* (2012), *New Chinese-Language Documentaries* (2015) and *Filming the Everyday* (2018).

ACKNOWLEDGEMENTS

We are incredibly grateful to staff at Routledge, and in particular to Natalie Foster, for responding so enthusiastically to the proposal for a new monograph series *Remapping World Cinema: Regional Tensions and Global Transformations*, and to this ambitious flagship volume. Natalie has shown nothing but encouragement, support and sound advice, without which bringing to publication such an ambitious volume might well have been impossible.

In the early stages the Companion represented a collaborative effort between the Centre for World Cinemas and Digital Cultures at the University of Leeds and B-Film: The Birmingham Centre for Film Studies at the University of Birmingham. With Alex Marlow-Mann's move to the University of Kent, the Centre for Film and Media Research came on board and so we have three important centres of research to thank for their support in this venture.

We thank all our contributors for their excellent contributions, their impeccable time-keeping and their engagement from the outset with the vision and strategy of the Companion. Where relevant, contributors have included funding and research-related acknowledgements in their individual chapters.

Our gratitude is also due to Esther Santamaría-Iglesias, who took on the enormous task of compiling a thorough and reader-friendly index for the entire volume with great skill and effort.

Finally, we wish to thank our students, past, present and future, to whom this book is dedicated. Someone said recently, "If you believe you're a citizen of the world, you're a citizen of nowhere." We believe the opposite is true. And we have World Cinema to prove it.

Rob Stone, Paul Cooke, Stephanie Dennison
and Alex Marlow-Mann
April 2017

INTRODUCTION

The longitude and latitude of World Cinema

Rob Stone, Paul Cooke, Stephanie Dennison and Alex Marlow-Mann

A coordinated view of World Cinema is one that plots the geographical range of films and filmmakers, their movements and audiences against the cultural, technological and political dynamics that create barriers and breakthroughs. The task of remapping the cinemas of the world on a spinning globe is doomed to inexactitude, however, because of the flux, drag and effervescence that constitutes a busy network of ebb and flow, of centripetal and centrifugal impulses that constantly reshape the form and function of the cinemas of the world. Yet the evolution of maritime navigation can offer a schema of how local tensions and worldwide transformations interact and can be negotiated. To adequately describe a location and situate it in its global context, one has to specify not only its "horizontal" distance from other locations but also its "vertical" distance between the Earth's poles. At the same time, one must negotiate the Earth's bulging, misshapen, somewhat egg-like structure with curving seas and a slowly shifting gravitational field, further complicated by local discrepancies and arbitrary irregularities. Simply locating a multitude of "African" cinemas in a continent is inexact and disorienting; merely tracking a film on its international trajectory is blinkered; examining the impact of technology in one area without reference to its effect on another is irresponsible. Territorialising cinemas is too easy. Instead, the task of (re-)mapping World Cinema requires new means of measurement and fresh tools for analysis.

Like the abandoned ship of Umberto Eco's *L'isola del giorno prima* (The Island of the Day Before, 1994)—which is gradually revealed to be an experimental laboratory for developing a sure means of measuring longitude and thus accurately navigating the world—this volume constitutes a vessel for developing new tools to navigate our way through World Cinema. And just as Eco's shipwrecked sailor learns that measuring time is crucial to calculating longitude, so we too pay crucial heed to historical developments and evolution in our process of remapping World Cinema for the twenty-first century. The *Routledge Companion to World Cinema* thus aims to be a touchstone publication for a crucial moment, when the industry, ideas and functions of film are in tremendous flux, not just from the effects of digital technologies and new screen media, but from economic and political changes that prompt us to question the very utility of the terms "world cinema" and "film". Bewildered and not a little frightened by recent political events, this volume constitutes an attempt to remap the territories of World Cinema and contemporary Film Studies in order to understand their history, enhance awareness of their current condition and plot trajectories for their development.

It is thus dedicated to delineating changes in the territories of World Cinema in terms of both longitudinal (historical, geographical, national, regional, transnational and global) and latitudinal (theoretical, industrial, thematic, aesthetic, technological and commercial) imperatives and parameters. To wit, therefore, its rationale and structure.

In aiming to revisit and, if necessary, revise outdated assumptions about national cinemas, this volume has been designed as a forum dedicated to challenging complacent views of hegemonic film cultures and replacing outmoded ideas about production, distribution and reception that incriminate the long-term underpinning of Film Studies by Orientalist understandings of non-Western cultural practices and products that are consumed in the West. Such a popular conceptualisation of World Cinema is analogous, as Stephanie Dennison and Song Hwee Lim note, to that of "World Music" and "World Literature", namely as non-situated cultural products that can be defined straightforwardly, and comfortably, as "Other" to the West (Dennison and Lim 2006: 1). In response, we asked our contributors to challenge this definition by taking into consideration the global activities and interchange of films and filmmakers. The rationale behind the design and construction of this volume was not simply a question of displaying an array of international or transnational subjects, nor even making broad claims for globalisation in its list of contents, but of revealing, exploring, explaining and considering commonalities and differences between the scale, engagement, strategies and anomalies of areas of filmmaking activity worldwide.

One might read this volume in linear fashion, but far better to keep checking latitude and longitude to plot a sure course through the landscapes of the world's cinemas. The *Routledge Companion to World Cinema* offers both a survey and an investigation into the condition and activity of contemporary filmmaking worldwide, often challenging long-standing categories and weighted—often politically motivated—value judgements, thereby grounding and aligning the reader in an activity of remapping which is designed to prompt rethinking. In so doing, this volume subscribes to the movement led by recent academic and critical writing on numerous aspects of World Cinema that has signalled a need to move away from discussion of traditional mechanisms for film production, distribution and consumption in order to identify a variety of cinemas that are resistant to the perceived cultural hegemony of Western culture in general, and Hollywood in particular. We thus took our cue (along with several of our contributors) from works such as Dennison and Lim's *Remapping World Cinema: Identity, Culture and Politics in Film* (2006) as well as *Cinema at the Periphery* (2010), edited by Dina Iordanova, David Martin-Jones and Belén Vidal, which uncovered multiple, diverse forms of cinematic creation that set the academic sector to arguing the case for accented, interstitial, intercultural, transnational, underground, minor or small cinemas.

This flux and fragmentation certainly offered a more dynamic and authentic view and understanding of World Cinema, but the task of herding all these splintering debates into a single volume required a new framework, one that took them all into account and found fresh focus in such divergence. The challenge of combining a cohesive overview with close analysis of such disparity demanded that we emphasise global transformations in terms of regional tensions, and vice versa. Each contributor was charged with this scholarly concern in relation to geographical and historical descriptions, analyses of the digital era related to film production, distribution and reception, and interest in the future of the discipline of Film Studies itself. Working together, we instigated what we hoped was a profound and timely re-examination of prevalent conceptualisations of World Cinema, while simultaneously calling into question the utility of the term through the act of remapping.

The contributors to this volume all reject the binary divide that sees "other" cinemas defined as non-Hollywood, a conceptualisation recently noted by Lucía Nagib, Chris Perriam and Rajindah

Dudrah in *Theorizing World Cinema* (2011) as perpetuating the unhelpful and erroneous attitude that puts all other cinemas into the position of victim; that is, "purely reactive manifestations incapable of eliciting independent theory" (xxii). Thus, armed with our new tools for remapping World Cinema, we set out to challenge traditional ways of coordinating (and therefore limiting) thinking on our subject. Obstacles were many. Following debate and decision, we set upon World Cinema as our subject, "world cinema" for the times that it was called into question, and "the world's cinemas" or "cinemas of the world" for when a less holistic, more cautious view was called for. We worried about whether the flood of American films in recent years has diluted or even washed away a wealth of national cinematography in Asia and Latin America, Africa, the Middle East, Europe and the former Soviet states. We explored symbolic and experiential dimensions of the impact and influence of new and established film cultures worldwide as they interacted, paying attention nonetheless to responsive filmmaking activities that included regional attempts to clone or counter what might be perceived as the global excesses of the Nollywood, Bollywood or Hollywood brands. Struggling to reach new understandings, we were nevertheless determined not to replace one hegemony with another. Rather, we recognise, for example, that popular entertainment films are made and distributed the world over and so we set out to identify and analyse worldwide trends in aesthetics, archetypes and narrative structures as well as their exceptions. Concurrently, we sought to explore and map the filmmaking activity that, in contrast to the mainstream circuits and distribution formats and platforms, is online, elsewhere and otherwise engaged—even if sometimes these activities are merely another reflection of the power dynamics that exist in physical reality.

In populating and shaping *The Routledge Companion to World Cinema* we also heeded the conclusions put forward by Rosalind Galt and Karl Schoonover in their *Global Art Cinema* (2010), that there are serious perils in thinking in terms of a simplistic geographical engagement of an international filmmaking community that is absorbed by dominant circuits of capital, stereotype, and imperialist vision. At the same time, one must also be mindful of the geographical specificities, and often very precisely situated realities and pragmatic demands of production and consumption. Consequently, we duly recruited Galt and Schoonover as contributors and thus our guides. In this way, the volume seeks to uncover the complex ways in which film is globalised, but also regional, defined by socio-political processes that illustrate the interconnectivity between global changes in political and economic power and all-encompassing digital transformations. What impact has this had upon the arguably worldwide sedimentation of people in terms of their status within an increasingly neoliberal world order? How does the current wave of political populism feed into or potentially change this order? All this affects changes in regional film policies, creative activities, community "uprisings" in film production and reception, and a broad, interactive use of new screen technologies that posit a collectively owned understanding of a place in that world. As a result, and in addition to fresh analysis of the meaning and importance (or otherwise) of geographical borders, this volume encompasses the remapping of economic, political, aesthetic and cultural assumptions to which World Cinema is subject.

Compiling this volume was its own voyage of discovery. As the volume began to cohere, we realised that cinemas of the world are defined not by any clichéd reaction against Hollywood by "other" cinemas but by something much closer to a network of challenges to homogeneity by which filmmakers and film-watchers experience, accept, or attempt to reject globalisation on their own terms. Thanks to new media, many peoples of the world can experience international communication and the marginalised can often find a voice, thereby setting examples and aspirations for those who do not yet have that access or possibility. Film can foster empathy and incite debate by highlighting interdependency and potential. Yet there are also many who lack the technology, who are "off the grid" (Andrew 2012) and unmapped, whose production and consumption of films is also a concern of this volume. Moreover, while the means of audio-visual production are in the hands of a growing proportion of the world's population, having a voice in the midst of internet traffic is all well and good, but who can hear it? Who controls the power of curation in cyberspace? So much remapping, with new information coming at us from all angles, meant that our new way of measuring and coordinating both the latitude and longitude of World Cinema had to convince our contributors of its relevance before our positioning of their chapters could demonstrate its coherence.

For this reason, *The Routledge Companion to World Cinema* is divided into two sections of twenty chapters each. The first is entitled Longitude and is concerned with geographical areas, ways of mapping or remapping the landscape and extent of World Cinema. This includes analysis of those films and cinemas that slip between the gaps of conventional geographic categories, revealing themselves as impossible to situate or equally at home in multiple geographic contexts. The second section is entitled Latitude and is concerned with new theoretical strategies pertaining to thematic and practical ways of understanding and negotiating World Cinema. Both sections investigate key themes and crucial areas of enquiry. Each of the forty chapters provides a survey of a topic, explaining why the issue or area is important, and critically discussing the leading views in the area. Contributors then develop their arguments and explain their understanding of the subject by analysing key films and engaging with the work of others, offering a new take on their topic. Each chapter includes definitions, historical perspectives and discussion of key critical issues.

The debate outlined by this volume is not over, but neither is it just beginning. Many of the contributors have been puzzling over their subjects for years. Consequently, our aim here is to provide a forum for them to share ideas, for cross-referencing and new comparative analysis. We thus drew together a group of scholars from a range of disciplines at a variety of career stages. These include many of the key scholars in World Cinema Studies, alongside emerging voices, oftentimes with new ways of approaching their topic, a "ground zero" approach to discovering and explaining just what is happening in the cinemas of the world, and why. We always intended that the expertise contained herein would be global and would contend with how filmmaking and the study of film is being transformed in countless ways by the internet, which truly internationalises research, distribution, access, fan-bases and the curriculum. We therefore cover areas such as contemporary distribution and reception studies in order to examine why and how film-watching is often no longer a time-consuming activity for a captive audience but an elliptical one for the solitary and easily distracted spectator; at the same time, we exhorted our contributors to effectively dialogue with each other in order to investigate why and how (and for how much longer) film-watching nonetheless remains a communal activity for a worldwide spectatorship. Moreover, we investigate the ways in which the traditional divide between "theory" and "practice" in Film Studies becomes increasingly blurred (if it was not always to some degree blurred) in the digital age. Contributors examine the ways in which the digital revolution has not only opened up new possibilities for film consumption, but also for production. Mobile phones can now capture images of a quality that would have been reserved for the high-end cameras of Hollywood less than a decade ago. A generation of "digital native" children straightforwardly negotiate editing tools to post their product on YouTube or any number of social networking platforms, aspiring to become the next PewDiePie, KSI or Porta dos Fundos, and in so doing they are challenging critical assumptions about the trajectory of film aesthetics along with the possibilities and politics of form (Kosoff and Jacobs 2015). Contributors explore the impact of such developments not only on the shape of the films being made and the way they are consumed, but also how this helps to transform the broader political and educational film infrastructure, the way the world envisages training and support for future generations of filmmakers and to what end. To what extent does this challenge the parameters of the debate that has accompanied the entire history of the medium between film as "art" versus film as "commerce" in a world where film policy might be as concerned with the medium's role as a "soft power asset", on the one hand, or as a tool to support international development on the other?

Previous and successive remappings of World Cinema have tended to emphasise the longitudinal and, to some extent, ignore its interaction with latitude. Unhelpful generalisations have thus descended, erasing nuance, difference and specifics. In response, *The Routledge Companion to World Cinema* had its work cut out to cram an entire planet's worth of filmmaking activity into only so many pages. It is not, therefore, and never could be, a Borgesian remapping of the world in the model of that which is elaborated in *Del rigor en la ciencia* (On Exactitude in Science, 1946), which is based on a 1:1 scale and thus renders a map as big as the world itself. We nevertheless worked hard to cover geographical and thematic areas of enquiry, illustrating and examining how cinema worldwide is at this very moment evolving beyond understandings of geographical territories, influence and populace, while simultaneously engaging with thematically motivated concerns that reflect global transformations and their effects on regional tensions.

Part I: Longitude

The usefulness of our coordinated view of World Cinema is artfully demonstrated by **Yingjin Zhang**—1 The cinematic and the real in contemporary Chinese cinema. Here, Zhang's coordinates are fixed longitudinally on China, one of the world's most significant film production centres and markets, and one that continues to challenge scholars in the West, and latitudinally on realism, explored more broadly in this volume by Lúcia Nagib (Chapter 25). Zhang demonstrates the importance of a situated reading of "the real" in order to understand film production in China over the last three decades, given that realism was an officially sanctioned concept for decades and "still carries negative connotations of cliché and propaganda". He argues that it is only since the 1980s that filmmakers in China have broken away from an "officially dictated vision of reality". The so-called Fifth Generation thus rediscovered the real through a "wordless contemplation of the natural landscape", which enabled them to distance themselves from the rhetoric of *realpolitik* and "to project a vision of national culture distinct from that endorsed by Communist historiography". The subsequent independent filmmakers of the Sixth Generation have in turn adopted a more subjective and individualised perception of the real, as summarised in director Lou Ye's phrase: "My camera doesn't lie." The Sixth Generation, then "conjure up improvised conditions of real life punctuated by alienation, contemplation and rebellion".

While Chinese cinema could be described as one of the staples of the World Cinema diet for festival programmers, audiences and researchers, **Jonathan Driskell**—2 Southeast Asian independent cinema: a World Cinema movement—recognises a "mismatch" between the cinematic output of the eleven countries that make up southeast Asia (including the significant Philippine and Malay cinemas) and the recognition they have received, both in terms of audiences and, for example, in key World Cinema texts of the late twentieth century. Driskell's contribution thus serves in part to fill a gap in scholarship on contemporary filmmaking in the region. In his chapter we see a number of features that resonate with filmmaking practices and experiences elsewhere in the world: the clear importance given to independent filmmaking by World Cinema festival programmers, the continued prominence of politically engaged films from the region in terms of circulation abroad, the increasing significance of European film festivals for both circulation and film funding, and regional funding and distribution/exhibition initiatives that stimulate individual industries but do not entirely mask the still problematic notion of lumping certain nations together in particular geopolitical groupings. Driskell observes that these regional initiatives have not as yet yielded any meaningful filmic reflections on the regions as imagined communities, mirroring observations made by Stephanie Dennison (Chapter 6) in relation to similar initiatives and failures in the imagined community of the Portuguese-speaking world.

The cinemas of Japan and Korea have often been discussed in conjunction with one another (see, for example, Bowyer and Choi 2004). However, in her chapter dedicated to the subject—3 Global intimacy and cultural intoxication: Japanese and Korean film in the twenty-first century—**Felicity Gee** argues that, historically speaking, the two cinemas have always been fairly distinct and independent and that their shared history is a problematic and conflicted one characterised by "ugly intimacies". It is only in the twenty-first century (and specifically following the 1998 "Open Door Policy/Good Neighbour Policy" summit that opened the doors to pan-Asian co-productions) that explicit interaction between the two became the norm. Subsequently, the twenty-first century witnessed the explosion of (transnational) Asian cinema on a global scale through such phenomena as the Korean blockbuster and J-Horror. This longitudinal shift towards a "global intimacy" between Japanese and Korean cinema is paralleled by a series of latitudinal shifts that reshaped the nature of these cinemas: the impact of corporate finance, the increasing importance of transmedia interactions, and the emergence of a "digital world in which local presence is no longer a prerequisite either for transnational collaboration or as a physical marker of national branding". Some have criticised these developments in terms of a loss of cultural specificity, identifying a "cultural odourlessness" in contemporary Japanese cinema and seeing the Korean blockbuster as Hollywood imitation. Yet, as Gee shows, phenomena such as J-Horror and Korean melodrama continue to rely heavily on culturally specific tropes. Contemporary Japanese and Korean cinema must therefore be understood in terms of "a circulatory exchange between the specific and the universal".

Given its commonly used moniker (Nollywood) it is unsurprising that scholarly and audience interest in Nigerian popular movie production (currently the second largest on Earth, behind only Bollywood) has, until relatively recently, been almost exclusively predicated on its relation to Hollywood. Rather than following the well-worn course of reading Nigerian film in contradistinction to US mainstream production, **Jeffrey Geiger**—4 Media refashioning: from Nollywood to New Nollywood—engages with an ongoing remediation of Nigerian movies. Geiger highlights the privileged space traditionally afforded celluloid in Film Studies analyses (cf. the close association between Nollywood and video production) and it is precisely this privileging of one media platform over another that he seeks to avoid via a discussion of media refashioning. Geiger's recognition of the danger in isolating film and/or video production in academic work is echoed elsewhere in this companion. For example, Anne Ciecko (Chapter 16) argues that Arab cinema studies should be part of a larger dialogue with audiovisual culture and digital media, while Mette Hjort (Chapter 40) highlights how Global North/South film support programmes will often be multidisciplinary in nature, thus promoting film as part of a broader cultural package. Geiger in his examination of Nigerian filmmaking also, crucially, seeks to "unsettle goal-oriented narratives of improvement" (to wit, Nollywood progresses to 35mm, gains footholds in the international film festival circuit and thus graduates to an acceptable form of filmmaking which is only then worthy of close analysis), and he highlights the demands of a certain way of reading certain World Cinema films (the legacy of Third Cinema theories and an insistence that African cinema is oppositional to dominant cinematic forms in its politics and ideology) and their negative impact on the reading of Nollywood to date.

The history, shape and momentum of the contemporary South African film industry, discussed by **Ian-Malcolm Rijsdijk**—5 Framing democracy: film in post-democracy South Africa—are, of course, strikingly different from those discussed by Geiger (Chapter 4) in relation to Nollywood, and later by Ciecko (Chapter 16) in relation to North African production, thus serving to remind readers of the importance of avoiding generalising about film production (or anything else) in relation to large geopolitical areas such as Africa. Rijsdijk's focus here is the impact of the so-called "born-free" generation on contemporary filmmaking and the extent to which they counter the post-apartheid narratives of the rainbow nation, renaissance and reconciliation. As well as providing readings of some of this new generation's key films, such as *Necktie Youth* (2015, South Africa, Sibs Shongwe la-Mer), Rijsdijk highlights the important role assumed by a local film festival (the Durban International Film Festival) in forging a sense of new South African cinema. Thus, the latitudinal relevance of Marijke de Valck's chapter on World Cinema's film festivals (Chapter 32) is clear here, but so too is Paul Cooke's chapter on Soft Power (Chapter 24), given that in practice contemporary filmmakers in South Africa are questioning what continues to be, at least abroad, a very attractive national narrative.

The contemporary film history of South Africa and the socio-political context in which films are currently being made arguably share more features in common with fellow BRICS nation Brazil than with other filmmaking cultures in Africa: hence the emphasis made by **Stephanie Dennison**—6 Brazilian cinema on the global screen—on the importance of testing out different ways of mapping cinema longitudinally. The latitudinal factors under consideration in her rethinking of contemporary Brazilian filmmaking are, in particular, film festivals and issues relating to transnationalism. While recognising that domestic film production is and always has been the principal focus of film policy in Brazil, a country with generous local sources of film funding, particularly when compared to many of its neighbours in South America, and while also recognising that the relatively large domestic market reacts positively to domestic film production of a more mainstream and popular type, Dennison acknowledges a new-found ease with which certain directors and film producers navigate the international film festival and film funding circuits, circuits that are explored further in this context by Dolores Tierney (Chapter 7). Dennison concludes her chapter by exhorting scholars and programmers to cease "requiring of Brazilian filmmakers and producers that they operate as the bearers of a national identity". The implication here is that by doing so we risk ghettoising or maintaining the invisibility of certain types of film production, such as transnational co-productions.

In the following chapter on Latin American cinema—7 Transnational filmmaking in South America—**Dolores Tierney** argues that over the past twenty years, individual national states have reduced or withdrawn their support for the film industry and filmmakers have had to turn to private and international sources of funding to fill the gap. This latitudinal shift in the mode of production employed by individual filmmakers and national cinemas has had a consequent longitudinal effect, facilitating the distribution and circulation of Latin American films internationally and propelling certain Latin American filmmakers (Alejandro González Iñárritu, Alfonso Cuarón, Guillermo del Toro, Fernando Meirelles, Walter Salles) into careers beyond national or regional boundaries. Latin America has thus been particularly marked by the "transnational turn" in contemporary cinema. Taking the Peruvian director Claudia Llosa as a case study of the "festival filmmaker", Tierney argues that the funding mechanisms for such a transnational arthouse cinema favour particular realist aesthetics, as examined by Lúcia Nagib (Chapter 25) and Marije de Valck (Chapter 32), which risks both homogenising cinemas from different national and cultural contexts and ghettoising Latin American cinema within the festival/arthouse circuit. There is therefore both a need to resist or find alternatives to the inadvertently neo-colonialist implications of such a model and to allow Latin American films to reach larger domestic and international audiences.

Mapping a "Caribbean cinema" is, as **Dunja Fehimović** notes, problematic not least because the notion of the Caribbean is itself open to multiple interpretations and definitions. Her chapter—8 Connected in "another way": repetition, difference and identity in Caribbean cinema—proposes that Caribbeanness can be located above all in the notion of "Créolité", the sense of belonging to a group characterised by a non-harmonious mix of cultural factors, which aligns her idea of Caribbean cinema with that of Rob Stone's "cinemas of sentiment" (Chapter 21). This finds expression through the search for a particular Caribbean aesthetic (for example, through a particular use of light) as part of a broader process of "Caribbeing". Ultimately, however, Fehimović argues that a "true Caribbeanness can only be found in and through contingency and relationality—in short, in openness to the rest of the world". Thus, she proposes approaching Caribbean cinema as "'cinemas of relation'—that is, cinemas that express their particularity and authenticity not through retrenchments in the national or the local or through straightforward opposition to a hegemonic 'centre' but by constantly making and reconfiguring multiple connections".

Rather than providing an overview of the workings of the contemporary Mexican film industry or of key films of the contemporary period, both of which can be found elsewhere in relative abundance, **Niamh Thornton**—9 Women's (r)evolutons in Mexican cinema—works in the spirit of this volume by considering the role of women (and as a corollary, race) in relation to one of the grand themes of Mexican cinema: the Mexican Revolution (1910). Thornton argues that through critical oversight, the presence of women filmmakers in the vast body of filmic work that deals with the revolution has been ignored in favour of more clear-cut and racially unproblematic women-centred narratives, such as those bound up with the Golden Age of Mexican melodrama. Thornton observes that "the particularities of women's lives and stories told on film concurrently have distinct peaks and troughs that have as much to do with changes in the industry and more equal and distributed access to the means of production as they have with struggles for legal rights". By realigning her coordinates, Thornton is able to provide both a nuanced reading of Mexican film history and a telling illustration of how women directors can be written out of national film narratives when we keep going back to the same set of limited coordinates. Mark Goodall (Chapter 30) likewise observes that the problematic nature of the representation of women in cult films has led to their ultimate exclusion from the canon, and we might also recall here our unchecked insistence in taking our lead, when it comes to discussions of gender and race in relation to cinema, from Hollywood (consider the importance we tend to give initiatives such as the Geena Davis Institute and the Oscars So White social media campaign for our understanding of women and race in relation to contemporary film, for example).

If the principal film producing countries of Western Europe appear to have already been fairly comprehensively defined and studied, **Paul Julian Smith**—10 Popular cinema/quality television: the audiovisual sector in Spain—demonstrates that even these cinemas are in flux and open to remapping. Taking as his point of departure the cultural bias traditionally assigned to cinema over television, Smith demonstrates how the increased salience of popular genres (such as the thriller) over conventional auteur cinema coupled with the rise of new "quality" television series such as *El tiempo entre costuras* (The Time in Between, 2013–2014, Spain) has led to a latitudinal shift, blurring distinctions between the two media and altering our conceptions of both Spanish cinema and television—even if the Spanish critical establishment has yet to fully embrace this change—thereby exemplifying such evolution in other European countries and parts of World Cinema too.

The tensions between the national, the regional and the transnational are central to **Olof Hedling**'s discussion of contemporary Scandinavian cinema—11 Contemporary Scandinavian cinema: between art and commerce. He examines the dramatic success story of "Nordic Noir" and, in particular, *Män som hatar kvinnor* (The Girl with the Dragon Tattoo, 2009, Sweden/Denmark/Germany, Niels Arden Oplev) in the light of Thomas Elsaesser's critical assessment of the increased marginality of European cinema and of Mette Hjort's typology of transnationalism. Paying particular attention to the role played by regional film funds and the kind of piecemeal, transnational funding strategies pioneered by Lars von Trier and Peter Aalbæk Jensen's company Zentropa, he demonstrates both the way *The Girl with the Dragon Tattoo* has been variously (and problematically) positioned as a Scandinavian, Swedish or Danish success, and also the fact that the film's global success is ultimately relative: "Scandinavian cinema can be said to be just as successful—or rather unsuccessful—as most non-English language cinemas on the international stage."

The uncertain future of the UK due to the process of Britain's withdrawal from the European Union is explored by **James Chapman**—12 British cinemas: critical and historical debates—where it takes its place among other uncertainty-related debates that have shaped the nature of British cinema, which has often found itself "betwixt and between" Europe and Hollywood. This has resulted in British cinema studies focusing on "the re-evaluation of directors, genres and periods in order to show that British cinema is a site where culturally significant films have been made". Chapman outlines the political economy of the British film industry, which highlights the very different nature of the industry's historical relationship with Hollywood, for example, whereby major US studios ultimately bankrolled the industry by the 1960s. He also reflects upon the very Europeanness of British cinema from the 1990s onwards, as a result of EEC and then EU funding initiatives, and of the involvement of European media conglomerates, such as the Dutch Polygram, in independent British production (namely the ultra-successful Working Title Films). Notwithstanding this potential negative impact of the UK leaving the European Union, Chapman does remind us that, since the British film industry "resembles many other medium-sized national cinemas in so far as distribution and exhibition are dominated by multinationals operating on a global scale", major successes can disguise the fact that "many British films fail to secure a full theatrical release". Thus, as with many of the cinemas examined in this longitudinal section, those same distribution and exhibition constraints that have dogged World Cinema for decades continue to exist.

One of the most noticeable developments in World Cinema since the new millennium is explored by **Elżbieta Ostrowska** and **Joanna Rydzewska**—13 Developments in Eastern European cinemas since 1989—that is, the unexpected success of Eastern European Cinema, which has redrawn the cultural map of Europe by moving the border eastwards and questioning the established axiology of the concepts of Western and Eastern European cinema. The origins of this change lie, of course, in the historical and political shake-up brought about by the break-up of the Soviet Union and the collapse of the former Communist States. This led to a dramatic (latitudinal) shift in the mode-of-production, as state-run and funded film industries gave way to a producer-driven free market system. Moreover, as far as a longitudinal mapping of Eastern European cinemas is concerned, this has had several effects: increasing diversification and localism and placing new significance on individual national cinemas, on the one hand, and on the other, the increased importance of pan-European or global production strategies and distribution strategies. Ostrowska and Rydzewska explore these tensions between the national and the transnational during a period of political and cultural transformation through three case studies: an analysis of the Romanian New Wave as a European film movement, how transnational co-productions have changed the cinema of Hungarian auteur Béla Tarr, and how the transnational labour market has affected the role of female directors and actors from the region without significantly altering representations of Eastern European women on screen.

Ostrowska and Rydzewska's analysis (Chapter 13) of the way the success of movements such as the Romanian New Wave has shifted conceptions of European cinema and moved the border eastward leads into **Lydia Papadimitriou**'s chapter—14 Cinema at the edges of the European Union: new dynamics in the South and the East. In the light of the referendum that resulted in movements to take the UK out of the European Union and the ongoing migrant crisis, she notes how, "despite the official emphasis on unification, cultural proximity, free movement of people and the gradual dissolution of boundaries, real and symbolic hierarchies have persisted within the EU", in particular between the (real and perceived) economic and social differences between the northern and southern countries, and between the original Western European members and the new Eastern European entrants. Focussing on two case studies (Greek cinema, the "Weird Wave" and its leading auteur, Yorgos Lanthimos in the south, and the new EU members Romania, Bulgaria and Croatia in the east), Papadimitriou explores the challenges faced by small and peripheral cinemas within the European context, arguing that "a new Balkan regionalism that would reinforce co-operation across the countries of South-Eastern Europe could help strengthen their marginal position, redefining the European project in more inclusive and polycentric ways, and enabling the region to project internationally".

Viviane Saglier addresses one of the most intractable problems for any mapping of World Cinema: how to deal with clearly significant film cultures that are not represented or defined by a strong or established state—15 The non/industries of film and the Palestinian emergent film economy. Traditionally both the film industry and Film Studies tend to assign nationality primarily on the basis of funding, but this becomes problematic in the case of disputed states or those without established funding mechanisms. The rise of a distinct Palestinian art cinema since the 1980s exemplifies these problems and contradictions perfectly. Most of its filmmakers were educated in the diaspora and its films are funded transnationally through European film funds and directed at the global festival circuit. This constitutes a paradox in that "on the one hand, the category of World Cinema allows Palestinian cinema to exist internationally as such despite the absence of financial support from the Palestinian proto-state [. . .] On the other hand, World Cinema constitutes the very discourse and economy that prevents Palestinian cinema from developing its own economic and industrial base by maintaining its dependence on European and external funding". Drawing on postcolonial theory, Saglier explores the possibilities for building a more independent film culture in such weak/non-states, through such devices as guerrilla filmmaking techniques and the role of film festivals in facilitating the building of a grass roots filmmaking culture and infrastructure.

In the following chapter—16 Locations and narrative reorientation in Arab cinemas/World Cinema—**Anne Ciecko** forewarns us that "within the larger map of World Cinema, the concept of Arab cinema (or Arab Cinemas [. . .]) is problematised by the concept of a world within a world, as well as the transdiscursive legacies of Occidentalism, Eurocentrism, nationalism, colonialism, and civilization". She then traces the impact of scholars and exhibitors both outside and within the region in defining what this cinema/these cinemas might be. Ciecko points to intersectionality as a potentially valuable way of "complicating constructions of Arab cinema and its storytelling functions". She refers to the recent proliferation of multi-strand narratives in World Cinema as a potential in terms of diversifying narrative possibilities. These films set in fixed (longitudinal) geographical spaces that incorporate a range of (latitudinal) viewpoints highlight issues of diversity and multifarious narrative possibilities in World Cinema, as well as the growing number of transnational "network narratives" (to borrow David Bordwell's term) that bear witness to individual filmmakers' attempts to represent global concerns (*Babel* [2006, France/USA/Mexico, Alejandro González Iñárritu] and *360* [2011, UK/Austria/France/Brazil/USA, Fernando Meirelles], to name two that are referenced in this companion), along with a steady trickle of multi-authored omnibus films that pretend to tackle grand themes from a global perspective (e.g. *Paris, je t'aime* [2006, France/Lichtenstein/Switzerland/Germany, Olivier Assayas, *et al.*]), and which are increasingly being driven by film festivals (e.g. *Venice* 70: *Future Reloaded* [2013, USA, Hala Abdallah, *et al.*] and *Asian Three-Fold Mirror: Reflections* [Japan/Cambodia/Malaysia/Phillippines, 2016, Brillante Mendoza, *et al.*]).

Madhuja Mukherjee—17 The forking paths of Indian cinema: revisiting Hindi films through their regional networks—is, like Alex Marlow-Mann (Chapter 26), concerned with the extent to which the emphasis on national cinemas tends to erase regional complexities and difference. Focussing on one of the largest, and linguistically and culturally most diverse, nations on Earth, India, she challenges the entrenched association between Indian cinema and the Bombay-based Hindi-language cinema of Bollywood. Adopting a historical perspective and focusing on the case study of New Theatres, she demonstrates how in the 1920s and 1930s Hindi language cinema emerged in a range of locations such as Calcutta (in Bengal) and Pune (in Maharashtra) and was inextricably tied to a process of modernisation associated with the Bhadralok (English educated, urbane, upper-caste, Hindu, gentry of Bengal). It was only with the Second World War, Independence and Partition that conditions changed, producing a regional shift towards Bombay and the rise of the so-called "Hindi socials". Regional tensions continued to manifest themselves in later films, however, as can be seen from an analysis of the shifting identity of the country's biggest star, Amitabh Bachchan. Moreover, recent years have witnessed a resurgence of the local which testifies to "the continuing dialogue between global Bollywood and local cultures [and] highlights the authorial, industrial and cultural transactions that still exist between the Hindi mainstream and its many others".

Geoff King's chapter—18 American indie film and international art cinema: points of distinction and overlap—on the points of convergence and divergence between the American "indie" films and international art cinema provides a clear example of the way in which a longitudinal/latitudinal approach can enhance our understanding of World Cinema. These two categories of cinema are clearly demarcated longitudinally (American versus international) and therefore it has often been assumed that the two are also entirely different latitudinally (in terms of aesthetics and thematics). This has resulted in a lack of scholarship addressing the similarities and intersections between the two phenomena, something that King's remapping sets out to redress. While both arthouse cinema and the American indie have been defined in opposition to the (Hollywood) mainstream through an emphasis on increased "realism", King notes how art cinema has traditionally been seen to lean more towards the experimental, and the indie more towards the commercial. This is sometimes seen as a product of different intellectual currents: existentialism and modernism in the case or art cinema, multiculturalism and postmodernism in the case of the indie. Yet he also notes how the differences between these two forms of cinema are less clear-cut than has traditionally been assumed, with examples of a serious/modernist approach displayed by certain indies and of a more playful/postmodern one in certain art films. King thus advances a relational methodology, which has parallels with Dunja Fehimović's approach to Caribbean cinema (Chapter 8).

If British cinema is frequently defined as "betwixt and between" Europe and the USA (Chapter 12), then the history of Canadian cinema is marked by its location "betwixt and between" the UK and the USA. What is apparent when reading **Chris Gittings**'s chapter—19 Canadian cinema(s)—is that Canada's relationship with the United States is of such overwhelming importance that it obliges us to put into perspective claims of US dominance coming from, say, those working in British cinema and Australasian cinemas. Canada has the added constraint of having too small a domestic audience to make movie-making viable without achieving some success abroad, although here too we would do well to recall that even Hollywood can no longer rely on its domestic market to hit its revenue targets. What Canadian contemporary film production as explored by Gittings can boast, however, is a remarkable number of latitudinal coordinates: women's film production (Studio D, set up in 1974, was the first publicly funded women's production unit in the world), realism (see Lucía Nagib's discussion of the seminal *Atanarjuat* (Atanarjuat: The Fast Runner, 2001, Canada) by Inuit director Zacharias Kunuk (Chapter 25), a history of creative exhibition techniques (John Grierson's National Film Board set up successful alternative exhibition spaces in regional libraries as early as the 1940s and currently make domestic films available via streaming), queer cinema (the films of high-profile directors John Greyson and Bruce la Bruce that ultimately enable Canadian film to brand itself on the World Cinema film festival circuit as queer; see also Rosalind Galt and Karl Schoonover (Chapter 28)), film festivals (The Toronto International Film Festival and its role in promoting Canadian film in the World Cinema distribution marketplace), and so on. But before we herald Canadian cinema(s) as the premiere success story in World Cinema, Gittings reminds us of a bleak statistic, to which many of the film cultures explored in this longitudinal section can relate: in 2015 Canadian films held only a 1.9 per cent market share of the Canadian box office. He also makes an observation that is echoed in a number of the longitudinal surveys included in this *Companion*: that diversity is largely absent from popular genres and that "arthouse cinema continues to be where we find indigenous, queer and transnational filmmakers".

In the final chapter in our Longitude section—20 Conventions, preventions and interventions: Australasian cinema since the 1970s—**Jonathan Rayner** draws attention to a strikingly similar set of influences on the cinemas of Australia and New Zealand to those on Canadian film (Chapter 19): i.e. British and American. One way these influences are being challenged is via the growth of international co-productions with Asian countries. Returning to the comparison with Canada, however, there does not appear to be such a stark divergence between popular genres and commercial success in foreign markets with, for example, typically Australian genres such as the Ocker comedy, the period film, the Gothic horror film and the male ensemble drama managing to find audiences both at home and abroad. That said, Rayner does acknowledge that tensions exist (of the kind we witness in British, Brazilian and many other cinemas in this section) between commercial and artistic concerns. Rayner acknowledges the huge impact on New Zealand filmmaking of the global success of the *Lord of the Rings* trilogy (2001–2003, New Zealand/USA/Germany, Peter Jackson) and informs us that capitalising on this success, which consists of "establishing the country as a post-production hub as much as an exotic location [is] at once a boon and a burden". He concludes his chapter by stating that "the achievements of Australasian cinema under [. . .] inauspicious or frankly hostile conditions have been to persist, to represent and broadcast a multiplicity of relevant cultural histories, narratives and identities", which provides a fittingly upbeat reflection with which to draw this longitudinal section to a close.

Part II: Latitude

Like several other writers in the Latitude section, **Rob Stone**—21 Cinemas of citizens and cinemas of sentiment: World Cinema in flux—seeks to remap World Cinema by challenging and updating some of the established categories and theories underpinning conventional thinking. Rejecting Benedict Anderson's notion of "imagined communities", which has been so fundamental for conceptions of national cinemas, he draws instead on Georg Sørenson's distinction between communities of citizens, which are defined by an exchange of "political, social and economic rights and obligations" and communities of sentiment, which are based on an ungovernable flow that extends via empathy to include those along a strata of common or similar cultural, social, linguistic, economic conditions, enabling "a historical identity based on literature, myths, symbols, music and art, and so on". While some have problematised national cinema through reference to the transnational or to accented, migrant, diasporic or small cinemas, Stone polemicises with writers such as Stephen Crofts by proposing a categorisation that does not depend specifically on the national. A "cinema of citizens" is top-down and inward looking and at its most extreme would coincide with a servile cinema centred on the state, while "cinemas of sentiment" exist in the interstices—online, in the margins, supported by film festivals, larger cultural movements and other funding streams—and are thus bottom-up, outward looking and more inclined to be critical. To demonstrate the ways in which such an alternative approach contributes to our remapping of World Cinema, Stone draws on films from a range of different geographic traditions, from Catalan to Chinese cinema, from African cinemas to Dhallywood, and from American Mumblecore to the Romanian New Wave (Chapters 1, 13, 18). Moreover, Stone recognises that, as Jürgen Habermas has argued, nations (and cinemas) are not fixed and static, but rather in flux, and therefore a cinema of sentiment can morph into a cinema of citizens and vice versa. Stone's model thus provides an invaluable new way of (re-)mapping cinema, which is particularly pertinent in the context of current debates about the legitimacy and limitations of the national cinema model.

If latitudinal theorisation has helped define and shape our understanding of the geographies of World Cinema. there are at least two ways in which one could embark on a exploring them anew: first, by applying existing theories to longitudinally different groups of films, and second, by developing new theories or deploying previously neglected ones. **David Martin-Jones**'s chapter—22 Transworld cinemas: film-philosophies for world cinemas' engagement with world history—sits at the intersection between these two strategies. He draws on the "trans" of transnational and the "world" or World Cinema, proposing the idea of "transworld cinemas [to] provoke new ways of thinking about films [,] classify[ing] or categoris[ing] films much as the field does currently for a national cinema, but with examples from across diverse cinemas". To do this, he argues for the need to move beyond the predominantly European philosophical traditions prevalent in film theory to explore new avenues. Specifically, he cites the Argentine philosopher Enrique Dussel's work on "transmodernity", which posits that the idea of modernity derives from the conquest of the Americas in 1492 and thus is inherently bound up with colonialism, and "contract theory", which "offers many different ways of thinking about new transworld groupings of films, from ecology (the Natural Contract) to gender (the Sexual Contract) to intercultural connections (the Racial Contract)". Martin-Jones' transworld approach brings together films from different geographic regions regardless of whether or not they share established links (for example, as co-productions) and in so doing reveals previously hidden points of similarity and difference, thereby remapping our understanding of World Cinema. Approaching films in this way also has an impact on how we understand history through film, a topic also explored by Vito Zagarrio (Chapter 34), shifting the emphasis from national histories to world history.

In the following chapter—23 Transnational cinema: mapping a field of study—**Deborah Shaw** outlines the shift in Film Studies to incorporate the so-called transnational turn that had initially influenced social and cultural theory. The belated incorporation of transnationalism into discussions of film was at first focused on migration, diasporic and (post)colonial cinemas, but now "there are few areas within Film Studies on which transnational cinema has not left its imprint". Indeed, many chapters in this volume, both longitudinal and latitudinal, reference the transnational. Shaw acknowledges that it is very much Anglophone film studies that is driving this interest in transnationalism. She thus provides a timely and necessary overview and summary of the arguments of key English-language texts on the transnational in relation to film, some of which (Higbee and Lim's, for example) were published in the ground-breaking *Transnational Cinemas* film journal that she founded. Higbee and Lim's "manifesto" is for the privileging of a "critical transnationalism", which involves the exploration of relations of post-coloniality, politics and power. Shaw concurs with the authors on critical transnationalism as offering a way forward from potentially woolly and catch-all definitions (after all, what film nowadays can accurately claim to exist exclusively in a national or sub-national context?), but she also makes the case for including Hollywood films in discussions of the transnational. Citing the example of the *Star Wars* trilogy and the investment of their young fans all over the world, she describes them as "differently transnational, belonging to separate ends of an economic and artistic scale and performing different functions, but we need to be cognisant of this diversity [. . .], yet not cast festival art films, or exilic and diasporic filmmaking as uniquely privileged sites of transnational filmmaking".

Paul Cooke steps up next to explore the changing geopolitical landscape of global film culture—24 "Soft power" and shifting patterns of influence in global film culture. His focus here is the BRICS grouping that emerged around the same time as Joseph Nye's soft power theory, which identifies the "power of attraction" as being potentially more influential in contemporary international relations than the "hard power" of "coercion or payments". Some of the BRICS nations (China and India in particular, but also Russia and to a lesser extent South Africa and Brazil) provide fascinating illustrations of using film as a soft-power asset, both in terms of film production and the development of national narratives on screen. As Cooke asserts, "Hollywood has long been a soft-power asset, regularly deployed by the government to support its drive to communicate the benefits of its value system, of democracy and the potential of the 'American Dream'". But the growing power and influence of Chinese production companies in Hollywood, and the concerted effort of the Indian government to harness the Bollywood phenomenon in order to promote a desired national narrative that appeals to the politically and economically influential Indian diaspora, demonstrate that a potential power shift is taking place in the filmmaking landscape spurred on by the soft-power ambitions of national governments.

Lúcia Nagib's chapter—25 Realist cinema as World Cinema—seeks to examine and problematise the premise that "realism" is the common denominator across World Cinema. For Nagib, problems arise in the barely challenged formulation of Thomas Elsaesser (2009) that European arthouse/auteur cinema (and by extension, World Cinema) has always defined itself against Hollywood on the basis of its greater realism. These problems include the "Hollywood (or Europe) versus the rest of the world" binary that much World Cinema theory seeks to avoid, including Nagib's own widely-cited formulations, as well as the implicit assumption that World Cinema depends on its "artistic and auteurist pedigree". Nagib instead proposes locating realism at the point of production and in address, therefore defining realist cinema by "an ethics of the real that has bound world films together across history and geography at cinema's most creative peaks". Films discussed in this context include *The Act of Killing* (2012, UK/Denmark/Norway, Joshua Oppenheimer), *In film nist* (This Is Not a Film, 2011, Iran, Jafar Pahini) and *Crime Delicado* (Delicate Crime, 2006, Brazil, Beto Brant). Nagib concludes by proposing "realist" cinema as a more accurate term than "world" or "modern" cinema to signify this ethics.

If transnational cinema (Chapter 23) constitutes one pole of our remapping of World Cinema, then regional cinema constitutes the other. Both problematise the predominance of the national as a means of geographically categorising cinema, pointing towards other scales of relationship and interaction. However, the national, the regional and the transnational should not be understood in opposition to one another, but rather as points along a continuum; individual films may orient themselves towards one end but few (if any) films are wholly and unequivocally national, regional or transnational. Drawing on a range of examples from around the globe, **Alex Marlow-Mann** poses the question of how one might define, theorise or study a regional cinema—26 Regional cinema: micro-mapping and glocalisation. Employing the concept of "glocalisation", he argues that the regional should be understood primarily not in relation to the national, but to the global, and thus the increased emphasis on regionalism in recent years should be considered a logical consequence of globalisation. While the "transnational turn" in Film Studies has done much to revise and enhance our understanding of film, he argues that its current seeming ubiquity risks homogenising disparate film cultures and obscuring difference. To counterbalance this disparity, Film Studies requires a "regional turn", one that allows for the "micro-mapping" of regional production realities, film cultures and the circulation of films.

While a large body of scholarship on women filmmakers and feminist theory has emerged since the 1970s, much of this originates in, and is centred upon, Europe or the West. Explorations of women's cinema have therefore tended to neglect the longitudinal in favour of the latitudinal. However, as **Kate Ince** argues—27 Global women's cinema—there have been moves to redress this balance and "In the twenty-first century, a literature suggesting that women's cinema be considered as (a) world cinema has begun to emerge". Ince thus maps the contours of this emerging field of study, as well as providing snapshots of women's filmmaking around the globe in the early twenty-first century. She notes the emergence of women filmmakers in a number of contexts from which they had previously been absent (most notably East Asia, and Central and Latin America), the continuing dearth of sub-Saharan female filmmakers, and the surprising role played by Middle Eastern (and in particular Iranian) women filmmakers, not to mention the important role of the diaspora in relation to women's filmmaking from various of these regions. Ince's essay is thus predicated on a "de-Westernisation" of women's cinema, which derives from the de-Westernisation of film studies pioneered by Saer Maty Bâ and Will Higbee that informs several chapters of this volume.

The intersection of queer sexualities with globality has become an increasingly visible flashpoint in world politics, but it is also present in culture, and particularly in World Cinema. In their co-written chapter—28 Provincialising heterosexuality: queer style, World Cinema—**Rosalind Galt** and **Karl Schoonover** ask whether "something like a coherent queer global style be identified?" In contrast to narrow definitions of queer cinema that focus only on Western forms and LGBT identities, the authors insist that "all non-normative modes of being and the texts that register them contribute to queer cinema and its global life". They argue that in queer film studies "to ignore short films and genres outside of art cinema is often to exclude the practices of queer women and of filmmakers in the Global South". Taking their inspiration from Dipesh Chakrabarty's influential work of postcolonial theory *Provincializing Europe* (2000), the authors aim to "reframe World Cinema *both* without installing Europe and America as the source of film style upon which all other iterations of film style are based *and* without assuming heterosexuality [. . .] as the necessary precondition and determinant of the cinematic experience". They further argue that Raymond Williams' concept of "structures of feeling" can be appropriated in order to think of style in relation to queer cinema because "looking for a queer structure of feeling in contemporary world cinema leads us to discern in cinematic styles the condensation of queer experiences that form resistant modes of being and indeed propose different worlds".

Turning our attention from films to their stars, it is fair to say that while some scholarly texts provide exceptions to prove the rule (Meeuf and Raphael 2013; Wing-Fai and Willis 2014; Bergfelder *et al.* 2016), most of the scholarly work that has been carried out on film stars focuses on white Americans. As **Ginette Vincendeau** observes—29 Stars across borders: the vexed question of stars' exportability—, "for many viewers and scholars alike, 'stardom' and 'the star system' have long been synonymous with Hollywood" and this fact is underlined by foundational work within star studies: "Whether we like it or not, the hold of (mostly white) English-speaking Hollywood stars on worldwide audiences continues apace." Vincendeau focuses on four French stars similar in age and profile: Jean Dujardin, Omar Sy, Audrey Tautou and Marion Cotillard. The differences in their star texts reveal the "complex way in which gender intersects with international celebrity culture and national identity". Vincendeau reveals the advantage held by the two female stars when it comes to "crossing over" given that the fashion and cosmetics sectors with which they are associated are marked as feminine and French. Thus Tautou and Cotillard are "able to channel a version of French identity that has worldwide recognition thanks to its synergy with globally exportable brands". Audience research discussed by Huw Jones (Chapter 39) confirms Cotillard as one of the few non-US box-office draws for European film audiences, while Vincendeau reveals that in order for stars to stand a chance at being globally recognised, they must be a "major success at home, [have] the skills to perform convincingly in the host language and the ability for the star to practise the 'international vocabulary' that characterises the contemporary star-system within the global culture of commodities".

Mark Goodall—30 Film fusions: the cult film in World Cinema—follows other chapters in this volume in their rejection of the notion of World Cinema as "an esoteric 'other' to mainstream (Hollywood) film culture". Cult cinema, which he reads as "both culturally specific and yet transglobal" incorporates the more familiarly cult mondo, exploitation and animation/manga traditions, as well as "transglobal cult films" such as *Shalimar* (1978, India/USA, Kishan Shah) and those defined by Goodall as "non-Western cinema that exists entirely independently of neo-colonial traditions". Here he focuses on *Macunaíma* (1969, Brazil, Joaquim Pedro de Andrade) and the horror films of Zé do Caixão (Coffin Joe). Thus, Goodall's focus in this chapter is on "individual works of world film art that can be interpreted as, and have organically become, through a variety of chance and random processes, 'cult'". Goodall concludes that "thinking about the established World Cinema canon, one could view cult films as the 'unruly child' of the European arthouse movement and the 'serious' national cinemas of the post-war global film epoch. Nevertheless, it is clear that the critical aspects that make cult cinema what it is—transgressive, disruptive and carnivalesque—are worth examining and enrich the cinematic output of a particular geographical space."

One of the characteristics of contemporary cinema to emerge from this volume is the emphasis on small or peripheral cinemas, alternative modes of productions that challenge the mainstream, and the increasing (geographic) diversity of World Cinema. However, the corollary to this process is the increasing dominance of an ever more circumscribed and repetitive global (Hollywood) mainstream most clearly embodied by superhero franchises. Such films are typically dismissed by critics for their repetitiveness, redundancy and supposed lack of ambition or imagination. Any understanding of their global dominance is typically couched in an analysis of box-office figures and ideas of cultural hegemony. Provocatively, in his chapter—31 Perpetual motion pictures: Sisyphean burden and the global screen franchise—**James Walters** wonders whether it is possible to advance a more positive interpretation of such films and thus a more productive explanation of their (global) appeal. Drawing on Albert Camus' alternative reading of the myth of Sisyphus, he argues that the significance of these films lies not in their lack of resolution or innovation, but rather in their emphasis on the endless and repetitive struggles faced by their protagonists. Such a reading, Walters argues, means that the films, apparently so far removed from the reality of their audience's lives, become significant in relation to the struggles of everyday life.

One of the key touchstones for many of the chapters in this volume is film festivals, testimony not only to their importance for the contemporary film industry and culture, but also of the role they play in localising cinema and thus shaping (longitudinal) conceptions of World Cinema. **Marije de Valck**—32 Screening World Cinema at film festivals: festivalisation and (staged) authenticity—traces the historical evolution of film festivals in relation to their role as shapers of World Cinema: from showcases of individual national cinemas in the inter-war and immediate post-war years, to promoters of new waves which were responsible for the "discovery" of new national cinemas and an enlargement of the World Cinema canon between the 1960s and the 1980s, and then as agents, facilitators and producers in the 1990s, playing an active role in shaping the World Cinema landscape. Such a role is not without its contradictions and limitations, above all in the implicitly neo-colonialist agendas that can limit, constrain or distort the cinemas from other parts of the world they hope to support (Chapter 7, 13, 14, 15). De Valck explores this in great detail through the case study of the Oscar-nominated film *Tanna* (2015, Australia, Bentley Dean and Martin Butler), arguing that its representation of the South Pacific Vanuatu island is characterised by a supposed "authenticity" that reveals itself to have been largely staged for the benefit of the festival circuit. While the emphasis on "authenticity" is closely tied up with the goal of promoting World Cinema that has characterised the film festival from its earliest days, the future of film festivals is nonetheless "tied up with a sustainable commitment to cultural diversity and a willingness to attend to its complexities".

The resurgence of interest in cinephilia is one of the most striking developments in Film Studies in the new millennium. However, as **Belén Vidal** observes—33 Cinephilia goes global: loving cinema in the post-cinematic age—there are numerous significant differences between the first and second waves of cinephilia. First, there has been a shift from scarcity to abundance, with films from all over the globe and from all periods of history now available at a click. Second, there has been a shift away from collective viewing in the cinema auditorium to individual viewing on a variety of home video and internet platforms. Third, cinephilia has lost its synchronicity with its object of love, as viewers cling to the films of yesteryear and become filled with nostalgia. And finally, there has been an increase in participation, which has challenged the Eurocentric nature of twentieth-century cinephilia, creating possibilities for technologically enabled "global synchronicity" and "new opportunities for a horizontal re-mapping of cinephilia".

Vito Zagarrio's treatment of the interaction between film and history adopts a dual focus: longitudinal (examining the shifts between the European debates of the 1970s to the Anglo-American scholars of the 1990s and beyond) and latitudinal (addressing how technological, historical and political changes have transformed both cinema's engagement with history and with Film Studies conception of the relationship between the two). In his chapter—34 Another (hi)story? Re-investigating the relationship between cinema and history—Zagarrio argues that while the first (principally European) film historians were concerned primarily with clear-cut historical narratives and placed a great emphasis on ideology, more recent scholars (particularly in Anglo-American contexts) have read films from a wide range of genres and dealing with different time periods (right up to contemporary reality) from a historical perspective: "Thus the question has shifted from being the identification and (ideologically driven) analysis of 'the historical film' to using the concept of film as history as a method to analyse a wide range of films and genres." This shift caught up with broader ideas and discourses around the rise of post-modernism, the "loss of the real" and the "unrepresentability of history", but also result from technological changes (in particular the rise of digital cinema and CGI) and are embodied above all in contemporary war films such as *American Sniper* (2015, USA, Clint Eastwood).

The term "archival cinema" gained prominence with the rise of digital cinema and refers broadly to analogue film from a historically remote period; its status as archival cinema is conferred primarily by viewer's expected recognition that it is based on "old film[s]". However, as **Paolo Cherchi Usai** explains—35 Archival cinema—any definition of archival cinema is inherently problematic given that the term means different things to different constituencies and in different geographic contexts. It can be used to refer to moving images on either celluloid or digital/electronic media (providing that the original archival source is on celluloid), to original footage (e.g. a newsreel) or reconfigured footage (e.g. a compilation film), to films preserved in an archive/museum or found footage and old home movies, and regardless of intent or the way in which it is used (as historical evidence or artwork, in a manner appropriate to its original purpose or antithetical to it). To explode the complexities and contradictions inherent in this status, Cherchi Usai surveys both the terminology used to refer to archival films in a number of languages, revealing different understandings of and relationships to archival films in a range of (longitudinally) diverse contexts, and drawing on an often surprising variety of films, prompting us to interrogate where the boundaries of archival cinema can or should be located. Finally, he proposes a new and as yet unanswered complementary question: whether or not there is (or can be) such a thing as a "digital archival film"?

In the next chapter—36 Digital cinemas—**Sean Cubitt** demonstrates how digital technologies have not only affected archives (Chapter 35) but have altered the terms of all the major areas of film: finance, production and post-production, distribution and consumption, meaning that now "cinema is digital from conception to delivery". In some instances (synchronising sound and visual edits hemispheres apart, and the production of animated films, for example) these new technologies permit a "radical globalisation of cinema production". However, Cubitt questions (as many other contributors in the volume do) whether new developments such as digital filmmaking bring genuine and greater democratisation to the filmmaking landscape. He also considers the impact of the digital capture of images on the analysis of realism, which, as we have seen across a number of chapters (1, 25) continues to lie at the heart of much discussion of World Cinema. Cubitt concludes that "we might understand digital cinema as a cinema that embraces its own ideological formation in the form of a significant ambiguity about its truth status".

Virginia Crisp echoes Cubitt's reflections on the shifting film landscape, whereby "nothing has changed, and yet everything has". Crisp suggests that while some new intermediaries or gatekeepers have appeared on the scene, many of the old ones (the traditional professional film distributors, for example) continue to hold on to their power. Thus, while she argues in her chapter—37 Access and power: film distribution, re-intermediation and piracy—that piracy and file sharing should be included within the definition of media distribution "and should be understood not as marginal practices but as central drivers of the global distribution of film", she also recognises that, given that US big-budget, proactively distributed movies dominate piracy and file sharing, "an era of limitless content, rather than putting the power in the hands of the consumer, returns power squarely to the gatekeeper". That said, Crisp also acknowledges that, crucially for our study of World Cinema, "before heralding the new dawn of an era of unprecedented choice, we must consider that not everyone has access to the same services, in the same way, and under the same conditions".

The advent of digital technology and Web 2.0 has been one of the most dramatic factors in the reshaping of World Cinema, as many of the contributions to this volume have shown. This is not limited to the circulation of films, but also to both the nature of original content and the way in which it is produced. Drawing on extensive interviews with creators, executives, technology integrators and policy makers, **Stuart Cunningham** and **David Craig** document this new "screen ecology", and its dramatic effects in their co-written chapter—38 The emerging global screen ecology of social media entertainment—the challenging of the dominant producers of moving image entertainment by new tech firms (Amazon, YouTube, Netflix), the rise of social media entertainment, the monetisation and professionalisation of previously amateur content creators, and the consequent dramatic shift in global reach.

Much research in the field of World Cinema still remains focused on the analysis of films as texts, and on the contexts in which they are produced. **Huw D. Jones**—39 Remapping World Cinema through audience research—underscores the insights that can be gained from "box-office figures, audience surveys and focus groups", along with new techniques in making use of the audience data now available online, such as webscraping and data-mining. Jones's focus here is on audience research in relation to the consumption of European film in countries of the European Union, but his chapter also includes reflections on films from both the USA and the so-called "rest of the world". Research of this kind to date has tellingly revealed, for example, that in relation to the "national" question, "theatre admissions for US films tend to be highest in small countries with a weak national film industry" and film audiences identify themselves along national, rather than transnational or global lines. Like Virginia Crisp (Chapter 36), Jones sees the positive in Video on Demand: in EU countries the relatively wide variety of films available via VoD currently debunks the myth that one of the main obstacles to greater consumption of non-Hollywood fare is lack of exhibition space. Even in the context of regular cinema-going, Jones reminds us that "even though [. . .] only 2 per cent of cinema admissions in Europe are for films from the rest of the world, this still represents about 20 million cinemagoers per year". And given the increase in scholarly interest in film festivals, it is interesting to note that, with the exception of high-profile auteurs such as Pedro Almodóvar, festival success features quite low down in terms of "bait to attendance", with "the story" and "genre/type of film" playing a more significant role in decisions to watch "foreign" films.

In the final chapter in this companion—40 Eyes on the future: World Cinema and transnational capacity building—**Mette Hjort** provides us with a case study of what she has usefully defined as "milieu-building transnationalism", with a view to looking beyond the peaks of cinematic creation "to the ground where the conditions for different types of film-related success are being prepared". Focusing on Nordic/African partnerships, and those stemming from Denmark in particular, she highlights the role of human rights thinking in the context of North/South collaborations with a focus on film. What is particularly striking, beyond the success stories (the films themselves, widening participation in filmmaking in Mali, Uganda and Burkina Faso, etc., post-production capacity building, and so on) and the constraints (e.g. security issues in the lands of Islamic Maghreb and "cultural differences regarding hierarchy/authority and equality in professional interaction") is the fact that the wealth of film partnerships sponsored by the Danish Centre for Culture and Development (CKU) have ended. Hjort identifies this policy shift (one that is currently occurring in a number of other film cultures) as "symptomatic of neoliberal priorities, political expediency, and a diminished appetite for funding not only development work, but also culture".

In sum, while this volume provides us with much to celebrate, we also recognise the danger that changing political winds and technological shifts pose to the kinds of film production, distribution and consumption that its contributors have sought to hold up to the light. As the forty chapters demonstrate, the task of constantly remapping World Cinema is as Sisyphean as that explored by James Walters in relation to the struggles of superheroes (Chapter 31). Several of the contributors have extended their research into monographs already, such as Rosalind Galt and Karl Schoonover's *Queer Cinema in the World* (2016) and Geoff King's *Art Cinema: Positioning Films and the Construction of Cultural Value* (2018). Others are currently working on monographs that will appear in the complementary Routledge series *Remapping World Cinema: Regional Tensions and Global Transformations*, which is co-edited by the same team as this volume, and for which this Companion duly acts as a kind of flagship. These include David Martin-Jones on transworld cinemas, Felicity Gee on magical realism in World Cinema, Stephanie Dennison on Brazilian film culture, Dunja Fehimović on Caribbean cinemas of relation, and several others whose chapters are thus akin to trailers. Work on World Cinema never stops; but the need to pause occasionally, measure progress, and plot our future course is essential if we are to continue to understand the global reach and meaning of film, to contextualise its expression, and project our fears and ambitions onto World Cinema as a vehicle, platform and medium of human interconnectedness and the audio-visual communication of ideas, and as a global network extending via invitations to empathy. To this end, we chose our cover image from *Bu san* (Goodbye, Dragon Inn, 2003, Taiwan, Tsai Ming-liang) because it spoke to us of nostalgia and resolve, two elements that guided our hand in the selection of themes and contributors, whose respect for the past does not obviate recognition of the need for change, even though this may obliterate traditions. In *Goodbye, Dragon Inn*, a cinema in Taipei, Taiwan, is closing down and the occasion is marked by a screening of *Long men kezhan* (Dragon Inn, 1967, Taiwan, King Hu), a classic of the *wuxia* genre that fills patrons and employees alike with a love of film that extends to the ghosts in the cinema, who appear both enraptured and fearful, their fate caught up in that of the film and the building, their home that faces dereliction. For all the martial arts and swordplay action on the screen-within-the-screen, however, the cinema-within-the-cinema is hushed and somewhat mournful for the passing of the celluloid era. Nevertheless, if *The Routledge Companion to World Cinema* has been constructed and is read correctly by following its lines of latitude and longitude till coordinates meet, it will offer a guide of sorts, a plan of a kind, and a map of some resemblance to both the analogue lands below and the digital skies above what we lovingly refer to as World Cinema.

References

Andrew, D. (2012) "Off the Grid of Global Art", Keynote delivered to the SOCINE annual conference, São Paulo, Brazil.

Bergfelder, T., Shaw, L. and Vieira J. L. (eds) (2016) *Stars and Stardom in Brazilian Cinema*, New York and Oxford: Berghahn.

Bowyer, J. and Choi, J. (2004) *The Cinema of Japan and Korea*, London: Wallflower Press.

Chakrabarty, D. (2007) *Provincializing Europe: Postcolonial Thought and Historical Difference*, Princeton, NJ and Oxford: Princeton University Press.

Dennison, S. and Lim, S. H. (2006) "Situating World Cinema as a Theoretical Problem", in Dennison, S. and Lim, S. H. (eds) *Remapping World Cinema: Identity, Culture and Politics in Film*, London: Wallflower Press, 1–15.

Galt, R. and Schoonover, K. (eds) (2010) *Global Art Cinema: New Theories and Histories*, Oxford: Oxford University Press.

Galt, R. and Schoonover, K. (2016) *Queer Cinema and the World*, Durham, NC: Duke University Press Books.

Iordanova, D., Martin-Jones, D. and Vidal, D. (eds) (2010) *Cinema at the Periphery*, Detroit, MI: Wayne State University Press.

Kosoff, M. and Jacobs, H. (2015) "The 15 Most Popular YouTubers in the World", *Business Insider UK*, http://uk.businessinsider.com/the-most-popular-youtuber-stars-in-the-world/#15-ksi-1, 18 September.

Meeuf, R. and Raphael, R. (eds) (2013) *Transnational Stardom: International Celebrity in Film and Popular Culture*, New York: Palgrave Macmillan.

Nagib, L., Perriam, C. and Dudrah, R. (eds) (2011) *Theorizing World Cinema*, London: I. B. Tauris.

Wing-Fai, L. and Willis, A. (eds) (2014) *East Asian Film Stars*, Basingstoke: Palgrave Macmillan.

PART I

Longitude

1

THE CINEMATIC AND THE REAL IN CONTEMPORARY CHINESE CINEMA

Yingjin Zhang

Introduction: the cinematic and the real

In the cinematic landscape, the real is never a pure ontological entity transferred directly from the external world. At the birth of cinema, when the Lumière Brothers were thrilled at capturing reality in documentary shorts such as *L'Arrivée d'un Train en Gare de La Ciotat* (*Arrival of a Train at La Ciotat*, 1895, France), Georges Méliès would soon discover the cinematic capacity for manipulating images and visualising fantasies in fiction films such as *Le Voyage dans La Lune* (A Trip to the Moon, 1902, France). Méliès's fantasy and Lumière's reality were subsequently postulated as two distinct traditions in early cinema, although filmmakers tend to posit reality as their primary end and fiction as the means to that end; indeed, scholars believe the two traditions eventually merged in Hollywood's classical cinema (Katz 1994: 854, 927). Yet, with the advent of postmodernism, the real is increasingly seen as mediated by technological apparatus and human intervention, and "reality" is claimed as "always-already present in people's minds as textual fabrication, model, or simulation that in fact precede reality or even generate it" (Shaul 2008: 48). In documentary film studies, the tension between reality and representation is perceived as unresolvable in

> the perennial Bazin *vs* Baudrillard tussle, both of whom—from opposite perspectives—argue for the erosion of any differentiation between the image and reality, Bazin because he believed reality could be recorded, Baudrillard because he believes reality is just another image.
>
> *(Bruzzi 2000: 4)*

In contemporary Chinese cinema, this sense of the real as a creatively constructed image rather than a politically postulated, "objective" referent to the empirically verifiable external world would exert a tremendous impact on filmmaking in the post-Mao period (since 1976). After three previous decades of strict ideological control and oftentimes-brutal political repressions, in the early 1980s Chinese filmmakers gradually learned to expand their visions of the real beyond those authorised by the Communist Party. Thirty-five years since then, the real in Chinese cinema has appeared to pertain more to individual perception and interpretation than to ideological promulgation and political administration, although the party-state still maintains the power of propaganda and censorship. Given this situation, the cinematic landscape of the real has developed into a site of contention, and realities of various kinds have gone through continual reconstructions, often in relation to what is alleged to be unreal or no longer real.

On China's post-Mao screen, socialist realism—the "official brand" that "forgets realism's realist potential and capacity for critical questioning of established conventions and reality", has become "no longer real and is out of touch with the actual conditions of society" (Wang 2008: 498). With its formulaic typical characters and its teleological vision of history, socialist realism (Y. Zhang 2004: 202–205) was discredited by two prominent groups of Chinese avant-garde filmmakers. First, in the mid-1980s, the Fifth Generation of directors (e.g., Chen Kaige, Zhang Yimou), who were so named because they mostly came from the fifth class admitted to the Beijing Film Academy, began to distance themselves from the urban centre of *realpolitik* by directing their camera at the breath-taking rural *landscape* in an attempt to retrieve memories of Chinese national culture and history repressed in dominant Communist narratives. Second, in the early 1990s, the Sixth Generation (e.g., Zhang Yuan, Wang Xiaoshuai) started to delve into the *mindscape* of alienated urban souls so as to reinstate their own individual perceptions of the real; along the way they challenged both the official media's hackneyed versions of Chinese reality and the Fifth Generation's reinvented Chinese tradition in its "ethnographic cinema", which was popular in the international arthouse circuit for a while (Chow 1995; Y. Zhang 2002: 207–239). Entering the twenty-first century, several young independent directors (e.g., Jia Zhangke, Ying Liang) have reconstructed the cinematic real by revisiting rural and hinterland landscapes, but this time not to fix them as readily decipherable symbols of China or Chineseness but to project a precarious sense of landscape in motion.

The idea of "landscape in motion" derives from twin realisations that nature and culture specific to a locality are increasingly subjugated to transnational, translocal flows in the current age of globalisation and that sometimes the cinematic is the only means of capturing the real in transformation or even in ruins. The flows of capital and labour have further compelled independent directors to move toward the *ethnoscape*, which Arjun Appadurai defines as

> the landscape of persons who constitute the shifting world in which we live: tourists, immigrants, refugees, exiles, guest workers, and other moving groups and individuals [who] constitute an essential feature of the world and appear to affect the politics of (and between) nations to a hitherto unprecedented degree.
>
> *(1996: 33)*

In addition to ethnoscape, Appadurai delineates four other major spheres of globalisation: mediascape, technoscape, financescape and ideoscape. To reframe Appadurai's vision of current global flows for Chinese cinema, we can conceptualise the party-state sector of film enterprise as a propagandist ideoscape centred on politics and power, the commercial sector as a mediascape anchored on capital and profits, the art film sector as a mindscape inclined toward aesthetics and prestige, and the independent sector as an ethnoscape aligned with marginality and truth (Y. Zhang 2010: 43–48).

In what follows, I first discuss the Fifth Generation's rediscovery of "the real" by way of confronting the natural landscape, which enabled them to project a vision of national culture distinct from that endorsed by Communist historiography. Second, I analyse the Sixth Generation's passion for individual perception, their exploration of the mindscape of urban youths and their persistent claims to truth and reality. Third, I turn to a group of young independent directors who emphasise polylocality and the deliberate integration of fiction and documentary in their depiction of an ethnoscape of precarious mobility and private memory. By analysing landscape, mindscape, and ethnoscape as three intertwined tropes, as well as nature, truth, and polylocality as three focal concerns, this chapter seeks to advance our understanding of a complex, on-going process of negotiation between the cinematic and the real in contemporary Chinese cinema.

The Fifth Generation's landscape of nature: in search of national culture

Martin Lefebvre draws attention to two issues when approaching landscape and cinema. First, according to Sergei Eisenstein, landscape is "the least burdened with servile, narrative tasks, and the most flexible in conveying moods, emotional states, and spiritual experiences" (1987: 217). In other words, cinematic landscape enjoys certain autonomy from narrative and therefore induces interpretations and emotions that may not fit a film's plot-driven actions. Second, for cultural geographers, "landscapes do not exist independently of human investment toward space, which is one way of distinguishing them from the idea of 'nature' [. . . for nature] would likely continue to exist" without human intervention (Lefebvre 2006: xiii). It is through human actions that nature and the environment are transformed into the landscape. The etymology of "landscape" (along with its earlier versions, "landskip" and "landtskip") traces its suffix to "-shaft", "-scipe", "-ship" and other related terms such as "gesceape", "gescape", and "ishapen" all of which mean "to give form or shape". Lefebvre reasons that human perception through certain mental "framing" is what gives form to the otherwise "formless" natural environment: "With that frame nature turns into culture, land into landscape" (Lefebvre 2006: xv). Landscapes, therefore, reflect human experiences.

The Fifth Generation announced their arrival with two avant-garde films that feature the significance of landscape over that of narrative plot and dialogue. In *Yi ge he ba ge* (One and Eight, 1984, China, Zhang Junzhao) and *Huang tu di* (Yellow Earth, 1984, China, Chen Kaige), the experimental use of minimal plot and dialogue compels the viewer to contemplate

Figure 1.1 Communist soldier Gu Qing emerging into the horizon of Loess Plateaus in *Huang tu di* (Yellow Earth, 1984, China, Chen Kaige). ©Guangxi Film Studio.

the awe-inspiring barren landscapes in central China. *Yellow Earth*, in particular, presents the lands and ravines of Loess Plateaus along the meandering Yellow River in Shaanxi province (Figure 1.1). In sharp contrast to its overwhelming visual images, *Yellow Earth* contains very little in terms of narrative or character development, and its uncanny landscapes puzzled contemporary viewers who had been entrenched for decades in socialist realism that insisted on explaining every detail of a film.

Chen Kaige offered this instruction to his film crew: "in terms of cinematic structure, I want our film to be rich and variable, free to the point of wildness [. . .] The quintessence of our style can be summed up in a single word: 'hanxu'(concealment)" (Barmé and Minford 1988: 259). This style of *hanxu* was radical then in that it refused to restage the party-endorsed myths of the Chinese revolution, its prolonged shots of the natural landscape challenging the film establishment. Xia Yan, a ranking film bureaucrat and veteran screenwriter from the 1930s, admitted his discomfort: "I simply fail to understand how people so close to Yan'an could remain completely untouched by the new spirit that came from Yan'an" (Barmé and Minford 1988: 267)—Yan'an here being the Communist headquarters in the early 1940s. What is absent in *Yellow Earth* is the received historical wisdom—namely that Chinese peasants always awakened to their innate revolutionary spirit once they were mobilised by the Communists.

This absence is most powerfully staged in the film's final scene, where the Communist solider Gu Qing returns to a village devastated by drought. After a long sequence of an all-male crowd of superstitious peasants praying for rain to a dragon king statue, the taciturn boy Hanhan seems to catch sight of Gu and rushes against the frenetic crowd to greet him. However, through a series of cross cuts, Gu appears to be caught on the horizon, as if he were a mirage flickering between the empty sky and the parched land. The off-screen song sung by Cuiqiao, Hanhan's elder sister, only intensifies this optical illusion, for the viewer knows by this point that Cuiqiao was forced into an arranged marriage and was drowned while attempting to escape across the Yellow River, singing a revolutionary song without finishing the phrase "Communist Party", the organisation that would "save the people".

Two interpretations of the final sequence are worth contemplating. First, Esther Yau hints at an unyielding presence in *Yellow Earth*, namely a "simple Taoist philosophy which (dis)empowers the text by (non)affirming speaking and looking: 'Silence is the Roaring Sound, Formless is the Image Grand'" (1987–88: 32). This idea, taken from the Daoist classic *Dao de jing*, "great music has no sound (*dayin wusheng*), the great image has no form (*daxiang wuxing*)", supports the film's extensive use of silence and empty space, which works to empower the viewer to distance themselves from the illusion promulgated by the rhetoric of *realpolitik* and to reconnect with the real through the wordless contemplation of the natural landscape. Second, even though the Fifth Generation was initially fascinated with the Daoist rendition of landscape, their ultimate concerns remained with the human world. According to the film's cinematographer Zhang Yimou, their landscape images were designed to capture "the sustaining strength and endurance of a nation" (Barmé and Minford 1988: 259). Through wordless images and avant-garde techniques, the emergent Fifth Generation sought to articulate a new sense of the real radically different from the socialist construction of history and reality, ultimately aspiring to present a new representation of the Chinese nation.

In hindsight, it is ironic that the Fifth Generation first found their receptive audiences not inside China but overseas, and their growing international fame would soon undermine the radical manner in which they redefined the cinematic real through uncanny landscape. After *Red Sorghum* (Zhang Yimou, 1987) won the first Golden Bear for Chinese cinema at the 1988 Berlin Film Festival, natural and cultural landscapes took on a different meaning on the international screen. Increasingly, exotic cultural practices characterised Fifth Generation productions, and erotic sexuality became prominent. From *Ju Dou* (1989, China/Japan) to *Da hong deng long gao gao gua* (Raise the Red Lantern, 1991, China/Hong Kong/Taiwan), Zhang Yimou's overseas-funded art films of the period showed increasingly less open landscapes and more enclosed—even claustrophobic—spaces. Just as Zhang's screen protagonists quickly changed from rebels to conformists, his audiences were lured into a mesmerizing display of Orientalist motifs as quintessential images of "Chinese" culture. In the meantime, even the natural landscape had lost its transformative power at the hands of the Fifth Generation, and the stunning beauty of desolate terrains in western China provided but an empty stage for enacting an enigmatic tale of dedication, desire, and desperation.

The Sixth Generation's mindscape of youth: in defence of individual perception

In the early 1990s, the emergent Sixth Generation began to question cultural traditions reinvented by the Fifth Generation and lamented the lack of a "sense of reality" (*xianshi gan*) in Chinese filmmaking (Cheng and Huang 2002: 31). For them, to return to the real was to venture from history to reality, from the countryside to the city, from overloaded symbols to contingent situations, from gorgeous landscapes to precarious mindscapes (Z. Zhang 2007). For example, Sixth Generation filmmaker Zhang Yuan's way of recapturing the real was to draw inspiration from "real people and real events" (*zhenren zhenshi*), as he did in *Mama* (1991, China), which cast a real-life autistic boy and his agonizing mother forsaken by an indifferent society. Likewise, Wang Xiaoshuai cast a real-life artist couple in *Dongchun de Rizi* (The Days, 1993, China), which ends with a narcissistic moment when Dong (played by the Chinese artist and actor Liu Xiaodong) talks to himself in front of a mirror. Wang continued in this vein in *Jidu Hanleng* (Frozen, 1997, China), a fictional re-creation of the shocking suicide of Qi Lei, a Beijing performance artist, adopting a minimalist documentary style (*jilu fengge*). Indeed, documentary aesthetics are characteristic of the emergent Sixth Generation in general (in part constrained by their independent low-budget productions). Zhang Yuan, for instance, integrated into his fiction film, *Beijing za zhong* (Beijing Bastards, 1993, China), a large portion of documentary rehearsal footage of Cui Jian, the first rock star in China and a symbol of rebellion in the immediate aftermath of the 1989 Tiananmen Square Incident.

Nonetheless, it would be wrong to take early Sixth Generation films as exemplary of a desire for pursuing reality as it is. Just as the Fifth Generation was fascinated with the real beyond their natural landscapes, the Sixth Generation intended their documentary-like urban images to convey a specific type of truth characterised by psychological complexity. While acknowledging that *zhenshi* ("truth" or "the real") is the weapon each new generation of filmmakers uses to blaze a new path for themselves, Zhang Ming categorically dismissed any sense that his films are intent upon presenting "life as it is" (*xiang shenghuo benlai yiyang*) and questioned: "Who has ever captured the real? The real itself never exists in a work of art. What we have is the author's vivid imagination (*bizhen de xiangxiang*), his attitude, taste, sensibility, and personality" (2003: 28).

Among the Sixth Generation, Zhang Ming is not alone in highlighting the indispensable role of the artist's imagination and sensibility in reconstructing the real. Jia Zhangke likewise contends that what is important to a film is not the real itself but the "rendition of the perception of the real" (*chenxian zhenshi gan*), and he further claims that "the perception of the real may not always come from directly capturing the outside world, for it may possibly come from subjective imagination" (Jia *et al.* 2007: 24). Not surprisingly, Jia's word "imagination" (*xiangxiang*) echoes Zhang Ming's, while his term "subjective" dovetails with this assertion by Jiang Wen, a popular male star-turned-film director: the more an artist is subjective, the better the film becomes, because "everything is subjective, and objectivity resides in subjectivity" (Cheng and Huang 2002: 77).

For the Sixth Generation, *zhenshi* is inevitably filtered through subjective perception, and their cinematic real therefore emerges as a series of mindscapes. What Jia Zhangke seeks to convey in his underground trilogy—*Xiao Wu* (Pickpocket, 1997, China/Hong Kong), *Zhantai* (Platform, 2000, Hong Kong/China/Japan/France), and *Ren xiao yao* (Unknown Pleasures, 2002, China/Japan/South Korea/France)—is the "condition of life" (*shenghuo zhuangkuang*) as he experienced it in his hometown (Cheng and Huang 2002: 326). Similarly, Zhang Ming aims to capture in *Wu shan yun yu* (Rainclouds Over Wushan, 1995, China) the "mode of life" (*shengming zhuangtai*) of his hometown, "the real existence (*zhenshi cunzai*) that escapes the naked eye but can be sensed spiritually" (Cheng and Huang 2002: 25, 34).

The subjective grounding of the Sixth Generation's individualised perception of the real brings us to the manifesto-like statement, "My camera doesn't lie", which has come to characterise this group with regard to truth and reality. The statement first appeared as Lou Ye's idiosyncratic justification of his neo-noir feature, *Suzhou he* (Suzhou River, 2000, Germany/China/France), which deals as much with lies and betrayals as with unreliable memory and vanishing idealism in an elusive mindscape of Shanghai. Nonetheless, Lou argues that, as a filmmaker, he himself did not lie, despite all his tricks of cinematic doubling, narrative suspense, and optical illusions. After all, *Suzhou River* was started first as a documentary project (Y. Zhang 2002: 329–330) because Lou wanted to record the "real look" (*zhenshi mianmao*) of life along this once polluted river hidden behind the shining façade of a globalizing Shanghai (Cheng and Huang 2002: 258). Regardless of its documentary and fictional components, the film *Suzhou River*, to quote Lou Ye (Cheng and Huang 2002: 265), "can express my true impression (*zhenshi yinxiang*) of the Suzhou River. My camera doesn't lie (*sahuang*)". If we think through the implications of Lou's phrase, the real (*zhenshi*) for him relies first on "my impression" (as individual perception) and then "my camera" (as cinematic technology), which finally produces "my truth" (as coded in the filmic text).

The first-person possessive pronounced in the statement "my camera doesn't lie" foregrounds the agency given to the artist, whose individual perception of the real acquires a dynamic role in cinematic representation and who facilitates the integration of mindscape with landscape in the resulting film. Significantly, Jia Zhangke's and Zhang Ming's perceptions of the real in terms of *zhuangkuang* or *zhuangtai* (circumstance, condition, situation), as cited above, reveal a conception of the real as contingent, variable, and multivalent, rather than as an essence whose interpretation is reserved by the party-state (as in socialist realism) or whose symbolism is fixed in the natural landscape (as the Fifth Generation would have it). For the Sixth Generation, the mindscape of *zhenshi* is open to contradiction, and such contradiction is often scripted into an enigmatic "urban dreamscape", where "phantom sisters"—two lookalike female characters played by the same actress—challenge the male artist's ability to decipher a radically changing world (Z. Zhang 2007: 344–387), such as we see in *Suzhou River* and *Yue shi* (Lunar Eclipse, 1999, China, Wang Quan'an).

Independent directors' ethnoscape of polylocality: in the name of private memory

In the new century, there is a veritable shift of emphasis from the mindscape of the artist (often singular) to the ethnoscape of ordinary people (always plural) in a reconfiguration of *zhenshi* in Chinese cinema. Jia Zhangke's *Shijie* (The World, 2004, Chinea/Japan/France) is a study of labour migration set in Beijing. Rather than insisting on the artist's subjective perceptions

Figure 1.2 Migrant worker Han Sanming looking over the Yangtze River in *Sanxia haoren* (Still Life, 2006, China/Hong Kong, Jia Zhangke). ©Xstream Pictures/Shanghai Film Studios.

of the real as the early Sixth Generation did in the 1990s, Jia Zhangke and his younger colleagues tend to project their visions onto a series of ethnoscapes, of people who are forced to move around in search of opportunities. To be sure, such ethnoscapes are equally open to contradiction, just as the Sixth Generation's mindscapes from the 1990s were. This awareness of contradiction is evident in Jia Zhangke's description of what he perceives to be the reality of the Three Gorges area, the setting of the Yangtze River in his *Sanxia haoren* (Still Life, 2006, China/Hong Kong)—that is, a reality fraught with the absurd coexistence of "rationality and irrationality, progressiveness and backwardness, misery and optimism, vitality and repression" (Jia *et al.* 2007: 19) (Figure 1.2).

Two scenes in *Still Life* best illustrate Jia's imaginative merger of landscape and mindscape into a new ethnoscape. In the first, the male protagonist Han Sanming holds up a RMB banknote, which bears the picture of the Kuimen Gorge as national scenery, against the actual landscape he can see. Incidentally, Han first looks at the other side of the banknote, which bears a benevolent image of Mao Zedong, the supreme leader whose poetic vision of a man-made lake among mountains was partially responsible for the world's largest engineering project, the Three Gorges Dam. When Han flips over the banknote and the parallel landscapes on the banknote and in the background come into view, we realise that not only has the water level risen considerably higher but that Jia's creativity lies not so much in this visual comparison but in its symbolic evocation of political power over the natural landscape. Economic development, aided by national politics and transnational capital, has irreversibly changed the natural and cultural landscape of the area, resulting in over a million people being relocated and ancient relics being forever lost to the water.

In the second scene, which follows immediately after Han's puzzled look at the altered landscape, a flickering UFO flies across the Kuimen Gorge scenery, as if disturbed by the enormous change taking place in nature. Jia Zhangke's creative insertion of this surreal moment ties together two parallel narratives of troubled marriages. The scene continues with the UFO, but the onscreen character now is Shen Hong, a nurse from Jia's hometown province Shanxi. Other surreal moments in *Still Life* include a scene in which an oddly shaped concrete structure suddenly takes off like a rocket when no one is looking, and another when Han, on his way back to Shanxi with a group of local prospective coal miners, is dumbfounded to see a tiny human figure walking on a tight rope between two hazardous buildings that are set to be demolished.

Such surreal moments in *Still Life* serve as Jia Zhangke's attempt to delineate a landscape in motion or in ruins, which is staged now through the interaction of people on the move. At the beginning of the film, Han Sanming travels south from Shanxi and joins the local workers in demolishing deserted buildings in the soon-to-be-flooded ancient river town of Fengjie, and by the end of the film he is leading a group of workers north to Shanxi, where the prospective income from life-threatening coal-mining is higher than the already dangerous demolition jobs in Fengjie. By referencing the polylocality in China's changing labour market in the age of globalisation (including the industrial hubs of Guangdong further south and the financial centre of Shanghai to the east), *Still Life* hints at an ethnoscape in motion, where the locals may no longer be able to stay long term; their frustrated emotions constitute a desolate mindscape mirrored by the landscape in ruins.

Yet, Jia Zhangke is not alone in reconstructing a new sense of the real through an ethnoscape of polylocality. Just as Jia's fiction film *Still Life* uses elements of documentary, Ying Liang's *Ling yi ban* (The Other Half, 2006, China) stages documentary-like scenes in order to capture contradictions in a globalizing China. *The Other Half* follows Xiaofen, a secretary in a law office whose observation offers a rare kaleidoscopic view of the changing ethnoscape in Zigong, an inland city of Sichuan province. Many clients seek legal advice for their troubled marriages, and their cases vary from gold digging (a young wife intent on divorcing her rich husband without his prior knowledge) and domestic violence (an abused wife prohibited from divorcing her army husband due to a legal code protecting military marriages) to wasted youth (an old lady eager to divorce her husband on the grounds of theirs being a "loveless" arranged marriage that has lasted for decades) and child custody (a mother trying to convince her young son to accuse her ex-husband of child abuse). As more clients join these women in front of the camera to bare their souls to the viewer, it becomes obvious that *The Other Half* aims at enumerating widespread social problems in a series of animated talking-head interviews. As the camera captures people from different age groups and social backgrounds eagerly stating their cases, the viewer gradually comes to terms with a dismal reality that is taking place in and through these staged interviews.

Sure enough, the staged on-camera interviews in *The Other Half* add a feel of authenticity to the ethnoscape in transformation, and the actual television news footage of the military police enforcing the evacuation order following an explosion in a local chemical plant contributes to the film's reality effect. Moreover, the invisible poisonous fume that emerges from the plant serves as a metaphor for an inland city plagued by such widespread social problems as public health hazards, environmental pollution, traffic accidents, unemployment, gambling, drinking, teenage pregnancy, prostitution, human smuggling, robbery and murder. The film engineers a further twist to its blurred line between documentary and fiction when Xiaofen herself talks to the camera and seeks a legal opinion about her boyfriend, a murder suspect who has disappeared. The untimely death of her friend, a prostitute who dreamt of migrating to the United States, casts an ominous shadow on Xiaofen's fate. Suffering from chronic asthma, Xiaofen collapses on a bridge at the end of the film, and the long take of a deserted, eerily quiet city under an evacuation order is disturbed by a cell phone message from her boyfriend, who has travelled to Shanghai and started a restaurant business there.

Polylocality is a defining feature of the ethnoscape in transformation in a globalizing China. Rather than translocality, which implies a connection and movement between two or more localities, polylocality points to both the multiplicity of localities out there and the condition of unevenness in which localities are brought into translocality in radically different ways

(Y. Zhang 2010: 6–9). In *The Other Half*, Xiaofen falls down in the midst of poisonous fumes, while her boyfriend starts a new life in Shanghai and her father works on the faraway northwestern frontier of Xinjiang. By mixing documentary and fiction, films such as *The Other Half* and *Still Life*—and we can further cite Jia Zhangke's *Er she si cheng ji* (24 City, 2008, China/Hong Kong/Japan) in this regard, which features on-camera interviews with real-life and fictional characters, as well as his *Tian zhu ding* (A Touch of Sin, 2013, China/Japan/France), which consists of four fictional segments based on real-life tragic events—provide us with a unique way of reconstructing the globalizing China as an enormous ethnoscape in the midst of drastic transformation. Significantly, this time around the reconstruction of the real is filtered through the private memory not of an individual artist but of ordinary characters who never pretend to comprehend entirely what is happening to them or how they relate to the large-scale transformation of China in the age of globalisation.

Conclusion: the real versus realism

Despite radically different perceptions in the past three decades, what is remarkable about the cinematic and the real on China's post-Mao screen is that, in most cases, it is no longer superimposed from above but is tactically constituted from below. In the 1980s, the real was posited as an ontological entity and projected onto the natural landscape so as to keep its distance from the urban centre of *realpolitik*, a distance that empowered the Fifth Generation to reconstruct images of national culture and history beyond the Communist rhetoric. In the 1990s, the real was reconceptualised in an *existential* mode and internalised in the shifting mindscape of the urban youth, whose frustrations and pursuits enabled the Sixth Generation to conjure up improvised conditions of real life punctuated by alienation, contemplation, and rebellion. In the new century, the real is to be found in the process of verbal reminiscences of, or silent meditations on, things past and present, and these individual reminiscences and meditations find resonance in documentary-like observational images of historical traces left behind—or sometimes literally swallowed up—by a fast-moving society, as represented by independent filmmakers in a series of ethnoscapes in transformation.

Significantly, whereas Chinese independent filmmakers have consistently mobilised the claim to the real, they have also consistently avoided the topic of realism (either as *xianshi zhuyi* or *xieshi zhuyi*). One immediate reason is that realism, as an officially sanctioned concept in China for several decades in the mid-twentieth century, still carries negative connotations of cliché and propaganda (as in "socialist realism" or its equivalents, such as "revolutionary realism"). Another reason is that, rather than being restricted by certain aesthetic modes of representation, independent filmmakers aspire to remain creative with their own perceptions and renditions of the real, integrating those methods otherwise classified as contradictory or incompatible (e.g., both documentary and surreal in *Still Life*), and drawing on a wide array of cinematic genres and techniques, including animation (as in *The World*), or even resorting to television footage (as in *The Other Half*). For this generation, the real exists not only in mobility but also in mobilisation—mobility because they must actively chase after the real, and mobilisation because they must resort to a variety of cinematic means available to them. While a few scholars have explored the use of realism by independent Chinese filmmaking (McGrath 2008; Wang 2008), young filmmakers' consistent preference for *zhenshi* and *jishi* (documenting the real) is yet to enjoy detailed scrutiny. Here *zhenshi* and *jishi* work to keep alive an imaginative space in which these filmmakers can articulate their own visions of the past, present, and future. Their preference for the real (as something to be creatively retrieved and reconstructed) over realism (as an over-determined concept or a hackneyed formula) has enabled, and will continue to enable, them to project challenging new cinematic landscapes, mindscapes and ethnoscapes.

References

Appadurai, A. (1996) *Modernity at Large: Cultural Dimensions of Globalisation*, Minneapolis, MN: University of Minnesota Press.

Barmé, G. and Minford J. (eds) (1988) *Seeds of Fire: Chinese Voices of Conscience*, New York: Hill & Wang.

Bruzzi, S. (2000) *New Documentary: A Critical Introduction*, London: Routledge.

Cheng, Q. and Huang, O. (eds) (2002) *Wode sheyingji bu sahuang: xianfeng dianying ren dang'an—shengyu 1961–1970* Beijing: Zhongguo youyi chuban gongsi.

Chow, R. (1995) *Primitive Passions: Visuality, Sexuality, Ethnography, and Contemporary Chinese Cinema*, New York: Columbia University Press.

Eisenstein, S. M. (1987) *Nonindifferent Nature*, Herbert Marshall (trans.), Cambridge: Cambridge University Press.

Jia, Z., Rao, S., Zhou, Y. and Chen, X. (2007) "Sanxia haoren" (Still life), *Dangdai dianying* 2: 24.

Katz, E. (1994) *The Film Encyclopedia*, 2nd edn, New York: HarperCollins.

Lefebvre, M. (ed.) (2006) *Landscape and Film*, London: Routledge.

McGrath, J. (2008) *Postsocialist Modernity: Chinese Cinema, Literature, and Criticism in the Market Age*, Stanford, CA: Stanford University Press.

Shaul, N. B. (2008) "Morphing Realities: The Current Status of the Real in Film and Television", *Framework* 49 (1): 48–54.

Wang, B. (2008) "In Search of Real-Life Images in China: Realism in the Age of Spectacle", *Journal of Contemporary China* 17 (56): 497–512.

Yau, E. (1987–88) "*Yellow Earth*: Western Analysis and a Non-Western Text", *Film Quarterly* 41 (2): 32.

Zhang, M. (2003) *Zhaodao yizhong dianying fangfa*, Beijing: Zhonggguo guangbo dianshi chubanshe.

Zhang, Y. (2002) *Screening China: Critical Interventions, Cinematic Reconfigurations, and the Transnational Imaginary in Contemporary Chinese Cinema*, Ann Arbor, MI: Center for Chinese Studies, University of Michigan.

—— (2004) *Chinese National Cinema*, London: Routledge.

—— (2010) *Cinema, Space, and Polylocality in a Globalizing China*, Honolulu: University of Hawaii.

Zhang, Z. (ed.) (2007) *The Urban Generation: Chinese Cinema and Society at the Turn of the Twenty-First Century*, Durham, NC: Duke University Press.

2

SOUTHEAST ASIAN INDEPENDENT CINEMA

A World Cinema movement

Jonathan Driskell

Introduction

As a number of writers have commented (Hanan 2001; Baumgärtel 2012a), there has been something of a mismatch between the healthy cinematic output of Southeast Asia and how little international recognition these cinemas have achieved. Although the cinematic histories of the eleven countries that make up Southeast Asia—Brunei, Cambodia, East Timor, Indonesia, Laos, Malaysia, Myanmar, the Philippines, Singapore, Thailand, Vietnam—have been varied, from nation to nation and at different points in time, the region has much to boast about. Philippine cinema, for instance, has been the third largest in the world at many points in its history, in terms of the number of films released per year, coming only after Hollywood and "Bollywood". During the golden age of Malay cinema, British Malaya had some of the most impressive cinema attendance figures in the world: "It is [. . .] said that the film-going public in British Malaya was the highest per head in the world at that time [the 1950s], which also explains why Hollywood was eager to cultivate the Malayan film market" (Kahn 2006: 129). Even Cambodia, which is rarely considered to be a major filmmaking nation, produced over 400 films during its golden age, which lasted from the 1960s to the mid-1970s, though most of these were destroyed after the Khmer Rouge seized power in 1975.

The region has produced a wealth of popular genres and a host of stars who in the domestic market have rivalled those coming from Hollywood: in Thailand Mitr Chaibancha dominated the box office in the 1950s and 1960s until his untimely death in 1970, when he fell out of a helicopter while filming a stunt; the multi-talented P. Ramlee, a star–director–writer–musician–composer from the 1950s–1970s is still a national icon in Malaysia; the Philippines has produced countless "love teams" (star pairings who appear together in film after film) and truly stellar stars, such as Nora Aunor, whose phenomenal appeal is narrativised in Ishmael Bernal's *Himala* (Miracle, 1982, Philippines). The region has also produced critically acclaimed cinema, some of which has gone on to receive international recognition at major film festivals. The "New Philippine Cinema" directors, such as Lino Brocka, Mike de Leon and Ishmael Bernal, achieved success during the 1970s and 1980s, with Brocka being nominated for the Palme d'Or at the Cannes Film Festival in 1980 for *Jaguar* (1979, Philippines) and again in 1984 for *Bayan Ko: Kapit Sa Patalim* (Bayan Ko, 1984, Philippines/France). From Thailand Euthana Mukdasanit won the best film award at the Hawaii International Film Festival in 1985 for *Peesua lae dokmai* (Butterfly and Flower, 1985, Thailand). Rithy Panh has also been gaining recognition since the mid-1990s for his films about the Khmer Rouge regime in Cambodia, such as *Neak Sre* (Rice People, 1995, Cambodia/France/Switzerland/Germany), *S-21, la machine de mort Khmère rouge* (S-21: The Khmer Rouge Killing Machine, 2003, Cambodia/France) and *L'image Manquante* (The Missing Picture, Cambodia/France, 2013), which won the Un Certain Regard prize at the 2013 Cannes Film Festival.

In spite of this, there was, until quite recently, relatively little academic interest in Southeast Asian cinema, either from academics working in the region or from film scholars in the West—there are some exceptions, including early pieces by scholars such as Annette Hamilton (1992; 1992a), amongst a few others. This marginal place is evident from books on World Cinema and film history. For instance, *The Oxford Guide to Film Studies* (Hill and Church-Gibson 1998) includes a section on World Cinema that has chapters on Indian, Chinese, Hong Kong, Taiwanese, Japanese, African and South American cinemas, but nothing specifically on any Southeast Asian cinemas. Similarly, Geoffrey Nowell-Smith's *The Oxford History of World Cinema* (1996) includes a short section on Indonesian cinema, but no other cinemas from the region. However, in the last decade or so this has been changing, with a wealth of work emerging, including no fewer than five books, two of which focus on independent cinema, the main topic of this chapter: *Film in South East Asia: Views From the Region* (Hanan 2001), *Le Cinéma d'Asie du Sud-Est* (*Southeast Asian Cinema*, Margirier and Gimenez 2012), *Film in Contemporary Southeast Asia: Cultural Interpretation and Social Intervention* (Lim and Yamamoto 2012), *Glimpses of Freedom: Independent Cinema in Southeast Asia* (Ingawanij and McKay 2012) and *Southeast Asian Independent Cinema* (Baumgärtel 2012). There has also been the establishment of the Association of Southeast Asian Cinemas Conference (ASEACC) and an online film journal devoted to Southeast Asian cinema, *Criticine* (though this has ceased publishing new material, in large part owing to the death of its founder, Alex Tioseco, in 2009). There are many reasons for this increased interest in Southeast Asia, including developments in Film Studies, such as the turn to World Cinema, peripheral cinemas and film history, as well as broader developments in academia, such as the rise of "area studies" and postcolonial studies.

The region has also witnessed a new independent cinema, occurring most strongly in Malaysia, Thailand, Singapore, the Philippines and Indonesia, though Vietnam, Laos and East Timor have all also been included in discussions, albeit to a lesser extent (Lam 2012; Norindr 2012; Bexley 2012). Emerging across the region in the late 1990s and early 2000s, some of the earliest films were *Everything Will Flow* (Punlop Horharin, 2000) and *Dokfa nai meu-man* (Mysterious Object at Noon, 2000, Thailand/Netherlands, Apichatpong Weerasethakul) from Thailand, *Lips to Lips* (2000, Malaysia, Amir Muhammad) from Malaysia, *Still Lives* (1999, Philippines, Jon Red) from the Philippines, and *Stories About Love* (2000, Singapore, Chee Kong Cheah, James Toh and Abdul Nizam) from Singapore – though even earlier than that Eric Khoo was pioneering Singaporean independent cinema with such films as *Mee Pok Man* (Singapore 1995) and *Shier Lou* (12 Storeys, Singapore, 1997). Owing to the accomplishments of independent cinema, the region's cinematic output is beginning to gain more international recognition. The Thai director Apichatpong Weerasethakul has had considerable success at Cannes: *Sud sanaeha* (Blissfully Yours, 2002, Thailand/France) won the Un Certain Regard prize in 2002, *Sud Pralad* (Tropical Malady, 2004, Thailand/France/Germany/Italy) (Figure 2.1) won the Prix du Jury in 2004 and *Loong Boonmee raleuk chat* (Uncle Boonmee Who Can Recall His Past Lives, 2010, Thailand/UK/France/Germany/Spain/Netherlands) won the Palme d'Or in 2010. Similarly, Filipino director Brillante Mendoza won the best director prize at Cannes in 2009 for *Kinatay* (Butchered, 2009, France/Philippines). More recently, Anthony Chen's *Ilo Ilo* (2013, Singapore/Japan/Thailand/France) won the Camera

Figure 2.1 One of Thai director Apichatpong Weerasethakul's Cannes successes: *Sud Pralad* (Tropical Malady, 2004, Thailand/France/Germany/Italy), which won the Prix du Jury in 2004. ©Downtown Pictures/ TIFA.

d'Or at Cannes in 2013. These are just some of the Southeast Asian films that have performed well at film festivals in recent years—there are many others.

This new, critically acclaimed mode of filmmaking suggests that the region's independent cinema is a film movement of sorts. Since the earliest years of cinema, many movements have emerged: German Expressionism, Soviet Montage, Poetic Realism, Italian Neorealism, French New Wave, New German Cinema, Cinema Novo, and Dogme 95, to name just some. While the whole idea of the film movement could be viewed as a highly Westernised construct, borrowing as it does from European art history, movements continue to be a dominant way of understanding the history of cinema as well as national cinemas and, indeed, World Cinema. Lúcia Nagib (2011), for instance, structures her book *World Cinema and the Ethics of Realism* around world cinema movements.

This chapter will give an overview of the Southeast Asian independent cinema and will addresses a number of core questions: In what ways is this cinema independent? What is the cinematic and social significance of these films? How have they been discussed in the literature on Southeast Asian cinema? To what extent can these films be seen as part of a pan-Southeast Asian film movement? In exploring this, I mainly draw on the canon of early independent films that emerged in the late 1990s and early 2000s, in order to offer a general introduction to the subject, though I also use some more recent examples and refer to some of the region's newer, emerging filmmakers.

A new cinema

At the centre of film movements is the idea that they represent something new, a break with previous ways of making films, usually through challenging established approaches to film production and form, but also often through their encapsulation of an emerging zeitgeist—in the way that the French New Wave formed part of the period's new youth culture, for example. As a new type of independent filmmaking that emerged suddenly and rapidly gained success,

Southeast Asian independent cinema would appear to conform to this idea. It should be noted, however, that the presence of independent cinema in the region is not entirely new. There were previous waves of independent cinema in a number of countries, such as in the Philippines where the collapse of the studio system in the 1960s and 1970s saw a huge rise in independent film productions.

We should begin, then, by exploring the specifics of this new type of cinema, which we can start to do by examining what exactly this independent cinema is independent *from* (see also Lent 2012). A key issue to consider here is how independent cinema must negotiate two main forces: the state and the existing market, or, more broadly, global capitalism.

On the one hand, in countries across Southeast Asia, the state supports the domestic industry through quotas and protectionism, ensuring that local films are screened, and that they are funded. This also means that the national film product is state controlled, to varying degrees, which naturally impacts upon the nature of the films made. As Hernandez points out, government funding often comes with "strings attached" (2012: 230). Governments also exercise control of the cinema through censorship. This has brought about some revealing censorship stories—*Babe* (1995, Australia/USA, Chris Noonan), for example, was banned for a while in Malaysia, a Muslim country, owing to its non-halal protagonist (it does not help that the word babe is coincidentally quite close to the Malay word for pig, *babi*). Censorship regulations have been a particular obstacle for Independent filmmakers in the region, many of whom have had their films banned or heavily censored. Singaporean director Royston Tan made *Cut* (2004, Singapore), a short satirical film about censorship in the country, as a response to the heavy censorship of his debut feature *15* (2003).

At the same time, independent cinema must negotiate the existing structures of the market, which creates a dominant, profit-driven or "mainstream" cinema. In Southeast Asia this is partly made up of Hollywood, which, like elsewhere, invariably secures a large portion of the market; other "international" cinemas, including Bollywood, which is particularly popular in Malaysia; as well as the domestic mainstream cinemas of each country. These cinemas can have something of a strangle-hold on domestic markets. The Indonesian filmmaker Nia Dinata has commented that the Group21 cinema chain has a monopoly on exhibition in Indonesia, making it difficult for alternative films to reach a large audience (Baumgärtel 2012d: 206). Both the state and the existing industrial structures, then, embody ways in which cinema is controlled and contained.

How, then, do the independent cinemas of Southeast Asia exist independently of this? This is not always clear-cut as some films and filmmakers will work partially, though not fully, within these established systems. Miriam Lam (2012) gives an example of this, explaining how Vietnamese independent films are better termed semi-independent because of how they tend to involve collaboration between transnational/diasporic groups and the Vietnamese state. In other contexts, independent filmmakers have found ways of circumventing some of these established sources of power, mainly through what Khoo Gaik Cheng refers to, in her discussion of the Malaysian independent cinema, as a "do-it-yourself" philosophy (2007). Central to this is the rise of digital filmmaking, which is seen by many (e.g. Hernandez 2012) as being one of the key catalysts for the emergence of this cinema as it enables filmmakers to work with much smaller budgets—not just because digital video is cheaper than film stock, but also because they can use smaller crews and can film more easily on location. Indeed, such technology also affords greater freedom, with some filmmakers adopting "guerrilla filmmaking" strategies, such as shooting without permits (sometimes at prohibited locations). It should be noted that while this do-it-yourself approach is potentially liberating, enabling a whole new generation of filmmakers who may otherwise have been excluded from making films, some have also expressed concerns that such a situation has in some cases brought about a lowering of quality (Baumgärtel 2012f).

The do-it-yourself philosophy also extends to distribution and exhibition, with independent filmmakers finding alternative avenues for the screening of their work. While some manage to secure limited screening runs in mainstream multiplexes, many films are considered to have too narrow an appeal. Other screening opportunities include film clubs and private screenings, as well as national and international film festivals, and online exhibition—many Southeast Asian independent films can be viewed on sites such as YouTube or Vimeo.

These production, distribution and exhibition methods are linked to differences in the kinds of films that are made. Independent cinema in Southeast Asia is, like independent cinemas elsewhere, largely an "auteur" cinema, in which the director is central. As Baumgärtel comments:

> The flexibility and autonomy that digital video afforded these filmmakers calls to mind Alexandre Astruc's notion of the *camera-stylo* (the camera pen), where filmic images become a means of writing just as flexible and subtle as written language and where the director is the sole author of the film.
>
> *(2012a: 7)*

As a consequence, independent cinema exhibits formal and thematic variety, with these directors making films according to their own personal visions. There are significant differences, for example, between the films of Amir Muhammad, whose documentary *Lelaki komunis terakhir* (The Last Communist, 2006, Malaysia/Netherlands), about Chin Peng, the leader of the Malayan Communist Party, includes humorous musical numbers, and those of Apichatpong Weerasethekul, whose films offer slower, more abstract reflections on everyday life. The independent cinema of the region also uses a diverse range of forms, such as the short film, the documentary and the feature-length narrative film, while also drawing on a host of genres such as comedy, melodrama and the historical film.

While this variety makes it difficult to establish a clear list of features belonging to independent cinema, there are common aesthetic tendencies. For instance, there is an emphasis on realism, owing to the emphasis on cheaper shooting methods, including the use of location shooting and non-professional actors rather than established stars (though some actors have gone on to become stars, such as Coco Martin in the Philippines, where he is known as the "king of the indies"). The use of digital video enables multiple takes, creating a greater emphasis on improvisation, long-takes, spontaneity and chance, again common features of a realist aesthetic. Even directors who do not use digital video, such as Yasmin Ahmad in Malaysia or Nia Dinata in Indonesia, often work within the conventions of realism through their use of everyday spaces and stories. This emphasis on realism is a common feature of World Cinemas (Nagib 2011), which are often seeking to define themselves in opposition to the seemingly fantastical and "escapist" genres often found in Hollywood. Beyond the conventions of realism, many independent films engage in formal play and experimentation. Perhaps most famously Lav Diaz has pushed the boundaries of cinematic expression through his creation of monumentally *long* films. His most recent work, *Hele sa hiwagang hapis* (A Lullaby to the Sorrowful Mystery, 2016, Philippines/Singapore), which won the Alfred Bauer Prize at the 2016 Berlin International Film Festival, is eight hours long.

Many Southeast Asian independent films are also distinct from the mainstream through their social, political and ideological outlook. Again, we must take care not to sum up the politics of these films as a whole, as the output is diverse and many independent films retain regressive features, in terms of gender, sexuality and class politics, while others push established boundaries of representation. For instance, while many independent films in the Philippines shine light on the problem of poverty in the country, making these films distinct from some of the country's romantic comedies featuring popular "love teams", there have been accusations that some of these involve a somewhat exploitative relationship with such subject matter. Brillante Mendoza's films, for example, have been labelled by some as "poverty porn" for the way in which they take Western, middle-class film festival audiences on exhilarating and sensationalist journeys into the slums and underworld of the Philippines, such as in *Butchered*, a film about a gang murder of a prostitute (Baumgärtel 2012e).

And yet, independent films frequently broaden the range of representations offered in the countries they come from. This often involves focusing on groups of people who are neglected in the mainstream. For instance, we see working class lives in *Punggok rindukan bulan* (This Longing, 2008, Malaysia, Azharr Rudin), marginalised ethnic groups such as the Igorots in *Batad sa paang palay* (Batad, 2006, Philippines, Benji Garcia) and queer sexualities in films such as *Arisan!* (The Gathering, 2003, Indonesia, Nia Dinata). In Malaysia independent cinema has also done much to challenge the nation's ethnic politics. Whereas mainstream films have for decades focused almost exclusively on Malay stories and characters (Malays are the politically dominant ethnic group, making up around 60 per cent of the nation), independent cinema includes films focusing on other Malaysian ethnic groups such as the Indians and Chinese, as well as work that deals with interethnic stories, such as *Sepet* (Chinese Eye, 2004, Malaysia, Yasmin Ahmad) – a love story about a Malay girl and a Chinese boy. It is of note that *Sepet*, like many other independent films from the region, also features a strong female character and offers a more female-centred point of view.

Independent cinema also often deals more overtly with political issues. While the region has a range of political systems, it suffers from a number of common recurring problems, such as corruption, authoritarianism and political repression. Many independent filmmakers have seized on the opportunity to challenge this, such as Amir Muhammad who has made a number of political documentaries, including *Malaysian Gods* (2009, Malaysia), *The Last Communist* and *The Big Durian* (2003, Malaysia). In Singapore, Martyn See has risked being put in jail for making films about the difficulties faced by Singapore's opposition politicians, such as *Singapore Rebel* (2005), about Dr Chee Soon Juan, leader of the Singapore Democratic Party.

Since its emergence in the late 1990s and early 2000s, independent cinema has served as a valuable new type of filmmaking. However, while we can see many points of similarity from across the region, are these sufficient for us to characterise independent cinema as a pan-Southeast Asian film movement? In order to explore this more fully, it is necessary to examine Southeast Asian independent cinema's regional identity.

A regional cinema

Most writers on the Southeast Asian independent cinema will at some point consider the question of whether these films can be taken together as a pan-regional cinema, which also impacts upon the extent to which we can view them as part of a discrete "movement", in so far as movements must possess a certain amount of unity. Southeast Asia is a contentious and much debated term in a range of disciplines, including politics, anthropology, and Southeast Asian studies. On the one hand, there are clear ways in which these countries have a shared heritage. For instance, most of the countries were colonised by Western powers: Brunei, Malaysia, Myanmar and Singapore by the UK; Indonesia by the Dutch; East Timor by the Portuguese;

Vietnam, Cambodia and Laos by the French; the Philippines by the Spanish and then the USA. The only country that was not colonised was Thailand, though even it became heavily Westernised during the colonial period. Nowadays the region is brought together in some respects through the existence of the Association of Southeast Asian Nations (ASEAN), the regional political organisation that brings about cooperation between its eleven member states, while also forging cultural links through events such as the ASEAN Football Championship.

At the same time, as Adam Knee (2011: 357) discusses, some question the validity of the term Southeast Asia, arguing that it is "loaded with ideological baggage and is removed from the actual people and experiences (and in some case scholars) of the countries in question, the product of Western thinking and Cold War priorities, which it still residually supports". In addition, for some people Southeast Asia is an arbitrary marker that fails to carve out a coherent and discrete territory encompassing a shared identity for the people who live there. This stems from the fact that Southeast Asia is a richly diverse region, containing a wealth of religions (including Islam, Buddhism, Hinduism and Christianity), ethnic groups (too many to mention, though in addition to "indigenous" groups there are strong Indian and Chinese populations), cultural influences from the former colonisers, the Arabic World, India and China, and many languages (most countries in the region have several widely spoken languages). There are also huge economic differences between the countries, with Singapore at one extreme, as a fully developed nation, and countries such as the Philippines at the other, where large portions of the population live in poverty.

With these issues in mind, to what extent can we speak of an independent pan-Southeast Asian cinema? On the level of production some initiatives have been set up to foster connections between filmmakers from across the region, such as the S-Express Short Film Festival, which brought together Yuni Hadi (from Singapore), Amir Muhammad (Malaysia) and Chalida Uabumrungjit (Thailand), representing, as Knee discusses, "a particularly exemplary instance of a festival self-consciously working to foster a regional filmmaking community" (2011: 361). More recently, the Malaysian director Tan Chui Mui has set up the New Next Wave filmmaking workshops, which involve film personnel from across Southeast Asia mentoring young Malaysian filmmakers. At the same time, such linkages are sparse and sporadic. Pen-ek Ratanaruang has stated that while he has met and is familiar with the work of Amir Muhammad, along with some other filmmakers from the region, he does not often watch their films (Baumgärtel 2012b: 200). In a similar vein, the Singaporean director Eric Khoo has rather bluntly said "In terms of Malaysian films, I am not too keen on them. I like the recent horror films. The Philippine films—I have not watched that many recent ones" (Baumgärtel 2012c: 226). Moreover, while we can see some similarities in many (though far from all) of the region's independent cinemas in terms of production methods and a realist sensibility, aimed at presenting an "authentic" picture of the world, there is little reflection on a specifically Southeast Asian identity within this work, aside from perhaps in narratives that explore Southeast Asia's tropical spaces, particularly its jungles (Knee 2011: 358), or "border films" such as *This Longing*, which is set in Johor Bahru at the border of Malaysia and Singapore and deals with the relationship between these two countries, though this is a special case as Malaysia and Singapore have historically been close and were even part of the same country between 1963 and 1965.

Instead, many of the region's independent films turn their lens towards an examination of the nations they come from. Indeed, while the two books on Southeast Asian independent cinema to some extent offer a regional overview, most of the chapters focus on specific nations—exceptions include Hernandez's piece on the origins of Southeast Asian independent cinema (2012). This is also replicated on the level of production. While filmmakers in the Philippines and Indonesia produced "manifestos" for their independent cinemas, there is not a broader manifesto for the region as a whole (unsurprisingly). This is symptomatic of a larger level of collaboration on the national level: in Thailand there is Thaiindie, a group of Thai independent filmmakers; in the Philippines there is IFC (Philippine Independent Filmmakers' Multi-Purpose Cooperative); Malaysia has a couple of independent film companies, Doghouse73 Pictures and Da Huang Pictures. Indeed, the collaboration between filmmakers on a national level is often overt. Ratanaruang comments on how Thai filmmakers often help each other out (Baumgärtel 2012b: 200) and this is something we can also see in individual films. *Todo Todo Teros* (2006, Philippines, John Torres) includes cameos by a host of individuals associated with Filipino independent cinema, such as the critic Alex Tioseco and the filmmakers Khavn de la Cruz, Regiben Romana and Lav Diaz.

In addition, these films often deal with nationally specific issues, using realism in order to provide "truer" visions of the nation and challenge the exclusions and omissions of the mainstream. For instance, independent cinema in Malaysia has provided a more realistic vision of the country's linguistic identity. Reflecting its multiculturalism, Malaysia is a multilingual nation in which people may speak Malay, English, "Manglish" (English combined with words, and sometimes grammar, taken from other Malaysian languages, especially Malay), various Chinese dialects (Mandarin, Hokkien, Cantonese, Hakka), Tamil, and indigenous languages, among others. However, until recently, the government defined Malaysian cinema as films that are in at least 90 per cent Bahasa Malaysia, the national language. With the advent of independent cinema, there has been a fuller exploration of the nation's linguistic reality, with films featuring a range of languages, as well as—importantly—a mixture of languages, in keeping with the nation's *rojak* (Malay for mixed) culture. As we have seen, the region's independent cinemas often share a concern for representing a broader range of people and places, and for interrogating social and political issues. While this unites these cinemas, it also potentially divides them, in so far as each nation explores its own nationally specific issues. Indeed, these films will often only truly make sense to an audience that is familiar with the intricacies of the country they come from. For example, in order to fully understand Malaysian films such as *Chemman chaalai mal* (The Gravel Road, 2005, Malaysia, Deepak Kumaran Menon) and *Jagat* (2015, Malaysia, Shanjhey Kumar Perumal), which deal with problems facing the Malaysian–Indian community, one would benefit from an understanding of how the films draw on—and challenge—local stereotypes about Malaysian–Indians. To take things to an even more local level, Benedict Anderson has argued that while "Cannes juror Quentin Tarantino can admire *Sat Pralaat*'s ambiguities and highly sophisticated narrative technique", the film is in many respects addressing a rural audience of *chao baan* (villagers) familiar with the characters and atmospheres of the countryside environments he depicts (2012: 159).

It is true that the Southeast Asian independent cinema also reaches beyond the nation, but this is often done by also reaching beyond Southeast Asia. First, funding for these films will sometimes come from international bodies, such as the Hubert Bals Fund as part of the Rotterdam Film Festival and the Asian Public Intellectuals Fellowship of the Nippon Foundation, which have funded the work of a number of independent filmmakers, such as Amir Muhammad, Lav Diaz and Anocha Suwichakornpong, among others (Hernandez 2012: 231). Collaborations and subject matter may also go beyond the nation, too. For instance, Ratanaruang has made films with Japanese elements, such as *Ruang rak noi nid mahasan* (Last Life in the Universe, 2003, Thailand/Japan/Netherlands), for which Christopher Doyle was his cinematographer. As Khoo has argued, some scholars are too eager to pigeonhole the Malaysian independent filmmakers as being solely concerned with representing their nation (and in particular its ethnic politics). She argues that James Lee's films are "less interested in capturing the racial alienation of the Chinese minority in Malaysia" and are more concerned with "universal themes confronting the modern subject living in an urban, global, capitalist society" (2012: 122). Moreover, Southeast Asian independent films also find a large part of their audience overseas at international film festivals, evident from the major festival successes listed above.

Conclusion

The problems involved in discerning a set of clear, pan-regional qualities within Southeast Asian independent cinema makes it difficult for us to view it as a fully homogenous film movement. These films are in many respects part of a global trend in digital independent filmmaking, which connects them with the Danish film movement Dogme 95, for example, as much as it does with each other. Of course, the film movements of World Cinema have rarely been entirely homogenous. As Lúcia Nagib has commented, when we use World Cinema as a method it becomes a way of "cutting across film history according to waves of relevant films and movements, thus creating flexible geographies" (2006: 31). Southeast Asian independent cinema as a film movement marks out one such flexible geography. Although far from being homogenous, films from across the region share production, distribution and exhibition methods, formal features, and thematic and ideological concerns.

Moreover, Southeast Asian independent cinema has had a significant impact on the development of indigenous film cultures. It has created new approaches to filmmaking and storytelling that have challenged the dominance of Hollywood as well as the respective nations' mainstream cinemas. In a number of respects, independent cinema has also been a source of influence *for* the mainstream cinemas. In the Philippines, for example, the studio ABS-CBN has created a company called Cinema One that now produces independent films so as to capture this market, and in Malaysia there is evidence of an opening up of representations. For decades the nation's mainstream "national" cinema consisted of mono-ethnic Malay movies—one of the reasons why Khoo (2006) has termed it a "cinema of denial", for denying the nation's multiculturalism. However, there is evidence that this is changing—2016 saw the release of *Ola Bola* (2016, Malaysia, Chiu Keng Guan), a multi-ethnic film about the Malaysian national football team's campaign to qualify for the 1980 Olympics, which has already become the nation's highest grossing film of all time. Moreover, one of the main contributions that independent cinema has made is that it has explored issues often ignored or avoided in the mainstream, including under-represented people and groups, as well as taking on major political issues in what are in many respects still quite repressive societies.

Although academic work on the cinemas of the region was being produced before the emergence of the independent films, there has been a recent increase in such scholarly activity. Independent cinema was one of the catalysts for the creation of ASEACC, as is acknowledged in the call for papers for the Fifth Conference, held in Manila in 2008, which focused specifically on the region's independent filmmaking:

> The first decade of the 2000s has seen a stunning upsurge of independent cinema in a number of Southeast Asian countries. This development has been one of the motivations of the Annual Southeast Asian Cinemas Conference (ASEACC), and this year we want to focus completely on the issue of identity.

Not only has this resulted in independent cinema receiving more attention, as is evident from the wealth of books and papers that have been published on this subject in recent years; it has also meant that other aspects of the region's cinema have been brought to the fore.

Among many other topics, the region's popular film history is also starting to receive more attention, evident, for example, from a recently published special issue of *Plaridel*, the journal of the University of the Philippines' School of Mass Communication, which focuses on Southeast Asian horror cinema (Ancuta and Campos 2015). One of the independent cinema's many important contributions and accomplishments, then, is that it has played a role in pushing the development of Southeast Asian cinema studies, a discipline that in turn promises to cast even more light on the region's rich cinema history and culture.

References

Ancuta, K. and Campos, P. (2015) "Locating Southeast Asian Horror: Special Issue", *Plaridel* 12 (2).

Anderson, B. R. O'G. (2012) "The Strange Story of a Strange Beast: Receptions in Thailand of Apichatpong Weerasethakul's *Sat Pralaat*", in Ingawanij, M. A. and McKay, B. (eds) *Glimpses of Freedom: Independent Cinema in Southeast Asia*, Ithaca, NY: SEAP, 149–163.

Baumgärtel, T. (ed.) (2012) *Southeast Asian Independent Cinema*, Hong Kong: Hong Kong University Press.

—— (2012a) "Introduction: Independent Cinema in Southeast Asia", in Baumgärtel T. (ed.) *Southeast Asian Independent Cinema*, Hong Kong: Hong Kong University Press, 1–10.

—— (2012b) "'I love making films, but not getting films made': Interview with Pen-ek Ratanaruang", in Baumgärtel T. (ed.) *Southeast Asian Independent Cinema*, Hong Kong: Hong Kong University Press, 191–200.

—— (2012c) "'I do not have anything against commercial films': Interview with Eric Khoo", in Baumgärtel T. (ed.) *Southeast Asian Independent Cinema*, Hong Kong: Hong Kong University Press, 213–226.

—— (2012d) "'I want the people of Indonesia to see a different point of view, whether they agree with it or not': Interview with Nia Dinata", in Baumgärtel T. (ed.) *Southeast Asian Independent Cinema*, Hong Kong: Hong Kong University Press, 201–211.

—— (2012e) "'An inexpensive film should start with an inexpensive story': Interview with Brillante Mendoza and Armando Bing Lao", in Baumgärtel T. (ed.) *Southeast Asian Independent Cinema*, Hong Kong: Hong Kong University Press, 155–170.

—— (2012f) "The Downside of Digital: A German Media Critic Plays Devil's Advocate", in Baumgärtel T. (ed.) *Southeast Asian Independent Cinema*, Hong Kong: Hong Kong University Press, 141–149.

Bexley, A. (2012) "Independence and Indigenous Film: The Framing of Timor-Leste", in Ingawanij, M. A. and McKay, B. (eds) *Glimpses of Freedom: Independent Cinema in Southeast Asia*, Ithaca, NY: SEAP, 137–147.

Hamilton, A. (1992) "The Mediascape of Modern Southeast Asia", *Screen* 33 (1): 81–92.

—— (1992a) "Family Dramas: Film and Modernity in Thailand", *Screen* 33 (3): 259–273.

Hanan, D. (ed.) (2001) *Film in South East Asia: Views from the Region*, Vietnam: SEAPAVAA.

Hernandez, E. M. P. (2012) "The Beginnings of Digital Cinema in Southeast Asia", in M.A. Ingawanij, M. A. and McKay, B. (eds) *Glimpses of Freedom: Independent Cinema in Southeast Asia*, Ithaca, NY: SEAP, 223–236.

Hill, J. and Church-Gibson, P. (eds) (1998) *The Oxford Guide to Film Studies*, Oxford: Oxford University Press.

Ingawanij, M. A. and McKay, B. (eds) (2012) *Glimpses of Freedom: Independent Cinema in Southeast Asia*, Ithaca, NY: SEAP.

Kahn, J. S. (2006) *Other Malays: Nationalism and Cosmopolitanism in the Modern Malay World*, Singapore: NUS Press.

Khoo, G. C. (2006) *Reclaiming Adat: Contemporary Malaysian Film and Literature*, Singapore: UBC/ Singapore University Press.

—— (2007) "Just Do-It-(Yourself): Independent Filmmaking in Malaysia", *Inter-Asia Cultural Studies* 8 (2): 227–247.

—— (2012) "Smoking, Eating, and Desire: A Study of Alienation in the Films of James Lee", in Ingawanij, M. A. and McKay, B. (eds) *Glimpses of Freedom: Independent Cinema in Southeast Asia*, Ithaca, NY: SEAP, 121–135.

Knee, A. (2011) "In (Qualified) Defense of 'Southeast Asian Cinema': Text of Keynote Talk for the 6th Annual Southeast Asian Cinemas Conference, Ho Chi Minh City, Vietnam, July 1–4, 2010", *Asian Cinema* 22 (1): 357–366.

Lam, M.B. (2012) "Circumventing Channels: Indie Filmmaking in Post-Socialist Vietnam and Beyond", in Ingawanij, M. A. and McKay, B. (eds) *Glimpses of Freedom: Independent Cinema in Southeast Asia*, Ithaca, NY: SEAP, 13–19.

Lent, J. A. (2012) "Southeast Asian Independent Cinema: Independent of What?", in Baumgärtel, T. (ed.) *Southeast Asian Independent Cinema*, Hong Kong: Hong Kong University Press, 13–19.

Lim, D. C. L. and Yamamoto, H. (eds) (2012) *Film in Contemporary Southeast Asia: Cultural Interpretation and Social Intervention*, London; New York: Routledge.

Margirier, G. and Gimenez, J. (2012) *Le cinema d'Asie du Sud-Est*, Lyon: Asiexpo Edition.

Nagib, L. (2011) *World Cinema and the Ethics of Realism*, New York: Continuum.

—— (2006) "Towards a Positive Definition of World Cinema", in Dennison, S. and Lim, S. H. (eds) *Remapping World Cinema: Identity, Culture and Politics in Film*, London: Wallflower Press, 30–37.

Norindr, P. (2012) "Towards a Laotian Independent Cinema?", in Lim D. C. L. and Yamamoto H. (eds) *Film in Contemporary Southeast Asia: Cultural Interpretation and Social Intervention*, London; New York: Routledge, 41–52.

Nowell-Smith, G. (ed.) (1996) *The Oxford History of World Cinema*, Oxford: Oxford University Press.

3

GLOBAL INTIMACY AND CULTURAL INTOXICATION

Japanese and Korean film in the twenty-first century

Felicity Gee

Introduction

Since the economic downturn of 1997 (the so-called Asian Financial Crisis (AFC)), films from mainland China, Korea, Japan, Taiwan and Hong Kong have enjoyed considerable success throughout East Asia, and, increasingly, on a global scale. Once the dictate of international film festival jurors and critics, changes to trading conditions, industry infrastructure and the rise of social media and internet-driven business have expanded the reach of these national cinemas. In particular, Japanese and South Korean (hereafter Korean) films have attracted worldwide attention, sometimes on a blockbuster scale (see Bong Joon-ho's *Snowpiercer*, 2013, South Korea/Czech Republic/USA/France); and, thanks to clever marketing strategies, DVD sales of "quality" or "extreme" films have found increasingly knowledgeable audiences. Genres such as horror, period, classroom and family dramas, melodrama, science fiction, crime, slow cinema, and violent revenge narratives have characterised the field, but these labels are simply insufficient to define the work. The twenty-first century has seen a rise in queer subject matter, female directors, and films addressing *zainichi* (or Korean residents in Japan) and "outsider" perspectives from both regions; and tastes, styles, ancillary marketing and a "newly emerging geography of digital cinema" (Wada-Marciano 2012: 45) have diversified the industries and intoxicated the marketplace.

In 2005, Third Window Films announced their pledge to bring "quality Asian cinema" to British viewers' homes via a range of DVDs that reach "beyond long-haired ghost films and mindless Hollywood action copies, sourcing the finest works in new *Far Eastern* Cinema" (Third Window Films (undated), author's emphasis). One example is *New Directors from Japan* (2014), which showcases films by young, "unique" directors Kosuke Takaya, Nagisa Isogai and Hirobumi Watanabe, providing the only means of distribution for their work either in Japan or abroad. Overall, Third Window's aim, it seems, is to circumnavigate the inevitable lull in interest in the 1990s imports branded under Tartan's now defunct "Asia Extreme" label (as discussed by Stringer 2007, Dew 2007, Wada-Marciano 2009) by offering a re-branded alternative to an educated audience (these particular films ruminate on themes such as global capitalism, sexual perversion, and obsessive sibling rivalry). While various studies have noted the cultural specificity of recent Japanese and Korean cinema—the folkloric and literary roots, the oblique references to the atomic bombs, the performance styles originating from traditional *butoh* or *kabuki*, the technological environment of modern Tokyo or Seoul, the vengeful *onryo*—(Hand 2006; Phu 2010) they have also acknowledged the transnational impulse that defines their reception, and ultimately, their cross-cultural afterlife in the form of co-produced re-makes. Julian Stringer notes how, in the case of Japan, "it becomes possible to engage with some of the complex inter-media and cross-cultural relations forged in recent years, both inside and outside Japan, among remade, recycled and re-circulated, and popular as well as highbrow, cultural artefacts" (2007: 298). In the case of Tartan Asia Extreme, this intertextuality accounts equally for the international awareness of Korean films of this period, such as Park Chan-wook's *Gongdong gyeongbi guyeok JSA* (JSA: Joint Security Area, 2000, South Korea) and *The Vengeance Trilogy* (2002–2005, South Korea) or Kim Ki-duk's *Seom* (The Isle, 2000, South Korea) and *Nabbeun namja* (Bad Guy, 2001, South Korea).

The popularity of parallel industries such as gaming, comic books, fan magazines, television and music, and the easily packaged extremes of cuteness and horror/violence, has only served to fuel film successes. Arguably, the sustained success of Japan's soft power, for example, is largely thanks to ancillary products and cute (*kawaii*) anthropomorphic characters and fashion styles (such as gothic-lolita) that can be found in the most unlikely shops (as well as specialist ones) the world over. Sharon Kinsella offers that in Japan "Individualism generally and youth culture in particular have been interpreted, first and foremost, as a form of wilful immaturity or childishness" (1998: 291), and certainly the adoration surrounding *cosplay* (character fancy dress) or characters such as Sanrio's Hello Kitty shows that the catharsis of being childish has caught on. Syncretised with the ubiquitous rush of social media's recycled or quoted images, the thrill of danger, violence or commodity fetishism, and the paradox of fame and anonymity that twenty-first-century life brings, *kawaii* culture is also a lasting component of recent films such as *Samaria* (Samaritan Girl, 2004, South Korea, Kim Ki-duk), *Shimotsuma monogatari* (Kamikaze Girls, 2004, Japan, Tetsuya Nakashima), *Kiraware Matsuko no isshô* (Memories of Matsuko, 2006, Japan, Tetsuya Nakashima), *Kokuhaku* (Confessions, 2010, Japan, Tetsuya Nakashima), *Ai no mukidashi* (Love Exposure, 2008, Japan, Sion Sono), *Sakuran* (2006, Japan, Mika Ninagawa) and *Herutâ sukerutâ* (Helter Skelter, 2012, Japan, Mika Ninagawa) in which a postmodern mix of styles and attributes meld tradition and consumerism, and tread a line between parody and pastiche.

Global hits such as Psy's 2012 *Gangnam Style*, Studio Ghibli's animated films, Nintendo games, *Pokémon*, the films of Park Chan-wook, Kiyoshi Kurosawa, Kim Ki-duk, Naomi Kawase, Hirokazu Kore-eda, Kinji Fukasaku, Takashi Miike; and the international renown of novels such as Han Kang's *The Vegetarian* (2015) or Haruki Murakami's fiction have all contributed to an awareness of Japanese and Korean cultural outputs, and more specifically, to a cine-literacy that is reliant upon a range of artistic, industrial and consumerist practices, but which has historically evolved unevenly across the two nations.

More recent evolutions in new and trans media, and the democratizing potential of making film digitally, can shed new light on the affective and creative ways in which the Japanese and Korean film industries respond to global cultural flows, and in which filmmakers approach their subjects. Aihwa Ong notes that an analysis of global cultural flows does not necessarily account for "their embeddedness in differently configured regimes of power" (1999: 4), and Koichi Iwabuchi echoes this sentiment, proposing that "Globalisation processes will continue to relentlessly capitalise on intra-Asian cultural resonance, at the same time reproducing unequal cultural power relations in multiple and multilayered ways" (2002: 210). In terms of global consumption, older trends embedded within the structure of the international film festival match Iwabuchi's and Ong's observations. The much-cited "opening up" of Japanese cinema to the

West with Kurosawa's *Rashomon* (1950, Japan) taking the Silver Lion at the Venice Film Festival in 1951, encouraged an exoticist cinephilia that was based on region and auteur value. Yet it was only after forty-one years of competing at Venice that a Korean director won the Golden Lion (Kim Ki-duk for his eighteenth feature film, *Pietà*, 2012, South Korea, a dark portrait of a son atoning for his sins). What is interesting is how "East Asian" art cinema has evolved in symbiotic relation to the international film festival (Busan [Pusan] International Film Festival, 1996–present, is a key example—see Gateward 2007) and the rise of independent distributors and lobbyists for national cinemas (see Galt and Schoonover 2010). Dudley Andrew's evaluation of the "duality" (regional/polyglot audience) resulting from festivals' autonomous selection process (2010: vii) is echoed in Leo Ching's assertion that regional markets are inherently complicit in globalisation, allowing "the contending forces of global integration and local autonomy [to] converge" (2000: 244).

This chapter briefly consolidates the historical links and "ugly intimacies"[1] that existed between Japan and Korea in the past, and how these continue to shape their respective cultural industries. More specifically, it draws on key films, filmmakers, genres and trends that can be said to define "Japanese" and "Korean" cinema in the twenty-first century, and their place in an increasingly intimate and culturally intoxicated marketplace. It also takes for granted the continued project of "De-Westernizing" film studies (after Bâ and Higbee 2012) and reflects upon recent scholarly debates surrounding the mapping of increased reverse cultural flows (from East Asia to Hollywood) and intra-regional flows (within East Asia) (see, for example Ciecko 2006, Galt and Schoonover 2010, Lee 2011a, Gates and Funnell 2012) and the wider discussion on national, transnational, diasporic, regional and hybrid cinemas that weave through this book.

Japan and Korea: global intimacy and the other

Often thrown together under the umbrella of East Asian cinema, there is undoubtedly a *global intimacy* in the ways in which Japanese and Korean films and filmmakers negotiate their intertwined geopolitics, and in their—often very subtle—self-effacing humour in the face of horror. However, a mutual reciprocity in terms of style and influence is at marked odds with the roles played out in stories of battle, political and cultural displacement, diasporic communities, enforced prostitution, and mass migration in which the roles of oppressor and oppressed are nationally defined. These histories tell of inequality and suffering: the systematic invasion of Korea by Japan (1592–1598); colonial rule of Korea by Japan (1910–1945); the occupation of Japan by the United States, from 1945 to 1952; the Korean War which divided the country into Northern and Southern territories, from 1950 to 1953; the violent Gwangju uprising (Democratic Uprising) of 1980 and ongoing issues involving *zainichi* rights. In addition, both regions also foster an ambivalent relationship with the US expressed through ongoing issues relating to constitutional rights, US military presence, commerce and industrial regulation, and ideological differences. Scholarship focused on Japanese and Korean cinema, and their interrelation, has burgeoned, and most recently reflects the speed and diversity with which films are created in relation to socio-political concerns, but also to competitive market share (both local and global). A range of perspectives represented in the diverse work of Aaron Gerow, Isolde Standish, Michael Raine, Frances Gateward, Abé Markus Nornes, Julian Stringer, Yuriko Furuhata, Rayna Denison, Tony Rayns, Jinhee Choi, Mitsuyo Wada-Marciano, Mark Schilling, Chris Berry, Dal Yong Jin, Lee Dong-hoo, Mika Ko, Yomota Inuhiko, Koichi Iwabuchi, Darcy Paquet, Misuhiro Yoshimoto, and Jasper Sharp, among many others (including the *Journal of Japanese and Korean* Cinema, 2009, edited by David Desser) illustrate the impossibility of a mono-cultural approach. As well as established forms of criticism focused on auteur theory and genre, the international enterprise of East Asian film studies fosters diverse approaches to non-heterogeneous and diasporic experience from within cosmopolitanism, and on the inclusion/exclusion that global circulation engenders.

Mika Ko's invaluable work on "otherness" in *Japanese Cinema* (2010) raises the perennial question of identity emerging from years of cultural displacement and migration following Korea's double separation from Japan and North Korea. She reminds us that the opposing perceptions of "*nihonjinron* [discourses of Japaneseness] and the *kokutai* or unified national body" (2010: 62) on the one hand, and "no such thing as a coherent unified Korean identity" on the other (2010: 126) divide the experience of belonging along lines of privilege and discrimination that are complex and individual. Myung Ja-kim argues that Kim Ki-duk's filmmaking, in addressing miscegenation and shameful pasts, pushes for an acceptance of difference, whereby "Prejudice against a marginalised group, whether it is related to class, race, ethnicity, or gender, is another projection of the psyche of the colonised victim, signifying the need for the other" (2010: 260). Similarly, socio-politically motivated scholarship over the past decade discusses how the Korean "renaissance" (Choi 2010), or "New Korean Cinema"—which presents "its dazzling colours to the world in multiple versions [. . .] across diverse territories" (Stringer 2005: 7)—and a renewed interest in melodrama, documentary and heritage films also coincides with recent political debates on *jeongsindae* (comfort women, or military prostitutes) deployed to entertain, respectively, the Japanese and American soldiers, and the Korean army.

Such emotional scars are clear to see in many contemporary films such as the monumental hit *Amsal* (Assassination, 2015, South Korea, Choi Dong-hoon) depicting Korean independence fighters, monochrome biopic *Dongju* (Dongju: The Portrait of a Poet, 2015, South Korea, Lee Joon-ik) which portrays the life of the eponymous resistance poet, Korean–Japanese co-production *Mai wei* (My Way, 2011, South Korea, Kang Je-Gyu) or even the long-lasting legacy of the original *kaiju eiga* (monster film) *Gojirā* (Godzilla, 1954, Japan, Ishirô Honda), and in films centred around issues of borders and border-crossings: *Hwanghae* (The Yellow Sea, 2010, South Korea/USA/Hong Kong), *Swiri* (Shiri, 1991, South Korea, Je-kyu Kang), *2009 loseuteu maemorijeu* (2009: Lost Memories, 2002, South Korea, Lee Si-myung) or the 2002 television drama *Friends* (a co-production between Tokyo Broadcasting System (TBS) in Japan and Munhwa Broadcasting Company (MBC) in Korea). The cross-cultural flows that resulted in greater cross-pollination between the Japanese and Korean industries did not truly emerge until the twenty-first century, bringing the two nations into a close proximity that had not really been seen since the days of colonialism. What Dal Yong Jin and Dong-hoo Lee term "cultural regionalisation", the "process of change from relative heterogeneity and lack of cooperation towards increased cooperation, integration, convergence, coherence and identity in culture within a given geographical space" (2012: 27) has been greatly propelled by the region's reciprocal interest in soft power. Convergent cultural identities are also reinforced through the family drama, a central tenet of both cultures in which "the family confers a sense of Asian values widely shared between South Koreans and other Asians: values such as filial piety and parental responsibility, kinship and loyalty, cohesion and harmony" (Teo 2013: 174). Each in her own way is also defined through the layered psycho-geographies built up over years of invasion and migration, and ring-fenced by an insular and defensive attitude and (at various points in history) literal barriers to international trade: an "island mentality" or "complex" (*shima-guni konjō*) in the case of Japan, and the "hermit kingdom" of Korea during the isolationist period of the Joseon Dynasty (1392–1897), each designed to strengthen the nation against threat while maintaining key state ideologies. Surely we can see echoes of these ideas in the behavioural traits of the *hikikomori* (stay-at-home), a social condition in Japan (seen as an illness rather than a choice) that confines young adults to their rooms, shunning the outside world; or similarly in the figure of the *otaku*, the often obsessive gaming or *manga* fan who seemingly lives a myopic existence glued to their media of choice (see Barral 1998; Kinsella 1998; Napier 2006). The result of effectively shutting out the rest of the world had enormous repercussions in the historical past, and traces are still clearly evident in the language, behaviour, beliefs, and the still (transnational co-productions notwithstanding) largely mono-cultural spaces portrayed in the films of both regions.

During the colonial period, Japan instigated a slogan promoting the ideology that "Japan and Korea are one" (*naisen ittai*), a sign of "cosmetic multiculturalism" (Ko 2010), a superficial integration that masked the real plight of the colonised and deterritorialised. Such historical attempts to gloss over oppression and inequality offered a pseudo-transnational "togetherness" that functioned at political and economic levels, but which has continually been challenged by filmmakers. More recent developments in relations between the two regions have replaced this problematic colonial slogan with a range of governmental policies that aim to address the painful memory of Japanese rule and its enslavement of Korean nationals. A key turning point was in 1998, when the "Open Door Policy/Good Neighbour Policy" summit held between President Kim Dae Jung and Prime Minister Keizo Obuchi led to Korea opening its doors to Japanese popular culture, thereby ensuring a platform for pan-Asian co-production, diversification of the motion picture, publishing, music and television industries, and opportunities to build greater understanding between the two countries. Recent Japanese films present worlds governed by mythical or romantic elements to create an embodied filmic experience through which to experience the "other", in most cases a *zainichi*.

GO (2000), for example, is a popular novel written by Kaneshiro Kazuki (2000), a third generation Korean living in Japan, which investigates the subject of nationality focalised through a *zainichi* high school student. A year later, it was made into a critically acclaimed film of the same title, directed by Isao Yukisada and starring Japanese heartthrob Yōsuke Kubozuka as the main protagonist Sugihara. This casting is significant in that Kubozuka appeals to both Korean and Japanese audiences, and his star persona thereby supersedes the more negative and incendiary connotations of Sugihara's outsider status. In line with popular Korean and Japanese films of the early 2000s, the film enlists the tropes of teen romance and violent, stylised, revenge narratives (the film's intense anger is located within a presumed "Korean" sensibility) in order to highlight the discrimination that determines Sugihara's path. Sugihara falls in love with Japanese student Sakurai, who manages to break the pattern of her parents' prejudice against North Korea and to reciprocate his love. The film asks its audience to identify not with one side or the other, but with a shifting scale of emotions that are tied and untied to their protagonists. On one level, this encouragement to identify with the constraints and unfairness of discrimination that continues for *zainichi* in Japanese society seems positive, however, as Iwabuchi warns, "a young [Korean] person who reads manga does not necessarily forget the political implications of the past" (2015: 20). Progress is often slow and, perhaps superficial: "In many cases, the use of minority groups in Japanese films has simply provided a 'multicultural gloss', whereby minority cultures have become the object rather than the subject of representation and consumption" (Ko 2010: 172). Mark Schilling has referred to the 1990s as a creative and hopeful decade in Japanese film history, a decade that saw a boom in cinema-going, and the rise of the multiplex in rural, suburban and city centres, but no real rise in the overall market share (1999). What is particularly striking about this period is that against the failing economy, in the wake of the AFC, the industry saw a rise in the number of new directors, a rise in the number of small theatres and "the stubborn vitality" of the independent film sector buoyed by private and corporate finance (Schilling 1999: 24). Directors such as Hirokazu Kore-eda, Naomi Kawase, Takeshi Kitano, Takashi Miike, Tetsuya

Nakashima, Shunji Iwai, Shinji Aoyama, Sion Sono, Hideo Nakata, Hayao Miyazaki created a buzz around the domestic film, despite the domination of foreign imports at the box office. However, back in the late 1990s *Hallyu* (the Korean Wave) and "things Korean [were] not fashionable in a narrative of the cosmopolitan atmosphere of contemporary Japan" (Yomota 2003: 84) because "Koreans [had] been too close a presence for Japanese to build them into a positive stereotype in cinema" (Yomota 2003: 87). This was all to change (as has been discussed in Gateward 2003; Choi 2010; Kim 2011; Dal and Dong 2012; Dal 2016) when the sheer force of *Hallyu* washed over film industries and audiences the world over.

The jaw-dropping success of K-film in the twenty-first century

While Japanese cinema has enjoyed a longer period of consumer and critical attention internationally thanks to a sustained interest in auteur cinema (led not only by *Cahiers du cinéma* in the 1960s, but also thanks to the work of Noël Burch and Donald Richie), this millennium has seen the Korean film industry take the lead, garnering its place in the global imagination. In 1986, the Korean Motion Picture Law (MPL) allowed direct distribution by major Hollywood studios, combined with a reduction in the screen quota for domestically produced films, paving the way for a greater Hollywood share of the market. Clearly the Korean market needed to change, and the industry began to harness the potential of conglomerate money to distance itself from the films of the 1980s. The government's realisation that economic growth and global acumen could be achieved through cultural products meant that change happened in all areas. For example, the Korean Film Archive (KFA) in Seoul (1974) and the North Korean film archive in Pyongyang (1961) were established late into the twentieth century; but in the era of New Korean Cinema, the movement of the KFA to the $2 billion Seoul Arts Complex (completed in 1993) and its upgrade from a non-profit to a government affiliated foundation in 2002; the restructuring of the Korean Motion Picture Promotion Corporation (KMPPC), into the Korean Film Council (KOFIC) and the explosion of cinemas and festivals into the 2000s show an unprecedented investment in the industry. As Jinhee Choi (2010) has pointed out, the boom in financial and governmental support was matched by increased visibility and renown on the international film festival circuit. Certainly, as all writers on contemporary Korean cinema since the 2000s have described, the combination of a willing government, *chaebols* (large, often family-owned, business conglomerates) with money to burn, directors with a greater freedom to express criticism of the past, the creation of a regional trend, and a booming star culture that spans music, film, television and promotional goods (crossover stars such as Song Joong-ki, Lee Byung-hun, Son Ye-jin or Hai Ji), propelled Korea to a success that, in terms of visibility and box office takings, clearly surpassed that of Japan.

By 2005 Korea had become "the fifth largest theatrical market in the world, with $890 million in box-office receipts" (Choi 2010: 2). This "awe-inspiring" rise in economic fortunes at the turn of the millennium (Jeong 2011: 110) is coupled with a rise in conglomerate and venture capital flowing into the film industry, enabling "386 Generation" directors to make commercially viable films for mass audiences. The term 386, while referring to the speed of an Intel computer chip, also refers to a generation in their thirties, born in the 1960s and witness to the political turmoil of the 1980s, a term, that as Choi points out, is more political than "Baby Boomer" (2010: 4). Under Kim Dae-jung's presidential steer, directors such as Park, Bong, Lee Chang-dong, Gina Kim, Im Kwon-taek, Hong and Ing Sang-soo flourished and the era of the Korean blockbuster arrived: "In both the People's Republic of China and the Republic of Korea, the rise of blockbuster consciousness is linked to dismantling trade protectionism under intense lobbying from the US" (Berry 2003: 218). The rise of the big-budget blockbuster has certainly attracted record audiences for Korean films domestically, but has also garnered success in regional markets and at American, Latin American, and European film festivals.

In 2008, Christina Klein examined the reasons "Why American Studies Needs to Think about Korean Cinema, Or, Transnational Genres in the Cinema of Bong Joon-ho". Selecting a director who is responsible for one of the highest grossing films in Korean box office history (*Gwoemul* [The Host, 2006, South Korea]), which, even in 2016 remained in the top five behind James Cameron's *Avatar* [2009, USA] and Kim Han-min's naval epic *Myeong-ryang* [The Admiral: Roaring Currents, 2014, South Korea]), Klein examines the "ambivalent" and schizophrenic relationship with Hollywood genre film that is tested in Bong's *The Host,* and *Salinui chueok* (Memories of Murder, 2003, South Korea). Largely considered an auteur of the blockbuster, Bong's films are slickly produced, spectacular, meta-generic, and involve increasing levels of domestic and international investment, as is the case with 2013's *Snowpiercer* starring Tilda Swinton and John Hurt, and shot in a range of transnational locations. Korea's quest for a cinema that pushes national concerns, while remaining capable of attracting a mass audience, inevitably relies upon the most globally successful storytelling means, as Nikki J. Lee suggests: "Korea's pursuit of indigenous movie blockbusters has turned it into an international producer and distributor of localised global movies" (2011b: 61), whereby "Korean filmmakers use Hollywood's archives to navigate through their own globalised cultural economy" (Klein 2008: 873). A case in point would be Tartan's highly sexualised packaging of Je-Kyu Kang's 2003, mega-hit *Shiri* (universally accepted as Korea's first blockbuster) for its Asia Extreme DVD series in Europe featuring an image of lead actor Yunjin Kim tantalizingly holding a gun, placed above the *Empire* magazine tagline: "A mix of *Nikita* and *Die Hard*". The explosive domestic success of *Shiri* milked the film's global signifiers, highlighting sex, spectacle, the violent pursuit of a threat to national security and something of the thrill and the banality of the *Die Hard* franchise (1988–2013, USA).

Figure 3.1 Working within and against the boundaries of genre allows for resistance and creativity that is culturally specific: *Ah-ga-ssi* (The Handmaiden, 2016, South Korea, Park Chan-wook). ©Moho Film/Yong Film.

However, the notion of a K-blockbuster is not always considered favourably, with sceptics labelling the trend "Copywood" (Dal 2005; Klein 2008; Suh 2008), seeing the "K" of the "Korean" blockbuster as a cheap add-on marking it as imitation. However, as far as directors Park and Bong are concerned, working within and against the boundaries of genre allows for resistance and creativity that is *particular*. More recently, Park attended the UK premiere of his film *Ah-ga-ssi* (The Handmaiden, 2016, South Korea) (Figure 3.1), an adaptation of Sarah Waters' acclaimed novel *Fingersmith* (2002), and reiterated for the audience the significance of generic codification in the film's mise-en-scène (Q&A, London International Film Festival, October 2016). Within the confines of a gothic tale characteristic of those penned by the Marquis de Sade, or Sacher von Masoch, Park emphasises the imagined superiority of the Japanese way of life that remains like an "invisible" trace (Kim 2012: 426) in post-war Korea—cultural superiority embodied in art objects, literature and language. Waters' lesbian feminist text becomes a pretext for an exploration of a composite Korean identity based on trauma and revenge—Park's political and stylistic auteurist preoccupations.

Twenty-first-century diversification

"Global mass cultural formats [. . .] also work as an inter-nationalised interface that highlights the specific nationality of cultures and [. . .] propagates the idea of the nation as the unit of global cultural encounters in which people are urged to participate" (Iwabuchi 2002: 13). We need look no further for a better exemplar of this than 2016's global obsession with *Pokémon Go*, the hybrid game-child of Niantin, Pokémon and Nintendo that syncretises the "real" space of Google maps with those of a virtual game and film franchise, and connects its players via Android and iPhone mobile devices across the globe. Rayna Denison's work outlines the ways in which conglomerates have altered the landscape of film production over the past decade as part of the wider media systems networks, and examines how big name companies such as Fuji TV network, or WOWOW TV channel, produce high-budget film franchises as part of "already-profitable textual networks" through adaptations, re-makes, and serialised films (2016: 68). Participation via ancillary products and tie-ins is also on the rise: Kadokawa publishing company promotes the hybrid form of a book-magazine, or "mook" (*mukku*) to stimulate active participation, and expansion of the films themselves. This particular brand of popular filmmaking most importantly, for Denison, provides a way of investigating local and transnational products within a "transmedia intertextuality" that operates at the level of global technology and consumption (2016: 88). Similarly, media brands trade on the notion of consumers buying into a lifestyle, or "world", that has generated impressive results for Studio Ghibli and director/TV star (*tarentō*) Takeshi Kitano/Beat Takeshi's "Office" (see Napier 2006; Davis and Yeh 2009). Such strategies have become the rule rather than the exception for producing and marketing films in Japan, even for independent films, which also rely on conglomerate funding. What is particularly striking about such enterprises is that the role of film is undiminished despite the equally high profile of each of the associated texts (manga, TV anime series). One example of this is the *Umizaru* series directed by Hasumi Eiichirō and based on a manga by Satō Shūhō (1998–2001) (and examined by Denison), which demonstrates clearly how the high concept film helps to sell the franchise: "Scale has consequently become the central concept around which such preplanned serial productions are organised" (2016: 85). On the PonyCanyon Inc. webpage for the fourth film in the series—*Brave Hearts: Umizaru* (2012, Japan, Eiichirô Hasumi)—taglines urge the viewer to jump aboard a sinking ship and make ready for: "A maritime thriller on a spectacular scale!" in which the titular *umizaru* coastguards risk everything to save those on board (with advanced special effects and surround sound). Similarly, Fujiko F. Fujio's robot cat

Doraemon, a much-loved children's manga character, has become a hugely popular franchise, with the most recent film (the thirty-sixth, a remake of *Doraemon: Nobita no Nihon tanjô*, Nobita and the Birth of Japan, 1989, Japan, Tsutomu Shibayama) described by the *Asahi Shimbun* as "the latest Doraemon blockbuster", exceeding all previous records to become the biggest to date (2 June 2016). This impressive feat follows hot on the heels of *Stand by Me Doraemon* (2014, Japan/USA, Tony Oliver, Ryuichi Yagi and Takashi Yamazaki), which was released in over 50 countries, and did especially well in China, Hong Kong, Korea, Thailand, and Italy. Despite the fondness for the character as a national symbol, the animated films form part of what Iwabuchi terms "*mukokuseki* cultural forms"—or a cultural "odorlessness", whereby a likeable image of "modern 'Japaneseness'" supplants the "historically constituted, problematic, and uneven relationship with other Asian countries" of the imperial and colonial past (2002: 53). Denison's analysis of a regional market benefitting from a transmedia form of global intimacy is compelling and offers a realistic reading of a collaborative back-and-forth that nevertheless retains the "cool" branding of the local.

Meanwhile, with the title of his latest monograph on the contemporary Korean media markets, Dal moves forward to *Hallyu 2.0*, and a digital world in which local presence is no longer a prerequisite either for transnational collaboration or as a physical marker of national branding: "K-pop powerhouses are hiring Western composers, and game corporations use social networking sites as their platforms for global game users. The increasing role of social media and digital technologies has consequently prompted adjustments in corporate policies" (2016: 173). Dal describes the significance of Kim Young-sam's government-led KII initiative in 1995 to "construct an advanced nationwide information infrastructure consisting of communications networks, internet services, application software, computers, and information products and services", which was designed to enable Korea's survival in "the digital mode of global capitalism" (2016: 155–156), and raises one of the most pertinent questions of the 2010s: What does it mean when the contraflows between Western and non-Western regions have become more symmetrical due to computer and smartphone use? In answer, capitalism still favours the West—Apple and Android still own the lion's share of software.

Between "nation branding" and "cultural odorlessness"

Lastly, the facets of the wider "brand" of J and K-films in the twenty-first century are comprised of a number of recurring generic styles and thematic preoccupations; and within these a number of key terms, or concepts mobilise to illustrate specific feelings or experiences that are tied to ideas of national identity that pits particularity against "cultural odorlessness" (Iwabuchi 2002; Okada 2012), a circulatory exchange between the specific and the universal that has bolstered both Japanese and Korean film industries since the 1990s. Many of these films display the generic markers of earlier decades; many also enjoy a postmodern romp through genre parody and pastiche that leads to more culturally hybrid forms. In Korean cinema, for example, although crime and horror genres have proved extremely popular, more traditional national tropes explored through trauma and melodrama nearly always underpin the protagonists' quests for self-knowledge.

> Not only is Korea still scarred and traumatised by its colonial era and the Cold War, but—given the continuing US military presence and occasional threats of war from North Korea—it has yet to claim a true postcolonial and post-Cold War identity.
>
> *(Kim 2011: 212)*

In Korea, the Golden Age of melodrama (McHugh and Abelmann 2005) is characterised by a paradoxical tension bridging consumerist desires flailing in the wake of Western modernisation and "a collective trauma in the national psyche and pride, which was deeply connected to the nation's neo-Confucian tradition and to the ideals of Korean masculinity" (Jeong 2011: 2). The exquisite pain evoked in melodramatic discourse, such as that expressed in Yu Hyon-mok's 1961 film *Obaltan* (The Aimless Bullet, South Korea) proved irresistible to Korean audiences. A bleak portrayal of the Seoul slums shot in high contrast black and white, focalised through a displaced North Korean working-class family, *The Aimless Bullet* reverberates with tremulous emotions. Chol-ho's mother's anguished cries of "Let's get out of here!" Yong-ho's violent outrage at being cast in a film solely for his war scars, and Myong sook's despair, which turns her to prostitution and into the arms of American soldiers, find no means of escape beyond hopeless dreams. *The Aimless Bullet* endures as a marker of a key moment in Korean (film) history, a "refraction" (Choi 2010: 10) of the multiple experiences and processes that it captures. Moreover, it works through the "impossibility of a belief in the nation as a place of collective belonging" (Cho 2005: 101), locating national pride in the individual, or the coincidental drift of the characters, rather than the country itself. McHugh and Abelmann consider melodrama to be the most suitable vehicle with which to represent Korea's turbulent history and the "lived impact" (2005: 4) that the war, deterritorialisation, poverty, emasculation, and female labour had on the people. In 2016, following the December 2015 agreement between Japan and Korea, in which Japan apologised and agreed to award reparations to the remaining victims of enforced prostitution, a documentary film entitled *Gwi-hyang* ("Spirit" Homecoming, 2016, South Korea, Cho Jung-rae) topped the domestic box office, showing a continued interest in the subject, and the desire for global recognition for the women subjected to these horrors (Kahng 2016). Naturally it is a highly problematic task to try to define a national cinema according to stereotypical characteristics or essentialist generalities; however, certain cultural particularities necessarily contribute to an understanding of life in a region, affecting the ways in which it is represented on screen. For example, words exist in both the Korean and Japanese languages that are used to signify a mood, atmosphere or affect that is particular to the wider culture of each country. The folksong Arirang, for example, derives from an indigenous oral tradition that evokes *han* (or *haan*)—feelings that are closely associated with loss, pain, yearning and nationhood.

> You are going over Arirang hill
> My love, you are leaving me

Although Arirang's refrain might seem wistful, evoking rural scenes imbued with melodramatic longing, it is also a uniting chorus that expresses "The quintessentially Korean emotion of suppressed rage and sorrow" (Klein 2008: 881). It is worth noting that Kim Ki-duk employed the folksong in his low-budget, quasi-documentary *Arirang* (2011, South Korea) as a musical motif to express a series of particularly traumatic events, thus demonstrating the interconnectedness of national identity and suffering. *Han,* or *haan* (Son 2000), is part of the Korean psyche, both a philosophy and "an irresolvable grudge born of colonial occupation and wartime partition" (Davis and Yeh 2009: 16), which, as a rather complex nebula of feelings, resonates anew in every person. *Han* does not have a direct translation in English, but its cinematic realisation shows a tendency for outward expression; revenge or quest narratives; and unresolved crimes, feelings, memories that favour darkness over light. Although *han* may be represented through stories of individual trauma and revenge—from the ruinous and ruined female protagonists who transgress domestic rules in *Jayu buin* (Madame Freedom, 1956, South Korea, Han Hyeong-Mo) and *Hanyo* (The Housemaid, 1960, South Korea, Kim Ki-Young and 2010, South Korea, Im Sang-soo) to more familiar cult hits such as *Oldeuboi* (Oldboy, 2013, South Korea, Park Chan-wook) or *The Yellow Sea*—it is "not simply the private emotion of a person who has suffered a lot; it is a pervasive 'collective' emotional state among Koreans" (Yoon and Williams 2015: 41). Yoon and Williams also point out that one of the principal fascinations with the term is that within its negativity it also carries hope and inner strength, a need to overcome. Often in Korean films the figure of an observer appears in order to provide a position of calm, a mediating space to allow characters experiencing *han* to be momentarily released from their pain: Hee-jung's older female friend in *Ji-geum-eun-mat-go-geu-ddae-neun-teul-li-da* (Right Now, Wrong Then, 2015, South Korea, Hong Sang-soo) or the little girl in the ultimate scene of Bong's *Memories of Murder* each serve to provide space for the main character's reflection. We might see the uncensored bursts of grief, rage, or love in Korean films as something connected to *han*, a cathartic on-screen release or "*han*-venting" (Yoon and Williams 2015: 117). Despite the relative fluffiness of Korean rom-coms such as Yeopgijeogin geunyeo (My Sassy Girl, 2010, South Korea, Kwak Jae-young) or the comedic parody *Nam-ja sa-yong-seol-myeong-seo* (How to Use Guys with Secret Tips, 2013, South Korea, Lee Won-suk), the majority of Korean romantic comedies, even the happier ones, seem to harness the contradictory mood of *han*, ensuring that sickness (*Seulpeumboda deo seulpeun iyagi*, More than Blue, 2009, South Korea, Won Tae-Yeon, *Nam-ja-ga sa-rang-hal dae*, Man in Love, 2014, South Korea, Han Dong-wook), disability (*O-jik geu-dae-man*, Always, 2011, South Korea, Song Il-gon), crime and adversity (*Urideul-ui haengbok-han shigan*, Maundy Thursday, 2006, South Korea, Song Hae-sung), and numerous other themes, including immigration, class issues, and suicide, failure and repression, always interpenetrate the central conceit of love.

The heroic concept of *chamara* (to grit one's teeth and bear it) finds an equivalent in the Japanese *gaman suru*, where there is no option but to withstand adversity, never giving up. While *han* is particular to the history of the Korean peninsula and often turns to violent revenge, Japan's fifteen-year occupation drove film narratives towards a "cultural inversion" whereby the "tragic hero" archetype not only framed suffering within localised historical precedents, it also facilitated a project of forgetting (Standish 2011: 150). I would argue that, to an extent, the tendency towards escapism and forgetting in post-war Japanese film has been replaced in more recent works with a spiritual or metaphysical quest to overcome. Films such as *Miike's Chûgoku no chôjin* (The Bird People in China, 1998, Japan), Kiyoshi Kurosawa's *Kishibe no tabi* (Journey to the Shore, 2015, Japan/France), or Kawase's *Futatsume no mado* (Still the Water, 2014, Japan/France/Spain) explore the open-ended questions raised by reincarnation, rural superstitions, a school for flying, and the relationship between nature, metaphysics and humankind (Figure 3.2). As Kyoko confesses to the Shaman in Kawase's film: "I can't understand my mother's suffering—her body is gone, but her thoughts fill up the world." In Kurosawa's *Tokyo Sonata* (2008, Japan/Netherlands/Hong Kong) and *Journey to the Shore*, home is always far away, somehow enigmatic and elusive, and Kurosawa's particular brand of biting social realism (present also in his earlier horror-inflected work) observes a society obsessed with outward appearance and decency. Since the golden days of Yasujiro Ozu and Kenji Mizoguchi, an understated "*gaman*" (forbearance) has taken hold of characters facing the ills of the modern world. The iconic scene in Mizoguchi's *Sansho Dayu* (Sansho the Bailiff, 1954, Japan), in which Anjū silently commits suicide, exemplifies the calm and poise with which, similarly, characters in contemporary Japanese films and dramas resign themselves to fate. As Japanese students related to me at the height of the 2007 Korean drama boom in Japan, it was actually the animated expressions of emotion in these television episodes that they preferred to the outwardly controlled expressions of love in many Japanese dramas. Critics too, are often bewildered by the more subdued

Figure 3.2 *Futatsume no mado* (Still the Water, 2014, Japan/France/Spain, Naomi Kawase) explores the relationship between nature, metaphysics and humankind. ©Eddie Saeta S.A./Kumie.

sentiment in recent Japanese films. The criticism levelled at Naomi Kawase's most recent film *An* (Sweet Bean, 2015, Japan/France/Germany), for example, finds its *gaman*, social awkwardness and titular sweetness to be unrealistic and kitsch. Peter Bradshaw writes in *The Guardian* of "feeling exasperated by the sentimentality and stereotype being served up" (2015).

Conclusion

On 11 March 2011, following a 9.0 magnitude earthquake and a 15-metre tsunami, Fukushima, Miyagi and Iwate prefectures in the North of Japan's Honshu island were affected by widespread radiation, which occurred as a direct result of the loss of power to the region. The day after the initial devastation caused by the natural disaster, a leakage of radioactive materials was discovered outside the gate of one of the three nuclear reactors at the Fukushima Daiichi plant. A month later initial estimates of the radioactive damage to the area rose from level 5, to level 7, a severity not seen since the Chernobyl disaster in 1986. Statements from both the government and the Tokyo Electric Power Company (TEPCO) during the month after the disaster failed to reassure citizens on facts, or strategies for coping. In fact, it emerged that deception and saving face seemed initially more important than testing and evacuating affected areas.

Similarly, the national handling of the sinking of the *MV Sewol* ferry in the Yellow Sea off the South Korean peninsula, on 16 April 2014, in which 294 passengers died, and ten are still missing (many of whom were high school students) caused national outrage. The reports following the disaster laid blame at the hands of the ferry company, the crew, and the coastguard, and subsequent investigations have been severely hampered by political and bureaucratic infighting. What links these two tragic events is the way in which they have galvanised action in communities living across Japan and Korea, and the catalyst they have provided for creative responses to the crises through filmmaking. In two democratic countries, where speaking out is still difficult, films such as Lee Sang-ho and Ahn Hae-ryong's *Da-ee-bing-bell* (The Truth Shall Not Sink with *Sewol*, 2014, South Korea) and Toshi Fujiwara's *Mujin chitai* (No Man's Zone, 2012, Japan, one of many films dedicated to this topic) have given voice and visibility to people directly affected by the consequences of these events. I will end this chapter with a line from *No Man's Zone*: "Images of destruction are always hard to digest." The film considers the lack and/or abundance of images in our lives that are mediated through screens. How can a film make invisibility—radiation, the dead—visible, and what relationship might its words and images have to the idea of a nation and its people? Despite the flows of power and monetary exchange that these two national industries have witnessed and enjoyed, the images that are left for the viewer in the range of films produced carry within them the traces of history, culture and emotion that resist assimilation into a global product, and instead invite the viewer to participate in an exchange that connects the experience of the particular with that of the personal, home and belonging with affective experience.

Note

1 The term "ugly intimacies" is inspired by an international symposium held at University of California, Berkeley, and organised by Karen Vallgårda and Padma D. Maitland, 17 May 2016.

References

Andrew, D. (2010) "Foreword", in Galt, R. and Schoonover, K. (eds) *Global Art Cinema: New Theories and Histories*, Oxford: Oxford University Press, v–xii.

Bâ, S. M. and Higbee, W. (eds) (2012) *De-Westernising Film Studies*, New York: Routledge.

Barral, É. (1998) *Les enfants du virtuel*, Paris: Denoel.

Berry, C. (2003) "What's Big about the Big Film? 'De-Westernizing' the Blockbuster in Korea and China", in Stringer, J. (ed.) *Movie Blockbusters*, London: Routledge, 217–229.

Bradshaw, P. (2015) "An Review", *The Guardian*, 14 May, www.theguardian.com/film/2015/may/14/an-review-naomi-kawase-cannes-film-festival-2015.

Ching, L. (2000) "Globalizing the Regional, Regionalizing the Global: Mass Culture and Asianism in the Age of Late Capital", *Public Culture* 12 (1): 233–257.

Cho, E. (2005) "The Stray Bullet and the Crisis of Korean Masculinity", in McHugh, K. and Abelmann, N. (eds) *South Korean Golden Age Melodrama: Gender, Genre, and National Cinema*, Detroit, MI: Wayne State University Press, 96–116.

Choi, J. (2010) *The South Korean Film Renaissance: Local Hitmakers, Global Provocateurs*, Middletown, CT: Wesleyan University Press.

Ciecko, A. T. (ed.) (2006) *Contemporary Asian Cinema*, New York: Berg.

Dal, Y. J. (2005) "Blockbusterization vs. Copywood: The Nation-State and Cultural Identity in Korean Cinema", *Journal of Media Economics and Culture*, 3 (3): 46–72.

—— (2016) *New Korean Wave: Transnational Cultural Power in the Age of Social Media*, Urbana and Chicago, IL: University of Illinois Press.

Dal, Y. J. and Dong, H. (2012) "The Birth of East Asia: Cultural Regionalization through Co-Production Strategies", *Cinema and Media Studies* 32 (2): 26–40.

Davis, D. W. and Yeh, Y. (eds) (2009) *East Asian Screen Industries*, London: BFI.

Denison, R. (2016) "Franchising and Film in Japan: Transmedia Production and the Changing Roles of Film in Contemporary Japanese Media Cultures", *Cinema Journal* 55 (2): 67–88.

Dew, O. (2007) "Asia Extreme: Japanese Cinema and British Hype", *New Cinemas: Journal of Contemporary Film* 5 (1): 53–73.

Galt, R. and Schoonover, K. (eds) (2010) *Global Art Cinema: New Theories and Histories*, Oxford: Oxford University Press.

Gates, P. and Funnell, L. (eds) (2012) *Transnational Asian Identities in Pan-Pacific Cinemas: The Reel Asian Exchange*, New York: Routledge.

Gateward, F. (2003) "Youth in Crisis: National and Cultural Identity in New South Korean Cinema", in Lau, J. (ed.) *Multiple Modernities: Cinemas and Popular Media in Transcultural East Asia*, Philadelphia, PA: Temple University Press, 114–126.

Gateward, F. (2007) "Introduction", in Gateward, F. (ed.) *Seoul Searching: Culture and Identity in Contemporary Korean Cinema*, Albany, NY: State University of New York Press, 1–12.

Hand, R. J. (2006) "Aesthetics of Cruelty: Traditional Japanese Theatre and the Horror Film", in McRoy, J. (ed.) *Japanese Horror Cinema*, Edinburgh: Edinburgh University Press, 18–28.

Iwabuchi, K. (2002) *Recentering Globalization: Popular Culture and Japanese Transnationalism*, Durham, NC: Duke University Press.

—— (2015) *Resilient Borders and Cultural Diversity: Internationalism, Brand Nationalism, and Multiculturalism in Japan*, Lanham, MD: Lexington Books.

Jeong, K. Y. (2011) *Crisis of Gender and the Nation in Korean Literature and Cinema: Modernity Arrives Again*, Lanham, MD: Lexington Books.

Kahng, J. H. (2016) "Film Depicting Horrors Faced by Comfort Women for Japan Army Tops Korea Box Office", 3 March, www.reuters.com/article/us-southkorea-comfortwomen-film-idUSKCN0W50HN.

Kaneshiro, K. (2000) *Go!*, Tokyo: Kodansha.

Kim, K. H. (2011) *Virtual Hallyu: Korean Cinema of the Global Era*, Durham, NC: Duke University Press.

—— (2012) "Virtually Alive or Questionably Dead?: The Ambivalence of Modern Korean Identity in Literature and Cinema", *Crosscurrents: East Asian History and Culture Review* 1 (2): 419–429.

Kinsella, S. (1998) "Japanese Subculture in the 1990s: Otaku and the Amateur Manga Movement", *Journal of Japanese Studies* 24 (2): 289–316.

Klein, C. (2008) "Why American Studies Needs to Think about Korean Cinema, Or, Transnational Genres in the Cinema of Boon Joon-ho", *American Quarterly*, 60 (4): 871–898.

Ko, M. (2010) *Japanese Cinema and Otherness: Nationalism, Multiculturalism and the Problem of Japaneseness*, London: Routledge.

Lee, N. J. (2011a) "Localised Globalization and a Monster National: The Host and the South Korean Film Industry", *Cinema Journal* 50 (3): 45–61.

—— (2011b) "Questions of Cultural Proximity and the Asian Popular: South Korean Audiences Watching Zhang Yimou's Martial Arts Blockbusters", in Gates, P. and Funnel, L. (eds) *Transnational Asian Identities in Pan-Pacific Cinemas: The Reel Asian Exchange*, New York: Routledge, 101–114.

McHugh, K. and Abelmann, N. (eds) (2005) *South Korean Golden Age Melodrama*, Detroit, MI: Wayne State University Press.

Napier, S. (2006) "The World of Anime Fandom in America", *Mechademia: Emerging Worlds of Anime and Manga* 1: 46–63.

Okada, J. (2012) "Cultural Odor in the Global Order: Globalization and the Raced Japanese Body", in *Transnational Asian Identities in Pan-Pacific Cinemas: The Reel Asian Exchange*, New York: Routledge, 46–59.

Ong, A. (1999) *Flexible Citizenship: The Cultural Logics of Transnationalism*, Durham, NC: Duke University Press.

Phu, T. (2010) "Horrifying Adaptations: Ringu, The Ring, and the Cultural Contexts of Copying", *Journal of Adaptation in Film and Performance* 3 (1): 43–58.

Schilling, M. (1999) *Contemporary Japanese Film*, Boston, MA: Weatherhill

Son, C. H. (2000) *Haan of Minjung Theology and Han of Han Philosophy: In the Paradigm of Process Philosophy and Metaphysics of Relatedness*, Lanham, MD: University Press of America.

Standish, I. (2011) *Politics, Porn and Protest: Japanese Avant-Garde Cinema in the 1960s and 1970s*, New York: Continuum.
Stringer, J. (2005) "Introduction", in Shin, C. and Stringer, J. (eds) *New Korean Cinema*, New York: New York University Press, 1–13.
—— (2007) "The Original and the Copy: Nakata Hideo's *Ring* 1998", in Phillips, A. and Stringer, J. (eds) *Japanese Cinema: Texts and Contexts*, New York: Routledge, 296–307.
Suh, H. (2008) "South Korea's Film Dilemma in the U.S. Market: 'Copywood' or Asian New Wave?", *Asian Cinema* 19 (2): 270–280.
Teo, S. (2013) *The Asian Cinema Experience: Styles, Spaces, Theory*, London: Routledge.
Third Window Films (undated) http://thirdwindowfilms.com/about.
Wada-Marciano, M. (2009) "J-Horror: New Media's Impact on Contemporary Japanese Horror Cinema", in Choi, J. (ed.) *Horror to the Extreme: Changing Boundaries in Asian Cinema*, Hong Kong: Hong Kong University Press, 15–38.
—— (2012) *Japanese Cinema in the Digital* Age, Honolulu: University of Hawaii Press.
Yoon, K. K. and Williams, B. (2015) *Two Lenses on the Korean Ethos: Key Cultural Concepts and Their Appearance in Cinema*, Jefferson, MI: McFarland.
Yomota, I. (2003) "Stranger than Tokyo: Space and Race in Postnational Japanese Cinema", Gerow, A. (trans.), in Lau, J. (ed.) *Multiple Modernities: Cinemas and Popular Media in Transcultural East Asia*, Philadelphia, PA: Temple University Press, 76–89.

4

MEDIA REFASHIONING

From Nollywood to New Nollywood

Jeffrey Geiger

Introduction

Rather than pursue characterisations of Nollywood[1] as a maverick industry advancing on the global stage, or as slapdash movies for the masses, this chapter engages with an ongoing media refashioning, or remediation, of Nigerian movies. This approach aims to keep in mind both the "then" and "now" of the movement as well as its diversity—the flows and ebbs that began with its video origins in the early 1990s (usually traced to Kenneth Nnebue's *Living in Bondage* [1992, Nigeria]), moving into an era of popular and widely bootlegged VCDs, then in 2006 unexpectedly lauded as the third largest film producer in the world. By 2009, according to a UNESCO report, Nollywood had overtaken Hollywood to become the second largest globally in terms of films produced (United Nations 2009). More recently delineations of a "new Nollywood" have been taking shape, structured around moves towards transnational collaborations, larger budgets, and international success both in terms of festival visibility and positive reviews.

This chapter further draws on a scholarly turn away from the long-standing resistance to seeing Nollywood movies as texts worthy of serious study—the latter task once largely limited to sociological or economic approaches. Nollywood video films' often excessive, lurid content and themes, coupled with rough technique betraying rapid production, have led to lambasting by critics not only overseas but in Nigeria and across the continent (Krings and Okome 2013: 11). There have been notable exceptions to a prevailing scepticism—including the work of Onookome Okome, Jonathan Haynes, Moradewun Adejunmobi, John C. McCall and Brian Larkin—though a long-dominant stance, alongside concerns about content, has been embedded in presumptions of cinematic "quality" and the need to raise up Nollywood's production values to accepted "international industrial standards" (Barrot 2009: 58). A *New York Times* review by Matt Steinglass typified this viewpoint, calling Nollywood movies "too much of a not-very-good thing" (2002: 16).

Another *New York Times* feature ten years later, on the director Kunle Afolayan, seemed to soften this stance, yet it again invoked established attitudes about an "immature industry", arguing,

> most of the [Nollywood] movies themselves are awful, marred by slapdash production, melodramatic acting and ludicrous plots. Afolayan, who is 37, is one of a group of upstart directors trying to transcend those rote formulas and low expectations. His breakthrough film, the 2009 thriller *The Figurine* was an aesthetic leap: while no viewer would confuse it with *Citizen Kane*, to Nigerians it announced the arrival of a swaggering talent keen to upset an immature industry.
>
> *(Rice 2012: MM26)*

Side by side with concerns about the video movement's "erroneous and banal" images of Nigerian life (Krings and Okome 2013: 10), arguably conventions of "good taste" that have dominated national cinema discourses have further underpinned the critical marginalisation of less auteur-centred, non-state-supported (until recently), popular movements such as Nollywood (Geiger 2012). As Laura Hubner outlines, such perceptions of "taste" and "quality" still inhere in practices of film analysis, "because evaluation lies at the root of all (film) analysis, and is embedded within critical theory, [and] we inevitably get tied up in it, often at the moment we are trying to step back and assess it" (Hubner 2011: 218). Haynes rightly argued, in 2010, that it was time to put aside debates about Nollywood quality and begin to "roll out the full disciplinary apparatus of film studies and apply it to the video films", since "we have hardly begun describing them in the normal ways applied to other film cultures" (2010: 13). As publications such as Krings' and Okome's *Global Nollywood* demonstrate, the process of addressing Nollywood movies as complex narrative, aesthetic, stylistic and cultural productions in their own right is well under way.

Yet Nollywood continues to be in a state of flux, with industry trends heralding a "new Nollywood" era marked by collaborative financing and larger budgets, with films helmed by directors such as Obi Emelonye, Stephanie Orereke, and Afolayan (Ekunno 2011; Haynes 2014). This shift in part indicates growing confidence in Nollywood's global marketability, particularly beyond Nigeria and a west African diaspora; it also reflects the sheer will and ambition of its practitioners. Crucial to defining this new Nollywood are what Krings and Okome identify as the denser transnational dimensions of economic, technical and cultural co-production; further, these are films "often set in the diaspora and targeting mainly cinema audiences" (Krings and Okome 2013: 19). I would pause on this last point: that new Nollywood is characterised by moves towards celluloid production and theatrical projection—what media theorists would call *media transition*, though not the kind that results from phasing out or transforming "old" technologies in the face of new media developments. Strictly speaking, Nollywood really never produced "films" at all: almost all movies starting in the early 1990s were made using video, then drew on increasingly accessible digital technologies. The term "video film" has been employed to indicate a form of production and distribution (usually on cheap, easily duplicated—and pirated—VCDs, screened in informal settings, with streaming video more recently) very different from national cinema or Hollywood models. Yet with Jeta Amata's *The Amazing Grace* (2006, Nigeria/UK) and productions such as Afolayan's *Araromire* (The Figurine, 2009, Nigeria)—among films cited as marking the arrival of new Nollywood—a number of productions have departed from low-budget conventions in prioritising 35mm and theatrical release.

In navigating the territory of "new" practices beyond video, this chapter briefly discusses a highly visible example of new Nollywood, Biyi Bandele's 2013 adaptation of Chimamanda Ngozi Adichie's celebrated novel *Half of a Yellow Sun*, which deals with the Biafran independence movement and civil war. Bandele's project was publicised as the film that would confirm

Nollywood had finally graduated to an international stage, achieving long-sought-after mainstream respectability—or the "dream of a new Nollywood with functional storylines, quality pictures and ingenious directing" (Odulaja 2014)—shedding the stigma associated with rapidly produced video films. As one critic put it:

> with its big budget and pedigree cast and crew, *Half of a Yellow Sun* (2013, Nigeria/UK) signals nothing less than the Nigerian film industry's ambition to transcend the African market—and to transcend the perception of "Nollywood" as an assembly line churning out low-budget, straight-to-video fare.
>
> *(Greenberg 2014)*

But whatever efforts have been made to maintain distance between the so-called new Nollywood and the rest of Nollywood, I would suggest that this "new" is not simply about better-quality, transnational celluloid productions transcending low-budget entertainments, but a question of media transition; and thinking about media might help us to think in greater depth about processes of collusion, overlapping and borrowing in different media, and about both the shifts and continuities in perception that mark transitions from one medium to another. Both as a symptom of new Nollywood and a literary adaptation, a film such as *Half of a Yellow Sun* offers an example of media interference at a number of levels, inviting us to explore issues of narrative strategy and audience response arising through transitions from literature to film, from print to screen consumption, and, more broadly, from video/digital home viewing media to "new" trends in celluloid and cinema exhibition.

"New" Nollywood: frameworks

It should perhaps come as no surprise that the new Nollywood remains haunted by perceived shortcomings of Nollywood's past and present, and that numerous practitioners and critics have seemed eager to draw a line between Nollywood and its new incarnation. Yet media transitions can be as much about negotiating and reviving legacies of the past as they are a means of asserting definitive change. Indeed, labels circulating alongside new Nollywood, such as "Nigerian New Wave cinema" and "new Nigerian Cinema", recall more traditional concepts of the cinematic. This very language seems to invoke an aura of national cinema models (the French New Wave, Iranian New Wave, New Taiwanese Cinema, etc.) and celluloid traditions as much as it helps to indicate how Nigerian filmmaking relates to its pasts and potential futures. Alessandro Jedlowski succinctly notes:

> Those who propose the term *new Nollywood* tend to emphasize a relation of continuity between the video-boom era and the new releases and argue that the emergence of this new trend is a direct consequence of the video phenomenon. On the other hand, those who prefer the term *new Nigerian Cinema* underline the specificity of this new trend and its distance from the defining aspects of the video phenomenon (low-budget production, straight-to-video modes of distribution, popular and populist narratives, and aesthetics).
>
> *(2013: 37)*

Jedlowski prefers the term "New Wave" as a kind of middle ground: a means of marking continuities with the video film phenomenon while addressing the structuring differences of recent trends. There is an undeniable logic to this, though the identifying features of a sustained Nigerian New Wave are still emerging, while Nollywood video films on digital platforms continue to reach new audiences.

While I draw here on "new Nollywood" as a means of specifying trends identified by Krings and Okome, I am not endorsing one term or another. What I hope to emphasise is a refashioning of Nollywood along the lines of media refashioning, or remediation, articulated by Jay David Bolter and Richard Grusin. Here, remediation is effectively contingent on processes of "new" media remaking or refashioning the old:

> No medium today, and certainly no single media event, seems to do its cultural work in isolation from other media, any more than it works in isolation from other social and economic forces. What is new about new media comes from the particular ways in which they refashion older media and the ways in which older media refashion themselves to answer the challenges of new media.
>
> *(Bolter and Grusin 1998: 15)*

This process applies whether a case of a film adapting a book, or of newly marketed devices altering established practices (such as digital reproduction remediating video, which itself remediated celluloid). I am however drawn to the term refashioning here, rather than remediation. According to the *Oxford English Dictionary*, the prefix "re" comes from Latin meaning "again" or repetition, further indicating movement "back" or "backward"; "fashion" is both a process of making, and also a custom of style (that also has tendency to be "in" or "out"). New Nollywood trends (fashions?) demonstrate processes that at least partially track backwards as well as forwards (as in old media reappearing to refashion established new media practices), even as we see these different media interfering and working parallel with each other. In this sense, the "distance" that lies between the video-digital/televisual aspects of Nollywood and the celluloid/cinematic of new Nollywood (or "new Nigerian Cinema" as Jedlowski defines it) might be less well defined than the word "new" suggests.

My intention here is to avoid terminology that implies the isolation, or even privileging, of different media platforms. Thinking about media refashioning might help us to steer the discussion away from presumptions of "transcendence" provided by cinematic aesthetics. It might further unsettle goal-oriented narratives of improvement that have structured discussions, in industry and critical circles, of moves towards bigger budgets, international stars, and, crucially, 35mm. In this sense, the narrative that associates attaining international production standards with presumptions of quality would seem wrapped up in an agreed sense of cinematic aesthetics, experience, and "realism" that is essentially paradoxical: both a forward-moving progress narrative and a somewhat backward-looking glance towards "proper" cinema.

This "going back to cinema" (Jedlowski 2011: 85), or cinematic drive, further recalls a legacy that has haunted debates about Nollywood video film and that persists in discussions of new Nollywood: questions of Third Cinema and the ways that African cinema's stylistic and narrative strategies should engage with agendas for political and social change. The politics of resisting the conventions of Western films (most significantly, Hollywood) while promoting cultural memory and identity—as articulated by the Third Cinema theorist Teshome Gabriel—once dominated academic discussions of African cinema, stressing the filmmaker's obligation to produce art forms that advance postcolonial self-determination by embracing "the twin aspects of filmic experience—namely, style and ideology" (Gabriel 1982: xi). The term "oppositionality" has characterised this approach: opposition to Western conventions of production and consumption while decolonising an inherited, colonising mindset.

Third Cinema's calls for stylistic and ideological oppositionality, however, relied on a fairly stable, agreed sense of what constituted the cinematic apparatus and filmic experience. The emergence of phenomena such as Nollywood lit a fuse under presumptions of a "right" course of action for African cinema, and of what constituted politically effective filmmaking.[2] As Jyoti Mistry and Jordache Ellapen suggest, Nollywood manifests "opportunistic" commercial strategies, and "rarely do Nollywood films consider revisionist colonial histories"; more often they are "informed by immediate social and cultural concerns facing the local community" (Mistry and Ellapen 2013: 51). Their images have generated "mistrust and controversy" across the African continent, with a perceived negative impact on other regional media and entertainment industries (Krings and Okome 2013: 11). Yet they are also products of complex interrelations between remediation, innovative distribution, mass consumption, and the uneven postcolonial emergence of African culture industries. Rather than presenting a united or uniform message about colonial legacies, Nollywood has manifested a complex dynamic; it has been telling numerous different kinds of stories through accessible if often tricky and labyrinthine narratives, and is immediately recognisable for a hands-on, low-budget, rough and tumble style.

A number of commentators have stressed this more intricate version of Nollywood: that as an object of critical enquiry it is difficult to pin down, bluntly characterise, or easily dismiss. Jude Akudinobi notes that, "whether seen as a touchstone or scourge for African cinema, Nollywood is a complicated cultural, artistic, commercial, and transnational phenomenon", that is "always in a state of flux, constantly reworking proven formulas and reformulating conventions of the 'popular'" (2015a: 133–134). For Okome, Nollywood does manifest a social agenda: it can engage what Françoise Bayart called Africa's "ironic chorus"; it "performs the 'discontent' of Africa's postcoloniality" (Okome 2007: 8–10). The video films are thus "social texts" and forms of public performance, watched and interacted with in sites that range from street market stalls to informal video parlours and private homes (Okome 2007: 7).

In terms of media and Nollywood's predominantly televisual mode of consumption, then, moves towards new Nollywood's cinematic remaking perhaps could promise a return to the calls of Third Cinema for anti-commercial, political aesthetics and practices. The recent cinematic (re)turn, however, also might produce the opposite effect: needing greater economic success due to larger budgets, these films rely on high ticket costs and DVD sales, with theatres tending to be located in multiplexes and urban shopping malls open "only to specific segments of the population" (Jedlowski 2011: 85). The films themselves further differ from mainstream Nollywood "by incarnating the dreams and fears of an elite middle class rather than those of a large popular audience" (Jedlowski 2011: 85). The production contexts, distribution, and content of *Half of a Yellow Sun* raise many of these larger questions about new Nollywood and its relations to Nollywood's defining features, and even to the political aims of African Third Cinema.

Half of a Yellow Sun (2013): new media/old media

In terms of inception and production, Biyi Bandele's adaptation of *Half of a Yellow Sun* exemplifies most of the characteristics of new Nollywood as described by Krings and Okome (2013: 19). The film drew on innovative approaches to funding that resulted in a budget exceeding expectations for a Nigerian film. Executive producer Yewande Sadiku noted in interviews that accumulating funds for the project was a challenge that required rethinking her financial expectations and strategies. Seventy to eighty percent of the budget (which topped out at 1.6 billion naira, or roughly ten million dollars) came from Nigerian investors, with foreign partners that included the British Film Institute (Ogunlesi 2013).

Even while attempting to distance itself from run-of-the-mill Nollywood productions, the film's pre-release publicity and reception reveal how contingent new Nollywood has been on the video film movement and its popular networks. The film was early on hailed as destined to mark out a new era for Nollywood, with promotional materials and online discussions expressing belief that it would finally assuage concerns about "poor quality" Nigerian movies. One commentator noted that Nollywood fans seeking more professional looking productions and international recognition would finally hear "their prayers [. . .] answered; we'll pray no more": Nollywood had arrived to produce "its most expensive movie yet" (Baffour 2013). Deeply embedded in discussions of Bandele's production as it moved forward were debates about Nollywood's status and the directions in which Nigerian filmmaking needed to travel in order to overcome its critical, theatrical, and award-circuit marginalisation. As Nadia Denton, author of *The Nigerian Filmmaker's Guide to Success: Beyond Nollywood*, asserted:

> There's an emerging class of Nigerian filmmaker [who] don't want their films to just go out on DVD into the market, like they traditionally have, but they want to do the festival circuit, internationally. They want to get Academy Award nominations. They want the world's vision of Africa to be quite different. And they're working tirelessly, in terms of the aesthetic and the quality of their films, to try to raise the bar.
>
> *(Joyner 2014)*

Underlining such elevated expectations, the film debuted at the Toronto International Film Festival (TIFF)—a rare case of a Nigerian feature at a major festival of this stature outside of Africa.

But *Half of a Yellow Sun*'s status as new Nollywood might be examined in more depth. Bandele did not come up through the ranks of jobbing Nollywood networks; he is a London-based, established novelist and playwright who worked with the Royal Court Theatre and the Royal Shakespeare Company. Though *Half of a Yellow Sun* was his cinema debut, in a number of ways it can be seen to follow auteurist tendencies that have reinforced national cinema models (and have been revived in African cinema) (Buscombe 1981; Sanogo 2015). Bandele not only directed but wrote the adaptation, with little interference or guidance from Adichie. Indeed, Bandele stated that Adichie "had absolutely no involvement whatsoever", and stressed he avoided being overly dogmatic with respect to faithfulness to the novel (Beesley 2014). He further articulated his role as a writer-director transforming a text into a new medium: "in changing to different mediums you cannot be literal", he noted, "if you're translating German or French into English, you have to use idioms and it's exactly the same with cinema" (Beesley 2014). Here the writer–director, working along lines described by Walter Benjamin as the task of the translator, can discover means of harmonising the resultant text with its original (Benjamin 1996 [1923]: 257), while outlining the distinctiveness both of the new medium and of creating cinematic art.

While in global terms ten million dollars is a relatively modest budget for an ambitious transnational project, the film's international visibility, the status of Adichie's book, and Nollywood's internet buzz greatly boosted interest. After completion, it became clear that cultural and political pressures were higher on this kind of theatrical release than Nollywood had yet encountered: due to revisiting sensitive issues relating to Nigeria's early independence era and the fragmentations of the Biafran war, a seemingly nervous Nigerian Film and Video Censors Board delayed release within the country due to "objectionable" scenes (BBC 2014). It was finally released in Nigeria in August 2014, nearly eleven months after its Toronto debut.

The film broke box office records on its first weekend of release in Nigeria, and won the Golden Dhow at the Zanzibar International Film Festival. Still its reception among Nollywood fans was mixed. A chief criticism related to casting, reducing a well-known, award-winning Nigerian actress such as Genevieve Nnaji to a small role while elevating actors born and working outside Nigeria to starring roles. Some Nollywood supporters found fault with the inauthenticity of accents and the pronunciation of the Igbo language: "Anika Noni Rose as Kainene retains her American accent. And unforgivably [Thandie] Newton is unable to say 'kedu'—this last is particularly troubling" (Aigbokhaevbolo 2014). Indeed, for a film largely funded by Nigerian investors and shot domestically (at Tinapa Studios in Cross River State, with sequences done at Shepperton Studios in London), reducing emerging and familiar Nigerian actors to minor roles, as happened to OC Ukeje as well as to Nnaji, might seem a means of distancing the production from Nollywood associations and roots, if not necessarily from Nigeria itself.

If casting decisions hint at an implicit, if partial, distancing of the production from familiar Nollywood faces and practices, interestingly reviews generated outside Nigeria frequently

Figure 4.1 Promotional poster for *Half of a Yellow Sun* (2013, Nigeria, Biyi Bandele). ©Soda Pictures.

isolated the cast's performances as the film's strongest element. For Peter Bradshaw writing in *The Guardian*, the film is "well intentioned and certainly very well cast" (Bradshaw 2014), while for Guy Lodge in the same newspaper, it is "rescued by uniformly strong performances, with Thandie Newton on seething, career-best form" (Lodge 2014). As the film's promotional poster demonstrates, the international appeal not just of the actors but of the credentials they brought with them—"Academy Award nominee" and "BAFTA winner" are displayed above the leads' names—would have been considered crucial to bolstering the film's festival and award-circuit appeal.

The poster's imagery and text fuel audience expectations of cinematic grandeur: this is clearly not cheaply made, Nollywood-style entertainment. The imagery works to encapsulate the narrative and visual expansiveness, and star power, of big screen productions (Figure 4.1). The eye-catching credentials listed above Chiwetel Ejiofor's and Newton's names further announce, and brand, the production as occupying an international and cinematic, rather than localised and televisual, realm. The film's title is framed by sample reviews and a catchphrase ("divided by war, united by love") positioned against a collage of five dramatic scenes that dissolve into and appear to emerge from each other. Somewhat strangely, one version of the poster (featured on the region 2 DVD) calls the film "the greatest love story on film since *Gone with the Wind*" (James 2014), the latter film without doubt part of the classic cinematic canon, though frequently associated with Hollywood's history of racial stereotyping and nostalgic portrayals of antebellum slavery. The breadth of a classic Hollywood epic is captured in a wide shot of landscape, with

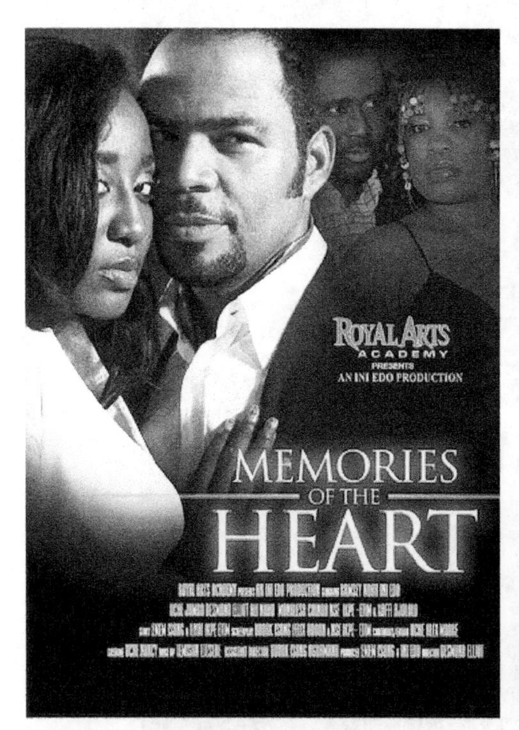

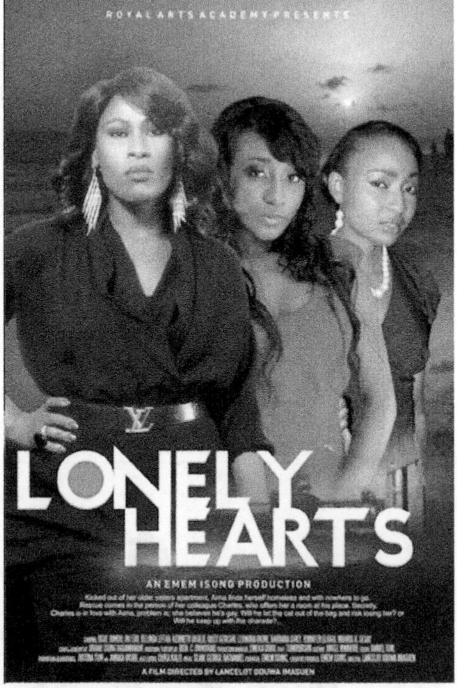

Figure 4.2 *Memories of the Heart* (2010, Nigeria, Desmond Elliot). ©Royal Arts Academy.

Figure 4.3 *Lonely Hearts* (2013, Nigeria, Lancelot Oduwa Imasuen). ©Royal Arts Academy.

figures framed on one side by the flames of war, on the other by the setting sun, redolent of the cinematographic "golden hour" or what Jack Cardiff called the "magic hour" (Cardiff 1996). This dissolves into a two-shot of Kainene (Rose) and Richard (Joseph Mawle) dancing, which itself is set against the dominant shot: a close up of Odenigbo (Ejiofor) and Olanna (Newton) at their wedding, promising a narrative of epic romance alongside epic conflict. Overall, the collage signals a sweeping story lensed through cinematic aesthetics: it is visually composed along the lines of the renaissance altarpiece or fresco, where the viewer is invited to interrelate smaller panels crowned by a larger figure or figures (usually "Christ in Majesty"); it also evokes the cinematic technique of the lap dissolve.

The *Half of a Yellow Sun* poster markedly differs from much Nollywood promotional imagery, which tends to feature lead actors in close up or medium shots, usually facing the camera in a form of direct address to the audience (Figure 4.2 and Figure 4.3). This practice reflects an emphasis in the video films on developing strong central characters (which can lead to sequels) and promoting global transmedia stars in the Nollywood system (Tsika 2015: 51). It also follows conventions of small screen shooting, recalling the interactivity and intimacy of televisual consumption, as Nollywood video films have generally been made for a market that centres on domestic (and often distracted and interrupted) viewing habits (Adejunmobi 2015: 123).

Given *Half of a Yellow Sun*'s promotional efforts to connote an epic and rarefied cinema experience, it is telling of new Nollywood's still-fragile critical status that, when surveying Western media outlets, we find critics locating its chief problems in replicating offenses commonly ascribed to Nollywood. Perhaps invoking the Nollywood video film's historical relations to the soap opera, Bradshaw continues: "the film is often stately and sluggish with some very daytime-soapy moments of emotional revelation. At other times, it looks more like a filmed theatrical piece" (Bradshaw 2014). Similarly, for Lodge, the film is "a soapy step down from its literary source", and a "surface-level saga" (Lodge 2014; 2013). The *Los Angeles Times* refers to it as a "choppy melodrama" (Abele 2014). Indeed, Latin American soap operas or *telenovelas* had a significant influence on Nollywood from its beginnings, and were popular in Nigeria from the late 1980s through the mid-1990s, particularly when a dispute between the Nigerian Television Authority and its sponsors during the 1990s hindered Nigerian production (Aminu 2009). As Haynes puts it, "soap operas (both domestic and imported) [. . .] make up a large part of [Nollywood's] DNA" (2007: 139).

Writing after a TIFF screening, Zeba Blay followed a further line of critique that, while not always severe, compared the film unfavourably to its literary source. Blay suggests the film lacks the stylistic inventiveness and subtlety of Adichie's book while relying "too heavily on melodramatic dialogue and an emotionally manipulative score" (Blay 2013). The film version is a compressed and chronologically linear version of the novel, attempting to encompass the prodigious expanse of Adichie's story while providing a coherent and easily digested narrative within a rather lean 107-minutes running time. The novel is structured through three narrative focalisers, rendered in third person with elements of modernist free indirect discourse, styled to bring the reader closer to the characters' inner worlds. These primary figures are Olanna, daughter of a wealthy industrialist and Kainene's (non-identical) twin; Ugwu (John Boyego in the film), who is Odenigbo's bookish and observant houseboy; and Richard, a British expatriate obsessed with Igbo culture, who becomes romantically involved with Kainene. These diverse perspectives are reduced in the film to a primary focus on Olanna with a secondary focus on Kainene. The result of Bandele's streamlining—where the sujet, or organisation of the storytelling, is more closely aligned with the fabula, or actual story as it would exist in chronological order—is a significant change to Adichie's formal rendering of the complex and elusive processes of (re)constructing cultural and national history, and memory.

While divided between three focalisers, the novel's narrative is also divided between two historical moments in the 1960s, moving back and forth often unpredictably—time travelling to before and during the Biafran war—therefore invoking the ruptures and uneven constructions of history that result from personal and cultural traumas. Adichie's book is marked by historical retellings that diverge and overlap, with a wilful and at times disruptive inversion of chronological sequencing, undermining any neat cause and effect interpretations of military conflict or of those who become involved, and implicated, in it. At unexpected moments, the repressions of cultural and national memory are interrupted by eruptions of knowing or shock, marked out by a formal strategy of narrative elision and unsettling return: the sudden explosion of the air raid, or the news report announcing life-altering events, that crash into increasingly precious scenes of domestic calmness and the everyday.

The film aims for greater narrative transparency, which was perhaps considered necessary to its transnational success. This impression is reinforced by techniques such as the animated maps that link transitions to different scene locations and illustrate the characters' comings and goings—from Lagos to Kano, Nsukka to Port Harcourt—visually laying out the sprawling geography of Nigeria, presumably for those (non-Nigerian audiences) less familiar with it. Again, such moves would seem to go against the approach of the novel, which offers no illustrative map, and problematises the mapped zones of Nigeria and their common territorialisations through a novelistic structure that could be described more as a mosaic than a linear cause and effect pattern. As much as it deals with violent conflict and cultural division, Adichie's novel stresses connections and affiliations forged across zones of difference.

One important element maintained in the film is the enigmatic characterisation of Kainene. In the novel she is associated elliptically, via Richard, with the ancient Igbo roped pot—an unknowable, fetishised vessel that Richard (himself a rather fragile, decentred Western subject amidst the postcolony) is unable to fully comprehend or possess, yet to which he is irrepressibly drawn. When, in the novel, Richard is searching for Kainene as the war draws to a close, he shows people her photo hoping to jog their memories, although "sometimes, in his rush, he pulled out the picture of the roped pot instead" (Adichie 2006: 407). Kainene's disappearance and ultimate status as "missing" further underlines her elusiveness, the elusiveness of Nigeria itself to desiring Westerners such as Richard, and the ways the traumatic collective memory of the Biafran war is a kind of caesura, refusing definitive resolution. Bandele omits the image of the Igbo bronze pot, but retains Kainene's missing status, which for Akudinobi suggests "a parable of psychical repression, repositioning her [. . .] as an obstacle to amnesiac, nationalistic narratives of closure" (2015b: 281). Still, Bandele inserts a further closure in the form of end titles, where the book offered only intermittent inklings of the future (via fragments from Ugwu's book): we are informed that Richard returned to Nsukka, that Odenigbo and Olanna have remained together for decades, that Ugwu is a writer, and that Baby (Chiamaka) has become a doctor.

The film's narrative, structural and symbolic streamlining of the novel does not necessarily, however, mean that it lacks all subtlety. It offers skilful cinematic flourishes, such as the drawn out, overhead zoom to the couple lying in bed as Olanna reveals her infidelity to Odenigbo; the expertly controlled emotionalism of the key scene, in both book and film, where Odenigbo's mother (Onyeka Onwenu) remains behind as the war advances. Its cinematographic canvas (lensed by John de Borman) conjures up expansive vistas, again marking a change from Nollywood's televisual world of close ups, or what Haynes calls "fundamentally a cinema of faces, which need to be seen in close-up because we need to see the tears streaming down them or otherwise get close to the emotions generated by almost invariably melodramatic plots". Haynes continues, noting Nollywood offers "an aesthetic of immediate impact, plunging us into each moment and milking it for everything it is worth, rather than subordinating every element in the film to an overall sense of design" (Haynes 2007: 139). Bandele's production arguably does illustrate this latter sense of embedding elements within a larger cinematic design: the carefully controlled performance of Ejiofor, for example, almost effortlessly meshes with the note-perfect mis-en-scène of Odenigbo's Nsukka house, drenched in warm tones and carefully crafted lighting set-ups (the *New York Times* justifiably praised the film's "faultless art direction" [Kenigsberg 2014]).

Yet the film at the same time draws on an aesthetic of immediate impact that recalls Nollywood, also taking a cue from Adichie's novel. One of the effective techniques that Bandele adapts to the cinematic idiom is Adichie's command of the abrupt shift in tone, dictated by a sudden, usually violent event. In the book, a moment of bonding between mother and adopted child during bath time is shattered by the raised voice of Odenigbo announcing news of Major Nzeogwu's fierce coup attempt, foreshadowing the much more intense shocks and ruptures of impending war (Adichie 2006: 123). Another key moment, approximated in the film as closely as possible in terms of narrative content and tone, is the wedding scene, where the brief suspension of forward movement in anticipating taking a photograph is broken by an air raid. As the novel describes it:

> When Okeoma started his toast, she wiped her eyes and told the photographer standing behind the tripod, "Wait, wait, don't take it yet."
>
> Ugwu heard the sound just before they cut their cake in the living room, the swift *wah-wah-wah* roar in the sky. At first it was thunderous, and then it receded for a moment and came back again, louder and swifter.
>
> *(Adichie 2006: 202)*

In the film the scene begins with wide exterior shots of the wedding party advancing up the street, followed by a gathering in the living room, with "Hail Biafra" by Cardinal Rex Lawson permeating the diegetic space. Odenigbo and Olanna pause for a photograph as they cut the cake, standing in front of a large window that roughly approximates the aspect ratio of the cinema screen. As the photographer counts down, an explosion directly outside the window shatters the moment: war explodes into the domestic scene; political and national tensions erupt into private life. The music ("music has no borders" argues Professor Ezeka early in the novel [Adichie 2006: 110]) instantly stops; the tone lurches into sudden chaos as the guests flee in terror. The overall effect draws both on classic cinematic framing and editing techniques and an aesthetic of immediate impact that recalls Nollywood: we are plunged into the moment with physical and dramatic intensity.

Half of a Yellow Sun exemplifies the culturally specific yet also transnational, outward-looking tendencies of new Nollywood, as well as the latter's self-conscious efforts to reinstate the cinematic experience; yet in it we can also see how contingent new Nollywood has been on Nollywood itself. The film's reception in many markets further betrays an inbuilt critical tendency towards dismissing Nollywood, and the difficulties new Nollywood faces in shaking off the ghosts of the "old".

Conclusion

Yet if *Half of a Yellow Sun* comes from such a different world to Nollywood in terms of approach, budget, casting, distribution, and other defining elements, what is really left of Nollywood in the new incarnation?

In spite of poor box office takings outside of African markets,[3] Bandele's film arguably broke new ground with respect to budgeting in Nigeria and distribution overseas. Perhaps new Nollywood does not need a progress narrative of "transcending" the video film, but rather a position that embraces what I have been calling here Nollywood's ongoing refashioning: a cinematic continuum that draws together diverse approaches. Indeed, cinematic outputs are diversifying, from no budget to blockbuster, from small and miniature screens to IMAX and 3D, from wide international release to straight-to-YouTube series and shorts. Nollywood too is diversifying, with numerous films available on pay-per-view platforms such as Netflix, and South Africa's M-Net, featuring Nollywood channels, available across the continent. Launched in 2011, iROKOtv, widely referred to as the "the Netflix of Africa", is a dedicated site for accessing thousands of Nollywood and Ghanaian movies.

Nollywood's refashioning indicates, in many ways, that since the 1990s it has not been just a phenomenon waiting to progress towards higher quality cinema, but has always been what Leon Gurevitch, in another context, calls a "symptom of a mediated negotiation with, and expansion of, audiovisual functions that during the twentieth century came to be associated with the cinematic" (Gurevitch 2013: 175). This does not mean that, keeping new Nollywood in mind, we cannot or should not try to engage practices that constitute a particular experience of the cinematic, but at the same time we might recognise that a given medium's "identity" can only be defined in a difference-relation to other media: all media (including theatrically projected celluloid) are therefore in an *intermediate state* with reference to other media, not just emerging media (Geiger and Littau 2013: 3–4). This thinking might encourage further revising of goal oriented "beyond video" cinematic narratives, and perhaps holds the promise of locating Nollywood video films as central to cinema history, and new Nollywood cinema as a distinct manifestation of Nollywood.

Notes

1 The term "Nollywood" has problematic associations and has been contested almost since it appeared. As Carmen McCain points out, the term Nollywood "homogenizes a diverse industry" and tends to emphasise Lagos-based video production, potentially eliding the importance of Yoruba and Hausa productions (the Hausa industry, based in Kano, known for decades as "Kannywood"), as well as Edo film-making based in Benin City and that of nearby countries such as Ghana (McCain 2011).

2 Arguably, Gabriel himself incorporated this potential for change into his Third Cinema theory, later arguing: "One of the great mistakes of "left" politics has always been to imagine itself as pure and unambiguous in its oppositional stance. Rather than setting itself simply in opposition to capitalism, a composite politics, by its nature, works to disorganize the rigid "Us versus Them" structure upon which globalisation, imperialism, and other forms of oppression are based. Third Cinema, at its best, always drew its strength from this sense of complexity, diversity, and multiplicity" (Gabriel 2009).

3 An ambitious marketing campaign in the UK involved collaboration between the BFI and Kush Promotions, targeting Black audiences and media outlets. The film grossed just over £150,000 in thirteen weeks of release, which the managing director of the film's distributor, Soda Pictures, considered a "decent result" (Barratt 2014: 15).

References

Abele, R. (2014) "*Half of a Yellow Sun* Doesn't Add Up to a Satisfying Whole", *Los Angeles Times*, 23 May, www.latimes.com/entertainment/movies/la-et-mn-half-yellow-sun-review-20140523-story.html.

Adejunmobi, M. (2015) "African Film's Televisual Turn", *Cinema Journal* 54 (2): 120–125.

Adichie, C. N. (2006) *Half of a Yellow Sun*, London: Fourth Estate.

Aigbokhaevbolo, O. (2014) "*Half of a Yellow Sun* Not for Nigerians", *This is Africa*, 3 November, http://thisisafrica.me/half-yellow-sun-not-for-nigerians/.

Akudinobi, J. (2015a) "Nollywood: Prisms and Paradigms", *Cinema Journal* 54 (2):133–140.
Akudinobi, J. (2015b) "*Half of a Yellow Sun* by Biyi Bandele", *African Studies Review* 58 (2): 279–281.
Aminu, A. B. (2009) "Nollywood Can Be Saved If …" [interview with Mak 'Kusare], *Weekly Trust* (Abuja), 1 August, http://weekly.dailytrust.com.
Baffour, K. (2013) "*Half of a Yellow Sun* Confirmed as Nollywood's Most Expensive Movie", Naij.com, 1 August, www.naij.com/31426.html.
Barratt, J. (2014) "Insight Report: *Half of a Yellow Sun*", British Film Institute and Bigger Picture Research, www.bfi.org.uk/sites/bfi.org.uk/files/downloads/bfi-insight-report-half-of-a-yellow-sun-2014-10-20_0.pdf.
Barrot, P. (ed.) (2009) *Nollywood: The Video Phenomenon in Nigeria*, Bloomington, IN: Indiana University Press.
BBC News (2014) "*Half of a Yellow Sun* Approved by Nigeria Censors", BBC News website, 8 July, www.bbc.co.uk/news/world-africa-28212955.
Beesley, R. (2014) "Personalizing the Political: *Half of a Yellow Sun*", *Aesthetica* 58 (April/May), www.aestheticamagazine.com/personalising-the-political-2/.
Benjamin, W. (1996 [1923]) "The Task of the Translator", trans. Harry Zohn, in Bullock, M. and Jennings, M. W. (eds), *Walter Benjamin: Selected Writings, 1913–1926*, Cambridge, MA: Harvard University Press, 253–263.
Blay, Z. (2013) "TIFF 2013 Review: Biyi Bandele's Adaptation of *Half of a Yellow Sun* Misses the Mark", *IndieWire*, 12 September, www.indiewire.com/2013/09/tiff-2013-review-biyi-bandeles-adaptation-of-half-of-a-yellow-sun-misses-the-mark-165235/.
Bolter, J. D. and Grusin, R. (1998) *Remediation: Understanding New Media*, Boston, MA: The MIT Press.
Bradshaw, P. (2014) "*Half of a Yellow Sun* Review", *The Guardian*, 10 April, www.theguardian.com/film/2014/apr/10/half-of-a-yellow-sun-chimamanda-ngozi-adichie-film-review.
Buscombe, E. (1981) "The Idea of National Cinema", *Australian Journal of Screen Theory* 9 (10): 141–153.
Cardiff, J. (1996) *Magic Hour: The Life of a Cameraman*, New York: Faber.
Ekunno, M. (2011) "Nollywood and the New Cinema", *234Next*, 2 January, https://findingnollywood.com/2011/01/03/234next-nollywood-and-the-new-cinema/.
Gabriel, T. (1982) *Third Cinema in the Third World: The Aesthetics of Liberation*, Ann Arbor, MI: UMI Research Press.
—— (2009) "Third Cinema Updated: Exploration of Nomadic Aesthetics and Narrative Communities", *Articles and Other Works*, Teshome Gabriel.net, http://teshomegabriel.net/third-cinema-updated.
Geiger, J. (2012) "Nollywood Style: Nigerian Movies and 'Shifting Perceptions of Worth'", *Film International* 10 (6): 58–72.
Geiger, J. and Littau, K. (2013) "Introduction: Cinematicity and Comparative Media", in Geiger, J. and Littau, K. (eds), *Cinematicity in Media History*, Edinburgh: Edinburgh University Press, 1–18.
Greenberg, I. (2014) "Can *Half of a Yellow Sun* Bring Nollywood Closer to Hollywood?" *Lagos Today*, 12 September, www.lagostoday.org/can-half-of-a-yellow-sun-bring-nollywood-closer-to-hollywood/.
Gurevitch, L. (2013) "Cinema, Video, Game: Astonishing Aesthetics and the Cinematic 'Future' of Computer Graphics' Past", in Geiger, J. and Littau, K. (eds), *Cinematicity in Media History*, Edinburgh: Edinburgh University Press, 173–195.
Haynes, J. (2007) "Nollywood in Lagos, Lagos in Nollywood Films", *Africa Today* 54 (2): 131–150.
—— (2010) "What Is to Be Done? Film Studies and Nigerian and Ghanaian Videos", in Saul, M. and Austen, R. A. (eds), *Viewing African Film in the Twenty-first Century*, Athens, OH: Ohio University Press: 11–25.
—— (2014) "The New Nollywood: Kunle Afolayan", *Black Camera* 5 (2): 53–73.
Hubner, L. (ed.) (2011), *Valuing Films: Shifting Perceptions of Worth*, Basingstoke: Palgrave.
James, A. J. (2014) "Here Comes the Sun", *Nigerian Watch* (UK), 28 March, 7.
Jedlowski, A. (2011) *Videos in Motion: Processes of Transnationalization in the Southern Nigerian Video Industry: Networks, Discourses, Aesthetics*, PhD Thesis, University of Naples Orientale, https://orbi.ulg.ac.be/bitstream/2268/177490/1/PhD%20Dissertation%20-%20A.Jedlowski.pdf.
Jedlowski, A. (2013) "From Nollywood to Nollyworld: Processes of Transnationalization in the Nigerian Video Film Industry", in Krings, M. and Okome, O. (eds), *Global Nollywood: The Transnational Dimensions of an African Video Film Industry*, Bloomington, IN: Indiana University Press, 25–45.
Joyner, A. (2014) "New Nollywood? The Future of the World's Second Largest Film Industry", 1 April, *International Business Times*, www.ibtimes.co.uk/new-nollywood-future-worlds-second-largest-film-industry-1442857.

Kenigsberg, B. (2014) "In Nigeria, the Personal and the Political Clash: *Half of a Yellow Sun*", *New York Times*, 15 May, www.nytimes.com/2014/05/16/movies.

Krings, M. and Okome, O. (eds). (2013) *Global Nollywood: The Transnational Dimensions of an African Video Film Industry*, Bloomington, IN: Indiana University Press.

Lodge, G. (2013) "Toronto Film Review: *Half of a Yellow Sun*", *Variety*, 8 September, http://variety.com/2013/film/global/half-of-a-yellow-sun-review-toronto-1200603565/.

Lodge, G. (2014) "*Starred Up, Labor Day, Half of a Yellow Sun,* and More", *The Guardian*, 2 August, www.theguardian.com/film/2014/aug/02/dvds-downloads-starred-up-labor-day.

McCain, C. (2011) "Nollywood and Its Terminology Migraines", *Daily Trust* (Abuja), 30 July, www.dailytrust.com.ng.

McCall, J. C. (2007) "The Pan-Africanism We Have: Nollywood's Invention of Africa", *Film International* 5 (4): 92–97.

Mistry, J. and Ellapen, J. A. (2013) "Nollywood's Transportability: The Politics and Economics of Video Films as Cultural Products", in Matthias Krings and Onookome Okome (eds), *Global Nollywood*, Bloomington, IN: Indiana University Press, 46–69.

Odulaja, A. (2014) "*Half of a Yellow Sun* and Its Many Controversies", *NET* online, 25 August, http://thenet.ng/2014/08/net-special-a-look-at-half-of-a-yellow-sun-and-its-many-controversies/.

Ogunlesi, T. (2013) "Nigeria's Nollywood Seeks Overseas Acclaim", *Financial Times* (London), 10 October, https://next.ft.com/content/63d8674a-2440-11e3-a8f7-00144feab7de.

Okome, O. (2007) "Nollywood: Spectatorship, Audience, and the Sites of Consumption", *Postcolonial Text* 3 (2): 1–21.

Rice, A. (2012) "A Scorsese in Lagos: The Making of Nigeria's Film Industry", *New York Times* Magazine, 23 February, MM26-MM29.

Sanogo, A. (2015) "Certain Tendencies in Contemporary Auteurist Film Practice in Africa", *Cinema Journal* 54 (2): 140–149.

Steinglass, M. (2002) "When There's Too Much of a Not-Very-Good Thing", *New York Times*, 26 May, sec. 2, 16.

Tsika, N. A. (2015) *Nollywood Stars: Media and Migration in West Africa and the Diaspora*, Bloomington, IN: Indiana University Press.

United Nations News Center (2009) "Nigeria Surpasses Hollywood as World's Second Largest Film Producer", 5 May, www.un.org/apps/news/story.asp?NewsID=30707#.V0ImfvkrLIU.

5

FRAMING DEMOCRACY

Film in post-democracy South Africa

Ian-Malcolm Rijsdijk

> Could've been the rainbow, though.
>
> *(Necktie Youth)*

Introduction

In Sibs Shongwe La-Mer's 2015 film *Necktie Youth* (South Africa/Netherlands), a wealthy black mother and father discuss the news over breakfast. Parents of the film's protagonist Jabz, they are seated at opposite ends of an ornate dining table against a backdrop of tall bookshelves and luxurious drapes (Figure 5.1). After the mother bemoans the scandal-ridden politicians of the moment, the father responds, "There was only one Mandela, and even him it was just sheer luck." There follows a cutaway to a large gilt-framed portrait of Nelson Mandela staring serenely over the conversation, a kitsch icon (Figure 5.2).

Figure 5.1 A wealthy black mother and father discuss the news over breakfast in *Necktie Youth* (2015, South Africa/Netherlands, Sibs Shongwe-La Mer). ©Urucu Media/Whitman Independent/100% Halal.

Figure 5.2 A kitsch icon of Nelson Mandela stares down in the reverse shot of Figure 5.1. *Necktie Youth* (2015, South Africa/Netherlands, Sibs Shongwe-La Mer), set during the anniversary of the Soweto Youth Uprising of 1976. ©Urucu Media/Whitman Independent/100% Halal.

Throughout the film, South Africa's reconciled rainbow nation appears intermittently in a nostalgic haze of faux home-movie segments. Parents, and the idols of their political emancipation, lie on the periphery of the youthful protagonists' experiences as they carouse around Johannesburg in a Jaguar, drinking, taking drugs, having sex, and talking about why Emily, Jabz' white girlfriend, hanged herself and live-streamed her suicide on the internet. The film opens with Emily staging and completing her suicide while her mother talks on a cellphone inside the house, and closes with Jabz' parents coming upon their son's suicide.

In *Thina Sobabili* (The Two of Us, 2015, South Africa, Ernest Nkosi) Thulas, a small-time township gangster looks after his sister Zanele, protecting her from older, wealthy men while scrounging money to pay for her high-school education. He has lied to his sister, saying that their mother, Zoleka, is dead, while in reality she lives with her abusive partner across town. Zoleka finally returns to witness the aftermath of a fight that leaves Thulas dead in her arms. At the end of both films, parents appear powerless to save their abandoned children.

It would be tempting to suggest that these films—directed by young filmmakers, and featuring young people cast adrift in contemporary South Africa—represent a "New Wave" of South African cinema (Prendini Toffoli 2015; Motsaathebe 2015). There are several factors that support this, among them the emergence of film training at tertiary institutions in the past fifteen to twenty years, increased access to foreign markets for South African filmmakers, and transformations in digital distribution platforms. However, one needs to distinguish between the mere fact of "newness", and the deeper transformations in South African society that are changing the way filmmakers tell stories, the stories they are choosing to tell, and the ways people are watching them. As filmmaker Jenna Bass says: "I have to believe that South African audiences have been waiting for [. . .] a sea-change in cinema to start reflecting some kind of relatable truthfulness, even if it's bizarre and sometimes extreme" (Sebambo 2015). Bass expresses both the optimism and caution of the so-called "born frees", loosely defined as those young people who have grown up in post-apartheid South Africa. Political scientist, Robert Mattes describes how,

> Beginning in 1997, growing numbers of young people began to move through the ages of 16, 17 and 18 and enter the political arena with little if any first-hand experience of the trauma that came before [...] Their first political experience, possibly casting a vote in the 1999 election, was with a relatively normal, though clearly reform-minded, democratic political system.
>
> *(2012: 139)*

The "born-frees"—who constitute both the new generation of filmmakers and a substantial part of their potential audiences—are defined by a paradox: in an environment of supposed opportunity, "many born frees face the same, if not greater, levels of unemployment, poverty, inequality and hopelessness as their parents" (Mattes 2012: 140). Are they truly born free, or are they growing up with the burden of expectation born of the fact of political liberation?

This chapter will examine contemporary South African film drawing on two apparently contradictory concepts; first, what political scientist Colin Crouch has termed "post-democracy", and second, "democracy-to-come", developed by Jacques Derrida, but adapted to the South African context by Herman Wasserman. Is a "New Wave" of "born-free" South African filmmakers emerging, and what do they have to say about a country that is now post-apartheid and post-Mandela, uncomfortably reconciled, maturing yet unsettled by youthful protest? Is South African film experiencing a "post-nationalist shift" in which "nation building has become a less prominent, if not absent, motivation in filmmaking" (Tcheuyap 2011: 1), and are we defined by the genuine plurality of our narratives rather than a rainbow of many parts?

Before engaging with thoughts about South Africa's social and political present, it is important to note one key parameter of this discussion: I will examine feature films that constitute only a small percentage of what could be considered screen representations of the country. Tomaselli and Shepperson write that, "the potential for cinematic symbolic expression to mediate between a known and familiar past (even if the material and symbolic relations of this past have been almost totally rejected), and a desired but uncertain future, should not be underestimated" (2014: 111). However, balanced against this desire to tell the national story through the medium of film (particularly the fiction feature film) is the observation that, "although it is reasonable to suggest that many in South Africa are conscious of cinema, they do not experience it as a need due to their cultural experience under conditions of necessity" (2014: 113).

A fuller examination of South Africa's democratic character on screen needs to consider the complexity of broadcast television (national free to air and commercial), television audiences, and the increasing popularity of documentary film. My aim, therefore, is not to propose a cultural understanding of South Africa through its feature films, but rather to see how the social and political processes in the country are evident in the visual storytelling that is particular to the fiction feature film.

South Africa turns 21, or "the tunnel at the end of the light"

In 2014 South Africa celebrated the twentieth anniversary of its first democratic elections. It was the year that Mandela's autobiography *Long Walk to Freedom* finally made it to the cinema screen (a year after Mandela died) in a big-budget British–South African co-production (with British actor Idris Elba as Mandela). While there was a great deal of reflection on the momentous 1994 elections—marked by documentaries such as *Miracle Rising: South Africa* (2013, South Africa, Brett Lotriet Best) and *1994: The Bloody Miracle* (2014, South Africa, Bert Haitsma and Meg Rickards)—and continued public recognition of Mandela's role in the "peaceful transition to democracy" (Camay and Gordon, n.d.; Posel, 2014), the nostalgia in these films belied increasing volatility in the country: ongoing xenophobic violence, service-delivery protests, and deepening dissatisfaction with the government's response to the Marikana massacre of 2012. The murder by police of thirty-four miners at Marikana has developed into a potent symbol of state violence in contemporary South African political history, and is frequently paralleled with the massacre of black protestors by the apartheid government at Sharpville in 1960.

One can consider South Africa's cultural history since the unbanning of the African National Council (ANC) in 1990 as consisting of several eras. The period between 1990 and 1994 was an "interregnum" characterised by a heady mix of optimism, paranoia and violence or, put another way, Gramsci's "great diversity of morbid symptoms" (1971: 276). In the years following the first democratic elections, the metaphor of the "rainbow nation" drove the national narrative, symbolised by iconic moments such as Mandela's donning of the Springbok jersey at South Africa's triumphant Rugby World Cup Final of 1995, and represented by the Truth and Reconciliation Commission, the hearings of which began in 1996.

Mbeki's presidency was one of relative stability, though it was increasingly undermined by two dominant failures: Aids denialism (which delayed the roll-out of antiretroviral drugs at state institutions) and the festering arms deal scandal, where billions of Rands were paid out in a complex system of bribes between European arms manufacturers and locally connected businessmen and politicians (Feinstein 2007). The political legacy Mbeki hoped to leave was of an African Renaissance, "a rediscovery of ourselves [. . .] a voyage of discovery into our own antecedents, our own past as Africans [. . .] Unless we are able to answer the question: Who are we?, we shall not be able to answer the question: What shall we be?" (Gevisser 2007: 16). While striving for an economic and political awakening of the African continent, Mbeki faced the real fear of failing to meet the expectations of the majority of South Africans to bring about meaningful change in their lives beyond the democratic right to vote. This "dream deferred" (2007: 658) is what signals the volatile transition from the political era of Mbeki to the rousing populism of Jacob Zuma, who unseated Mbeki as president of the ANC in 2007 and became president of the country in 2009.

A discussion of the vicissitudes of Zuma's presidency and the alarming implosion of South Africa's economy and political dialogue in the past five years lies on the periphery of this chapter. The current political ferment, dominated by the student-driven protests and constitutional court rulings around the president and parliament, makes most statements about contemporary South Africa subject to swift irrelevance. However, what is relevant to this discussion is the increasingly widespread disaffection for the ruling party during Zuma's term in office, made manifest during local government elections in August 2016. While the factionalism within the ruling party, and the extraordinary nation-wide corruption that has characterised Zuma's presidency has prompted nostalgia for the ANC of Mandela, Sisulu and other elder statesmen, as South Africa celebrated its twenty-first birthday and democratic maturity, it is worth briefly considering Mandela's legacy.

In 1994, Rob Nixon wrote: "From the outset, the South African state seemed to fear that Mandela possessed a great talent for immortality" (1994: 175). To some extent, the same is true for the ANC governments that have succeeded Mandela: how to celebrate the popular national unification he championed while dealing with the rifts in class and race that have increasingly defined South African society in the post-Mandela years. Mandela's advanced age and rapidly deteriorating health meant that his death in December 2013 was expected; more significantly, however, it was regarded by some with great dread. What would happen afterwards? Would the reconciliation between black and white for which Mandela had worked so hard fall apart? As was the case during the interregnum, the reality was more banal than such dire predictions: there was no need to stock up on canned food, batteries and bottled water.

When I have posed the question of how we define our current cultural condition to my students in seminars—given that post-apartheid now appears too crudely temporal—a few original terms have arisen: post-millennial is popular, but feels too global; post-reconciliation is interesting as is the more theoretical construct of (de)reconciliation which suggests simultaneous attempts to reconcile and deconstruct a national narrative in which reconciliation has been an imperative. What is certain in these discussions with the so-called "born-frees" is that the cult of Mandela has gradually been eroded. As Nixon noted presciently at the time of the first elections:

> Mandela has found himself hard pressed to sustain an aura as a national politician equal to his international prestige as elder statesman. Indubitably, of the two, his internal authority will continue to come under greater pressure as South Africa enters the tunnel at the end of the light.
>
> *(1994: 190)*

Thus the paradox of Mandela. There is nostalgia for Mandela that emerges ever more frequently as people shake their heads at intemperate cabinet debates, and bemoan the lack of moral substance in the current ANC leadership. At the same time there is a recognition that reconciliation was too easily won by whites, that blacks made substantial compromises while the white business classes were not made to work hard enough in confronting both the evils of apartheid and the deep inequalities that it has perpetuated into the present (Roper 2013; Meintjies 2015). As one placard put it bluntly during #FeesMustFall protests in 2015: "My parents were sold dreams in 1994, I'm just here for the refund" (Serino 2016). During a flashback montage of a child's birthday party in the 1990s, the narrator of *Necktie Youth* notes wryly, "Could've been the rainbow, though". For these young protagonists, the rainbow nation and the African renaissance are the exhausted mantras of their parents' generation.

A democracy "only in frame"

Two approaches to democracy inform my analysis of contemporary South African film. The first is Colin Crouch's theory of post-democracy (2004), and the second is "democracy-to-come" an idea developed by Jacques Derrida over many years but addressed most recently in *Rogues* (2005).

In a young democracy such as South Africa in 1994, the right to vote was an act of both symbolism and agency. After being denied the vote for so long, those voting for the first time were enjoying one of the most fundamental rights of citizenship while many of those who had voted before felt that they were voting for the first time in genuinely free and fair elections. Beyond this symbolic act, everyone who voted did so with a sense that their vote counted, that they had agency in shaping the national political dispensation. Indeed, Crouch proposes that:

> Societies probably come closest to democracy in my maximal sense in the early years of achieving it or after great regime crises, when enthusiasm for democracy is widespread; when many diverse groups and organizations of ordinary people share in the task of trying to frame a political agenda which will at last respond to their concerns; when the powerful interests which dominate undemocratic societies are wrong-footed and thrown on the defensive; and when the political system has not quite discovered how to manage and manipulate the new demands.
>
> *(2004: 6–7)*

Crouch's thesis is built around four ideas: (1) the rise of global corporations that transcend the laws of the state; (2) the decline of manual working classes; (3) the failure of the separation of the state and corporate interests in the eyes of the public; and (4) the control of mass media by corporate interests in opposition to the supposed democratisation of public discourse brought about by the Internet.

Crouch's focus in 2004 was predominantly on European countries and crises in the politics of the left, though perhaps if he were writing today, South Africa would bear mentioning. For example, consider his claim that:

> Under the conditions of a post-democracy that increasingly cedes power to business lobbies, there is little hope for an agenda of strong egalitarian policies for the redistribution of power and wealth, or for the restraint of powerful interests.
>
> *(2004: 4)*

After twenty years of neoliberal economic policy that has pandered to the free market while retaining a partial grip on state-owned enterprises (power generation, telecoms, the national broadcaster), a generation of young people are leaving secondary school with uncertain job prospects while all around them are the spoils of profound economic prosperity. Free of the repressive laws of apartheid, they are also "less committed to democracy" (Mattes 2012: 144). "Born frees" "feel disconnected from democratic processes as embodied by politicians and political institutions [. . .] it's all the same, if you vote or not because nothing improves. Your vote does nothing" (Malila *et al.* 2013: 423). Such antipathy towards the structures of democratic process is a symptom of Crouch's post-democracy.

In the wake of claims of "state capture", R250 million spent on President Zuma's Nkandla homestead, and widespread nepotism linking relatives of cabinet ministers to lucrative business deals, Crouch's comment on corruption reads like an excerpt from South Africa's daily news: "Indeed, corruption is a powerful indicator of the poor health of democracy, as it signals a political class which has become cynical, amoral and cut off from scrutiny and from the public" (2004: 10). At this point, one can see Crouch's post-democracy sliding inexorably from a democratic ideal towards economic dystopia. From a participatory democracy, South Africa has become in Xolela Mangcu's words, a democracy "only in frame" (2015). What is particularly relevant in the South African context is, first, Crouch's observations that the conditions of democracy persist in the post-democracy (free and fair elections, relative freedom of the media); and that political compromises give way to more "flexible form(s) of political responsiveness" (20–21).

With the country's courts frequently handing down judgments opposing the state, a fiercely independent Public Protector in the person of advocate Thuli Madonsela, robust political opposition, and civic organisations challenging attempts to limit press freedom, South Africa's famously progressive constitution appears well defended. I interpret the "flexible forms of political responsiveness" in the South African context as including the growing diversity in political opposition and their challenges to the parliamentary status quo; and the emergence of citizen movements such as Abahlali baseMjondolo (shack-dwellers movement) and the "hashtag" student movements (#RhodesMustFall, #FeesMustFall) that began in 2015 and have now spread to universities in the global north.

For Engin Isin and Greg Nielsen, the two conventional concepts of citizenship—as legal status and practice "in which the latter is seen as the condition of the possibility of the former"—should be supplemented by a third concept: acts of citizenship described as "collective or individual deeds that rupture social-historical patterns" (2008: 2). "Acts of citizenship" is one way of describing Crouch's "political responsiveness", interventions against the state that highlight the failure of democracy, or, as Wasserman proposes in his analysis of the Marikana mine massacre of 2012, "the incomplete nature of the post-apartheid democracy that prevented [the miners] from realizing the promises of democracy" (2015: 383).

Wasserman draws on Derrida's concept of "democracy-to-come" to describe the "belief in the realization of democratic citizenship" in South Africa, "even if such an ideal seems elusive in [. . .] everyday experiences" (381). For Derrida:

> the "to come" not only points to the promise but suggests that democracy will never exist, in the sense of a present existence: not because it will be deferred but because it will always remain aporetic in its structure [...] Democracy is the only system, the only constitutional paradigm in which, in principle, one has or assumes the right to criticize everything publicly, including the idea of democracy, its concept, its history and its name.
>
> *(2005: 86, 87)*

Democracy insists on "heterogeneous collectivity" within a "homogenous unit" (the nation state), and proposes both equality and freedom, even if "freedom must always take place in relation to limits imposed by others" (Matthews 2013). In this understanding, democracy is not teleological, a perfect state that can be attained, but is always under way, constantly at risk of change and transformation from within. It is not without hope, though, for as Thomson notes, "democracy-to-come implies rather that even where there is less, or ever so little, democracy, a future for democracy still remains" (2005).

How can these concepts of democracy be usefully applied to an understanding of contemporary South African cinema?

"Born frees" and "independent cinema"

In her study of post-apartheid cinema, Lucia Saks examines the possibility of an "independent cinema" of autonomous filmmaking in post-apartheid South Africa, "one that is more critical, independent, and experimental, but still more organic to place, time, and people than one envisaged by the state" (2010: 154). Independence is framed, in one sense, through the lens of "counter cinema"—filmmaking that rejects the ideological closure and imperialist politics of Hollywood. More significantly, for Saks, independence is about autonomy, about filmmakers exercising their freedom as individual artists in the new dispensation of South African democracy: "It is not exactly, therefore, about national cinema, but about a nation's capacity to become a place for its own cinematic representations of the colliding worlds of its individuals" (2010: 159).

The contradiction this introduces is that autonomy allied with individuality draws this independent cinema away from the anti-apartheid counter cinema that "meant to root forms of representation in language speaking for, understood by, and in the name of all the people" (2010: 160). This "new counter cinema" suggests not only a fundamental break with the apartheid past (and the filmmaking conditions associated with it), but also a break with post-apartheid narratives of nation-building, reconciliation and wealth redistribution.

Saks and Treffry-Goatley note the growth of two approaches by the state to film production in post-apartheid South Africa: driving "an indigenous film industry which reflects the nation's own culture in its cinema and television" (in Saks 2010: 7) on the one hand, and, on the other, developing an industry—including a film service industry—that can compete internationally on economic terms. Treffry-Goatley argues that this latter neoliberal paradigm potentially threatens diversity in the industry because it is reliant on consumption and fiscal prudence (2010b: 50) as opposed to risk-taking and independent vision.

One can see this "double articulation" (Saks 2010: 7) in the following brief exercise drawn from the Durban International Film Festival (DIFF), the biggest in South Africa, which compares the opening film with the winner for Best South African Feature (for the past ten years). Though the tension between critical acclaim and commercial success is a feature of most major film festivals, DIFF normally opens with a South African film and strongly emphasises South African themes, thus attempting to fulfil both national and international cinema mandates.

Year	*Opening Film (director)*	*Best SA Feature Film (director)*
2006	*An Inconvenient Truth* (Davis Guggenheim)	*Conversations on a Saturday Afternoon* (Khalo Matobane)
2007	*Meisie* (Darrell Roodt)	*Heartlines* (Angus Gibson)
2008	*Jerusalema* (Ralph Ziman)	*Triomf* (Michael Raeburn)
2009	*Izulu Iami* (Madoda Ncayiyana)	*Shirley Adams* (Oliver Hermanus)
2010	*State of Violence* (Khalo Matobane)	*Live Above All* (Oliver Schmitz)
2011	*Otelo Burning* (Sara Blecher)	*Skoonheid* (Oliver Hermanus)
2012	*Elelwani* (Ntshaveni Wa Luruli)	*Zambezia* (Wayne Thornley)
2013	*Of Good Report* (Jahmil X. T. Qubeka)	*Durban Poison* (Andrew Worsdale)
2014	*Hard to Get* (Zee Ntuli)	*Love the One You Love* (Jenna Bass)
2015	*Ayanda* (Sara Blecher)	*Necktie Youth* (Sibs Shongwe la-Mer)

Figure 5.3 Durban International Film Festival (DIFF): opening films and winners of Best South African Film, 2006–2015.

Other than in 2006 (when the hot-topic eco-documentary *An Inconvenient Truth*, 2006, USA, Davis Guggenheim, opened the festival), all the other opening films have been South African productions with local directors and casts. They have also conformed to either genre conventions (crime dramas such as *Jerusalema*, [2008, South Africa, Ralph Ziman], *State of Violence* [2010, France/South Africa, Khalo Matabane], *Hard to Get* [2014, South Africa, Zee Ntuli]) or realist modes (*Meisie* [2007, South Africa, Darrell Roodt], *Izulu Iami* [My Secret Sky, 2008, South Africa, Madoda Ncayiyana]). One notable exception was in 2013, where *Of Good Report* (2013, South Africa, Jahmil XT Qubeka) was banned by the Film Publications Board (FPB) shortly before the opening night. This created a storm of controversy with many accusing the FPB of a return to the days of apartheid censorship, and became a notable non-event as the film was only screened at the festival's close. Drawing on Nabokov (and Kubrick's) *Lolita*, Qubeka's violent rural *noir* was also aesthetically adventurous, shot in black-and-white and featuring an unsettling score by Phillip Miller. Somewhat ironically, then, the one radical film chosen to open the festival in recent years was banned before it could be shown. Furthermore, the best South African film of that year was awarded to *Durban Poison* (2013, South Africa), directed by

Andrew Worsdale, whose 1987 film *Shot Down* (South Africa), which was also banned at the time of its release, is considered something of a cult experimental film of the late apartheid era.

The films that have taken home the Best South African Feature award have mostly been ground-breaking experimental films that have provoked and divided audiences. (The commercially oriented animation film *Zambezia* [2012, South Africa, Wayne Thornley] could be considered an anomaly, although it did represent a major step forward in South African animated film production.) For example, *Shirley Adams* (2009, South Africa/UA/UK) explicitly showcased Oliver Hermanus's European avant-garde influences, while his second film, *Beauty* (2011, South Africa/France/Germany), which won two years later, divided viewers at the festival with its unflinching depictions of repressed white Afrikaner homosexuality. Both films divided audiences and caused controversy. In the process they also established Hermanus as a significant filmmaker internationally.

In the past two years, commercially oriented genre films have opened the festival while provocative, personal films (*Necktie Youth* and *Love the One You Love* [2014, South Africa, Jenna Cato Bass]) have won over the jury. These films have also been distributed in innovative ways—for example, *Necktie Youth* was released simultaneously at the cinema and on iTunes—confirming Treffry-Goatley's proposal in 2010 that:

> an alternative production model exists that can potentially grant filmmakers greater freedom in cinematic production and dissemination. This model makes use of digital production and distribution technology and functions with less capital, less outside assistance and has a greater focus on the local market.
>
> *(2010a: 210)*

Examining the table of films from DIFF highlights three features of the contemporary South African filmmaking landscape. First, local commercial filmmaking is increasingly represented by distinct trends: a (largely white) Afrikaans niche market producing crowd-pleasing genre films; an award-winning service industry supplying crews and locations to major international television series and feature films; popular films that seek to represent new South African social realities (*Happiness Is a Four-letter Word* [2016, South Africa, Thabang Moleya]; *Ayanda* [2015, South Africa, Sara Blecher]; *Tell Me Sweet Something* [2015, South Africa, Akin Omotoso]); and independent filmmakers who gain traction with audiences and the national film agency National Film and Video Foundation (NFVF) after film festival success. Second, contemporary independent filmmakers are embracing digital technologies, experimental forms and alternative distribution strategies. Third, contemporary independent filmmakers are representing South African realities less in symbolic and archetypal forms, focusing more on how political and social realities operate in their character's psychologies and daily lives. Describing the motivations for her film *Love the One You Love*, Bass says:

> In 2013, I found myself incredibly disillusioned, not only with my career, but also with relationships, and where we were at in South Africa—probably like a lot of people of my generation. I felt that I'd been living in acceptance of so many illusions about the way that the world was supposed to be in terms of love, success, equality, justice and truth, and it seemed these things were all interlinked.
>
> *(cited in Sebambo 2015)*

Bass's film explores the relationships between two sets of characters living in Cape Town. In the first narrative, a "perfect" couple's relationship deteriorates. In the second, a middle-aged white man tries to understand why his girlfriend left him; his guide around the city (and on his journey to understanding) is a young coloured boy, the brother of his former girlfriend. In both narratives, there are elements of paranoia as the characters suspect that forces outside their control are conspiring against them.

The political elements of the films mentioned here are often indirect. Is Francois, the protagonist of Hermanus's *Beauty*, "a synecdoche for white male South Africa"? (Chetty 2011) What is the relevance of the Mandela facemasks that gradually infect Sandile's relationship with Terri in *Love the One You Love*? Few of the characters express explicit political sympathies, yet all of them are grappling with the shaping of their identities in a period of social and political volatility.

Saks's partial answer to her question of the possibility of a contemporary counter-cinema in South Africa is a conflict between "the anti-apartheid formulation of a revolutionary/critical cinema and the new dispensation, in which the critical goal is to be independent, and so, individual, a citizen exercising his or her right to freedom of expression" (2010: 168). It is this striving for independence of vision that characterises many independent films of the past five years, often in the face of prevailing political attitudes. Hermanus's third film, for example, *The Endless River* (2015, South Africa/France), the first South African film to screen in competition at the Venice Film Festival, confronts violent crime in South Africa head on, undermining national narratives of reconciliation.

Necktie Youth's narrator intones, "we watched everything get less hopeful for everyone". This hopelessness on the screen now finds its manifestation in protests by young South Africans who—though not much more hopeful—are taking to the streets and the Internet to do something about it.

Necktie Youth and "the view from the suburbs"

In the Oscar-winning South African film *Tsotsi* (2005, UK/South Africa, Gavin Hood) a young township gangster enters the leafy suburbs and opportunistically hijacks a car belonging to a middle-class black couple. The film makes frequent recourse to images that show the distinct divide between the wealthy and the poor as well as their close proximity in areas often separated only by a road or a stretch of veld. *Necktie Youth*'s protagonists could reside in the house that Tsotsi and his gang burgles. Though Jabz and September spend most of the film travelling around the city, they are dislocated within it. Over images of the inner city, the narrator says: "No-one from our side of town ever goes there."

The fragmentary form of *Necktie Youth* produces an aggregation of affect: juxtapositions of voice and image and instances of deliberately constructed mise-en-scène evoke a persistent awareness of difference that drives the characters' fatal aimlessness. Shortly after the scene where the portrait of Mandela appears, there is another painstakingly deliberate composition: as Jabz steals money out of his father's wallet, a portrait of Mahatma Ghandi is prominently and incongruously visible on the wall of his parents' bedroom.

Later, while Jabz and September take a taxi home late at night (Figure 5.4), September is drawn into conversation with the driver who, in a brief monologue, voices the disenchantment with president Zuma that is so much a part of current public discourse in South Africa: "Zuma does not give a shit about the people, the very people who put him there." As he speaks, the camera picks out a showroom of cars, the combination of sound and image situating the driver as a mouthpiece rather than a character. To reinforce the point, his opinions fade, replaced by Jabz' voiceover as he recalls his last conversation with Emily. The possibility of engaging with

Figure 5.4 Jabz and September take a taxi home: *Necktie Youth* (2015, South Africa/Netherlands, Sibs Shongwe-La Mer). ©Urucu Media/Whitman Independent/100% Halal.

the majority of the city's people is subsumed by internal reflection or, as September says, the next "every night casual flex" (pills, coke, alcohol, sex). Jabz and his friends are ambiguously represented as carefree and smart, yet depressed and ignorant. They are history-less with little notion of the struggle that has led to their privilege beyond icons (such as Mandela) who symbolise that struggle. Jabz' parents are the aspirational "black diamonds" thriving in the neoliberal free-for-all of South Africa's post-revolutionary capitalist democracy, Fanon's comprador bourgeoisie.

The film signals the historical dislocation of its young protagonists in the opening montage. While Emily's desperate phone message plays over shots of privileged middle-class Johannesburg life—gardeners blowing leaves, trimming hedges, domestic workers talking—what is playing on the TV inside the house is anachronous footage of apartheid-era protests. We soon learn it is 16 June, the anniversary of the 1976 Soweto uprising when black high school students rejected the language policies of the apartheid state. That crisis—inspired by its youth—redefined the country and is a rallying point for youth activism in the country today. Emily's suicide, on the other hand "set her mother's house on fire", in Jabz' words, triggering a chain of intensely personal and at times narcissistic reactions from her circle of friends. The date of Emily's suicide seems to be less her choice than director Shongwe-La Mer's.

Necktie Youth presents a range of disparities: between rich and poor, past and present, young and old. But more than that, these polarities remain unresolved and unresolvable: the shock of Jabz' suicide will lead to an identical cycle of emotional confusion and drug-fuelled disorientation to that which resulted from Emily's suicide. Which one of the group might be next?

In an interview with *Necktie Youth*'s auteur, Sibs Shongwe-La Mer, Michelle Lowenstein writes, "these 'born frees' were meant to be the epitome of the new South Africa and yet, for some reason, they are plagued by feelings of emptiness brought on by a lack of cultural identity" (2015). Her statement reveals a void that gets to the heart of the "born free" malaise: she can't identify a "reason" for the characters' feelings of emptiness, but frames it as an illness, something "brought on by a lack of cultural identity". This latter point suggests a historical dimension. To reframe Mbeki's question, who are we if we don't know where we've come from? But the narrator is dismissive of the past, or at least of the nostalgia for Sophiatown—a suburb of Johannesburg, celebrated for its black cultural life, that was destroyed by the apartheid regime—that celebrates "the sound of jazz sitting on the night like new perfume". Shongwe-La Mer accepts Lowenstein's existential invitation: his characters are protected from the failure of their present leaders to bring about change for the majority of South Africans by a combination of their wealth and identity as educated black South Africans. They might share the taxi driver's critique of the president, but they cannot muster up any anger, and they have no real experience of what to be angry about. "These kids face a classic existential problem. In the townships, people have to worry about getting food to live. Here, kids have everything handed to them. They lack a purpose [. . .] they don't know what to do" (in Lowenstein 2015).

Not very far away, Thulas and Zanele—the brother and sister at the centre of *The Two of Us*—would shake their heads at such self-reflection. While Zanele studies and dreams of finding a way out of the township (she wants to be an air hostess), Thulas broods and picks fights, protects his sister yet beats her when he thinks she is lying. Traumatised by witnessing the sexual abuse of Zanele as a baby by Skhalo (his mother's partner), he wages a battle with Zanele's friend Tumi, a sassy school friend who exploits her looks to get what she wants from men. Tumi wants Zanele to taste a bit of the good life, while Thulas wants to save her from predatory older men known as "blessers" (McVeigh 2016). Thulas hangs out with his unemployed friends, Mandla and Sbu, planning crimes, and beats up Sbu after he expresses an interest in Zanele. After rebuffing the eager (but penniless) Sbu, Zanele goes on a date with an older man. It turns out to be Skhalo, which leads to a violent and ancient climax: as their mother returns home after leaving Skhalo for good, Zanele stabs Thulas by accident as he and Skhalo scuffle. There is no postscript and no justice, only a mother on the margins of the story cradling her dead child. The denouement in *The Two of Us* is no less bleak than in *Necktie Youth*, except one senses that September and his mates could not care less about those inhabiting the "shit" parts of Johannesburg. The divisions between the films' geographies and their youthful characters' outlooks are starkly represented, and yet both are part of the same generation, those supposedly "born free".

One way of understanding the coexistence of these worlds in time and space is to consider the films as representations of a larger media landscape in South Africa. Steven Friedman argues:

> [T]he mainstream press, which also exerts a crucial influence on the way in which news is reported by other media, is neither the "eyes and ears" of the society, nor its watchdog: it performs both functions, not for all of society but for the suburban middle class [...] the freedom it seeks to guard is that of the middle class.
>
> *(2011: 107)*

It is this "view from the suburbs" that provides the context for Shongwe-La Mer's aimless protagonists and that keeps the world of Thulas and Zanele out of view. The youthful protagonists of both films are "born frees" but the opportunities for Jabz and September are real (Jabz can go to university if he chooses), whereas Zanele's dream of travelling the world is framed as fantasy as she takes a drive in a luxury car with an older suitor.

Conclusion

To what extent is this restless independence simply the product of young filmmakers seeking to redefine their art and shock the orthodoxies of the previous generation, to challenge their parents' faith and heroes? Young South Africans often hear how the country "won" its democracy in 1994, or how democracy began with the 1994 elections. Posel writes that, "in retrospect, it is difficult not to respond incredulously to these declarations of a redemptive rupture with the past or to think of the soaring hopefulness for a new way of being in South Africa as naïve" (2014: 71). The result of this initial "enthusiasm for democracy" (Crouch) is that democracy is positioned as something to be lost, eroded as the "miracle" wears off.

The older generation in these films of post-democracy South Africa is ineffectual and absent, or reacts violently against rejection by younger characters (Francois in *Beauty*, Skhalo in *The Two of Us*, and Parker Sithole in *Of Good Report*). For the younger generation—burdened with hope, exhausted by promises of reconstruction and development, and grounded in the reality of persistent race and class divisions as well as economic inequality—democracy is a worn ideal. While the characters of these films struggle with their fractured lives, many of them fatally, the films themselves are nevertheless evidence of vital new energies in South African film. A host of modestly budgeted, adventurous and confrontational films are finding young audiences and expressing unvarnished, personal views about the country's youth.

References

Camay, P. and Gordon, A. J. (n.d.) "South Africa Civil Society and Governance Case Study No. 1", in O'Malley, P. (comp.) *The National Peace Accord and its Structures*. Johannesburg: Co-operative for Research and Education (CORE), www.nelsonmandela.org/omalley/index.php/site/q/03lv02424/04lv03275/05lv03294/06lv03321.htm.

Chetty, K. (2011) *Skoonheid* [review]. Mahala, 11/08/2011, www.mahala.co.za/movies/skoonheid/

Crouch, C. (2004) *Post-Democracy*, Cambridge: Polity.

Derrida, J. (2005) *Rogues: Two Essays on Reason*, trans. Brault, P-A. and Naas, M., Stanford, CA: Stanford University Press.

Feinstein, A. (2007) *After the Party: A Personal and Political Journey Inside the ANC*, Johannesburg: Jonathan Ball Publishers.

Friedman, S. (2011) "Whose Freedom? South Africa's Press, Middle-Class Bias and the Threat of Control", *Ecquid Novi: African Journalism Studies* 32 (2): 106–121.

Gevisser, M. (2007) *Thabo Mbkei: The Dream Deferred*. Johannesburg: Jonathan Ball Publishers.

Gramsci, A. (1971) *Selections from the Prison Notebooks*, Hoare, Q. and Nowell Smith G. (eds and trans.) London: Lawrence & Wishart.

Isin, E. F. and Nielsen G. M. (2008) "Introduction", in Isin, E. F. and Nielsen, G. M. (eds) *Acts of Citizenship*, London: Zed Books, 1–12.

Lowenstein, M. (2015) "*Necktie Youth*: Issues of Cultural Identity," *The Citizen*, 21 September, http://citizen.co.za/780678/necktie-youth-issues-of-cultural-identity/.

McVeigh, T. (2016) "Village Girls Fight Scourge of the 'Blessers'—Whose Gifts Ruin their Lives," *The Guardian*, 24 July, www.theguardian.com/society/2016/jul/23/hiv-aids-africa-girls

Malila, V., Oelofsen, M., Garman, A. and Wasserman, H. (2013) "Making Meaning of Citizenship: How 'Born Frees' Use Media in South Africa's Democratic Evolution", *Communication* 39 (4): 415–431.

Mangcu, X. (2015) "SA Is Gone, My Countrymen", *City Press* 13 December, http://city-press.news24.com/Voices/sa-is-gone-my-countrymen-20151211.

Mattes, R. (2012) "The 'Born Frees': The Prospects for Generational Change in Post-apartheid South Africa", *Australian Journal of Political Science* 47 (1): 133–153.

Matthews, D. (2013) "The Democracy to Come: Notes on the Thought of Jacques Derrida", *Critical Legal Thinking*, 16 April, http://criticallegalthinking.com/2013/04/16/the-democracy-to-come-notes-on-the-thought-of-jacques-derrida/.

Meintjies, M. (2015) "EFF's Malema Takes Aim at 'Sellout Black Billionaires' in Oxford Address", *Business Day (BDLive)*, 26 November, www.bdlive.co.za/national/politics/2015/11/26/effs-malema-takes-aim-at-sellout-black-billionaires-in-oxford-address

Motsaathebe, G. (2015) "The Rise of Film Production and the Politics of the Star System in South Africa", *Communication* 41 (4): 444–458.

Nixon, R. (1994) *Homelands, Harlem and Hollywood: South African Culture and the World Beyond*, New York: Routledge.

Posel, D. (2014) "Madiba Magic: Politics as Enchantment", in Barnard, R. (ed.) *The Cambridge Companion to Mandela*. New York: Cambridge University Press, 70–91.

Prendini Toffoli, H. (2015) "SA Film Signals New Directions", *Mail & Guardian*, 17 December, http://mg.co.za/article/2015-12-17-sa-film-signals-new-directions.

Roper, C. (2013) "The Lies Mandela Taught Us", *Mail & Guardian*, 13 December, http://mg.co.za/article/2013-12-12-the-lies-nelson-mandela-taught-us.

Saks, L. (2010) *Cinema in a Democratic South Africa: The Race for Representation*, Bloomington, IN: Indiana University Press.

Sebambo, K. (2015) "Jenna Bass Says We're Seeing a Sea-change in South African Films", Design Indaba, 23 September, www.designindaba.com/articles/point-view/jenna-bass-says-we're-seeing-sea-change-south-african-films.

Serino, K. (2016) "How Apartheid Haunts a New Generation of South Africans", *The Atlantic* 21 September, www.theatlantic.com/international/archive/2016/09/south-africa-apartheid-mandela-born-free-university/500747/.

Tcheuyap, A. (2011) *Postnationalist African Cinemas*, Manchester: Manchester University Press.

Thomson, A. (2005) "What's to Become of 'Democracy to Come'?" *Postmodern Culture* 15 (3), http://pmc.iath.virginia.edu/text-only/issue.505/15.3thomson.txt.

Tomaselli, K. G. and Shepperson, A. (2014) "Transformation and South African Cinema in the 1990s", in Ukadike, N. F. (ed.) *Critical Approaches to African Cinema Discourse*, Lantham, MD: Lexington Books, 107–134.

Treffry-Goatley, A. (2010a) "The Representation and Mediation of National Identity in the Production of Post-apartheid, South African Cinema", PhD (University of Cape Town, 2010).

—— (2010b) "South African Cinema after Apartheid: A Political-Economic Exploration", *Communication* 36 (1): 37–57.

Wasserman, H. (2015) "Marikana and the Media: Acts of Citizenship and a Faith in Democracy-to-Come", *Social Dynamics* 41 (2): 375–386.

6

BRAZILIAN CINEMA ON THE GLOBAL SCREEN

Stephanie Dennison

Introduction

Brazil has one of the largest and most profitable audio-visual sectors in the world, and one of the most productive film industries in South America. It has regularly produced both "quality" films that appeal to arthouse audiences worldwide, and those that dialogue with the universally popular Brazilian soap operas (such Brazilian films regularly attract domestic audiences in excess of four million). The country has, in the twenty-first century, increased its profile in international relations and global economic affairs. Despite this, historically and more recently Brazilian films have not gained the exposure that they arguably merit, or rather, they have not received the attention of critics, festival programmers and academics that, I will argue here, they deserve.

World Cinema theory argues against the notion of Hollywood as having the central role in filmmaking and providing the standard industry model, to which all other film cultures are seen as peripheral (Nagib 2006a: 30). It rejects a binary view of filmmaking practices (Brazilian cinema, for example, in contradistinction to Hollywood). But, crucially here, it also argues against the exclusive reading of film industries as pertaining only to particular regions, and of the insistence of labelling as World Cinema only films from erstwhile "Third-World" regions that demonstrate political engagement (Dennison and Lim 2006). Taking inspiration in particular from Dudley Andrew (2006) and his formulation that World Cinema encourages us to think about different maps, in this essay I seek to redress the balance that tips heavily towards analyses of Brazilian films either in relation to Hollywood, as one-off anomalies, or as exclusively part of a particular imagined community. More often than not, when they are programmed at festivals or discussed by academics and critics, for example, Brazilian films are lumped together with "Latin American cinema", despite a number of quite stark differences between Brazil and the bulk of the other industries in Latin America (language spoken (Portuguese), size of industry, availability of state funding, size of domestic audience, lack of reliance on co-productions, and so on). Such lumping together arguably results in a form of erasure, whereby the distinctive features of Brazilian cinema are ultimately elided.

Much has changed in the last ten years in relation both to film culture within Brazil, how films are produced and funded, and to Brazilian cinema's reception abroad. This chapter seeks to document and comment on these changes. It will focus on issues relating to the reception and circulation of Brazilian films beyond Brazil, considering, for example, Brazilian film-makers and producers' increased impact on the World Cinema festival and funding circuits and how these circuits are navigated by them.

Brazilian film and the international festival circuit

In a provocative essay in *Remapping World Cinema: Identity, Culture and Politics in Film* (2006), Michael Chanan begins by taking to task the *Guardian* film reviewer Andrew Pulver for his demonstration of what Chanan claims is an all-too-familiar lack of historical memory on the part of critics when it comes to Latin American cinema (38). Pulver (2002: n.p.) had excitedly reviewed the Cannes out-of-competition film *Cidade de Deus* (City of God, 2002, Brazil, Fernando Meirelles and Kátia Lund), claiming that its virtuosity "belies the idea that we are looking at any kind of dispatch from a primitive movie-making backwater". Chanan's evident exasperation is understandable: the critic, as well as thinly veiling his prejudice, appeared to be unaware, for example, of the legacy of "el nuevo cine latinoamericano" (The New Latin American Cinema), the umbrella term for a series of film movements that emerged in Latin America in the 1960s and 1970s that revolutionised filmmaking processes and ideology in the so-called Third World and beyond, and that inspired filmgoers of the European film festival circuit at the time. What Chanan does not question, however, is Pulver's insistence on framing his review of a Brazilian film within the context of Latin American film production, whereby he claims that *City of God*, and another Brazilian film, *Central do Brasil* (Central Station, 1998, Brazil, Walter Salles) make up something he refers to as "la buena onda" (literally "the good wave"), a phrase seemingly coined to describe a new generation of Mexican filmmakers that emerged at the turn of the twenty-first century, and sloppily reproduced by Pulver to describe contemporary Latin American cinema.

Had Pulver been *au fait* with The New Latin American Cinema cited above, he may well have made reference to Cinema Novo, the Brazilian arthouse film movement that impacted on festivals such as Cannes in the 1960s.[1] But Cinema Novo is not the beginning of the story of Brazilian cinema's presence on a global stage. Brazil first made its mark on the European festival and arthouse circuit a decade earlier with Lima Barreto's "Western" *O Cangaceiro* (The Bandit, Brazil, 1953), the first Brazilian film to win at Cannes (the "Best Adventure Film" category). In the same year the less celebrated historical melodrama *Sinhá Moça* (The Landowner's Daughter, 1953, Brazil, Tom Payne) was both selected for the main competition at Berlin and won the Bronze Lion at Venice. Both were preceded by *Caiçara* (1951, Brazil) and *Tico-Tico no Fubá* (Sparrow in the Cornmeal, 1952, Brazil), both of which were directed by Adolfo Celi and were screened in competition at Cannes.

Far from being an "ironic anomaly" (Lopez 1998: 135), *The Bandit* and the three other films mentioned above were produced by the short-lived but historically important Vera Cruz studios. Vera Cruz (the original name given to Brazil when the Portuguese first reached the coast in 1500) was established in São Paulo in 1949 by a group of wealthy industrialists, with the aim of producing quality films that would also have commercial appeal. It modelled itself on Hollywood's MGM studio, adopting the industrial studio system. With the slogan "from the plateau of Piratininga to the screens of the world!", its vision was decidedly global in reach: its ambition was demonstrated by the successful recruitment of experienced industry personnel from Europe. It was headed up by Brazilian Alberto Cavalcanti whose directing credits included films produced in France, Germany, and for the GPO Film Unit and Ealing Studios in the UK. Because of the lavish costs of the production of its films, Vera Cruz exceeded what could be recovered at home and went bankrupt in 1954, after only five years.[2]

Ana Lopez (1998) provides a fascinating revision of the Vera Cruz phenomenon that both challenges the dominant reading of the studio's productions as purely imported and therefore un-Brazilian, and ponders as to why such a reading came about in the first place. She argues that "Vera Cruz is understood to have been merely a kind of necessary prelude, a historical footnote to, or maybe even a misguided digression from, the soon to emerge Cinema Novo movement" (128). To an extent, then, the domination of Cinema Novo has erased from international (and domestic)[3] film memory the fact that the fleeting Vera Cruz project was already, in the 1950s, placing Brazilian films in key film festivals in Europe. And even into the 1960s, when it is true to say that Cinema Novo dominated, in terms of Brazilian film production, the "big three" European festivals (Cannes, Berlin and Venice), it was Anselmo Duarte's popularly-inflected *O Pagador e Promessas* (The Given Word, 1962, Brazil) that secured for Brazil its one and only Palme d'Or. Luiz Zanin (2012) argues that it is a mystery how *The Given Word* ever won this award, given that it faced stiff competition from films by Buñuel, Antonioni and Bresson, among other consecrated names. Zanin astutely hints at its "charming whiff of the Third World" (2012) as a possible draw for jury members of the ilk of François Truffaut, as well as the excellent interpretations of the cast, and its technical quality, provided by H. E. (Chick) Fowle,[4] the British photographer renowned for his work on such iconic early British documentaries as *Night Mail* (1936, UK), and brought over to Brazil in the 1950s to work at Vera Cruz. In fact, Chick Fowle worked on five Brazilian films between 1951 and 1962 that competed at Cannes, all of which predated Cinema Novo's success abroad.

The filmmakers of the Cinema Novo movement sought to transform society by applying a new, critical and modernist vision of the nation, and to find a new cinematic language that better reflected Brazilian reality, as a challenge to what they considered the vacuous, derivative and industrially produced *chanchada* films, the music-hall inspired comedies that emerged in the 1930s and dominated film screens in Brazil until the 1950s. Many of the classic Cinema Novo films, and particularly those that found favour with European arthouse audiences, portrayed the cinematically unexplored backlands or *sertão* such as *Vidas Secas* (Barren Lives, 1962, Brazil, Nelson Pereira dos Santos), a scathing indictment of social injustice in Brazil's impoverished Northeastern interior which premiered at Cannes in 1963.

Writing in 1975, Julianne Burton observed that "First world critics have a fascination with the Brazilian cinema novo" (33). The European market was clearly important to Cinema Novo directors, not only in terms of sales and the promotion of films, but also strategically to help them deal with the dictatorship. After all, with the international praise of Cinema Novo, it was difficult for the dictatorship, with its "business as usual" posturing, at least up until 1968, to deny Brazilians the right to view the films at home (Figueirôa 2004: 45). Brazilian films in the 1960s were popular in France, for example, because their release coincided with a time when both *auteur* cinema and "sociological" films were particularly popular (Figueirôa 2004: 138). Cinema Novo also served the purpose in Europe of educating audiences, hungry for knowledge of other cultures, about Brazil (102). Glauber Rocha for one was acutely aware of the way Brazilian films were often consumed in Europe, and of Europeans' habit of turning to the culture of the underdeveloped world to satisfy their "nostalgia for primitivism" (Rocha in Johnson and Stam 1995: 69).

With the demise of the Cinema Novo in the early 1970s, Brazilian cinema did not simply disappear from global screens. In 1969 a majority State-owned distribution and production company, Embrafilme, had been set up with the express purpose of increasing the market share of Brazilian films both at home and abroad. And it was under the headship of Roberto Farias (1974–1979) that Embrafilme's budget was substantially increased and an aggressive policy of selling films abroad began (Gatti 2008: 46), with sales agents established in New York and Paris, and significant support offered for festival attendance by directors, for example. Successes at this time shifted decidedly away from the "whiff of the Third World" and "nostalgia for primitivism" referred to above,[5] and instead highlighted the sensual and carnivalesque side to Brazilian culture. Films included the light-hearted *Dona Flor e Seus Dois Maridos* (Dona Flor and Her Two Husbands, 1976, Brazil, Bruno Barreto), starring the "bombshell" Sônia Braga, a phenomenal success at home and subsequently distributed in the US. It was nominated for a Golden Globe (Best Foreign Film) in 1978 and was remade by Hollywood with the title *Kiss Me Goodbye* (1982, USA, Robert Mulligan), starring Sally Field and James Caan.

Even in the 1980s—a filmmaking period dominated in Brazil by soft and hardcore porn production, and one that has been largely edited out of Brazilian film history—one or two Brazilian films continued to be selected for the major European festivals almost every year, along with a healthy number of features screening and winning prizes at the increasingly important Havana festival of Latin American film. In 1989 the neoliberal Fernando Collor de Mello won the first direct presidential elections in nearly thirty years, and he quickly set to dissolving film institutions, starting in 1990 with Embrafilme. He was impeached and resigned amid a corruption scandal in 1992. As a consequence, film production was reduced to single figures for the first years of the decade, until the results of the new Audiovisual Law of 1993 could be seen from 1995 onwards. Remarkably, then, in the second half of the 1990s, with the return to production and State support for the film industry after the lost years of the ill-fated Collor administration,[6] regular appearances by Brazilian films on the international festival circuit were complemented by the much-sought-after Oscar nod. In this period Brazil secured three nominations in the space of four years for best foreign language Oscar, and *City of God* (Figure 6.1) was nominated in four different categories shortly after in 2004, demonstrating not only a return to strength of the industry after it practically ground to a halt in 1990, but also the increased influence and lobbying power of certain Brazilian directors and film producers within Hollywood, a subject to which I will return.

Figure 6.1 *Cidade de Deus* (City of God, 2002, Brazil, Fernando Meirelles and Kátia Lund) helped demonstrate the new vitality of Brazilian film. ©O2 Filmes/VideoFilme/Hank Levine Film/Globo Filmes/Lumière/Wild Bunch.

With the growth of the film festival circuit from the 1990s onwards, and particularly of festivals championing more independent productions, such as Rotterdam and Sundance, Brazilian films have continued to be successful. Both Rotterdam and Sundance (both the festivals and their associated film funding schemes) have been generous to Brazilian film,[7] helping to cement its reputation as a World Cinema player. The so-called Sundance Labs are of increasing importance in the creation of successful World Cinema films: in 2011, for example, six out of the twenty feature films in competition at the Sundance film festival came through the Sundance Institute's workshop programme. Writing in 2006, Lúcia Nagib argued:

> It is not mere coincidence that several of Brazil's most successful films abroad, such as *Central Station* (Walter Salles, 1998), *Me You Them* (Andrucha Waddington, 2000) and *City of God* (Fernando Meirelles and Kátia Lund, 2002) have received Sundance support for their films.
>
> *(2006b: 96–97)*

In her essay, Nagib argues that festival labs such as Sundance are influencing the kinds of stories being told by World Cinema in the twenty-first century, a cinema that is aimed at a new audience which is enlightened, comfortable with subtitles, keen to be instructed, but not necessarily fans of the experimental and less commercial end of arthouse production à la the late Portuguese filmmaker Manoel de Oliveira (Nagib 2006b: 96–97). In this context she discusses Walter Salles's *Central Station*, which underwent numerous rewrites at the Sundance lab before emerging to claim its place as one of the great and most successful World Cinema films of the late 1990s. Nagib points to the need for further discussion of the impact of seeking co-production funding and chasing festival opportunities on Brazilian (and by extension, other World Cinema) film production. She warns: "The recipe of the private hero, in a national cultural context, who goes through the experience of the improbable made convincing by a wisely constructed script generates interesting questions of authorship and nationality which deserve further attention" (Nagib 2006b: 98).

But the links between Sundance and the Brazilian film industry run deeper than what could be superficially appraised as a rather condescending meddling in plots, via funding and lab opportunities, with a view to producing some kind of homogenous global narrative. The number of high-profile Brazilian directors, producers and films connected to Sundance is striking, and suggests, in counterpoint to Nagib's argument, that film industry personnel from the former Third World can enjoy a symbiotic relationship with the Institute. By way of example, José Padilha, now widely known outside of Brazil as the director of the 2014 remake of *Robocop*, and creator of the Netflix smash hit series *Narcos*, began a close relationship with Sundance, which arguably set him on course for international recognition, when his debut feature documentary *Onibus 174* (Bus 174, 2002, Brazil, José Padilha and Felipe Lacerda) featured at the festival. His 2010 documentary *Secrets of the Tribe* (UK/Brazil/France) also screened at Sundance (Brazilian documentaries are a regular feature at the festival) and elicited further invitations: to hold the international premiere of his domestic box-office smash *Tropa de Elite: O Inimigo Agora é Outro* (Elite Squad: The Enemy Within, 2010, Brazil) there, as well as to serve on the festival jury.

As a result of the success of *Central Station* Robert Redford, founder of the Sundance Institute, encouraged Walter Salles to direct the first filmic adaptation of Che Guevara's *Motorcycle Diaries* (Williams 2007: 11), one of the most successful co-productions to come out of Latin America and arguably the next step for Salles, after filming two successful road movies (one national, one transnational) towards road-movie gold in the form of the opportunity to adapt Jack Keroac's *On the Road*. It is worth noting that both Walter Salles's *On the Road*

(2012, France/USA/UK/Brazil/Canada/Argentina) and the Brazilian co-produced *Frances Ha* (2012, USA/Brazil, Noah Baumbach) are regular features on Sundance TV movie schedules.

One of the biggest filmic talking points in Brazil of the last couple of years, Anna Muylaert's *Que Horas Ela Volta?* (The Second Mother, 2015, Brazil) premiered at Sundance in 2015 and picked up acting awards for the two leads, Regina Casé and Camila Márdila. It went on to pick up two more awards in out-of-competition sections of the Berlin film festival, a festival that has, since *Central Station* won the Golden Bear back in 1998, screened a large number of Brazilian films and has awarded prizes to José Padilha's *Tropa de Elite* (Elite Squad, 2008, Brazil)—Golden Bear, and Teddy awards ("the official queer award" at Berlin) to *Hoje Eu Quero Voltar Sozinho* (The Way He Looks, 2014, Brazil, Daniel Ribeiro) and Anna Muylaert's follow-up to *The Second Mother, Mãe Só Há Uma* (Don't Call Me Son, 2016, Brazil). Twelve Brazilian films screened at the Berlinale in 2017.

Brazilian players and global film production

Directors such as Salles and Meirelles are, to borrow Deborah Shaw's description of transnational directors, "fluent in transnational modes of narration, and are physical embodiments of cultural exchange" (Shaw 2013: 60). As defined by Shaw, they form part of a group of directors in Latin America "who work and seek funding in a range of national contexts, while they have their films distributed in a global market" (60–61). But while these "celebrity" transnational directors share company with the likes of Mexicans Alejandro González Iñárritu, Afonso Cuarón and Guillermo del Toro, we can also look elsewhere, to the producers, for example, for noteworthy examples of industry players taking on the globe. By way of example, in an article tellingly entitled "Brazil's RT Features Gives US Independent Films a Boost", John Hopewell (2016: n.p.), *Variety*'s chief international correspondent, declared that "to find one of the biggest impact players on the American indie scene, you have to go to São Paulo". Hopewell was referring to RT Features, the Brazil-based production company fronted by Rodrigo Teixeira,[8] whose list of recent indie credits is impressive, as Hopewell recognises, for any producer of any nationality: the aforementioned *Frances Ha*, *The Witch* (2015, USA/UK/Canada/Brazil, Robert Eggers), *Mistress America* (USA/Brazil, 2016, Noel Baumbach), to name only three from a long list of productions, both of US and Brazilian origin. *Variety* reported in 2014 that Teixeira and no less than Martin Scorsese were setting up an emerging talent fund (Keslassy 2014: n.p.), further illustrating the global importance of RT Features. In 2017 Teixeira will begin co-production on Brad Pitt's *Ad Astra* (Racy 2017).

The success of RT Features, and other production companies in Brazil with international profiles, such as Salles' Videofilmes (*On the Road*; *Jia Zhangke: A Guy from Fenyang*, 2014, Brazil/France, Walter Salles) and Meirelles' O2 Filmes (*Blindness*, 2008, Canada/Brazil/Japan, Fernando Meirelles; *360*, 2011, UK/Austria/France/Brazil/USA, Fernando Meirelles) highlight the danger in drawing the easy conclusion that producers based in emerging nations engage in international film production only when they need the financial support from more powerful partners based in Europe or (much less frequently) the USA to make local movies. By way of example of such a relationship, consider the influence of El Deseo (Spain), the Almodóvar brothers' production company that co-produces with key auteurs such as Lucrecia Martel and Paul Leduc in Latin America. According to Marvin D'Lugo (2013), El Deseo produces films with an "ambitious transterritorial aesthetic that seeks to engage audiences in Spain and Latin America in [. . .] the co-production of a transnational Hispanic identity" (D'Lugo 2013: 113). One of the motivating factors in this, far from straightforward financial transaction, is a "special affinity with Latin America" (D'Lugo 2013: 131), but what is clear is that this exploration of transnational Hispanic identity and special affinity appears to be, or at least it is most commonly read as, the prerogative of Europeans (the ex-colonial rulers, if you like). Similar arguments have been levelled against Ibermedia, the Hispanic and Latin American film production funding pool (Falicov 2013).

An excellent example of inversion of the supposed one-directional co-production power flow is Brazilian production company Conspiração Filmes and their key involvement in the "Spanish" film *Lope* (The Outlaw, 2010, Spain/Brazil/France, Andrucha Waddington). I use scare quotes here deliberately, as this, to all intents and purposes, is an excellent example of national cinema: a lavish, big-budget period film that recounts the adventures of one of the indisputable symbols of "Hispanidad" or Spanishness: Lope de Vega, the Golden-Age author. The film was nominated for a Goya, the principal Spanish film gong, in six different categories. Brazilian Conspiração contributed to the production with 20 per cent of the budget and crucially provided the (Brazilian) director, Waddington.

Brazil and international co-productions[9]

In Brazil, while the raw co-production numbers compare quite favourably to other Latin American countries (thirty-five in the period 2013–2014, for example), we need to bear in mind that over 100 Brazilian films are released every year, and of these, only around ten percent are international co-productions. In the period 2005–2014, most of these films were co-produced with Portugal (twenty-five), followed by France and Argentina (sixteen each) and then Spain (fifteen) (Rocha and Ibiapina 2016: 102–103). It is worth reflecting on this as, once again, facile assumptions can be made about the pull of old colonial ties in terms of contemporary cultural production, and in particular at a time when transnational/migratory stories are very much in vogue. It is likely that these assumptions are based partly on our understanding of the relationship which many film industries of former Spanish- and French-language colonies have with producers based in Spain and France. However, unlike the French and Spanish cases, there is a dearth of films that depict relations (historical or contemporary) between Portugal and its former South American colony. In fact, in terms of industry relations and transnational story-telling, there is much greater resemblance between Portugal's relationship with its former African colonies, and Francophone and Hispanophone cultural relations. Rather than pointing to a body of work that indicates cultural exchange, as promoted on paper by many of the State funding opportunities available to Brazilian and Portuguese filmmakers, many of the Brazilian/Portuguese co-productions of the last few years are opportunistic in nature, with finished products that rarely travel beyond the territory making the majority investment. Industry expert André Sturm suggests that Brazilian funding for such initiatives is relatively easy to secure (via funding calls that are far from competitive), and that after securing the funding it is equally easy for directors and producers to circumvent any stipulations regarding "cultural exchange" (in Rocha and Ibiapina 2016: 145–146). They simply need to have contacts in the Portuguese film industry, something that is inevitably facilitated by a common language, and perhaps attractive for those who are less adventurous when it comes to transnational film financing. For while film directors such as Walter Salles, Kleber Mendonça Filho and Karim Ainouz, for example, navigate the international film scene effortlessly with their impeccable language skills acquired through living and studying abroad, there are a great many cultural producers in Brazil who lack the confidence and experience to do business in any language other than Portuguese.

Since the "Cinema do Brasil" film promotional programme was set up in 2006, there has been a marked growth in both international co-productions and Brazilian film exhibition abroad. The programme's creator, André Sturm, appears to have been inspired to set up the initiative, which is run through Brazil's export agency APEX, after drawing the conclusion that big-screen exposure on the European festival circuit for countries such as Argentina was a direct result of making international co-productions with key players in Europe such as France, Spain and Germany (Rocha and Ibiapina 2016: 87).

As Brazil finds itself in one of its worst economic crises in years, it is questionable as to whether the level of investment in co-production will continue, particularly given the negligent results in terms of building a market for Brazilian product in Portugal for example. And we must also question the attraction of small amounts of Brazilian funding for foreign directors and producers to film in Brazil via co-production arrangements. It seems that even where formal coproduction treaties exist, film business can be hard to conduct in Brazil. The celebrated Argentine cineaste, Daniel Burman, said the following of his experience of working in Brazil:

> Speaking as a director and author, working in Brazil is both natural and fruitful. But, speaking as a producer, I don't know if I'll make any more co-productions. My two experiences of working in Brazil revealed a huge asymmetry between administrative processes in Brazil and Argentina. In Brazil, everything takes so long, everything seems so much more difficult. I don't want to say bureaucratic, but the time it takes to produce anything in Brazil means I'd rather stick to Argentina.
>
> *(Miranda 2014: n.p.)*

Conclusion

There are two final issues that need to be borne in mind in relation to this notable list of illustrations of Brazilian "presence" in the global marketplace. First of all, in terms of State legislation and support for the film industry, the priority is and has always been promoting film within the domestic market. With popular comedy films, such as those produced by Globofilmes, the film production and distribution arm of the mighty Globo media conglomerate, audience figures regularly hit four million, thus signalling that the internal market is large enough to provide considerable commercial success. This in great part explains why we have, for example, seen no significant attempt by Globofilmes to break into foreign markets, such as Portugal, where Globo TV soap operas continue to reign supreme.

Secondly, evidence suggests that legislators themselves in Brazil do not view Brazilian film culture's global presence as described above as in any way significant (Rocha and Ibiapina 2016: 169; Dennison and Meleiro 2017). As I have argued elsewhere, despite the presence of Brazilian films abroad, at least on the festival circuit, Brazil lacks a national film brand (Dennison and Meleiro 2017). Given the transnational profile of some of Brazil's key players (José Padilha; Walter Salles; Fernando Meirelles; Rodrigo Teixeira; Andrucha Waddington, for example), who are "hotwired into an international framework of distribution as never before" (Brookes 2002: n.p.) and given the less than effective legislation and funding in place to encourage a more consolidated international dissemination of Brazilian films, this is not entirely surprising. What we can say with confidence is that Brazil is actively contributing, whether consciously or not, to twenty-first-century World Cinema culture. Perhaps it is time that we ceased requiring of Brazilian filmmakers and producers that they operate as the bearers of a national identity (Ezra and Rowden 2006: 3) any more than we would make this requirement of a (US) Hollywood player.

Notes

1 Given the movement's natural leader Glauber Rocha's Latin Americanist vision, there is at least in this case some justification for reading Cinema Novo within the context of Latin American film production. See Zuzana Pick's aptly titled, *The New Latin American Cinema: A Continental Project* (1993).
2 For more information on the Vera Cruz project, see Shaw and Dennison (2007: 73–76).
3 Sheila Schvartman (n.d.) observes that as a result of the critical acclaim of the Cinema Novo, Brazilian cinema's myth of origin was set in the 1960s.
4 Russell and Foxon (2015). See BFI website.
5 There are, of course, always exceptions that prove the rule, and one worth mentioning here is Hector Babenco's Embrafilme-distributed and Gloden Globe-nominated *Peixote: A Lei do Mais Fraco* (*Pixote*, 1980), which dealt with the tough lives of street kids.
6 For more information, see Shaw and Dennison (2007: 81–9).
7 As we go to press, no fewer than fifteen films have been selected to screen at Rotterdam 2017.
8 Not to be confused with the "other" Brazilian Rodrigo Teixeira, co-creator of Magnopus and successful special effects consultant based in Los Angeles.
9 For a more detailed description of the current co-production scenario in Brazil, and in particular in terms of government initiatives and legislation, see Dennison and Meleiro (2017).

References

Andrew, D. (2006) "An Atlas of World Cinema", in Dennison, S. and Lim, S. H. (eds) *Remapping World Cinemas: Identity, Culture and Politics in Film*, London: Wallflower Press, 19–29.

Brookes, X. (2002) "First Steps in Latin", *Guardian*, 19 July, https://www.theguardian.com/film/2002/jul/19/artsfeatures.

Burton, J. (1975) "The Old and the New: Latin American Cinema at the (Last?) Pesaro Festival", *Jump Cut* 9: 33–35.

Chanan, M. (2006) "Latin American Cinema: From Underdevelopment to Postmodernism", in Dennison, S. and Lim, S. H. (eds) *Remapping World Cinemas: Identity, Culture and Politics in Film*, London: Wallflower Press, 38–51.

Dennison, S. and Lim, S. H. (2006) "Situating World Cinema as a Theoretical Problem", in Dennison, S. and Lim, S. H. (eds) *Remapping World Cinemas: Identity, Culture and Politics in Film*, London: Wallflower Press, 1–15.

Dennison, S. and Meleiro, A. (2017) "Brazil, Soft Power and Film Culture", *New Cinemas* 14 (1): 17–30.

D'Lugo, M. (2013) "Pedro Almodóvar's Latin American 'Business'", in Dennison, S. (ed.) *Contemporary Hispanic Cinema: Interrogating the Transnational in Spanish and Latin American Film*, London: Tamesis, 113–135.

Ezra, E. and Rowden, T. (2006) "General Introduction: What Is Transnational Cinema?" in Ezra, E. and Rowden, T. (eds) *Transnational Cinemas: The Reader*, New York: Routledge, 1–12.

Falicov, T. (2013) "Ibero-Latin American Co-productions: Transnational Cinema, Spain's Public Relations Venture or Both?" in Dennison, S. (ed.) *Contemporary Hispanic Cinema: Interrogating the Transnational in Spanish and Latin American Film*, London: Tamesis, 67–88.

Figueirôa, A. (2004) *Cinema Novo: A Onda do Jovem Cinema e Sua Recepção na França*, Campinas: Papirus.

Gatti, A. P. (2008) *Embrafilme e o cinema brasileiro*, Centro Cultural Sao Paulo: E-book.

Hopewell, J. (2016) "Brazil's RT Features Gives US Independent Films a Boost", *Variety*, 12 February, http://variety.com/2016/film/global/brazil-production-company-rt-features-1201701634/.

Keslassy, E. (2014) "Martin Scorsese, RT Features Launch Film Fund (EXCLUSIVE)", *Variety*, 16 May, http://variety.com/2014/film/news/martin-scorsese-rt-features-launch-film-fund-exclusive-1201183816/.

Lopez, A. M. (1998) "The São Paulo Connection: The Companhia Cinematografica Vera Cruz and *O Cangaceiro*", *Nuevo Texto Critico* 9 (22): 127–154.

Miranda, A. (2014) "*O mistério da felicidade* é a segunda coprodução de Daniel Burman com o Brasil; e pode ser a última", *O Globo* 8 October, http://oglobo.globo.com/cultura/filmes/o-misterio-da-felicidade-a-segunda-coproducao-de-daniel-burman-com-brasil-pode-ser-ultima-14173583#ixzz4Ve9rL58Y.

Nagib, L. (2006a) "Towards a Positive Definition of World Cinema", in Dennison, S. and Lim, S. H. (eds) *Remapping World Cinemas: Identity, Culture and Politics in Film*, London: Wallflower Press, 30–37.

—— (2006b) "Going Global: The Brazilian Scripted Film", in Harvey S. (ed.) *Trading Culture: Global Traffic Local Cultures in Film and Television*, Eastleigh: John Libby, 95–103.

Pick, Z. M. (1993) *The New Latin American Cinema: A Continental Project*, Austin, TX: University of Texas Press.

Pulver, A. (2002) "Follow That Chicken", *Guardian* 24 May, https://www.theguardian.com/film/2002/may/24/cannes2002.cannesfilmfestival1.

Racy, S. (2017) "Brasileiro Vai Produzir Novo Filme de Brad Pitt", *Estadão Cultura*, 9 February, http://cultura.estadao.com.br/blogs/direto-da-fonte/brasileiro-vai-produzir-novo-filme-de-brad-pitt/.

Rocha, F. and Ibapina, D. (2016) *Cinema Brasileiro e Co-produção Internacional*, Curitiba: Appris.

Rocha, G. (1995) "An Esthetic of Hunger", in Johnson, R. and Stam, R. (eds), *Brazilian Cinema: Expanded Edition*, New York: Columbia University Press, 69–71.

Russell, P. and Foxon, S. (2015) "Born in 1915: Eight Great British Documentary Filmmakers", British Film Commission website, www.bfi.org.uk/news-opinion/news-bfi/features/born-1915-eight-great-british-documentary-filmmakers.

Schvartman, S. (n.d.) "Humberto Mauro e a memória do cinema nacional", *Revista Tropico*, www.revistatropico.com.br/tropico/html/textos/1412,1.shl.

Shaw, D. (2013) "Deconstructing and Reconstructing Transnational Cinema", in Dennison, S. (ed.), *Contemporary Hispanic Cinema: Interrogating the Transnational in Spanish and Latin American Film*, London: Tamesis, 47–65.

Shaw, L. and Dennison, S. (2007) *Brazilian National Cinema*, London and New York: Routledge.

Williams, C. (2007) "Los Diarios de Motocicleta as Pan-American Travelogue", in Shaw, D. (ed.) *Contemporary Latin American Cinema: Breaking into the Global Market*, Plymouth, MA: Rowman & Littlefield, 11–27.

Zanin, L. (2012) "50 anos da Palma de Ouro a *O Pagador de Promessas*", *Estadão Cultura*, 24 May, http://cultura.estadao.com.br/blogs/luiz-zanin/50-anos-da-palma-de-ouro-a-o-pagador-de-promessas/.

7
TRANSNATIONAL FILMMAKING IN SOUTH AMERICA

Dolores Tierney

Different forms of transnational filmmaking have been a feature of Latin American film production since its inception, an eagerly sought out option since the 1970s, and an increasing necessity since the late 1980s and early 1990s (García Canclini 1997: 256). What has changed in Latin America over the last twenty years to make the transnational mode so key has been a shift in the way the state funds and organises Latin America's national industries. As the state has lessened or completely withdrawn financial support for the different national filmmaking endeavours, filmmakers have had to seek funding opportunities privately and often abroad from Europe and the United States. At the same time, media conglomerates and quasi-state cultural organisations in Europe and the US, as well as some individual auteurs such as Pedro Almodóvar, have looked to Latin America to develop new markets and to seek out cultural renewal (D'Lugo 2003: 104; Donoghue 2014). This dismantling of state protection for national filmmaking and exposure to global market forces has had both detrimental and beneficial effects on its major national industries. On the one hand, these measures have decimated production numbers and further increased the hold Hollywood films have on the domestic box office. On the other hand, these measures have facilitated both the distribution and circulation of *some* films and creative and technical personnel across borders and into global film markets and metropolitan production venues *and* initiated a series of artistically innovative but also commercially successful films. Although the state has, in the course of these twenty years, returned to a position of dominance in support for filmmaking in the three major national traditions (Brazil, Mexico, Argentina), and production numbers have recovered, contemporaneously, state support (via a system of grants, loans, subsidies, tax incentives and screen quotas) only accounts for a *part* of a film's complex financial structure. At some point in their development, production, post-production or distribution, Latin American films may benefit from a form of financial support that comes from outside its national borders, whether it is funding from a European or US institution or from a Motion Picture Academy member company with these latter agencies proving essential in order to secure distribution both domestically and abroad. These differing forms of transnational support are actively encouraged and sought out by the state. Prominent filmmakers have also emerged as key players in this transnationalised cinematic sphere. Acting as mediators between the art and commerce of filmmaking, and using the leverage their transnational careers have afforded them, Latin America's most famous transnational directors (Iñárritu, Cuarón, del Toro, Meirelles, Salles) and their production companies (Esperanto Filmoj, VideoFilmes, Tequila Gang, Cha Cha Chá,

O2 Filmes) have played an active role in fomenting the film cultures in their respective nations (D'Lugo 2003: 103).

This chapter argues for the importance of understanding the region's contemporary filmmaking output within this framework of transnationalism. To better understand how contemporary transnational Latin American cinema works across the region, this chapter begins by tracing the concept of transnational cinema as it has emerged in film studies and in particular how it is situated within broader discourses around Latin American national cinemas. It goes on to explore the cinema in which these discourses are employed—arthouse cinema—looking at films from Latin America's arthouse resurgence, arguing that these exemplify how transnational flows of capital and creativity impact on Latin American cinema. It focuses in particular on two films by Peruvian director Claudia Llosa—*Madeinusa* (2006, Peru/Spain) and *La teta asustada* (The Milk of Sorrow, 2009, Peru/Spain)—as representative of a key paradigm of transnational cinema: the festival-funded film. Centring on Llosa's films, but also drawing on other arthouse films from Latin America, this section lays out the histories and cultural politics of the funding bodies that finance films from the Global South. It explores what the links are between these films' transnational funding structures and their aesthetic features and what the study of Llosa's films and the art cinema resurgence brings to the understanding of transnational cinema in Latin America.

A core point of enquiry of a new journal from Intellect, *Transnational Cinemas* launched in 2010, and the subject of several prominent recent anthologies (Ezra and Rowden 2006; Ďurovičová and Newman 2010; Lefere and Lie 2016), the concept of cinematic transnationalism has gained increasing currency in contemporary studies of global and postcolonial cinemas, particularly in the way it offers a means of theorising the movement, and displacement, of cinemas, directors, actors and film personnel across national and regional borders as well as a way of describing "production and distribution practices, sources of funding, casting decisions, [and] thematic concerns" (Hjort 2010: 12). In Latin American film scholarship, the concept of cinematic transnationalism has become central to contemporary theorisations of the region's cinemas in ways that explore cinematic practices, cycles, particular films, or periods that in some way "exceed" the aesthetic, geographical and political borders that historically define its national cinemas. These include a recent issue of *Transnational Cinemas* dedicated to Latin American transnational cinema (Barrow and Falicov 2013), work on inter-American filmmaking in the classical era (Fein 1998; Tierney 2011); work on the transnational careers of the classical era's film personnel between Latin America, Hollywood and Europe (López 1998, 2000; Tierney 2012), a focus on the contemporary "transatlantic traffic" of co-productions between Latin America and Spain/Europe (Smith 2003; Hoefert De Turégano 2004; Falicov 2007, 2010; Villazana 2008, 2009; MacLaird 2008–2009; Triana-Toribio 2013) and several recent anthologies that explore both the transnationality of the Mexican classical era (Irwin and Ricalde 2013) and the diverse transnationality of individual films (Bermúdez 2011; Dennison 2013).

As these examples illustrate, the transnational is a hold-all term, capable of describing a range of complex extra-national practices in contemporary and earlier modes of funding, production and distribution of films. It is precisely its multivalence however, that presents problems for some theorists. First, as such an elastic concept in an industry that has always "operated on a regional, national and transnational basis" (Higson 2000: 67), the concept of the transnational risks the kind of plurality where it can simultaneously "mean anything and everything" (Hjort 2010: 12) *and* consequently, nothing in particular. Second, its expandability threatens to homogenise the very important diversities between national cinemas, flattening out differences between them, while simultaneously connecting them in a globally networked film economy. It is precisely the political and cultural displacement of the nation that the use of the term transnational suggests that is at the core of some Latin American film scholars' exception to it.

While critics in Europe and other parts of the world have identified a number of difficulties with the concept of a national cinema (Higson 2000; Ďurovičová 2010) some scholars of Latin American cinema make the case for its continued relevance (King 2000: 255; 2004: 304; Page 2009: 9). John King, for instance, argues that "the nation remain[s] the principle site for both the production and the reception of movies" (2004: 304) but does not take into account how, with the piecemeal funding that most contemporary films involve, the nation itself becomes a multiple, determined and transnational site, crisscrossed by currents of global commerce and international funding. What is at stake in the retention of the national as the only valid paradigm for exploring Latin America's national cinemas, is an anti-colonial and nationalist stance *against* the colonising tendencies of Hollywood and other first world cinemas. What is understandably problematic about the transnational for these theorists is that it seemingly emphasises the few films—the relative blockbusters with evident transnational pedigree, *Amores perros* (2000, Mexico, Alejandro González Iñárritu); *Y tu mamá también* (2001, Mexico, Alfonso Cuarón); *El secreto de sus ojos* (The Secret in Their Eyes, 2009, Argentina/Spain, Juan José Campanella), and *Nueve reinas* (Nine Queens, 2000, Argentina, Fabián Bielinsky)—at the expense of the many—the small arthouse films that are more overtly "national" but that struggle to get production funding and, once completed, to find distribution in their own national markets and internationally (King 2004: 304; Page 2009: 9–10) *and* that it celebrates the transnational capital that is so often a prominent feature of these films, and its continued exploitation of Latin America's (cultural) resources.

For these critics, the transnational masks the very real difficulties of film production in Latin America, *and* creates an apolitical form of criticism that finds value in commercial success and ignores the very specific conditions of economic exploitation currently threatening Latin American national filmmaking endeavours. While these critics are correct about the problems faced by Latin American filmmakers, what they do not take into account in their drawing up of a national/transnational dichotomy is that those "national" films focused on in scholarship that are "state supported" in their respective countries have simultaneously also benefited from, and are in fact dependent on several sources of transnational funding and, as the rest of this chapter will argue, these transnational funding bodies are not insignificant in determining the aesthetic and cultural identities of the films. It is worth noting that many of the films Joanna Page (2009) explores in her monograph, where she argues for the use of a national (rather than transnational) cinema paradigm, have also benefitted from transnational funding—in the form of monies from film festivals, cultural institutions, television stations and funding agreements located in Europe, the US or transatlantically between Spain and Latin America: *Los guantes mágicos* (The Magic Gloves, 2003, Argentina/France/Germany/Netherlands, Martín Rejtman), Hubert Bals Fund/Fonds Sud/Arte; *Géminis* (The Twins, 2005, Argentina/France, Albertina Carri), Fonds Sud; *Bolivia* (2001, Argentina/Netherlands, Adrián Caetano), Hubert Bals and *Rapado* (Skinhead, 1992, Argentina/Netherlands, Martín Rejtman), Hubert Bals.

Transnational filmmaking in Latin America has historically and contemporaneously taken on a multiplicity of forms. In one of its most frequently cited forms, the official state-backed co-production between European cultural institutions (or television stations benefitting from grants given by the state) and producers from Latin America, two or more countries "collaborate in the process of financing and producing a film" (MacLaird 2008–2009: 51). International co-productions have produced some of Latin America's greatest critical and commercial successes; *El crimen del Padre Amaro* (The Crime of Father Amaro, 2002, Carlos Carrera) was a co-production between Mexico, Spain, Argentina and France and grossed $27 million. They have equally produced some of its worst failures; *El coronel no tiene quien le escriba* (No One Writes to the Colonel, 1999, Arturo Ripstein) was a co-production between Mexico, France and Spain and a commercial flop. In another of its most frequently cited forms transnational cinema is equated with the Latin American blockbusters that have overt transnational status because they are either directly financed, developed or distributed by companies/cultural institutions from beyond the geospatial limits of the continent: *Amores perros*; *Diarios de motocicleta* (The Motorcycle Diaries, 2004, Argentina/USA/Chile/Peru/Brazil/UK/Germany/France, Walter Salles); *Y tu mamá también*, *Cidade de Deus* (City of God, 2002, Brazil/France, Fernando Meirelles and Kátia Lund).

While theorists most commonly frame and sometimes judge co-productions and the continents' blockbusters as properly transnational, they tend to frame arthouse films as national in as much as they fit within the prescriptive textual and ideological features of national cinema (an auteurist, realist "quality" cinema) (Higson 1989: 37, 41). They are, however, in some ways, not that dissimilar. Latin America's most well-known arthouse directors (Llosa, Lucrecia Martel, Lisandro Alonso, Fernando Eimbcke, Amat Escalante, Carlos Reygadas) are similarly involved in a transnational dynamic. Their films add another critical dimension to the idea of transnational cinema in Latin America, presenting an alternative form of transnationalism not strictly reliant on a straight commercial transaction but on something else instead. How we understand the dimensions of this transnationalism is still, nevertheless dependent on the funding structures of these arthouse films and the national situation of filmmaking in their respective industries.

Until the early 1990s, the category of film most commonly funded by Latin America's different national film institutes was a realist, auteurist, arthouse cinema. But since the depletion of state funding cinema and the dismantling of state film protection in the early 1990s, many independent Latin American filmmakers, if they cannot raise money from private sources, are often in need of transnational support whether from a European institution, funding body, multilateral funding agreement or television station, or from the US, via Sundance or a Motion Picture Academy member company. This patchwork of funding with or without state support has become a typical scenario for the most successful recent Latin American arthouse films (Figure 7.1).

Funding initiatives mostly linked to European and US festivals have increasingly become part of the funding structures of Latin American arthouse films and in some cases have actually played a role in developing and sustaining key movements with "[a]lmost all" of el nuevo cine argentino (The New Argentine Cinema) films receiving "sponsorship from one of these sources" (Aguilar 2011: 12). Established in the 1980s, 1990s, and early 2000s many of these funding initiatives, particularly the European ones—Rotterdam Film Festival's Hubert Bals award, Fonds Sud Cinema award, Fribourg Film Festival's Visions Sud Est, the Sundance Institute, its awards and its screenwriting lab, the Global Film Initiative, Berlin Film Festival's World Cinema Fund, Cine en construcción (jointly organised by the San Sebastián Film Festival and the Latin American Film Festival of Toulouse), and the Cannes Film Festival's Cinéfondation—are Government supported, usually by monies earmarked for foreign aid (Falicov 2010: 3; MacLaird 2011; Ross 2011: 261; Campos 2013: 15). Awards are made to facilitate development, production, post-production and distribution, and usually range from €10,000 or $10,000 up to $200,000, with average production awards ranging from €50,000 to €100,000 per film. Given that, based on the reported budget of a handful of films, the average Latin American arthouse film costs around €1,000,000, the winning of multiple funding awards is required to successfully realise any single production. For instance Eimbcke's *Lake Tahoe* (2008, Mexico/Japan/USA), Reygadas's *Batalla en el cielo* (Battle in Heaven, 2005, Mexico/Belgium/France/Germany/Netherlands) and Escalante's *Los bastardos* (The Bastards, 2008, Mexico/France/USA) were all funded by a system of support that included both funding from the Mexican state (through IMCINE, its funding bodies FOPROCINE or FIDECINE and in the case of *Lake Tahoe*, the tax incentive law 226 also known as EFICINE) and funding from a variety of festivals and their funds. *Battle in Heaven*

		Festival Funding						
	Gov. Funding	**Visions Sud Est**	**World Cin Fund**	**Sundance/ NHK**	**Hubert Bals**	**Fonds Sud**	**European TV**	**Ibermedia**
Perú								
Claudia Llosa								
Madeinusa (2006)	√			√			√ Canal+, TVE	
La teta asustada (2010)	√	√	√				√ TVE	√
Mexico								
Fernando Eimbcke								
Lake Tahoe (2008)	√			√				
Carlos Reygadas								
Japón (2002)	√				√			
Batalla en el cielo (2005)	√				√	√	√ Arte France	
Stellet Licht (2007)	√		√				√	
Post Tenebras Lux (2012)	√					√	√Arte France	
Amat Escalante								
Los bastardos (2008)	√					√		
Heli (2013)				√		√	√Arte	
Argentina								
Lucrecia Martel								
La ciénaga (2001)				√				√
La niña Santa (2004)						√		√
La mujer sin cabeza (2008)						√	√ Arte France	
Lisandro Alonso								
Lalibertad (2001)	√postprod					√		
Liverpool (2006)		√			√			√
Jauja (2015)	√		√					

Figure 7.1 Funding structures of selected arthouse successes 2002–2015.

received funds from Hubert Bals and Fonds Sud while *The Bastards* received funds from Fond Sud. *Lake Tahoe* was developed through Sundance/NHK scriptwriting lab.

What is significant about the financial assistance offered by foreign institutions, film festivals and their related competitions is not necessarily the amount: Fonds Sud's award for Martel's *La mujer sin cabeza* (The Headless Woman, 2008, Argentina/France/Italy/Spain) was €90,000 of a total budget of €1.71 million, World Cinema Fund's award for Alonso's *Jauja* (Land of Plenty, 2014, Argentina/Denmark/France/Mexico/USA/Germany/Brazil/Netherlands) amounted to €50,000. What is important about this assistance is the "access [it affords] to *other* economic resources" (Aguilar 2011: 12, emphasis added). Winning one funding competition singles-out scripts or incomplete features as attention-worthy for other festivals and ultimately distributors (MacLaird 2011: 3). Ironically, in Argentina in particular, these "other [. . .] resources" whose interest is often piqued by foreign financial assistance has included its National Film Institute (INCAA), as the story of how Alonso's *La libertad* (Freedom, 2001, Argentina) was completed illustrates. Not being able to even apply to INCAA because of its script based funding application (which is the same with most funding competitions in Europe and North America) during pre-production or production, Alonso made the film with $30,000 of family money and only received state support (of $70,0000 post-production funds) when a Cannes' delegate (on a scouting trip to Argentina) expressed interest in showing the film in "Un Certain Regard" section of the Festival (Matheou 2010: 293). In the case of Argentina, it is not just foreign funding that has nudged its national institute towards greater support of its small arthouse cinema. As Aguilar points out, the state was forced into it "in light of the impact of these movies on the festival circuit and their prestige among critics" (2011: 12). Similarly, in Mexico, the national film institute IMCINE was pushed towards greater support of its independent sector, by the "positive reception [on the funding and festival circuit]" of directors such as Reygadas (*Japón* [2002, Mexico, Germany/Netherlands/Spain]; *Battle in Heaven; Stellet Licht* [Silent Light, 2007, Mexico/France/Netherlands/Germany]; *Post Tenebras Lux* [2012, Mexico/France/Netherlands/Germany]) who was "originally turned down for state support" (MacLaird 2011: 2).

Multi-lateral agreements made between national film institutes is also a key source of funding. The largest of these is Programa Ibermedia. Ibermedia is the main coproduction film fund between Spain and Latin America. Established by CAACI (Conference of Ibero-American Audiovisual and Film Institutes) and the heads of national film institutes in 1997, the fund includes Spain, Portugal and twelve other member countries (Peru, Bolivia, Brazil, Chile, Colombia, Cuba, Mexico, Panamá, Argentina, Puerto Rico, Uruguay, and Venezuela) (Falicov 2007: 21–22). Additionally, from October 2016 Italy has been admitted to Ibermedia (De Marco 2016). Each country makes a minimum contribution of $100,000 with some countries making larger contributions. In 2007, these country contributions were as follows: Mexico ($500,000), Brazil ($300,000), Peru, Argentina, Colombia, Cuba, and Portugal ($100,000 each) (Falicov 2007: 22). Until the economic crisis, Spain's contribution to the Ibermedia fund was as much as $3,500,000 a year (Anon. 2015). Since 2007, the minimum contribution has risen to $150,000 with some of the larger Latin American economies increasing their contribution beyond that in 2015: Brazil ($800,000), Argentina ($500,000) and Venezuela ($600,000) (Anon. 2015). Despite its ongoing economic crisis, Spain remains marginally the largest contributor, giving $850,000 in 2015 (Anon. 2015). All the member countries can compete via production companies to receive monies from Ibermedia's different funds; a script development fund, a co-production fund, a training grant and a distribution grant (Falicov 2007: 21–22) for a pot that is worth in 2015 $4,700,000 (Anon. 2015). Ibermedia has supported the production of many films of the art cinema renaissance including *La Ciénaga* (The Swamp, 2001, Argentina/France/Spain/Japan, Lucrecia Martel) and *Liverpool* (2008, Argentina/France/Netherlands/Germany/Spain, Lisandro Alonso). It has also supported the distribution of films within Latin America. Macondo Cine Video was awarded funds to distribute *Whisky* (2004, Uruguay/Argentina/Germany/Spain, Juan Pablo Rebella and Pablo Stoll) in Mexico and Atlanta Films was funded to distribute Martel's *La niña santa* (The Holy Girl, 2004, Argentina/Italy/Netherlands/Spain) (Falicov 2007: 22).

Since the 1980s, European television companies have also played a large role in funding co-productions with Latin America. Between 1986 and 1992, Spanish television invested more than $20 million in co-productions with Latin American countries (Hoefert de Turégano 2004: 17). Coinciding with the withdrawal of state support across the region this represented a sum larger than all the "Latin American governments combined" (Hoefert de Turégano 2004: 17). The publicly owned TVE (Television española) has been the most active in establishing co-productions with Latin America. Canal+ España, the second most important television network for Spanish film production has also been active in co-productions in the region

(Campos 2013: 15-6). In France, in addition to public channels France 2 and France 3's participation in co-productions with Latin America, the work of the (Franco-German) private cable channel Arte France and its various subsidiaries also stands out (Campos: 2013: 15–6). It has given partial funding to three of Reygadas' films; *Battle in Heaven*, *Silent Night* and *Post Tenebras Lux*, to Martel's *The Headless Woman*, and to Amat Escalante's *Heli* (2013, Mexico/Netherlands/Germany/France). As Minerva Campos points out, the support films receive from these television channels is more than direct investment and promotion. It also includes exhibition and distribution (2013: 16). Under current legislation in Spain, film funding from television (or telecommunications companies) is mandated by government quotas obliging television operators to buy or coproduce Spanish and European movies. These quotas in turn benefit projects co-produced with Latin American nations (Hopwell 2013). Since the economic crisis, and with Spain producing fewer big films Spanish companies are looking to other industries to co-produce with (Hopwell 2013).

Filmmaking in Peru: *Madeinusa* and *The Milk of Sorrow* as festival films

Peru is one of Latin America's smaller national filmmaking endeavours in which production has been sporadic and only really began in earnest in the late 1970s (Middents 2009: 1–2). As in Brazil, Mexico and other countries in the region, in the early 1990s, the state withdrew all support for the film industry, replacing its *ley de cine* (cinema law)—which had guaranteed exhibition for locally produced films, and limited the exhibition of foreign films through quotas—with a new law that remains current (Martínez 2008: 10; Fowkes 2016; Ames Ramello 2017). This law "establishes competitions for film grants but does not ensure any other mechanism for film preservation, distribution or internet promotion" (Ames Ramello 2017). Although these grants give money towards productions and screen writing, the small amounts they represent mean that contemporary films can only be made on an artisanal basis; shooting with digital cameras, small production crews and often (but not always) non-professional actors (Martínez 2008: 18; Ames Ramello 2017), and can often take five years to reach completion (Fowkes 2016). *Madeinusa* and *The Milk of Sorrow* as well as other Peruvian successes of the last decade (Josué Méndez' *Días de Santiago*, Days of Santiago, 2004, Peru) Daniel and Diego Vidal Vega's *Octubre* (October, 2010, Peru), which were all partially funded by these grants, were made following some if not all of these artisanal modes (Matheou 2010: 383). In May of 2011, CONACINE, the state directory body for film, was absorbed into the Ministry of Culture and the office of DICINE (Dirección de Industrias Culturales) was created (Bedoya 2011; Ames Ramello 2017).

Madeinusa takes place over one Easter weekend in an isolated Andean village Manayaycuna where during the time period of "Tiempo Santo" (Holy Time) God is dead and therefore sin does not exist. The villagers are hence free to do whatever they want; steal, drink or have sex with whoever they like, even if it is, in Madeinusa's father's case, his own daughter. The film follows the eponymous protagonist (Magaly Solier) through her weekend of duties as the Virgin Mary and her encounter with Salvador, a young engineer from Lima trapped in the village on his way to another town. *The Milk of Sorrow* takes place in a *pueblo joven* (slum) outside Lima. It tells the story of Fausta (Solier) a migrant from an Andean village, who is afflicted with the "milk of sorrow" (or more literally "the frightened breast"), a psycho-somatic illness believed to be passed through breast milk to the children of women raped during the violence of the 1980s. Fausta is so fearful of life, of men and of sexual attack that she will not go out alone and has, as a precautionary measure, inserted a potato into her vagina. When her mother, Perpetua, dies and she needs money to bury her, she is forced to take a job as night housekeeper at the house of a reclusive pianist and composer, Aída (Susi Sánchez).

Like many prominent films of the recent arthouse resurgence, Llosa's films reflect the multiple funding sources that have become typical and necessary in Peru and across Latin America. For instance, in addition to money it received from CONACINE ($100,000), *The Milk of Sorrow*, which was re-released after its Oscar nomination (the first ever for a Peruvian film), received awards from two European funds Berlin's World Cinema Fund (€50,000) and Fribourg's Visions Sud Est (CHF50,000), as well as majority (80 per cent) funding from Ibermedia which was divided equally between two Spanish production companies, Wanda Vision and Oberón. *The Milk of Sorrow* also received support from the Departement de Cultura del la Generalitat de Catalunya and Televisió de Catalunya. *Madeinusa* similarly received $10,000 from the Sundance/(Japanese television network) NHK script writing competition which facilitated the script's development at a scriptwriting lab (Matheou 2010: 377). TVE provided funding and support for both *Madeinusa* and *The Milk of Sorrow*. Canal+ España awarded a $125,000 prize to *Madeinusa* for best script at the Festival of New Latin American Cinema in Havana in 2004 (Matheou 2010: 376).

In addition to *Madeinusa*'s and *The Milk of Sorrow*'s transnational funding structures making them useful objects of study for this chapter, the narratives of their productions typify the difficulties and problems of filmmaking for Latin American filmmakers *and* illustrate the processes by which transnational funding may alleviate some of these problems. *Madeinusa* and *The Milk of Sorrow* both took several years to make and, despite high profile awards including the Golden Bear at the Berlin International Film Festival, received poor theatrical distribution in the US. They circulated mainly in Peru where, thanks to a grass roots screening tour run by Llosa herself, *Madeinusa* was a "smash hit" (Barrow 2013: 211) and *The Milk of Sorrow* attracted 250,000 spectators (Middents 2013: 158) and on what Piers Handling, Director of the Toronto Film Festival, has called, the "alternative distribution network": the festival circuit (in Turan 2002: 8).

Madeinusa and *La teta asustada*'s narratives, extra-filmic conditions and aesthetics are also useful to this chapter because they offer a means of scrutinising the same processes of cultural transformation and transculturation that are central to critical debates about transnational funding. These debates acknowledge the utility of festival funds to cash-strapped Latin American filmmaking endeavours, particularly in the variety of filmmaking activities they fund and facilitate (talent campuses, script development, preproduction, completion, striking prints, exposure, and, in the case of those with markets attached, distribution deals) (Falicov 2010: 4–6; Triana-Toribio 2013: 90–92). They also point out how the funds are potentially and sometimes inevitably characterised by a neo-colonial power dynamic (Campos 2013: 16). As Tamara Falicov suggests, these festival funds are effectively "exploiting the cultural resources of the South to enrich the global festivals of the North" particularly because the awarding of completion funds is often about "producing [innovative] content for [what are essentially competing] festival[s]" (2010: 5). Significantly, Llosa's films premiered at the festivals that funded them, *Madeinusa* at Sundance in 2006 and *The Milk of Sorrow* at Berlin in 2009. Falicov further suggests that the neo-colonial power dynamic is redoubled when these festival funding bodies make prescriptive demands of scripts from the Global South or influence the content and style of these films by only funding films that fit aesthetic criteria appealing to Western audiences (2010: 5).

Llosa has never suggested she experienced such direct prescriptive demands from the various bodies who funded her films (Matheou 2010: 377), though other directors such as Martel have (Oubiña 2009: 2). It is nevertheless important to ask whether the style of the films Llosa and other directors of Latin America's art cinema renaissance are producing under the guise of these festival/European-funded films may not be indirectly prescribed. It has, after all been suggested that "a transnational aesthetic" is effectively produced in the film-festival circuit, through funding and a larger "system" of facilitation and encouragement (Falicov 2010: 5).

To date, how this "transnational aesthetic" might translate cinematographically has not been the focus of academic study. Instead, scholars have looked at the festival prescribed content in these films. Miriam Ross, for instance, usefully suggests the framework offered in festival-funded films "adheres to what film festival audiences have come to expect of developing world modes of being: poverty and limited social structures" (2011: 264). But if we consider this "transnational aesthetic" in cinematographic terms, what is striking is that Llosa's *Madeinusa* and *The Milk of Sorrow* and other favourites of the festival circuit—Alonso's *Freedom* and *Liverpool*, Caetano's *Bolivia*, Eimbcke's *Lake Tahoe* and Escalante's *Sangre* (2005, Mexico/France), *The Bastards*, and *Heli*—all share a common use of neo-realist modes (location shooting, non-professional actors, an artisanal mode of production, a focus on the quotidian). This realism as a project can be connected both with a broader realist revival in world cinema of which Latin America's transnational cinema is a part, and a "historical chain of film cycles" starting from neo-realism but continuing through the European new waves, into the Latin American new cinemas of the 1960s and the Dogme '95 movement (Nagib and Mello 2009: xiv).

There is of course, a broad spectrum of approaches and realisms within these and other festival-funded successful art cinema directors, ranging from the transcendental realism of Reygadas to the haunting realism of Llosa and Martel who both explore the repressed/not yet come to terms with histories of their respective countries: in *The Milk of Sorrow* the violent conflict between the Peruvian Army and the terrorist group *The Shining Path*, and in *The Headless Woman* the dirty war of Argentina's dictatorship (1976–1983). Given that realism is an important element of these and many other films of the continent's festival funded arthouse renaissance it is possible that it has become an "unspoken" prescriptive demand determining which films get funded by these European and US funding bodies. In this way realism (as opposed to other aesthetic modes that have previously trended in global cinemas such as allegory) becomes the favoured mode not just because it fits within the norms of European art cinema (Bordwell 2002) and of national cinema (as described by Higson) but also because it is the most effective means for communicating the "poverty" and "limited social structures" that Ross argues is what audiences and the festivals that wish to attract them "have come to expect of developing world [films]" (2011: 264).

For instance, in *The Milk of Sorrow*, many scenes in the *pueblo joven* play out in realist master shots that enable the signalling of the very overcrowded living conditions Fausta and her family experience (Figure 7.2). In one of these scenes Fausta's cousin, Máxima (Maria del Pilar Guerrero) argues with her father about the length of the train on her wedding dress. Pairing the master shot with another key realist technique, the framing in depth, other characters, including her brother Jonatan and mother, move from background into foreground and in and out of the composition as they too participate in the discussion and the holding up of the dress. The tableau framing and depth of field emphasise that the "room" in which this scene plays out is in fact the dusty yard in front of the very small house in which the family live.

In *Madeinusa*, a similarly realist master shot is also used to point towards the insanitary conditions in which Madeinusa and the other villagers in Manayaycuna live (Figure 7.3). Early on the camera focuses on Madeinusa's necessary daily ritual of spreading rat poison around the house. When she finds a dead rat and throws it away we cut to a long shot, that frames Madeinusa beside the house and the rat in the extreme foreground. A similarly composed long shot of the house, with a still living but evidently poisoned rat in the foreground appears towards the end of the film. The rat's death throes, its stomach rising and falling rapidly, foreshadow Madeinusa's revenge, when she poisons her father for raping her and breaking her mother's earrings.

Figure 7.2 Key realist techniques of master shot and framing in depth are employed to represent the overcrowded living conditions in the *pueblo joven* in *La teta asustada* (The Milk of Sorrow, 2009, Peru/Spain, Claudia Llosa). ©Generalitat de Catalunya—Institut Català de les Indústries Culturals (ICIC)/Ministerio de Cultura/Oberón Cinematográfica/Televisió de Catalunya (TV3)/Televisión Española (TVE)/Vela Producciones/Wanda Visión S.A.

Figure 7.3 The use of a master shot and framing in depth to signal the insanitary conditions in an Andean village in *Madeinusa* (2006, Peru/Spain, Claudia Llosa). ©Oberón Cinematográfica/ Vela Producciones/Wanda Visión S.A.

Seeming confirmation about the neo-colonial influences these festival-funded films may reflect, and concerns that they are really addressed to Western (festival) audiences are evident in some of responses to Llosa's films from Peruvian criticism. For instance, as Peruvian scholar Natalia Ames Ramello indicates, the film's wholly invented central conceit of "Tiempo Santo", particularly the variety of bacchanalian festivities that villagers can take part between 3pm on Good Friday (the hour of Christ's "death") and dawn on Easter Sunday (his "resurrection") results in the depiction of Peru's indigenous peoples and Andean culture through the stereotypes of the dominant Eurocentric discourse: drunkenness, crime and incest. Even though "Tiempo Santo" involves mixing "real local traditions" such as "floral carpets" and Catholicism with fictional rituals such as "the human clock" and the permission to misbehave, Ames Ramello suggests that the representation of the village is actually much less a realist depiction and much more the reflection of Peru's dominant classes' anxieties about the perceived "backwardness" of Andean culture (Ames Ramello 2012: 4, 6; Matheou 2010: 380). Local criticism like that of Ames Ramello emphasises Llosa's position as part of the social class (of white Peruvians) that is critiqued in both films (César Hildebrandt, quoted by Middents 2013: 158). This criticism of Llosa is potentially redoubled by the fact that her film education, like that of some of her filmmaking compatriots (Méndez) was acquired "in the West". She studied for a Master's degree in scriptwriting in Madrid.

However, Llosa mitigates these criticisms of her films through narratives that are self-consciously constructed to show awareness of the dominant classes' colonialist gaze and its problematic representational tropes and by doing so, offer a counter perspective. For instance, both *Madeinusa* and *The Milk of Sorrow* dramatise and critique the encounter between an indigenous Peruvian (Solier) and a white Peruvian of European descent; Salvador the *limeño* engineer who is confined in Manayaycuna during the Easter weekend festivities and Aída, Fausta's employer. Madeinusa, sees Salvador, as a manifestation of the Europeanised/Americanised culture she fantasises about—the trinkets of which she keeps in a box, including a magazine called *Maribel* and some beaded earrings that had belonged to her mother. She tells her sister that Salvador "has light eyes, like in the magazines". When she has sex with him, she points out that he has her name on his tee-shirt (misrecognising the label which is ironically the likely origin of her name "Made in USA"). His response to her observation "You shouldn't be called Madeinusa, but Rosa or Carmen" shows his ignorance of the fact that these Spanish names are equally inauthentic for her and a marker of the country's original colonisation.

The Milk of Sorrow also emphasises the Eurocentric impulse to (mis)name (control/map) indigenous Peru. Aída (played by Spanish actress Sánchez which heightens the film's postcolonial critique) calls Fausta's a variety of names other than her own. She is inspired to compose again by the Quechua melodies Fausta sings around the house and gets the very shy Fausta to sing these songs to her by promising to give her the pearls from a broken necklace. Fausta (who is aptly named) agrees to this pact because she needs money to transport her mother's dead body back to their Andean village for burial. However, at the film's denouement, Aída performs one of Fausta's Quechua melodies at a concert and then afterwards, when Fausta comments on the performance (in a way that oversteps prescribed class and ethnic boundaries) puts her out of the car, refusing to pay her the promised pearls.

With narratives about cultural encounters and cultural theft both films are self-conscious parables about the tensions between an already hybridised indigenous and a Europeanised Peru; both dealing in different ways with transculturation. The narrative of *The Milk of Sorrow* in particular gestures towards an awareness of the problems of transnational (festival) funding because it also involves a narrative that is about the exploitation of indigenous cultural capital (Fausta's Quecha songs) for the benefit of an (ethnically) European (local) elite (Aída's piano concert). On the grounds of their own self-consciousness *Madeinusa* and *The Milk of Sorrow* in many ways anticipate the criticisms that were made in Peru about the films and their director. Llosa's awareness of the neo-colonised gaze and its problematic desire to folklorise Peru's indigenous and mestizo population (Salvador's comments on what Madeinusa should be called, Aída's continual inability to remember Fausta's name) in part redeem the films, in that they acknowledge the problematic nature of their own representations.

These considerations aside, it is ultimately on their cinematic realist credentials that Latin American arthouse films such as *Madeinusa* and *The Milk of Sorrow* present cultural capital to the film funds, television stations and festivals of the North that provide the monies for their development or completion. This cultural capital is often referred to in the mission statements of the various funding bodies as cultural "expression" or "diversity" (Fonds Sud 2016). In addition, Llosa's films offer what (European) film festival audiences expect "poverty and limited social structures" (Ross 2011: 264) in a mode (art cinema realism) designed to appeal to those same audiences. However, as self-conscious meditations on the transnationalised cultural sphere that highlight both the advantages (the enabling of Peru's struggling cinematic culture, the circulation of Peruvian culture across borders) and the drawbacks (the reification of local narratives within tropes and stereotypes of art cinema) of these transnationalised funding structures *The Milk of Sorrow* and *Madeinusa* maintain a stance that is importantly political and critical in their realism.

Conclusion

This chapter's focus on Llosa's films and Latin America's art cinema resurgence has outlined the financial and aesthetic aspects of transnational Latin American cinema from a transatlantic perspective: analysing how funding and cultural imperatives operate between mostly Europe and Latin America (and sometimes the United States). Looking to the future however, scholarship's emphasis on these transnational festival films and their impact on their national industries is likely to need re-evaluating. After all, the mostly European festival network on which these films circulate does nothing to ameliorate the structural problems of poor distribution and unfair competition (from Hollywood) that most of these films (excepting Llosa's) experience in their respective domestic markets. Additionally, as industry commentators such as Nick Roddick suggest, the reach of even the big festivals has to be called into question. He suggests big festivals are really nothing more than "elegantly constructed events at which an international elite of journalists can stock up on the best of world cinema" (2012: 15). It is therefore imperative to explore ways of extending the distribution and circulation of Latin America's diverse transnational art cinema beyond the small number of journalists (and academics) so that it may reach larger domestic and also international audiences.

References

Anon. (2015) "Ibermedia mueve fichas y depura recursos", *El telégrafo*, 30 July, www.telegrafo.com.ec/cultura1/item/ibermedia-mueve-fichas-y-depura-recursos.html.

Ames Ramello, N. (2012) "Analysis of the Representational Logic of Race in *Madeinusa* (Claudia Llosa 2006)", unpublished essay.

—— (2017) Email correspondence with author.

Aguilar, G. (2011) *New Argentine Cinema: Other Worlds*, London: Palgrave Macmillan.

Barrow, S. (2013) "New Configurations for Peruvian Cinema: The Rising Star of Claudia Llosa", *Transnational Cinemas* 4 (2): 197–215.

Barrow, S. and Falicov, T. (2013) "Latin American Cinema Today: Reframing the National", *Transnational Cinemas* 4 (2): 143–145.

Bermúdez Barrios, N. (2011) *Latin American Cinemas Local Views and Transnational Connections*, Calgary: University of Calgary Press.

Bedoya, R. (2011) "Páginas del diario de Satán", 20 May, http://paginasdeldiariodesatan.blogspot.co.uk/2011/05/el-fin-de-la-autonomia-de-conacine.html.

Bordwell, D. (2002) "The Art Cinema as Mode of Film Practice", in Fowler, C. (ed.) *The European Cinema Reader*, London: Routledge, 94–102.
Campos, M. (2013) "La América Latina de 'Cine en Construcción'. Implicaciones del apoyo económico de los festivales internacionales", *Archivos de la Filmoteca* 71: 13–26.
D'Lugo, M. (2003) "Authorship, Globalization, and the New Identity of Latin American Cinema: From the Mexican 'Ranchera' to Argentinian 'Exile'", in Dissanayake, W. and Guneratne, A. (eds) *Rethinking Third Cinema*, London and New York: Routledge, 103–125.
De Marco, C. (2016) 'Italy joins Ibermedia,' 25 October, http://cineuropa.org/nw.aspx?t=newsdetail&l=en&did=319019 December 2016.
Dennison, S. (2013) *Contemporary Hispanic Cinema: Interrogating the Transnational in Spanish and Latin American Film*, London: Boydell Brewer.
Donoghue, C. B. (2014) "Sony and Local-Language Productions: How Conglomerate Hollywood Is Changing Localization Strategies and Its Approach to the Global Film Market", *Cinema Journal*, 53 (4): 3–27.
Ďurovičová, N. (2010) "Preface", in Ďurovičová, N. and Newman, K. (eds) *World Cinemas: Transnational Perspectives*, New York and London: Routledge, ix–xv.
Ďurovičová, N. and Newman, K. (2010) *World Cinemas: Transnational Perspectives*, New York and London: Routledge.
Ezra, E. and Rowden, T. (2006) "General Introduction: What Is Transnational Cinema?" *Transnational Cinema: The Film Reader*, London and New York: Routledge, 1–12.
Falicov, T. (2007) "Programa Ibermedia and the Cultural Politics of Constructing an Ibero-American Space", *Spectator* 27 (2): 21–30.
—— (2010) "Migrating from South to North: The Role of the Film Festival in Funding and Shaping Global South Film and Video", in Elmer, G., Davis, C., Marchessault, J. and McCollough, J. (eds) *Locating Migrating Media*, Lanham, MD: Lexington Books, 3–22.
Fein, S. (1998) "Transnationalization and Cultural Collaboration: Mexican Film Propaganda during World War II", *Studies in Popular Latin American Culture* 17: 105–128.
Fonds Sud (2016) "Overall Objective", 14 October, www.filmfrasor.no/sorfond/about.
García Canclini, N. (1997) "Will There Be a Latin American Cinema in the Year 2000? Visual Culture in a Postnational Era", in Stock, A. M. (ed.) *Framing Latin American Cinema: Contemporary Critical Approaches*, London and Minneapolis, MN: University of Minnesota Press, 246–258.
Higson, A. (1989) "The Concept of a National Cinema", *Screen* 30 (4): 36–46.
—— (2000) "The Limiting Imagination of National Cinema", in Hjort, M. and MacKenzie, S. (eds) *Cinema and Nation*, London and New York: Routledge, 63–74.
Hjort, M. (2010) "On the Plurality of Cinematic Transnationalism", in Ďurovičová, N. and Newman, K. (eds) *World Cinemas, Transnational Perspectives*, New York and London: Routledge, 12-33.
Hoefert de Turégano, T. (2004) "The International Politics of Cinematic Coproduction: Spanish Policy in Latin America", *Film & History: An Interdisciplinary Journal of Film and Television Studies* 34 (4): 15–24.
Hopwell, J. (2013) "Spain Reaches Out for Amigos to Partner in Film Production", *Variety*, 19 April, http://variety.com/2013/film/global/spain-looks-looks-partners-in-film-production-1200391619/.
Irwin, R. and Ricalde, M. (2013) *Global Mexican Cinema: Its Golden Age*, London: BFI.
King, J. (2000) *Magical Reels: A History of Cinema in Latin America* London: Verso.
—— (2004) "Cinema in Latin America", in King, J. (ed.) *Cambridge Companion to Latin Modern Latin American Culture*, Cambridge: Cambridge University Press, 282–313.
Lefere, R. and Lie, N. (2016) *Nuevas perspectivas sobre la transnacionalidad del cine hispano*, Leiden: Brill.
López, A. M. (1998) "From Hollywood and Back: Dolores Del Rio, A Trans(National) Star", *Studies in Latin American Popular Culture* 17: 5–32.
—— (2000) "Crossing Nations and Genres: Travelling Filmmakers", in Noriega, C. (ed.) *Visible Nations: Latin American Cinema and Video*, London and Minneapolis, MN: University of Minnesota Press, 33–50.
MacLaird, M. (2008–2009) "Co-producing IberoAmerican Culture: *Sólo Dios sabe*'s Transcontinental Journey", *Lucero: A Journal of Iberian and Latin American Studies* 18 (19), 51–59.
—— (2011) "Funding and the Auteur: Comparing the Objectives of National, Regional, and International Production Grants", Society for Cinema and Media Studies Annual Conference, New Orleans, March.
Martínez, G. (2008) "Cinema Law in Latin America: Brazil, Peru and Colombia", *Jump Cut: A Review of Contemporary Media*, 50, 2 September, www.ejumpcut.org/archive/jc50.2008/LAfilmLaw/text.html.
Matheou, D. (2010) *New South American Cinema*, London: Faber.

Middents, J. (2009) *Writing National Cinema: Film Journals and Film Culture in Peru*, New England: Dartmouth College Press.

—— (2013) "The First Rule of Latin American Cinema Is You Do Not Talk about Latin American Cinema: Notes on Discussing a Sense of Place in Contemporary Cinema", *Transnational Cinemas* 4 (2): 147–164.

Nagib, L. and Mello, C. (2009) *World Cinema and the Ethics of Realism*, London: Bloomsbury.

Oubiña, D. (2009) "La vocación de alteridad (festivales, críticos y subsidios del nuevo cine argentino)", in J. Pena Pérez (ed.), *Historias extraordinarias: Nuevo cine argentino 1999–2008*, Madrid: T&B Editores, 15–23.

Page, J. (2009) *Crisis and Capitalism in Contemporary Argentine Cinema*, Durham, NC: Duke University Press.

Roddick, N. (2012) "Festival or Famine", *Sight & Sound* 22 (2): 15.

Ross, M. (2011) "The Film Festival as Producer: Latin American Films and Rotterdam's Hubert Bals Fund", *Screen* 52 (2): 261–267.

Smith, P. J. (2003) "Transatlantic Traffic in Recent Mexican Films", *Journal of Latin American Cultural Studies* 12 (3): 389–400.

Tierney, D. (2011) "Emilio Fernández 'in Hollywood': Mexico's Postwar Inter-American Cinema, *La perla/The Pearl* and *The Fugitive*", *Studies in Hispanic Cinemas* 7 (2): 81–100.

—— (2012) "Latino Acting on Screen: Pedro Armendáriz Performs Mexicanness in Three John Ford Films", *Revista Canadiense de Estudios Hispánicos* 37 (1): 111–134.

Triana-Toribio, N. (2013) "Building Latin American Cinema in Europe: Cine en Construcción/Cinéma en construction", in Dennison, S. (ed.) *Contemporary Hispanic Cinema: Interrogating the Transnational in Spanish and Latin American Film*, London: Boydell & Brewer, 89–112.

Turan, K. (2002) *Sundance to Sarajevo: Film Festivals and the World They Made*, Los Angeles, CA: University of California Press.

Villazana, L. (2008) "Hegemony Conditions in the Coproduction Cinema of Latin America: The Role of Spain", *Framework: The Journal of Cinema and Media* 49 (2): 65–85.

—— (2009) *Transnational Financial Structures in the Cinema of Latin America: Programa Ibermedia in Study*, Germany: VDM Verlag.

8

CONNECTED IN "ANOTHER WAY"

Repetition, difference and identity in Caribbean cinema

Dunja Fehimović

Introduction: defining Caribbean cinema

There is no defining Caribbean cinema. This task, fundamental to the project of the present chapter, rests on another essential question: What is the Caribbean? Rather than constituting a basis for further intellectual enquiry and artistic creation, however, this deceptively straightforward interrogative is at the heart of unresolved debates and repeated attempts at (self-)definition by Caribbean writers, artists, intellectuals and filmmakers. If we start from the decision, reassuringly grounded in the physical realm, to equate the Caribbean with the geographical feature of the Caribbean basin, we are soon thwarted by the realisation that there are in fact five interconnected basins, covering the islands in the Caribbean Sea and touching on the mainland territories of Central America, Venezuela and Colombia. If this is the case, then should we consider these mainland territories, for example, as Caribbean? Where might we draw the imaginary line between the Caribbean and South or Central American "sections" of the relevant countries? With all this in mind, we might ask, where does Caribbean cinema begin, and where does it end? Which routes does it follow and what forms does it take?

As we delve into this problem, adding racial, linguistic, historical, and cultural criteria to our geographical categories, the Caribbean "in theory" increasingly starts to clash with the Caribbean "in practice", so that inconsistencies emerge and criteria become unclear. Suriname, Guyana and French Guiana, for example, are far more commonly included in investigations of the Caribbean and its cinema than Colombia and Venezuela. The first major study of its kind, Mbye Cham's edited volume, *Ex-iles: Essays on Caribbean Cinema*, begins by acknowledging that "the Caribbean covers a much wider geographic, cultural, linguistic and racial expanse than covered in this book" (1992: xiii). Cham chooses to focus on the cinemas of Guadeloupe, Martinique, the "Netherlands Antilles" (Curaçao, Suriname, Aruba), Haiti, Jamaica, Trinidad and Tobago, and their diasporas. He justifies the exclusion of Cuba, Venezuela, Puerto Rico, and the Dominican Republic by brief reference to the "significant and fine body of critical works" on these areas (Cham 1992: xii), though it seems that this is only really the case with Cuba. Meanwhile, he omits Britain's Caribbean diaspora because it is discussed in another edited volume, *Blackframes: Critical Perspectives on Black Independent Cinema* (Cham and Andrade-Watkins 1988). In this way, Cham, not unlike other scholars, obtains a corpus of Caribbean cinema by negation. A particularly illustrative example of the gap between theory and practice is provided by prominent Guadeloupian filmmaker Christian Lara, whose five requisites for Caribbean film have proven influential: "the director should be from the Caribbean, the subject matter should be a Caribbean story, the lead actor/actress should be from the Caribbean, Creole should be used, the production unit should be Caribbean" (in Tallon 1983). Apart from the fact that "the Caribbean" floats vaguely, undefined, through these stipulations, it is telling that, for some critics, many of Lara's films are themselves "severely limited in their Caribbeanness" (Cham 1992: 11) according to these same criteria.

The ontological uncertainties implicit in these discussions have confounded thinkers not only at the level of the Caribbean as a whole, but also at that of individual Caribbean nations. In a lecture delivered in 1939 and first published the following year, Cuban anthropologist and sociologist Fernando Ortiz took geography as the point of departure for his definition of Cubanness. However, the simple statement with which he began—"Cuba is an island"—was soon troubled by the realisation that "Cuba is an archipelago, that is, a conjunction of many islands, of hundreds of them" (2008: 1, translations author's own). On both the broader and the narrower scales, what begins as a single referent soon starts to multiply, spinning out of control and beyond our grasp. Prefiguring "lines of flight" (Deleuze's term (Deleuze and Guattari 2013) denotes the possibility of unpredictable, potentially liberating mutation), on the one hand, and the transnational turn in cultural and film studies on the other, the Caribbean, its cultures, and its cinemas condemn the enquirer to "an unending search", forever opening onto "other possible voyages, other possible routes" (Benítez Rojo 1996: xi). Just as the Caribbean expands ever outwards in trade, migratory and other routes from its putative roots in the Caribbean basin, so Caribbean cinema constitutes an "expanded" (Huyssen 2002) and ever-expanding field.

These geologically and geographically based enquiries, though refusing to yield absolute definitions, form the substratum of a particularly productive and influential meditation on the Caribbean: Antonio Benítez Rojo's *The Repeating Island: The Caribbean and the Postmodern Perspective* (all quotations here refer to James E. Maraniss's translation of the second edition, published in 1996). The Cuban-born writer begins with a "concrete and easily demonstrated" fact: "the Antilles are an island bridge connecting, in "another way", North and South America" (1996: 2). Benítez Rojo's reference to "las Antillas", a term more often used to denote the Francophone Caribbean, itself repeats in another way the instability of the signifier of the Caribbean which we have already seen with reference to geography, reminding us of the region's characteristic linguistic and cultural plurality. Concluding that its connective quality gives the region "the character of an archipelago" (1996: 2), Benítez Rojo reconfigures the insights of Martiniquan writers Édouard Glissant, Jean Bernabé, Patrick Chamoiseau, and Raphaël Confiant in the key of Chaos theory, which had then recently emerged to posit intimate, unseen connections between the minute and the vast, suggesting that "within the (dis) order that swarms around what we already know of as Nature, it is possible to observe dynamic states or regularities that repeat themselves globally" (1996: 2). Like Benítez Rojo, therefore, this chapter "aspires to be repetitive rather than definitive" (1996: xi), tracing a Caribbean cinema that emerges through the differential repetition of particular characteristics, anxieties, and themes: identity, independence, fragmentation, connection, and consumption.

Glissant's most influential texts, *Caribbean Discourse* ([1981] 1989) and *Poetics of Relation* ([1990] 1997) elaborate a vision of the Caribbean—albeit with an undeniable focus on Martinique in particular—that rejects totalising projects of knowledge and teleological metanarratives of History and Progress, and is instead characterised by multiplicity, ambivalence and disorder. Writing three years later, Bernabé, Chamoiseau and Confiant adopted and adapted Glissant's ideas to produce a manifesto of sorts: *In Praise of Creoleness* (1993). Renouncing the "two incumbent monsters" (1993: 80) of Europeanness (colonisation and the mental alienation of the colonised subject) and Africanness (erected as a new ideal by the Négritude movement led by fellow Martiniquan Aimé Césaire), these authors pointed to Glissant as a foundational thinker of "Caribbeanness" (1993: 83). The cultural heart of Caribbeanness, for Bernabé and colleagues, is *Créolité*: being part of a group that results from "a nonharmonious (and unfinished therefore nonreductionist) mix of linguistic, religious, cultural, culinary, architectural, medical, etc. practices" belonging to the different peoples (Amerindians, Europeans, Africans, Arabs, Asians) brought together by colonisation (1993: 92). In this concept, and in key moments in all of these texts, a particular differential repetition starts to emerge: a "true" Caribbeanness can only be found in and through contingency and relationality—in short, in openness to the rest of the world. As such, Caribbean identity is allied with movement rather than stasis, Becoming rather than Being. This vision is antithetical to any classic "Introduction to", and finds its expression more through a series of tentative, unstable connections than through the comfort of clear definitions, delimitations, and conclusions.

If the Caribbean is characterised by "open specificity", "kaleidoscopic totality", and "the nontotalitarian consciousness of a preserved diversity", "[t]o define" becomes "a matter of taxidermy" (Bernabé *et al.* 1993: 89, 88). To the practical resistance of the Caribbean to straightforward definition, then, we now add a political resistance to *definition* as a kind of "bringing to an end". The external imposition and fixing of meaning is a form of symbolic violence associated with death and likened, in the *Éloge*, to "cultural amputation" (1993: 104)—dividing the subject on whom it is imposed. In his two seminal explorations of colonisation and its psychological consequences, *Black Skin White Masks* ([1952] 1967) and *The Wretched of the Earth* ([1961] 2004), the Martiniquan-born Frantz Fanon explored the related phenomenon of the colonised subject's mental alienation:

> Because it is a systematic negation of the other person and a furious determination to deny the other person all attributes of humanity, colonialism forces the people it dominates to ask themselves the question constantly: "In reality, who am I?"
>
> *(2004: 250)*

In *Black Skin, White Masks*, Fanon memorably uses the example of a young black Antillean watching a Tarzan film in Europe: his *de facto* identification with Tarzan becomes much more difficult as the surrounding (white) audience automatically identifies him with the black savages on screen. Through this "conclusive experience" (1967: 152–153) it becomes evident that the black subject, like the colonised subject more broadly, is subjected to and by the knowledge and representational systems of the coloniser. He is thus split from himself—a condition memorably described by Bernabé, Chamoiseau, and Confiant as a state of being "fundamentally stricken with exteriority", only able to "perceive [. . .] one's world [. . .], with the eyes of the other" (1993: 76).

This is far from being a surpassed stage of development. In addition to a common past of colonisation, much of the Caribbean continues to occupy complex and often uncomfortable positions in relation to former (and newer) "colonisers"; this is the case of France's Overseas Departments (*département d'outre-mer* or *DOM*) in the Caribbean—Guadeloupe, Martinique and French Guiana; the British Overseas Territories, including Anguilla, the Cayman Islands and Montserrat; and Dutch territories such as Aruba, Curaçao and Sint Marteen. From the negotiation of its independence between Spain and the US at the Treaty of Paris, to US military interventions allowed by the Platt Amendment, to more recent attempts to bring down the Revolution, Cuba has a long history of struggles for national sovereignty. Meanwhile, the oxymoronic quality of Puerto Rico's official name, *Estado Libre Asociado de Puerto Rico* (the Commonwealth of Puerto Rico, but literally "The Associated Free State of Puerto Rico") indicates its ambivalent, problematic status vis-à-vis the US.

The Caribbean in cinema

Given the manifestation of these formative experiences of colonisation, post-, and neo-coloniality in distorted self-perception and uncertain identity, we must think not only about Caribbean cinema, but also, and—given the fact that "filmmaking in the Caribbean by Caribbean people" is a relatively recent phenomenon (Cham 1992: 1)—perhaps first, about the Caribbean *in* cinema. Artistic, literary and filmic representations can cement and contribute to the effects of colonisation, reinforcing the Caribbean subject's mental alienation and "exteriority" by imposing the deathly stasis of reductive stereotypes. As Aimé Césaire has noted, the kinds of foreign films to which the Caribbean is exposed contribute greatly to the fact that "[t]he Antillean being is a human being who is deprived of his own self, of his history, of his traditions, of his beliefs" (in Sephocle 1992: 360). Typing "Caribbean film" into an internet search engine, I find myself scrolling through dozens of pages before I can locate a result that does not relate to Jerry Bruckheimer's multi-million-dollar film franchise, *Pirates of the Caribbean* (2003–2017). The film series' origins in a theme-park ride designed by Walt Disney on the basis of a hodgepodge of "general Pirate narratives" (Petersen 2007: 67) speaks eloquently to the way in which it exoticises and objectifies the region for capitalist consumption. Like Disney's ride, which first opened to the public in 1967, the film exemplifies "the Disneyland simulacrum" (Baudrillard [1981] 1994), recreating "a history that never truly existed" (Petersen 2007: 64)—one that is, moreover, problematically "blanketed in whiteness" (with the one exception of an archetypal tragic *mulata*—Calypso/Tia Dalma [Thomas 2014: 187]).

While cinematic exploitations of the Caribbean often reinforce existing problematics of sovereignty, identity and self-worth, they also shore up the "superiority" of "the West". Tellingly, Mimi Sheller's analysis of the construction of Western Europe and North America's modernity through the consumption of Caribbean environments, commodities, bodies, and cultures opens with a cinematic metaphor: "Despite its indisputable narrative position at the origin of the plot of Western modernity, history has been edited and the Caribbean left on the cutting-room floor" (2003: 1). The remaining frames and sequences have tended to foreground stereotypes of the exotic or folkloric, usually only portraying locals as "picturesque native types or servants of one sort or another: human exotica, local color" (Thelwell 1992: 177). It is unsurprising then, that this complex intersection of consumption, commodification, identity, and alienation might feature in Caribbean films from the Caribbean. Indeed, it comes memorably to the foreground in Jamaica's first fiction feature, *The Harder They Come* (1972, Jamaica). Released in the years following the island's independence, Perry Henzell's film quickly established itself not only as the foundation of a "national" cinema, but also, for many, as "the quintessential Caribbean film" (Paddington and Warner 2009: 100). Its portrayal of country boy Ivan's move to Kingston, foray into the music industry, and involvement in the drug trade was pioneering in its celebration of working-class Jamaican culture and language (Creole/Patois/Patwa), but also attracted criticism at home for its "representation of ganja consumption and [. . .] 'glamorous' Jamaican gangsters"—stereotypes that normally plagued foreign depictions of the island (Ceccato 2015).

Kenneth Harris reads the film in terms of racial, sexual and commodity fetishism to conclude, somewhat cynically, that its underlying purpose is "the commodification of reggae for white consumers" (1992: 214). Despite the film's prominent soundtrack and its protagonist's musical aspirations (rising international reggae star Jimmy Cliff played Ivan and sang on the soundtrack), this reductive view overemphasises the film's collusion in fetishisation; after all, the protagonist's spectacular death warns that (mis)identification with (foreign) images—in Ivan's case, with the cowboys he watches at the cinema (specifically Sergio Corbucci's *Django*, 1966, Italy: a spaghetti western that thus also revolves around (mis)identification with foreign images)—is a mirage that will end in violence, be it symbolic—alienation and "mimicry" (Bhabha 1994), or literal—death. The film quickly became a "cult classic" abroad, where it appealed, ironically, for its attractive and exotic "Jamaicanness" (Paddington and Warner 2009: 101), but it was particularly important in Jamaica, where for the first time a film had "reveal[ed] [the] country to itself" (Césaire in Sephocle 1992: 365). Though some critics have interpreted its use of Hollywood techniques as a kind of betrayal to the black Jamaican experience (Yearwood 2000: 161), its enthusiastic acceptance by national audiences and filmmakers alike confirms Bruce Paddington and Keith Warner's suggestion that "Caribbean film continues to survive and its identity, as with the Caribbean itself, has been forged as a result of these interactions and negotiations" (2009: 92). In this way, Victoria Marshall's designation of Jamaican film as "likkle but tallawah" (1992: 99) (a Jamaican Patois phrase meaning "small but strong") remains valid today, as Henzell's classic continues to provide inspiration for a steadily growing number of Jamaican cineastes (not least Storm Saulter, whose *Better Mus' Come*, 2010, Jamaica, is a kind of indirect sequel to Henzell's film).

"[A] country without images is a country that does not exist"

Given the evident implication of cinema with hegemonic geopolitical systems and racial, sexual, and gender inequalities, it is perhaps hardly surprising that artistic modes, from visual art to poetry and cinema, have sought to reclaim the Caribbean through an ongoing quest for authenticity, a search for self on individual, national, and regional levels. In such a context, cinema is important because, in the words of prominent Cuban filmmaker and intellectual Julio García Espinosa, "[a] country without images is a country that does not exist. All that we do, all that we want to do, is to have the right to be the protagonists of our own image" (in López 2007: 186). In Cuba, the foundation of the Instituto Cubano de Arte e Industria Cinematográficos (ICAIC—The National Institute of Cinematographic Art and Industry) shortly after the 1959 Revolution bore witness to a political commitment to national sovereignty and a cultural commitment to the development, promotion, and celebration of national culture and identity. The films ICAIC has produced have varied widely in their themes, aesthetics, and approaches, but a common thread of critical questioning can be found in their portrayals of Cuban history and reality, the quintessential example of which is arguably Tomás Gutiérrez Alea's *Memorias del subdesarrollo* (*Memories of Underdevelopment*, 1968, Cuba).

Set during the 1962 missile crisis, the film explores the tense uncertainty of the post-Revolutionary, Cold War period through the psychological paralysis of the white, bourgeois intellectual Sergio, who remains on the island after all of his friends and family have left. Speaking eloquently about his country's underdevelopment, in which "nothing has continuity, everything is forgotten [and] people aren't consistent" (all translations my own), Sergio nonetheless fails to identify his own faults, which ironically take the form of another of his pronouncements on underdevelopment: "the incapacity to relate things, to accumulate experience, and evolve". Although he is aware that he is experiencing the birth of a new era, and critiques the old, bourgeois order to which he used to belong, he also bitterly repeats the same stereotypes that mark Cuba as part of the underdeveloped "tropics", recalling the multiple forms of consumption of the Caribbean: "That's what backward countries are for: to kill things, to fish, and to sunbathe. There you have her, the beautiful Cuban *señorita*."

As Julianne Burton points out, the film's opening sequences combine documentary footage and fiction to simultaneously reference and undermine cinematic representations of Cuba—and the Caribbean—according to stereotypes of exoticism, sensuality, rhythm and racial otherness ([1977] 1990: 236). Working through a dialectics of identification and distanciation, the film is exemplary in its questioning of notions of modernity, development, coloniality, Caribbeanness, and Cubanness. According to Ana López's influential reading, for example, "*Memorias* should also be considered as the first Cuban film of exile, marking the disarticulation of an 'inside' space for nationness and the re-articulation of a transnational (or at least, north–south) mode of a more ambivalent 'Greater Cuban' identity" (1995: 7).

As Cham has pointed out, outside of Cuba, the emergence of Caribbean films in the 1970s and 1980s was a product of similarly significant social, political, and economic developments, such as Jean-Claude Duvalier's dictatorship in Haiti, Michael Manley and Edward Seaga's governments in Jamaica, and the nascent pro-independence movements of Guadeloupe and Martinique (1992: 2). Though Cuba is historically unique in the Caribbean in terms of the level of state support dedicated to local filmmaking, official backing and funds also proved crucial to the production of Euzhan Palcy's *Rue cases nègres* (Sugar Cane Alley, 1983, Martinique/France)—a Martiniquan film which has similarly acquired the status of a "classic". Adapted from Joseph Zobel's novel (1950), the film owes its creation in large part to the personal, political, and financial support of Aimé Césaire, who was serving on the Regional Council of Martinique at the time, and whose cultural initiatives (such as SERMAC—Service Municipal d'Action Culturelle) Palcy credits with laying the foundations for her film's success (in Givanni 1992: 295). Set in the 1930s, *Rue Cases-Nègres* deals with slavery's aftermath through the story of young José and his grandmother, Amantine (Figure 8.1). The two live next to a sugarcane plantation, but when José is presented with a scholarship to a city school, they must both face new difficulties in Fort-de-France. In line with Nègritude's goals of reclaiming blackness and African heritage as sources of pride and strength, the film uses the protagonist's only father figure, the

Figure 8.1 *Rue cases nègres* (Sugar Cane Alley, 1983, Martinique/France, Euzhan Palcy) deals with slavery's aftermath through the story of young José and his grandmother. ©NEF Diffusion/Orca Productions/SU.MA.FA.

storyteller Medouze, to highlight the importance of Africa to the development both of José and of Martinique (Antoine-Dunne 2010: 103).

Importantly, this political and cultural commitment to a recovery of African heritage also manifests itself through a particular aesthetic. Indeed, the film's use of light "adds to the creation of an image grounded in an idea of blackness, in particular, since light intensifies the concentration on skin colour, especially in the portrayal of Medouze and José" (Antoine-Dunne 2010: 103). Its focus on a Caribbean, tropical light has a long creative tradition, the latest interpretation of which is perhaps to be found in the films and theorisations of contemporary Trinidadian filmmaker, Yao Ramesar. Reflecting on the Caribbean sun as "a centrifugal force and aesthetic" in regional cinema, Ramesar has developed a natural approach to lighting that he believes favours dark skin-tones and resonates psychologically with local audiences (in Chong 2015: 127). Over time, and through the production of feature films such as *SistaGod* (2006, Trinidad and Tobago, Yao Ramesar) and *Haiti Bride* (2014, Trinidad and Tobago/ Haiti, Yao Ramesar) (Figure 8.2), this practice has crystallised into a very deliberate quest to develop an "eyealect": a Caribbean "visual vernacular" (in Chong 2015: 122) that corresponds with the region's many linguistic variations. This aesthetics is thus part of a wider philosophy of filmmaking that Ramesar calls "Caribbeing"—a commitment "to reflect our realities in life and our culture on screen" (in Raphael 2014) that we might apply to many of the films discussed here. Importantly, Ramesar's focus on representing and celebrating Caribbean identity on screen does not constitute a retrenchment in some narrow sense of self. Rather, his claim that his work is "creolisation squared" (in Chong 2015: 122) resonates with the ideas of open, unfixed Caribbeanness and *Créolité* explored above.

More specifically, we might align Ramesar's approach with Gilberto M. Blasini's insightful exposition of a "Caribbean cinematic créolité" (2009). Analysing the syncretic and never complete process of creolisation in relation to "the tactical inscription of diasporic African cultures into cinematic texts", Blasini shows how blackness and Africanness become "symbolic sites where social, cultural, and political elements converge and transform into a discourse that can be called 'Caribbean *créolite*'" (2009: 71, 73). His reading of key films such as Palcy's *Sugar*

Figure 8.2 *Haiti Bride* (2014, Trinidad and Tobago/Haiti, Yao Ramesar) illustrates a very deliberate quest to develop an "eyealect", a Caribbean "visual vernacular". ©Caribeing.

Cane Alley, and Curaçaoan filmmaker Felix de Rooy's *Almacita di Desolato* (Almacita, Soul of Desolato, 1986, Netherlands Antilles/Netherlands) demonstrates the way in which a focus on the specific and apparently narrow quickly starts to open out, as "*créolite* not only documents the continual transformations of the Caribbean but also reinvents its geocultural scope by expanding beyond the Antilles" (2009: 73). The syncretic content, form, and aesthetics of these films encourage us to make connections with the south-eastern coast of the USA, the north-eastern coast of South America, and the Caribbean diaspora's host countries, amongst other places. In this way, a turn to specificity soon becomes a call for connection, as it grows increasingly difficult to categorise and contain Caribbean cinema according to national, regional or other criteria.

This problem of categorisation is evident in the emergent canon examined here—a Cuban film that has been associated with Latin America and the *New Latin American Cinema* movement of the 1960s and 70s, a Martiniquan story that speaks broadly to the postcolonial experience, a Jamaican "classic" in critical dialogue with Hollywood practices and images, and a Trinidadian–Haitian exploration of "Caribbeing", all of which are of uncertain or mixed genre. Unsurprisingly, then, the question of where studies of such films *fit* has manifested itself in scholarship on Caribbean cinema, which, with the exception of a few more comprehensive volumes, is scattered among collections or texts dedicated to more or less broad concepts such as Third Cinema, World Cinema, Francophone Cinema, or Black Cinema. This fragmentation of the scholarly corpus is apt in its reflection of the geographic, cultural, and linguistic fragmentation that characterise the Caribbean, and it can at times encourage readers and viewers to adopt a relational perspective that reflects on the understandings of Caribbeanness outlined here. However, some of these approaches also limit connections and comparisons in a way that—albeit unwittingly—reinforces the historic marginalisation of Caribbean cultures.

Caribbean cinemas as "cinemas of relation"

We have seen this debate play out in more general terms around "Third" or indeed, "World Cinema", whose frequent construction in opposition to the hegemonic forces of Hollywood or "mainstream" commercial film reinforces the kind of binary that has long relegated the Caribbean to the margins of history and civilisation. However, recent explorations of Caribbean cinema have sought to redress this imbalance; by "not only recovering but also reimagining the parameters of the missing archives of the Caribbean's transnational history with motion pictures" (Francis 2014), issue 17 of *SX Salon* proposes a new angle that focuses on Caribbean film archives. A special issue of online journal *Imaginations* entitled "Caribbean Cinema Now" (2015) gathers scholarly presentations from the tenth anniversary of the Trinidad and Tobago Film Festival (TTFF) to "[indicate] a more optimistic outlook for the future of Caribbean film studies" (Hambuch 2015). Meanwhile, a special issue of *Caribbean Quarterly* seeks "a multifaceted approach to the Caribbean as a whole", juxtaposing essays on diasporic film with studies of "national" or local films (Antoine-Dunne 2015: 4).

While acknowledging the importance of critiques of centre/periphery theories by critics such as Teshome Gabriel (1982) and Ella Shohat and Robert Stam (1994), we must acknowledge that the categories of "Third" and "World" cinema are useful in the way that they force us to recognise the inequalities and imbalances that shape Caribbean geopolitical and economic realities, and, therefore, cinemas. After all, Caribbean nations and dependencies are small, and limited internal markets mean that film production is expensive and therefore often impracticable. The "isolation" of much of the Caribbean makes it more expensive and challenging to obtain necessary equipment and technology. While the dissemination of video and digital technologies has greatly improved this situation, the still-difficult access to the latest equipment is further complicated by the fact that many elements, from training to post-production facilities, are unlikely to be available close to home. As a result, production capacity is further restricted, and the pool of qualified and experienced individuals remains small. Those who have the requisite skills and know-how often stay abroad, where there are more funds, more networks—in short, more opportunities to produce. At the same time, the absence of a local film *industry* proper is both cause and effect of the dominance of Hollywood productions and foreign-owned cinema complexes in many parts of the Caribbean. Given these characteristics, we might usefully see much of the region in light of Mette Hjort and Duncan Petrie's discussion of "the cinema of small nations" (2007). Importantly, the category of "small nation" relies on relation and relativity, since physical, political and economic "size" can only be determined in comparison with something else (2007: 2).

Given the importance of the relational in Caribbean culture, Erling Bjöl's suggestion that "a small state should be [. . .] considered shorthand for a state in its relationship with greater states" (in Yoo 1990: 12) could be put to productive use in an analysis of Caribbean cinema. However, the characteristic of "small nationhood" also risks resonating too strongly with the binaries often common to ideas of Third and World Cinema—binaries that paradoxically restrict rather than facilitate relationality. Alert to Paul Willemen's warning that the international focus in Western cinema studies tends to result in the neo-colonial imposition of Euro-American paradigms on non-Western films (2006: 34), we might therefore adapt Bjöl's thought to do greater justice to the intellectual history and creative reconfigurations of the region. Taking the lead from Glissant's *Poetics of Relation*, I propose a renewed exploration of Caribbean cinemas as "cinemas of relation"—that is, cinemas that express their particularity and authenticity not through retrenchments in the national or the local or through straightforward opposition to a hegemonic "centre" but by constantly making and reconfiguring multiple connections. In the cinema of relation, "each and every identity is extended through a relationship with the Other" (Glissant 1997: 11). Such a reframing makes the important political move of shifting Caribbean cinema from the margins to a position, if not of centrality, then of exemplarity, where its rhizomatic (rather than arborescent, hierarchical) roots and routes speak eloquently to the state of an increasingly transnational cinema in an increasingly globalised world. This approach would therefore reflect the identification—signalled by writers such as Bernabé, Chamoiseau and Confiant, that the Caribbean is "the anticipation of the relations of cultures, of the future world whose signs are already showing" (1993: 88).

Conclusion

This redefinition necessitates, in further and more extensive studies of Caribbean cinema, the adoption of a more thoroughly comparative approach, less limited by the linguistic or geographic parameters that have characterised scholarship to date. In this sense, Kristian Van Haesendonck and Theo D'haen's tellingly entitled *Caribbeing: Comparing Caribbean Literatures and Cultures* (2014) provides a potential model to follow, in which it becomes clear that a comparative aspect is indispensable if we are to discover similarities and differences between various sites of Caribbeanness, and do justice to the suggestive overlaps and disjunctures between Caribbeanness, *Créolité*, postcolonialism, and globalisation. Working thematically, the collection shifts the diasporic from its habitual position of marginality or supplementarity, integrating it into explorations of "Caribbeing"—defined (in a different but not incompatible way to Yao Ramesar's idea) as a "state-of-being where the very name Caribbean is overdetermined with new meanings that exceed a clearly delimited geographical space" (2014: 11).

Such a move outwards to perceive Caribbean cinemas in multiple relations with others echoes the desire for connection evidenced by initiatives such as the CaribbeanTales Incubator and

Worldwide Distribution company (Simpson 2015), or recent calls by Cuban filmmakers for a film law that will allow them to reconnect with Latin America and the Caribbean (Anon. 2015). However, it is also hampered by the precarious and limited availability of Caribbean cinema; the same problems that plague production affect distribution, so that (with the exception of Cuba) local films are rarely shown in cinemas, and even then have short runs, while only very few are available for purchase on official DVDs. More common, but still limited, is circulation via bootleg copies, internet streaming, illegal download, and USB (in Cuba, entertainment circulates through the so-called "paquete semanal", or "the weekly package"). Although dedicated film festivals such as TTFF and CaribbeanTales do provide opportunities to see Caribbean productions, it is an irony befitting the region's complex history and geopolitics that the distribution, circulation and consumption of Caribbean cinema is currently characterised by both (industrial, commercial) isolation but also the kind of multiple, unofficial, unpredictable connections fostered by digital media and the internet. Nevertheless, if these modes of circulation were to be harnessed to allow a study of these films and their itinerant, rhizomatic afterlives, the examination of an "expanded" Caribbean cinema might reinforce the ongoing reconfiguration of "World Cinema" as a study of cinemas of relation, emphasising migrations, returns, connections, and relationships in film history, practice, distribution, consumption, narrative and aesthetics. Such a film studies would undoubtedly benefit from the new perspectives afforded by a characteristically Caribbean "errantry" (Glissant 1997: 18), revealing cinemas to be intimately connected, albeit "in another way".

References

Anon. (2015) "Por una nueva ley de cine en Cuba", *Cine Cubano, La Pupila Insomne*, 1 November, https://cinecubanolapupilainsomne.wordpress.com/2015/11/01/por-una-nueva-ley-de-cine-en-cuba/.

Antoine-Dunne, J. (2010) "Sound and Vision in the Caribbean Imaginary", *Journal of West Indian Literature* 18 (2): 95–114.

—— (2015) "Introduction: Back and Beyond—The Context", *Caribbean Quarterly* 61 (2–3): 1–6.

Baudrillard, J. (1994) *Simulacra and Simulation*, Faria Glaser, S. (trans), Ann Arbor, MI: University of Michigan Press.

Benítez Rojo, A. (1996) *The Repeating Island: The Caribbean and the Postmodern Perspective*, Maraniss, J. E. (trans.), 2nd edn, Durham, NC; London: Duke University Press.

Bernabé, J., Chamoiseau, P. and Confiant, R. (1993) *Éloge de La Créolité/In Praise of Creoleness*, Taleb-Khyar, M. B. (trans.), Éd. bilingue français–anglais, Paris: Gallimard.

Bhabha, H. (1994) *The Location of Culture*, London: Routledge.

Blasini, G. M. (2009) "Caribbean Cinematic Créolité", *Black Camera* 1 (1): 70–90.

Burton, J. ([1977] 1990) "Memories of Underdevelopment in the Land of Overdevelopment", *Cineaste* 8 (1): 16–21. Reprinted in Chanan, M. (ed.) *Memories of Underdevelopment*, New Brunswick, NJ; London: Rutgers University Press, 232–246.

Ceccato, S. (2015) "Cinema in Jamaica—The Legacy of *The Harder They Come*", *Imaginations: Journal of Cross-Cultural Image Studies* 6 (2): 54–67.

Cham, M. B. (ed.) (1992) *Ex-Iles: Essays on Caribbean Cinema*, Trenton, NJ: Africa World Press.

Cham, M. B. and Andrade-Watkins, C. (eds) (1988) *Blackframes: Critical Perspectives on Black Independent Cinema*, Cambridge, MA: MIT Press.

Chong, D. P. (2015) "Alighting on a Language of Caribbean Film: A Conversation with Yao Ramesar", *Caribbean Quarterly* 61 (2–3): 119–133.

Deleuze, G. and Guattari, F. (2013) *A Thousand Plateaus: Capitalism and Schizophrenia*, Massumi, B. (trans.), London: Bloomsbury.

Fanon, F. (1967) *Black Skin, White Masks*, Markmann, C. L. (trans.), London: Pluto Press.

—— (2004) *The Wretched of the Earth*, Philcox, R. (trans.), New York: Grove Press.

Francis, T. (2014) "Unexpected Archives: Seeking More Locations of Caribbean Film", *SX Salon* 17, 22 October, http://smallaxe.net/wordpress3/discussions/2014/10/22/unexpected-archives/.

Gabriel, T. H. (1982) *Third Cinema in the Third World: The Aesthetics of Liberation*, Ann Arbor, MI: UMI Research Press.
Givanni, J. (1992) "Interview with Euzhan Palcy [1988]", in *Ex-Iles: Essays on Caribbean Cinema*, Mbye, B. C. (trans.), Trenton: Africa World Press, 286–307.
Glissant, É. (1989) *Caribbean Discourse: Selected Essays*, Dash, M. J. (ed. and trans.), Charlottesville, VA: University Press of Virginia.
—— (1997) *Poetics of Relation*, Wing, B. (trans), Ann Arbor, MI: University of Michigan Press.
Hambuch, D. (2015) "Introduction: Caribbean Cinema Now", *Imaginations: Journal of Cross-Cultural Image Studies* 6 (2), http://imaginations.csj.ualberta.ca/?p=7880.
Harris, K. (1992) "Sex, Race, Commodity and Film Fetishism in *The Harder They Come*", in Cham, M. B (ed.), *Ex-Iles: Essays on Caribbean Cinema*, Trenton, NJ: Africa World Press, 211–219.
Hjort, M. and Petrie, D. J. (eds) (2007) *The Cinema of Small Nations*, Edinburgh: Edinburgh University Press.
Huyssen, A. (2002) "High/Low in an Expanded Field", *Modernism/Modernity*, 9 (3): 363–374.
López, A. M. (1995) "Memorias of a Home: Mapping the Revolution (and the Making of Exiles?)", *Revista Canadiense de Estudios Hispánicos*, 20 (1): 5–17.
—— (2007) "Cuba: A Porous National Cinema", in *The Cinema of Small Nations*, Hjort, M. and Petrie, D. J. (eds), Edinburgh: Edinburgh University Press, 179–197.
Marshall, V. (1992) "Filmmaking in Jamaica: 'Likkle but Tallawah'", in Cham, M. B. (ed.) *Ex-Iles: Essays on Caribbean Cinema*, Trenton, NJ: Africa World Press, 98–105.
Ortiz, F. (2008) "Los Factores Humanos de La Cubanidad", *Perfiles de La Cultura Cubana* 2: 1–15, www.perfiles.cult.cu/articulos/factores_cubanidad.pdf.
Paddington, B. and Warner, K. Q. (2009) "The Emergence of Caribbean Feature Films", *Black Camera* 1 (1): 91–108.
Petersen, A. (2007) "'You Believe in Pirates, Of Course ...': Disney's Commodification and 'Closure' vs. Johnny Depp's Aesthetic Piracy of 'Pirates of the Caribbean'", *Studies in Popular Culture* 29 (2): 63–81.
Raphael, C. (2014) "Robert Yao Ramesar: Caribbean Film Takes Off", *The Trinidad Guardian Newspaper*, www.guardian.co.tt/news/2014-01-05/robert-yao-ramesar-caribbean-film-takes.
Sephocle, M. L. (1992) "Interview with Aimé Césaire", in Cham, M. B. (ed.), *Ex-Iles: Essays on Caribbean Cinema*, Trenton, NJ: Africa World Press, 359–369.
Sheller, M. (2003) *Consuming the Caribbean: From Arawaks to Zombies*, London; New York: Routledge.
Shohat, E. and Stam, R. (1994) *Unthinking Eurocentrism: Multiculturalism and the Media*, London: Routledge.
Simpson, H. (2015) "The Caribbean, On Screen: A Conversation with Frances-Anne Solomon", *Imaginations: Journal of Cross-Cultural Image Studies* 6 (2): 98–111.
Tallon, B. (1983) "L'An II Du Cinéma Antillais [Interview with Sarah Maldoror and Christian Lara]", *Autrement* 49: 242.
Thelwell, M. (1992) "The Harder They Come: From Film to Novel", in Cham, M. B. (ed.) *Ex-Iles: Essays on Caribbean Cinema*, Trenton, NJ: Africa World Press, 176–210.
Thomas, T. (2014) "Race and Remix: The Aesthetics of Race in the Visual and Performing Arts", in Navas, E., Gallagher, O. and burrough, x. (eds), *The Routledge Companion to Remix Studies*, London: Routledge, 179–191.
Van Haesendonck, K. and D'haen, T. (eds) (2014) *Caribbeing: Comparing Caribbean Literatures and Cultures*, Amsterdam: Rodopi.
Willemen, P. (2006) "The National Revisited", in Vitali, V. and Willemen, P. (eds) *Theorising National Cinema*, London: BFI, 29–43.
Yearwood, G. L. (2000) *Black Film as a Signifying Practice: Cinema, Narration and the African American Aesthetic Tradition*, Trenton NJ: Africa World Press.
Yoo, C. Y. (1990) *The International Relations of Korea as a Small State*, Baltimore, MD: Johns Hopkins University Press.

9

WOMEN'S (R)EVOLUTIONS IN MEXICAN CINEMA

Niamh Thornton

Introduction

Women's Cinema is an elastic and slippery term. It can mean film for or by women, cinema with women's stories at its centre or with powerful female stars and/or significant female protagonists, and encompasses many genres, techniques, aesthetic concerns and approaches. A look at mostly Anglophone feminist film criticism that traces developments in industry and extra-industrial practice, production, and representation from the 1970s on reveals as much (see, for example, Pietropaolo and Testaferri 1995; Jayamanne 1995; Humm 1997; Rich 1998; Chaudhuri 2006; and Hollinger 2012). The stories told, who created them, and how they were distributed and consumed is central to much of their analysis. This writing necessarily cannot capture the full picture and is looking and listening from a particular vantage point, but reflects the complicated, differentiated, and knotty issues that affect industrial and creative practice and its consumption. As access to basic rights (such as education, universal suffrage, economic independence, and so on) is variable from one nation state to another, the particularities of women's lives and stories told on film concurrently have distinct peaks and troughs that have as much to do with changes in the industry and more equal and distributed access to the means of production as they have with struggles for legal rights.

For my purposes, as the high profile faces of filmmaking, the actor and director are useful means of examining cinema, not least because insufficient work has been carried out on the other roles to be able to map out a complete trajectory. The story of women in film is as complicated, faltering, and densely circumscribed by access and circumstance as is the case for women in any professional career in the last hundred or so years. Much as with other creative fields, it is tempting to ascribe an upward trajectory to women's involvement in filmmaking, to draft neat lines around the movements that have emerged, and ignore the forms of storytelling that do not fit easily into preconceptions about women-centred narratives. But this does not allow for the inequalities that still stymy much of this history and persist into the present day.

Given that it is a costly endeavour that requires close collaboration with (often) large teams of people, figuring through who holds the power over the final product in filmmaking can be tricky. The lively debates that regularly take place around awards ceremonies evidence this and often privilege the above-the-line workers, not least the performers and directors.

This approach puts much onus on individuals and their successes and failures, or our success or failure as audiences and critics in recognising their achievements rather than focusing on a complex inter-relationship between industry conditions, historic developments and individual attainment. As a consequence of the dearth of research into women's creativity from multiple levels of filmmaking it is currently impossible to provide a complete picture of the development and evolution of their roles. Therefore, this chapter will consider directors and actors, taking into account figures with differentiated access to the industry, and examine their output in relation to the social, industry, and production conditions in which they were working.

This chapter will consider Mexico as a case study because of its simultaneously unique and representative position in global cinema and focus on war films, because of their popularity as a genre in Mexican cinema, but one that is not conventionally thought of in terms of women's cinema. Over the course of its long history Mexican filmmaking has dominated the Spanish-language market, often working in parallel and, sometimes, in tandem with Hollywood. This allows a look at an industry that has been, simultaneously, a financial powerhouse in some markets and a successful arthouse producer in others (McKee Irwin, Castro Ricalde *et al.* 2013). Previously in Mexican scholarship, important work of recuperation and recognition of Mexican filmmakers and stars has been carried out by film historians and scholars that focuses on two key periods: the so-called Golden Age of the studio period 1930s–1950s (Joanne Hershfield 1996, 2000 and 2008) and the 1970s and 1980s which saw the emergence of feminist directors concerned with women's narratives (Elissa Rashkin 2001 and Patricia Torres San Martín 2004). Both of these periods are important touchstones for how women's filmmaking has evolved and will be expanded upon here. Building on their work yet taking a different frame, this chapter will shift the focus onto a key historical moment, the Mexican Revolution (1910–1920), in order to allow space to draw out the larger picture, challenge preconceptions about women's presence in bellicose films, and consider how women's film has evolved in Mexico.

Conventionally in film historiography, war films are not closely associated with women filmmakers. War films represent moments of national crisis, provide an unusual perspective on women's stories, and, as a consequence, they have considerable capacity to afford unique insights into women's participation in cinema as cast and crew. Despite this, through critical oversight, their presence has been ignored in favour of more clear-cut women-centred narratives. In Mexico women direct, write and feature in films of the Revolution as key characters and in starring roles and, yet, as with other cinemas, this is seen as anomalous or denigrated rather than taken as an opportunity to follow how women's presence is a recurrent feature of a national preoccupation. This chapter will draw on this rich strand as a productive means of considering women's filmmaking in Mexico from a greatly neglected perspective through a chronological exploration of the development of women's creative output on screen and the changes in the industry.

Film and the Mexican Revolution

The Revolution, writ large and in upper case to designate its foundational status, was a defining conflict in Mexican political and cultural life. It resulted in seismic population changes, millions dead, and led to the birth of the current political system whereby a single party, the Partido Revolucionario Institucional [Institutional Revolutionary Party] (PRI) has held power almost uninterruptedly for nearly 75 years over the course of the twentieth and twenty-first centuries.

For this to succeed, there was a concerted effort by the party to take ownership of the Revolution and strengthen its claim to have been the principal actors in over-turning the old order and, thereby, to have brought about political and social change. Film has been integral to this nation building agenda whereby the PRI has actively funded and supported creative representations of the Revolution. As a consequence, there are more than 250 films of the Revolution of multiple genres and periods and it continues to be a focus and setting for films up to the present day (Vazquez Mantecón 2010: 17). Following on from Susan Dever (2003), "Revolution" must be understood to refer to multiple referents: a bellicose period (1910–1920); a process (1920–1942); and a trope continually renewed and recycled for political and socio-cultural ends. In this way, the presence of women on and off screen in films of the Revolution is part of an iterative creative process of nation building that has also seen many opportunities for divergent and unique challenges to the status quo.

The first films of the Revolution were documentaries distributed as newsreels or for campaigns (see Pick 2010). There are a few extant and they have considerable indexical and aesthetic value. In critical studies of the films of the Revolution, *Vámonos con Pancho Villa!* (Let's Go With Pancho Villa, 1936, Mexico, Fernando de Fuentes) is presented as the archetypical and high point of the early fiction films (Pick 2010: 7). It was one of many studio-made films from the 1930s onwards that were often adaptations of novels of the Revolution or modelled on the tropes of these, which focused on bands of brothers going off to battle, paying little attention to women characters. The prestige attached to this film was determined by critical frameworks deployed by a series of filmmakers in the 1960s and 1970s keen to find aesthetic and narrative antecedents that did not cleave to the generic tropes of more popular, often female-centred stories of the 1930s–1950s. The premise of canon formation of Revolutionary films was that they consisted of films centred on male enterprise and were frequently devoid of women.

In the early twentieth century, Mexico developed a highly successful industry that was, in part, modelled on the Hollywood studio system and was part-financed and supported by successive governments that produced popular films for local and international audiences. The peak period for the studios was between the early 1930s and the late 1950s and is often referred to in the literature as the Golden Age of Mexican cinema (see Hernández Rodríguez 1999; Tierney 2007: 1–2). During the Golden Age, female stars had a significant presence. In a cinema that favoured melodrama as a "dominant genre", with a particularly Mexican inflection, the woman's film had a significant place (Mistron 1984: 47). Iconic roles often identified with well-known stars are the lasting legacy of this era, yet few are included in lists or academic studies that ascribe prestige to the films. In a book about the best-paid actor of the period and a woman who repeatedly appeared in films set during the Revolution, María Félix, critic and author Paco Ignacio Taibo lays this out in idiosyncratic style when he delineates key characteristics associated with female stars of the period, and indicates how Félix defied convention (Taibo 2004: 16–17). Unlike other critics and historians of Mexican cinema, Ignacio Taibo highlights their performance styles rather than indicating archetypal roles. There is no mention of what John Mraz concisely summarises as, "the mother, the Indian and the shrew" (2009: 9), to which must be added the numbers of prostitutes, soldiers and sacrificing wives that many of these women (and others) played, which Alicia Vargas Amésquita explores in her writing (2010). Exceptionally, and as an early proponent of star studies in Mexico (his work was originally published in 1985), Ignacio Taibo foregrounds their individual strengths and the popular reading of their star texts. His list is but a sample of significant stars who were integral to this period of filmmaking. Where few female directors emerged during the Golden Age, the performances of the female actors of this period were integral to the construction of womanhood and were opportunities to either establish fixed representations of women in Mexican society or to challenge these.

The Golden Years: 1930–1958

Two films set during the Revolution that play at either end of the good/rebellious woman spectrum also star two of the biggest film stars of the era: the conformist woman of *Flor silvestre* (Wild Flower, 1943, Mexico, Emilio Fernández) starring Dolores del Rio and Pedro Armendáriz, and the tension between conformity and dissent in *La cucaracha* (The Soldiers of Pancho Villa, 1959, Ismael Rodríguez, Mexico) starring Félix, del Rio and Fernández. Both films are indicative of critical reception of the women in film from the Golden Age. *Wild Flower* has garnered many plaudits and critical acclaim with its "maudlin, melodramatic plot" (Mistron 1984: 51). It is the story of a woman who sacrifices much for her country and the future of her child, where "the revolution is seen as the painful birth of a new generation of families who are able to live in the more just and equitable society envisioned and created by those who came before" (Mistron 1984: 51). This was del Rio's first role on her return from Hollywood and is structured as an extended flashback narrated by José Luis/Armendáriz who is telling her son the reasons why she has sacrificed so much to create a better future. José Luis Armendáriz is her husband who defied his wealthy father in marrying Esperanza and then becomes a leader in the Revolution. Esperanza operates as the impetus for José Luis' rebellion against his father and can be read as a proxy for the people for whom he has gone into battle. Given the nature of women's activities in the Revolution as nurses, cooks, laundresses, companions, prostitutes, and combatants, Esperanza's presence alongside her husband is typical of how women are represented in the films of the Revolution (Soto 1979). Hers are the more respectable responsibilities of cooking and cleaning, not unlike the domestic chores expected of her in peacetime. She is upset by the losses of war, but accepts the need for Revolution as a necessary process of attaining a better future for her son. The representation of Esperanza's acceptance of loss and self-sacrificing love for her child is a repeated trope in the films that reiterate the significance of Revolution as the foundational national narrative.

Where *Wild Flower* has been lauded for privileging and fetishising conformity and sacrifice, *The Soldiers of Pancho Villa* both deploys these tropes and plays with its opposite. As a consequence, *The Soldiers of Pancho Villa* has been largely reviled by critics. Del Rio revisits her role as self-abnegating woman while Félix switches between being a cross-dressing combatant and a supportive camp companion. The plot is concerned with the love triangle between La Cucaracha (Félix), Isabel (del Rio) and Colonel Antonio Zeta (Emilio Fernández). Zeta first pursues La Cucaracha, a combatant who also has a reputation for drinking, fighting, and having multiple sexual relationships with men. After he seduces her, she briefly adopts new responsibilities and moves from being a combatant to the domestic chores associated with women. Her clothes also shift from what is coded as masculine attire to the skirts, shawls and blouses similar to those of the other women. These transformations do not remain fixed. La Cucaracha has not been tamed through seduction. Unable to fit in with the other women or leave her drinking and fighting behind, she soon returns to battle and loses Zeta. He is then seduced by Isabel, which results in tension between the women until La Cucaracha discovers she is pregnant whereby her wardrobe changes again and she blends in with the other women.

Through plot twists and wardrobe changes Félix's performance shifts between masculine coded open body gestures and closed guarded feminine movements. The absence of moral lessons mean that the film opens up spaces for gender non-conformity in a genre that is generally understood to be highly conservative. This ambiguity can be attributed to the leads and their star texts. As I have written elsewhere, Félix had a public life that defied convention (Thornton 2013). She had multiple romantic partners, led an extravagant lifestyle and was the centre of many public scandals. In contrast, del Rio had a glamorous, but quiet life generally conforming to the traditional Mexican idea of a good woman. Their star texts are inscribed in any reading of these films and are further reinforced through their performances. Not only is it significant that La Cucaracha is an unmarried mother of the new Mexican child of the Revolution, but also that Félix's star text refuses conformity to mores of the state in the same way that del Rio's Esperanza in *Wild Flower* can only ever be self-sacrificing and traditional because of how her star text is to be understood in the light of her other performances.

Extravagant and outspoken, Félix was an outlier who became the best paid star (male or female) of the industrial era, but is the least researched by scholars, while del Rio also attained considerable fame and success she did so by conforming to an idealised form of womanhood that has led to considerable critical attention. Stars of the Golden Age, such as del Rio, appear to attract critical attention through conformity to type and narrow ideas of taste and prestige, because value is given to films by particular male auteurs. In contrast, women directors are evaluated differently from their male contemporaries.

Women had great difficulty in entering the director's union, therefore it was a role dominated by men. Just two female directors managed to break into the profession with any success during this period: Matilde Landeta (1910–1999) and Adela Sequeyro (1901–1992). Landeta and Sequeyro were pioneers who made genre films that reveal distinct creative decisions, but cannot be easily read as auteurs. As a consequence, like some of their male contemporaries working in industrial cinema, they have been overlooked. Unlike the male directors they had to overcome barriers unique to women. Their careers have been recuperated by film historians such as Patricia Torres San Martín (2004), but rarely appear in traditional film historiography because of their gender and the somewhat stop start nature of their careers. In the interest of space I shall focus on one of Landeta's films as exemplary of how women filmmakers of this era found ways to critique the Revolutionary project while working from within an industrial context.

B. Ruby Rich, in her construction of a revisionist history of Latin American cinema, picks out *La negra Angustias* (1949, Mexico, Matilde Landeta) because, for her, it functions as an "anomaly" (1995: 173), which challenges the categories and labels ascribed to Latin American cinema where its "entire history [. . .] has come to be judged by the yardstick of its early classics" (1995: 168). Rich's focus is on reassessing Latin American cinema and moving it away from the strictures of New Latin American cinema and the attendant emphasis on political and socially conscious filmmaking. Rich's reading brings attention to a neglected filmmaker, but does not recognise that, in many respects, *La negra Angustias* conforms to local filmmaking practices, techniques, and thematic concerns that "managed, in imperfect and sometimes surprising ways, to reflect on the revolution as a disruptive and contradictory event" (Pick 2010: 4). The plot follows the coming of age of Angustias (María Elena Marqués) and her participation in the Revolution and elevation to the position of colonel. She is a young woman who bears the multiple stigmas—in Mexico of that time—of being an illegitimate child of rape and of mixed White and Black race (she is described as *mulata* in the book and film). There are few films with Black Mexicans at their centre, which places the narrative focus at a vanguard. However, the decision to cast a White actor and black her up reveals a racial insensitivity that should not be ignored, but is not unusual for this time.

The casting of Marqués as Angustias confuses the racial concerns of the film. She was a star whose roles often emphasised her purity through accentuating her Whiteness in a country that still privileges pale skin. An example of such a role is in *Doña Bárbara* (1943, Mexico, Fernando de Fuentes and Miguel M. Delgado), where she is, also, the child of a rape, a "primal scene that organises the narrative" of both films (Arredondo 2011: 76). In *Doña Bárbara* she vies with her mother—the eponymous Doña Bárbara played by Félix—for the love of a man, whose narrative and allegorical role is that of civilizing the people and place. Given this antecedent and other similar roles, Marquéz is difficult to read as *mulata*. As a product of the studio system that relied on a star system that lacked stars of colour, the casting of Marquéz is a flawed attempt at exploring race. Although others did not explore Blackness, *La negra Angustias* could be compared to star films where White actors browned up to perform indigeneity. Two examples of these can be found in del Rio as the eponymous *María Candelaria* (1944, Mexico, Emilio Fernández) and Félix in *Maclovia* (1948, Mexico, Emilio Fernández). Neither are films of the Revolution, a type of film that rarely included race as a self-conscious theme.

While the focus on race in Revolutionary films may be rare in Mexican cinema, *La negra Angustias* shares other commonalities with studio films of the time. It is an adaptation of a Novel of the Revolution, one that the critic Seymour Menton (1954) compares to two other novels: *Doña Bárbara* by Rómulo Gallegos (1947), a canonical Regional Novel, and the iconic and foundational Novel of the Revolution, *Los de abajo* (The Underdogs, 1915) by Mariano Azuela (Azuela 1996). As reliable sources of ready-made and popular narratives or texts that provide prestige to the film, adaptations have been common in Mexican cinema since the early period (Thornton 2016). In addition, there are other strong female roles that have significant military responsibility, such as those starring Félix, *The Soldiers of Pancho Villa* and *La generala* (1971, Mexico, Juan Ibáñez), that had space for characters who were "ambiguous and contradictory" (Dávalos Orozco 1999: 46). As with the Félix star vehicles and other films that address the contemporary anxieties around women's demands for rights in the 1940s and onwards, *La negra Angustias* tackles issues of sexuality and orientation in ways that allow a space for a nuanced exploration of these. Rich may over-declare how anomalous Landeta is, but rightly credits her with having "laid the groundwork for the Latin American women's films of the 1980s, which began to incorporate women's struggles for identity and autonomy" (1995: 174). Rich, here, is referring to the women directors who made low budget independent films that I will discuss below.

Years of rebellion and change: the 1960s and 1970s

By the 1960s increasing numbers of women in Mexico, as elsewhere, were shifting from working in informal sectors and conforming to traditional domestic roles to attaining greater legal rights and access to secondary and university education that was expected to lead to professional careers. Feminist magazines provided a forum for sharing ideas and debating issues, as did labour movements, and activist and social solidarity groups. In 1968 there were worker and student protests that culminated in a massacre on 2 October, days before the opening of the Olympic games staged in Mexico City. Many students filmed the protests and unrest, and several films, largely documentaries, were consequently made from this footage. As was the case in many other countries, 1968 was utterly transformative socially, culturally and politically and marked filmmaking by those involved in the protests and their creative output for decades to come.

At this time studio filmmaking went into decline for multiple reasons including: the rising popularity of television, the lack of investment in cinema theatres, changes in government support, and a decline in audiences because of the formulaic nature of the output. The shift also took place thanks to the confluence of social, political and cultural changes in the 1960s. A small, but vocal, group of critics, filmmakers and academics began to write about film in the *Nuevo cine* (New cinema) journal (see Noble 2005). They organised screenings of international arthouse and experimental films, held discussion groups, and created awards and festivals with the aim of fomenting a cinema culture distinct to that of the studios. The first Mexican film school opened in 1963 which provided a new generation with the technical and intellectual skills that previously were only acquired through apprenticeships and had required membership of the studio-affiliated unions.

A small number of women attended film school at this time, but it would take some years for there to be a critical mass. The feminist scholar Elissa J. Rashkin found records from the Centro Universitario de Estudios Cinematográficos (University Centre for Cinematic Study, CUEC), for only two female students between 1963 and 1970 and only three graduates from 1975 to 1980 at the *Centro de Capacitación Cinematográfica* (Centre for Cinematic Training) (2001: 68). Both are prestigious institutions. One of the select few to complete her studies and gain a foothold in the industry in the 1960s was a formidable pioneering figure in Mexican cinema, Marcela Fernández Violante. Hers is an unusual trajectory in relation to both her contemporaries and the history of women filmmakers in Mexico. While her male contemporaries were getting support from the government-backed film bank and sidestepping the unions associated with the studio films, she was the first woman admitted to the director's union and worked on both studio-based projects and films supported by the Universities as well as being the director of the CUEC from 1984 to 1988. She worked hard to revive interest in her female predecessors, such as Landeta, but has received scant attention because she too has an anomalous place in Mexican film history.

Rashkin has described Fernández Violante as "an always-controversial figure [, who] can perhaps best be described as a maverick" for her outspoken manner in interviews and for inhabiting an unusual "borderline between industrial and university cinema" (2001: 77). Despite receiving awards for her work, her industrial and university prominence, and the repeated recognition of her importance in film histories, especially as a representative of a growing number of women filmmakers, Fernández Violante's work is little studied by academics. This is for a variety of reasons: her early work, while independent in aesthetic, thematic and narrative terms, was made within the studio system unlike her male contemporaries; unlike many other women filmmakers, her films cannot be easily categorised as feminist; and she often tackles historical figures who are out of political favour. In sum, her output is difficult to place along the lines of previous studies of this period of male or female Mexican filmmaking.

Fernández Violante directed two films of the Revolution: *De todos modos Juan te llamas* (The General's Daughter aka. Whatever You Do It's No Good, 1975, Mexico) and *Cananea* (1978, Mexico). The first is set during the short-lived *Cristero* Rebellion (1926–1929) and the second in the run-up to the Revolution. The *Cristero* Rebellion was a religious war between the state and a small group of radical priests and lay people who wanted to challenge the government's decision to reform the relationship between the church and the state (see, Meyer 2008). The film centres on the family of General Guajardo (Jorge Russek, voiced by Federico Romano), an authoritarian figure who has a difficult relationship with his wife, Beatriz (Patricia Aspillaga) and three children, Armanda (Rocio Brambila), Andrés (uncredited), and Gabriel (uncredited). Encouraged by a rousing speech from the pulpit by the priest, the village women beat Beatriz to death in front of Armanda. Traumatised by this, Armanda turns to her cousin, Colonel Gontrán Bonilla (Juan Ferrara), in whom she has evident amorous interest. He, in turn, despite being a serving officer, is disillusioned with the state's turn from the ideals of the Revolution. The unfolding of the narrative is tragic and leads Armanda to escape the small village for an uncertain future in Mexico City. The original Spanish title, *De todos modos Juan te llamas*, rendered in the alternate title *Whatever You Do It's No Good*, alludes to the fact that this story is not just about Armanda's coming of age and sexual awakening, it is about a family falling apart. In the nuanced and complicated realisation of this story, this family can both act as an instance of how outside, public political forces play on family life and as an allegory of the Mexican state and its failings.

Bonilla is seen reading a book by one of the intellectual leaders of the Revolution, the anarchist Ricardo Flores Magon. His story is fictionalised in *Cananea*, where he is renamed Baca Calderón (Carlos Bracho). In Fernández Violante's words, it attempts to "portray anarchists as the conscience of society, but not as the solution to society's problems" (Burton 1986: 200). Baca Calderón arrives in a mining town controlled by the US citizen, Colonel William Greene (Steve Wilensky), who has gone from a struggling miner in the deserts of Northern Mexico to a wealthy businessman. While Baca Calderón is shown as having a significant role in organising labour, he is also a flawed individual who has much to learn about class difference and leadership. His successes are mired with poor communication skills and a willingness to impel others to their death in pursuit of his cause. At the same time, Greene is portrayed as a sympathetic but flawed businessman, whose greed has blinded him to the needs of his workers. Both films are instances of looking at the Revolution from an alternate perspective. They are complex and nuanced, yet have received little attention because Fernández Violante falls outside of the usual mould for women in Mexican film.[1]

Talent among the trash: the 1970s and 1980s

In the 1970s and 1980s, popular cinema became dominated by straight-to-video releases, B-movie horrors and superhero films, what Victoria Ruétalo and Dolores Tierney have labelled Latsploitation (2009), on the one hand, and, due to the potential to shoot cheaply independent of the studio system, it opened up a space for alternative filmmaking practices and gave opportunities to those who had been heretofore marginalised to take up a place behind the camera, on the other hand. There were few films about the Revolution made during this period. Just as in other filmmaking countries, women were getting opportunities to make films and doing so in a multiplicity of styles. Directors, such as María Novaro, Busi Cortes, Marisa Sistach, Eva López Sánchez, Dana Rotberg and Guita Schyfter emerged during this period (see Rashkin 2001). Researchers, such as Rashkin, concerned with women's filmmaking, have privileged these filmmakers because they represent a remarkable moment of artistic output and the important act of recuperation and historiography has been "a formidable challenge to a long-standing cinematic tradition of female objectification, erasure, and displacement" (2001: 2). Writers on this period, like Rashkin, have focused on directors, but I want to include actors in this discussion because they prove a fruitful contrast with stars of the studio system.

Two actors who are productive to consider because they illuminate female performances from the 1970s up to the present day are María Rojo and Diana Bracho. Rojo started in television on soap operas, then had her first film role in *Los cachorros* (The Cubs, 1973, Mexico) by the independent filmmaker Jorge Fons, with whom she would later work with on the first fiction film about 1968, *Rojo amanecer* (Red Dawn, 1989, Mexico). Rojo has performed in films that tackle thorny political themes, such as *Bajo la metralla* (Under Fire, 1983, Mexico, Felipe Cazals), the aforementioned *Red Dawn* and, more recently, *La dictadura perfecta* (The Perfect Dictatorship, 2014, Mexico, Luis Estrada). Bracho had some walk-on roles as a child, worked in television, and had her first major role in *El castillo de la pureza* (The Castle of Purity,

1973, Mexico, Arturo Ripstein), who is himself the son of a major film producer. Many of her extended family were involved in filmmaking including her father, the director Julio Bracho, and her aunts, Andres de Palma and del Rio, and her roles have been wide-ranging. They include performances in arthouse films by male auteurs, such as Fons and Ripstein; on early films by women directors; in television soap operas; and genre films. One of her recent roles is as Félix in a short entitled *María Bonita* (Eternal Beauty, 2015, Mexico, Amanda de la Rosa Frisccione). Both Bracho and Rojo have become heavily identified with strong female roles and employ a naturalistic performance style drawn from their time working in theatre. In particular, in critical analysis of their roles, their performances in films by women filmmakers are favourably analysed and, because of their perceived congruity in aesthetics they have become linked with the aforementioned growth in female directors who operated outside of the studio system during the 1980s and 1990s.

The misperception that the 1980s in Mexican cinema was a period of decline in quality is, in part, because women filmmakers were seen to be marginal in their approaches, and because there is an over-emphasis on external validation (sales or awards) on the success of the film industry. Both Rojo and Bracho acted in films by women or where female characters were part of a strong ensemble cast. An example of this is the aforementioned and under-valued *Under Fire* in which Rojo appeared. It is an adaptation of *Les justes* (The Just Assassins), a 1949 play by Albert Camus. The action and events in the play are transposed from 1905 plot to assassinate the Grand Duke Sergei Alexandrovich by a group of Russian Socialist Revolutionaries to the attempted kidnap of a corrupt politician in Northern Mexico by a group of armed Socialist Revolutionaries. In *Under Fire* the account of the attack transmitted via the media is distorted and portrayed as a narco gang dispute. Male and female members of the group are on equal footing, that is, they have shared responsibilities and are shown to be as competent with weaponry, they vie for power and distrust one another equally. It is a highly charged political film that is illustrative of the choice Rojo has made in her career to pick challenging roles that crossed genres and styles.

There is a deliberate naturalism to Rojo's performance as María in *Under Fire*. This is reinforced by naturalistic lighting, few cuts with long takes, and frequent medium to long shots. To an extent, the audio-visual techniques employed by Cazals are auteurist touches that seek to achieve a heightened and, somewhat sordid, realism. These are also evident in his earlier film *Los Poquianchis* (1976, Mexico), a film based on a true story of a prostitution ring involved in serial murders. It is another ensemble piece with performances by both Rojo and Bracho. They are actors who employ restrained performances, despite their start in television soaps, a genre associated with excess in movement, tone, and voice all in service of heightening emotion. They keep their gestures to a minimum, are expressive only in moments of drama or action, and modulate their voices to convey subtle emotional responses. This contrasts greatly with studio stars such as Félix's full use of her vocal range, expansive gestures, and capacious movement through the mise-en-scène. To an extent some of these elements were peculiar to Félix, but there are commonalities with other actors of the studio era.

Bracho and Rojo's naturalistic performative style suited the male auteurs of the 1970s, who wanted to move away from studio-style aesthetics, and the realist approach to genre narrative by the women directors of the 1980s. Rojo's naturalistic performances are distinct from the melodramatic performances associated with the female-centred films made by the studios up to the 1950s. Few independent women filmmakers made films of the Revolution starring women. Rojo has only had a small role in a film of the Revolution, *Zapata en Chinameca* (Zapata in Chinameca, 1987, Mexico, Mario Hernández) about the final days of the Revolutionary leader, Emiliano Zapata. This is worth remarking upon because of her significance as an actor and the disregard for films of the Revolution because of their association with studio films. Women filmmakers appeared to move away from the Revolution as a setting, theme or context during the 1970s and 1980s in favour of contemporary stories. After a two-decade decline, the 1990s saw a renewed interest in the Revolution.

NAFTA and internationalisation: the 1990s and 2000s

The 1990s saw another shift in the film industry after the signing of the North American Free Trade Agreement (NAFTA) between Canada, Mexico and the US, which stipulated that Mexico must decrease state investment in cinema. Funding was reliant on private sources, the most lucrative of which was via transnational co-productions with US studios. A key example of a financially lucrative film following this model is *Como agua para chocolate* (Like Water for Chocolate, 1992, Mexico, Alfonso Arau, 1992), set during the Revolution. Directed by Arau, it was adapted by Laura Esquivel, his then-wife, from her eponymous bestselling novel. This collaboration brings to the fore questions of auteurship (and authorship) and how we ascribe ownership to creative work.

Both the film and novel form of *Like Water for Chocolate* are well-studied texts. The novel heralded a publishing Boom in Mexican women's writing (Hind 2010). On the back of its success, in Mexico, more women were getting published and promoted by publishing houses and there was a new interest in women-centred narratives. Also, due to the sales of the novel in translation, it saw increased attention paid to the broader category of Latin American writing by women at a global level. Both novel and film have been categorised as magical realist, a label that is often mistakenly deployed as a placeholder for the exotic, strange and surreal. In *Like Water for Chocolate* it is a conceit employed to blur distinctions between the living and the dead and sees fantastic occurrences take place in what is to be understood as realist narratives. The novel has received considerable attention for its form. It is the fictional recovery of a missing piece of the narrator's personal history using recipes that celebrate the domestic and supposedly mundane aspects of the everyday set against the dramatic backdrop of the Revolution. The film is less experimental, yet, unusually for a film of the Revolution, it privileges the domestic by focusing on the family drama over the potentially action-filled war taking place beyond their purview.

It is practice in adaptation studies to privilege the source text and to measure the adaptation in terms of its faithfulness. When the scriptwriter is the original author, faithfulness is taken as read, even more so in this case where the creative team were husband and wife. Consequently, the film can be ascribed with Esquivel's authorial imprimatur. It is often noted that *Like Water for Chocolate* marked a turning point in Mexican filmmaking because of its sizeable international box office earnings. What few highlight is that the most significant Mexican film of the 1990s was a woman-centred, woman-authored popular genre film of the Revolution. Ignacio Sánchez Prado (2014) has studied how this then led to a growth in Romantic films for a bourgeois, largely female audience. Such subsequent films rarely make it to the international arthouse or film festival circuit, but do have considerable domestic audiences (see Sánchez Prado 2014).

Despite its box office earnings *Like Water for Chocolate* did not result in an upswing of films by or about women, nor of a renewed interest in films set during the Revolution. One of the few other films of the Revolution from the mid-1990s attempted to go further in its radical critique of the Revolutionary project. Starring Diana Bracho, *Entre Pancho Villa y una mujer desnuda* (Between Pancho Villa and a Naked Woman, 1995, Mexico, Sabina Berman and Isabelle Tardán) is based on a play written by Berman. The film tells the story of Gina (Bracho), a businesswoman who is undergoing a personal crisis after Adrián (Arturo Ríos), her lover, leaves her just when he appeared to have decided to commit to their relationship. Troubled by this change and influenced by a theory that all Mexican men model themselves on the Revolutionary leader, Pancho Villa's machismo, she decides to "act like a man" herself and takes a younger lover, Ismael (Gabriel Porrás), to whom she refuses to commit. Gina is torn between the two men. In an extra twist that provides an element of screwball comedy, Villa (Jesús Ochoa), provides advice to both Gina and Adrián. His hyper-masculine heroic manner is straight out of the studio era films, which clashes with the naturalism of the performances and settings inhabited by the other characters. The farce is to be found in the incongruous intervention of Villa as synonym for Revolutionary ideology in a woman's love life. Gina realises that this model of masculinity is redundant and is not what she really wants. This film is illustrative of the shift away from narratives clearly set during the Revolution at this point in Mexican filmmaking and, although largely ignored in film analysis, has a significant meta-critical role on the stylistic tropes of Mexican films of the Revolution.

The 1990s and 2000s are often read as a period of renaissance for Mexican film. In terms of scale and range, this is not the case. In the 1990s the volume of films made plummeted and there was a shift towards transnational film productions from the early 2000s following a pattern that can be seen around the world. The release of *Amores perros* (2000, Mexico, Alejandro González Iñárritu) heralded this new period whereby the so-called three amigos, Alfonso Cuarón, Guillermo del Toro and Iñárritu have attained international attention and moved from the national to the inter- and transnational stage (see Shaw 2013). This has been followed by a select number of (mostly male) auteurs gaining international attention such as Carlos Reygadas, Amat Escalante and Gerardo Naranjo. These successes have been limited to a small number of individuals, whose reference to the Revolution has been tangential, thematic, or meta-textual, at least up until the 2010 centenary commemorations.

In a return to a more sideways look at the Revolution reminiscent of Berman and Tardán's *Between Pancho Villa and a Naked Woman* two women directors contributed to the anthology *Revolución* (2010, Mexico): Patricia Riggen's *Beautiful and Beloved*, about a woman's decision to bury her grandfather in Mexico with his gun from the Revolution, and Mariana Chenillo's story of a young woman's struggle to pay for a new front tooth in *The Estate Store*. *Revolución* is made up of ten shorts and was released to commemorate the centenary of the Revolution. Gael García Bernal and Diego Luna's production company Canană were behind the project. Luna asked the filmmakers to respond to the question, "Where is the Revolution today?" (Ellis 2010).

The Estate Store is set in contemporary Mexico. Yolanda (Mónica Bejarano) is a young woman working on the shop floor of a large supermarket. She has a false tooth and wants to save up to get an implant in time to go out on a date with the floor manager. In advance of her appointment, which she must pay for in cash, instead of being given her full pay she is given in-store vouchers. She complains and loses her job. The title refers to the practice of indentured slavery common on large plantations from colonial era onwards and invites the viewer to draw a correlation between this and the exploitation inherent in transnational capitalism. One of the aims of the Revolution had been to free workers from this oppressive practice prevalent during colonial times. As Maricruz Castro Ricalde (2014) convincingly argues, *The Estate Store* is an insightful exploration of the effects of neoliberal economics on the individual, which can be read as a form of neocolonialism, and presents another failed promise of the Revolution.

In Riggen's *Beautiful and Beloved* Mexican-American Elisa (Carmen Corral) comes to terms with her Mexican-ness through having to smuggle her dead grandfather back to Mexico, as she is unable to afford to do so by legal means. The film is named after the song "Beautiful and Beloved Mexico", composed by Chucho Monge. It is a patriotic *ranchera* whose lyrics explicitly reference the desire to be repatriated after death "if I die far from you" (Ramírez-Pimienta 2010: 32).

The "you", here, is Mexico. Riggen's most successful film to date, *La misma luna* (Under the Same Moon, 2007, Mexico/USA), also had immigration as a central narrative concern: a child wanting to reunite with his mother. *Beautiful and Beloved* employs music to create a sentimental portrait of the loss and longing of migration. Riggen has consistently worked outside of Mexico, like the "Three Amigos"; her most recent project is *Los 33* (The 33, 2015, Chile/USA), about the Chilean miners who were trapped for seventeen days after an explosion. Where Riggen draws on elements of comedy and melodrama in her filmmaking, Chenillo's approach is more subtle, employing a realist aesthetic, yet both are keen to make explicit the affective consequences of Revolution. Just as it is impossible to describe a male aesthetic, the two shorts by these two directors demonstrate how women in film are influenced by the patterns and developments in the Mexican film industry as well as responding to the demands of inter- and transnational cinema.

Conclusion

The history of Mexican film is told as one of volume and quality. Success is measured by external awards (Cannes, Oscars) and influential historians or critics' valorisations according to their taste. Women are largely overlooked in this framing of the story. In a country that has had a significant film industry with a range of talented creatives, it is tempting to tell the story in broad sweeps that ignore disparities and disruptions. Women's involvement in film, whether as cast or crew, is a welcome complication to neat historiography and a necessary challenge for scholarly research.

Films of the Revolution are a productive means of looking at Mexican women in film as they allow for a reflection upon consistencies and differences. These examples go against the grain in contemporary critical analysis, as women are not usually associated with war narratives. In the Mexican context there is such a volume of films of the Revolution as well as variation in generic and aesthetic approaches that it allows for useful comparisons across time periods and styles. Critical attention to women in film should look for women in the expected and unexpected places because many of the models for examining women's place in cinema are modelled on Hollywood cinema. Women's cinema is still a contentious label because there is insufficient research into the many ways they have participated in the industry and those who do get attention conform to pre-existing patterns. It is productive to follow the career trajectories of global women filmmakers and to look at those who fit easily within existing frameworks. It is also important to consider those other anomalous figures in order to find alternative movements and yet, to avoid the temptation to create neat categorisations that allow for simple brushstrokes. In the case of Mexican cinema, taking the Revolution as the focal point is a way into considering a particularly productive nation-building project from the perspective of women creatives and the multiple approaches they have taken to tackle it in film.

Note

1 I have previously written on *Cananea* (Thornton 2013) and *General's Daughter* (Thornton 2017).

References

Arredondo, I. (2011) "Watching Rape in Mexican Cinema", in Barrios, N. B. (ed.) *Latin American Cinemas: Local Views and Transnational Connections*, Calgary: University of Calgary Press, 175–198.

Azuela, M. (1996) *Los de abajo*, Mexico City: Fondo de Cultural Económica.

Burton, Julianne (1986) *Cinema and Social Change in Latin America: Conversations with Filmmakers*, Austin, TX: University of Texas Press.

Castro, R. M. (2014) "Revolución y neocolonialismo en La tienda de raya de Mariana Chenillo", *Cinémas d'Amérique latine*, 22, http://cinelatino.revues.org/861: 129–139.

Chaudhuri S. (2006) *Feminist Film Theorists: Laura Mulvey, Kaja Silverman, Teresa de Lauretis, Barbara Creed*, London: Routledge.

Dávalos Orozco, F. (1999) "The Birth of the Film Industry and the Emergence of Sound", in Hershfield, J. and Maciel, D. R. (eds) *Mexico's Cinema: A Century of Film and Filmmakers,* Wilmington, DE: SR Books, 17–32.

Dever, S. (2003) *Celluloid Nationalism and Other Melodramas: From Post-Revolutionary Mexico to Fin de siglo Mexamérica,* New York: State University of New York Press.

Ellis, C. (2010) "Gael García Bernal and Diego Luna Stage Their Own Revolución", *The Huffington Post*, 17 November, www.huffingtonpost.com/cynthia-ellis/diego-luna-and-gael-garci_b_784008.html.

Gallegos, R. ([1947]2005) *Doña Bárbara*, Madrid: Catédra.

Hernández Rodríguez, R. (1999) "Melodrama and Social Comedy in the Cinema of the Golden Age", in Hershfield, J. and Maciel, D. R. (eds) *Mexico's Cinema: A Century of Film and Filmmakers*, Wilmington, DE: SR Books, 101–121.

Hershfield, J. (1996) *Mexican Cinema/Mexican Woman, 1940–1950,* Tucson, AZ: The University of Arizona Press.

—— (2000) *The Invention of Dolores del Rio*, Minneapolis, MN and London, University of Minneapolis Press.

—— (2008) *Imagining la chica moderna: Women, Nation, and Visual Culture in Mexico, 1917–1936,* Durham, NC and London: Duke University Press.

Hind, E. (2010) "Six Authors on the Conservative Side of the Boom Femenino, 1985–2003: Boullosa, Esquivel, Loaeza, Mastretta, Nissán, Sefchovich", in Finnegan, N. and Lavery, J. (eds) *El Boom Femenino Mexicano: Reading Contemporary Women's Writing*, Newcastle-Upon-Tyne: Cambridge Scholars Press, 48–71.

Hollinger, K. (2012) *Feminist Film Studies*, London: Routledge.

Humm, M. (1997) *Feminism and Film*, Indianapolis, IN: Indiana University Press.

Jayamanne, L. (ed.) (1995) *Kiss Me Deadly: Feminism and Cinema for the Moment*, Sydney: Power Publications.

McKee I., Castro Ricalde, R. and M. with Szurmuk, M. Álvarez, I, and Sužnjević, D. (2013) *Global Mexican Cinema: Its Golden Age "el cine mexicano se impone"*, London: BFI Palgrave.

Menton, S. (1954) "La negra Angustias, una Doña Bárbara mexicana", *Revista Iberoamericana* XIX (38): 299–308.

Meyer, J. (2008) *The Cristero Rebellion: The Mexican People Between Church and State 1926–1929*, Cambridge: Cambridge University Press.

Mistron, D. (1984) "A Hybrid Subgenre: The Revolutionary Melodrama in the Mexican Cinema", *Studies in Latin American Popular Culture* 3: 47–56.

Mraz, J. (2009) *Looking for Mexico: Modern Visual Culture and National Identity*, Durham, NC and London: Duke University Press.

Noble, A. (2005) *Mexican National Cinema,* London and New York: Routledge.

Pick, Z. M. (2010) *Constructing the Image of the Mexican Revolution: Cinema and the Archive*, Austin, TX: University of Texas Press.

Pietropaolo, L. and Testaferri, A. (eds) (1995) *Feminisms in the Cinema*, Indianapolis, IN: Indiana University Press.

Ramírez-Pimienta, J. C. (2010) "Chicago lindo y querido si muero lejos de ti: el pasito duranguense, la onda grupera y las nuevas geografías de la identidad popular mexicana", *Mexican Studies/Estudios mexicanos* 26 (1): 31–45.

Rashkin, E. J. (2001) *Women Filmmakers in Mexico: The Country of Which We Dream,* Austin, TX: University of Texas Press.

Rich, B. R. (1995) "An/Other View of New Latin American Cinema", in Pietropaolo, L. and Testaferri, A. (eds) *Feminisms in the Cinema*, Indianapolis, IN: Indiana University Press, 168–192.

—— (1998) *Chick Flicks: Theories and Memories of the Feminist Film Movement*, Durham, NC and London: Duke University Press.

Ruétalo, V. and Tierney, D. (eds) (2009) *Latsploitation, Exploitation Cinemas and Latin America*, London: Routledge.

Sánchez Prado, I. (2014) *Screening Neoliberalism: Transforming Mexican Cinema, 1988–2012*, Nashville, TN: Vanderbilt University Press.

Shaw, D. (2013) *The Three Amigos: The Transnational Filmmaking of Guillermo del Toro, Alejandro González Iñarritu and Alfonson Cuarón,* Manchester: Manchester University Press.
Soto, S. A. (1979) *The Mexican Woman: A Study of Her Participation in the Revolution, 1910–1940,* Palo Alto, CA: R & E. Publications.
Taibo, P. I. (2004) *María Félix: 47 pasos por el cine,* Mexico: Ediciones B.
Thornton, N. (2013) *Revolution and Rebellion in Mexican Cinema,* New York: Bloomsbury.
—— (2016) "Writing Cinema: The Communicating Vessels of Literature and Film", in Nogar, A., Ruisánchez Serra, J. R. and Sánchez Prado, I. (eds) *A History of Mexican Literature,* New York: Cambridge University Press, 411–425.
—— (2017) "Re-Framing Mexican Women's Filmmaking: The Case of Marcela Fernandez Violante", in Martin, D. and Shaw, D. (eds) *Latin American Filmmakers: Production, Politics, Poetics,* London: I.B. Tauris, 197–216.
Tierney, D. (2007) *Emilio Fernández: Pictures in the Margins,* Manchester: Manchester University Press.
Torres San Martín, P. (ed.) (2004) *Mujeres y cine en América Latina,* Guadalajara: Universidad de Guadalajara.
Vargas Amésquita, A. (2010) "Si Adelita se fuera con otro", in Garza Iturbide, R. and Lara Chávez, H. (eds) *Cine y Revolución: La Revolución Mexicana vista a través del cine,* Mexico City: Instituto Mexicano de Cinematografía/Cineteca nacional, 149–163.
Vazquez Mantecón, Á. (2010) "La presencia de la Revolución mexicana en el cine: apuntes hacia un análisis historiográfico", in Garza Iturbide, R. and Lara Chávez, H. (eds) *Cine y Revolución: La Revolución Mexicana vista a través del cine,* Mexico City: Instituto Mexicano de Cinematografía/Cineteca nacional, 13–27.

10

POPULAR CINEMA/QUALITY TELEVISION

The audio-visual sector in Spain

Paul Julian Smith

Industry, academy, theory

In 2013 the Spanish auteurist film journal *Caimán* (previously *Cahiers du Cinéma España*) published a special supplement on the "Other Cinema" in Spain. Transparent in their attempt to confer prestige and create cultural distinction, the various critics praised a young cohort of austere, low budget filmmakers taken to be distinct from an assumed Spanish commercial mainstream.

In 2014 Belén Esteban, arguably the most controversial figure to emerge from Spanish reality TV and its vulgar celebrity culture, was sent by national network Tele5 to Morocco in order to investigate social conditions in Spain's southerly neighbour (Tele5 2014). Right-thinking commentators were horrified by this latest evidence of *telebasura* (trash TV).

It would seem, then, that cultural gatekeepers still have no difficulty in enforcing the long-standing dichotomy between elite art cinema and trash mass TV. Yet other sources suggest otherwise. The annual survey of OBITEL, the Ibero-American survey of television fiction in 2013, was on the topic of social memory, a theme particularly appropriate for Spain. And the Spanish section of the report, coordinated by Charo Lacalle, was entitled "Fiction Resists the Crisis." Lacalle records positive factors in the Spanish TV sector: average daily viewing in 2012 reached a new record of 246 minutes (OBITEL 2013: 280), with series fiction as the most popular format, occupying 21.8 per cent of the schedule.

Showing proof of audience fidelity to local drama, swashbuckling romance *Águila Roja* (Red Eagle, 2009–, Spain) was the most watched programme for the fourth year running (2013: 282), in spite of government cuts to RTVE's budget that limited the length of its season (2013: 285). No fewer than 32 different local titles were broadcast, with a total of 36 per cent being set "in the past" or "historic" (2013: 296); and the top ten exhibited a wide range of genres (from adventure and drama via mini-series and dramedy to comedy and fantasy) (2013: 299). Social questions treated by these shows, said to be "highly topical", include prejudice against women and gays, the insecure job market, the housing crisis, and euthanasia (2013: 300). Of the only two titles that failed to connect with the national audience, significantly one was a failed version of the classic US sitcom *Cheers* (1982–1993, USA) (2013: 384), suggesting that foreign formats hold little attraction for viewers in Spain. Spanish TV drama thus both explored the country's past, connecting with social memory, and reflected on the present, engaging with urgent contemporary issues. This is a valuable combination that is not to be found in all territories. Nevertheless, analysis of the audio-visual sector in Spain, particularly a comparison of popular cinema and quality television, offers a valuable case study for understanding the shift in the cultural status of television relative to an aesthetic revolution that challenges the privilege of cinema and creates new tensions in World Cinema.

If the Spanish television drama so eagerly consumed by mass audiences should not be tarred by the brush of *telebasura* reality programming, Spanish cinema, conversely but consistently, cannot solely be identified with the art movies promoted so determinedly by *Caimán*. In spite of media concentration on the precarious Other Cinema (whose audiences are as low as its budgets), the seventh annual edition of "Spanish Film Screenings" (otherwise known as "Madrid de Cine") which I attended in the capital on 18–20 June 2012, at the height of the economic crisis, told a more complex story. Intended as the major professional event for the promotion of Spanish film to foreign buyers and specialist journalists, "Madrid de cine" is organised by FAPAE (the producers' association), ICAA (the film academy), and other bodies including the Madrid tourist authority. There was once more a "padrino" ("godfather") for the event. This year it was Enrique Urbizu (director of *No habrá paz para los malvados* [No Rest for the Wicked, 2011, Spain], at the time the most recent feature to gain the best film award at the Goyas or Spanish Oscars). Representing Spanish national cinema, Urbizu gave delegates an evocative and informative talk on "the light of Madrid" high above the city in the tower of the Cibeles Palace.

In spite of a dramatic fall in production, things at Madrid de Cine seemed surprisingly positive. A FAPAE report at the event suggested that, out of a total of 199 features made in 2011 (the fourth highest figure in Europe), the number of titles screened abroad had increased (by 21 per cent), as had the number of countries in which they were seen (by 15 per cent). In Mexico alone distribution had risen to 36 titles, higher than ever before. Ironically, then, just as Spain boasts a greater number of tourists than it does inhabitants, so its cinema earns twice the income abroad than it does at home (in 2011 the figures were €185 million abroad versus just €90 million domestically).

Although Spanish cinema may be fully globalised, what I argue here, however, is that Urbizu's audience-friendly feature marked the beginning of an unanticipated trend: the reconnection of Spanish cinema with its own public. It did so via the neglected but popular genres of romantic comedy and thriller. As we shall see, the so-called *género negro* (police or detective drama) is a unique example of commercial film that is held by influential taste communities to be compatible with cultural distinction.

Independent of these industrial or quantitative trends, recent academic research, qualitative by nature, has also suggested that the dominant paradigm of auteur cinema/popular TV might be under pressure. Sally Faulkner's *A History of Spanish Film* (2013) goes beyond the auteur canon, rereading the history of Spanish film by focusing on a new corpus of titles that are placed between high and low culture. Similarly, Vicente J. Benet's *El cine español: una historia cultural* (2012) locates distinguished auteurs such as Víctor Erice and Carlos Saura in their social context and juxtaposes them with supposedly trashy sexploitation and youth movies. Meanwhile Samuel Amago's *Spanish Cinema in the Global Context* (2013) likewise combines analysis of the artistic taste for reflexivity with the less cerebral trends current in the popular genres and the movie marketplace. In recent television studies, meanwhile, Manuel Palacio has offered a minute study of the TV of the transition, arguing convincingly for the medium's decisive role at that decisive time as a kind of pedagogy of democracy in a new Spain (2012). This is a vital function that Palacio, the doyen of Spanish television studies, had previously highlighted in his general history of Spanish television (2001).

Beyond the academic sphere, there are signs that Spain is finally acknowledging the shift in the cultural status of television relative to cinema, which allows for the adoption of an aesthetic attitude toward the long despised medium. After decades of virulently attacking TV, *El País* has boasted since 2012 in Natalia Marcos a specialist reviewer of television fiction (previous columnists limited themselves to humorous political commentary), albeit one whose perspective is restricted mainly to US dramas. Local television fiction was vigorously defended from the Left when it was dismissed by a Partido Popular politician as being simply a way to "pass the time". Spanish series now have an established festival (in Vitoria) and regularly host movie-style premieres in one-time picture palaces on Madrid's Gran Vía. Meanwhile the TV screenwriters association vigorously campaigns for recognition of their members' creative work. Tentative mechanisms of legitimation have thus emerged for the medium of television fiction.

If we pull back from such anecdotal signs of change in the Spanish audio-visual habitus, we might turn, or return, to current developments in the long-running scholarly debate on quality TV. From Europe, Milly Buonanno has recently contested the overwhelming academic focus on the HBO canon, characterised as it is by novelty, edginess, narrative complexity, and cinematic ambition (2014: 9). This bias, she suggests, has served to conceal European traditions of quality that are based rather on cultural prestige and respectability (2014: 19). The new trend in favour of aesthetics in Anglo-American TV studies (Jacobs and Peacock 2013), meanwhile, has scholars arguing against the use of "cinematic" as a term of praise for quality television and championing a sensitivity to the distinctive qualities of the electronic medium, even as that medium is newly placed in the privileged aesthetic situation that was once reserved for high culture.

Adopting a yet more theoretical perspective toward the Spanish context of crisis (financial, political, cultural), we might also appeal here to Bourdieu. The latter speaks in the context of post-May 68 France of the "dispossession" and "maladjusted expectations" of the former cultural elite. These terms are defined by Bourdieu's exegete Ivan Ermakoff as, respectively, "a situation where people do not get what they feel they are entitled to" and one where people "cannot fulfil their aspirations" (2013: 98). Like Bourdieu's *soixante-huitards* before them, then, the established film community in Spain employ a perverse negative strategy characterised by the "adherence to a behavioural script at odds with the strategic imperatives imposed by shifting constraints". In Ermakoff's words the once privileged but newly dispossessed "draw on their stock of culturally shaped expectations and on their experience of past practices [. . .] highlight[ing] the relative salience of symbols and past events in the collective memory of the group" (2013: 101).

The annual Goya ceremonies that combine self-defeating protests of entitlement with appeals to once uncontested symbols of an august past (ritual attacks on government policy and acts of mourning for deceased eminences) follow Bourdieu and Ermakoff's pattern. Historically this strategy, which I suggest has now been challenged by the emergence of quality genre film, has promoted a disconnection of the Spanish public from a dispossessed and maladjusted film establishment.

Televisual cinema?

In what remains of this chapter I will propose a new paradigm for the Spanish audio-visual sector at this time of changing habitus. First, I argue for the salience of a new cinema hostile to earlier auteur or current "other" film, a popular school that is steeped in televisual culture, but cannot be reduced to it. Second, I argue for the importance of a new quality television that sets itself apart from ordinary TV through aesthetic and social ambitions that might be

Figure 10.1 *No habrá paz para los malvados* (No Rest for the Wicked, 2011, Spain, Enrique Urbizu), starring José Coronado, is an internationalised production with clear local referents. ©AXN/Audiovisual Aval SGR/Canal+ España/Generalitat Valencian/Instituto de Crédito Oficial/Instituto de la Cinematografía y de las Artes Visuales/Lazonafilms/Manto Films/ Telecinco Cinema.

called (*pace* the aestheticians) cinematic, but draws still on the specificities of a medium now fortified by its convergence with the internet and social media. I focus in film on the thriller as a relatively rare and problematic genre; and in television drama on a (more broadly defined) law and justice genre, which is also little practised in Spain.

My first text is Urbizu's already mentioned *No Rest for the Wicked*, a brutally efficient thriller which both swept the boards at the Goyas and attracted a domestic audience of almost 700,000 (Figure 10.1). When a corrupt cop (José Coronado, veteran of quality TV series such as Tele5's pioneering *Periodistas* (Journalists, 1998–2002, Spain) drunkenly shoots three dead in a Madrid nightclub, he sets off a double hunt: his own for the sole witness to his crime and that of a woman judge who takes on the murder investigation.

With its expert suspense and action sequences, *No Rest for the Wicked* might seem to be a fine example of that internationalised production that is content to follow the US lead. But this slick genre film has clear local referents. In an early sequence Coronado stands in a wasteland in front of the four new skyscrapers that have come to symbolise the unsustainable boom and bust of the Spanish economy. And it is a shock to see an actor warmly remembered as a dashing leading man now so battered and grizzled. Moreover, half way through the film, the thriller veers into politics as the criminal cop blunders into the preparations for an Islamist terror atrocity similar to that which struck Madrid in 2004.

In interview at Madrid de Cine, Coronado noted the close connection between the three media of film, television and theatre across which jobbing actors now move at will. Likewise, Urbizu's practice shows that skilled directors can make apparently abstract genre films that draw on a US TV aesthetic and yet connect closely with the concerns of local cinema audiences: one actor noted, also at the Screenings, that the film's title had been borrowed for placards in street demonstrations during the continuing economic crisis. Genre cinema thus proves to be an invaluable means for addressing urgent socio-political concerns as it moves upmarket and embraces quality scripting, performance and cinematography.

Following this template, three years later *El Niño* (The Kid, 2014, Spain/France, Daniel Monzón) combined Goya-winning technique (for both special effects and sound) with genre conventions. This drug smuggling thriller thus boasts big budget action, beginning in medias res with a taut chase sequence and indulging throughout in frequent helicopter and boat pursuits set and shot in the picturesque Straits of Gibraltar. Newcomer Jesús Castro as the titular youth who will become initiated into narcotics trafficking across the watery border is presented unapologetically for our visual pleasure. This is especially true of a skinny-dipping sequence that the neophyte actor repeatedly claimed in interview to find especially trying. Confirming this appeal to facile visual pleasure at the expense of more challenging subject matter, the young Spaniard's cross-cultural romance with a young Moroccan woman is sketchily and unconvincingly depicted.

It is precisely through casting, however, that *The Kid* establishes its claim, beyond the genre limitations of popular cinema, to quality. Castro is paired with gruff Luis Tosar as his police nemesis, a consecrated actor trailing Goya wins not least as star of prison drama *Celda 211* (Cell 211, 2009, Spain/France), the previous feature from director Daniel Monzón. Likewise, a pliant press stressed the lengthy preparation time spent in pre-production (some five years), a labour intended to serve as guarantor of the second movie's cultural capital. *El País* even praised the character development displayed by Tosar's clichéd troubled police officer (Ordoñez 2015), appealing to a psychological complexity that, beyond the dynamic plotting of the thriller, is often held to be a criterion for artistic quality in cinema.

Yet, striking a balance with the rival television medium, Jesús Castro would later be cast in the second season of police drama *El Príncipe* (2015–2016, Spain) on Tele5, the most popular free to air national network in Spain. And in fact, as we shall see, the latter's first season had fully anticipated the feature film in both its North African setting and focus on geopolitical tensions between Spain and Morocco. Highly accessible and pleasurable, then, *The Kid* is an extreme case of my new paradigm: a popular genre film that engages newly emergent mechanisms of legitimation to achieve a degree of that cultural distinction once reserved for auteur or "other" cinema.

The Kid was swiftly followed in theatrical release and critical consecration by serial killer movie *La isla mínima* (Marshland, 2014, Spain) by Alberto Rodríguez, hitherto known for youth films sometimes starring Spanish television's biggest crossover star, Mario Casas (*7 vírgenes*, 7 Virgins, 2005, Spain; *Grupo* 7, Unit 7, 2012, Spain). As period fiction is ubiquitous on television but relatively rare in a feature sector where budgets are now reduced by the crisis, *Marshland's* setting in the Transition to democracy already engages a televisual register. TVE's storied *Cuéntame* (Tell Me, 2001–, Spain) has explored the period for over a decade; and *La chica de ayer* (Yesterday's Girl, 2009, Spain), broadcast by private free to air network Antena 3, had been a time travelling police drama set in the same post-Franco era. Moreover, corrupt cop Javier Gutiérrez had been intimately known to Spanish audiences over the preceding five years as the sidekick in TVE's highest rated series, the already mentioned period romance *Red Eagle*.

Beyond format and casting, the serial killer genre, rarer of course in Spain than in the US, is indigenised here by its placing in a precise temporal and spatial context that owes much to television's perceived closeness to a local audience. Gutiérrez's character is thus not simply a bent cop whose conduct of a multiple murder case of young women is not to be trusted; he is also a veteran of the Francoist security forces who, it is revealed, took part in extra-judicial killings.

Moreover, as in *The Kid*, a transnational-style criminal plot is transformed through a distinctive Andalusian location, in this case the treacherous and picturesque marshland of Doñana.

Frequent aerial shots of this distinctive landscape, with its intricately geometric patterns of land and water, are used both for aesthetic effect (the film won the Goya for best cinematography once more) and narrative function (the placing of lost characters in an extreme and disorientating environment). The film uses this very precise setting as part of a general critique of the Transition in an invocation of historical memory that would be amenable to Left-leaning and telephobic taste-makers at newspapers such as *El País*. Indeed, in a reality effect that reinforces *Marshland's* expert recreation of the period through production design, the opening credits show documentary footage of the time.

Yet the casting once more of *niño du jour* Jesús Castro in a sinister co-star role distances *Marshland* once more from the past practices of period filmmaking now identified with a dispossessed and maladjusted film establishment. The presence of new intermediatic star Castro, plus his fellow TV-recognisable cast, thus reconfirms *Marshland*'s clear connection with my new paradigm of audience-friendly, but expertly realised, genre cinema.

In these thrillers, then, the televisual mode is engaged in part through the familiarity of the actors, who serve to domesticate a somewhat distant Hollywood genre. But these features remain cinematic in the tensions they display between their generic constraints and their continued aspiration to aesthetic and thematic ambition. As we shall now see, the same perilous equilibrium is seen in three recent television series that fall broadly into the law and justice genre, one that is as problematic in Spanish TV as it is in Spanish cinema. Here, so-called cinematic television (the label applied to special or event programming) takes over the aspiration to national narrative once embodied by auteur cinema without abandoning the seriality that is the defining characteristic of long-form TV drama.

Cinematic TV?

Educated Spaniards would no doubt be surprised to learn that my first example of quality television is Antena 3's drug-dealing drama *Sin tetas no hay paraíso* (You Don't Get to Heaven Without Tits, 2008–2009, Spain), a rare Spanish adaptation of a Colombian original. After all, the Latin American *telenovela*, which was once widely shown in Spain, is now spurned by critics and audiences alike as a low quality import. Inspired no doubt by the knowingly salacious title (and sometimes showing little knowledge of the actual content of the series that ran for three seasons between 2008 and 2009), politicians and academics alike have attacked the show for its supposed reactionary ideology. Thus we are told that it imposed impossible standards of female beauty, promoted the desirability of violent crime and sex, and reduced women, mesmerised by fatally attractive gangster lovers, to Cinderella-style passivity.

Yet significantly enough the changes made by the Spanish producers to the original Colombian format reveal television's new aspirations to psychological and narrative complexity in the former country. The main plotline remains teenage Catalina's relationship with the criminal kingpin known as El Duque. But the complication here is that she is in love with him and he treats her tenderly, among other things opposing her desire for the breast implants referred to in the series title. (Conversely the Colombian series begins with a brutally pragmatic episode in which the young heroine fails to make the grade as a prostitute because of her ostensibly deficient cup size.) Indeed, in the star-making role for Miguel Ángel Silvestre as El Duque, his oft displayed physique, warmly appreciated by female fans, displaces female anatomy as a source of visual pleasure for the viewer.

Unexpectedly, once more Antena 3's adapters set this central and newly romantic story amid multiple new plot strands that complement and complicate its meaning. Thus they invent a police inspector who is obsessed with taking down the seductive narco capo but serves as a problematic embodiment of the law in that he is himself addicted to prescription drugs. Catalina's family, now elevated to lower middle class from the humble deprivation they endured in Colombia, includes a single mother whose tentative romance with a factory owner (played by distinguished film veteran Fernando Guillén Cuervo) provides as reciprocal and respectful a version of heterosexual romance as any feminist academic could hope for. El Duque's conflict with the incoming Colombian narcos who call him "españolito" gives rise to uncommon reflections on a crisis-ridden Spain's newly submissive relationship with Latin America.

Beyond these narrative and thematic complexities, technical credits are also high. There are frequent well-chosen exteriors, placing a transnational plot within a recognisable Madrid setting. For example, the lovers tryst in the Parque de Occidente with the Palacio Real standing proudly behind them or enjoy a hotel room with an ominous view of the hulking Telefónica tower on the city skyline outside. When El Duque is forced to flee his home territory, three episodes are even set and shot in the Colombia that remains exotic to Spanish viewers.

Yet the Madrid locations also suggest that the series, in spite of its cinematic complexity and scope, aims for televisual closeness and domesticity. After a difficult day Catalina makes her daughter a "Spanish omelette", national comfort food. Fans proudly recognise the actress who plays Catalina's frenemy Yéssica (who grooms her young classmates as precocious prostitutes) as a Galician, just like them (María Castro would later go on to play the more sympathetic protagonist of *Vive cantando,* 2013–2014, Spain, a softer-focused musical drama). Silvestre for his part, fielding obtrusive enquiries about his physique and nude scenes to the Spanish press (as "kid" Jesús Castro was later to do), invokes his own workaday origins in Valencia. The production and reception of this show, then, are fully indigenised in a way attempted by the localising thrillers I studied in the first half of this chapter, but one that was able to extend deeper and longer into audience affections over three top-rated seasons.

You Don't Get to Heaven Without Tits' feminisation of the audience is reinforced in a very different example of quality TV, *El tiempo entre costuras* (The Time in Between, 2013–2014, Spain, Iñaki Mercero/Norberto López Amado/Iñaki Peñafiel) (Figure 10.2). Invoking the mini-series that is for Buonanno the epitome of European-style authoritative canons of quality, this period

Figure 10.2 *El tiempo entre costuras* (The Time in Between, 2013–2014, Spain, Iñaki Mercero/Norberto López Amado/Iñaki Peñafiel), starring Adriana Ugarte, offers some of the most glamorous and intensely pleasurable visuals ever seen in Spain ©Antena 3 Televisión/Boomerang TV.

romance, a literary adaptation, ran for just eleven feature length episodes. And exploiting the convergence of film and TV aesthetics, it offered some of the most glamorous and intensely pleasurable visuals ever seen in Spain, whether on big or small screen.

The Time in Between is a big budget historical drama about a seamstress-cum-spy. Although broadcast by Antena 3 once more, it is made by Boomerang, an independent production company less known but more versatile than its rivals. Initially a period piece may not seem so novel. Antena 3's schedule is itself awash with costume drama with daily serials *Amar en tiempos revueltos* (To Love Is Forever, 2005–, Spain) and *El secreto de Puente Viejo* (The Secret of Puente Viejo, 2011–, Spain) occupying some three hours each afternoon in the post-lunch "sobremesa" slot. In their quest for event programming, however, so alien to the daily rhythm of soap and *telenovela*, Antena 3 kept their prestige serial under wrap for almost twelve months, waiting for the right date and building anticipation. The broadcaster was rewarded with an extraordinary rating, averaging five million, and a 25.3 per cent share over the course of the series.

The key innovation (and attraction) of *The Time in Between* is that it is quite literally a costume drama. Initially alone and unaided, the protagonist comes to run the most fashionable dressmaking studio in her native Madrid, where she has moved after a period in Morocco. Much action in later episodes takes place in Lisbon, where Sira seduces a businessman in league with the Nazis. Her true love, however, is a freedom fighter whom she pretends to disdain in order to protect his life. But more frequent and dramatic scenes show the normally self-controlled Sira hugging and sobbing with a female English friend ("Love hurts, darling!").

As Sira sacrifices her relationships with her lover and long lost father to her somewhat mysterious espionage mission, it might appear that the series is simply a remake of the Hollywood woman's movie: she is a Mildred Pierce who has swapped a baking dish for a sewing machine. The theme of the absent father and uncertain paternity seems similarly taken straight from Latin American *telenovela*, even though that genre is, as mentioned earlier, no longer successful in Spain.

However, three elements move *The Time in Between* onto a different level. The first is the extraordinary care given to mise-en-scène. Every shot is perfectly composed and curated, from (of course) the parade of exquisite costumes to the luxurious authentic locations. Even when Sira is forced to waylay a chicken truck for a secret mission (her pencil skirt means she needs to be carried on board in the driver's arms) she drapes her hair in a cerise chiffon scarf. But given the fact that the narrative focuses precisely on fashion as women's work and feminine guiles (Nazi ladies also come into Sira's orbit drawn by her unparalleled skill with a needle), the extravagant display of wardrobe, apparently incongruous in the context of war-torn Europe, is thematised and does not feel superfluous to the plot.

A second related element after the sumptuous look is the performance by star Adriana Ugarte, who is perfectly (and differently) coiffed and attired in each scene. As we have seen in the case of *You Don't Get to Heaven Without Tits*, Spanish series are normally ensemble by nature. It is thus highly unusual that one actor should carry a whole drama on her elegantly-clad shoulders. Moreover, Ugarte, who is in almost every shot, gives a highly controlled performance that could not be further from the melodramatics of classic Hollywood or modern *telenovelas*. She brings a sobriety and intensity to a potentially soapy plot whose distinction is intensified by the remarkably leisurely pace of a narrative that seems (like Sira herself) somehow suspended in time.

This brings us to the final characteristic of the show: its relation to history. The grand narrative of the Civil War and Nazism is glimpsed only tangentially through costume, women's work (which comes down to the same thing here), and female psychology, both individual and collective (Sira gathers a crowd of faithful followers at her studio). In spite of this indirect engagement with historical context, then, *The Time in Between* could be read as a revival of

Spain's mini-series of the 1970s and 1980s, which were invariably literary adaptations of the classics. Like, say, TVE's *Fortunata y Jacinta* (Fortunata and Jacinta, 1980, Spain/France), a prestigious adaptation of the novel by Benito Pérez Galdós, *The Time in Between* boasts unusually high production values that are (as mentioned earlier) currently inaccessible to Spanish directors in feature film, whose budgets have (as also mentioned earlier) been cut with the crisis.

The ample Antena 3 budget transforms everyday television into an aesthetic object offering intense visual pleasure. But where the classic serials of the Transition served (as Palacio has shown) to educate Spaniards in the new responsibilities of democracy, the moral of *The Time in Between* is more diffuse and private, focusing as it does on female self-realisation, both emotional and economic. *The Time in Between* thus bids for a quality demographic, which, unlike the family audience still sought by most Spanish series, coincides with the tastes of adult, childless, and professional women. It is telling that after Sira suffers a miscarriage she is not tempted to have another child.

In the same year as Antena 3's *The Time in Between*, Tele5 broadcast expert police series *El Príncipe* (2014–2016, Spain), also set in North Africa, in this case the Spanish enclave of Ceuta. *El Príncipe*, named for a real life neighbourhood, engages not only with the drug dealing we saw in *You Don't Get to Heaven Without Tits* but also (and I believe this is unprecedented) with Islamist terrorism. And the casting of José Coronado as a corrupt cop means that he brings with him memories of his very similar role in feature film *No Rest for the Wicked*. Yet *El Príncipe* also stages a complex and involving love affair between another Christian cop (who is in fact an undercover secret agent, played by Álex González) and a Moslem teacher (Hiba Abouk), the first time that a Spanish actor of Arab descent had been offered an above the title role in a TV series or indeed film. This theme is explored at once more subtly and sexily than in the similar thriller *The Kid*, which was released after *El Príncipe*'s first season was shown.

By dealing with one of the most charged topics in contemporary Spanish politics and society, jihadism and the relation with a Moslem minority little represented in the media, *El Príncipe* clearly aspired to the status of national narrative. And its aesthetics are also of the highest quality. Rather than shoot on (dangerous) site, the production team employed the Digital Backlot supplied by Stargate Studios, known for quality US shows *Mad Men* (2007–2015) and *The Walking Dead* (2010–), and used, it was claimed, for the first time in Europe. The high-speed car chase sequence with which the first episode opens would not be envied by *The Kid*. And the labyrinthine plot, with its expert cliff-hangers and reversals, is based on a script that, rarely in Spain, was preconceived as an artistic whole, one in which every beat is perfectly placed.

Yet it is precisely at this point that *El Príncipe*, an ostentatious example of cinematic TV in its aesthetic, is most televisual. Its narrative effect depends wholly on the seriality of long-form television and its emotional payoff on viewers' continuing cohabitation with its characters (some of the most sympathetic of whom turn out to be terrorists). Indeed the series' density makes the subsequent feature *The Kid* feel shallow and hollow ("child's play", perhaps) by comparison. And *El Príncipe*'s mediation on cross-cultural romance (and violence) charts the complexities of both in a way no Spanish film has to date.

Conclusion

It was in the wake of *El Príncipe* that Tele5 squandered their newly acquired prestige by sending to Morocco, in the footsteps of their prize-winning fictional police officers, despised reality star Belén Esteban. It might appear, then, that each medium will return to its own level. Yet I have argued that, in this new media paradigm for Spain, the emergent genre cinema also appeals to the televisual virtues of closeness or locality in order to indigenise the foreign genre of the thriller;

and, that when viewed on a wide screen TV, the aesthetics of the features and series I have treated fully converge. It is significant that after *Marshland* triumphed at the Goyas its producer Mikel Lejarza described his company Atresmedia (parent company of Antena 3) as a "group committed to cultural creation" and to "the management of audiovisual content" (in general) for an audience that he had no hesitation in calling "intelligent" (Premios Goya 2015).

Spanish television drama has thus achieved a distinctive brand of quality that hybridises Buonanno's European virtue of cultural respectability (seen in *The Time in Between*) with the more novel and edgy American tone (seen in *El Príncipe*), both of which seem to chime with viewers. And after the problematic period I cited via Madrid de Cine at the start of this chapter, Spanish cinema also achieved a historically large share of its home market in 2014, due in part to the last two films I discussed here. More surprisingly yet, the press, including *El País,* celebrated their genre status as thrillers, praising both the commercial and the artistic success of the year's cinema (Ordoñez 2015).

But I would suggest, finally, that, rejecting the dispossession and maladjustment of the film establishment as they have in the appreciation of an expert popular cinema, viewers and scholars of Spanish media (as well as those of many other nations) should also pay closer attention to current TV series: expertly crafted national narratives that attract audiences larger and longer lasting than any feature film.

References

Amago, S. (2013) *Spanish Cinema in the Global Context*, New York and London: Routledge.

Benet, V. J. (2012) *El cine español: una historia cultural*, Barcelona: Paidós.

Buonanno, M. (2014) "Quality Television and Transnational Standards", lecture presented at Graduate Center, CUNY, November 21.

Caimán (2013) "El otro cine español", Special Supplement, *Caimán* 19 (70).

Ermakoff, I. (2013) "Rational Choice May Take Over", in Gorsky, P. S (ed.), *Bourdieu and Historical Analysis*, Durham, NC: Duke University Press, 89–106.

Faulkner, S. (2013) *A History of Spanish Film: Cinema and Society 1910–2010*, London: Bloomsbury.

Jacobs, J. and Peacock, S. (eds) (2013) *Television Aesthetics and Style*, New York: Bloomsbury.

OBITEL (2013) "Memoria social y ficción televisiva en países iberoamericanos", *OBITEL. Observatorio iberoamericano de la ficción televisiva,* https://blogdoobitel.files.wordpress.com/2011/04/obitel-2013-espanhol.pdf.

Ordóñez, M. (2015) "Hora punta del cine español", *El País*, 7 February, http://cultura.elpais.com/cultura/2015/02/04/babelia/1423068329_126196.html.

Palacio, M. (2001) *Historia de la televisión en España*, Barcelona: Gedisa.

Palacio, M. (2012) *La televisión durante la Transición española*, Madrid: Cátedra.

Premios G. (2014) "La forja de una carrera", 13 March, http://premiosgoya.academiadecine.com/actualidad/detalle.php?id=471.

Tele5 (2014) "Los ojos de Belén: Marruecos", *Tele5*, 2 February, www.telecinco.es/losojosdebelen/a-carta/ojos-Belen-Marruecos-T01xC05_2_1748280198.html.

11

CONTEMPORARY SCANDINAVIAN CINEMA

Between art and commerce

Olof Hedling

Introduction

In a recent essay, Thomas Elsaesser gives a harsh verdict on the state of European cinema today. From a geopolitical position in which "the new 'marginality' of Europe" is assumed, a number of "negative qualifications associable with European cinema" are put forward. Among those are that the continent's cinema is:

> artificially kept alive with government subsidies, Council of Europe directives [...] and cheap television co-production deals; bolstered by being co-opted for cultural tourism and city branding; speaking on behalf of no constituency, and for the most part, speaking to no public other than festival audiences, loyal cinephiles and university students.
>
> *(Elsaesser 2015: 19)*

This judgment, moreover, may be seen as a development of one of the themes underlying the same author's earlier work, *European Cinema: Face to Face with Hollywood* (2005), which has been designated as "the most important book on European cinema to emerge in recent years" (Harrod *et al.* 2015: 6–7). Here, one of the main arguments is that European cinema has experienced what, to use a football analogy, is described as "relegation": it has dropped in rank, to become just another sub-set under the generic label of "World Cinema" (Elsaesser 2005: 497).

However, despite Elsaesser's efforts and many productive suggestions, what precisely was meant by demoting European cinema to the supposedly less prestigious status of "World Cinema" remains somewhat elusive. As has been argued in response: "World Cinema is a contested concept and its boundaries are as yet unclear" (Berghahn and Sternberg 2010: 38). Nevertheless, inspired by Elsaesser, Berghahn, Sternberg and others have offered a few tentative suggestions, such as that "migrant and diasporic cinema marks the World Cinema turn in European cinema" and, not least, that "the concept of World Cinema implies transnational connections on the level of film production, financing, distribution and reception" (Ibid.: 36, 38). While transnational cinema is, in turn, thought to comprise "different aspects of film production, distribution and consumption which transcend national film cultures", it seems generally to be presumed that the concept of national cinema is in a state of flux (Ibid.: 22; Higson 1989).

In what follows, Scandinavian cinema over the last two decades or so will be scrutinised from the perspective suggested by the viewpoints outlined above. Scandinavian film will be placed in the contemporary European context, revealing that some of the "negative qualifications" put forward by Elsaesser to some extent seem to hold true, while others, perhaps paradoxically, may in fact be viewed as, in a way, beneficial. Additionally, processes such as transnational exchange, globalisation, internationalisation, increasing migration and the role of diaspora will also be explored. Here, Mette Hjort's proposed typology of the different kinds of transnationalism pertaining to audio-visual production will serve as a stepping stone to illuminate not only the forces propelling contemporary Scandinavian film production specifically but, more generally, a great deal of film production in Europe and globally as well (2009).

A Swedish success?

In 2009 the principal "Swedish" box-office successes in domestic theatres were, by far, the three feature-length films adapted from domestic crime writer Stieg Larsson's so-called Millennium trilogy. The first instalment of the series is a story about a disillusioned investigative journalist who, thanks to the help of a highly introverted and asocial computer hacker, succeeds in solving the disappearance of a woman while simultaneously exposing an internationally oriented Swedish business magnate as a corrupt criminal.

Män som hatar kvinnor (The Girl with the Dragon Tattoo, 2009, Sweden/Denmark/Germany, Niels Arden Oplev)—hereafter *The Girl*—went on to sell more than 1,217,000 tickets in domestic cinemas in a country of less than ten million people (SFI 2010: 22). It also attracted audiences of almost one million in Denmark and slightly over 500,000 in Norway, despite the fact that the neighbouring countries only have a population about half the size of Sweden. Altogether the film sold 1.8 million tickets in the tri-national Scandinavian region within its first thirty days of release—a record (Stenport and Traylor 2015: 80).

The film also exported very well outside of the Nordic region, in territories such as France, Germany, Spain and the UK. In the latter market, the film was even theatrically distributed in both dubbed and subtitled versions and was, perhaps paradoxically, presented with a BAFTA Film Award as the best "Film Not in the English language" in 2011. A 2014 research report ranked the film second behind the French box office sensation, buddy comedy *Intouchables* (The Untouchables, 2011, Olivier Nakache and Eric Toledano), among a very limited group of non-English language European films released between 2005 and 2012 that were very successfully distributed in Europe in territories outside of their domestic market (Jones 2014).

On a parallel note, the film's success in the Nordic region did not follow established patterns. Despite claims that Scandinavia is "a film and television culture with a strong affinity between the three countries", in reality, studies demonstrate that "[t]he exchange of films between the Nordic countries doesn't indicate a natural cultural connection with an obvious audience interest in films from the neighboring countries" (Bondebjerg and Redvall 2013: 127, 140). It is therefore truly remarkable that *The Girl*, according to the European Audiovisual Observatory's Lumière database, attracted more Danish cinemagoers than any film made in the country's domestic language during the two decades since 1996.

The film's runaway success obviously did not go unnoticed in Sweden. The Swedish Film Institute (SFI), the main national Swedish film support agency and one of the film's funders, thus exclaimed in its annual report:

> The massive success of the Millennium trilogy in 2009 put Sweden on the international film map. Internationally, the phenomenon was termed "Swedish noir" [...] today the three films in the trilogy are the biggest export success in Swedish film history.
>
> *(SFI 2011: 26)*

However, making the film a matter of national pride in this fashion—using the descriptive moniker "Swedish" rather than the more established "Nordic Noir", or the previously common "Scandinavian crime"—is somewhat unconvincing and problematic, given that the film clearly illustrates the contemporary problems involved in "pigeon-holing films by nationality" (Jones 2015: 2). Accordingly, Norwegian, German and Danish funds made a considerable contribution to the financing of the film, as did the Nordic Film and Television Fund (NFTF; a co-production fund created in 1990). Moreover, while this version of *The Girl* was shot in Swedish on wintry, cold and occasionally dark domestic locations (with the exception of two scenes set in Australia and the Caribbean which were filmed in the south of Spain), was based on a Swedish literary work and starred Swedish actors, it was also supported by the Danish Film Institute as well as by Danish public broadcaster DR. The Danish financial involvement was not, of course, merely a sign of some altruistic confidence in the production *per se*; rather, it was conditioned by the fact that the production included a considerable Danish contribution of artistic and craft expertise, with virtually all the so-called "A-functions" behind the camera being handled by Danes, including a Danish director, director of photography, producer, editor, sound designer, production designer and music composer. In addition, the film's script was also written by two Danish screenwriters.

The producer's decision to employ an abundance of Danish above-the-line personnel was presumably not motivated by the idea that the Danes were much more artistically proficient at their crafts than their Swedish counterparts. Rather, the incentive for the strategy appears to have been that it gave the producers means to access significant funding from both the aforementioned NFTF and the Danish state by exploiting the Danish film support directive which posits that a film is still eligible for public film subsidies even if it lacks a Danish setting and is not in the Danish language, provided that key members of the crew are Danish. This directive dates from the 1980s and was prompted, among other factors, by national *auteur* par excellence Lars von Trier's penchant of shooting in English, using international actors and almost always situating his plots either abroad or in non-defined locations (Hjort 2005: 12).

The Girl was consequently an international co-production, shot and post-produced at particular locations in Sweden, including at the geographical sites of two major regional film funds. These funds had presumably inserted localisation clauses stipulating that part of the shooting or post-production was to take place in the fund's vicinities with a certain part of the production personnel being locally or regionally registered in exchange for the fund co-financing the venture (Hedling 2010a: 336).

Moreover, by using the practice, common in Scandinavia since the early 1990s, of exploiting the film and its two sequels to produce a spin-off extended TV-serial—which included more footage, re-edited and divided into episodes and broadcast later—the producers additionally secured significant funding from several TV sources in various countries, while simultaneously ensuring that the final product was diversified and marketable in more than one way. Indeed, at least one scholarly text refers to *The Girl* as a "Swedish TV adaptation", comparing it to HBO shows such as *Game of Thrones* (2011–, USA/UK, David Benioff and D.B. Weiss) and *The Wire* (2002–2008, USA, David Simon) (Byg and Torner 2013: 119).

The interest among broadcasters in financing film can be traced back to the deregulation of the television sector in Scandinavia in the late 1980s, when the era of public broadcasting

Figure 11.1 Violence against women: Noomi Rapace and Peter Andersson in *Män som hatar kvinnor* (The Girl with the Dragon Tattoo, 2009, Sweden/Denmark/Germany, Niels Arden Oplev). ©Yellow Bird.

monopolies ended. As private actors entered the market, competition for programming increased. Ever since, television companies—public and private, Scandinavian, as well as repeatedly German ones—have been frequent suppliers of film funding. For complex reasons, having to do with public film funding regulations, the wishes of television companies to exploit material as much as possible, together with thoughts about convergence and synergy, this development has occasionally, as in the instance of *The Girl*, resulted in material being presented in both television and film formats. In various ways one may consequently speak of how film and television have increasingly merged during the last couple of decades. In terms of Nordic Noir productions, the practice has been examined as a "pan-Scandinavia media concept" (Hedling 2010b: 129–143).

The Girl was therefore not a "Swedish" film in the bounded, differentiated and perhaps outdated sense the SFI attempted to appropriate it as. Going back to Andrew Higson's original stipulations about what constitutes a national film, *The Girl* hardly qualifies as national cinema defined in either "economic" or "textual" terms (Higson 1989: 36). With its crime investigation/rape-revenge plot, conventional, linear narration, overriding themes of sexualised violence, the oppression of women and the iniquities of contemporary capitalism, its genre, form and themes appear perhaps "Western" rather than particularly Swedish (Figure 11.1). Thus, the film can be considered an example of that increasingly common entity, a "Scandi-pudding" with additional German funding, constructed around the idea of convergence and synergy between film, television and internationally distributed bestselling crime literature. The German co-funding, which has been an almost constant in Nordic Noir productions during recent decades, moreover, can be ascribed to a peculiar German attraction that has come to project Sweden and Scandinavia as in some sense "pleasurable" (Vonderau 2010: 148). Simultaneously, the production is also part feature film and part TV serial and as such very much a "borderless, transnational filmmaking" product that "is in many ways typical of contemporary European cinema" (Higson 2015).

The transnationalism of the present

In a critique of the ambiguous ways in which the term transnational has been repeatedly used, Mette Hjort has attempted to outline what she calls a "typology of transnationalisms" in connection with contemporary audio-visual production (2009: 12–33). Hjort's palpable purpose is to more specifically illuminate and contextualise the concept. She consequently identifies nine specific types of cross-border collaboration, several of which help to shed light on the various aforementioned production strategies employed during the making of *The Girl* as well as revealing the powers, interests, aspirations and motifs of the entities that put up the funds and that propel current transnational film and, to some extent, dramatic television production in Scandinavia.

First, the Danish, Swedish, Norwegian and German co-interests in the film and television series may be described as affinitive transnationalism. With regard to this type of transnationalism, cooperation is the outcome of cultures being alike with "similarity understood in terms of ethnicity, partially overlapping or mutually intelligible languages, and a history of interaction giving rise to shared core values, common practices, and comparable institutions" (Hjort 2009: 17). German co-productions with Scandinavia and especially Sweden have been common at least since the 1970s. Since the early 1990s and with regard to Nordic Noir content, collaborative networks, ways of cooperation and pre-supposed division of production tasks have gradually been developed that eventually have smoothed out glitches typically associated with Euro-puddings, such as for instance dubbing (Bergfelder 2005: 327). Between the Nordic partners there is also a shared experience regarding difficulties that are typical of the audio-visual contexts in many small nations, or to minor cinemas in more general terms, a context that the NFTF, moreover, was originally set up in part to remedy.

Second, *The Girl* can be said to straddle two of Hjort's types of transnational collaboration, what she terms "milieu-building transnationalism" and "modernising transnationalism". The former type can be seen in the case of the Swedish, mainly publicly supported, regional film funds that acted as co-producers on the film and television series and thus guaranteed that a certain portion of the production would and did take place in the respective geographical areas. In this instance, attracting a production of comparatively large scale—from a Nordic, and perhaps even European, perspective—and markedly dominated by Danish creative talent may be seen in conjunction with the funds' aims of developing an artistically innovative and economically viable production environment or, to put it differently, a self-sustaining audio-visual cluster (Hedling 2010a: 335). In short, the hope may have been that members of what has been described as the internationally celebrated Danish thriving film milieu would complement those in Stockholm and Trollhättan—the southwest Swedish former industrial town where one of the funds is located—and thus add some constructive features (Elsaesser 2005: 14). Viewed from another perspective, it can equally be suggested that the Danish led crew and the mainly Swedish cast sought out these centres to jointly develop solutions to "problems that hamper the development of thriving film milieus" (Hjort 2009: 19).

However, to bolster the audio-visual milieu is not the only objective of these regional film funds. As a result of the end products coming out of them as well as the general climate projected as a result of the audio-visual production, they also serve the function of marketing the location and raising visibility, promoting a process of reinvention that also has significant economic implications. Accordingly, at least one motive behind starting the funds was to aid societal transition in areas that were marred by unemployment, economic distress and post-industrial decline (Hedling 2010a: 335). Being associated with the resulting symbolic cultural capital was consequently part of the regions' and towns' attempt to become, simply put, more modern. Attracting audio-visual production to particular locations in Scandinavia has in fact become such a large-scale operation that it has occasionally led to government ministers becoming involved in hands-on negotiations with global media majors regarding production location (Rossing Jensen 2015). Such was the case, for instance, with Universal and Working Title's production of the first instalment of Norwegian bestselling author Jo Nesbø's series about Oslo detective Harry Hole, *The Snowman* (2017, UK, Tomas Alfredson).

Third, the collaboration between different partners in various, if closely situated, nations may be deemed what Hjort calls "opportunistic transnationalism". Here purely economic thinking takes precedence and the selection of partners, the blend of cast and crew and locations are considered in such a way so as to maximise possible economic opportunities. As implied above, this appears to have very much been on the producers' mind as the project was set up. The main production company behind *The Girl*, Yellowbird, established its own subsidiaries in several countries, in part as a way to anchor themselves to national public funders. This strategy is now well established and had already been pioneered by Scandinavian production houses beginning with Lars von Trier and Peter Aalbæk Jensen's company Zentropa, started in Copenhagen 1992. According to their website, Zentropa at present have more than ten subsidiaries in almost as many countries, all with the word Zentropa in the company name and with the purpose, one assumes, of making them eligible for public funding, which is almost always in some way limited along national lines. One employee explained the strategy thus: "We traipse about Europe like gypsies and set up camp wherever we happen to find financing opportunities and the best locations" (quoted in Hjort 2009: 20). Local, regional and national economic incentives consequently appear a central part of what Dina Iordanova has described as "the intensifying migratory dynamics and the transnational essence of contemporary cinema" that "make it necessary to re-evaluate the concepts of belonging and commitment to a national culture" (2003: 149).

Like Zentropa, Yellowbird and the producers of *The Girl* had a long history of setting up similar Nordic Noir transnational projects, while also being pioneers in terms of bringing the Germans on board, something that they had started with as early as the early 1990s. In short, the various personnel and location strategies employed during the production of *The Girl* display great resourcefulness on the part of the producer in generating the greatest opportunities for eligibility for funding from as many transnational co-production funds, national public service broadcasters, national film support agencies and different regional funds as possible.

In other words, purely economic thinking, often seen as an undesirable distinguishing trait of Hollywood's traditional way of operating, has become extremely important in Europe and Scandinavia as well, despite the continent's sometimes supposed heritage of a more creatively inclined and altruistic production culture (Elsaesser 2005: 494). This particular economic thinking however is not quite of the relatively transparent Hollywood kind, traditionally based on profit maximisation while keeping costs down. Rather, several national and international, regional and local organisations and agents negotiate diverse interests such as national prestige, the benefits of international collaboration, local and regional visibility and economic regeneration as the supposed paybacks of financing and accommodating international and domestic productions.

Further sides of the transnational and migratory coin

The kind of transnational partnerships, migratory movements and regional interaction propelled by various impetuses for cross-border collaboration exemplified by the production of *The Girl*, have become increasingly standard practice in Scandinavia during the last two decades or so. And even if various Nordic Noir projects have been at the forefront of this development, what can be described as "film production as usual"—in other words, the making of art films, national epics and a long line of domestic comedies and dramas—has adopted similar cross-national cooperation strategies. For instance, the Danish director Suzanne Bier's well-received, genre-driven romantic comedies such as *Den skaldede frisør* (Love Is All You Need, 2012, Denmark/Italy/

France/Germany/Sweden/Japan/Norway) starring Pierce Brosnan, and relationship melodramas like *Brødre* (Brothers, 2004, Denmark/UK/Sweden/Norway), starring Connie Nielsen, testify to an ever-increasing transnational working practice and a global consciousness from the point of view of production, outreach and subject matter. While also having worked in Hollywood on occasion, Bier's "Danish" films such as *Efter brylluppet* (After the Wedding, 2006, Denmark/UK/Sweden) and the Academy award winner *Hævnen* (To a Better World, 2010, Sweden/Denmark/Norway) consequently thematise Danes, and frequently Swedes, working abroad, while the films engage with social issues pertaining to global conflicts and inequalities. Hence, they put assumptions about Scandinavian life, Swedishness and Danishness into stark relief.

However, in recent years, further forms of exchange and more extreme examples of migratory patterns and entanglements in the Scandinavian audio-visual production environment have emerged that barely existed a few years ago. In mid-November 2011, a local newspaper in the city of Malmö in the southernmost part of Sweden posted a two-minute audio-visual snippet on its homepage. The occasion was that sixteen days of location work for the romantic horror sequel *1920—Evil Returns* (2012, India, Bhushan Patel), a Bollywood movie and reputedly an Indian remake of *The Exorcist* (1973, USA, William Friedkin), was being conducted in the vicinities (Figure 11.2). Some of the principal crew and several of the film's stars were interviewed, all praising the natural splendour of the locations and the landscape as well as the hospitability they encountered. Two local filmmakers, provided through the regional film fund and the Öresund Film Commission, and employed by the Indian production as location managers, also gave enthusiastic testimony about the collaboration. Not least, they stressed the event as a regional breakthrough and how local sights and historical treasures now got exposure among the massive audiences of the sub-continent across the globe. The economic potential, including paving the way for tourism, was profound. On the one hand, of course, Bollywood movies are constantly filming in Europe, with the UK, the Alps and Italy used repeatedly. On the other, for Southern Sweden, isolated by the Baltic Sea from the Continent and on the margins of Europe, this was a first. In general, the event was received as an encouraging part of larger global developments.

Locations in Scandinavia have, of course, occasionally been used in international productions through the years, either for short sequences or more substantial parts of films, such as the Stockholm-shot Robert Mitchum espionage thriller *Foreign Intrigue* (1956, USA,

Figure 11.2 Bollywood promoting southern Sweden. Tia Bajpai and Aftab Shivdasani in *1920—Evil Returns* (2012, India, Bhushan Patel). ©ASA Production & Enterprises/BVG Films.

Sheldon Reynolds). Similarly, Alfred Hitchcock's *Topaz* (1969, USA) includes Copenhagen settings. However, as Lars von Trier's English language productions *Dancer in the Dark* (2001, Denmark/France/Sweden/Italy/Germany), *Dogville* (2003, Denmark/Sweden/UK/France/Germany/Netherlands/Norway/Finland/Italy) and *Manderlay* (2005, Denmark/Sweden/France/UK/Germany) brought Hollywood nobility such as Nicole Kidman, Lauren Bacall and James Caan to the streets of the post-industrial town of Trollhättan—the setting of the regional film fund Film Väst—a buzz started to surround audio-visual production in a way that had not previously existed in Scandinavia.

More recently, the BBC's decision to produce its television adaptations of crime writer Henning Mankell's novels about Kurt Wallander, starring Kenneth Branagh, on authentic locations in Ystad, Southern Sweden, as well as media conglomerate Sony's decision to have David Fincher shoot his remake of *The Girl with the Dragon Tattoo* (2011, USA/Sweden/Norway) in the Swedish capital, were widely covered in the news. The latter even spurred a television documentary by public service broadcaster SVT (Swedish Television). Here, the experiences of the people in a small northern community, as Fincher, Daniel Craig and Rooney Mara came to the village for a few days of location work, was told very much in terms of global developments reaching even remote parts of sparsely populated northern Scandinavia. One of Stockholm's larger museums similarly launched The Millennium Tour, a guided walking tour through the locations used in the story.

From an industrial perspective, interviews with Swedish crew members were also published, stressing the productive process of knowledge transfer regarding, for instance, forms of organisation, division of work, problem solving, communication and means of efficiency. Working on such an unusually large (for Scandinavia) film resulted in useful production skills, treasured by the local filmmaking community (Cederskog 2011). Interestingly, little evidence of a discourse of cultural imperialism with regard to either production was palpable. Accordingly, no one pointed to the fact that all of the Wallander novels had already been adapted in Swedish. Similarly, the fact that a fairly recent version of the same story Fincher was about to tell already existed was obviously mentioned, but without much antipathy. A certain resentment regarding the American film's supposedly less convincing portrait of what was considered the novel's prevailing sense of feminist resignation was perhaps the one area where the Fincher film came up for criticism (Larsson 2014: 116–117).

The Indian film crew, the BBC and Sony were welcomed to various degrees as a fresh source of skilled jobs in a glamorous industry, as vehicles for local place marketing and as agents of recognition of Swedish culture and its visual qualities, signalling a breakthrough on a limited but nonetheless global stage. In sum, these various attitudes can be seen as a symptomatic Scandinavian response to what sociologist David Hesmondhalgh has proposed about how the "cultural industries have moved closer to the centre of the economic action in many countries and across much of the world" (2013: 2).

However, there have also been less forgiving attitudes toward recent developments within the audio-visual production sector, what can be called a certain resistance to globalisation. Of late, a few Scandinavian productions have started to migrate abroad, mainly to be shot in the Baltic countries or in Eastern Europe, in places such as Prague, Budapest and Sofia. This is of course due to the fact that this practice reduces production costs. These films and television series—for instance the mainly Norwegian *Kon-Tiki* (2012, Norway/UK/Germany/Sweden/Malta/Denmark, Joachim Rønning and Espen Sandberg), the mainly Danish *Flammen & Citronen* (Flame and Citron, 2008, Denmark/Germany/Norway/France/Sweden/Finland/Czech Republic, Ole Christian Madsen), the television series *1864* (2014–, Denmark/Norway/Sweden/Germany, Ole Bornedal) and the mainly Swedish *Den allvarsamma liken* (A Serious Game, 2016, Sweden,

Pernilla August)—have all been produced on a certain scale as runaway productions in locations where labour and services are less expensive than in Scandinavia. Moreover, with tax breaks or various forms of financial incentive, production costs are further diminished as a result of using these locations. Consequently, these productions could only be made on location in Scandinavia on a less ambitious scale or not at all. This, obviously, is opportunistic transnationalism in its most crystalline form.

Until very recently, when Norway finally subsumed, the Scandinavian countries did not participate in the contest of enticing runaway audio-visual production through tax breaks or other forms of economic incentives (Rossing Jensen 2015). Such incentives have obviously been introduced in many European territories. This so-called "subsidy race" has been under investigation by the EU Commission (EAO 2014: 10). As a result of the increasing number of Scandinavian runaways, however, calls for the introduction of incentives have emerged. Consequently, in the last few years, people within the film business and particularly those attached to regional film funds have attempted to influence the national government in the direction of supplying schemes that would make production in Sweden more attractive. At the 2015 Cannes film festival, regional film fund Film Väst accordingly presented a report, written by the British consultancy firm Olsberg-SPI but financed by the fund, which called for the introduction of incentives (Olsberg-SPI 2015).

Another way of attempting to keep domestic production at home and, on occasion, attracting international shoots, is of course film funds. When public film funds were set up in Sweden in the 1990s, and later to a lesser extent in Norway and Denmark, they were swiftly able to attract a majority of the domestic production as well as several of von Trier's productions by supplying approximately 10–25 per cent of the budget (Hedling 2010a: 335). Similarly, a film fund was started in Copenhagen 2013 in an attempt to counter the drift of productions away from the Danish capital. Beside domestic productions and Scandinavian television series, the fund has so far additionally been able to attract part of the shoot of the comparatively high profile, international production *The Danish Girl* (2015, USA/UK/Denmark/Belgium/Japan, Tom Hooper).

Compared to tax incentives, however, the strength of film funds appears limited. They simply do not seem to have the means to attract the kind of films made in Europe's runaway centres such as London, Berlin, Prague and Budapest. For now, at least, Scandinavia consequently appears somewhat on the margins as a European film production location and as a film community and there is certainly the risk of ever more of its domestic production becoming runaways. Voluntarily or not, film funds and production service providers in Scandinavia have had to become aware of what has been termed "the unstable and unequal partnership between a footloose international production economy and situated local actors and intermediaries" (Goldsmith and O'Regan 2005). In the context of such a global situation, it is difficult to predict the future geographical developments of a comparatively small film production environment in terms other than a continuation and expansion of the trends exhibited over the past few years.

Conclusion

To return to *The Girl*, the film is by far the greatest success in terms of international audiences that Scandinavian film has experienced during the last few decades. Moreover, films in the same vein such as *Hodejegerne* (Headhunters, 2011, Norway/Denmark/Germany, Morten Tyldum) and a number of television series of the Nordic Noir variety have noticeably registered with spectators outside of the Scandinavian region. Similarly, in terms of critical acclaim, reviews and festival awards, we can also observe a concurrent increase in interest, especially in Danish cinema (Elsaesser 2005: 14). Dogme 95, the maverick figure of Lars von Trier, regular domestic market shares of 25 per cent and more, as well as internationally recognised actors such as Nikolaj Coster-Waldau and Mads Mikkelsen have been interpreted as signs of a particularly vital, domestic film culture, ever ready to renew itself.

All of these achievements, however, can be questioned in a number of ways. First, the aforementioned examples can be seen as just the small tip of an iceberg, the atypical outcomes of a body of work that for the most part may be regarded as mediocre and not very attractive to audiences. Second, the accomplishments have seemingly not translated into any of the Scandinavian film industries becoming less dependent on public support. In fact, these film industries very much remain a benefits culture and, if on-going discussions are anything to go by, will continue to be so for the foreseeable future. Third, the relative international success of the Nordic Noir titles has been called into question. In relation to its theatrical run in the US, *The Girl* has been described as "effectively a low-budget film in the US context [. . .] when the film travels across the Atlantic, it arguably transforms into an upmarket art film, screening primarily in urban centres and college towns rather than ubiquitously at suburban multiplexes" (Stenport and Traylor 2015: 80). Similarly, the same film's performance compared to Fincher's remake in the UK was also commented on in slightly critical terms: "It was successful *for a foreign language film* and, to some extent, because it emulated the conventions of Hollywood" (Mazdon 2015: 209, italics in the original). In the same vein, it has been remarked that while "the increasing transnational distribution and reception of Nordic Noir represents an indisputable advance [. . .] the reception, particularly in the US and the UK, testifies to a situation where the effect of cultural discount still lingers on" (Hedling 2014). In short, Scandinavian cinema can be said to be just as successful—or rather unsuccessful—as most non-English language cinemas on the international stage. Thus, it can, indeed, to a degree at least be seen as just another sub-set under the generic label of "World Cinema". Returning to Elsaesser's argument about the "negative qualifications associable with European cinema", several of these hold true even with regard to a film such as *The Girl* and to Scandinavian cinema in general. Government subsidies, Council of Europe directives, television co-production deals, cultural tourism and city branding indeed all matter greatly in getting projects under way. Occasionally, however, and contrary to Elsaesser claims, some of these films also speak to a public other than festival audiences, loyal cinephiles and university students.

References

Bergfelder, T. (2005) "National, Transnational or Supranational Cinema? Rethinking European Film", *Media, Culture, Society* 27 (3): 315–331.

Berghahn, D. and Sternberg, C. (2010) "Locating Migrant and Diasporic Cinema in Contemporary Europe", in Berghahn, D. and Sternberg, C. (eds) *European Cinema in Motion: Migrant and Diasporic Film in Contemporary Europe*, London: Palgrave, 13–49.

Bondebjerg, I. and Redvall, E. N. (2013) "Transnational Scandinavia? Scandinavian Film Culture in a European and Global Context", in Palacio, M. and Türschmann, J. (eds) *Transnational Cinema in Europe*, Zürich and Berlin: Lit Verlag, 127–145.

Byg, B. and Torner, E. (2013) "Divided Dirigisme: Nationalism, Regionalism, and Reform in the German Film Academies", in Hjort, M. (ed.) *The Education of the Filmmaker in Europe, Australia, and Asia*, New York: Palgrave Macmillan, 105–126.

Cederskog, G. (2011) "När jag mötte Hollywood ..." [When I Met Hollywood ...], *Dagens Nyheter*, 20 December, www.dn.se/kultur-noje/film-tv/nar-jag-motte-hollywood-/.

EAO (2014) *The New Cinema Communication (Iris Plus 2014–1)*, Strasbourg: European Audiovisual Laboratory.

Elsaesser, T. (2005) *European Cinema: Face to Face with Hollywood*, Amsterdam: Amsterdam University Press.

—— (2015) "European Cinema into the Twenty-First Century: Enlarging the Context?", in Harrod, M., Liz, M., and Timoshkina, A. (eds) *The Europeanness of European Cinema: Identity, Meaning, Globalization*, London: I.B. Tauris, 17–32.

Goldsmith, B. and O'Regan, T. (2005) *The Film Studio: Film Production in the Global Economy*, Lanham, MD: Rowman & Littlefield.

Harrod, M., Liz, M. and Timoshkina, A. (2015) "The Europeanness of European Cinema: An Overview", in Harrod, M., Liz, M. and Timoshkina, A. (eds) *The Europeanness of European Cinema: Identity, Meaning, Globalization*, London: I.B. Tauris, 1–16.

Hedling, O. (2010a) "The Regional Turn: Developments within Scandinavian Film Production", in Larsson, M. and Marklund, A. (eds) *Swedish Film: An Introduction and Reader*, Lund: Nordic Academic Press, 334–345.

—— (2010b) "Historien om ett brott. Kriminalfilmsserier som regionalt och panskandinaviskt mediekoncept", in Agger, G. and Waade, A. M. (eds) *Den skandinaviske krimi: Bestseller og blockbuster*, Göteborg: Nordicom, 129–143.

_____ (2014) "Notes on Nordic Noir as European Popular Culture", *Frames Cinema Journal*, http://framescinemajournal.com/article/notes-on-nordic-noir-as-european-popular-culture/: 201v214.

Hesmondhalgh, D. (2013) *The Cultural Industries* (3rd edn), London: Sage.

Higson, A. (1989) "The Concept of National Cinema", *Screen*, 30 (4): 36–47.

_____ (2015) "The Cultural Politics of European Cinema" (blog post), 3 July online, http://mecetes.co.uk/the-cultural-politics-of-european-cinema/

Hjort, M. (2005) *Small Nation, Global Cinema*, Minneapolis, MN: University of Minnesota Press.

—— (2009) "On the Plurality of Cinematic Transnationalism", in Ďurovičová, N. and Newman, K. (eds) *World Cinemas, Transnational Perspectives*, New York and Abingdon: Routledge, 12–33.

Iordanova, D. (2003) *Cinema of the Other Europe: The Industry and Artistry of East Central European Film*, London: Wallflower Press.

Jones, H. (2014) "Which Feature Films Travel within Europe? A report by Dr Huw Jones for the MeCETES team meeting. Presented at the University of Copenhagen, 14 March 2014", 3 July, www.academia.edu/7440414/Which_Feature_Films_Travel_within_Europe

Jones, H. D. (2015) "The Cultural and Economic Implications of UK/European Co-production", *Transnational Cinemas* 7 (1): 1–20.

Larsson, M. (2014) "En queerfeministisk utopi?: Sexualitet i Millenniumserien", in Hedling E. and Wallengren, A-K. (eds) *Den nya svenska filmen: Kultur, kriminalitet & kakafoni*, Stockholm: Atlantis, 111v126.

Mazdon, L. (2015) "Hollywood and Europe: Remaking *The Girl with the Dragon Tattoo*", in Harrod, M., Liz, M., and Timoshkina, A. (eds) *The Europeanness of European Cinema: Identity, Meaning, Globalization*, London: I.B. Tauris, 199–212.

Olsberg-SPI (2015) *A Production Incentive for Sweden*, 5 November, http://filmvast.se/wp-content/uploads/2015/05/A-Production-Incentive-for-Sweden-final-draft-2015-05-11.pdf.

Rossing Jensen, J. (2015) "Norway Introduces 25% Rebate for International Film and TV", *Cineuropa*, 8 October, http://cineuropa.org/nw.aspx?t=newsdetail2016-03-07. &l=en&did=299934.

SFI (2010) *Filmåret i siffror 2009*, Stockholm: Svenska Filminstitutet.

—— (2011) *Filmåret i siffror 2010*, Stockholm: Svenska Filminstitutet.

Stenport, A. W. and Traylor, G. (2015) "The Eradication of Memory: Film Adaptations and Algorithms of the Digital", *Cinema Journal* 55 (1): 74–94.

Vonderau, P. (2010) "Inga Lindström and the Franchising of Culture", in Hedling, E., Hedling, O. and M. Jönsson (eds) *Regional Aesthetics: Locating Swedish Media*, Stockholm: Kungliga biblioteket, 141–152.

12
BRITISH CINEMAS
Critical and historical debates

James Chapman

> As, geographically, Britain is poised between continents, not quite Europe, and very far from America, so from certain points of view the British cinema seems to hover between the opposite poles of France and Hollywood. Our directors and producers never or rarely have the courage to tackle, in an adult manner, the completely adult subject; yet they lack also the flair for popular showmanship that is characteristic of the American cinema.
>
> *(Anderson 1949: 113)*

Introduction

British cinema has always had a reputation as being somehow betwixt and between: on the one hand it lacks the artistic kudos of European—especially French and Italian—cinemas, while on the other hand it cannot match the zest and popular appeal of Hollywood. Jacques Rivette put it a different way when he remarked: "British cinema is a *genre* cinema, but one where the genres have no genuine roots [. . .] On the other hand it isn't an *auteur* cinema either, since none of them have anything to say" (quoted in Hillier 1985: 32). A consequence of this sense of being neither one thing nor the other is that much of the academic criticism of British cinema has often been couched in defensive terms: there is still a perceived need to make the case for studying British cinema. Hence the critical and historical discourses of British cinema studies have generally focused on the re-evaluation of directors, genres and periods in order to show that British cinema is a site where culturally significant films have been made.

Like all national cinemas, some of the debates around British cinema are culturally specific while others are more general issues common to most Western film industries. As an Anglophone cinema it is particularly affected by the presence of Hollywood: political and cultural concerns over the "Americanisation" of British audiences have been a consistent theme since the 1920s (Glancy 2014). The familiar debates that structure critical discourses around most non-US film industries—art cinema or entertainment cinema, *auteur* cinema or genre cinema, indigenous cinema or international cinema—have been overlaid in Britain with an often fiercely contested debate over questions of quality and taste that for a long time has determined which films are seen as representative of the national cinema. This chapter will focus on three areas that are central to understanding British cinema: the political economy of the film industry, especially the extent to which it is still appropriate to speak of a "British" film industry; the nature of British film culture, particularly the prominence of realism as the dominant aesthetic and how this has affected which films have been deemed culturally and artistically significant; and the role of British cinema as a vehicle of national projection in the construction—and latterly also the interrogation—of ideologies of "Britishness".

The political economy of the British film industry

America's presence in the British film industry extends back to the period before the First World War when US distributors embarked upon an expansionist strategy of overseas sales, and was consolidated by the 1920s when American films accounted for around 80 per cent of those shown in British cinemas (PEP 1952: 43). In contrast to the US film industry, which had integrated the practices of production, distribution and exhibition, the British industry was under-capitalised and fragmented. The British film industry never achieved the degree of vertical integration seen in the USA: the Associated British Picture Corporation (founded in 1933) and the Rank Organization (from the early 1940s) were the only two British companies operating as combined producer–distributor–exhibitors on the model of the US "majors" and even then only Rank (for a relatively brief period in the mid-1940s) positioned itself as in competition with Hollywood in the international market (Street 2002). American distributors have accounted for the lion's share of the British market since the interwar period, while the institutional links between British distributors and Hollywood have meant that American films have generally been favoured at the expense of the domestic variety.

The British production sector has historically experienced periods of boom and bust: a pattern emerges whereby occasional high-profile successes have led to over-production and consequent heavy losses. The Anglophone Hungarian producer Alexander Korda was the first to make a breakthrough in the international market during the sound era with his historical drama *The Private Life of Henry VIII* (1933, UK, Alexander Korda). The film's success prompted Korda to embark upon an ambitious production strategy with a cycle of increasingly expensive films that were notable for their cultural and aesthetic ambition but failed to replicate the original success: hence Korda was forced to scale back his production activities and sell the studio he founded (Denham) to his rival J. Arthur Rank. The Rank Organization in turn set its sights on the world market at the end of the Second World War and tried to out-Hollywood Hollywood in the production of "prestige" films such as *The Red Shoes* (1947, UK, Michael Powell and Emeric Pressburger) and *Hamlet* (1948, UK, Laurence Olivier); but the critical kudos it gained from backing such relatively high-brow fare did not make up for the losses sustained in its production programme and accordingly Rank was forced into a policy of cost-cutting and retrenchment. Other independent producers, including Woodfall Films in the 1960s, Lord Grade in the 1970s and Goldcrest in the 1980s, have similarly failed to sustain ambitious programmes. Grade's *Raise the Titanic!* (1980, UK/USA, Jerry Jameson) and Goldcrest's *Revolution* (1985, UK/Norway, Hugh Hudson) both suffered losses heavy enough to sink the companies.

The economic instability of the British production sector has brought about different strategies for supporting it from government. The Cinematograph Films Act of 1927 was the first instance of state intervention: it was a protectionist measure that introduced a minimum "quota" of British films mandatory for all exhibitors and distributors. The impetus behind the Act—popularly known as the Quota Act—was both economic (to boost British production) and cultural (to promote the treatment of British subjects and themes rather than leaving the screen representation of Britain in the hands of Hollywood). The quota remained in force in one form or another until the early 1980s when it fell foul of the free-market doctrine of the

Conservative government of Margaret Thatcher. The other major official measures to bolster the industry came from the Labour government of the late 1940s. In 1949 the National Film Finance Corporation (NFFC) was set up to assist producers in raising production finance. The NFFC provided so-called "end money" that allowed producers to raise capital via bank loans and advances from distributors: in total it assisted over 750 films until it was abolished in 1985 (Street 1997: 16). The Eady Levy was a further attempt to assist the domestic industry: this was a levy on sales of cinema tickets in order to create a fund that was then shared among producers and distributors in relation to the box-office returns of their films. It amounted in effect to a subsidy for box-office success and it drew criticism for the fact that American companies were among the chief beneficiaries: it too was abolished in 1985.

The post-war period saw profound changes in the political economy of the British film industry. Indeed, the idea of a genuinely "British" industry had been largely eroded by the end of the 1950s as wholly British-owned producers such as Ealing Studios wound down and more films were produced with American investment. Hollywood studios had been investing in British production since the 1930s—MGM set up its own British studio in 1937—but this practice became more common after the Second World War when a combination of factors including a favourable exchange rate following the devaluation of Sterling in the late 1940s and the subsidies available via the Eady Levy encouraged the trend for so-called "runaway" productions shot overseas as nominally domestic films (Stubbs 2009). The production ecologies of such runaways were varied: they ranged from co-productions between British and American producers such as *The Third Man* (1949, UK/USA, Carol Reed) and *The African Queen* (1951, UK/USA, John Huston) to films that were to all intents and purposes top-line Hollywood films made in British studios by the British subsidiaries of US studios such as Disney's *Treasure Island* (1950, UK/USA, Bryon Haskin), Warner's *Captain Horatio Hornblower, RN* (1951, UK/USA, Raoul Walsh) and MGM's *Ivanhoe* (1952, UK/USA, Richard Thorpe). Columbia's *The Bridge on the River Kwai* (1957, UK/USA, David Lean), *The Guns of Navarone* (1961, UK/USA, J. Lee Thompson) and *Lawrence of Arabia* (1962, UK/USA, David Lean) were essentially international pictures that just happened to be produced by British companies even though in some cases they were shot largely overseas. In the 1960s United Artists—which depended upon independent producers for all of its product—led the way in British production when it backed a number of successful British films including *Tom Jones* (1963, USA, Tony Richardson) and the James Bond series. The Bond films, which began with *Dr. No* (1962, UK, Terence Young), represent the archetypal Anglo-American production alliance in their combination of British cultural capital (the source novels of Ian Fleming and most of the technicians involved in making the films, which have usually been based at Pinewood Studios) and US dollars. By the end of the 1960s it was estimated that 90 per cent of the production finance for British films came from America (Walker 1974: 16).

The 1960s was a boom period for British cinema when the phenomenon of "Swinging London" attracted foreign *auteurs* including François Truffaut (*Fahrenheit 451*, 1965, UK), Roman Polanski (*Repulsion*, 1965, UK) and Michelangelo Antonioni (*Blow-Up*, 1966, UK) to make films in Britain. However, the apparent renaissance of British filmmaking in the 1960s could not disguise the fact that the long-term trends in the British film industry since the Second World War were the decline of cinema attendances and the contraction of the production sector. Annual cinema attendances had declined steadily for a decade following their peak of 1,635 million in 1946 but had still remained above pre-war levels until the end of the 1950s when they experienced a precipitous decline with half the cinema-going audience disappearing between 1956 (1,101 million per annum) and 1960 (500 million per annum) (Wood 1980). As elsewhere, the reasons for the decline of cinema-going were complex and cannot be explained solely by the rise of television (though that was undoubtedly a major factor): they also included changing patterns of leisure and consumption, and the decline of inner cities where most cinemas were located. A consequence of declining cinema attendances (and hence diminishing revenues) was the contraction of the production sector which by the 1980s had shrunk to its smallest size since the mid-1920s.

At the same time as encouraging American investment in the production sector, however, the British film industry has also looked to collaborate with European partners. The first example of this was the "Film Europe" movement of the late 1920s: a series of informal agreements between different European studios that saw the exchange of personnel—Alfred Hitchcock, for example, directed his first two pictures in Germany in 1925–1926—and the production of multiple-language features such as E. A. Dupont's stagey early talking picture *Atlantic* (1929, UK). The "Film Europe" movement was an attempt to counter the economic and cultural hegemony of Hollywood by pooling the resources of under-nourished national cinemas: it flourished briefly but fell apart following the arrival of the talkies—"polyglot" multiple-language films proved too expensive to recoup their costs—and the rise of European Fascism which promoted more narrowly nationalistic and highly ideological film cultures than the idealistic internationalism of "Film Europe" (Higson and Maltby 1999). European co-productions were scarce during the 1930s but they re-emerged after the Second World War when Britain made bilateral co-production agreements with Italy, France and the Federal Republic of Germany. The Cinematograph Films Act of 1960 established a framework whereby co-productions could be classed as British quota pictures.

Britain's belated entry into the European Economic Community (EEC) in 1973 saw co-productions with European partners expand significantly, though some films, such as the espionage thriller *Permission to Kill* (1975, UK/Austria/USA, Cyril Frankel), attracted the derisory label of "Europuddings". From the late 1980s, however, the European Commission launched a number of initiatives to support filmmaking across the EEC and its successor the European Union (EU). Ken Loach, Britain's most critically (if not commercially) acclaimed filmmaker of the 1990s and 2000s, directed a series of low-budget realist dramas including *Riff-Raff* (1991, UK), *Land and Freedom* (1995, UK/Spain/Germany/Italy/France), *Carla's Song* (1996, UK/Spain/Germany) and *The Wind That Shakes the Barley* (2006, Ireland/UK/Germany/Italy/Spain/France/Belgium/Switzerland), all of which were supported by EU funding. At the other end of the scale Britain's most successful independent producer of the 1990s, Working Title Films, responsible for major box-office hits such as *Four Weddings and a Funeral* (1994, UK, Mike Newell) and *Notting Hill* (1999, UK/USA, Roger Mitchell), was a subsidiary of the Dutch media conglomerate PolyGram. Indeed, it might be argued that British cinema was never more "European" than it was during this period: Loach's films, in particular, were held in high esteem by European critics and won major prizes at the Cannes, Venice and Berlin film festivals. It remains to be seen what the consequences will be for British cinema of the United Kingdom's decision in 2016 to leave the European Union.

The contemporary British film industry resembles many other medium-sized national cinemas in so far as distribution and exhibition are dominated by multinationals operating on a global scale and the domestic production sector now more resembles the cottage industry of the early years of cinema than the golden age of the Rank Organization. It is an industry where occasional major successes—including Working Title's Hugh Grant-starring romantic comedies and 'heritage' films such as *Elizabeth* (1998, UK, Shekhar Kapur) and *The King's Speech* (2011, UK/USA/Australia, Tom Hooper)—disguise the fact that many British films fail to secure a full theatrical release. And the definition of what constitutes a British film has become increasingly blurred so that a mainstream Hollywood vehicle such as the swashbuckling fantasy *Pirates of the Caribbean: On Stranger Tides* (2011, USA/UK, Rob Marshall) met the British Film Institute's "cultural test" of a British film, while the science fiction drama *Gravity* (2013, UK/USA, Alfonso Cuarón) was claimed by the British media as a British film on account of its special effects work having been done in Britain. The increasing fluidity over how a national cinema can be defined was summed up thus by the veteran director Lewis Gilbert: "You should be able to define a British film in the same way you can define a British Premier League football team—one where 60% of the players are foreign" (*Screen International*, 8 January 1999: 32).

British film culture and questions of quality and taste

The dominant mode or style of British cinema has been realism: this has been the preferred aesthetic of many British filmmakers and critics. Hence the most acclaimed filmmaking practices in British cinema history have been the documentary movement (especially during the 1930s and 1940s) and social-realist feature films such as the "New Wave" cinema of the late 1950s/early 1960s—exemplified by *Room at the Top* (1959, UK, Jack Clayton), *Saturday Night and Sunday Morning* (1960, UK, Karel Reisz), *The Loneliness of the Long Distance Runner* (1962, UK, Tony Richardson) and *This Sporting Life* (1963, UK, Lindsay Anderson)—and the work of directors such as Ken Loach and Mike Leigh. It is impossible to exaggerate the significance attached to the documentary movement in British cinema history. Documentary—associated principally with a group of filmmakers who clustered around the austere Scots Presbyterian John Grierson in the 1930s—was seen as a socially purposeful film practice committed to portraying the real lives of ordinary people that was qualitatively different from the fictions of Hollywood or the British studios. The post-war Arts Enquiry (a survey on behalf of the Dartington Hall Trustees written by members of the documentary movement) asserted unequivocally that "documentary is Britain's outstanding contribution to the film" (Arts Enquiry 1947: 11). Although it has since been pointed out that documentary itself was a relatively marginal mode of film practice at the time, whose audiences were on the whole quite small (Swann 1989), it has nevertheless exerted an influence on British film culture out of all proportion to its popular appeal. The influence of documentary can be seen in the films of Ealing Studios—often claimed as the most quintessentially British studio of all—and in the cycle of popular war movies during the 1950s such as *The Cruel Sea* (1953, UK, Charles Frend) and *The Dam Busters* (1955, UK, Michael Anderson) which exemplified a merger between the narrative conventions of the feature film on the one hand and the style and technique of documentary on the other.

John Ellis (1996) has shown how the preference for realism emerged during and after the Second World War—often characterised as British cinema's "golden age"—which he sees as a critical project to support the development of a British "quality" cinema distinct from the artificial glamour of Hollywood. The dominant critical discourse of the 1940s—exemplified by broadly "middle-brow" film critics such as C. A. Lejeune (*The Observer*), Dilys Powell (*The Sunday Times*), William Whitebait (*The New Statesman*), Richard Winnington (*News Chronicle*) and Arthur Vesselo (*Sight and Sound*)—promoted an idea of "quality" cinema based on realist narratives and aesthetics. The overwhelming preference was for films with unsensational stories, believable characters and a sober, pared-down visual style such as *This Happy Breed* (1944, UK, David Lean), *The Way to the Stars* (1945, UK, Anthony Asquith) and *Brief Encounter* (1945, UK, David Lean). There was also a critical investment in quality literary adaptations that showcased the creative imagination of British filmmakers, such as Laurence Olivier's *Henry V* (1944, UK) and David Lean's *Great Expectations* (1946, UK) and *Oliver Twist* (1948, UK).

It is no coincidence that ever since the 1940s, the two genres most associated with "quality" British cinema have been the social-realist drama and the classic literary adaptation.

The preference for realism has had important consequences for the historiography of British cinema. The standard histories of British cinema have on the whole privileged periods and movements when realism has been in the ascendancy, particularly the Second World War and the new wave—which, like its French counterpart, flowered briefly, emerging at the end of the 1950s and generally held to have run its course by 1963—but have neglected other film styles and genres characterised by non-realism or fantasy. The most persistent metaphor of recent British film historiography has been the idea of the "lost continent"—a term coined by Julian Petley to describe "the repressed side of British cinema, a dark, disdained thread weaving the length and breadth of that cinema, crossing authorial and generic boundaries, sometimes almost entirely invisible, sometimes erupting explosively, always received critically with fear and disapproval" (Petley 1986: 98). The "lost continent" represents the disrespectable side of British cinema—exemplified by *film noir*-style thrillers, horror movies and low-brow comedies such as the *Carry On* series—in contrast to the respectable world of documentary and prestigious adaptations of Charles Dickens or Jane Austen.

A critical project of British film studies over recent decades has been the exploration of this "lost continent". The chief beneficiaries of this historical revisionism have been once-popular but critically despised genres such as the Gainsborough costume melodramas of the mid-1940s—exemplified pre-eminently by *The Wicked Lady* (1945, UK, Leslie Arliss)—and the Hammer horror cycle beginning with *The Curse of Frankenstein* (1957, UK, Terence Fisher) and *Dracula* (1958, UK, Terence Fisher). The Gainsborough melodramas are now championed for their transgressive gender politics and for flaunting the conventions of visual authenticity in their flamboyant and expressive mise-en-scène which mobilises the past for symbolic effect rather than being tied to a strict discourse of historical authenticity (Harper 1994; Cook 1996). And Hammer horror has been claimed both as a distinctively British genre with (contrary to Rivette) genuine cultural roots in the tradition of English Gothic literature (Pirie 1973) and as a site for exploring changing social and sexual mores that anticipated the cultural revolution of the 1960s (Hutchings 1993).

The exploration of the "lost continent" of British cinema has also brought about the critical rehabilitation of filmmakers such as Michael Powell and Ken Russell, disregarded for what the critical orthodoxy regarded as their melodramatic excess and flamboyant visual style. Powell is the filmmaker whose reputation has undergone the fullest reassessment. The conventional account of Powell's career saw it as a gradual trajectory from the documentary-influenced style of films such as *The Edge of the World* (1937, UK) and the wartime propaganda features *49th Parallel* (1941, UK) and *One of Our Aircraft is Missing* (1942, UK) to the allegorical fantasy of *A Matter of Life and Death* (1946, UK)—which Richard Winnington described as "even farther away from the essential realism and true business of the British movie than their two recent films *I Know Where I'm Going* and [*A*] *Canterbury Tale*" (Winnington 1949: 69)—the melodrama of *Black Narcissus* (1947, UK) and the extreme stylisation of *The Tales of Hoffmann* (1951, UK), and finally culminating in the sordid psycho-sexual horror of *Peeping Tom* (1960, UK) that provoked such a hostile backlash from the critics that it was blamed for ending Powell's career. Yet, following decades of sympathetic reassessment (Christie 1985; Moor 2005), a new orthodoxy has emerged that casts Powell as one of British cinema's great visual stylists and (along with his writing partner Emeric Pressburger) as one of its most visionary filmmakers, while *Peeping Tom* is now understood as a serious examination of emotional repression (in its way a critique of the traditional style of British films) and as a metaphor for the voyeuristic impulse of the filmmaking process.

British cinema and the projection of Britishness

The principal ideological project of British cinema throughout much of its history has been the projection of national identity (Richards 1997). The potential value of film as a medium of national projection was recognised from early in its history. This idea informed the debate around the Cinematograph Films Act of 1927 and was the subject of Stephen Tallents's highly influential pamphlet *The Projection of England* (1932) in which he argued that "we must master the art of national projection and must set ourselves to throw a fitting presentation of England upon the world's screens" (Richards 1984: 248). This became the self-appointed role of the leading British producers of the 1930s and 1940s. Alexander Korda's London Film Productions, for example, produced a series of expensively mounted historical/costume films such as *The Scarlet Pimpernel* (1934, UK, Harold Young) and *Fire Over England* (1937, UK, William K. Howard), while its triptych of British Empire films—*Sanders of the River* (1935, UK, Zoltan Korda), *The Drum* (1938, UK, Zoltan Korda) and *The Four Feathers* (1939, UK, Zoltan Korda)—sought to present the imperial project as a progressive civilizing mission that brought British values to the rest of the world. Michael Balcon followed a similar path during his period as head of production at the Gaumont-British Picture Corporation, producing films such as *The Iron Duke* (1934, UK, Victor Saville) and *Rhodes of Africa* (1936, UK, Berthold Viertel and Geoffrey Barkas), though when he moved to Ealing Studios at the end of the decade he became more associated with films that poked gentle fun at the British character. In particular, the postwar cycle of Ealing comedies—including *Passport to Pimlico* (1949, UK, Henry Cornelius), *Whisky Galore!* (1949, UK, Alexander Mackendrick), *The Lavender Hill Mob* (1951, UK, Charles Crichton) and *The Titfield Thunderbolt* (1953, UK, Charles Crichton)—characterised the British people as a nation of eccentrics. Balcon averred that "the comedies reflected the country's mood, social condition and aspirations" (Balcon 1969: 158). They are acclaimed for their celebration of community action (*Passport to Pimlico, Whisky Galore!*) but at the same time have been criticised for their nostalgic conservatism (*The Titfield Thunderbolt*).

The projection of nationhood is of course always ideologically charged: national identity is itself an ideological construct and its meaning in film has often been contested. Nowhere is this more evident than in the cycle of "heritage" films that have divided critics over their representations of class and nation. The heritage cycle—it is largely a critical term rather than one that has any currency in the film industry itself—comprises costume dramas of the 1980s and 1990s such as *A Passage to India* (1984, UK/USA, David Lean), *A Room With A View* (1986, UK/USA, James Ivory), *Maurice* (1987, UK, James Ivory), *Howards End* (1992, UK/Japan/USA, James Ivory) and *The Remains of the Day* (1993, UK/USA, James Ivory). All but the first were made by the producer-director team of Ismail Merchant (Indian) and James Ivory (American)—again demonstrating the fluidity of the concept of the national in contemporary British cinema—and all but the last were adapted from the novels of E. M. Forster. With their languid pace and highly pictorialist visual style, these films belong squarely within the tradition of the quality literary adaptation. Yet they have sharply divided opinion. For their critics, heritage films are nostalgic and backward-looking: they employ their period trappings as a means of distracting audiences from real social problems. Hence Andrew Higson argues that the films "construct such a delightfully glossy visual surface that the ironic perspective and the narrative of social criticism diminish in their appeal for the spectator" (Higson 1993: 120). Jeffrey Richards, however, regards this critique as "short-sighted" and argues that the films "are profoundly subversive" in so far as "they provide a continuing and comprehensive critique of the ethic of restraint, repression and the stiff upper lip" that has traditionally been seen as a defining characteristic of British national identity (Richards 1997: 169).

It would be fair to say the projection of Britain in British films was often not a very realistic one. A frequent complaint during the 1930s was that too many British films were West End dramas or Art Deco musicals and that the working classes (a group that made up the majority of the cinema-going public) were largely absent except as comedy caricatures. As John Grierson complained in 1932:

> It is not satisfactory to face the world with British films which are, in fact, provincial charades of one single square mile within the Empire [...] There is an unknown England beyond the West End, one of industry and commerce and the drama of English life within it, which is barely touched.
>
> *(Richards 1984: 245)*

It was left to documentary to explore this "unknown England" in short films such as *Industrial Britain* (1931, UK, Robert Flaherty) and *Night Mail* (1935, UK, Harry Watt and Basil Wright). Excursions by feature films outside the London metropolis were rare until the New Wave filmmakers adopted the practice of shooting on location around the factories and terraced houses of northern industrial towns: even *Love on the Dole* (1941, UK)—John Baxter's film of Walter Greenwood's Depression-era novel—was shot largely in the studio. It is probably fair to say that the films of the British New Wave were the first to put Grierson's "unknown England" on the screen in all its grim and unfettered glory.

The increasingly fragmented nature of the film industry in Britain over recent decades has seen the emergence of more regionally diverse filmmaking practices. This process began with the setting up of regional filmmaking collectives such as Amber Films of Newcastle (1969), the Edinburgh Film Workshop (1977), the Birmingham Film and Video Workshop (1981) and the Derry Film and Video Collective (1984) which adopted alternative documentary practices and positioned themselves outside the institutional production and distribution structures of the mainstream film industry. Amber's *Seacoal* (1985, UK, Murray Martin and Amber Production Team)—a one-off venture into fictional feature film production albeit one that was based on actual experiences—exemplifies a practice of regionally specific filmmaking that bears favourable comparison with acclaimed television dramas such as the BBC's *The Boys from the Blackstuff* (1981, UK). Since the 1980s the introduction of regional government subsidies (the Scottish Film Production Fund was created in 1982, for example) and the advent of Channel 4 (the fourth terrestrial television channel which began broadcasting in 1982 with a mandate for "alternative" provision) provided a stimulant for independent filmmakers. The emergence of small-scale but culturally distinct filmmaking traditions in Scotland, Wales and Northern Ireland has challenged the hegemony of the once-dominant English/British cinema. These traditions exemplify Stephen Crofts's definition of regional cinemas existing both within and as alternatives to a national cinema (Crofts 1993: 57). Northern Ireland further exemplifies a sub-state cinema caught between two alternative national cinemas: it can be seen as a part of both British cinema and Irish cinema. Scottish cinema has been the most visible through the films of writer-directors such as Bill Forsyth and Bill Douglas. The international profile of Scottish cinema received a major boost in the 1990s with the success of *Shallow Grave* (1994, UK, Danny Boyle) and *Trainspotting* (1996, UK, Danny Boyle) (Figure 12.1).

Another consequence of the fragmentation of the film industry in Britain has been the greater visibility for hitherto marginalised social groups. Again this process began through the film collective movement, exemplified by groups such as the London Women's Film Group (1973), the Black (Afro-Caribbean) collective Ceddo (1981), Asian collective Retake (1982) and the Black Audio Film Collective (1984). The breakthrough for filmmakers from ethnic

Figure 12.1 The international profile of Scottish cinema received a major boost in the 1990s with the success of *Trainspotting* (1996, UK, Danny Boyle). ©Channel Four Films/Figment Films/ The Noel Gay Motion Picture Company.

minority backgrounds came through figures such as the British-Pakistani writer Hanif Kureishi (*My Beautiful Laundrette*, 1985, UK, Stephen Frears) and the Ghanaian-born documentarist John Akomfrah (*Handsworth Songs*, 1986, UK), though the most commercially successful director has been a British-Asian woman, Gurinder Chadha, whose films *Bhaji on the Beach* (1993, UK) and *Bend It Like Beckham* (2002, UK/Germany/USA) explore the hybridity of ethnic cultures in contemporary Britain in suggesting that it is possible to be both British and Asian. Chadha's most successful film has been *Bride & Prejudice* (2004, UK/USA/India), a delirious mixture of Jane Austen and the conventions of "Bollywood" that included funding from British, American and European sources. A tradition of women directors in British cinema can be traced back to the careers of Muriel Box and Wendy Toye in the 1950s, and to Mary Field and Jill Craigie in the documentary field, though perhaps only Sally Potter, through films such as *Thriller* (1979, UK) and *Orlando* (1993, UK/Russia/Italy/France/Netherlands), has succeeded in making overtly feminist films that have bridged the gap between the avant-garde and the mainstream.

Conclusion

The historical trajectory of British cinema has seen a transition from a hegemonic national cinema in the 1930s and 1940s—the period that marked the height of cinema-going as a social practice in Britain—to a more fragmented contemporary film culture characterised by its diversity and hybridity. The emergence of regional and other alternative film practices suggests that it is no longer appropriate to think in terms of one British cinema but rather of British *cinemas* in the plural. This also applies to the critical discourses: there is no longer a single critical construct of British cinema but rather a range of cinemas that allow space for fantasy and melodrama to coexist alongside the documentary-realist tradition within a national filmmaking tradition that need not be narrowly defined by one aesthetic practice. A film culture that includes talents as diverse as David Lean, Carol Reed, Ken Loach and John Akomfrah is not one that suggests a monolithic view of national identity. In fact, British cinema has arguably been one of the film cultures most open to—and certainly enriched by—exile and émigré filmmakers, from Alexander Korda in the 1930s to Ang Lee with *Sense and Sensibility* (1996, USA/UK) and Shekhar Kapur with *Elizabeth* (1998, UK). Some of the most acclaimed dissections of the English class system—including *The Servant* (1963, UK), *Accident* (1967, UK) and *The Go-Between* (1971, UK)—were by the exiled American director Joseph Losey. British cinema (in all its forms) need no longer be seen as caught between Hollywood and Europe but rather as a subject worth exploring—and celebrating—in its own right.

References

Anderson, L. (1949) "Alfred Hitchcock", *Sequence* 9: 113–123.

Arts Enquiry (1947) *The Factual Film: A Survey Sponsored by the Dartington Hall Trustees*, London: Geoffrey Cumberlege/Oxford University Press.

Balcon, M. (1969) *Michael Balcon Presents ... A Lifetime of Films*, London: Hutchinson.

Christie, I. (1985) *Arrows of Desire: The Films of Michael Powell and Emeric Pressburger*, London: Waterstone.

Cook, P. (1996) *Fashioning the Nation: Costume and Identity in British Cinema*, London: British Film Institute.

Crofts, S. (1993) "Reconceptualising National Cinema/s", *Quarterly Review of Film and Video* 14 (3): 49–67.

Ellis, J. (1996) "The Quality Film Adventure: British Critics and the Cinema 1942–1948", in Higson, A. (ed.), *Dissolving Views: Key Writings on British Cinema*, London: Cassell, 66–93.

Glancy, M. (2014) *Hollywood and the Americanization of Britain: From the 1920s to the Present*, London: I. B. Tauris.

Harper, S. (1994) *Picturing the Past: The Rise and Fall of the British Costume Film*, London: British Film Institute.

Higson, A. (1993) "Re-presenting the National Past: Nostalgia and Pastiche in the Heritage Film", in Friedman, L. (ed.) *British Cinema and Thatcherism: Fires Were Started*, London: UCL Press, 109–129.

Higson, A. and Maltby, R. (eds) (1999) *"Film Europe" and "Film Europe": Cinema, Commerce and Cultural Exchange, 1920–1939*, Exeter: University of Exeter Press.

Hillier, J. (ed.) (1985) *Cahiers du Cinéma Vol.1. The 1950s: Neo-Realism, Hollywood, New Wave*, Cambridge, MA: Harvard University Press.

Hutchings, P. (1993) *Hammer and Beyond: The British Horror Film*, Manchester: Manchester University Press.

Moor, A. (2005) *Powell & Pressburger: A Cinema of Magic Spaces*, London: I. B. Tauris.

Petley, J. (1986) "The Lost Continent", in Barr, C. (ed.) *All Our Yesterdays: 90 Years of British Cinema*, London: British Film Institute, 98–119.

Pirie, D. (1973) *A Heritage of Horror: The English Gothic Cinema, 1946–1973*, London: Gordon Fraser.

Political and Economic Planning (1952) *The British Film Industry: A Report on Its History and Present Organisation, with Special Reference to the Economic Problems of British Feature Film Production*, London: Political and Economic Planning.

Richards, J. (1984) *The Age of the Dream Palace: Cinema and Society in Britain 1930–1939*, London: Routledge & Kegan Paul.

—— (1997) *Films and British National Identity: From Dickens to "Dad's Army"*, Manchester: Manchester University Press.

Street S. (1997) *British National Cinema*, Abingdon and New York: Routledge

—— (2002) *Transatlantic Crossings: British Feature Films in the USA*, London: Continuum.

Stubbs, J. (2009) "The Eady Levy: A Runaway Bribe? Hollywood Production and British Subsidy in the Early 1960s", *Journal of British Cinema and Television* 6 (2): 1–20.

Swann, P. (1989) *The British Documentary Film Movement, 1926–1946*, Cambridge: Cambridge University Press.

Walker, A. (1974) *Hollywood, England: The British Film Industry in the Sixties*, London: British Film Institute.

Winnington, R. (1949) *Drawn and Quartered: A Selection of Weekly Film Reviews and Drawings*, London: The Saturn Press.

Wood, L. (ed.) (1980) *British Film Industry: A Reference Guide*, London: British Film Institute.

13

DEVELOPMENTS IN EASTERN EUROPEAN CINEMAS SINCE 1989

Elżbieta Ostrowska and Joanna Rydzewska

Introduction

At the 2016 Cannes Film Festival, Romania could boast the third largest number of films shown, after only the US and France. Out of its six entries, *Bacalaureat* (Graduation, 2016, Romania/France/Belgium) won its director Cristian Mungiu the Best Director Award, while *Câini* (Dogs, 2016, Romania/France/Bulgaria/Qatar) by Bogdan Mirică won the FIPRESCI Award (Zeitchik 2016). The 2016 Cannes story is only the latest in a series of successes for Romanian films over the past decade since Cătălin Mitulescu won the Palme d'Or for his short film *Traffic* (Romania) in 2004. In the subsequent four years—between 2005 and 2009—the five main prizes at the Cannes Film Festival went to Romanian films, solidifying their claim to be the next European movement—The Romanian New Wave (hereafter: RNW) as critics have termed it—after von Trier and Vinterberg's Dogme 95.

The success of Eastern European films at the arguably most prestigious European film festival is significant, given that as recently as 2000 not a single film was produced in Romania (Uricaru 2012: 427). The crisis of film production was endemic in the region in the 1990s following the break-up of the Soviet Bloc, which freed a number of states from Soviet domination but left them economically, politically and socially lagging behind the rest of Europe, and the film industry was no exception (Wood and Iordanova 2000; Iordanova 2002; Imre 2005). The lack of funding in the 1990s that followed the transformation from the communist state-owned system to the producer-driven free market drove Eastern European cinema near to collapse. It is the accelerated re-structuring of their financing model throughout the 1990s into an interface between national and transnational enterprise, however, that led to the Europeanisation of Eastern European films. At the time of writing, Eastern European films are sponsored by a host of European production companies, as in the case, for example, of the Paris-based Why Not Productions, which has recently produced both the award-winning *Graduation* and *Dupa dealuri* (Beyond the Hills, 2013, Romania/France/Belgium, Cristian Mungiu), but also such European arthouse hits as *De rouille et d'os* (Rust and Bone, 2012, France/Belgium, Jacques Audiard) and *I, Daniel Blake* (2015, UK/France/Belgium, Ken Loach). Nevertheless, the role of the national institutes has also been central in enabling the success of Eastern European films. Indeed, the Romanian Law of Cinematography introduced in 1999 (analysed below) was so successful that Poland introduced its own Act on Cinematography and created the Polish Film Institute in 2005, which led to the international success of such Polish films as *W imię* (In the Name of. . ., 2013, Poland, Małgorzata Szumowska), *Ida* (2013, Poland/Denmark/France/UK, Paweł Pawlikowski) and *Zjednoczone stany miłości* (United States of Love, Poland/Sweden, Tomasz Wasilewski). Identifying directorial talent through national funding, fostering films' transnational universal themes aimed at international arthouse audiences and international forms of distribution, including film festivals' visibility and international funding, and authorial freedom as a function of directors' own private production companies are all emblematic of the Romanian New Wave's success, and underpin a transformative financing model across Eastern Europe.

The example of Romania, on the one hand, illustrates how the break-up of the Soviet Bloc led to the increased diversification, localism and enhanced significance of national cinemas in Eastern Europe. On the other hand, it shows how the return to the national is countered by the creation of pan-European, post-national or indeed worldwide configurations fuelled by globalisation, the advancement of the neoliberal market economy, the expansion of new social media, and increased migration (Imre 2012: 2). In securing a place in the canon of (Western) European film movements, along with such well-established "moments" in national cinemas as German Expressionism, Italian Neo-Realism and the French New Wave, the Romanian New Wave (RNW) has inserted Eastern European cinema onto the contemporary Film Studies map of European cinema, from which it has too often been erased. The RNW thereby redraws the cultural map of Europe by moving the border eastwards, and questions the established axiology of the concepts of (Western) European and Eastern European cinema, where "European" has more often than not stood for certain privileged countries such as France, Germany or Italy (although the exact countries of European cinema can be difficult to establish without risking a debate). Given Eastern Europe and Eastern European cinema's entrenched real and perceived marginalisation, as a result of political isolation behind the Iron Curtain and their geographical location on the periphery of what has traditionally been regarded as Europe, the fact that Eastern European cinema is starting to achieve the same kind of recognition and inclusion as more westerly-located countries points to its increasing Europeanisation.

There is consequently a great need to reassess the position of Eastern European cinema. While its marginal and subordinate position has often been acknowledged in academic writing (Wood and Iordanova 2000; Iordanova 2003; Hames 2004; Imre 2005, 2012; Portuges and Hames 2013), including from a postcolonial perspective (Mazierska *et al.* 2013), a study of the ways in which Eastern European cinema has joined the European mainstream is long overdue. In order to redress this imbalance, one goal of this chapter is to argue that since around 2000 Eastern European cinema has become subject to accelerated processes of transnationalisation. Contrary to the received wisdom that the year 1989 was the watershed for the emergence of a new paradigm, this chapter proposes that the financial collapse of the Romanian film industry in 2000 and its subsequent industry developments that led to the rise of the Romanian New Wave after the year 2000 can be used as a lens for understanding the changes in Eastern European cinema more generally. A second more complex goal is to assert that there remains a discrepancy between reality and perception as, both inside and outside, Eastern Europe and its cinema are still viewed and treated as marginal and subordinate to the West.

This chapter will therefore look first at how historical and political events and European thought have shaped the idea of Eastern Europe and the concept of Eastern European cinema vis-à-vis the West, and the way the collapse of communism in 1989 and recent extension of the European Union have redefined the geographical reality of Eastern Europe and its cinemas, but not necessarily how they are perceived. Using postcolonial theory with an emphasis on production studies, the chapter then looks at continuity and change in Eastern European cinema across a trio of case studies that link pre-1989 isolation and marginalisation with current transnationalism. The section on the cinema of Béla Tarr analyses how a new industrial mode of co-production has given Tarr transnational opportunities and consequently facilitated a change of style of his films; the section on Eastern European female directors and actresses assesses how the transnational labour market has given real opportunities to this group, who nevertheless remain discriminated against in terms of representation on screen. The final section advances a definition of the Romanian New Wave as a European movement that has not been previously defined in a systematic way, and brings the Europeanisation and transnationalism of Eastern European cinema together.

Across the three case studies, this chapter argues that the main impetus for the new direction of Eastern European films comes from changes in the mode of production that had a profound impact, not only on the levels of yearly film production but also on the aesthetic and thematic preoccupations of films, and, most significantly, on access to foreign markets and distribution channels, following international co-financing and screening at film festivals.

The idea of Eastern Europe

The notion of "Eastern Europe" is by no means straightforward. As Larry Wolff argues in his seminal book, *Inventing Eastern Europe: The Map of Civilization on the Mind of the Enlightenment* (1994), it dates from the Enlightenment when Western intellectuals, travellers, and writers created a discourse about the eastern half of the continent in a manner similar to that of the Orient analysed by Edward Said. Consolidated over centuries, this mental map was "a paradox of simultaneous inclusion and exclusion, Europe but not Europe" (Wolff 1994: 7). These ambiguities became more complex after the Second World War when most of the countries identified as Eastern European formed the Eastern Bloc controlled by the Soviet Union. First, after 1961, the former Yugoslavia's affiliation with the Non-Aligned Movement provided relative independence from the Soviets. Then, terms such as "East Central Europe" and "Central Europe" were proposed which excluded the region made up of Poland, Czechoslovakia and Hungary as historically and culturally distinct from the rest of the Eastern Bloc, especially from the Balkan countries (Iordanova 2003; Hames 2004). With the realignments of 1989 and the break-up of Yugoslavia, the geopolitical borders between the West and East of Europe changed radically. In joining NATO in 1999 and the EU in 2004, Poland, along with Hungary, the Czech Republic and Slovakia, nominally shifted to "Europe". By contrast, the Balkan countries, especially those that were part of former Yugoslavia, were relegated to the European frontiers.

Given the ongoing political shifts of borders and membership of supranational entities such as the European Union and NATO, it is not easy to pinpoint the exact dividing line between Western and Eastern Europe today. Depending on how it is defined, Eastern Europe may now encompass as many as twenty or as few as four countries. Where the lines are drawn clearly has implications for how we study Eastern European cinema (Coates 2000; Hames 2004; Iordanova 2003, 2005; Imre 2012). Nevertheless, notwithstanding ongoing fluctuations of the notion of Eastern Europe, it is still firmly present in contemporary socio-political and cultural discourse. Although it disconcertingly echoes Western colonial hegemony, is associated with period of Soviet oppression, and operates within geopolitical processes of exclusion and inclusion, the category of Eastern Europe still identifies a distinct region within Europe which has a shared history and culture, including cinema.

The Eastern European mode of production in the 1990s: from state-subsidised to a producer-driven film production system

Commentators agree that the major change exerting a profound impact on the cinemas of the region in the 1990s was a move away from state subsidised and unit-based studio film production to a free market dominated by producers; this contributed to a significant drop in film production across the region (Wood and Iordanova 2000; Iordanova 2003). The move to a capitalist economy and revenues-based approach left some directors unable to readjust from their high-status as auteurs and national prophets, whose function was not just to entertain but to offer a direct intervention into historical reality. Others embraced opportunities to obtain international funding. The gap produced by the withdrawal of state funds was filled in the 1990s by pan-European funding bodies such as Eurimages (the Council of Europe's Fund), MEDIA (the European Community Programme), bilateral agreements between countries (especially with France), and a French programme aimed specifically at Eastern Europe: Fonds ECO (Fonds d'aide aux co-productions avec les Pays d'Europe Centrale et Orientale).

These funds had two immediate effects on Eastern European cinema. First, they facilitated integration and ensured the visibility of Eastern European auteurs, and second, they aligned Eastern European cinema with the global trend of free movement of creative personnel across borders (Jäckel 1998; Iordanova 2002). The ECO contributed to the making of sixty-five feature films between 1990 and 1997, furthering the careers of such established auteurs as the Romanian Lucian Pintilie with *Balanta* (The Oak, 1992, France/Romania), the Russian Vitali Kanievsky with *Samostoyatelnaya zhizn* (An Independent Life, 1992, UK/Russia/France) or Lithuania's Sarunas Bartas with *Few of Us* (1996, Portugal/France/Germany/Lithuania) (Jäckel 2003: 63). The ECO fund ended in 1996, mainly because several Eastern European film industries were showing signs of recovery (Jäckel 2003: 63). However, European international funds could also generate new problems, particularly for new talent, emphasising, as they have done, the persistence of authorship in Eastern European cinema. Specifically, the changes in the Eurimages schemes towards the end of the 1990s started to focus more on the commercial potential of the project and took into account the previous track-record of the director in allocating the funds. This favoured "established 'auteurs'" and created "an emerging class of internationally renowned [. . .] bankable 'auteurs'" from Eastern Europe (Iordanova 2002: 520). Béla Tarr is a good case in point.

The persistence of auteurism: Béla Tarr's cinematic journeys

Although for more than forty years Eastern European cinema developed under the strict control of communist states, a framework of national and auteur cinema shaped production throughout this time. After 1989 these auteurist and national tendencies became even more pronounced due to the disappearance of state control.

Béla Tarr is one of the most notable contemporary Eastern European film auteurs. In his monograph on the Hungarian filmmaker, András Bálint Kovács highlights the consistency of themes, characters and style throughout Tarr's career (2013: 1). However, while formal discipline and aesthetic minimalism characterise his whole oeuvre, his approach to the cinematic image and its relationship to reality has undergone an evolution as a result of international funding. His films from the late 1970s and 1980s, such as *Családi tüzfészek* (Family Nest, 1977, Hungary), *Szabadgyalog* (The Outsider, 1980, Hungary), *Panelkapcsolat* (The Prefab People, 1982, Hungary) and *Öszi almanac* (Almanac of the Fall, 1984, Hungary), depict the oppressive socio-political situation of Hungary in the era of late communism by means of specific cinematic strategies such as the predominance of close-ups and long takes. In his films from the late 1980s and early 1990s, such as *Kárhozat* (Damnation, 1987, Hungary) and *Sátántangó* (Satantango, 1994, Hungary/Germany/Switzerland), Tarr evokes the crisis and stagnation of late communism and the early post-communist period. He approaches his subject through a specific historical situation, yet simultaneously transforms it into a universal myth. Both films use monochrome photography, painterly compositions, and minimalistic mise-en-scène to diminish scenic realism and replace it with visual abstraction. This aesthetic is maintained in Tarr's last three films made in the 2000s, *Werckmeister harmóniák* (Werckmeister Harmonies, 2000, Hungary/Italy/Germany/France), *A londoni férfi* (The Man from London, 2007, Hungary/Germany/France) and *A torinói ló* (The Turin Horse, 2011, Hungary/France/Germany/Switzerland/USA), which he announced would be his last film.

Kovács considers the aesthetic evolution of Tarr's oeuvre to be a maturation of his style. However, this approach diminishes the significance of a thematic shift in his work, specifically, a gradual withdrawal from the topical and a turn towards the perennial. These thematic changes occurred precisely at a time when the Hungarian director was searching for new production opportunities, and reflect a more transnational sensibility. Tarr made his debut in the Balázs Béla Studio, a small filmmaking unit named after Eastern Europe's most famous film theorist that emerged in 1958 as a spontaneous initiative on the part of film students and young filmmakers, and that was later modestly supported by state funding. His subsequent projects, consisting of short films, TV plays, and feature films, received finance from the state film school, Hungarian television, Társulás studio (a film unit organised by another group of Hungarian filmmakers), and Mafilm, the biggest film production company in Hungary. Finally, for *Damnation* he secured finance from several sources not directly involved in film production. As Kovács emphasises, *Damnation* was the first Hungarian full-length feature produced outside of the state-regulated film industry (Kovács 2013: 10).

As his first independent production, *Damnation* offered Tarr much more artistic freedom and control, which resulted in substantial aesthetic refinement, and, consequently, led to his first

Figure 13.1 *Sátántangó* (Satantango, 1994, Hungary/Germany/Switzerland) marked the beginning of the transnational phase of Hungarian auteur Béla Tarr's career. ©Mozgókép Innovációs Társulás és Alapítvány/Von Vietinghoff Filmproduktion (VVF)/Vega Film.

international film-festival success. *Damnation* introduced three main novelties to Tarr's work: poetic dialogue, a setting that consisted of realistic components, mutually arranged in such a way as to create a "non-existent and completely set-like world", and, finally, complex camera movement coordinated with the composition (Kovács 2008:14). Following this, Tarr managed to secure international finance (including from Eurimages) for his next project, *Satantango*, a seven-and-a-half-hour film that marked the beginning of a transnational stage in his career (Figure 13.1). From that point on, all Tarr's films received support from various European sources, were distributed internationally, and achieved considerable success at film festivals.

While making *Satantango* and two later films, Tarr continued to work with his previous team, of whom Agnes Hranitzky was the most significant member. The cast were Hungarians who spoke their dialogue in their native language, and the local alcoholic drink, Palinka, played an important role, not merely as a simple realist scenic prop, but also as a metaphor for an existential crisis. Ultimately, in *Satantango* the vernacular becomes fragmented and de-contextualised, a directorial choice that moves it from the realm of the national into the transnational. The latter manifests itself either as a mosaic of vernacular cultures or as images of a humanity abstracted from their socio-political and cultural determinants.

The Turin Horse represents Tarr's final point in this trajectory. It features characters who are passive and who barely interact with socio-cultural reality and focuses on mundane and everyday rituals such as clothing, eating and cleaning, which are repeatedly shown in their real-time duration. Furthermore, the characters speak minimally and their dialogue does not propel the narrative. The visual, stripped of any local references, subordinates the verbal (Figure 13.2). Instead, *The Turin Horse* utilises intertextual references to Western art, for example paintings by Mantegna, Georges de La Tour and Vincent van Gogh, as if attempting to re-establish a symbolic link between Eastern and Western European cultures (see Pethő 2016; Quandt 2012). Likewise, the film's prologue, which recalls Friedrich Nietzsche's traumatic witnessing of a carthorse being whipped on the streets of Turin, inscribes the film firmly within the European philosophical tradition.

Figure 13.2 Non-places: a humanity abstracted from their socio-political and cultural determinants in *A Torinói Ló* (The Turin Horse, 2011, Hungary/France/Germany/Switzerland/USA, Béla Tarr). ©TT Filmmûhely/Vega Film/Zero Fiction Film/Movie Partners In Motion Film.

Tarr's late films de-emphasise geopolitical localities and replace these with non-places, as proposed by the French anthropologist Marc Augé (1995), or the Deleuzian "any-space-whatever" (Deleuze 1986: 105–126). This gradually changing use of space again marks a trajectory from the national to the transnational. His early works feature the claustrophobic spaces of typical communist housing projects, spaces that satisfy Augé's description of "places" being "relational, historical and concerned with identity" (1995: 77). In Tarr's films from the 2000s, by contrast, "non-places" predominate. Although Augé links these "non-places" with sites of global commerce, whereas Tarr's films are set exclusively in non-modern localities, neither evokes concrete or discrete identities. Ultimately, these films conjure the melancholic non-places of post-communism where endless repetition of everyday activities and gestures are withdrawn from both larger historical narratives and a recognisable geopolitical order. Transnationalism in Tarr's films is more about being "nowhere" than "everywhere". The fact that post-Wall Europe is a borderless space of free movement remains redundant for those who are both unable and unwilling to move anywhere.

Tarr's films from the 2000s transgress the limits of national Hungarian and Eastern European cinema, not only by means of specific textual strategies but also in terms of their mode of exhibition and distribution. As already mentioned, since *Damnation* his films have circulated in the film festival circuits, gaining significant attention from the international arthouse film audience. His success in these circles is perhaps because his films epitomise all the basic characteristics of a specific sub-genre of festival films: "seriousness/minimalism in vision and sound; their open and demanding narrative structures; their intertextuality [. . .] and, finally, their subject matter, including controversy as well as freedom" (Wong 2011: 68). Tarr's films have successfully participated in the European Film Festival network that provides space for the circulation of European art cinema. Unlike in the late 1950s and early 1960s, European art cinema does not function within the framework of national cinemas, but emerges as a transnational phenomenon. Tarr's artistic trajectory, while not unique, was until the end of the 1990s mostly open to well-established auteurs such as István Szabó or Krzysztof Kieślowski. After 2000, a younger generation of filmmakers began to emerge, including Polish Paweł Pawlikowski (*My Summer of Love*, 2004, UK), Ukrainian Myroslav Slaboshpytskyi (*Plemya* [The Tribe, 2014, Ukraine/Netherlands]), Hungarian Lásló Nemes (*Saul fia* [Son of Saul, 2015, Hungary]) along with a number of female directors discussed below.

Migrant Eastern European women behind and in front of the camera

New models of international financing and transnational mobility have created opportunities for Eastern European female personnel, actresses and directors, but they have not dismantled the Western representational regime, which still perceptually assigns Eastern Europe and especially Eastern European women a subordinate position. The postcolonial framework clearly highlights the binary power structure in representation, where the West still defines the East; however, it is countered by the global processes of mobility and the fragmentation of financing that enable Eastern European female directors to produce their own films and seek funding from national and international bodies.

Although this extra- and intra-textual mobility is by no means gender specific, female cinematic journeys vividly reflect the complex process of fluctuation within European identities and cinemas. Mark Betz's identification of the "wandering women" in European modernist cinema as "engaged in a quest for meaning [. . .] of [within] a changing Europe" may still be relevant in the post-communist era (2009: 95). As both subjects and objects of cinematic representation, the figure of the Eastern European "wandering woman" reveals deep fissures and cracks in the body of this supposedly "unified" Europe.

Cinematic images of Eastern European migrant women feature in post-1989 films made in both Eastern and Western European cinema, for example, *Prostytutki* (Prostitutes, 1997, Poland, Eugeniusz Priwieziencew), *A Szerencse lányai* (Daughters of Happiness, 1999, Poland/Germany/Hungary, Márta Mészáros), *Masz na imię Justine* (Your Name Is Justine, 2004, Poland/Luxembourg, Franco De Pena) and *La sconosciuta* (The Unknown Woman, 2006, Italy/France, Giuseppe Tornatore), *A mi madre le gustan las mujeres* (My Mother Likes Women, 2002, Spain, Daniela Féjerman and Inés París) or *Habitación en Roma* (Room in Rome, 2010, Spain, Julio Medem). Although the mobility of female characters constitutes "a broad representational continuum", this theme predominantly manifests itself in two opposing forms, the "traveller" and the "trafficked" (Engelen and Heuckelom 2013: x). In the latter case, a disenfranchised Eastern European woman, whose country is in the midst of an economic crisis engendered by the rampant implementation of Western capitalism, is either forced or lured to leave. She becomes a victim of capitalism as her body is used as an object of exchange. It is significant that Western European cinema features this negative variant of female mobility with more frequency than films made in Eastern Europe. These dual figures of the exploited female worker and the prostitute reveal economic and social inequalities in a "unified" and border-free Europe. They serve the purpose of political and social criticism and simultaneously demonstrate that the West/East division is still extant. The geopolitical order of "unified" Europe is presented as being implicitly hierarchical, with a stable "centre", the West, and a centrifugal "periphery", the East, a fact that ultimately reinforces ethnic stereotypes (the masculine variant being the violent Eastern European gangster).

The majority of films concerning victimised Eastern European women are made by (Western) male directors (Tarr 2010: 175). They often utilise the device of the inter-ethnic romance narrative. One of the best known of these is *Ondine* (2009, Ireland/USA, Neil Jordan) featuring Polish actress Alicja Bachleda-Curuś and Colin Farrell. It exploits the familiar motif of a "damsel in distress" who is ultimately saved by a (Western) man, a trope that reinforces both patriarchal and Western supremacy. Though performing in the role of a helpless Eastern European woman, Bachleda-Curuś is herself a truly cosmopolitan actress working in the film industries of her native Poland, various European countries and Hollywood. In turn, Katia Golubeva, a Russian–Lithuanian–French actress, epitomises international success and recognition in the arena of international art cinema due to her appearances in films directed by Bruno Dumont, Claire Denis and Leos Carax. Among other Eastern European actresses who have achieved significant transnational recognition are Lithuanian–Russian Ingeborga Dapkunajte, *Mission: Impossible* (1996, USA, Brian de Palma), and Serbian Branka Katić, *Captain America: The Winter Soldier* (2014, USA, Anthony Russo and Joe Russo). Although they personally and professionally move fluently across transnational cinematic space, these performers seem to experience a representational glass ceiling in that they are often type-cast in the roles of victimised and helpless Eastern European women.

Very few filmmakers have attempted to dismantle or subvert the cultural persistence and narrative attraction of the ethnically stereotyped Eastern European woman. Of these few, one of the most effective is Mimi Chakharova, a Bulgarian filmmaker living in the US. Her strategy in her film *The Price of Sex* (2011, USA/United Arab Emirates/Bulgaria/Moldova/Turkey), for example, is to use a form of investigative documentary to reveal the passivity and occasional complicity of Western law enforcement agencies in the trafficking of Eastern European women. Despite these sporadic attempts to resist the representational pattern of subjugated Eastern European female characters, they usually fit into Thomas Elsaesser's category of the "subnational", associated with categories such as "migrants", "refugees" and "asylum seekers", who constitute the very opposite of the supra-national cosmopolitan elite (2005: 116). These two valuing categories of "hyphenated nationals", as Elsaesser calls them, are useful tools with which to approach the issue of female cinematic mobility and uncover the postcolonial framework within which they operate. The films portray Eastern European women as "sub-nationals", given voice on screen by "supra-national" Eastern European female film professionals. Importantly, these actresses and directors do not work within the category of exilic or diaspora cinema but mostly engage with specific co-production projects (Iordanova 2010: 50). Thus they represent what Jane Mills calls "sojourner cinema", that is, work "made by filmmakers who are not involuntarily relocated in another country but who choose to travel across national borders and who do not relocate permanently" (Mills 2014: 142). Among these filmmakers are a significant number of women.

Polish director Agnieszka Holland's case demonstrates a gradual shift from "exilic cinema" (she chose to stay in France after Poland's introduction of martial law in 1981 and made films such as *Bittere Ernte* (Angry Harvest, 1985, Germany) and *To Kill a Priest* (1988, France/ USA) to "sojourner cinema". Since 1989 she has engaged with film and television projects in various countries, including co-productions such as *Europa Europa* (1990, Germany/ France/Poland), *Copying Beethoven* (2006, USA/Germany/Hungary) and *In Darkness* (2011, Poland/Germany/Canada), and has directed the acclaimed HBO TV shows *The Wire* (2002–2008, USA) and *Treme* (2010–2013, USA). Yet she always returns to Poland. Holland's younger compatriot Małgorzata Szumowska embraced the category of "sojourner cinema", and the opportunities for international co-productions that have emerged since 2000, from a very early stage in her cinematic career. As early as 2004 she directed a segment called "Crossroads" within the portmanteau film *Visions of Europe*, which she also co-produced— the film brought together a number of European directors, including Eastern European Béla Tarr, Sarunas Bartas and Damian Kozole, to explore the topic of the European Union. She has very successfully secured funds from the Polish Film Institute and various trans-European producers, and her films circulate widely on the film festival circuit; her *33 sceny z życia* (33 Scenes from Life, 2008, Germany/Poland) won a Special Jury Prize at the 2008 Locarno International Film Festival, while *W imię . . .* and *Cialo* (Body, 2015, Poland) were presented at numerous film festivals and both won Silver Bears in Berlin. Even though *Elles* (2011, France/Poland/Germany) was slightly less successful, its model of financing follows the model that has been developed so successfully in the case of the Romanian New Wave. It mixes funds from the national body The Polish Film Institute and from various international bodies, including the European Union's MEDIA Programme, and uses the filmmaker's own production company, Shot-Szumowski. It also references European arthouse films by casting Juliette Binoche in the main role. Apart from producing her own films, Szumowska has also co-produced well-known European films such as Lars von Trier's *Antichrist* (2009, Denmark/Germany/France/Sweden/Italy/Poland), through Zentropa International Poland. Similarly, the Bosnian filmmaker Jasmila Žbanić has pursued a border-crossing path and a model of producing her own films, co-producing the films of others, and securing national and international funds. For example, *Grbavica* (Esma's Secret – Grbavica, 2006, Bosnia and Herzegovina/Croatia/Austria/Germany) was sponsored, among others, by the Bosnia and Herzegovina Ministry of Culture and Sport and Ministry of Culture, the Republic of Croatia and Eurimages Council of Europe. Although her films are mostly concerned with local themes concerning the Bosnian war and its aftermath, they evidently resonate with an international audience, as proven by their international critical acclaim and box office success.

The Romanian New Wave: European cinema, co-productions and film festivals

The recent phenomenon of the Romanian New Wave also brings into focus many features that characterise post-1989 Eastern European cinema and its move towards Europeanisation and transnationalism, such as cinematic representations of the collapse of communism, the examination of life under communism, pan-European co-productions, and the increasing role of international film festivals in promoting low-budget national cinema productions.

The grouping of generationally defined directors who ostensibly share thematic and stylistic similarities has always been contentious, especially when, as in the case of the Romanian New Wave, they do not produce a manifesto. Nevertheless, the unprecedented success of Romanian films on the arthouse festival circuits (especially the Cannes Film Festival which uses national identity as a primary selection criterion) and among critics has created such a cachet for Romanian films that they have been collectively labelled the Romanian New Wave (Scott 2008). *Moartea domnului Lăzărescu* (The Death of Mr Lazarescu, 2005, Romania) by Cristi Puiu and *California Dreamin' (Nesfarsit)* (California Dreamin', 2007, Romania, Cristian Nemescu) won top prize in Un Certain Regard and in the next three years the Palme d'Or went to *A fost sau n-a fost?* (12:08 East of Bucharest, 2006, Romania) by Corneliu Porumboiu, *4 luni, 3 saptamâni si 2 zile* (4 Months, 3 Weeks and 2 Days, 2007, Romania/Belgium) by Cristian Mungiu (Figure 13.3 and a short film *Megatron* (2008, Romania, Marian Crişan).

The directors who form the core of the movement—Cătălin Mitulescu, Cristian Mungiu, Radu Muntean, Corneliu Porumboiu, Cristi Puiu and the late Cristian Nemescu—and their films share a remarkable number of characteristics (Scott 2008; Nasta 2013; Pop 2014). The majority of these directors were born in the late 1960s and early 1970s and are so-called "children of the Decree 770", the 1966 law forbidding any form of abortion in Romania (Scott 2008; Pop 2014: 25). They share the generational experience of living under an extreme version of communism, enduring the truly tragic effects of the abortion decree and witnessing the only violent ending of a communist regime in Eastern Europe, all of which are prominent

Figure 13.3 The Palme d'Or win of *4 luni, 3 saptamâni si 2 zile* (4 Months, 3 Weeks and 2 Days, 2007, Romania/Belgium, Cristian Mungiu) at the Cannes Film Festival helped propel the Romanian New Wave into the international limelight. ©Mobra Films.

Figure 13.4 Minimalist stylistic choices of the Romanian New Wave in *Dupa dealuri* (Beyond the Hills, 2013, Romania/France/Belgium, Cristian Mungiu). ©Mobra Films/Why Not Productions/Les Films du Fleuve/France 3 Cinéma/Mandragora Movies.

themes in their films. These directors also went to the National University of Drama and Film (U.N.A.T.C), where they experienced the tutorship of the older generation of Romanian directors and collectively rebelled against the old ways of representation. In particular, the Romanian New Wave's insistence on realism is not only an aesthetic choice, and verisimilitude is not its only motivation; rather, it is an ethical choice to present the truth (Scott 2008). The directors of the Romanian New Wave take an ethical and revisionist stance against the former mendacious ways of representing reality (governed by censorship under communism) and against the older generation of directors, some of whom may have compromised with the communist regime. In that sense, the RNW displays striking parallels with another European movement, Italian neo-realism, which took a moral and aesthetic stance against fascism (Hayward 2000: 202).

Cristi Puiu's *Marfa si banii* (Stuff and Dough, 2001, Romania), the film often cited as the precursor to the Wave, announced a set of hallmarks of the movement: a thematic focus on stories set amid everyday life under communism (even if they explore the historical event of the 1989 revolution, it is through personal experience), an emphasis on the grim facts of quotidian existence, and minimalist stylistic choices: plain, available lighting; unobtrusive natural sound; hand-held camera; everyday décor, and an austere, neo-realist style with a penchant for the Bazinian essence of realism (long takes, deep focus, limited editing and static camera positions) (Scott 2008; Nasta 2013; Pop 2014) (Figure 13.4). The stylistic convention of "unflinching realism" is a logical choice when making films based on real events under financial restrictions, and it is to the directors' credit that they have made a virtue out of necessity. While small budgets let directors avoid "market censorship", the aesthetic and stylistic similarities of the films are also due to the minute scale of the Romanian cinema industry that forces the directors to rely on the same pool of available talent, such as the screenwriter Răzvan Rădulescu, who wrote or co-wrote a number of critically acclaimed films: *The Death of Mr Lazarescu, 4 Months, 3 Weeks and 2 Days*, Radu Muntean's *Hîrtia va fi albastră* (The Paper Will Be Blue, 2006, Romania) and *Marti, după Crăciun* (Tuesday, After Christmas, 2010, Romania) and *Pozitia copilului* (Child's Pose, 2013, Romania, Calin Peter Netzer); the cinematographer Oleg Mutu (*The Death of Mr Lăzărescu, 4 Months, 3 Weeks and 2 Days* and *Beyond the Hills*); the editor Dana Bunescu; and actors, with Luminita Gheorghiu as the muse of the movement.

As the RNW reaches its twelfth year (2004–2016), a span of time that tends to herald the death of any European movement, we can begin to understand the reasons for this unparalleled success story from Eastern Europe. As mentioned at the beginning of this chapter, industry changes have had the most profound impact on the Europeanisation of Eastern European cinema, and the trajectory of Romanian cinema from "year zero" of no film production in 2000 to the definitive recent inclusion of the RNW into the canon of European movements best exemplifies this. Romania introduced the new Law of Cinematography in 1999, modelled on the French law, which "regulated the relationship between the private production companies and the state source of funding, mostly in the form of state interest-free loans for private companies" (Uricaru 2012: 435). The system allocates up to 50 per cent of the film cost from the Romanian National Centre for Cinematography (Centrul Național Cinematografei, CNC) based on a points system for the quality of the screenplay, the track record of the production company, and the director's previous international success at film festivals that validates "the decisive role of the international film festivals" (Uricaru 2012: 434). While virtually all later films of the RNW have been sponsored by the CNC (e.g. *4 Months, 3 Weeks and 2 Days, Tuesday, After Christmas, Beyond the Hills*), the establishing films of the movement did not benefit from the state system of funding (and were produced independently) because the system puts a premium on previous film festivals' awards (see Iordanova). However, many of the directors of the RNW formed private production companies as early as 2000, which helped them raise funds from international sources and gave them a degree of artistic freedom and control. Famously, Cristi Puiu's Mandragora produced *The Death of Mr Lazarescu*, the first film of the movement, after the CNC refused to sponsor it, while Corneliu Porumboiu's 42Km Film produced the second film of the movement, *12:08 East of Bucharest* (and co-produced all of his films) and Cristian Mungiu's Mobra Films produced three of his films. A combination of private production companies, therefore, initially enabled the creativity of the RNW directors to emerge. Later financial boosts from the state-owned CNC built upon this foundation to establish the Romanian New Wave as a truly European movement.

Both the CNC requirement of previous festival awards to sponsor film projects and international co-productions have also ensured that thematically the Wave is a transnational phenomenon aimed at international arthouse audiences. Despite the fact that the films are set in a recognisable Romanian reality, themes and images of communism and its fall have become the defining moments of recent European history and belong to a pan-European heritage. The transnational nature of the phenomenon at the interface of the national and international is also evident in the RNW's reliance for its own definition on international festival circuits that paradoxically insist on defining in national terms those films that do travel well across borders. It is this interaction between national and international funding, national milieus and European themes, and effective international film festival strategies that has brought Romanian cinema to the attention of worldwide audiences.

Conclusion

The three case studies presented illustrate the impact of changing models of finance on Eastern European cinema since 1989. Béla Tarr's cinematic career serves as a primary instance of the persistence of auterism in the cinema of the region, but also of Eastern European cinema's general shift from an emphasis on the national to the transnational. National and European funds and the availability of globalised production opportunities have also opened up the cinematic space of Europe for female Eastern European filmmakers who, as argued, have experienced unprecedented freedom of artistic movement and frequently display an entrepreneurial approach to producing films. However, the positive experience of film practitioners' mobility across, and beyond, Europe is contrasted with the representation of its negative counterpart in the "trafficking of women", a dominant theme in the Eastern European narratives of feature films made by Western, mostly male, filmmakers. If Eastern European female filmmakers fully contribute to recent "sojourner cinema", transgressing essentialist notions of national identity, cinematic representations of women from the region are still linked with the negative stereotype of a woman who is forced to travel and is sexually exploited. The two radically opposed forms of the cinematic mobility of Eastern European women are both a symbol and a symptom of, on the one hand, the Europeanisation of Eastern European cinema and, on the other, entrenched perceptual divisions in Europe. Finally, the Romanian New Wave is a stellar example of the Europeanisation of Eastern European cinema, and a collective cinematic trajectory from the national to the transnational in terms of mode of production, based on funding from national and international bodies (both private and the European Union), and co-production by directors' own companies.

Critical insistence in Romania and elsewhere that a number of films can be seen as both examples of auteur cinema and national cinematic movements prove that seemingly old-fashioned critical categories are still valid. To sum up, Eastern European cinema participates in the new development of European globalised and transnational cinemas but at the same time it manifests the persistence of national and auteurist frameworks.

References

Augé, M. (1995) *Non-Places: Introduction to an Anthropology of Supermodernity*, Howe, J. (trans), London/New York: Verso.

Betz, M. (2009) *Beyond the Subtitle: Remapping European Art Cinema*, Minneapolis, MN; London: University of Minnesota Press.

Coates, P. (2000) "Shifting Borders: Konwicki, Zanussi and the Ideology of 'East-Central Europe'", *Canadian Slavonic Papers* 42 (1–2): 87–98.

Deleuze, G. (1986) *Cinema 1: The Movement*, Tomlinson, H. and Habberjam, B. (trans), Minneapolis, MN: University of Minnesota Press.

Elsaesser, T. (2005) "Double Occupancy and Small Adjustments: Space, Place and Policy in the New European Cinema since the 1990s", in *European Cinema: Face to Face with Hollywood*, Amsterdam: Amsterdam University Press, 108–130.

Engelen, L. and Heuckelom, K. (2013) *European Cinema after the Wall: Screening East-West Mobility*, Lanham, MD: Rowman & Littlefield.

Hames, P. (2004) "Introduction", in Hames, P. (ed.), *The Cinema Central Europe*, London and New York: Wallflower Press, 1–13.

—— (ed.) (2004) *The Cinema Central Europe*, London and New York: Wallflower Press.

Hayward, S. (2000) *Cinema Studies: The Key Concepts*, London: Routledge.

Imre, A. (ed.) (2005) *East European Cinemas*, London: Routledge.

—— (ed.) (2012) *A Companion to Eastern European Cinemas*, Chichester: Wiley-Blackwell.

Iordanova, D. (2002) "Feature Filmmaking Within the New Europe: Moving Funds and Images across the East-West Divide", *Media Culture and Society* 24 (4): 517–536.

—— (2003) *Cinema of the Other Europe: The Industry and Artistry of East Central European Film*, London/New York: Wallflower Press.

—— (2010) "Migration and Cinematic Process in Post-Cold War Europe", in Berghahn, D. and Sternberg, C. (eds) *European Cinema in Motion. Migrant and Diasporic Film in Contemporary Europe*, Basingstoke: Palgrave, 50–75.

Jäckel, A. (1998) "Cooperation Between East and West in Europe: Film Policy and Integration. From Hope to Disenchantment?", in Columbus, F. (ed.), *Central and Eastern Europe in Transition, Vol. II*, New York: Nova Science Publishers, 41–68.

—— (2003) *European Film Industries*, London: Palgrave Macmillan.

Kovács, A.B. (2008) "The World According to Béla Tarr", *KinoKultura* 7, February 2008, www.kinokultura.com/specials/7/kovacs.shtml.

—— (2013) *The Cinema of Béla Tarr: The Circle Closes*, London and New York: Wallflower Press.

Mazierska, E, Kristensen, L. and Näripea, E. (2013) *Postcolonial Approaches to Eastern European Cinema: Portraying Neighbours on Screen*, London: I.B. Tauris.

Mills, J. (2014) "Sojourner Cinema: Seeking and Researching a New Cinematic Category", *Framework* 55 (1): 140–164.

Nasta, D. (2013) *Contemporary Romanian Cinema: The History of an Unexpected Miracle*, New York: Wallflower Press.

Ostrowska, E. and Rydzewska, J. (2007) "Gendered Discourses of Nation(hood) and the West in Polish Cinema", *Studies in European Cinema* 4 (3): 187–98.

Pethő, Á. (2016) "The 'Chemistry' of Art(ifice) and Life: Embodied Paintings in East European Cinema", in Mazierska, E., Mroz, M. and Ostrowska, E. (eds), *The Cinematic Bodies of Eastern Europe and Russia: Between Pain and Pleasure*, Edinburgh: Edinburgh University Press: 239–256.

Pop, D. (2014) *Romanian New Wave Cinema: An Introduction*, Jefferson, TX: McFarland & Company.

Portuges, C. and Hames, P. (eds) (2013) *Cinemas in Transition in Central and Eastern Europe after 1989*, Philadelphia, PA: Temple University Press.

Quandt, J. (2012) "Bleak house", *Artforum International* 50: 77–78, http://login.ezproxy.library.ualberta.ca/login?url=http://search.proquest.com.login.ezproxy.library.ualberta.ca/docview/921277498?accountid=14474.

Scott, A. O. (2008) "New Wave on the Black Sea", *The New York Times Magazine*, 20 January, www.nytimes.com/2008/01/20/magazine/20Romanian-t.html?_r=0.

Tarr, C. (2010) "Gendering Diaspora: The Work of Diasporic Women Film-Makers in Western Europe", in Berghahn, D. and Sternberg, C. (eds), *European Cinema in Motion. Migrant and Diasporic Film in Contemporary Europe*, Basingstoke: Palgrave, 175–195.

Uricaru, I. (2012) "Follow the Money—Financing Contemporary Cinema in Romania", in Imre, A. (ed.), *A Companion to Eastern European Cinemas*, Chichester: Wiley-Blackwell, 427–452.

Wolff, L. (1994) *Inventing Eastern Europe: The Map of Civilization on the Mind of the Enlightenment*, Stanford, CA: Stanford University Press.

Wong, C. (2011) *Film Festivals: Culture, People, and Power on the Global Screen*, New Brunswick, NJ: Rutgers University Press.

Wood, N. and Iordanova, D. (2000) "Introduction to Eastern European Cinema", in Taylor, R., Wood, N., Graffy, J. and Iordanova, D. (eds), *The BFI Companion to Eastern European and Russian Cinema*, London: BFI Publishing, 1–4.

Zeitchik, S. (2016) "Romania Continues an Unlikely Cinematic Domination at Cannes, with a Pair of Rival Directors", *The New York Times*, 25 May, www.latimes.com/entertainment/movies/la-et-mn-cannes-romania-new-wave-movies-mungiu-puiu-20160525-snap-story.html.

14

CINEMA AT THE EDGES OF THE EUROPEAN UNION

New dynamics in the South and the East

Lydia Papadimitriou

Introduction

The late 2000s saw the European Union face a significant financial crisis, unprecedented in its history. Almost a decade after the introduction of the single currency in January 2002, a debt crisis hit the Eurozone, leading to financial recession, fiscal austerity, social upheaval and political tensions, especially in the most indebted countries. Often referred to by Anglophone media in the early 2010s with the derogatory acronym PIGS, these countries—with the ambivalent exception of the "I" that could equally stand for Ireland—all belonged to European South: Portugal, Italy, Greece and Spain. An implicit internal border between the ostensibly diligent and thrifty North and the lazy and profligate South surfaced, reproducing deeply entrenched stereotypes.

Despite the official emphasis on unification, cultural proximity, free movement of people and the gradual dissolution of boundaries, real and symbolic hierarchies have persisted within the EU. Aside from a North–South divide, distinctions between Western and Eastern Europe also remain. While the EU's enlargement has increasingly brought into the fold a number of countries from the ex-communist bloc, economic and other discrepancies among citizens and states have endured. The UK's referendum vote in June 2016 to exit the EU was largely motivated by such discrepancies, translated into the fear of an intensified influx of economic migrants. The uneven and, until such developments concealed, dynamic between centre and periphery within the EU, is still present (Imre 2012: 6–7).

Tensions have also been evident around the EU's Eastern external edges too. In 2013, geopolitical considerations led to clashes in the Ukraine, an ex-Soviet republic internally divided between pro-Europeans and pro-Russians. In a series of localised conflicts reminiscent of Cold War tensions, the southeastern region of the Crimea fell into war, thus raising fears of a further escalation of violence in close proximity to the EU. More recently, since 2015, over a million refugees from Syria and other warring regions of the Middle East have been crossing the Mediterranean to reach European lands. This refugee crisis has drawn attention to the permeability of Europe's external borders, rekindling a number of questions about European values and reinforcing divisions and distinctions within Europe that led—among other things—to the UK's Brexit vote. The countries of the European South and East have become passageways for the more prosperous, desirable and increasingly out-of-bounds Central and Western Europe.

The above indication of points of tension within—and beyond—the EU suggests some of the different ways in which the edges of the Union can be conceptualised (Cooper 2015). This chapter aims to throw light on recent developments in the cinemas of geographical regions that could be considered as the (internal) edges of the EU. It will focus on the financially troubled South of Europe (mainly Greece), and it will also introduce the cinemas of the most recent entries in the EU, all of which used to belong to the Eastern Bloc: Bulgaria (joined in 2007), Romania (2007) and Croatia (2013). As all these countries, including Greece, are known to belong to the Balkans, this chapter will also explore the concept of Balkan cinema and argue for its potential in empowering these peripheral cinemas. The chapter takes its cue from an intellectual drive that emerged in the 2000s to discover and validate the marginal, the small, and the peripheral in world cinema (Hjort 2005; Iordanova *et al.* 2010; Giukin *et al.* 2014). Drawing attention to films and cinematic traditions that are often overlooked challenges entrenched hierarchies in Film Studies—and beyond. In exploring recent cinematic developments in the chosen national and transnational contexts, the chapter will also engage with the, sometimes contested, role of European institutions in fostering and promoting its small cinemas. It will focus both on aspects of production and financing, as well as distribution and exhibition that enable the circulation of such films—including film festivals.

Cinema in Greece and the European South since the crisis

In an article on the cinemas of Portugal, Greece and Spain, Kourelou, Liz and Vidal (2014) compare developments in the respective countries of their focus and highlight structural similarities among them. They stress that, while financial unsustainability and extensive reliance on state funding has placed these cinemas in a chronic condition of crisis, the significant reduction of national public subsidies for cinema since 2010 led to a creative resurgence among filmmakers and to the adoption of more collaborative, independent, and non-profit based modes of production. While celebrating this creativity-under-duress, the authors also highlight that it has encouraged filmmakers to turn outwards and seek more "opportunities for internationalization" (2014: 147). These, crucially, include the role of film festivals (Cannes, Berlin, Venice, San Sebastian, Karlovy-Vary) in opening paths for circulation and recognition, but also in enabling networking and facilitating co-productions.

As the authors indicate, all three of these national cinemas have enjoyed increased international visibility in the years since the crisis. This has been fostered by a combination of media-triggered interest in the countries, together with a refreshed and distinctive cinematic output, in addition to the supportive role of the international film festival system. However, despite such structural similarities the three national cinemas have rarely been considered in comparative terms. This is partly because, in practice, there has been relatively little overlap between their cinemas in terms of actual filmmaking collaborations or stylistic similarities. While noting the presence of certain parallels in the recent cinematic development of countries of the European South, I will now focus on Greek cinema, as a particular instance of a "small cinema" that has indirectly benefited from the crisis in terms of both output and visibility, and grown to occupy a more prominent position within discourses of European and world cinema. Focusing mainly on the work of the director Yorgos Lanthimos, which has reached significant international prominence and critical acclaim during these years, I will explore the dynamic between the national and the transnational, as well as that between centre and periphery—or, to put it otherwise, the European core and its edges.

As I have argued elsewhere (Papadimitriou 2014a), 2009 represents a nodal point for contemporary Greek cinema, mainly because of the release of Yorgos Lanthimos' *Kynodontas*

(Dogtooth, 2011, Greece). The film premiered at Cannes, was shown in, and received awards from, many more festivals, and, most significantly, for the first time since 1977, it represented Greece at the Oscars with a nomination for Best Foreign Language Film. While *Dogtooth* brought Greek cinema to the attention of the festival circuit, the deepening of the crisis and the increased international media coverage instigated further interest in the film and, to a certain extent, in Greek cinema more broadly. An influential article in *The Guardian* explored the "weird wave of Greek cinema", and asked whether the "brilliantly strange" films of Lanthimos and Athina Rachel Tsangari are "a product of Greece's economic turmoil" (Rose 2011). Despite quoting the two filmmakers' scepticism regarding the existence of such a wave, the article suggested causality between the "troubled country" and the "inexplicably strange" films that had recently emerged from Greece—while also acknowledging the existence of a number of Greek films that do not quite fit that label.

The term "weird wave" has since often been challenged for being inappropriate and intrinsically negative; however, its suggestiveness has led it to dominate academic and critical discussions of recent Greek cinema and helped create value from a cinema that historically has had limited international presence. Indeed, the main two internationally known directors of Greek cinema in the past were Mihalis Cacoyannis (1921–2011) and Theo Angelopoulos (1935–2012). Cacoyannis helped define a particular exotic image of Greekness, associated with uninhibited emotional and libidinal expression (*Stella*, 1955, Greece; *Zorba the Greek*, 1965, USA/Greece), while also tapping into established Greek cultural capital through his adaptations of ancient Greek tragedies (*Electra*, 1962, Greece; *Iphigenia*, 1977, Greece). It is worth noting that the film that established his international reputation was *Zorba the Greek*, an American, rather than a Greek, production (20th Century Fox) with a transnational cast (Anthony Quinn, Alan Bates), and spoken in English. A few years later, Angelopoulos challenged the tourist image of the country by focusing on the "other Greece" of grey skies, abandoned mountain villages, and political post-war divisions, while also making extensive, albeit more indirect, use of Greek myths (*Anaparastasi,* Reconstruction, 1970, Greece; *O Thiassos*, The Travelling Players, 1975, Greece; *To Vlemma tou Odyssea*, Ulysses' Gaze, 1995 Greece/France/Italy/Germany/UK/ Federal Republic of Yugoslavia/Bosnia and Herzegovina/Albania/Romania). Like Cacoyannis, he developed transnational collaborations, evident mainly in the international cast of his later films (Harvey Keitel in *Ulysses' Gaze*, 1995; Bruno Ganz in *Mia aioniotita kai mia mera*, Eternity and a Day, 1998, Greece/France/Germany/Italy), and the extensive use of European funding and co-production opportunities.

The international breakthrough of *Dogtooth* in 2009 introduced a new Greek director as well as a new brand for Greek cinema—the "weird wave"—while, as noted above, the release of the film at the outset of the crisis made it easier to render it emblematic of a broader cinematic turning point for the nation. However, aside from the fact that *Dogtooth* was not a product of the *financial* crisis in Greece—although its subject matter and form can and have been plausibly connected to the country's political, social and even moral crises—it is highly questionable whether Lanthimos will continue to represent *Greek* cinema. This is both because he has distanced himself from the crisis-ridden Greek context and relocated to London, pursuing an international career; but also because even his Greek-language films (including *Dogtooth*) intentionally repress signs of Greekness and utilise instead an allegorical and oblique storytelling style with widely recognised, rather than culturally specific, references and archetypal conflicts. We have, in other words, the case of a transnational filmmaker who moved from the edges to the centre in search of financial opportunities, better working conditions, and a broader audience; but who, also, in the process of this move has detached himself from the association with a (peripheral) national cinema.

It is interesting to note how, unlike other directors whose formative years took place outside Greece (for example, Cacoyannis and Angelopoulos studied in London and in Paris respectively), Lanthimos was originally a "home-grown" filmmaker. His film education took place at the Stavrakos School in Athens (the only film school in Greece at the time) while during most of the 1990s and 2000s he worked extensively for the then flourishing audio-visual sector in Greece, shooting commercials, music videos and shorts, as well as his first independently produced feature, *Kinetta* (2005, Greece). With a strong reputation as a gifted director in the Greek media industry, and with the modest but significant festival success of his first feature, Lanthimos was able to secure enough public and private funding from within Greece to make *Dogtooth* (Papadimitriou, 2014b). This was just before the financial crisis. By the time of his third feature, *Alps* (2011, Greece), state funding (from the Greek Film Centre and the Greek State Television) was limited, and private financing even more restricted, so despite the success of his previous film, financially he struggled to complete it.

At this point, faced with the option to remain in a country in crisis or relocate, Lanthimos chose the latter and moved to London, from where he sought financing for his fourth feature film (and the third co-scripted with Efthymis Filippou). Shot in Ireland, with a budget that was twenty times larger than before, *The Lobster* (2015) is an English language, internationally cast, Irish, British, Greek, French, and Dutch co-production that received the Jury Prize at the 2015 Cannes Film Festival and has since then been widely distributed as an arthouse film. Firmly established by this stage as a director with international credentials, for his next project he has been able to secure "one of the most sought-after projects in the marketplace" (Jaafar 2015), a project developed by Film4 and the British Film Institute, *The Favourite.* A more mainstream project, the film is a costume drama set in eighteenth-century Britain, with no Greek involvement aside from Lanthimos' own. At the same time, Lanthimos has been developing another international co-production scripted by Efthymis Filippou, *The Killing of a Sacred Cow*, suggesting a desire to maintain the semi-absurdist and distinctively stylised brand identity of the films that emerged from this collaboration. Lanthimos' Greekness, however, is becoming increasingly less prominent.

The above discussion shows, first, that for cinema from the edges to circulate more widely, it needs to be validated through institutions and pathways that involve the centre: major film festivals, international stars, and powerful distributors. However, while this process takes place, the centre attracts and assimilates selected aspects of the edge: key talent relocates to the international and European metropolises to access more opportunities, while particular brands of national cinema—such as the Greek Weird Wave—matter mainly in the context of international art cinema promotion and circulation. In many ways this reflects the process of globalisation which, while open to fluidity, mobility, and the disruption of certain hierarchies, ultimately reinforces the centre and its interests—even if the centre is, arguably, partly transformed in the process.

Before concluding my discussion of Greek cinema as a peripheral European cinema, I would like to return briefly to a national frame of reference and throw some light on the production and reception of Greek films in Greece. I will demonstrate that, while overall film production has increased since the crisis, the pattern of reception of national films is strongly underscored by a popular/art dichotomy. I will then highlight the role of European institutions in supporting small and/or peripheral national cinemas in Europe.

Paradoxically, the total number of films made in Greece in the years since the crisis has increased: while 27 films were produced in 2010, data from the Greek Film Centre indicate a notable increase to 40 in 2013 and 46 in 2014. Of these films, however, only a small number has been released theatrically, and only a handful of these had a significant box office presence.

The most commercially successful Greek films in this period have been the two films by writer, director and star Christophoros Papakaliatis' *An . . .* (What If . . ., 2012, Greece) and *Enas Allos Kosmos* (Another World, 2015, Greece). Employing multi-stranded narratives that refer to the crisis but also elements of genre, Papakaliatis' films attract audiences with their combination of high-production values, star appeal, and an honest, if at times didactic, address. Another notable box office success has been *Mikra Anglia* (Little England, 2013, Greece), veteran director Pandelis Voulgaris' tale of a doomed romantic triangle set on the island of Andros in the early parts of the twentieth century. Apart from a few exceptions, the vast majority of commercially successful Greek films in this period (just like before) have been quickly produced comedies, often capitalising on television stars and reproducing well-worn popular scenarios.

As the above examples suggest, international acclaim and festival awards for Greek films do not necessarily translate into domestic box office success, even though they certainly contribute towards the films' visibility. Indeed, the films that make it to the larger festivals (Cannes, Berlin, Venice) tend to reach the top ten of Greek films released domestically. For example, Yannis Economides' physically and verbally violent *noir* set in crisis Athens, *Stratos* (2014, Greece/Germany/Cyprus) and camp melodramatic road movie about two half-Greek brothers, Panos H. Koutras' *Xenia* (2014, Greece/France/Belgium) were ranked fifth and sixth respectively in the Greek box office for Greek films. This nonetheless translated to roughly 16,000 and 15,000 admissions for each, and therefore not numbers that can guarantee financial sustainability in commercial terms. Such non-correspondence of critical and commercial success is not unique to Greek cinema, and is due to the limited audience appeal of films with challenging or "feel bad" topics, little—if any—use of genre, and self-conscious aesthetics, as opposed to more generically mainstream, melodramatic or comedic entertainment-orientated films. Despite its national and international notoriety, *Dogtooth*, for example, had around 40,000 admissions on its initial theatrical release in 2009—while Papakaliatis' popular *What If . . .* attracted over 450,000 people three years later.

Small countries with a language not widely spoken outside their national boundaries, and therefore with a disadvantage for exportability, face particular challenges in sustaining their cinematic production: their national market is limited and they often encounter fierce competition from better capitalised (mostly American) films. Partly in response to this problem, after the Second World War a number of Western European countries set up national funding bodies to support national production (and often its promotion to international festivals too), especially for films deemed culturally significant. By the late 1980s European institutions followed suit: Eurimages, the Council of Europe's support fund for European cinema, was established in 1988. Its aims are both cultural and industrial: to support (mainly through co-productions) films that promote European values while also fostering cross-European co-operation among professionals and aiming to broaden the audience basis of European films (Jackel 2003: 76–80). Eurimages is open to all 47 members of the Council of Europe, and it also accepts associate members (Eurimages 2016). Participation is optional and requires annual contributions—the UK, for example, joined in 1993 and withdrew in 1996 (Ibid.: 76–77). While offering benefits to larger members, the fund has been especially supportive of smaller and peripheral participating countries. According to Melis Behlil, Eurimages has significantly helped Turkey boost the international visibility of New Turkish Cinema, while also strengthening creative collaborations and co-productions, not least among its geographical neighbours—in this case Greece (Behlil 2012: 512–513).

In contrast to Eurimages, the MEDIA programme, established in 1987, is open to members of the EU and the European Economic Area (Creative Europe 2016). In its current reincarnation (2014–2020) as a sub-programme of Creative Europe its primary orientation is economic rather than cultural, aiming to enhance the "EU's competitive position in international trade" (Schlesinger 2015: 10). The limited resources (especially of Eurimages) and the separation of support for production and distribution, are among the criticisms expressed about these programmes (Iordanova 2002; Jackel 2003: 79–80). Overall, however, it is widely accepted that they have played a significant role in supporting cinemas from the European periphery and particularly, in "reinvigorate[ing] media production in the former Socialist states" (Imre 2012: 5).

European enlargement and the Balkans: Romania, Bulgaria and Croatia

The radical geopolitical transformations brought about by the end of the Cold War resulted in the EU's enlargement. The reunification of Germany in 1990 led to the immediate integration in the European Community of what had been East Germany, while 2004 saw a significant enlargement of the—by then renamed—EU to include ten new countries, eight of which had been part of the Soviet Bloc. Three years later, in 2007, Romania and Bulgaria joined, marking an eastward expansion of the Union. Croatia followed in 2013, becoming the second ex-Yugoslav country to become a full EU member.

Aside from their post-socialist past, the three most recent entries also share a different common identity: they all belong to the Balkans. A term laden with negative connotations of fragmentation, poverty and violence, its literal meaning refers to the geographical space that covers the territories of Romania, Bulgaria, Albania, the former Yugoslavia, but also Greece and (the Westernmost part of) Turkey. As Iordanova (2006: 1) has argued, despite appearing to be a project of "connecting a disconnected space", a regional approach to the cinema of the Balkans is very rewarding, as it brings to the surface an "astonishing thematic and stylistic consistency" among films produced in different national contexts. The 1990s wars of secession in the former Yugoslavia brought the attention of the international media to the area, and reinforced entrenched prejudices; but it also triggered a wave of creative work and scholarship on the topic, including foundational writings on Balkan cinema (Iordanova 2001). The restoration of peace and the entry of Balkan countries into the EU has changed the internal dynamics of the region and opened up opportunities for regional cultural redefinitions. Although the new challenges brought about by the recent waves of migration from further East risk further marginalising the Balkans in the context of Europe, a regional approach can both help revise perceptions and strengthen actual collaborative practices.

The disconnectedness of the Balkans has been evident in the past in the various political, religious and linguistic barriers that have hindered the circulation of the cinemas from this region across neighbouring countries. Save from the films that broke through to the West (or that circulated within the socialist bloc), cinemas in these countries developed and circulated predominantly within a national framework. During the 1990s the films from this region that gained prominence in the West generally concerned the crisis in Yugoslavia. At the height of the Bosnian war, in 1995, the two top winners of the Cannes Film Festival were Emir Kusturica's *Underground* (1995, Federal Republic of Yugoslavia/France/Germany/Bulgaria/Czech Republic/Hungary), a carnivalesque recounting of the history of Yugoslavia, and Theo Angelopoulos' *Ulysses' Gaze*, a Homeric Balkan road-movie concluding in Sarajevo. Other notable films from this period include Micho Manchevski's *Before the Rain* (1994, Republic of Macedonia/France/UK), Srdjan Dragojevic's *Lepa sela lepo gore* (Pretty Village, Pretty Flame, 1996, Federal Republic of Yugoslavia) and Goran Paskaljevic's *Bure baruta* (Cabaret Balkan, 1999, Federal Republic of Yugoslavia/Republic of Macedonia/France/Greece/Turkey)—all dealing with the consequences of ethnic tensions in the former Yugoslavia.

With the conclusion of the wars, attention to the region as a whole waned while the emphasis shifted towards the process of integrating these countries within the EU. This also had an impact on cinema, as funding from Europe became increasingly available to filmmakers, while the festival circuit opened paths for some directors and offered visibility to their national cinema. In the rest of this chapter I will briefly discuss recent developments in the cinemas of Romania, Bulgaria and Croatia, while also highlighting the extent of their trans-nationalisation both within the region and across Europe. I will place emphasis on the most prominent expressions of their cinemas, and situate them in the context of their national and international reception.

Of the three, Romanian cinema stood out in the 2000s, mainly through the emergence and wide acclaim of what became known as the Romanian New Wave (Nasta 2013: 139–200). The term refers to a group of films made by a generation of filmmakers who started working in the post-communist period and made films that conveyed in a suggestive and original way the experiences of the transition period, while also throwing new light to the Ceauşescu era. The films are characterised by a minimalist realist aesthetic: they focus on the everyday, they use understated acting, few if any narrative ellipses, long takes, tableau-like compositions, near-static shots, no extra-diegetic music score and—at times—dry humour (157). The three directors that best represent this aesthetic are Cristi Puiu (*Moartea domnului Lăzărescu*, The Death of Mr Lazarescu, 2005, Romania), Corneliu Porumboiu (*A fost sau n-a fost?*, 12:08 East of Bucharest, 2006, Romania) and Cristian Mungiu (*4 luni, 3 saptamâni si 2 zile*, 4 months, 3 weeks and 2 days, 2007, Romania/Belgium). All three won awards at the Cannes Film Festival, with Mungiu becoming the first Romanian Palme d'Or winner. A dark tragi-comedy about a dying man caught in a highly dysfunctional hospital system (*Lazarescu*); a dry satire about whether the revolution of 1989 started in a small provincial town or not (*East of Bucharest*); and an exploration of sexual exploitation and body commodification through the problem of illegal abortions during the Ceauşescu era (*4 months*)—all three films portrayed aspects of the recent past or of contemporary life in Romania in a fresh and subtle manner that attracted the interest of Western cinephile audiences, and launched critical writings about the Romanian New Wave (Nasta 2013).

Despite representing a break from previous cinematic approaches, such as Lucian Pintilie's more symbolic and obliquely expressive films (e.g. *Balanta*, The Oak, 1992, France/Romania), these films did not develop in a vacuum. Mircea Daneliuc, for example, had already employed a semi-documentary style in his work, often weaved with a degree of self-reflexivity (*Proba de microfon*, Microphone Test, 1980, Romania). That the new directors developed a pared-down cinematic language to convey their experience of a country in post-socialist transition (that also stylistically matched the limited financial resources available) helped identify them as a critical mass and facilitated the international circulation of their films. The films benefitted from a revamped system of state funding in 2003, and a number of them also managed to attract European funds (for example, *4 months, 3 weeks, 2 days* received support from the Hubert Bals Fund of the Rotterdam Film Festival). Despite critical acclaim, the films, however, were not box office successes in their native Romania, as audiences tend to prefer escapist (and mostly American) fare. It is worth noting, though, that the international success of *4 months, 3 weeks, 2 days* triggered inventive initiatives for parallel showings outside the commercial exhibition circuit, such as, for example, travelling screenings around the country (Nasta 2013: 198).

Like most Eastern European countries, during communism Romania had a significant studio infrastructure, as all film production was state funded. Referred to as the Balkan *Cinecittà*, during the 1960s the Buftea Studios hosted many European co-productions, mainly with France and Italy (Ibid.: 233). As the regime became more isolationist the studios were closed to Western productions, but, just like elsewhere in post-socialist Eastern Europe, they were later bought and renovated by Western private multinational companies. Acquired by Romanian-American Castel Films, the old Buftea studios were revamped and are now among the largest sound studios in Europe, attracting Western productions once more (Imre 2012: 2–3; Nasta 2013: 233). This offers economic benefits to the country, as it keeps the local workforce employed and skilled, but it does not necessarily lead to a strengthening of national film production or to opportunities for above-the-line personnel (such as screenwriters, directors, actors).

Aside from the similar acquisition of the Boyana studios in Bulgaria by an American company specialising in action films (Iordanova 2008: 11), other parallels also emerge between the two countries, such as the privatisation of the state-owned cinemas and the rise of the multiplexes. In Bulgaria, the attempt to attract audiences in refurbished single screen cinemas failed, and by the mid-2000s most of these closed, often leaving small cities without a cinema (Bulgarian Cinema 2014: 31–34). In contrast, the new multiplexes located in shopping malls thrived, boosting overall cinema attendance in the country, which, in 2013, reached record-breaking numbers (Ibid.: 23–25). Here, as elsewhere, the tendency has been for few big-budget, mostly American, titles to attract the largest audiences; however, interestingly, in the early 2010s a few Bulgarian commercial titles became runaway hits, reaching the top of the box office in the country.

On top of this list is *Mission London* (2010, Bulgaria/UK/Hungary/Republic of Macedonia/Sweden, Dimitar Mitovski), the third highest grossing film in Bulgaria since 1998 with 375,000 admissions—preceded only by James Cameron's global hits *Avatar* (2009, USA) and *Titanic* (1998, USA) (Ibid.: 28). A farcical comedy set in London, the film focuses on the semi-absurd series of events triggered by the decision of the Bulgarian president's wife to host an important reception in the British capital on the occasion of the country's entry into the EU. The film relies on national stereotypes, self-critically portraying the Bulgarians as brutish, but also the British as naïve and the Russians as mafiosi. Underlining the new European and cosmopolitan orientation of the country, it also suggests that "if everyone is flawed, then Bulgaria can easily become part of the dysfunctional European family" (Nedyalkova 2015: 118). Through its use of satire, parody and slapstick, and genre elements of romance and crime, *Mission London* released anxieties and fantasies experienced by the country's desired Europeanisation.

Since the early 2000s, the prospect of Bulgaria's entry in the EU led to the requirement that state supported films display a European orientation. The 2003 Film Industry Act introduced as its top criterion for subsidising a film its "artistic potential within the context of European cultural diversity", demonstrating a desire to "overcome the small national inferiority complex, cultural and business isolationism" that characterised aspects of national culture in the past (Ibid.: 99). This largely explains why, despite its commercial emphasis, *Mission London* received 35 per cent of its budget from a state subsidy. Despite being a European co-production with stakes from the UK, Hungary, Macedonia and Sweden, the film's commercial appeal was almost exclusively among Bulgarians. Its domestic box office returns are estimated at 1.3 million euros, a figure that matches its estimated total budget. It is notable that the second largest domestic box office hit, *Love.net* (2011, Bulgaria, Ilian Djevelekov), a Bulgarian version of *Love Actually* (2003, UK/USA/France, Richard Curtis), was also supported by the state; it received 66 per cent of its one million euro budget from state funds (Ibid.: 235).

Despite being controversial, the state's policy to support films with commercial potential in the domestic market has brought some positive returns for the domestic industry (Ibid.: 104). At a different end of the market, the last decade saw a number of distinctive documentaries produced in Bulgaria—mostly by Agitprop. Often utilising humour to highlight eccentricities triggered by the post-socialist transition, the films have challenged previously established documentary practices in Bulgaria and appeal to a European sensibility, thus successfully attracting co-production funding and festival awards (Ţuţui 2015: 218–221). Examples include Andrey Paounov's *Georgi i peperudite* (Georgi and the Butterflies, 2004, Bulgaria/Canada/Finland/Netherlands/Norway/UK/USA), an optimistic and playful portrait of a psychiatrist who dreams of having an eccentric farm for his patients; Boris Despodov's *Corridor#8* (2008, Bulgaria), a highly engaging absurdist series of vignettes around the development of a major road that would connect Bulgaria to some of its Balkan neighbours; and, more recently, *The Last Black Sea Pirates* (2013, Bulgaria, Svetoslav Stoyanov), that focuses on a group of ex-convicts and petty thieves on a tiny island off the Bulgarian coast and their attempts to fight the government while seeking a hidden treasure. The eccentric topics and exotic locations have helped attract attention to these films, but it is arguably the inventiveness and consistency of their cinematic approach that has placed Bulgaria in a leading position in the field of creative documentaries in the Balkans.

Bulgaria has recently seen a surge of first features directed by women, all gaining international attention. Maya Vitkova's *Viktoria* (2014, Bulgaria/Romania) is an exploration of the love–hate relationship of Bulgarians with their country, told through the symbolic tale of a girl born without a belly button in 1979. The film premiered at the Sundance Film Festival in January 2014 and triggered significant controversy when it was not selected to represent its country for the Oscars (Holdsworth 2014). Kristina Grozeva and Petar Valchanov's *Urok* (The Lesson, 2014, Bulgaria/Greece) was awarded the Best New Directors' Award at its world premiere in San Sebastian later that year. A micro-budgeted co-production with Greece, the film suspensefully explores the moral dilemmas of a provincial schoolteacher who tries to teach a lesson to a thieving pupil. Svetla Tsotsorkova's *Jajda* (Thirst, 2015, Bulgaria), a sensuous and symbolic tale of an isolated family in rural Bulgaria disturbed by the arrival of two well diggers, also opened at San Sebastian and travelled the festival circuit to critical acclaim.

The challenges faced by other Eastern European countries in terms of their transition to a market economy were even more intense in the case of Croatia (and most of the other ex-Yugoslav countries), because of the war and the fragmentation of the socialist federal country. Structural change was particularly slow and until the introduction of a new law in 2007, funding processes depended on centralised state mechanisms (Kurelec 2012: 44–48). With a population of 4.5 million, Croatia is a very small national market, and relies extensively on co-productions with the other countries of the former Yugoslavia—a practice established during communism. Indicatively, of the 15 feature-length feature films produced in Croatia in 2015, ten were co-productions, of which seven involved other ex-Yugoslav countries (Croatian Audiovisual Centre 2016).

One of the few films produced exclusively with state funds from Croatian television and that managed to combine popularity at home with acclaim at international festivals is Vinko Brešan's 1996 comedy *Kako je poceo rat na mom otoku* (How the War Started on My Island, 1996, Croatia). The film presents the events that triggered the war on a Dalmatian island as a conflict between a fun loving Mediterranean culture and an oppressive central authority. It became a huge domestic box office hit, attracting an audience of 350,000 (about 8 per cent of the population), a number only surpassed by *Titanic*, and established Brešan as Croatia's most prominent director. Despite relying on comic stereotypes, the film humanises the main Serb antagonist, thus avoiding nationalistic simplifications and appealing to a political consensus (Pavičic 2012: 53). Brešan's more recent *Svecenikova Djeca* (The Priest's Children, 2013), a co-production between Croatia, Serbia and Montenegro, takes on the sensitive topic of the Catholic Church, a very powerful institution in independent Croatia, and comically exposes its hypocritical stance on birth control.

The 1990s wars in Yugoslavia brought to the surface nationalism and religious intolerance, but the increasingly European orientation of the region reinforces cosmopolitanism, as well as a new Balkan regionalism. In films from the ex-Yugoslav countries, the traumas of the war are still a recurrent topic, but there is an emphasis on finding ways forward. Dalibor Matanić's highly acclaimed *Zvizdan* (The High Sun, 2015) is a Croatian–Serbian–Slovenian co-production that portrays the absurdities, tragedies and dead-ends of inter-ethnic hatred through three interconnected love stories in which the same two actors play different couples across three decades somewhere near the Croatian/Serbian border. The weaving of the three stories and characters in a way that transcends personal and national identities stresses the interchangeability of victims and perpetrators, and sets foundations for new beginnings.

Conclusion

The ongoing challenges facing Europe, most recently illustrated by the UK's vote to exit the EU, will inevitably lead to further redefinitions of the dynamic between centre and periphery, and shift both geographical and axiological boundaries. While European funding mechanisms (Eurimages, MEDIA) have already provided support for countries of the periphery, opportunities for a truly international career remain limited for those based far from the centre (as suggested by the case of Lanthimos). A new Balkan regionalism that would reinforce co-operation across the countries of South-Eastern Europe could help strengthen their marginal position, redefining the European project in more inclusive and polycentric ways, and enabling the region to project internationally. While national specificities may gradually erode in the context of globalisation, cinema can function as a means for further collaborations, across the local, the regional, the European—and beyond.

References

Behlil, M. (2012) "East Is East? New Turkish Cinema and Eastern Europe", in Imre, A. (ed.) *A Companion to Eastern European Cinemas*, Oxford: Wiley-Blackwell, 504–516.

Bulgarian Cinema 2014: Facts/Figures/Trends (2014) Sofia: Bulgarian National Film Center and Creative Europe.

Cooper, A. (2015) "Where Are Europe's New Borders? Ontology, Methodology and Framing", *Journal of Contemporary European Studies* 23 (4): 447–458.

Creative Europe (2016) 4 August, http://eur-lex.europa.eu/legal-content/EN/TXT/?qid=1408546810627&uri=CELEX:32013R1295.

Croatian Audiovisual Center (2016) 6 February, www.havc.hr/eng/croatian-film/croatian-film-catalogue?category=1&length=3&year=.

Eurimages (2016) 4 August, www.coe.int/t/dg4/eurimages/About/CriteresAdhesion_en.pdf.

Giukin, L., Falkowska, J. and Desser, D. (eds) (2014) *Small Cinemas in Global Markets: Genres, Identities, Narratives*, London: Rowman & Littlefield.

Hjort, M. (2005) *Small Nation, Global Cinema: The New Danish Cinema*, Minneapolis, MN: The University of Minnesota.

Holdsworth, N. (2014) "Bulgaria's Oscar Nominee Criticised for Director's Role on Selection Committee", *The Hollywood Reporter*, 9 August, www.hollywoodreporter.com/news/bulgarias-oscar-nominee-criticized-directors-730973.

Imre, A. (2012) *A Companion to Eastern European Cinemas*, Oxford: Wiley-Blackwell.

Iordanova, D. (2001) *Cinema of Flames: Balkan Film, Culture and the Media*, London: BFI.

—— (2002) "Feature Film-making within the New Europe: Moving Funds and Images Across the East-West Divide", in *Media, Culture and Society* 24 (4): 515–534.

—— (2006) *The Cinema of the Balkans*, London: Wallflower Press.

—— (2008) *New Bulgarian Cinema*, St Andrews: College Gate Press.

Iordanova, D., Martin-Jones, D. and Vidal, B. (eds) (2010) *Cinema at the Periphery*, Detroit, IL: Wayne State University Press.

Jaafar, A. (2015) "Rachel Weisz in Talks to Reunite with Yorgos Lanthimos in *The Favourite*", *The Deadline*, 15 October, http://deadline.com/2015/10/rachel-weisz-yorgos-lanthimos-the-favourite-emma-stone-olivia-colman-1201584014/.

Jackel, A. (2003) *European Film Industries*, London: BFI.
Kourelou, O., Liz, M. and Vidal, B. (2014) "Crisis and Creativity: The New Cinemas of Portugal, Greece and Spain", *New Cinemas* 12 (1–2): 133–151.
Kurelec, T. (2012) "Institutions, Infrastructure, Industry: Croatian Film or a Battle for Survival", in Vidan, A. and Crnković, G. P. (eds) *In Contrast: Croatian Film Today*, Oxford: Berghahn, 41–48.
Nasta, D. (2013) *Contemporary Romanian Cinema: The History of an Unexpected Miracle*, New York: Wallflower Press.
Papadimitriou, L. (2014a) "Locating Contemporary Greek Film Cultures: Past, Present, Future and the Crisis", *Filmicon: Journal of Greek Film Studies* 2: 1–19.
—— (2014b) "In the Shadow of the Studios, the State and the Multiplexes: Independent Filmmaking in Greece", in Erickson, M. and Baltruschat, D. (eds) *The Meaning of Independence: Independent Filmmaking around the Globe*, Toronto: Toronto University Press, 113–130.
Pavičic, J. (2012) "From a Cinema of Hatred to a Cinema of Consciousness: Croatian Film after Yugoslavia", in Vidan, A. and Crnković, G. P. (eds) *In Contrast: Croatian Film Today*, Oxford: Berghahn, 49–56.
Rose, S. (2011) "Attenberg, Dogtooth and the Weird Wave of Greek cinema", *The Guardian*, 27 August, www.theguardian.com/film/2011/aug/27/attenberg-dogtooth-greece-cinema.
Schlesinger, P. (2015) "Some Reflections on 'Creative Europe'", 26 January, http://culturalbase.eu/documents/6.%20SCHLESINGER.%20Creative%20Europe.pdf.
Ţuţui, M. (2015) "New Bulgarian Documentary", in Giukin, L., Falkowska, J. and Desser, D. (eds) *Small Cinemas in Global Markets: Genres, Identities, Narratives*, London: Rowman & Littlefield, 215–230.

15

THE NON/INDUSTRIES OF FILM AND THE PALESTINIAN EMERGENT FILM ECONOMY

Viviane Saglier

World cinema's binaries

This chapter seeks to position the framework of World Cinema with respect to film productions that are not understood as forming a cohesive film industry—despite efforts at organising film-making practices—because they are not supported by a strong state. I argue for an epistemology of world cinema that would bypass state powers as the primary lens to read industrial formations, and for a critical study of top-down processes of legitimisation. In his general introduction to *Critical Approaches to World Cinema* (Hill 2000), John Hill reasserts the worldwide economic predominance of the US film industry (here condensed to Hollywood), which to him explains the emphasis of critical writings on the topic. From this observation derives Hill's definitional focus of his co-edited volume on World Cinema with Church Gibson, which "is devoted to non-Hollywood cinemas, both in the sense of films that are made geographically outside Hollywood and films which have adopted a different aesthetic model of filmmaking from Hollywood" (Hill 2000: xiv). The conceptualisation of World Cinema within this binary tends to perpetuate power relations already in place by directly deducing the theoretical importance of an object of study from the latter's economic, political and diplomatic influence. Moreover, the emphasis falls on Hollywood to set a standard for what constitutes a proper film industry. The developing film industries in the Global South, small nations, and beyond have, however, defended a variety of positions in regards to Hollywood films and their strong presence locally. These industries in the making have also crafted their own strategies with respect to their particular needs and economic contexts. To echo Lúcia Nagib, instead of arguing for an oppositional definition of World Cinema, how can we theorise World Cinema from within—from the point of view of these film productions and more largely from film economies that have been described as World Cinema (Nagib 2006)?

Placing World Cinema at the centre of our study poses yet another fundamental problem. Going back to the history of the term reveals that it constitutes the basis for another hegemony, with its own production of legitimising discourses. Marijke de Valck reminds us that European international film festivals started establishing the economic and aesthetic category of World Cinema in the late 1960s, as they were undergoing a restructuration and increasingly included films from all around the globe. These festivals (Cannes, Berlin, Venice among others) offered Third World film productions better visibility in the European market, which was more lucrative for them than distribution in Third World networks. In turn, from the 1980s onwards, film festivals systematically promoted Third World film productions, the "discovery of new talents", and "New Waves", through the term "World Cinema" in order to enhance their own prestige and distinguish themselves from other festivals, a process that was backed by the economy of prizes and awards (de Valck 2007: 94). This new focus led some film festivals to become actively involved in the production of Global South films and thus contribute to the formation of these new waves of art cinema that feed the festival circuit and appeal to a transnational market, as has, for example, been the case with the renowned Hubert Bals Fund at the International Film Festival Rotterdam since 1988 (Ostrowska 2010: 145; Chan 2011: 254), now supported by the Dutch Ministry of Foreign Affairs. Similarly, the Berlinale's World Cinema Fund (WCF, est. 2004) provides production and distribution aid to what, in the organisers' phrase, are "countries with a weak production infrastructure" (World Cinema Fund 2016). European film festivals' cinema funds, very often backed by national financial support, are part of Europe's larger effort to develop co-productions with Global South countries through initiatives such as the European Union's MEDIA program.

World Cinema thus responds to an economic model whereby European funding typically supports small projects coming from contexts that are not considered to be driven by proper industries, and for the benefit and the expansion of the European market, by setting conditions around working techniques, crew members, shooting locations, targeted audiences, representational politics and style. Tamara Falicov rightfully observes that, although film festivals' funding:

> has helped further cultural production in countries with medium, small or non-existent film industries, there have been persistent cultural politics stemming from colonial legacies that continue to plague the film-funding dynamic, especially in countries in Africa and other former colonial territories.
>
> *(Falicov 2010: 3)*

A more acute curiosity about those postcolonial contexts, as well as new industrial formations, which include the rise of global film festivals outside of Europe (in East Asia or the Gulf, for example), ask us to expand the category of World Cinema to indeed understand the workings of world cinema economies outside of the Hollywood/non-Hollywood binary on the one hand, and the European/non-European binary on the other.

Towards non/industries of film

To refer back to the World Cinema Fund's quotation, what does a "weak production infrastructure" mean? How can we unpack the complexity of emerging or alternative film economies beyond such definitive statements? By privileging the European perspective, World Cinema has obscured the historical mechanisms by which film cultures and developing film industries are shaped within small nations, proto-states and other undermined political and economic formations in the Global South and beyond. This chapter focuses on the term "non/industry" to attend to a non-normative definition of film industries that does not rely on the legitimacy of political, economic and diplomatic structures; "non/industry" describes both this indecisive moment that sees the formation of multiple independent groups and enterprises, and the underlying aims of such groups to eventually consolidate a film industry whose future shape is still to be determined. The agency of the various actors invested in building film economies lies in the space between the "non" and the "industry". Emergent film economies are temporal objects as much as spatial ones, and they demand a theorisation and a methodology that acknowledge the negotiations, uncertainties and failures that contribute to shaping them.

For example, Rasha Salti's investigation of Syrian cinema results in listing paradoxes, the main one being that "if, objectively, Syrian cinema does not bear any of the attributes associated with [. . .] an industry, [. . .] it is nonetheless very difficult to discount the cogent body of work produced by Syrian filmmakers as a mere collection of 'Syrian films and Syrian filmmakers'" (Salti 2006: 1). Since 1963, Syria's scarce film production has been almost entirely funded by the state from a non-commercial perspective and has relied upon a dysfunctional network of film theatres. This cinema is traditionally highly experimental and sophisticated, critical of the state, and very successful abroad, although not so much seen at home. How to describe this in-between economy? Questioning the field of media industry studies, Nitin Govil comes to the conclusion that the term "film industry" has for too long been considered to be obvious, and has therefore remained unchallenged. He takes the example of the Mumbai film industry, which the Indian state did not recognise as such before 1998, although it had the capacity for production and distribution of one, as well as a division of cultural labour. Govil adds, "however, industry status always seemed elusive, relegating Indian cinema to a kind of 'not-yet' Hollywood" (Govil 2013: 176). How can we then study and theorise these film economies that are "not-yet Hollywood" (or not-yet European)? Govil proposes to examine the Indian commercial cinema industry as "re-cognised: not as a pre-existing structure of calculation but as a way of figuring things out" (Govil 2013: 176). Similarly, Tesjawini Ganti insists that no assumption can guide the study of media industries. Stemming from her ethnographic work on the production aspect of the same recognised post-1998 Mumbai industry, she asserts that "we must expand our understanding of what an 'industry' is and not presume certain organisational structures, division of labour, or financial arrangements from the outset" (Ganti 2014: 17). The study of non/industries challenges World Cinema's assumptions of what counts as industry, but it also reflects on how the economic structure of the category World Cinema has been negotiated within non/industries.

The case of Palestinian cinema

Palestinian cinema offers a perfect example to illustrate these debates because it is representative of the rise of World Cinema, while the conditions of its very existence and definition challenge any fixed categorisation. With films such as *Yadon ilaheyya* (Divine Intervention, 2002, France/Morocco/Germany/Occupied Palestinian Territory, Elia Suleiman), *Paradise Now* (2007, Occupied Palestinian Territory/France/Germany/Netherlands/Israel, Hany Abu-Assad), *Milh Hadha al-Bahr* (The Salt of This Sea, 2008, Occupied Palestinian Territory/Belgium/France/Spain/Switzerland, Annemarie Jacir), *Lamma shoftak* (When I Saw You, 2013, Occupied Palestinian Territory/Jordan/Greece/United Arab Emirates, Annemarie Jacir) (Figure 15.1), *Omar* (2013, Occupied Palestinian Territory, Hany Abu-Assad), Palestinian cinema has been very successful abroad in the global art cinema circuit, particularly since the early 2000s, but it has more often than not relied upon foreign aid to support pre-production, production and post-production. It is however not so popular at home in the proto-state of Palestine, established by the widely contested Oslo peace process in 1993. While officially meant to lay the basis for national institutions, the peace process eventually allowed the perpetuation of the occupation through the fragmentation of the remaining Palestinian territory into various zones of governance and increased Israel's control over the local economy (Turner 2014). Film culture and its accessibility in Palestine have thus been consistent with the economic, political and geographic landscape shaped by the various stages of Israeli occupation. National cultural funds are insignificant; commercial film theatres exist in limited numbers but they all tend to privilege American blockbuster productions; and film education is still marginal despite private attempts

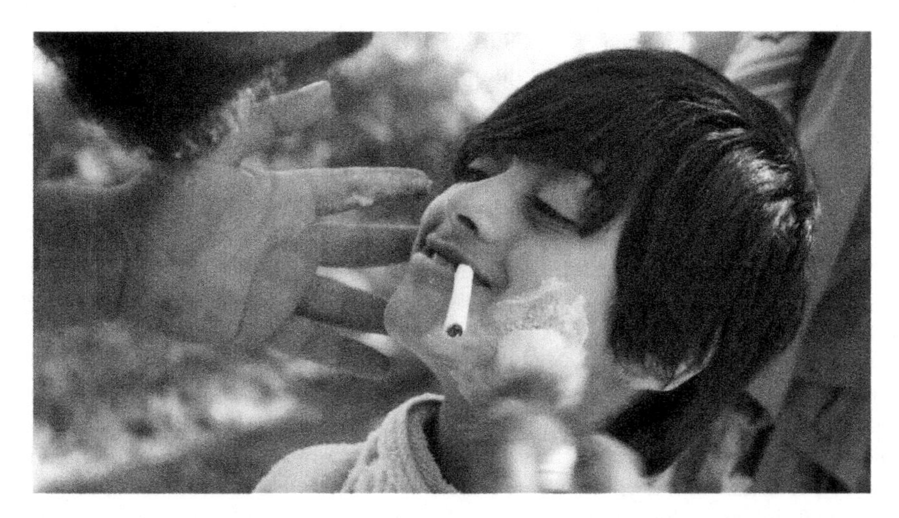

Figure 15.1 *Lamma shoftak* (When I Saw You, 2013, Occupied Palestinian Territory/Jordan/Greece/United Arab Emirates, Annemarie Jacir) was one of a number of Palestinian films to find success on the global festival circuit. ©Philistine Films/Faliro House Productions.

such as filmmaker Rashid Masharawi's Cinema Production Centre (active from the mid-1990s to the early 2000s), the A.M. Qattan Foundation (founded 1993), and programs in development in various universities. Many of the most celebrated Palestinian filmmakers of recent years were educated in the diaspora, such as Elia Suleiman, Annemarie Jacir (both in the US), and Hany Abu-Assad (in the Netherlands), whose films were mentioned above. Palestinian cinema thus needs to be comprehended within various geographical spaces that transcend the current borders, and extend to wherever Palestinians are. The violent history of this people has seen them displaced within and outside the West Bank and Gaza, within and outside present-day Israel, also referred to as historic Palestine, and in exile with or without refugee status and within and outside the region.

Despite their dispersion, Palestinian filmmakers have made a point of shooting their films in occupied Palestine, thus contributing to building a community there, where the fragmentation of the territory, the submission of the local economy to Israeli rule, the lack of independent institutions and daily military violence have made such initiatives very difficult. George Khleifi and Nurith Gertz situate the emergence of Palestinian art cinema in the 1980s with the symptomatic return of Belgium-exiled filmmaker Michel Khleifi to historic Palestine in order to shoot his first film *Al Dhakira al Khasba* (Fertile Memory, 1980 Belgium/France/Occupied Palestinian Territory) (Gertz and Khleifi 2008), an intimate documentary about two Palestinian women of different generations and their struggle with both the occupation and their place in Palestinian society. This periodisation coincides with the rise of World Cinema in the A-list festival circuit. As was typical of that time and now, in the absence of any possible support from the then-sole representative of the Palestinian people, the Palestinian Liberation Organisation (PLO), *Fertile Memory* was coproduced by the Belgian Ministry of the French-Speaking Community, the German television channel ZDF and the French National Centre for Cinema (Centre National de la Cinématographie, CNC). Khleifi's next film, *Urs al-jalil* (Wedding in Galilee, 1987 France/Belgium/Occupied Palestinian Territory), received similar financial support and achieved great recognition, as it was awarded the International Critics Prize in Cannes in 1987.

Palestinian–British film producer, filmmaker and chairman of the eponymous foundation Omar al-Qattan explains how Khleifi's Europe-backed film projects in the West Bank generated new possibilities for making films that would be properly Palestinian, that is to say in this context, that would be made by a Palestinian film crew under the supervision of a Palestinian director (al-Qattan 2006). Until then, most Palestinian film workers were employed in Israeli crews as second- or third-tier technicians, and their skills were as a result limited. In fact, despite the lack of Palestinian funding, Khleifi qualified his first film as a "Belgian–French–Palestinian co-production" (Naficy 2000: 59). Such claims are significant in the face of Israel's constant efforts at erasing the Palestinian presence, history and culture, through sheer dismissal or co-optation. For example, Gertz and Khleifi recount how an Israeli distributor offered to promote Cannes-awarded *Wedding in Galilee*, but only under the condition that Galilee disappear from the title and the film be considered Israeli (Gertz and Khleifi 2008).

Sometimes, the process of defining Palestinian cinema according to the filmmaker's identity would come in direct tension with the source of funding. This would become apparent during the film's circulation in international film festival networks where the country of origin refers to the state from where the funding originates. In her attempt to anticipate another co-optation of Palestinian success in the World Cinema economy, Palestinian citizen of Israel Suha Arraf recently registered her film *Villa Touma* (2014) with the Venice Film Festival as Palestinian although she received financial support from the Israeli establishment, an institution that to her represents an occupying power. Her gesture ultimately questioned the prominence of funding and state formations over the artist's identity and other forms of political community in the classification of a film's origins in the particular context of the occupation (Anderson 2014). The Israeli government considered this an affront and threatened to demand that Arraf return the $580,000 she received for the film's production (Strickland 2014). Partly bending under pressure, Arraf resolved to list the film as "stateless" (Strickland 2014), thus reasserting the independence of Palestinians from the occupying state. This example asks how we can think of Palestinian production through state categories (which condition understandings of film industries) that do not reflect the Palestinian political reality on the ground. One of the biggest challenges posed to anyone ready to approach Palestinian production as more than "a mere collection of Palestinian films and filmmakers", as Rasha Salti put it with respect to Syrian cinema, is precisely the lack of national institutions to provide a clear-cut and predetermined understanding of the workings of the Palestinian film economy. More broadly, and as Kay Dickinson reminds us:

> As Hamid Dabashi argues, these conundrums provoke a serious ontological debate for film culture: "The very proposition of a Palestinian cinema points to the traumatic disposition of its origin and originality. The world of cinema does not know quite how to deal with Palestinian cinema precisely because it is emerging as a stateless cinema of the most serious national consequences."
>
> *(Dickinson 2010: 142)*

As a result, I want to point here to a paradox constitutive of World Cinema that the Palestinian example, with its multiple epistemological instabilities, reveals. On the one hand, the category of World Cinema allows Palestinian cinema to exist internationally as such despite the absence of financial support from the Palestinian proto-state. That is the reason why Michel Khleifi can claim to have directed Palestinian films. On the other hand, World Cinema constitutes the very discourse and economy that prevents Palestinian cinema from developing its own economic and industrial base by maintaining its dependence on European and external funding. Moreover, as Salah Mohsen, who promotes the rights of Palestinians in Israel, remarks in the case of the *Villa Touma* controversy, "it is very common for Israeli films [here read 'any world cinema production'] to receive European funding, but no one demands that they be classified as European films" (cited in Strickland 2014). In other words, and to respond to concerns I raised in the introduction to this chapter, while World Cinema is fed by European funding and co-production agreements that seal economic power relations, it is its being promoted as "world" and non-European that guarantees its circulation in the international art cinema circuit and transnational markets, and success of the festivals that produce and screen it. In addition, this rather general tension is here superimposed onto the political framework of the occupation, which takes shape in parallel, and sometimes very closely so, with European policies and World Cinema's mechanisms. The challenge that awaits the Palestinian filmmaking community is thus to take advantage of its newly acquired visibility in order to gain some independence from the current networks of funding and their ascendency, within the conditions of possibility defined by the occupation.

Independent cinema and the non/industry

For Gertz and Khleifi, today's Palestinian cinema results from the development of Palestinian art cinema in the 1980s. Along with most Palestinian filmmakers and scholars, they claim that there is still no Palestinian film industry because there is no fully fledged Palestinian state despite the 1993 Oslo Accords. The ensemble of Palestinian film productions has therefore been designated through various appellations that the two scholars list as follows: "'Independent Cinema,' 'Palestinian Cinema from the Occupied Lands' (Farid no date; Mdanat 1990) 'Post-Revolution Cinema,' or 'Individualistic Cinema' (Shafik, 2001)" (Gertz and Khleifi 2008: 33). In turn, filmmaker and scholar Sobhi al-Zobaidi writes in 2008, after the second Intifada, about a "new and independent cinema, [. . .] independent from the authorities of state, religion and commerce [. . .] which is best understood as individual cinema" (al-Zobaidi 2008). Al-Zobaidi's conflation of independence and individualism highlights the consequences of working almost completely outside the nation-state framework. On the one hand, the absence of Palestinian state supervision and thus control gives the freedom for filmmakers to operate without compromising their views; on the other hand, there is no structure to help local artistic collaboration and each cultural worker is individually competing for funding, technical resources, and visibility. This independence from the state only hides another dependence, namely on external funders. Looking at the evolution of Palestinian World Cinema and the kinds of pressure exercised by this funding model in the late 1980s and 1990s, al-Qattan for example laments "the emergence of a simple (simplistic) aesthetics and preference for individual(istic), harmless and generally apolitical and sanitised subject matters" (al-Qattan 2006: 117).

How can we reconcile this understanding of independent cinema with the first signs of increased collaboration between Palestinian film workers that underlie the project that some members of the local film community (including Omar al-Qattan) openly claim will build a film industry in the long term? From the mid-2000s onwards, individual or groups of filmmakers started establishing their own production companies, such as Idiom Films, Collage Productions, Odeh Films, Philistine Films, or Pal Cine productions. Some individuals (although very few) have also made successful attempts at minimising European involvement in their films' production, by counting on Arab solidarity networks and the Palestinian diaspora. In 1993, Rashid Masharawi's *Hatta Ishaar Akhar* (Curfew, 1993, Israel/France/Occupied Palestinian Territory/Germany/Netherlands) was called "the first truly Palestinian film" because it was made with a Palestine-based production company (Gertz 2004: 24). More recently, Hany Abu Assad's *Omar* (2013) has benefited from the large support of Palestinian businessman Waleed Zuaiter, who provided 95 per cent of the necessary budget for the film while Enjaaz, Dubai Film Festival's post-production fund, supplied the remaining 5 per cent. The framework of independent cinema tends to ignore that Palestinian cinema was also supported, particularly during and after the Second Intifada, by the international news industry and the NGO economy, both of which directly took part in the crafting of the Palestinian proto-institutions after 1993. Moreover, a significant number of film festivals simultaneously started to emerge in Palestine at this time, stemming from various local collectives that negotiated in different ways their involvement with a multiplicity of foreign funding sources. Examining Palestinian cinema as a non/industry of film allows us to reflect upon independent cinema's modes of production. The latter must be situated within a broader industrial context, as well as an affective history in which "Palestinian [. . .] memory is mostly composed of an uninterrupted flow of uncertainties, insecurities, wars, and a general and detailed sense of destruction" (al-Zobaidi 2008).

Second Intifada cinema

During the Second Intifada (roughly 2000–2005), negotiations and making-do were at the heart of filmmaking tactics. This constituted a mode of production in itself, despite a weak infrastructure. This is worth acknowledging especially since other, more urban, infrastructures were so central to both the control of the population under occupation and the possibilities available for filmmaking. Kay Dickinson highlights the importance of roads and cars in cinema at a moment when flying and permanent checkpoints were multiplying, curfews were being reinforced, and the construction of the Separation Wall was moving forward. USAID-funded roads became an integral part of the landscapes Palestinians filmed but also defined the conditions of film production under the economy of the occupation. As for cars, Amahl Bishara reminds us in her analysis of Hany Abu-Assad's *Ford Transit* (2003 Occupied Palestinian Territory/Israel) that the shared taxis (*servees*) used as public transportation were given by the Israeli authorities to collaborators, who re-sold them to taxi drivers (Bishara 2015).

Identifying a trend of films under the umbrella appellation of "road (block) movies", Dickinson explains the tension prompted by relocating the road movie genre to the Palestinian context of the Intifada. While road movies generally champion freedom and resist the notion of "home", their Palestinian iteration reveals the many impediments to movement and reasserts Palestinians' claim to the land (Dickinson 2010: 139). In Mohanad Yaqubi's *Around* (2006, Occupied Palestinian Territory), a group of friends documents their ten-and-a-half hour journey from Jenin to Ramallah (only 63 km apart) to get their weekly pizza without going through checkpoints; conversely, Sobhi al-Zobaidi's *Obor kalandia* (Crossing Kalandia, 2002, Occupied Palestinian Territory) shows the ordeal people went through to cross checkpoints; while in Nahed Awwad's *Going for a Ride?* (2003, Occupied Palestinian Territory), still images of cars destroyed by Israeli tanks invading Ramallah are testament of forced immobilisation and revive the ghosts of past lives.

For Dickinson, Palestinian attempts at travelling around the occupied land also expose the guerrilla nature of Palestinian cinema (Dickinson 2010: 146). A film such as Annemarie Jacir's docu-fiction *Like Twenty Impossibles* (2003, Occupied Palestinian Territory), among many others, reveals how Palestinian filming and driving, the very documentation of movement, are perceived as a double threat by Israeli soldiers. In Nida Sinnokrot's *Palestine Blues* (2005, USA/Occupied Palestinian Territory), the filmmaker puts a hole in a bag to secretly film crossing through the Qalandiya checkpoint from Ramallah to Jerusalem. At that time and after, the journeys necessary to reach filming locations were also dependent on the drivers' skills in avoiding roadblocks. In an article in the monthly magazine *This Week in Palestine*, filmmaker

Najwa Najjar recounts the logistical nightmare of planning her feature film *Al-mor wa al rumman* (Pomegranates and Myrrh, 2008, Occupied Palestinian Territory), and how shooting in several locations required constant adaptation (Najjar 2008).

Taking guerrilla filmmaking seriously as a mode of production inscribes this reflection on non/industries into a double theoretical lineage that challenges in various ways the rhetorics of World Cinema. On the one hand, Ramon Lobato's study of what he coins "the shadow economies of cinema" expands phenomena that should be worthy of scholarly and economic attention beyond legal and legitimate forms of distribution, towards activities that are unmeasured, unregulated and extra-legal—which also conceptually applies to other forms of production and consumption. Lobato aims to "offer a different way of thinking about the innumerable practices of film viewing that are integral to everyday life around the world but marginal to film studies as a discipline" (Lobato 2012: 1). In contrast, World Cinema works both as an economic category that evens out the multiplicity of film production strategies in order to reassert an uncritical dependence on European and Western funding, and an epistemological category that defines this funding model as what makes these films legitimate objects of study, because they are recognised as art cinema, and as such, are supposedly politically neutral and universal.

On the other hand, the tradition of guerrilla cinema is rooted in the 1960s and 1970s struggles for decolonisation. For Argentine filmmakers and theoreticians Fernando Solanas and Octavio Getino, guerrilla cinema is the shape that a proper anti-capitalist and anti-bourgeois third cinema takes when it adjusts the mode of film production to an economy of decolonisation. For them, the third cinema of liberation, which uses guerrilla tactics, should make "films that the System cannot assimilate and which are foreign to its needs, or [. . .] films that directly and explicitly set out to fight the System" (Solanas and Getino 1969). Auteur, or art cinema, which they call "second cinema" cannot fit these requirements. The Palestinian context of the Second Intifada responds to some of the features outlined by Solanas and Getino in their famous manifesto. However, the Palestinian economy of decolonisation is one that includes uprisings within broader financial and power networks that are in constant negotiation with each other.

From the news industry to the non/industry of film

Many filmmakers active during the Second Intifada came from, or had been educated in, the diaspora, and they sought to found a film community in Palestine as much as build a local crew (Jacir 2008: 16). At the beginning of her self-reflexive documentary *Zaman al-akhbar* (News Time, 2002, Occupied Palestinian Territory), Lebanese-born Palestinian filmmaker Azza el-Hassan's voiceover reports that it is really hard to constitute a film crew during the Intifada because all the technicians are busy working with news agencies. Commenting on the predominance of the news as a mode of image-making, she summarises the situation as such in the film: "This is not the time to be doing films. This is news time." In fact, as scholar, filmmaker, and festival organiser Alia Arasoughly observes, many technicians as well as local filmmakers had previously been trained with the international TV crews established in the West Bank and Gaza to document the uprisings since the first Intifada in 1987. Their contracts were cheaper for these agencies, and provided the film training Palestinians could not find at home. For Arasoughly, the very understanding of film became subordinated to standards developed for TV. By the end of the Second Intifada, news had shaped both the Palestinians' relation to representations *of* themselves, and the production of these representations *by* themselves (Arasoughly 2013). Universities also perpetuated this logic by including audio-visual training within departments of media-journalism, as was the case at the prestigious Bir Zeit University in 2002 or the Institute of Modern Media at Al-Quds University as early as 1996.

The cinema of the second Intifada, and even more so the cinema that followed it, sought to reclaim the tools to narrate Palestinian stories beyond news-oriented documentary cinema, thus developing a trend that would be more experimental and/or interested in fiction, while also in negotiation with the guerrilla tactics mentioned above. Such projects, including the ones currently encouraged by the production company Idioms Films, tend to require a significant budget and subject filmmakers to a more ambitious mode of production and a distribution market closer to the demands of art cinema. However, the economy supposed to support this kind of production has not always empowered the community's narratives in the way some might have hoped. In 2004, a local team organised an ambitious festival, the Ramallah International Film Festival (RIFF), which aimed to attract the foreign community in order to give opportunities for exchange. At the time, the festival was criticised (including by the young team of Idioms Film in their short *Carnaval*, 2005, Mohanad Yaqub, Occupied Palestinian Territory) for highlighting Palestinian filmmakers who were already famous in international circuits and leaving younger generations in the shadow. Other festivals have evolved in parallel to the world cinema economy, targeting instead the human rights industry that has flourished since the Oslo Accords. Although such festivals are dependent on European funding in the same way the more industry-oriented festivals tend to be, these festivals have a range of relationships with the world cinema economy, from avoiding world cinema films in favour of local productions (Shashat Women's Film Festival) and encouraging partnerships with European Youth festivals active in the world cinema economy (International Young Filmmaker Festival), to attempts at using the resources that this economy offers to build opportunities for the local filmmakers (Gaza's Karama Human Rights festival).

Film festivals have thus worked as important proto-institutions in the reviving of a culture of cinema that had been interrupted by the forced closures of theatres during the first Intifada, and which had been complicated by a continuous lack of freedom of movement that limited social gatherings. Film festivals provide a good example of the non/industry of film in Palestine because they are unstable events that have adapted to an unstable environment. Cancellations, postponements, make-up screenings, changes of location, are only a few of the characteristics in the practice of film festivals in general that make them both precarious and flexible events. In many ways, due to this structural precariousness, film festivals are particularly adapted to the hostile environment of the occupation in Palestine, where, among other things, checkpoints, curfews, interruptions of screenings, confiscation of film material, and denial of guests' entry destabilise pre-set programs and constantly threaten such events' very existence.

In Palestine, however, these conditions tend to be imagined in tension with the standards set by global festivals. The type of industry-focused festivals one finds in Palestine (invariably industry focussed) tend to be heavily influenced by the notion of global art cinema and World Cinema. This is in large part due to the organisations that tend to preside over these events, organisations that are one of the only sources of funding available to Palestinian artists in the current post-Oslo and aid-driven economy. Moreover, local film festivals have become the dominant platform for the screening of Palestinian and art films because they have allowed the Palestinian non/industry to grow through a network that so many Palestinian filmmakers had already joined internationally. In addition to film screenings, most Palestine-based festivals include training roundtables, Q&As and workshops (scriptwriting, filming, editing, sound) that complement education given in the new film programs. At various levels, and in many different ways, these festivals have provided a hub for local and international film communities, and a forum for the various actors of the film industry (film distributors, TV buyers, foreign cultural institution representatives, producers, filmmakers, actors etc.) to meet. They often build partnerships with other foreign film festivals and local universities, putting representatives from

Palestinian national institutions into dialogue with the local film community with the aim of reaching out to remote audiences. As a result, they have contributed to the creating of links between communities, a crucial step if Palestine is ever to build a fully fledged film industry.

Film festivals are thus central to imagining a future for the Palestinian local film economy within the context of a non/industry of film and in negotiation with the global financial networks of global art cinema. Many events have identified themselves as actively working towards building a film industry through the local enhancement of film culture and thanks to the relative integration into the international art cinema scene. For example, the Al-Kasaba International Film Festival (2006–2010) welcomed Cannes festival director Thierry Frémeaux in 2009 to give an opportunity for local artists to learn the ropes and join the global art cinema circuit; the organisation FilmLab: Palestine launched "Days of Cinema" in 2014 as part of its plan to "effectively promote film art and film culture in Palestine with the greater aspiration of creating a productive and dynamic film industry, including through training workshops, residencies, and co-productions" (Film Lab: Palestine 2016). These festivals' connections to the global circuits are mostly made possible by their financing through the same European institutions and foreign national cultural institutes also behind many European film festivals, and which profit from opening new markets in Palestine.

Days of Cinema is a good example of this, as its partnership with numerous Danish institutions has inflected the event's programming. Denmark benefits from a strong presence in the Palestinian territories via the Danish House in Palestine (DHiP) and the Danish ministry of affairs' Centre for Culture and Development (CKU). In this particular case, Denmark's financial involvement led to the screening of five Danish films in the Days of Cinema 2015 and a workshop to present the Aarhus film lab in the 2014 edition. Partnerships with other Arab countries have not been as successful. In 2015, while many speakers were invited to join from the region in order to discuss possibilities for building independent regional Arab networks and South/South collaborations, most were denied entry at the border controlled by Israel. The conversation therefore shifted towards topics that European speakers could offer, representatives of institutions such as the World Cultural Fund (also a partner of the event) that, conversely, were allowed in by the occupier.

Conclusion

The example of the Palestinian non/industry of film illustrates the necessity of finding tools to account for the agency and struggles of undermined economic, political and diplomatic actors on the local and international scene. Contexts where a strong state is absent and political tensions constant, a situation to be found in many countries in the Global South and beyond, can be included in research on World Cinema if we expand the conceptualisation of the term beyond the binaries examined in my introduction. World Cinema becomes a more useful category if we reflect on the various levels at which it operates: epistemological, economic and political. Taking this multiplicity of layers into consideration allows us to draw a new map of world cinema that enhances paradoxes, negotiations and power relations.

References

al-Qattan, O. (2006) "The Challenges of Palestinian Filmmaking: 1990–2003", in Dabashi, H. (ed.) *Dreams of a Nation*, London and New York: Verso, 110–130.

al-Zobaidi, S. (2008) "Tora-Bora Cinema", *JumpCut: a Review of Contemporary Media*, 50, www.ejumpcut.org/archive/jc50.2008/PalestineFilm/.

Anderson, J. (2014) "The Hand That Feeds Bites Back", *New York Times*, 16 October, www.nytimes.com/2014/10/19/movies/israel-and-suha-arraf-differ-on-nationality-of-villa-touma.html?_r=0.

Arasoughly, A. (2013) "Film Education in Palestine Post-Oslo: The Experience of Shashat", in Mette Hjort (ed.) *The Education of the Filmmaker in Africa, the Middle East, and the Americas*. Basingstoke: Palgrave, 99–123.

Bishara, A. (2015) "From Dust to Concrete: Infrastructural Change, Intractability, and the Colonial Road Movie", *American Anthropologist* 117 (2): 398–401.

Chan, F. (2011) "The International Film Festival and the Making of a National Cinema", *Screen* 52 (2): 253–260.

de Valck, M. (2007) *Film Festivals: From European Geopolitics to Global Cinephilia*, Amsterdam: Amsterdam University Press.

Dickinson, K. (2010) "The Palestinian Road (Block) Movie: Everyday Geographies of Second Intifada Cinema", in Iordanova, D., Martin-Jones, D. and Vidal, B. (eds) *Cinema at the Periphery*, Detroit, IL: Wayne University Press, 137–155.

Falicov, T. L. (2010) "Migrating from South to North: The Role of Film Festivals in Funding and Shaping Global South Film and Video", in Elmer, G., Davis, C. H., Marchessault, J. and McCullough, J. (eds) *Locating Migrating Media,* Latham, MD: Lexington Books, 3–22.

Film Lab: Palestine (2016) 25 August, http://flp.ps/flp/.

Ganti, T. (2014) "The Value of Ethnography", *Media Industries Journal* 1(1): 16–20.

Gertz, N. (2004) "The Stone at the Top of the Mountain: The Films of Rashid Masharawi", *Journal of Palestine Studies* 34 (1): 24–36.

Gertz, N. and Khleifi, G. (2008) *Palestinian Cinema: Landscape, Trauma, Memory*, Edinburgh: Edinburgh University Press.

Govil, N. (2013) "Recognizing 'Industry'", *Cinema Journal* 52 (3): 172–176.

Hill, J. (2000) "General Introduction", in Hill, J. and Church Gibson, P. (eds) *Critical Approaches to World Cinema,* Oxford and New York: Oxford University Press, xiv–xv.

Jacir, A. (2008) "Letter from the Editing Room", *This Week in Palestine* 117: 16–19.

Lobato, R. (2012), *Shadow Economies of Cinema*, London: BFI.

Naficy, H. (2000) *An Accented Cinema: Exilic and Diasporic Filmmaking*, Princeton, NJ: Princeton University Press.

Nagib, L. (2006) "Towards a Positive Definition of World Cinema," in Dennison, S. and Song, H-L. (eds) *Remapping World Cinema: Identity, Culture and Politics in Film*, London and New York: Wallflower Press, 30–37.

Najjar, N. (2008) "Making a Feature Film in Palestine", *This Week in Palestine* 117: 12–14.

Ostrowska, D. (2010) "International Film Festivals as Producers of World Cinema", *Cinéma & Cie: International Film Studies Journal* X (14–15): 145–150.

Salti, R. (2006) "Critical Nationals: The Paradoxes of Syrian Cinema", *Kosmorama* 237.

Solanas, F. and Getino, O. (1969) "Towards a Third Cinema: Notes and Experiences for the Development of a Cinema of Liberation in the Third World", in Corrigan, T., White, P. and Mazaj, M. (eds) *Critical Visions in Film Theory*, Boston and New York: Bedford/St. Martin's, 924–938.

Strickland, P. O. (2014) "Suha Arraf On Her 'Stateless' Palestinian Film", *The Electronic Intifada*, October 9, https://electronicintifada.net/content/suha-arraf-her-stateless-palestinian-film/13936.

Turner, M. (2014) "The Political Economy of Western Aid in the Occupied Palestinian Territory Since 1993", in Turner, M. and Shweiki, O. (eds) *Decolonizing Palestinian Political Economy: De-Development and Beyond*, Basingstoke: Palgrave, 32–52.

World Cinema Fund (2016) *World Cinema Fund Supported Films* 2005–2015.

16

LOCATIONS AND NARRATIVE REORIENTATIONS IN ARAB CINEMAS/WORLD CINEMA

Anne Ciecko

Introduction

This chapter begins with a cinematic disappointment: a cautionary tale of the sparse landscape of a national/domestic film culture giving way to foreign interests and global aspirations, and a seeming desert of imagination. The Doha Film Institute in Qatar, together with a Tunisian film and television producer, teamed up to make a 55 million dollar production, *Day of the Falcon* (aka. *Black Gold*, 2011, France/Italy/Qatar/Tunisia, Jean-Jacques Annaud) that was almost universally panned upon its release (Ritman 2014). Located in an indeterminate Arabia, and filmed in Qatar and Tunisia, *Day of the Falcon* was directed by French filmmaker Jean-Jacques Annaud and starred a mostly non-Arab cast headed by Antonio Banderas and Freida Pinto in lead roles in a lavishly derivative, Arab-themed historical desert epic about the rise of the modern oil industry. Based on a 1957 book by Swiss writer Hans Reusch titled *South of the Heart: A Novel of Modern Arabia*, the ambitions of its film adaptation for grandiose global entertainment elided dimensions of cultural verisimilitude in favour of outmoded tropes and Orientalist stereotypes. The film failed to connect with contemporary audiences, and apparently contributed to the infrastructural implosion of the nascent Qatari film industry, and the squelching of dreams of an international Arab breakthrough blockbuster (Mintzer 2011; Pulver 2012). As this chapter examines and as Lina Khatib insists in her book *Filming the Modern Middle East*: "While it is important to study how the West represents the East, it is even more crucial to see how the 'Orient' represents itself'—or allows itself to be represented (Khatib 2006: 4).

Cultivating desert landscapes

The most immediate and nostalgic referent for *Day of the Falcon* is David Lean's T. E. Lawrence biopic *Lawrence of Arabia* (1962, UK/USA), a celebrated and canonical film about a problematic "Arab" poseur; in the words of Jack Shaheen, author of a critical compendium of representations of Arabs in Hollywood, *Lawrence of Arabia* "may contain compelling cinematography and engrossing performances, [but] as [Arab] history [it] receives a failing grade" (2001: 290). The film is paradoxical in its combination of reductive representations of tribal Arabs, coupled with a critique of colonialism (Caton 1999: 19). David Lean and his team shot the film in Morocco, a country that has served as locations for many international films, starting in the early decades of the twentieth century when European and American films featured locations from North Africa and the Middle East, and also frequently depicted "passive groups of the colonized" (Orlando 2011: 7). Alongside Peter O'Toole as Lawrence, Mexican-born Hollywood star Anthony Quinn plays Auda abu Tayi, the Bedouin leader of the Arab revolt; Quinn is later cast as Libyan tribal leader Omar Mukhtar, who fought Mussolini's troops in the deserts of Libya in *Lion of the Desert* (1980, Libya/USA, Moustapha Akkad). Aiming for authenticity, and partially funded by Libyan revolutionary leader Muammar Gaddafi, *Lion in the Desert* was actually filmed in the deserts of southern Libya. For Aleppo-born director Akkad, who became a major Hollywood player as producer of the *Halloween* slasher horror franchise, *Lion in the Desert* was the second of an unfinished Arab epic trilogy he had planned to complete before his tragic death in a 2005 hotel bombing in Amman, Jordan. It was a means of recuperating pan-Arab cinematic identity and promoting cultural understanding (Ciecko 2010: 14).

Perhaps the most globally visible dunes of the Arab world landscape are those recontextualised in the Star Wars franchise's mythical desert planet Tatooine, constructed of images filmed mostly in real-world locations in southern Tunisia. Tunisian landscapes and locations in movies such as *Star Wars: Episode IV—A New Hope* (1977, USA, George Lucas), *Raiders of the Lost Ark* (1981, USA, Steven Spielberg) and *The English Patient* (1996, USA/UK, Anthony Minghella), among others, inspired the National Office of Tunisian Tourism to capitalise on topographical iconicity made famous by foreign blockbusters and epics (Ben Bouazza and Schemm 2014). Instead, Tunisian filmmaker Nacer Khemir's "Desert Trilogy"—*El haimoune* (Wanderers of the Desert, 1984, Tunisia/France), *Le collier perdu de la colombe* (*The Dove's Lost Necklace*, 1991, France/Italy/Tunisia) and *Bab'Aziz* (Bab'Aziz—The Prince Who Contemplated His Soul, 2005, Switzerland/Hungary/France/Germany/Iran/Tunisia/UK)—mines a personal and collective image-repertoire of memory, folklore, Sufi mysticism and Arab Islamic representation more generally, in his examinations of the Arab desert and the Arab wanderer (Shafik 2007: 53). Locations find new currency as genres become culturally relevant. For example, after the 2003 military invasion in Iraq and subsequent occupation, Jordanian desert landscapes have served as displaced stand-ins or surrogates for the country-under-siege in foreign films, war movies such as *The Hurt Locker* (2008, USA, Kathryn Bigelow) and *Battle for Haditha* (2007, UK, Nick Broomfield). Writing on recent generations of Arab road themes in films and audio-visual culture, Laura Marks observes the relative absence of geographical deserts in current Arab filmmaking and video art, asserting that "the new desert is the Arab highway" in filmic works of "asphalt nomadism" (Marks 2015: 153). However, *Theeb* (2014, United Arab Emirates/Qatar/Jordan/UK, Naji Abu Nowar) is one case of contemporary national/pan-Arab cinema that reclaims the region, the physical desert, Arab history and the nomadic figure. A co-production of Jordan, United Arab Emirates, Qatar and the UK, it focuses on a Bedouin boy's coming of age and struggle for survival in the Wadi Rum desert during the First World War era, in the period following the Arab Revolt. Drawing inevitable comparisons, some critics have referred to *Theeb* as an Arab corrective or companion piece to the cinematic imaginary of Lean's *Lawrence of Arabia*. *Theeb* also extends Arab cinema's discursive journey into the international image market and critical acclaim as Jordan's first ever nominee for the Best Foreign Language Film Oscar at the Academy Awards.

Charting the Arab cinematic world(s)

Within the larger map of world cinema, the concept of Arab cinema (or Arab cinemas, plural, e.g., *les cinémas Arabes* as they are frequently called in French) is problematised by the concept of a world within a world, as well as the transdiscursive legacies of Occidentalism, Eurocentrism, nationalism, colonialism and civilisation. There is "not one school, form, structure, or style" to Arab cinema (Ghareeb 1997: 119, cited in Mellor 2011: 103). Because of the heterogeneity of "communities, peoples, states, governments, societal forms", as well as the diversity of languages (including multiple Arabic dialects), religions and sects, ethnicities and cultures, the Arab world is not a monolith; however, there are some common cultural topography and historical parallels across the cinemas of Arab nations (Shafik 2007: 1–2). Arab cinema does not have the same specific continent-focused valences of Asian cinema and African cinema, as member states of the "Arab world" or the Arab League of nations and territories (Algeria, Bahrain, Comoros, Djibouti, Egypt, Iraq, Jordan, Kuwait, Lebanon, Libya, Mauritania, Morocco, Oman, Palestine, Qatar, Saudi Arabia, Somalia, Sudan, Syria, Tunisia, United Arab Emirates, Yemen) intersect with or are contained within the two largest continents. However, the Arab world or Arab nations construction generally maintains a sense of shared Arab identity (political, linguistic, cultural) informed by the ideological project(s) of Arab nationalism. Some, but not all, of these sovereign Arab nations and territories are also frequently encapsulated in the transcontinental configuration of the "Middle East" that additionally includes non-Arab nations such as Iran, Cyprus and Turkey. Collected studies of Arab cinema and, or within, the Middle East configuration include editions by Gugler (2011), Ginsberg and Lippard (2010), Devi and Rahman (2014), among others. In making a further distinction, some scholars such as Hafez (2006) favour the linguistic and cultural inflections of the term "Arabic Cinema".

As an extension of the challenge of naming and locating, "Arab cinema", like Asian cinema and African cinema, may also include transnational and global diffusions and amalgamations of personnel, productions and representations as part of the category. Arab films and filmmakers have variously asserted or contested the nation-state and national/cultural identity. Arab films may represent interstitial and contested spaces; reappropriate and subvert cinematic stereotypes; engage with exilic, diasporic, and glocalised experiences. Arab cinema employs a wide array of ever-more-hybridised genre and iconographic conventions, yet the category (like Asian cinema and African cinema) can function discursively like a meta-genre, as in the case of Arab film festivals (such as the multi-site Arab Film Festival in multiple California cities inaugurated in 1996, the largest and oldest such festival in the United States, and the Biennial of Arab Cinema at the Institute du Monde Arab in Paris/Biennale des cinémas arabes à Paris) and distribution companies and networks (e.g. Arab Film Distribution, which "promotes and distributes the cinemas of the Arab world in North America" (Arab Film Distribution website), initially established in partnership with the Seattle Arab and Iranian Film Festival in 1990). For film scholarship, overlapping categories such as "beur" cinema (a colloquial vernacularisation of the word Arab, a term for films made by Maghrebi immigrants and their descendants, especially in the French context) and *le cinéma de banlieue* (depicting multi-ethnic experiences in the periphery of French cities) provide a means for "reframing difference" and intersectionality in Arab and African diasporic cinemas in particular national–cultural contexts (Tarr 2005).

In historicising Arab cinema, scholars and programmers have negotiated the perceived chronology of world cinema. For example, in the mid-1990s, discourse of the "centennial" of cinema became pervasive, frequently attributed to the "originary" discourses of the French brothers Lumière, the "pioneering" short films they and their team produced *(actualités),* and their combined camera, printer and projector invention (*Cinématographe*). Using as a starting point the 1896 production and exhibition in Cairo of films made in Egypt by Lumière collaborator Alexandre Promio, the Film Society of the Lincoln Center in New York City presented, in 1996, a showcase of 41 films from throughout the Arab world, then the largest such representation of Arab films in the USA (including films from Algeria, Egypt, Kuwait, Lebanon, Morocco, Palestine, Syria, and Tunisia), co-curated by Richard Peña and Alia

Arasoughly. In tandem with this project, Palestinian filmmaker, scholar and programmer Arasoughly edited and translated essays in a collection titled *Screens of Life: Critical Film Writing from the Arab World* (1996).

Complexities of Arab cinema as a category are evident in English-language scholarship dedicated to Arab cinema, in the establishment of new film festivals, in filmmaker manifestos, and in reflexive documentary engagement. The earliest book-length study of Arab cinema to appear in English is *The Cinema in the Arab Countries* (1966), a translation of the anthology prepared for the United Nations Educational, Scientific, and Cultural Organization (UNESCO). With most entries drawn from reports by Arab critics and filmmakers presented at round-table conferences on Arab culture and cinema in Egypt and Lebanon between 1962 and 1966, the volume was overseen by French writer and researcher Georges Sadoul, who also produced encyclopaedias of films and directors, and multi-volume histories of cinema, including *Histoire du cinéma mondial, des origines à nos jours* (1949). Additionally, it contains recommendations of the Arab League concerning film and television from meetings in Jordan and Syria in 1965 and 1966. Ambitiously reflective of the movement toward more pan-Arab inclusivity, *The Cinema in the Arab Countries* reports on Arab cinema in terms of larger film cultural activities (production, exhibition, marketing, and distribution) and inter-artistic relations (shadow shows, theatre, television, music). The book was published by the Interarab Centre of Cinema and Television in Beirut, that had, in its earlier incarnation as The Arab Film and Television Centre, previously sponsored multiple conferences on Arab cinema and culture and published the proceedings (Armes 2010: 30). *The Cinema in the Arab Countries* was published the same year as the inaugural Carthage Film Festival in Tunisia, devoted to Arab and African cinema, and considered to be the oldest film festival on the African continent. Adding coalition-building Third World and Third Cinema discourses into the mix, Arab filmmakers participated in the writing of their own versions following Latin American ground-breakers, Glauber Rocha's 1965 manifesto "Aesthetics of Hunger" and Julio Garcia Espinosa's "For an Imperfect Cinema" in 1969 (Daulatzai 2012: 57). New film cinema club organisations and journals were formed in Egypt and Morocco including Jamaat al-Cinema al-Jadida (The New Cinema Group) established in Cairo (Khouri 2010: 57; Daulatzai 2012: 57). In December 1973, Algiers was the site for the Third World Film-Makers Meeting sponsored by the Algerian National Office for Cinematographic Commerce and Industry and the Cultural Information Center, and attended by filmmaker delegates from Africa and Latin America including filmmakers from Algeria and Morocco. This gathering resulted in an influential manifesto of cinema against imperialism and neo-colonialism, "Resolutions of the Third World Film-Makers Meeting, 1974" (2004), followed up by a charter adopted at the Second Congress of the Fédération Panafricaine des Cinéastes (FEPACI) in Algiers, The Algiers Charter on African Cinema" (1975). Subsequent to *The Cinema in the Arab Countries*, key scholarly and documentary interventions explore Arab cinema as both distinct and politically and geoculturally intersectional—as in the case of Egyptian cinema and North African/ Maghrebi cinema, frequently distinguished from Francophone Sub-Saharan African cinema and institutions such as the film festival, FESPACO (Festival panafricain du cinéma et de la télévision de Ouagadougou, established in 1969). In their book *Arab and African Film Making*, Lizbeth Malkmus and Roy Armes discuss four geographical areas: "sub-Saharan Africa, the Arab West (or Maghreb), Egypt and the Arab East (or Mashreq) [that] all share the mark made on their political, economic and cultural developments by colonialism" (1991: 3). Tunisian filmmaker, screenwriter, and critic Férid Boughedir signals connections and divisions in the form of his documentary diptych, *Caméra d'Afrique* (Twenty Years of African Cinema, 1983, Tunisia/France) and *Caméra Arabe* (1987, Tunisia).

Situating the *Caméra Arabe*

Subtitled "The Young Arab Cinema", *Caméra Arabe* offers a narrative account (with voiceover by Boughedir), asserting that Arab cinema, or rather the films watched by the Arab public, was/were, for more than forty years, dominated by melodramas and musical comedies from Cairo studios. Egypt is "the oldest and largest film industry in the Arab world [and] the only Arab country that was able to establish a local film industry even before national independence" (Hillauer 2005: 35). This commercial hegemonic model was confronted by cultural change marked by the rise of Gamal Abdel Nasser, accompanied by a new realist cinema (with its exponents Salah Abou Seif, Henri Barakat, Kamel El Cheikh, Tewfik Saleh, Shadi Abdessalam, and "unclassifiable innovator" Youssef Chahine). For Boughedir, the liberation of the nations of Tunisia, Morocco and Algeria—the independence of Arab North Africa and the Third World more generally—encouraged the birth of a new cinema that was "totally different from its great Egyptian elder", celebrating the past struggle and the dignity of the oppressed. He cites as a landmark the Algerian war film *Rih al-awras* (The Winds of the Aures, 1967, Algeria, Mohammed Lakhdar-Hamina), made just five years after Algerian independence, that was followed by a wave of independent auteurs from North Africa and the Middle East who "struggled to give passion and voice to their own countries and dreamt of an alliance which would bring the lost family together again, and which would retrieve the lost grandeur and unity of Arab civilization". However, Boughedir marks the Six-Day War defeat in 1967 and Nasser's resignation thereafter as having a cataclysmic impact on the Arab psyche, as expressively reflected in Youssef Chahine's drama *Al-asfour* (The Sparrow, 1972, Egypt/Algeria) set during the Six Day War, a film that inspired other Arab filmmakers to grapple head-on with crises of subjectivity and the recovery of memory.

Boughedir emphasises the importance of international film festivals as showcases for World Cinema, including the Carthage Film Festival as a forum for Arab and African cinema, and the Cannes Film Festival as a World Cinema showcase and platform for international recognition. He also underscores the necessity of negotiating multiple worlds in promoting Arab cinema, while also retaining commitment to the Arab experience. *Caméra Arabe* celebrates the Palme d'Or prize win at Cannes for Algerian film *Chronique des années de braise* (Chronicle of the Years of Fire, 1975, Algeria, Mohammed Lakhdar-Hamina) which depicts Algeria's struggle for independence; however, it also includes an excerpted interview with Lakhdar-Hamina, who describes his commitment to his land, people and their passions, and his unwillingness to leave Algeria to take any of the multiple opportunities in the West that came his way after his Cannes win, even though he had fallen out of favour with the Algerian regime. Boughedir asserts that the new Arab cinema could not find an exhibition circuit, with screens dominated by foreign films; therefore, festivals in the Arab world starting with the Carthage Film Festival (and later the Damascus Film Festival in 1972) became important regional/international vehicles for Arab and African filmmakers.

The Palestinian plight due to the 1948 war, exodus and displacement—coupled with atrocities of occupation after the Six-Day War—became a rallying point for Arab filmmakers. Two films mentioned in *Caméra Arabe* provide particularly potent representations of the Palestinian experience and its impact on larger Arab consciousness. Egyptian filmmaker Tewfik Saleh directed and co-scripted the Syrian-financed drama *Al-makhdu'un* (The Dupes, 1973, Syria), an adaptation of Palestinian writer Ghassan Kanfani's 1962 novella *Men of the Sun* about the tragic struggles of desperate Palestinian refugees travelling to Kuwait for work. Because of its production circumstances, content and commitment, film scholar Viola Shafik, author of the afore-referenced landmark study of history and cultural identity in Arab cinema, calls *The Dupes* "a Pan-Arab production par excellence" (Shafik 2007: 155). Demonstrating the ways the past is located in the present (and vice versa), Lebanese filmmaker Borhane Alaouié's *Kafr kasem* (The Massacre of Kafr Kassem, 1975, Syria/Lebanon) dramatises the real-life events of the 1956 massacre of Palestinian civilians in the titular village. In an interview in *Caméra Arabe*, Israeli-born Palestinian filmmaker Michel Khleifi, living in exile in Belgium, muses about ways to represent Palestinian or Arab experience using cinema. Boughedir alludes to other Arab cinema manifestos, including the "Manifesto of the Palestinian Cinema Group" (1973) which called for a radical reformation of Arab cinema that has "for too long delighted in dealing with subjects having no connection to reality or dealing with it in a superficial manner" (Palestinian Cinema Group 1973: 273). Scholarship on Palestinian cinema, and Arab cinema more generally, has analysed the audiovisual delineations of visible and invisible borders, barriers, checkpoints and walls; interstitial spaces of exile and displacement; trauma, memory and dreams of a nation (Dabashi 2006; Gertz and Khleifi 2008). For scholar Kay Dickinson, road blocks have become part of what she calls the "everyday geographies" of post-year-2000 Palestinian film, "Second Intifada Cinema" (2010: 137–155). In building an infrastructure for expanded Arab cinema, Shashat Women's Cinema, a registered NGO founded by Alia Arasoughly in Ramallah, Palestine in 2005, coordinates an annual film festival, considered the longest-running women's film festival in the Arab world, and works toward capacity building, especially support of women, in the filmmaking sector (Hjort 2013: 102).

A final location *Caméra Arabe* explores is that of gendered subjectivity and agency. Boughedir asserts that part of the recovery process of Arab cinema is in the recognition, beyond the desire for a unified Arab subject, of Arab humanity and fractured identities. Films such as *Ahlam al-Madina* (Dreams of the City, 1984, Syria, Mohammad Malas), *Rih essed* (Man of Ashes, 1986, Tunisia, Nouri Bouzid), *Hadduta misrija* (An Egyptian Story, 1982, Egypt, Youssef Chahine) and *Traversées* (Crossing Over, 1983, Tunisia/France/Belgium, Mahmoud Ben Mahmoud) all deal in some way with a sense of collective defeat and a crisis of Arab masculinity, as well as the confrontation of memory and past faith in the Arab nation. *Omar Gatlato* (1977, Algeria, Merzak Allouache) is an international festival prize-winner that also drew record domestic audiences in Algeria (Armes 2005: 105). Through its savvy and uncondescending depiction of the vulnerable machismo of the pop culture-loving title character, it resonated with its exploration of the contradictions, pressures and absurdities of contemporary society and traditional values.

The historical recovery and recognition of Arab women filmmakers is also a critical project of world film scholarship and criticism. In her vitally interventionist *Encyclopedia of Women Filmmakers* (2005), Rebecca Hillauer notes that Lebanese filmmaker Heiny Srour's documentary *Saat al-tahrir dakkat* (The Hour of Liberation Has Arrived, 1974, UK/Lebanon/France) is not only the first film directed by an Arab woman to be screened at Cannes, but also the first film by any woman to be screened at the festival (Hillauer 2005: 25). While there are relatively few women filmmakers discussed in the documentary *Caméra Arabe*, a clip of Tunisian screenwriter and director Néjia Ben Mabrouk is included; she critiques male filmmakers' compulsion to either idealise women or represent them as full of gloom. *Caméra Arabe* also incorporates an extract from *Poupées de roseau* (Reed Dolls, 1981, Morocco), a woman-centred drama about a pregnant widow who ends up losing custody of her children, directed by Jilali Ferhati and written by Farida Benlyazid, who would go on to become an active film and television director (Gauch 2016: 196). In Boughedir's voiceover, the work of dynamic Lebanese filmmaker Jocelyne Saab is praised as taking risks in depicting street level realities of the civil war in Lebanon. Later in her career, in a broader pan-Arab filmmaking nexus, Saab would face another set of challenges with censorship in making her daring Cairo-set 2005 Egyptian/Lebanese/French co-production about female sensuality and the impact of forced female circumcision, *Dunia* (Kiss Me Not on the Eyes, 2005).

Caméra Arabe also reflexively integrates the agency of Arab women filmmakers, as it is edited by Tunisian filmmaker Moufida Tlatli who would go on to direct *Samt el qusur* (The Silences of the Palace, 1994, Tunisia/France), a powerful dramatic feature that provocatively asserts that national independence did not necessarily liberate women (Hillauer 2005: 19).

Pointing to the future (and to the past): multiplying narratives

In this chapter, I have suggested that intersectionality may be a valuable way of complicating constructions of Arab cinema and its storytelling functions. The recent proliferation of multi-strand narratives in world cinema is illustrative of the ways a single narrative feature film can open up diversifying narrative possibilities. In contemporary Arab cinema, it serves as a means to tease out myriad differences including cultural and racial/ethnic perceptions, regionalism and nationality, class and occupation, age and generation, and ideological and religious perspectives. *City of Life* (2009, United Arab Emirates, Ali F. Mostafa), *Sukkar banat* (Caramel, 2007, France/Lebanon, Nadine Labaki), and *Omaret yakobean* (The Yacoubian Building, 2006, Egypt/France, Marwan Hamed) are three disparate examples of multi-strand Arab filmmaking centred in a specific city location—Cairo, Beirut and Dubai, respectively—that create Arab cinema in cosmopolitan narrative spaces of globalisation. *City of Life* intertwines the lives of an Air Emirates air hostess from Romania, an Indian cab driver with Bollywood aspirations, two young male Arab Emirati friends from different economic backgrounds, and an anonymous cyclist (apparently of Southeast Asian heritage), who wordlessly frames the narrative from the perspective of street-level reality, and offers the possibility of hope and good luck for the disenfranchised. *Caramel*, referencing depilatory beauty ritual, intersects five Lebanese women in the location of a beauty shop in Beirut: Labaki's character who is having an affair with a married man, a Muslim wife-to-be who is not a virgin, a tomboy salon worker who experiences lesbian desire, an aging aspiring actress, an older dressmaker who sacrifices romantic love to focus on the care of her invalid sister. Centring on social mores, tensions in families and romantic relationships, and moral choices, *Caramel* refocuses attention from memories of the Lebanese Civil War that pervade much of contemporary Lebanese cinema, including the local hit musical comedy/drama *Bosta* (2005, Lebanon, Philippe Aractingi) in which Labaki played a central acting role. *The Yacoubian Building*, an adaptation of a best-selling novel by Alaa al-Aswany with reportedly the highest budget of any Egyptian film to date, features a pantheon of some of Egypt's most popular stars including the beloved Adel Emam, Tunisian-born Hend Sabry (who started her career in Moufida Tlatli's aforementioned 1994 feminist classic *The Silences of the Palace*), and veteran actress/chanteuse Yousra, in a trenchant critique of corruption in Egyptian politics and society. The film, named after a building that houses all classes from impoverished roof dwellers to debauched penthouse pashas and politicians, touches on an array of taboos including sexism and sexual exploitation of workers and wives, homosexuality and repression, religious hypocrisy, and the rise of fundamentalism and extremism. *The Yacoubian Building* employs multi-strand narration also as a vehicle for intertextuality as it references the melodramatic excess of Golden Age Egyptian melodrama and the multivalent politics of Egyptian television serials (Abu-Lughod 2004). While this expensive formula has not yet proven sustainable beyond the commercial success of *The Yacoubian Building,* with shifting local audience tastes toward more modest fare, Egyptian production and distribution company Good News Group has envisioned an integrated corporate structure across media and entertainment industries, and has been seeking out international co-financing partnerships (Jafaar 2010).

It can be argued that the future of all World Cinema is in co-partnerships, whether in terms of financing and modes of production, or in terms of imagining audience appeal through some sense of veracity that registers on multiple local, national and global levels. Arab cinema, like World Cinema, does not exist in a vacuum, or in a single location. Some future trajectories of Arab cinematic storytelling (and Arab film criticism and scholarship) and Arab/global film cultures can be found in extensions of cinema via new transmedial platforms, video-sharing, social mediations, multimedia artistic explorations and performances, pirate and hacking operations, citizen journalism, and diaristic documents. Arab cinema studies should be part of a larger dialogue with audiovisual culture and digital media. Research tends to focus mainly on the narrative fiction feature film intended for theatrical release as the standard-bearer of Arab Cinema/World Cinema, but scholarly work such as Laura U. Marks' *Hanan al-Cinema: Affections for the Moving Image* (2015) and *Unfoldment and Infinity: An Islamic Genealogy of New Media Art* (2010) offers compellingly rigorous and expansive contextual and theoretical frames for engaging with time, space, and embodiment in Arab experimental film and video works of all lengths, genres and formats. The structure of the "anthology" can also serve as an exciting vehicle for promoting a polyphony of independent Arab film/media voices in pan-Arab omnibus films and compilations such as *Resistance[s] I* and *II* and *III*, a multi-volume DVD project launched by the Paris-based label lowave. Another necessary site for representational expansion is created by queer Arab cinemas (and non-binaristic approaches to gender)—reading Arab film history against the grain to fill in the lacunae created by repression and censorship, but also recognising courageous queer independent and underground voices (Hassan 2010).

Arab cinema is also becoming an urgent contemporary discursive location for refugee cinema, with long histories of grassroots film/media training in camps and community centres. There is a need to document narratives of heroic process as well as product. For example, filmmakers and educators Maysoon Pachachi and Kasim Abid, who had previously run workshops in Ramallah and the West Bank, co-founded the Independent Film and Television College (IFTC) Baghdad in 2004 to provide free-of-charge intensive courses. Over the years, the College has helped train talented Iraqi documentary filmmakers including Hiba Bassem from Kirkuk who made an award-winning short called *Baghdad Days* (2005). However, IFTC has also shut down periodically because of violence, destruction and safety risk; or relocated students to Damascus. There Pachachi also ran a photography project with Iraqi refugee women in Syria that yielded a documentary film *Open Shutters Iraq* (2008, Iraq, Maysoon Pachachi), as well as a book, and photographic exhibitions (Clarke 2009; Dolberg 2010).

Another challenge that contemporary Arab cinema contends with is the potential "effacement" of film history in the heralding of emerging film cultures. Nascent Arab cinemas are vulnerable to the celebratory possibilities and limits of what I call "first film" discourses. The convergence between Arab cinema and world cinema, and corresponding media coverage, is evident in the understandably effusive response to the "World Cinema Audience Award" at the Sundance film Festival for the 2008 Jordanian film *Captain Abu Raed* (2008, Jordan, Amin Matalqa) or the first-ever submission of an officially Saudi film for the Best Foreign Language Film category of the Academy Awards for *Wadjda* (2012, Saudi Arabia/Netherlands/Germany/Jordan/United Arab Emirates/USA, Haifaa al-Mansour). However, decontextualised replication of "first film" assertions can lead to the sense that cinemas of Arab countries begin with Western discovery in the most reductive sense. Therefore, the following can make the field of inquiry more dialogic: recovery and documentation of lost film histories; the translation and circulation of film scholarship, journalism and criticism across linguistic and cultural boundaries; and attention to larger contextual questions of film culture and production/exhibition/distribution/reception. All narratives (including this attempt to narrativise Arab cinema, related scholarship, and film cultural initiatives) are necessarily elliptical. Another potential dialogic direction for World Cinema studies is the exploration of anecdotes, ephemera, affective investments, authorial subject positions, and nostalgia, in experiences of cinema (films already made and those not yet realised) and the world. Multiple testimonials can enrich the public extradiegetic discursive realm of Arab cinema and, indeed, World Cinema's offscreen locations. For example, first-hand experiences have informed this chapter on Arab cinema. Here are just a few: Jocelyne Saab at the NETPAC film conference and festival of Asian and Arab film in Delhi, where she told me about her travails making *Dunia* in Egypt; seeing *The Yacoubian Building* in Cairo and being invited by a local festival-goer to visit the building that inspired the novel/film; watching Ali Mostafa's award-winning graduation short in Dubai several years prior to his debut feature *City of Life*; happening upon Nadine Labaki and her team shooting *Caramel* at the Mayflower Hotel in the Hamra neighbourhood of Beirut and being told by a crew member that "everybody" already knows the first-time filmmaker/insta-auteur before finding out that this was true among young people in the region because of Labaki's well-known previous work as a music video director; interviewing a very young Naji Abu Nowar and his producer Nadine Toukan in Amman almost a decade before *Theeb* (2014), when they were trying to get his based-on-a-true-story script about an urban serial killer off the ground. As we know, his acclaimed first feature would become, instead, a Bedouin western, a truly epic desert journey.

References

Abu-Lughod (2004) *Dreams of Nationhood: The Politics of Television in Egypt*, Chicago, IL: University of Chicago Press.

Arab Film Distribution website, www.arabfilm.com.

Arasoughly, A. (1996) *Screens of Life: Critical Film Writing from the Arab World*, St-Hyacinthe, Quebec, CA: World Heritage Press.

Armes, R. (2005) *Postcolonial Images: Studies in North African Film*, Bloomington, IN: Indiana University Press.

—— (2010) *Arab Filmmakers of the Middle East: A Dictionary*, Bloomington, IN: Indiana University Press.

Ben Bouazza, B. and Schemm, P. (2014) "Tunisia Turns to 'Star Wars' to Boost Tourism", *Huffington Post*, 30 April, www.huffingtonpost.com/2014/04/30/tunisia-star-wars-tourism_n_5242531.html.

Caton, S. C. (1999) *Lawrence of Arabia: A Film's Anthropology*, Berkeley, CA: University of California Press.

Ciecko, A. (2010) "Akkad, Moustapha (1935–2005)", in Ginsberg, T. and Lippard, C. (eds) *Historical Dictionary of Middle Eastern Cinema*, Lanham, MD: The Scarecrow Press, 14.

Clarke, C. (2009) "Heroes and Handicams", *The Guardian*, 30 April, www.theguardian.com/film/2009/may/01/maysoon-pachachi-iraq-baghdad-film.

Dabashi, H. (2006) *Dreams of a Nation: On Palestinian Cinema*, London/New York: Verso.

Daulatzai, S. (2012) *Black Star, Crescent Moon: The Muslim International and Black Freedom Beyond, America*, Minneapolis, MN: University of Minnesota Press.

Devi, G. and Rahman, N. (eds) (2014) *Humor in Middle Eastern Cinema*, Detroit, IL: Wayne State University Press.

Dickinson, K. (2010) "The Palestinian Road (Block) Movie: Everyday Geographies of Second Intifada Cinema", in Iordanova, D., Martin-Jones, D. and Vidal, B. (eds) *Cinema at the Periphery*, Wayne State University Press.

Dolberg, E. (ed.) (2010) *Open Shutters Iraq*, London: Trolley Books.

Gauch, S. (2016) *Maghrebs in Motion: North African Cinema in Nine Movements*, Oxford: Oxford University Press.

Gertz, N. and Khleifi, G. (2008) *Palestinian Cinema: Landscape, Trauma and Memory*, Edinburgh: Edinburgh University Press.

Ghareeb, S. (1997) "An Overview of Arab Cinema", *Critique* 6 (11): 119–127.

Ginsberg, T. and Lippard, C. (eds) (2010) *Historical Dictionary of Middle Eastern Cinema*, Lantham, MD: Scarecrow Press.

Gugler, J. (ed.) (2011) *Film in the Middle East and North Africa: Creative Dissidence*, Austin, TX: University of Texas Press.

Hafez, S. (2006) "The Quest for/Obsession with the National in Arabic Cinema", in Vitali, V. and Willemen, P. (eds), *Theorizing National Cinema*, London: British Film Institute.

Hassan, O. (2010) "Reel Queer Arabs", *Film International* 43 (8), http://filmint.nu/?p=1295.

Hillauer, R. (2005) *Encyclopedia of Women Filmmakers*, Cairo: American University in Cairo Press.
Hjort, M. (2013) *The Education of the Filmmaker in Africa, the Middle East, and the Americas*, Basingstoke: Palgrave Macmillan.
Jafaar, A. (2010) "Good News to go international", *Variety*, 15 February, http://variety.com/2010/film/markets-festivals/good-news-to-go-international-1118015246/.
Khatib, L. (2006) *Filming the Modern Middle East: Politics in the Cinemas of Hollywood and the Arab World*, London: I.B. Taurus.
Khouri, M. (2010) *The Arab National Project in Youssef Chahine's Cinema*, Cairo: American University in Cairo Press.
Malkmus, L. and Armes, R. (1991) *Arab and African Film Making*, London and New Jersey: Zed Books.
Marks, L. U. (2010) *Enfoldment and Infinity: An Islamic Genealogy of New Media Art*, Cambridge, MA: MIT Press.
—— (2015) "Asphalt Nomadism", in *Hanan-al Cinema: Affections for the Moving Image* Cambridge, MA: MIT Press, 147–169.
Mellor, N. (2011) "Arab Cinema", in Mellor, N., Ayish, M., Dajani, N. and Rinnawi, K. (eds), *Arab Media*, Cambridge: Polity, 67–84.
Mintzer, J. (2011) "Black Gold: Film Review", *The Hollywood Reporter*, 9 November, www.hollywoodreporter.com/review/black-gold-film-review-259456.
Orlando, V. (2011) *Screening Morocco: Contemporary Film in a Changing Society*, Athens, OH: Ohio University Press.
Palestinian Cinema Group (1973/2014) "Manifesto of the Palestinian Cinema Group", in MacKenzie, S. (ed.) *Film Manifestos and Global Cinema*, Chicago, IL: University of Chicago Press, 273–275.
Pulver, A. (2012) "Black Gold—Review", *The Guardian*, 23 February, www.theguardian.com/film/2012/feb/23/black-gold-review.
"Resolution of the Third World Film-Makers Meeting, Algiers, December 5–14, 1973" (2004) in Shepherdson, K. J. (ed.), *Film Theory: Critical Concepts in Film and Media Studies*, Volume 3, Abingdon: Taylor & Francis, 325–334.
Ritman, A. (2014) "Whatever Happened to the Qatari Film Industry?" *The Guardian*, 6 March, www.theguardian.com/film/2014/mar/06/qatari-film-industry-doha-festival-black-gold.
Shafik, V. (2007) *Arab Cinema: History and Cultural Identity* [revised ed.], Cairo: American University in Cairo Press.
Shaheen, J. (2001) *Reel Bad Arabs: How Hollywood Vilifies a People*, New York: Olive Branch Press/Interlink.
Tarr, C. (2005) *Reframing Difference: Beur and Banlieue Filmmaking in France*, Manchester: Manchester University Press.

17

THE FORKING PATHS OF INDIAN CINEMA

Revisiting Hindi films through their regional networks

Madhuja Mukherjee

Introduction

This essay sets out to remap Hindi popular cinema by locating its regional trajectories and questions conventional accounts of Indian cinema that present a narrative of a fixed and definitive Hindi language cinema produced in Bombay. Indian films of the 1920s employed inter-titles in a variety of languages (English, Hindi, Gujarati, Bengali), as is evident not only from surviving films but also from the *Indian Cinematograph Committee Report* (ICCR 1927–1928), and were produced and circulated across multiple locations throughout India (on the ICCR see Jaikumar 2003). Furthermore, studies of film studios have demonstrated that the production of Hindi-language cinema was not, in fact, limited to Bombay, but rather that in the 1920s and 1930s studios were set up in disparate places such as Calcutta (in Bengal) and Pune (in Maharashtra) (see Bhaumik 2001; Mukherjee 2008). Consequently, the meteoric growth of Bombay-based Hindi melodramas in the 1950s, followed by the emergence of the blockbuster model that relied on famed stars such as Amitabh Bachchan, formulaic narratives and generic hybridity in the 1970s and the transnational success of Bollywood in the 1990s, can be explained through reference to a complex web of industrial conditions and historical evolutions (on Bachchan see Prasad 1998, and on Bollywood see Rajadhyaksha 2002). By addressing crucial debates and studies on Indian cinema and focusing in particular on the complicated regional production and circulation of Hindi cinema, this chapter argues for an alternative, and more geographically complex, historiography of Indian cinema.

The generic diversity of Indian cinema in the 1920s–1930s

Ashish Rajadhyaksha's landmark 1987 essay on the "Phalke Era" analysed the ways in which the idea of Indian modernity was forged through the mythological films produced by D. G. Phalke in Mumbai during the 1910s and 1920s, and in so doing laid the ground for new approaches to studies of Indian cinema. Subsequently, more recent research has stressed the popularity of other genres and the transnational flows of Hollywood films across Indian territories during this period. For instance, Nitin Govil and Eric Hoyt (2014) have shown how *The Thief of Bagdad* (1924, USA, Raoul Walsh) became a huge international success largely due to United Artists' distribution networks throughout Asia, while research by Valentina Vitali (2008) and Anupama Kapse (2014) have drawn attention to the vibrant presence of action and stunt films in India during the silent era.

In his dissertation on the growth of the Bombay film industry between 1913 and 1936, Kaushik Bhaumik (2001) discusses the dynamic dialogues between Hindi films, the so-called regional language films in Bengali, Punjabi, Gujarati, Marathi and the like and the popular cinema of Hollywood. By drawing on diverse sources, including the ICCR and Bhaumik's critical map of Indian films, this chapter highlights their multiple paths, especially their regional and cosmopolitan networks, and the fact that in the 1920s colonial India was regularly exposed to a wide range of American (and European) films. The production of Hindi films, which had (and have) pan-Indian distribution and exhibition networks, was actually dispersed across different sectors of British India and thus both culturally and economically divided. Such cultural interactions and economic explorations in relation to Indian modernity may be read in the light of Miriam Bratu Hansen's assertion that:

> cinema was not only *part and symptom* [italics added] of modernity's experience and perception of crisis and upheaval; it was also, most importantly, the single most inclusive cultural horizon in which the traumatic effects of modernity were reflected, rejected or disavowed, transmuted or negotiated.
>
> *(Hansen 1999: 62)*

Thus, as Anupama Kapse discusses, films such as *Diler Jigar* (1931, India, G.P. Pawar) presented "new social, psychic, and artistic possibilities" (Kapse 2014: 224). Building on such studies of early cinema, I will now explore how modernity was refracted through cinema and the manner in which popular cinema became both "part and symptom" of the modernity project, advanced to a great extent by the Indian bourgeoisie (on the project of Indian bourgeoisie see Chatterjee 1994).

Modernity, New Theatres and the 'literary mode': Hindi cinema in Calcutta in the 1930s

In the early 1930s, the concept of an idealised Indian cinema was expounded and quickly became inextricably linked with debates about modernity (see Mukherjee 2012a), nationhood and nationalism and the process of becoming 'modern' (see Niranjana *et al.* 1993). For example, as quoted in the report of the *Indian Film Industry's Mission to Europe and America* (published by the Motion Picture Society of India, Bombay, July–December 1945) during his Presidential address at the 51st session of the Indian National Congress in 1938, the nationalist leader Subhas Chandra Bose said:

> We should make India and her culture known to the world [...] If we could send out cultural and educational films made in India, I am sure that India and her culture would become known and appreciated by people abroad.
>
> *(Bose, quoted in Motion Picture Society of India, Bombay 1945: 2)*

Thus, not only was a nation being "imagined", but certain cultural forms such as cinema were being employed as a vehicle for national modernity. While both Soviet and (pre-1933) German nationalist models were pivotal in such debates, in India, the *Bhadralok*—English educated, urbane (upper-caste, Hindu) gentry of Bengal—became the bearer of such imaginings (see, for example, Kaviraj 1995). A thorough study of debates on cinema suggests that the aspiration to material supremacy (through education, scientific development and industrial growth) and spiritual sovereignty (involving culture and "the woman's question") could effectively be integrated into the cinema, since film was perceived as a technologically driven "art" form with "cultural" implications. Cinema could simultaneously project technical sophistication, an "imagined" Indian culture, and (a mythologised) history. In fact, a number of film reviews, editorials, letters to the editor, and pieces of studio news published in the influential journals such as *Film India, Film Land* and *Varieties Weekly* and others illustrate how issues of modernity, technology, industry, culture, language, artistic forms and gender were collapsed into the cinematic frame. In effect, cinema was seen as both a cultural product and project that had to be located within a larger international context, specifically in times of war and nationalism.

One may locate the emergence of New Theatres Ltd (henceforth NT) within the context of such debates. NT was established in Calcutta (Bengal), in 1931, by Birendra Nath Sircar, an Engineer trained in Glasgow, the son of the Advocate General of Bengal, and thus exemplary of the Bhadralok. From its inception until 1955, NT built technologically advanced studios, hired proficient (foreign) technicians, well-known authors, artists, musicians and directors (some of whom were active National Congress members), and produced films in Bengali, Hindi, Urdu and other languages. Sircar's early productions were immediately seen as an example of the Bhadralok's successful adoption of a popular form that had immense economic and cultural possibilities. During the inauguration of Chitra, NT's principal theatre in north of Calcutta, in November 1930, Subhas Chandra Bose urged Sircar, his employees, and the public to "to give less importance to foreign language films and focus on films made in Bengali" (see Mukherjee 2008). NT's other main cultural site, New Cinema, was inaugurated in Central Calcutta in 1932 by the well-known author, Sarat Chandra Chattopadhyay, who was also a National Congress leader and whose writings often seemed to "fill out" Bose's ideological considerations (see Sarkar 1987). Chattopadhyay was closely linked with NT's productions and the studio gained substantial pan-Indian popularity and respectability via adaptations of his novels. The links between active national politics, economic struggles, the growth of small scale industrial operations and debates on culture, technology and the positioning of the Bhadralok as the agency of change thus constitute crucial points of departure in the attempt to understand how cinema was imagined as a vehicle of modernity.

The association with Bose's and Chattopadhyay, together with the involvement of eminent musicians, technicians and authors, including Noble laureate Rabindranath Tagore, posit NT's activities in the wider political–cultural map. Moreover, Sircar's social status played a crucial role in establishing NT's position of respectability. NT was perceived as an "emblem of culture" and was often pitted against companies which produced films with physical action or comedies. As the writings of well-known journalist, writer and filmmaker K. B. Abbas (1939) make clear, companies such as NT and Prabhat Film Co., Poona, which made progressive-realist and "Saint films" in Hindi and Marathi, fulfilled the nationalist model of an ideal cinema (on Prabhat see Geeta Kapur 2000). Specifically, NT's "literary style", which was achieved through the adaptation of novels, complex characterisation, a manner of narration that portrayed character's interiority through meandering narratives, complicated dialogue, application of thoughtful background music, the creation of realistic settings and so on, contributed to its high status (see Mukherjee 2008). NT often quoted European authors such as Goethe and Voltaire in its advertisements and placed its elephant logo (comparable only to MGM's roaring lion) above the names of directors and popular actors establishing a distinctive identity (Mukherjee 2009).

Such a revisionist history of NT reveals that the Hindi market was not entirely dominated by production companies based in Bombay, such as Bombay Talkies, Wadia Movietone and

Ranjit Studios. Rather, NT and Prabhat Film Co., not only created a dent in the Northern and Western territories but also pioneered narrative and musical patterns and introduced a new visual iconography. This influence can be observed throughout the 1940s even though the studios located in the regions declined and then closed down in the 1950s. It is at this point that Bombay re-emerged as the principal site of Hindi film production, eventually becoming the "port of arrival" for many artists and reinforcing the widely known Hindi "Socials" (see Vasudevan 1989).

The decline of Calcutta studios and the rise of the Bombay brand in the 1950s

By the mid-1930s NT became a benchmark of idealised cinema. For instance, an anonymous reviewer in *Film World* (February 1934) emphasised that NT films were of "very high standard", the dialogue used "natural accent" and deployed "flawless" technique. However, *Film India* (January 1939) reviewed *Street Singer* (1938, India, Phani Majumdar), one of NT's biggest hits (with their pan-Indian singing sensations K. L. Saigal and Kanan Devi nee Bala), as "amateurish" and unsatisfactory, while *Lagan* (1941, India, Nitin Bose) was described as "nothing" compared to "the old standard of New Theatres" (1941, June, *Film India*). Nonetheless, such a narrative of the gradual decline of the ideal NT film is simplistic and misleading. For while NT had become principally associated with what have been termed "literary" films, in actual fact a number of its films did not fit within the framework (see Mukherjee 2011a and 2014). Moreover, the Hindi film market was bifurcated by multiple tendencies and some of the most popular Hindi films of the period belonged to other genres: action-thrillers produced by Wadia Movietone such as *Hunter Wali* (1935, India, Homi Wadia); (quasi-)historicals produced by Minerva Movietone such as *Pukar* (Call, 1939, India, Sorab Modi), *Sikandar* (1941, India, Sorab Modi) and *Jailor* (1938, India, Sorab Modi); Bombay Talkies' "socials" such as *Nirmala* (1938, India, Franz Osten), *Jhoola* (Swing, 1941, India, Gyan Mukherjee), *Naya Sansar* (New World, 1941, India, N R Acharya), *Kismet* (1943, India, Gyan Mukherjee); and big hits such as *Khazanchi* (1941, India, Moti B Gidwani) that incorporated a variety of popular tropes and reimagined the very notion of the popular. Moreover, during this period, Prabhat Film Co. had continued to produce "progressive" films directed by filmmakers such as V. Shantaram; Imperial Film Co. had produced India's first colour film, *Kisan Kanya* (1937, India, Moti B. Gidwani); and Mehboob Khan had made *Aurat* (Woman, 1940, India), portraying the iconic mother figure. While these films belonged to the all-inclusive Indian genre of the "Socials", some of them were also costume dramas set in the medieval period and thus adopted a distinct historical imaginary. The decline of the NT style, which had been one of the dominant modes in the 1930s and 1940s, must therefore be located in the complex mesh of political and cultural transformations of the period.

NT and the other studios in Calcutta, such as Sree Bharat Lakshmi Productions, began to disintegrate as a result of war and the volatile economic–political conditions of the 1940s (see Mukherjee 2009). During the Second World War, while Indian soldiers were fighting abroad, Eastern India lived in fear of bombing. Moreover, the Nationalist movement was at its peak and unprecedented communal riots soon ensued. Following the devastating Bengal famine in 1943 and nationwide bloodshed in 1946, both Independence and Partition took place in 1947 (see Sarkar 1984). Bengal experienced this traumatic transition in multiple ways and the film industry in Calcutta was severely affected. NT's economic and cultural dominance and the overall control of the big studios dwindled dramatically following these tragic events.

Nonetheless, 1940 witnessed an increase in industrial investment (in iron, steel, ammunitions, etc.) and this increased employment and the amount of money in circulation. Rapid migration from rural areas to the cities further increased the size of the cinema-going public and a new kind of money resulting from shady wartime deals popularly known as "black money" became easily available to the film industry (see Barnouw and Krishnaswamy 1980: 127–128). New strategies, including "one-film contracts" with the cast and crew became a common practice and although the cost of production increased four to six times, wartime deals brought easy and unaccounted capital (see Mukherjee 2009). Therefore, despite the scarcity of (imported) raw stock, and huge increases in cost of production (due to higher studio charges, star salaries, etc.), the industry experienced unprecedented growth and the number of films produced per year increased as a result of the expanded market. Popular films that previously ran for four to six weeks now ran for four to six months and NT had its biggest hit ever with *Wapas* (Back, 1943, India, Hemchandra Chunder). Thus, even when there was the risk of war and riots, there was no dearth of companies in cities such as Bombay, Calcutta, Madras (in South India) and Lahore (now in Pakistan). More than a hundred new companies—most of them with limited capital—were launched and production boomed, creating a huge demand for raw film, equipment, technicians, stars, and so on.

During the war, the studios suffered considerably due to a shortage of raw film stock, which was initially rationed and later available only on the black market. The big studios also suffered a severe financial crisis as hired personnel were quickly "bought" by the new companies with free-flowing capital. The patriarchal and vertical control of the studio owners no longer seemed viable. The situation was even more difficult in Bengal since partition meant that a large part of its market became a "foreign" market with the formation of (East) Pakistan. The removal of technical support from Europe as a result of the war, renewed control through censorship, the need to produce war propaganda films (which eventually flopped), the lack of raw film stock, and the scarcity of sufficient theatres to cater for the increased number of films produced all contributed to the disintegration of the studios. As for NT, directors such as Pramathesh Chandra (P.C.) Barua and Devaki Kumar Bose had already departed and with the war even respected technician–directors such as Nitin Bose and Bimal Roy left for Bombay. Furthermore, NT's production costs were far greater than the profits it could garner during this period and in 1955 the studio made its last films.

Conversely, by the 1940s, Bombay was the place to be (see, for example, Prakash 2010). Already in the previous decade Bombay had become a vibrant space for artistic encounters. Various groups and associations were established such as the Progressive Writers Association (1936), the Indian People's Theatre Association (1944) and the Progressive Artists Group (1947); moreover, in 1943 the headquarters of India's Communist Party was shifted from Lucknow (Central India) to Bombay. By the mid-1940s, there was a vibrant group of left-wing thinkers contributing to cultural life including eminent writers such as Saadat Hasan Manto, Krishan Chander, Ali Sardar Jafri and Ismat Chugtai, as well as performers and poets such as Sahir Ludhianvi, Majrooh Sultanpuri, Prem Dhawan, Shailendra and Kaifi Azmi. The presence of such figures contributed to the production of progressive films such as *Dharti Ke Lal* (Children of the Earth, 1946, India, K.A. Abbas) and *Neccha Nagar* (Lowly City, 1946, India, Chetan Anand). Additionally, the rapid economic growth in and around Bombay led to a migration towards the city, and the small-scale industries mushrooming in the Bombay suburbs produced greater possibilities for film production than in the city of Calcutta, which was only beginning to adjust to the millions of "refugees" who had arrived post-partition. Thus, the struggle over the Hindi film market was not solely the result of political change in the wake of the war and partition, but also the rapid development and subsequent stability of the Bombay production companies and the vibrant, left-leaning social and cultural scene in the city.

The rise and rise of the "Hindi Socials"

Ever since the mid-1930s, the genre labelled as the "Hindi Socials" had drawn on the discrete melodramatic tendencies pioneered by NT, Prabhat and Bombay Talkies. For example, India's first cinemascope film, *Kaagaz ke Phool* (Paper Flowers, 1959, India, Guru Dutt), is set during a moment of transition and describes the decline of the studio era and the way one director, Suresh (played by Dutt himself), negotiates these changes. It makes specific references to NT, contrasting films such as *Street Singer* and *Nartaki* (Dancer, 1940, India, Debaki Bose) as examples of the failing studio style with *Vidyapati* (1938, India, Debaki Bose) and *Devdas* (1935, India, P. C. Barua) as examples of an earlier golden age. Thus, the film tells the story of an era, interweaving Suresh's personal crisis with references to NT's films and history. In the process, Dutt fabricates intricate inter-textual links, employing creative mise-en-scène to allude to the dominant images of Barua's *Devdas*—shots of murky, sinister streets; the hero languishing in grief and pain; his visits to the brothel as in *Pyaasa* (Eternally Thirsty, 1957, India, Guru Dutt) (see Mukherjee 2011b).

In his reading of Hindi films of the 1950s, Ravi Vasudevan (1989) argues that Indian melodramas (and the "Socials") are dominated by two basic plot types. The "renunciation" plot, in which the hero rejects authority is exemplified by *Devdas* and *Pyaasa*; while *Awaara* (Vagabond, 1951, India, Raj Kapoor), *Deewar* (The Wall, 1973, India, Yash Chopra) and *Shakti* (Power, 1982, India, Ramesh Sippy) exemplify the second type which features an (Oedipal) "conflict" with an authorial father figure (see also see Vasudevan 2002). According to M. Madhava Prasad (1998), the social spaces articulated in such melodramas, and especially those of films from the 1960s, represent "a conflict between two ideologies of modernity, one corresponding to the conditions of capitalist development in the periphery and the other aspiring to reproduce the ideal features of the primary capitalist state" (Prasad 1998: 55). In examining the relationship between the transformation of cinematic institutions and the on-going struggle over the formation of the state, Prasad interprets films of the 1960s such as *Sangam* (Confluence, 1964, Raj Kapoor) as "feudal family romances" (Prasad 1998: 64) that narrativise negotiations between the newly formed nation-state and the conventions of existing community structures. Equally importantly, he highlights the tensions between spectatorship and citizenship embodied in such films.

Prasad goes on to demonstrate how, following the crisis of the Indian state after the death of India's first Prime Minister Jawaharlal Nehru and the meteoric rise of (his daughter) Indira Gandhi, which resulted in the rule of decree barring elections and civic rights in 1975, the film industry reconstituted itself "formally" through a process he describes as the "aesthetics of mobilization" (Prasad 1998: 138–159). By this point the democratic revolution had been "indefinitely suspended" and the cinema addressed the new context through "three distinct aesthetic formations—the new [state sponsored, developmental] cinema, middle-class [commercial] cinema, and the popular cinema of mobilization" (Prasad 1998: 118). Valentina Vitali (2008) also explores the cinema's response to this "moment of disaggregation" vis-à-vis the state, by comparing low-budget action films with films featuring Amitabh Bachchan, the biggest star of the period. An analysis of the interactions between "A-movies" and "B-movies" reveals how the cinematic scene was actually "highly hybrid", creating a "transnational category [in which] the national and regional forms" (Vitali 2008: 186) retained their distinctive characteristics.

Prasad's complex readings of the relationship between the state and cinematic forms call attention to the multiple courses within the industry. For instance, he identifies two types of

"Middle Class Cinema"; the first emerges from the culture of progressive realism in the films of Prabhat, while the second derives from the NT style, reproducing a realist aesthetic but working within a populist mode. As a result, there were two types of middle class cinema, one "asserting the national role" and the other attempting to produce "an exclusive space of class identity" (Prasad 1998: 163). More central to the concerns of this essay is his reading of middle-class cinema's:

> overwhelming dependence on Bengali culture [and the NT style] for its narrative and iconographic material as well as filmmaking talent [...] [and the ways in which] the industry found in those narratives a ready supply of "difference" which could be re-presented.
>
> *(Ibid.: 164–165)*

Films by Bimal Roy such as *Parineeta* (The Married Woman, 1953, India), *Do Bigha Zamin* (Two Acres of Land, 1953, India), *Biraj Bahu* (1954, India), *Devdas* (1955, India), *Parakh* (1960, India) and by Hrishikesh Mukherjee, such as *Anuradha* (Actress, 1960, India), *Anupama* (1968, India), *Satyakam* (1969, India), *Anand* (Bliss, 1971, India), *Bawarchi* (The Chef, 1972, India), *Chupke Chupke* (Hush Hush, 1975, India) (Figure 17.1]), all belong to such practice.

It is worth noting that the principal action hero of the period, Amitabh Bachchan, also performed in a number of Hrishikesh Mukherjee films, and that the exclusion of his middle-class roles (and his own English educated background) raise a series of questions around the construction of his star persona and point towards a possible new reading of industrial networks.

Figure 17.1 Films such as *Chupke Chupke* (Hush Hush, 1975, India) were dependent on Bengali culture, and the NT style, for their narrative and iconographic material.

During this period his persona was based primarily on elements such as forbidding anger, the question of an unresolved past, a deep attachment to the mother, excessive gloom and physical suffering. Yet the concurrent success of *Zanjeer* (Shackles, India, Prakash Mehra) and *Abhimaan* (Pride, India, Hrishikesh Mukherjee) in 1973, *Hush Hush* and *Sholay* (Embers, India, Ramesh Sippy) in 1975, and *Alaap* (Overture, India, Hrishikesh Mukherjee) and *Amar Akbar Anthony* (India, Mammohan Desai) in 1977, complicate such a simplistic, one-sided reading of his persona. For example, *Hush Hush*, which is a reworking of the Bengali film *Chhadmabeshi* (Incognito, 1971, India, Agradoot), presents Bachchan as an English Professor and portrays several middle-class characters, themes and situations that reinforce middle-class endogamy. Moreover, through location shooting and the creation of familiar situations and situational dialogues, Mukherjee transposed realistic aesthetics to the commercial sector. Particularly significant in this regard are the uses of music and the treatment of situation-specific songs.

The nature and functions of the "Middle Class Cinema" described by Prasad are dealt with explicitly in *Guddi* (1971, India, Hrishikesh Mukherjee). Here both the audience and the protagonist, Guddi, who is herself obsessed with popular cinema, are taken on a journey that leads them to become (seemingly) more rational and educated film-goers. Thus, the film addresses issues such as the problem of the reality-effect vis-à-vis tropes of popular cinema and the rise of stars following the disintegration of the studios. Such subjects are developed through a series of scenes in which Guddi is gradually reformed. Mukherjee represents the film industry in terms of visionary directors and good-hearted actors (especially those playing villains) and crews, thereby, as Prasad argues, "softening" the critique of popular cinema by portraying it as an enterprise. Moreover, the film draws attention to the use of playback, and the role of musicians, writers, technicians and the like. Not only does the film make use of actors from the early talkie period like Master Shiraj, but also features contemporary stars like Dharmemdra (playing himself), who escorts Guddi and her fiancé to a dilapidated studio, which, he claims belonged to Bimal Roy. As the camera tracks to draw attention to the remains of the past, Dharmendra's voice-over describes how they had shot landmark films such as Roy's *Bandini* (Captured Female, 1963, India), *Do Bigha Zamin* (1953, India) and *Madhumati* (1958, India), in the same studio. "Who remembers those names", he laments, before adding, "our names will be forgotten too." Aside from the fact that Mukherjee aspired to produce an idealised audience (or "citizen-subjects") in the new nation, his allusions to his own reformist films such as *Anupama* (1966, India) and those of Bimal Roy underline a longer trajectory of realist aesthetics that includes Roy's *Do Bigha Zamin*, a landmark and popular adaptation of *Ladri di biciclette* (Bicycle Thieves, 1948, Italy, Vittorio De Sica) scripted by Mukherjee, as well as his seminal work for NT such as *Udayer Pathey* (Towards the Light, 1944, India, Bimal Roy). The persistence of such "Bengali" elements alongside the dominant melodramatic mode, not only illustrates the industry's negotiation of the process of the formation of the national state, but also demonstrates how the promise of modernity evoked in the early period was kept alive and perpetually deferred.

Writing about *Kalapani* (Deported, 1958, India, Raj Khosla), which is a reworking of the Bengali film *Sabar Upore* (Beyond Everything, 1955, India, Agradoot) Prasad suggests that:

> The loss of thematic and iconic integrity that the Bengali "social" genre undergoes in the hands of the Bombay film industry has many causes. [...] The result was the creation of a new form which, in spite of the "nationalization" of the Hindi film industry in Bombay, would henceforth and for a long time retain these regional features.
>
> *(Prasad 2011: 78)*

The concluding section thus extends this proposition and examines this process of "nationalisation" and the "inscribing" of regional cultural features in contemporary cinema to reveal what we could term the "forking paths" of mainstream Hindi films.

The local in the global

With nationwide inflation in the 1980s, the production system in Bombay weakened considerably and, after a decade of astounding successes, even Amitabh Bachchan's films began to fare poorly at the box office. Moreover, amidst rapid political changes after Prime Minister Indira Gandhi's assassination and as his popularity began to wither, Bachchan stepped into politics, becoming a Member of Parliament. But the 1980s also witnessed the successful re-entry of producers from Southern provinces, with Tamil and/or Telugu companies producing a number of Bachchan vehicles such as *Andha Kanoon* (The Law Is Blind, 1983, India, T. Rama Rao), *Mahaan* (Great, 1983, India, Prakash Mehra and S. Ramanathan), *Geraftaar* (1985, India, Prayag Raaj) and *Akhree Raasta* (The Last Option, 1987, India, Bhagyaraj).

The media culture was also changing rapidly, with the arrival of new colour TV channels in 1982 and the introduction of cassette and videotapes in the music industry (see Manuel 1993). One of the biggest successes of the decade was a smaller-budget film, *Disco Dancer* (1982, India, Babbar Subhash), which, together with *Kasam Paida Karne Wale Ki* (I Swear by My Father, 1984, India, Babbar Subhash) and *Dance Dance* (1987, India, Babbar Subhash), comprised a loose "trilogy" that effectively introduced new musical (and media) forms, such as disco (see Mukherjee 2012b). The success of such smaller-budget films emphasises the influx and spread of new media and music cultures during this period, and one could suggest that the Bachchan film *Agneepath* (Path of Fire, 1990, India, Mukul S. Anand), which co-starred the lead from the disco trilogy, Mithun Chakraborty, was a response to these industrial (and political) changes.

Anurrag Kashyap's magnum opus *Gangs of Wasseypur* (2012, India), which was made and released in two parts, responds to these intense negotiations, while also harking back to the "B-movie" phase of Hindi cinema (see Mukherjee 2015) (Figure 17.2). The films are set in a quasi-real space in Jharkhand (formerly part of Bihar, India), and deal with the nexus between the coal mafia and politicians through a narrative that encompasses a broad historical arc and three generations of characters. Interestingly, the memory of Bachchan's star-persona (as well as those of Sanjay Dutt and Salman Khan) functions as a powerful structural device in the film. For example, the story of Faizal Khan, the protagonist of part 2, models his life on the estranged father–son narrative of *Trishul* (Trident, 1978, India, Yash Chopra). Indeed, it is by weaving a mesh of cross-references that Kashyap crafts a potent story that provides a commentary both on public cultures and their import within social histories. The films also evoke the memories of the "B-movies" of the 1980s and 1990s and of disco, employing the title song of *Kasam Paida Karne Wale Ki* when Sardar Khan, the protagonist of part 1, decides to confront his father's murderer, Ramadhir Singh. The use of the song, performed by a Mithun Chakraborty lookalike, makes the sequence both intensely comic and emotionally tense. The repeated use of camp cultural references give Kashyap's films added complexity, drawing attention to problematic issues in cultural and social history. Moreover, it is well-known fact that the film's music director, Sneha Khanwalkar, travelled across Bihar and the Hindi heartland (in the North of India) in order to collect local music and sounds. Thus, one of the most popular songs in the films, "Womaniya", was recorded in Patna, Bihar, using two local

Figure 17.2 The epic *Gangs of Wasseypur* (2012, India, Anurrag Kashyap) harked back to the disco and B-movies of the 1980s while also drawing on popular songs collected in Bihar and the Hindi heartland in the North of India.

singers, while the singers in the female chorus were formally untrained women discovered in a local temple. In an interview dated 1 August 2012 on the web channel BollywoodHungama.com, Khandwalkar suggested that:

> The voices in every state [of India] have a different grain, you can tell immediately [where they are from] [...] now technology allows [local recording] [...] you can even go to a house and record [...] in the studios you lose this energy [...] for "Womaniya" we recorded live [...] everything is mixed [...] It's fun.

Kashyap's films may be described as an extension of multiplex films that address the concerns of the *neo*-middle classes (see Gopal 2011). However, alongside such films, Kashyap's productions, such as the widely discussed small-budget films *Queen* (2013, India, Vikas Bahl) and *Masaan* (Crematorium, 2015, India, Neeraj Ghaywan), which received a certain degree of international acclaim, focus on local settings. These films also make use of regional differences in speech, dialect, community practices (including subjects such as caste discrimination) and a range of sub-cultural practices. One could argue that this renewed regional focus is a product both of personal concerns of the filmmakers, industrial renegotiations and the renewed interest of global media in local events and cultures.

This continuing dialogue between global Bollywood and local cultures highlights the authorial, industrial and cultural transactions that still exist between the Hindi mainstream and its many others. Indeed, in recent years there have been many popular films such as *Kahani* (Story, 2012, India, Sujoy Ghosh) and *Piku* (2015, India, Shoojit Sircar) that were not only largely shot in Calcutta but also featured substantial involvement on the part of the Bengali film industry in terms of both cast and crew, and therefore is considered quasi-Bengali productions.

Conclusion

This essay has focused on New Theatres and its legacy in order to present a revisionist history of Hindi cinema. However, a similar argument can be made in relation to Marathi language films, drawing attention to the extent to which Prabhat Film Co. created a dent in the Hindi film market during the 1930s and to which Dada Kondke's *tamasha*-style popular cinema, in films such as *Pandu Havaldar* (Constable Pandu, 1975, India), exerted a considerable influence on Hindi popular cinema (on Marathi cinema, see Ingle 2015). The more one examines the historical evolution of industrial structures, the more it becomes clear that the modes of production of Hindi cinema are manifold and the films it has produced complex and full of fissures. Moreover, what may at first appear to be the sudden and unexpected emergence of the "local" (places, themes, characters, idioms, cast and crew) within the framework of contemporary global Bollywood is in actual fact the contemporary manifestation of a cultural practice that has been vibrant from the very earliest days of Indian cinema.

References

Abbas, K. A. (1939) "These Three! ...", *Film India*, May 1939.

Barnouw, E. and Krishnaswamy, S. (1980) *Indian Film* (2nd edn), New Delhi: Oxford University Press.

Bhaumik, K. (2001) *The Emergence of the Bombay Film Industry, 1913–1936*, unpublished PhD thesis: University of Oxford.

Chatterjee, P. (1994) *The Nation and Its Fragments: Colonial and Postcolonial Histories*, New Delhi: Oxford University Press.

Gopal, S. (2011) *Conjugations: Marriage and Form in New Bollywood Cinema*, Chicago, IL: University of Chicago Press.

Govil, N. and Hoyt, E. (2014) "Thieves of Bombay: United Artists, Colonial Copyright, and Film Piracy in the 1920s", *BioScope* 5 (1): 5–27.

Hansen, M. B. (1999) "The Mass Production of the Senses: Classical Cinema as Vernacular Modernism", *Modernism/Modernity* 6 (2): 59–77.

Ingle, H. (2015) "Multiplex Exhibition and the New Marathi Cinema", *Journal of the Moving Image*, 13: 30–63.

Jaikumar, P. (2003) "More than Morality: The Indian Cinematograph Committee Interviews (1927)", *The Moving Image* 3 (1): 82–109.

Kapse, A. (2014) "Around the World in Eighty Minutes: Douglas Fairbanks and Indian Stunt Films", in Bean, J., Kapse, A. and Horak, L. (eds) *Silent Cinema and the Politics of Space*, Indianapolis and Bloomington, IN: Indiana University Press, 210–234.

Kapur, G. (2000) *When Was Modernism, Essays on Contemporary Practice in India*, New Delhi: Tulika Books.

Kaviraj, S. (1995) *Unhappy Consciousness Bankim Chandra Chattopadhyay and the Formation of Nationalist Discourse in India*, Delhi: Oxford University Press.

Manuel, P. (1993). *Cassette Culture: Popular Music and Technology in North India*, Chicago, IL: Chicago University Press.

Motion Picture Society of India, Bombay (1945) "Report on Indian Film Industry's Mission to Europe and America", July–December 1945.

Mukherjee, M. (2008) *The New Theatres Ltd: 'The Cathedral of Culture' and the House of the Popular*, unpublished PhD thesis: Jadavpur University.

—— (2009) *New Theatres Ltd: The Emblem of Art, the Picture of Success*, Pune: NFAI.

—— (2011a) "Bengal Elephants (in Blues and Greys): Revisiting the Meandering Course of the Studio Era", *Journal of Creative Communications* 6 (1–2): 149–162.

—— (2011b) "Remembering Devdas: Travels, Transformations and the Persistence of Images, Bollywood-Style", *Topia, Canadian Journal of Cultural Studies* 26: 69–84.

—— (ed.) (2012a) *Aural Films, Oral Cultures, Essays on Cinema from the Early Sound Era*, Kolkata: Jadavpur University Press.

—— (2012b) "The Architecture of Songs and Music: Soundmarks of Bollywood, a Popular Form and Its Emergent Texts", *Screen Sound Journal* 3: 9–34.

—— (2014) "Of Bhadramohila, Blouses, and 'Bustofine': Re-viewing Bengali High Culture (1930s-40s) from a Low Angle", in Sarmento, C. and Campos, R. (eds) *Popular and Visual Culture: Design, Circulation and Consumption*, Cambridge: Cambridge Scholars Publishing, 145–166.

—— (2015) "Of Recollection, Retelling and Cinephilia: Reading *Gangs of Wasseypur* as an Active Archive of Popular Cinema", *Journal of the Moving Image*, 13: 91–113.

Niranjana, T., Sudhir, P. and V. Dhareshwar (eds) (1993) *Interrogating Modernity: Culture and Colonialism in India*, Calcutta: Seagull Books.

Prakash, G. (2010) *Mumbai Fables*, Princeton, NJ: Princeton University Press.
Prasad, M. M. (1998) *Ideology of the Hindi Film: A Historical Construction*, New Delhi: Oxford University Press.
—— (2011) "Genre Mixing as Creative Fabrication", *BioScope: South Asian Screen Studies*, 2: 69–81.
Rajadhyaksha, A. (1987) "The Phalke Era: Conflict of Traditional Form and Modern Technology", *Journal of Arts and Ideas, Journal of Arts and Ideas*, 14–15: 47–78.
—— (2002) "The Bollywoodization of the Indian Cinema: Cultural Nationalism in a Global Arena", in P. Kaarsholm (ed.) *City Flicks: Cinema, Urban Worlds and Modernities in India and Beyond*, Roskilde: Roskilde University, 93–112.
Sarkar, S. (1984) *Modern India, 1885–1947*, Delhi: Macmillan India.
Sarkar, T. (1987) *Bengal 1928–1934, Politics of Protests*, Delhi: Oxford University Press.
Vasudevan, R. (1989) "The Melodramatic Mode and the Commercial Hindi Cinema: Notes on Film History, Narrative and performance in the 1950s", *Screen* 30 (3): 29–50.
—— (2002) "Shifting Codes, Dissolving Identities: The Hindi Social Film of the 1950s as Popular Culture", in Vasudevan, R. (ed.) *Making Meaning in Indian Cinema*, New Delhi: Oxford University Press, 99–121.
Vitali, V. (2008) *Hindi Action Cinema: Industries, Narratives, Bodies*, New Delhi: Oxford University Press.

18

AMERICAN INDIE FILM AND INTERNATIONAL ART CINEMA

Points of distinction and overlap

Geoff King

Introduction

How should we understand the relationship between American indie film and the broader realm of international art cinema? Both of these formations—each of which is a complex and often contested territory—are defined in large part in opposition to the dominant institution of Hollywood. But what do they have in common, and/or what markers of *difference* (in a neutral sense) or more value-laden *distinction* can be identified between the two? American indie film has largely been ignored in most academic accounts of art cinema, the international or global basis of which is often also marked in distinction from a US cinema sometimes seemingly conflated with Hollywood. Studies of indie have often viewed art cinema as a point of influence but the exact nature of the relationship has not been explored at any length or, I would suggest, with due acknowledgment of the multiple currents of each. This chapter will examine the relationship between the two formations at two main levels, closely related: the types of films involved (and the traditions on which these draw, including those associated with broader currents such as modernism and the postmodern) and the channels through which they circulate. If indie film is sometimes located in a position somewhere between art cinema and the more commercial mainstream, the argument here will be that it often draws on qualities associated with art cinema and that the lines between the two are often significantly blurred, even if some clear points of distinction can be identified and have been mobilised in certain discursive contexts.

Definitions

To start, we need a working definition of each of these categories. I am using the term "indie" here to signify a particular range of American independent cinema that came to prominence in the period from around the mid-1980s to early 1990s and that has remained a reasonably distinct category to date. Indie, in this usage, is often an abbreviation of "independent" but is not coterminous with everything that goes under the latter label when it is used to refer to *any* kind of filmmaking beyond the realm of the Hollywood studios. Independent, here, is an inclusive term that embraces a very wide range of different kinds of non-studio film. Indie is used to delineate a more specific type of cinema—although itself containing considerable variety—that became institutionalised in certain ways in this period. This is the kind of cinema associated with the names of filmmakers such as Jim Jarmusch, John Sayles, Todd Solondz, Hal Hartley, Steven Soderbergh, Kevin Smith, Quentin Tarantino, Nicole Holofcener and the Coen brothers; films such as *Stranger than Paradise* (1984, USA, Jim Jarmusch), *sex, lies, and videotape* (1989, USA, Steven Soderbergh), *Clerks* (1994, USA, Kevin Smith) and *The Blair Witch Project* (1999, USA, Daniel Myrick and Eduardo Sánchez); institutions such as the Independent Feature Project and the Sundance Film Festival; distributors such as October Films, Artisan Entertainment, Miramax and studio "speciality" divisions (including Miramax during its period under the ownership of Disney) such as Fox Searchlight and Sony Pictures Classics. A number of important distinctions can be, and have been, made between examples such as these but I would argue that they can be seen, collectively and broadly, to represent a particular field of cultural production, to use Pierre Bourdieu's term, in the conjunction of industrial, textual and discursive practices that they embody (Bourdieu 1993). One area of controversy is the status that should be accorded to the realm known as Indiewood, constituted primarily by the semi-autonomous speciality divisions created at some point by all of the studios to exploit parts of this market. Some commentators have also insisted on narrower uses of the term "indie", as distinct from "independent", even within this period and this broad terrain as I conceive it (for a discussion of this, see King (2014), "Conclusion").

"Art" cinema is a more diffuse category, generally used in relation to films from a longer historical period and from a much broader range of geographical locations. Exactly how art cinema is defined, and from what perspective, and how it might be understood in relation to broader notions of art and its cultural value, is a topic I explore at greater length in *Art Cinema: Positioning Films and the Construction of Cultural Value* (2018). Like "indie", the term is a marker of distinction from dominant industrial–commercial institutions, particularly Hollywood, that implies not just institutional difference but the production and consumption of films that are distinctive in particular ways, making claims of various kinds to a "higher" cultural status—as implied in the usage of the heavily loaded term "art" as the key feature of its designation. The many examples that might be included here would range from movements such as German Expressionism and French Impressionism to the particular consolidation of the category in the post-war era via Italian neorealism, the French *nouvelle vague* and many subsequent "New Waves" (more recently, for example, the Romanian and the Chinese) and similarly identified currents ranging across much of the globe. Both categories, usually restricted to the domain of feature-length narrative cinema, are best seen as broad and inexact, when subjected to close examination, but also as potent operational markers of particular regions of film culture in which strong investments are made by producers, consumers and the relevant interpretive communities—including, in some cases, investments in notions of distinction between the two or between aspects of one and the other. A definition of art cinema provided by Rosalind Galt and Karl Schoonover has much in common with how I would define indie, as a category "defined by its impurity" rather than any essence and describing "feature-length narrative films at the margins of mainstream cinema, located somewhere between fully experimental films and overtly commercial products" (Galt and Schoonover 2010: 6). A key difference between art and indie, however, is that the latter is often seen as tending some degrees more towards the commercial while some forms of art cinema lean more strongly towards the experimental end of the scale. How exactly this distinction is articulated is a key part of what follows.

To what extent, then, has each of these categories been considered or included in accounts of the other? Indie cinema has generally received little attention in major accounts of art cinema, for a number of reasons (a search of the index of the authoritative collection edited by

Galt and Schoonover, for example, reveals no entry for "indie" or "independent"; a section on "non-Hollywood models" exists as a sub-category of "United States", but the examples to which the references apply are works from the experimental avant-garde—and, in one instance, to a mixture of art and soft-porn qualities—rather than anything that would be included in the category of indie as employed here). As a category, art cinema has tended to be associated with an "international" or "global" territory (the term often preceded by one or other of these designations, or in some cases the narrower "European") in which America is not included. This is largely, it seems, because of a conflation, in this discursive context, of America and its globally dominant institution, Hollywood; so strong a pole of opposition is constituted by Hollywood, and so much has the term art cinema, consequently, come to be conjoined with geographical markers that seem often to imply anything-but-American. Studies of art cinema have also in some cases focused exclusively or primarily on what is often seen as the heyday of the form, in the 1950s and 1960s, a period before the emergence of indie as a consolidated entity. Art cinema has also sometimes primarily been associated with particular forms that display characteristics associated with modernism that are far less if at all prevalent in the indie sector—a point of distinction more central to the understanding of the relationship between the two offered by this chapter (a key source on art cinema in the context of modernism is Kovács (2007)). Indie film has also tended to be ignored or given little place in accounts of art cinema, I would suggest, because of a general tendency to position it less highly in prevailing film-cultural value hierarchies.

One exception to the tendency to separate out indie and art film is David Andrews' *Theorising Art Cinemas: Foreign, Cult, Avant-Garde and Beyond*, which employs a very broad definition of the latter that ranges from the avant-garde to the quality Hollywood film, including indie, on the basis of their shared, if variable, basis in the creation of comparative forms of cultural value (Andrews 2013). A key emphasis here is on the institutional basis of such definitions, and of the channels through which such films circulate and are valued as different from notions of the mainstream, an issue I return to below. This approach is valuable but comes, here, at the cost, I think, of closer engagement with some of the distinctive qualities of particular parts of this broadly conceived realm and some important process of differentiation that can be identified across its spectrum.

Aspects of art cinema have often been seen as contributing centrally to the particular range and blend of qualities associated with indie. I suggest elsewhere (King 2005) that art cinema is one major pole of influence on the sector, in textual dimensions such as the prevalence of low-key or more complex narrative strategies and in the use of both realist and expressive formal approaches (on which more below). Connections with overseas art cinema were also recognised by some early academic commentators, notably Annette Insdorf in an essay published in 1981 which suggests that makers of films of the period such as *Northern Lights* (1978, USA, John Hanson and Rob Nilsson) "treat inherently American concerns with a primarily European style", citing core art-filmmakers including Ingmar Bergman and François Truffaut as sources of inspiration (Insdorf 1981/2005: 29). Art cinema is also identified as an important influence on the independent sector by E. Deidre Pribram (2002). She usefully locates some examples of independent film as falling within categories of art film, although in this case the category "independent" is used more widely than usual, to include films that circulate within the same channels as American indies in the United States but that come from a wider range of national locations (a number of her primary examples are British films). This blurring of lines is useful as a way of breaking down some indie/art distinctions, and suggesting some overlapping of the two, but it leaves unclear exactly what qualifies for independent or art film status—as far as these can be understood institutionally as more or less distinct realms—in the first place. A more explicit account of the relationship between specifically American indie film and art cinema is offered by Michael Newman, although I would suggest that his approach over-states some points of difference and over-simplifies some aspects of the comparison between the two realms.

Newman's primary argument is that indie, as a distinctive film culture, "succeeds art cinema", at least within the repertoire of film cultures available in the United States (Newman 2011: 15). Indie is seen by Newman as "inheriting the social functions previously performed by foreign art films", as "a mode of filmmaking that those aspiring to certain kinds of status adopt as a common point of reference, a token of community membership" (Newman 2011: 15). That indie effectively supplanted art cinema to a large extent, in the sense of taking over much of the limited space available to broadly artistically leaning alternative narrative film in the American marketplace (and potentially beyond) seems clear enough. It did not do so entirely, however. Both indie and art films continue to circulate, through many of the same institutions. Within just the American context, then, or that of the broader circulatory sphere of both, we can still ask what *ongoing* relationship exists between the two, rather than seeing one as having replaced the other.

This brings us on to questions about differences between the two. For Newman, art and indie share certain qualities, particularly an emphasis on realism and authorship as major interpretive frameworks. But, he suggests, they also entail different viewing strategies that are rooted in two different contexts. Each is associated with the intellectual currents of its time: for art cinema, those of existentialism and modernism; for indie, "in place of existential angst and alienation we find the multiplicity and fragmentation associated with multiculturalism and postmodernism" (Newman 2011: 28).

Modernism, postmodernism and realism: distinctions and overlaps

The distinction made by Newman is useful up to a point, and cuts to some key differences that can be identified between the two fields, but it also risks over-simplification. It is true, as Newman suggests, that one key marker of difference between these categories is that art cinema includes many works that are more seriously challenging to the viewer than is anything like the norm in the indie sector; and that this can, indeed, be seen in terms of its greater commitment to qualities associated with modernism and some related intellectual currents identified in this account. Another useful distinction, one that acknowledges a wider range existing under the label of art cinema, is that made by András Bálint Kovács (2007) between what he terms "classical" and "modernist" strands within the broader realm of art film. This is a distinction that amounts to a difference in the nature and/or degree of difference from the norms of the mainstream-classical. For example:

> If an art film in general tends to present a complex situation that cannot be reduced to one or two well-defined problems [and on this basis departs from the norms of the conventionally classical] and therefore concentrates on the character's complex persona, what happens in modern art cinema is that this complex situation becomes ambiguous or impossible to define.
>
> *(Kovács 2007: 63)*

How far this difference is understood to map neatly onto distinct periods remains open to question. Kovács suggests that the era of modernist art cinema as such has ended, having gone into decline by the 1970s and 1980s. While some formal qualities associated with the modern continue to be found in subsequent art films, and continue to be available as options, he argues they are accompanied by "imported aesthetic phenomena [. . .] that are essentially uncommon to modernism" and drawn from the broader context of the postmodern (Kovács 2007: 47). Modernist art film, in this account, is film that responds specifically to the broader historical modernist art movement (associated particularly with the avant-garde upsurges of the 1920s and 1960s), one that is seen to have been replaced in more recent decades by that of the postmodern, an account broadly similar in this respect to that of Newman. In the field of art cinema, the outcome is seen by Kovács as a shift in favour of the classical variant of the form, or a fusion of the classical and modernist elements.

Whatever the overall balance might be considered to be, across the entire field of art cinema, films that display distinctly modernist characteristics continued to exist into the period in which indie came to prominence, and continue to do so today. This seems to complicate an association of either type with currents seen as prevailing only in one period or the other, as seems to be implied by Newman (2011) (even if they are viewed as more prevalent in a particular era). Multiplicity and fragmentation, for example, qualities Newman associates with the postmodern/indie conjunction, are qualities strongly to the fore in much of the work of Michael Haneke, a prominent figure whose work also retains dimensions that seem clearly modernist (challenging to the viewer, and marked as deeply "serious" in orientation) rather than postmodern (more playful) in character. Even if some of this can be viewed as an inheritance from the earlier period, such concerns seem equally appropriate to the social, political and/or cultural climate of the present, making any such distinction far less clear-cut. Modernist art cinema might be less prevalent after the period of its heyday, as suggested by Kovács, or might have less cultural reach and presence than it did in that period. To conclude that its era is "over", however, seems, again, overly to simplify the picture.

For Newman, a key characteristic of indie film is that it involves a sense of play, in its use of form, as opposed to the radical ambiguity (and all that this entails) often associated with art film (particularly in an influential account by David Bordwell (1985)). This might be true in some cases, but seems to me too great a generalisation. Elements of play might also be identified in some works of art cinema from the heyday of the 1960s, as in some of the earlier films of Jean-Luc Godard, for example (a different and harsher kind of play is also foregrounded at times in Haneke). It might be identified as a component of tendencies often associated with the postmodern, and is a quality found in some indie films (for example, the play with narrative sequence in *Pulp Fiction* [1994, USA, Quentin Tarantino]). But whether such a dimension should be seen as a *defining* quality of a broad arena—either indie film, say, or contemporary art or other currents labelled postmodern—seems to me to be doubtful and always to risk over-simplification. If play can also be identified in some art films from the period associated with modernism, there are also many examples of indie film (from the period associated with the postmodern) to which this does *not* seem to apply, including but not limited to those that share with art cinema a strong commitment to notions of serious socially conscious realism. If it is true that the most heavyweight of modernist approaches might rarely be found in the indie sector, I would suggest that more points of overlap can be established between some aspects of the two than Newman seems to imply.

Realism, modernism and postmodernism can usefully be identified as three broad tendencies in historical and/or contemporary art film practice, even if they are also components that might be mobilised to greater or less extents or degrees in particular cases from one period or another (and also if distinctions between concepts such as the modernist and postmodern might often be far from clear cut). One persistent strain of art cinema, particularly rooted in post-war Italian neo-realism, claims to present a more objectively realist picture of the world than is the norm in dominant commercial contexts such as Hollywood. Another can broadly be associated with wider artistic practices characteristically grouped together under the label of modernism, or at least some of these, including elements such as radical ambiguity or opacity, denial of emotional identification with character, and radical self-reflexivity. These are often taken, more or less directly, to embody thematic issues such as alienation, uncertainty and critique of forms of representation such as film and other media—concerns typically associated with what we might term the "heavyweight" end of art cinema, a category I examine in more detail elsewhere (King 2018). Familiar reference points here would be the work of figures such as Michelangelo Antonioni, Ingmar Bergman and Andrei Tarkovsky, but also many later filmmakers such as Haneke. Some of these thematic issues (particularly some forms of uncertainty about the relationship between the nature of reality and representation) can also be identified in currents associated with the postmodern, if with some important differences of emphasis, including in some cases a lighter stress on the playful rather than the bleakly nihilistic. If the style and content of one tendency makes claims to the status of objective realism, the others can be related to another key pole in prevailing notions of art, what Steve Neale terms "the other primary ideology of Art, the Romantic view that Art is subjective expression" (Neale 1981: 14).

Within the axes provided by these tendencies, some quite clear distinctions can usefully be made between art and indie. A strong vein of realism is a major component of many indie as well as art films. Heavier forms of modernism or focus on issues such as alienation are associated far more exclusively with the latter, however, while lighter varieties of play might be more common features of indie. The realist tendency remains an important part of indie film, however, which means that a considerable area of overlap exists between the two domains at this level alone. We might also identify some other tendencies that can be identified across the art–indie divide, including some forms of subjectively expressive filmmaking, often rooted in what might best be viewed as a kind of subjective realism, thus drawing on another major component of the wider artistic tradition. Another characteristic found in both spheres is the use of popular generic formats as vehicles for alternative or less mainstream approaches. In the indie sector, elements that have something in common with art cinema are very often mixed generally with more conventionally mainstream-oriented dimensions, usually associated with the "classical" Hollywood style. This is also true of many products of international art cinema, however, particularly that which falls into Kovács' category of the classical art film. Untypically for such a work, the main focus of which is European art film, Kovács does occasionally mention some examples from the indie sector (or that of its overlap with Hollywood), including his discussion of modernist narrative procedures in the work of David Lynch, Tarantino and the Coen brothers, although this is framed in the context of occasional space for such approaches in "quality Hollywood" production rather than with any acknowledgement of the specific terrain of indie itself (Kovács 2007: 60).

Even where we might find some important differences of degree—particularly degree of departure from the classical—the relationship between art and indie as a whole seems distinctly less than clear cut in a number of significant respects. If we were to map a spectrum that included both sectors, it would take the form of a continuum with considerable areas of overlap, even if many more examples from the art sector might be found at the "heavier", modernist end of the scale (beyond which, at the farthest reaches from the mainstream-commercial, we would find the realms of the fully avant-garde and experimental).

Making a case for continuity between the two realms in the case of films that make claims to the status of presenting more objectively realist views of the world seems relatively straightforward. That this is a major strand of art cinema, with an important emphasis on *social* realism, seems beyond argument. The dominant reference point for this tendency is the long-since canonised phenomenon of Italian neo-realism, as suggested above, a key point of reference usually for subsequent examples, among the more recent of which is the work customarily grouped under the labels of the Romanian and Chinese "New Waves" and the films of Jean-Pierre and Luc Dardenne. A similar strand is also easily identifiable in American indie film, from progenitors such as the works of John Cassavetes to a number of films that played a central role in the development of the sector in the 1980s (for example, *Heartland* [1979, USA, Richard Pearce] and *Working* Girls [1986, USA, Lizzie Borden]) to recent/contemporary examples such as the work of Kelly Reichardt and Ramin Bahrani (see King (2005): 63–84, 107–119; for a detailed analysis of the latter two, which includes their situation in the context of the international realist/neorealist tradition, see King (2014)).

It seems equally clear that there is no real equivalent in the indie sector of what we might term "hard-core" art cinema, in the sense of a sustained body of films that present themselves as the more "weighty", "intellectual", "difficult" or "forbidding" in character, often drawing on qualities associated with modernism and/or the overt exploration of themes such as the alienating nature of contemporary life. Plenty of such films are to be found among favourites of the art-cinema canon, just a few examples being: the social alienation manifested in Michelangelo Antonioni's *L'eclisse* (1992, Italy/France); the chilly ambiguities of Alain Resnais' *L'année dernière à Marienbad* (Last Year at Marienbad, 1961, France/Italy); the philosophical discourses found in films by Andrei Tarkovsky such as *Solyaris* (Solaris, 1972, USSR) and *Stalker* (1979, USSR); and more recent instances such as the alienation/abstraction of Michael Haneke's *Der siebente Kontinent* (The Seventh Continent, 1989, Austria) and the radical questioning of the position of the viewer in his two versions of *Funny Games* (1997, Austria; 2007, USA/France/UK/Austria/Germany/Italy), or the bleak minimalism of films by Béla Tarr such as *Sátántangó* (Satantango, Hungary/Germany/Switzerland) and *A torinói ló* (The Turin Horse, 2011, Hungary/France/Germany/Switzerland/USA).

The tendency to situate indie film as a "softer" or "safer", ultimately more commercially oriented cinema, has often been highlighted by the difference that remains in some examples that have been inspired, in some way or to some degree, by works of this kind of heavy weight. Thus Steven Soderbergh's characterisation of his film *The Limey* (1999, USA) as "*Get Carter* as made by Alain Resnais", a formulation that seems reasonably accurately to capture the positioning of the film mid-way between more conventional crime-revenge thriller and art film, or the same filmmaker's remake of *Solaris* (2002, USA) as a studio feature the qualities of which share a comparable location somewhere in between those of Hollywood norm and arthouse classic (on the former, see King (2011); on the latter, King (2009)). Or the aspects of Tarr—extended following tracking shots—employed by Gus Van Sant in the trilogy loosely comprised of *Gerry* (2002, USA), *Elephant* (2003, USA) and *Last Days* (2005, USA); films that include some such material that is formally radical by indie standards but without quite the intellectual weightiness of context associated with the work of the Hungarian director (King 2006).

What is the nearest we can find to the "heavyweight" variety of modernist-leaning art film in the indie sector? Among the strongest candidates would be the work of Jon Jost, a figure usually located outside the more institutionalised indie sector, however, in features ranging from *The Bed You Sleep In* (1993, USA) to *Over Here* (2007, USA), which employ oblique minimalist strategies to convey a sense of alienation or disconnection. It is precisely because of the radical nature of these films, by indie standards, that they have not really participated in the more concerted sphere of distributors, festivals, etc., that constitutes an important part of its field of cultural production and consumption. As I have argued elsewhere, a substantial gap exists in the indie sector between films of this nature—and, to some extent, the Van Sant films cited above—and those that more closely mix alternative and more classical components (King 2005: 138).

We might identify some other examples at the more art-leaning end of the indie spectrum—including, for example, the aspects of radical narrative uncertainty at the heart of David Lynch's *Lost Highway* (1997, USA/France), or the expressive digital textures of Harmony Korine's *Julien Donkey-Boy* (1999, USA)—but such cases are both relatively rare and still often less hard-core in their modernist or other non-mainstream strategies than some of the art films cited above.

The explanation for this absence might seem reasonably straightforward, a matter of the degree of commercial viability required within the particular constraints of the indie sector in its principal manifestations of recent decades. If the market for indie films in general can be a difficult one, that for the most demanding art films is likely to be all the more so. Given that the two markets overlap, however, both forming part of the broader "speciality" business in the United States (and often elsewhere), why might the more difficult varieties remain more prevalent elsewhere? The indie sector might have more commercial leanings, in general, as a result of factors specific to the American context, such as the existence of a more commercial, market-oriented culture. Financial subsidy at the national or supra-national level has, certainly, been a major factor in the support of art cinema historically, particularly in Europe and for many examples in the heyday of the immediate post-war decades. Limited support was received by some indie features in the latter decades of the twentieth century, through organisations such as the National Endowment for the Humanities, but this proved short-lived.

A stronger commercial imperative, coupled with expectations created by some notable break-out hits, might also help to explain what has often been seen as a leaning in the direction of qualities associated with the postmodern in the indie sphere. Approaches such as the playful, as identified by Newman, tend to be much easier to mix with larger commercial potential than the bleaker currents of modernist alienation (*Pulp Fiction* is, again, a good example here, among others, both in its qualities and its status as a cross-over success in the marketplace). That is to say, leanings in these kinds of directions might be dictated, or encouraged, as much by particular national-cultural contexts as by broader historical periodisation, although there are dangers of over-simplification in any such arguments (any attempt to make broader generalisations about such large fields of cultural production run this risk to some extent, including this one).

If the generally lighter quality of much indie film is associated with the more commercial US context, the heavier varieties of art cinema might be said to be rooted in locations that can be more hospitable to such material, for various reasons. This might be related to the more complex, storied histories, politics and cultural inheritances of the "old" world, for example, as applicable to locations such as Europe and Asia. These, or some of these, might also have stronger traditions in areas such as the kind of philosophical reflection that feeds into the hard-core tendency and that might be expected to find less traction—even that required for speciality varieties of cinema—in the United States. Heavier-weight varieties of art cinema might also be triggered in parts of the contemporary "developing" world by the more sharply drawn social contexts/crisis affecting some such places, where sufficient resources permit.

It would be a mistake, however, too closely to identify the international art sector with its most heavyweight, demanding or modernist-leaning exemplars. It is here, I think, that the degree of distinction from indie can sometimes be overstated. Considerably closer connections between the two can be identified in many cases, particularly within the kind of territory signified by Kovács' notion of the classical art film and/or examples in which aspects of art or indie are combined with more familiar genre frameworks. The latter is a familiar dimension of indie film, on which I have written at length elsewhere (King 2005). The valuation of indie, as something distinct from mainstream/Hollywood, might often include a disavowal of that seen as the generic, but many indies have worked within genre frameworks, even when seeking to complicate them or to put generic ingredients into contexts usually associated with the realist. The same can be said of many features that circulate within the realm of international art cinema. Within the broad context of the crime genre, for example, we could cite individual examples that stake or have been accorded varying claims to the status of art cinema, from the work of filmmakers as various as Akira Kurosawa, Jean-Pierre Melville, Jean-Luc Godard, Nuri Bilge Ceylan and Johnnie To.

Fields of circulation and consumption

A key point here is our understanding of art cinema as a field of circulation and consumption, mediated by various institutions and critical discourses, rather than being constituted by particular kinds of texts removed from this context (a key part of the intervention made by Neale (1981)). As Barbara Wilinsky argues, in a study of the history of the arthouse cinema in the United States, art film is best understood as "a dynamic and shifting concept created with pragmatic functions" within particular parts of the film business (Wilinsky 2001: 39). A key part of the discourse surrounding this realm is the myth of its non-commercial nature, as Wilinsky suggests, a notion propagated by those invested in the sector, including producers, distributors, exhibitors and viewers whose consumption of such work plays a part in their own marking of social distinction. This discursive separation from the commercial, a form of disavowal, is important to the success of art cinema *within* a particular commercial realm (Wilinsky 2001: 33–34). And from an early stage, as Wilinsky and others have suggested, one part of the appeal was less high-cultural in nature, art cinema often having traded also on its capacity to be more explicit in areas such as eroticism and violence. While art might often be positioned generally as higher-cultural in location than indie, in comparisons between the two, Wilinsky's account offers a useful shift of emphasis, in its focus on the extent to which art cinema has also tended in many cases to offer that which is marked as "different" from the mainstream "but not too different" (Wilinsky 2001: 39). The latter is a formulation that might also be used in relation to the American indie sector, suggesting again that what is involved in a comparison between the two is often a difference of degree; what we might term, if rather awkwardly, a difference in "not too different-ness".

Another key point that follows from Wilinsky's comment about the "dynamic and shifting" nature of art cinema—similar to the definition offered by Galt and Schoonover and to the way I would define indie—is that there is no *essence* of the form, or any type of art cinema that should especially be privileged over others that circulate within its realm. What often seems to happen is that particular types of art film *are* implicitly privileged over others, particularly those that engage most strongly with its social realist or modernist tendencies. This is understandable on more than one count. These are the types of art films that are positioned furthest from the norms of Hollywood (within the realm of feature-length narrative production rather than including the avant-garde). Given that distance from Hollywood is the single most prominent working ground of definition, greater distance might seem to imply more essential belonging to the category (that *difference* from Hollywood can itself be marked in numerous different ways is a good explanation of the variety found within the art film sector, as Neale suggests, even if this is bounded by particular institutional factors (Neale 1981: 15)).

Added to this is the differential investment in art films, as sources of distinction, on the part of those who participate one way or another in this sphere. The strongest sense of distinction is likely to be gained by—or by consuming, or having any other mediatory relationship with—films situated at the favoured pole. (In reality, the picture is likely to be more complicated, depending on exactly what combination of distinction-marking difference and more comfortably consumable familiarity/lesser-difference might appeal in any particular case.) Some films within the art-film sector might, therefore, seem "artier" than others, in what amounts to a competitive process of marking degrees of difference—one that includes the differences often asserted between art and indie as a whole. A division can thus be made between how we might understand this analytically—with art cinema as a wider and inessential category that might not be sustainable institutionally without its relatively more classical/mainstream components—and the manner in which such a category tends to function in on-the-ground processes of cultural distinction-marking.

Another key point of overlap between art and indie is the fact that they share, broadly, much the same arena of circulation and discursive articulation, including major festivals, approval by certain kinds of "serious" critics, exhibition primarily in arthouse theatres, and an emphasis throughout on the central role of the filmmaker as individual creative auteur. This remains the case, even if relatively less distinctive indie films have taken over some of the space within this realm that was formerly available to international art films, of whatever pitch those might be. This is why American indie and international art films are sometimes mixed together discursively *without* any particular distinction marking between the two, in forums the focus of which is dictated by the broadly defined "speciality" arena of circulation. The American indie-oriented website Indiewire, for example, often provides lists with headlines such as "The 12 Indies You Must See [fill in the gap for the period concerned, such as 'This Month']", the contents of which shift between American and overseas titles (for example, see Anon (2015)).

The role played by subtitles in international art film is another prominent factor in its differential positioning in relation to American indie when the two circulate in Anglophone contexts. Subtitles are key markers of distinction, often fetishised, as Mark Betz suggests, as markers of authenticity (and, by implication, difference from the mainstream) (Betz 2009). If we imagine the existence of two films circulating in the US or the UK or an English-language dominated festival context, one international art and one indie, that are otherwise much the same in the extent to which they depart from mainstream/classical conventions, the additional factor of subtitles (where these are required in non-English-language examples) would be likely to make the art film seem considerably more distinctive and specialised a product overall. Hence the extent to which dubbed versions of such films tend to be seen as "dumbed down", as Betz puts it, or generally rejected by those with strong investments in art cinema as a distinction-marking category. Part of their distinction is based in this dimension specifically on their status as markedly "foreign" or "exotic" within particular viewing contexts, and requiring viewers prepared to tolerate the distancing created by the presence of subtitles. This is another example of a point of distinction-marking that is undoubtedly often in play, in the evaluation and consumption of such films, but also based on an oversimplification. As Betz suggests, subtitling is no guarantee of something closer to any notion of the original artistic vision, however much it might generally be preferred as a marker of authenticity by many consumers of art films, as not all dialogue tends to be included (and quality of translation might be variable) and the process of reading titles imposes a form of attention on the viewer that obstructs the integrity of composition and mise-en-scène (Betz 2009: 91).

Many examples can be suggested of indie films that might seem a significant degree closer to the status of art cinema—if not the hard-core modernist variety—were they to be imagined (or themselves viewed, overseas) with subtitles. These might include the work of the likes of Jim Jarmusch, Todd Solondz and Todd Haynes, among many other contributors to the establishment of the indie sector from the 1980s and 1990s. At the same time, we might identify additional works that circulate in the international subtitled art sphere (outside their own countries of production) that embody characteristics widely associated with indie, for example the manifestly "quirky" aspects of films by figures such as Aki Kaurismäki (Finland) and Johnnie

To (Hong Kong) or the more general pitch of the films of Pedro Almodóvar (Spain), generally accorded the status of one of the auteur stars of the early twenty-first-century arthouse. Terms such as "quirky" and "offbeat" often contribute to the connotations of less heavyweight modality associated with indie films. They suggest something relatively weak, flimsy and superficial, compared with the weight, depth and steeliness often associated with heavyweight art films—but they are far from exclusive to the American indie sector.

Another ground on which art cinema seems often to be accorded higher status than indie is the notion that it (or privileged manifestations) offers a more serious expression or exploration of the nature of contemporary existence than tends to be argued in relation to the latter, in whatever particular historical currents either might be located. James Tweedie (2013), for example, reads art cinema "New Waves" such as those in France, Taiwan and China as figurations of various aspects of issues relating to major processes such as modernisation and globalisation, and the various hopes, fears or complications entailed by such developments. These cinematic movements *matter*, Tweedie implies, precisely because they engage in such weighty issues, both thematically and in their implications for the use of various formal strategies.

Tweedie offers a brief postscript that asks whether any equivalent new wave was experienced in America, concluding that if it was, it was very brief and soon became complicit in the world of corporate media (situated, in this account, in the moment between the writing of *The Graduate* [1967, USA, Mike Nichols] and its realisation on screen). The implication is that all that followed remained similarly complicit. Passing reference is made to a more recent "American independent cinema" (placed in scare quotes that imply a questioning of its independent status), but no comment is made at all about this sector as it developed from the 1980s, as if none of this has any scope to be read in any similar terms—either similar to the specific issues discussed in the rest of the book or as of any significance at all at this kind of level. Whether or not it might partake in any of the particular currents explored by Tweedie, indie film can clearly be read as an expression of particular socio-cultural/historical phenomena that might be accorded substantial significance. For Sherry Ortner (2013), for example, many indie films offer what amounts to a critique of the downside of neoliberal economic policies. Something similar is suggested by Claire Perkins (2016), who argues that indie films often take the contradictions and dissatisfactions of life under capitalism as their primary subject. Some of the issues considered by Tweedie might exist in a more heightened form in the case studies on which he focuses, particularly in the context of the epochal shifts undergone by both society/economy and cultural producers such as filmmakers in China in recent decades. These might also seem somewhat weightier, in their location in the context of such large-scale topics as globalisation and its discontents—compared, say, with satirical portraits of the mores of middle-class Americans, such as those examined by Perkins (2016). A difference of *tone* might sometimes be an important factor here, in the relative seriousness of modality presented by such cinemas or the seriousness with which they are taken by commentators, academic and otherwise. But any distinction between the two seems, again, to be one of degree rather than to be absolute—and in neither case do examples such as those cited typify the whole of the sector they might sometimes be taken to represent.

References

Andrews, D. (2013) *Theorising Art Cinemas: Foreign, Cult, Avant-Garde and Beyond*, Austin, TX: University of Texas Press.

Anon (2015) "The 12 Indie Films You Must See This January", *Indiewire*, 1 January, www.indiewire.com/article/the-8-indie-films-you-must-see-this-january-20150101.

Betz, M. (2009) *Beyond the Subtitle: Remapping European Art Cinema*, Minneapolis, MN and London: University of Minnesota Press.

Bordwell, D. (1985) *Narration in the Fiction Film*, London: Routledge.
Bourdieu, P. (1993) "The Field of Cultural Production, or The Economic World Reversed", in *The Field of Cultural Production*, Cambridge: Polity, 29–73.
Galt, R. and Schoonover, K. (2010) "Introduction: The Impurity of Art Cinema", in Galt, R. and Schoonover, K. (eds) *Global Art Cinema: New Theories and Histories*, Oxford: Oxford University Press, 3–30.
Insdorf (1981) "Ordinary People, European Style: Or How to Spot an Independent Feature", *American Film* 6 (10), September 1981, reprinted in Holmwood, C. and Wyatt, J. (eds) *Contemporary American Independent Film: From the Margins to the Mainstream*, London: Routledge, 27–34.
King, G. (2005) *American Independent Cinema*, London: I.B.Tauris.
—— (2006) "Following in the Footsteps: Gus Van Sant's *Gerry* and *Elephant* in the American Independent Field of Cultural Production", in *New Review of Film and Television Studies* 4 (2): 75–92.
—— (2009) *Indiewood: USA: Where Hollywood Meets Independent Cinema*, London: I.B. Tauris.
—— (2011) "Consciousness, Temporality and the Crime-Revenge Drama in *The Limey*", in Barton Palmer, R. and Sanders, S. M. (eds) *The Philosophy of Steven Soderbergh*, Lexington, KY: University Press of Kentucky, 91–106.
—— (2014) *Indie 2.0: Change and Continuity in Contemporary American Indie Film*, London: I.B. Tauris.
—— (2018) *Art Cinema: Positioning Films and the Construction of Cultural Value*, London. I.B. Tauris.
Kovács, A. (2007) *Screening Modernism: European Art Film, 1950–1980*, Chicago, IL: University of Chicago Press.
Neale, S. (1981) "Art Cinema as Institution", *Screen*, 22 (1): 11–40.
Newman, M. (2011) *Indie: An American Film Culture*, New York: Columbia University Press.
Ortner, S. (2013) *Not Hollywood: Independent Film at the Twilight of the American Dream*, Durham, NC: Duke University Press.
Perkins, C. (2016) "Life during Wartime: Emotionalism, Capitalist Realism and Middle Class Indie Identity", in King, G. (ed.) *A Companion to American Indie Film*, New York: Wiley-Blackwell, 349–367.
Pribram, E. D. (2002) *Cinema & Culture: Independent Film in the United States, 1980–2001*, New York: Peter Lang.
Tweedie, J. (2013) *The Age of New Waves: Art Cinema and the Staging of Globalization*, Oxford: Oxford University Press.
Wilinsky, B. (2001) *Sure Seaters: The Emergence of Art House Cinema*, Minneapolis, MN: University of Minnesota Press.

19

CANADIAN CINEMA(S)

Christopher E. Gittings

Introduction

The chapter provides an introduction to Canadian cinema(s) by delineating the simultaneously interconnected yet separate terrains of Anglo-Canadian, Québec, indigenous and transnational diasporic cinemas in Canada through the vectors of political economy, distribution, ideology and critical reception. Canadian cinema, what I am calling Canadian cinema(s), has long been a problematic object of study due, in part, to its variegated, multifaceted nature. Communications scholar Michael Dorland sees the heterogeneity of Canada's cinematic output, its shifting production "tendencies" over time—documentary, animation, experimental or feature film—as an early challenge for scholars working toward articulating some kind of unitary national cinema narrative (Dorland 1998: 3). Quebec academic Pierre Véronneau and future TIFF (Film Festival) director Piers Handling wrote in 1980 of the impossibility of grasping Canadian cinema: "It disappears in one area, crops up in another, moves from west to east, splits up, dies, is reborn etc." (Handling and Véronneau 1980: viii). Scholars such as Seth Feldman questioned the very existence of a Canadian national cinema due to the failure of distribution systems to deliver Canadian films to Canadian audiences, and exhibitors' dependence on lucrative Hollywood product at the expense of Canadian screen time (Melnyk 2004: 234). Dorland further clarified his 1998 position in a 2015 interview in which he stated "there isn't a Canadian cinema, but rather many Canadian cinemas", a perspective that is congruent with most contemporary understandings of the term national cinema as a problematic more than it is a straightforward hermeneutical category (Dorland 2016). Bill Marshall's *Quebec National Cinema* further advances both the notion of a plurality of cinemas within Canada and the concept of national cinema as a productive problematic: "Far from designating a stable object of investigation, let alone a master category grounding interpretations and analysis, [national cinema] represents a significant problem; [. . .] not a master hermeneutic but a master problematic" (Marshall 2001: 1–2). Similarly, my own monograph also works to trouble the narrow and provisional parameters of national cinema to reveal its constructed and contested terrain, a diachronic theatre for competing versions of nation at various stages of becoming, structured by the challenging discourses of decolonisation, multiculturalism, gender and class (Gittings 2002). In some ways Canada's national cinema was generated by what Dorland describes as an economy of talk before the artefact actually existed. The talk economy that imagined a feature film industry existing in the silent period and after

1968 was comprised of the voices of critics beginning as early as the 1910s and 1920s in publications such as *Canadian Motion Picture Digest*, governmental discourse emanating from the Canadian Government Motion Picture Bureau (CGMPB), the National Film Board (NFB) or the Massey Report's 1951 "Films in Canada", as well as academic discourse in the 1960s and 1970s (Dorland 1998: 13–18). For many academics and state bureaucrats, 1968, the year the newly minted Canadian Film Development Corporation (CFDC) (1967) tried to kick-start fiction feature filmmaking in Canada, marks the beginnings of a Canadian film industry. For the first time $10 million in federal funding, albeit a pitifully small amount, was available to producers to make fiction feature films.

Projecting immigration and settlement

Although widely thought of as beginning in 1968, fiction feature production has existed in Canada, in fits and starts, from the silent period forward. Moreover, a diverse array of other cinematic forms (shorts, documentary, experimental cinema and animation) was being produced prior to the 1960s. As much as the fiction feature was viewed by some as the Holy Grail of Canadian cinema, it is important to remember the distinctive history of developing Canadian cinema(s) by way of providing a wider context for understanding post-1968 policy and production. From its early beginnings in the age of imperial colonialism, through to the current era of globalisation, Canadian cinema(s) developed both domestic and international contexts for production and distribution. Shaped by first French then British incursions into the territories of Indigenous peoples, Canada became a territory dominated politically and economically by a white European invader/settler culture that generated the country's first institutions and industries, including cinema, in its own image. Early representations of the Canadian landscape were shot through a colonising lens that viewed Canadian terrain as empty territory to be taken by white British invader/settlers. Of course, the territory depicted was in the process of being stolen from Canada's First Nations. Underwritten by the Canadian Pacific Railway (CPR), English immigrant Richard Freer's films, including *Harnessing the Virgin Prairie* (1897), toured Britain in 1898. The government's Department of Trade and Commerce also recognised the utility of film for marketing Canada and Canadian products abroad; it created an in-house film unit, Exhibits and Publicity Bureau, in 1918 (Morris [1978] 1992: 131–132). The Bureau was to produce ten films a year to be distributed through Canadian Trade Commissions overseas (Morris [1978] 1992: 132). The Bureau's 1919 *Seeing Canada* series was highly successful with wide domestic distribution through Canadian Universal, international circulation by Imperial Pictures in Britain and theatrical and non-theatrical distribution in the United States, Australia, New Zealand, South America and Japan (Morris [1978] 1992: 134). Although the Bureau originally envisioned its films for foreign audiences, the domestic demand for Canadian films, a demand that, sadly, represented a rather singular moment in Canadian film history, led to the deal with Canadian Universal (Morris [1978] 1992: 134). By 1920, the CPR, a corporate entity that doubled as a state actor with its own Department of Colonization and Development, had incorporated a film production company, Associated Screen News, to further its and the nation's immigration and settlement agenda through newsreels but also, in collaboration with Canada's National Museum, a racialising ethnographic documentary short, *Nass River Indians* (1928, Canada, Marius Barbeau). Produced for the National Museum as part of the National Gallery of Canada's 1927 "Exhibition of Canadian West Coast Art, Native and Modern" (Jessup 1999: 49), the film is an example *par excellence* of Homi Bhabha's colonial discourse, the objective of which "is to construe the colonised as a population of degenerate types on the basis of racial origin, in order to justify conquest and establish systems of administration and instruction"

(Bhabha 1983: 23). Lynda Jessup's 2001 reconstruction of this lost film from two extant titles cut from it, *Saving the Sagas* (1928) and *Fish and Medicine Men* (1928) reveals ethnographer Marius Barbeau's representation of the Nisga'a of Northwestern British Columbia to be a "vanishing race" film trafficking in the worst kind of degenerate stereotypes. A tool of colonialism, the film, like many other ethnographic films of the period, represents itself as preserving the remnants of a dying culture, marking the assimilation and subsequent death of "primitive" Indigenous cultures overwhelmed by the modern technology of white Western European colonialism (Jessup 1999: 51–52). An image of a woman performing one of the supposedly "vanishing" Nisga'a cultural rites for the ethnographer's camera, a potlatch dance, is sexualised and debased by Barbeau's narrativisation of the woman's actions as soliciting a kiss or a drink (Jessup 1999: 59; Gittings 2002: 51). Another intertitle articulates quite clearly the film's assimilationist desire of "disappearing" "Indians" from the social terrain of the white nation in its ideologically charged interpretation of a medium shot of three young Nisga'a men in Western dress gathered around a radio, one wearing headphones: "The ways of the white man—and radio jazz—are sweeping away the colour of Indian life in British Columbia." This intertitle reveals the failure of the ethnographer's colonial imagination which could not conceive of Aboriginal cultures resilient enough to survive the cultural genocide unleashed upon them by first the British Empire and then the Canadian state; First Nations, Inuit and Metis people mastered communications technologies of radio, cinema and television and exploited them to represent their survival of colonialism through decolonising storytelling. As we shall see, Alanis Obomsawin, Zacharias Kunuk and Jeff Barnaby have met with great success representing the narratives of their living cultures through cinema. Most significantly, despite the horrors of the Indian Act the Nisga'a did not disappear; in 2000 the Nisga'a Lisims Nation became a self-governing Aboriginal territory.

Early fiction features such as Québec-produced *The Battle of Long Sault* (1913, Canada, Frank Crane, 1913), *Madeline de Verchères* (1922, Canada, J. Arthur Homier) and Halifax-based Canadian Bioscope's *Evangeline* (1913, Canada, E. P. Sullivan) were drawn from Canada's colonial history. *Evangeline*, adapted from American writer Henry Wadsworth Longfellow's poem of the Acadian expulsions, was the only profitable and critically acclaimed of these early features, due not only to the high production qualities but also, most certainly, the film's securing of American distribution. One of the perpetual obstacles to Canadian fiction-feature production throughout the twentieth century and into the twenty-first has been the country's small domestic market that has necessitated foreign distribution for economic viability. Moreover, the American domination of that small market's screens meant increasingly restricted access for Canadian films to Canadian screens, something most other national cinemas must also negotiate. Exhibitors then and now, are highly motivated to maximise box office receipts through Hollywood films and stars. One of the most successful Canadian fiction features arrived in 1919 with the domestic and international release of *Back to God's Country* (1919, Canada, David M. Hartford). With exteriors shot on a frozen Lesser Slave Lake in Alberta, interiors shot in California studios, and distribution handled by New York-based First National, this film, funded by local Calgary capital, anticipates the transnational turn Canadian cinema will take through co-production treaties in the late twentieth and early twenty-first centuries. Distributed throughout North America and Britain, Europe, Australia and Japan, *Back to God's Country* made $500,000 in the first year of its release yielding its Calgary investors a 300 per cent return (Morris [1978] 1992: 106–107). Starring the California-based Canadian screenwriter/actor/director Nell Shipman, who adapted the very popular American writer James Oliver Curwood's short story for the screen, the film's success was due in part to the international appetite for Curwood's narratives of the Canadian north and Shipman's star-making turn as the lead in the adaptation of Curwood's *God's Country and the Woman* (1915) (Morris [1978] 1992: 102). Unfortunately, the film's racialising depiction of Inuit women as intellectually challenged prostitutes, and of a Chinese man as an avaricious "yellow" figure of fun denigrated and murdered for his cultural differences in the film's opening saloon sequence, aligns with the conventional racial stereotyping all too present on the silent screen and in North-American society at this time (Gittings 2002: 21–32).

Quota-quickies: Hollywood branch plant production

Subsequent, sporadic attempts at fiction features in Canada over the next five decades failed both commercially and critically. The disastrous and very public failure of Canadian International Films' $500,000 First World War epic *Carry on, Sergeant* (1928, Canada, Bruce Bairnsfather) placed a chill on investment in, and production of Canadian features that lasted until after the Second World War (Morris [1978] 1992: 72). This fallow period in feature production was interrupted only by what came to be known as "quota quickies"; to circumvent the protectionist British Cinematograph Films Act (1927), Hollywood producers and talent migrated north to British Columbia to make B-grade pictures that would avoid British Empire tariffs on non-Empire films by posing as Canadian and therefore British Empire product. After the British quota legislation expired in 1938 there was no longer an economic incentive to have branch-plant Hollywood production companies operating in Canada making pallid imitations of Hollywood films; the production of Canadian features in British Columbia came to an abrupt halt.

The Canadian state's rejection of fiction feature production was established long before John Grierson and the founding of the NFB in 1939, a move that further entrenched documentary as the default mode of Canadian film production. By 1925, Ray Peck, director of the CGMPB, was already discouraging indigenous fiction feature production by Canadians in favour of Hollywood production companies setting up subsidiaries in Canada to gain access to the British empire market. Unlike countries such as France, Germany and the United Kingdom, Canada took no action to support domestic fiction feature production in the context of Hollywood's increasing global screen domination. Government bureaucrats like Peck continued to see film in fairly limited, utilitarian terms as a tool to promote trade and immigration, more of a propagandist medium for selling Canada and its goods to the world than what was to become one of the most important art forms of the twentieth century.

The National Film Board of Canada

Having defined the documentary form—"the creative treatment of actuality"— during his time at the UK's Empire Marketing Board film unit and later, the film unit at the General Post Office, Grierson was invited by the Mackenzie King government to come to Canada and write a report on the state of Canadian film production. At Grierson's insistence legislation based on his recommendations was drafted, tabled and passed as the National Film Act on 2 May 1939. The National Film Act gave the NFB the authority to "initiate and promote the production and distribution of films in the national interest and in particular to produce and distribute and to promote the production and distribution of films designed to interpret Canada to Canadians and to other nations" (Grierson quoted in Magder [1939] 1993: 52). Appointed to the role of Film Commissioner at the NFB, Grierson proceeded to implement his report. Following the absorption of the CGMPB by the NFB, the documentary-only vision of Grierson worked to delay the development of a feature film industry. Very much concerned by Canada's dependency on US film culture, Grierson complains, "when it comes to movies we have no emotional presentation of our own. It is another nation's effort and pride we see on our screen, not our own. We are on the outside looking in" (Grierson [1944] 1988: 55). Grierson's strategy to remedy this cultural deficit, however, was not for Canadians to produce Canadian features in Canada but for those interested in feature production to leave the country and make their "Canadian" film in New York or Hollywood; Canada would produce documentaries. Grierson imagined a more erudite, formally instructional Canadian cinema that would help shape Canadian identity and citizen subjects. The NFB as envisioned by Grierson met with incredible war-time success, producing two commercially and critically successful documentary series during the Second World War, *Canada Carries On* and *World in Action* which were both distributed theatrically and played in 90 per cent of Canadian theatres (Jones 1981: 36). Additionally, Grierson's NFB built a national audience for its films by rethinking the distribution issue that had plagued Canada historically to develop alternative exhibition windows for individuals and groups that were made accessible through volunteer projectionists and the twenty regional film libraries established by the board by 1942 (Jones 1981: 37). Ninety-two rural cinema circuits reached approximately a quarter of a million people a month by 1945 (Evans 1984: 162). Under Grierson's direction Canada became internationally recognised as one of the world's top producers of award-winning documentary films. An early effort, the war-time propaganda film *Churchill's Island* (1941, Canada, Stuart Legg), won the first Academy Award for Documentary Short Subject. Although possessing a fairly prescriptive and puritanical view of the documentary film and the work of the board, Grierson did bring animation to the NFB in 1941 by hiring fellow Scot Norman McLaren, an innovative artist whose anti-war stop-motion live or "pixeilation" animation classic *Neighbours* (1952, Canada) won the 1953 Academy Award for Documentary Short Subject and established the board's and Canada's international reputation for animated film. A new generation of animators developed at the NFB during the 1950s with such luminaries as Derek Lam and Arthur Lipsett emerging to make their own unique contributions alongside French-language animators such as Bernard Longpré, Yvonne Mallette, Pierre Moretti and Pierre Hébert. The 1970s saw many NFB animation shorts nominated for Oscars, a trend that continued amid government cuts to the board's budget with such twenty-first-century successes as the Academy Award winning *Ryan* (2004, Canada, Chris Landreth) and *The Danish Poet* (2007, Canada/Norway Toril Kove) (Handling *et al.* [2006] 2015).

After Grierson's departure in 1945, the board continued to make films that reflected government policy by communicating the state-sanctioned version of the nation to Canadians. If the films of the 1950s and 1960s do what Grierson believed NFB films should do, namely tell Canadians what they need to know and think (Grierson 1944: 64), they told them to know and think whiteness as a collective identity. It would take forty-six years before the NFB would shift its institutional structure to fund the representation of racial difference as an identifying coordinate of Canadianness under the New Initiatives In Film program of Studio D. Envisioned as The Woman's Studio in 1974, Studio D was the first publicly funded women's production unit in the world (Anderson 1996: 169). During the 1970s and 1980s, the NFB continued its mission of projecting state policy at moments when it underwent significant change with the Trudeau government's introduction of Multicultural policy of 1971 and parliament's passing of the Multicultural Act of 1988.

The most successful and best known film to come out of the NFB's Studio B experiments with the direct method is *Lonely Boy* (1961, Canada, Wolf Koenig and Roman Kroitor), a cinéma-verité style film representing several days in the maelstrom of fame and adolescent adulation experienced by teen singing sensation Paul Anka. Significantly, the auteur impulse renewed desires to make feature films at the board, both feature-length documentary and fiction features. From the English language unit emerged *Drylanders* (1963, Canada, Don Haldane), a fiction feature on pioneer life in Saskatchewan and from the French language unit *Pour la suite du monde* (For Those Who Will Follow, 1963, Michel Brault, Pierre Perrault), a *cinéma direct* documentary feature that re-enacted a traditional whale hunt on Quebec's l'Ile aux-Coudres. Both films were screened theatrically with *Drylanders* generating healthy box office receipts through its distribution deal with Columbia pictures and *For Those Who Will Follow* garnering critical praise at Cannes (Magder 1993: 99–100). Several other features were made at the NFB during the 1960s without the approval or knowledge of the board (Magder 1993: 100). One of the most beloved Canadian fiction-feature films of all time, *Mon oncle Antoine* (1971, Canada, Claude Jutra) was made as a co-production at the NFB and in association with private sector Gendon Films. The NFB has had a substantive influence on the Canadian feature's sense of social realism as it served as a type of film school for some of Canada's more significant feature directors in the 1960s, 1970s and 1980s. Not only Jutra, but also Don Owen who directed one of the early NFB fiction features *Nobody Waved Good-bye* (1964, Canada), Michel Brault whose *Les Ordres* (The Orders, 1974, Canada) was honoured for best direction at Cannes, Gilles Carle (*Les Plouffe* [1981, Canada], *Maria Chapdelaine* [1983, Canada/France]) and the prolific Denys Arcand, Cannes honoree and three-time Academy Award nominee for Best Foreign Film, who finally won the coveted gold statuette for *Les invasions barbares* (The Barbarian Invasions, 2003, Canada/France).

The NFB and its filmmakers continued to experiment with the technology of cinema throughout the 1960s and 1970s to develop a multiscreen projection system. Work by board directors Roman Kroitor, Colin Low and Hugh O'Connor produced the multi-screen project *In the Labyrinth* for the 1967 World's Fair in Montreal, Expo 67. Following the success of this film at Expo, Kroitor departed the NFB to co-create the 70mm large-screen format known as Imax with Graeme Ferguson and Robert Kerr. The NFB and its personnel continued to play a role in the development of Imax; the first Imax film, *Tiger Child* (1970), screened at Expo 70 in Osaka, was helmed by renowned NFB director Donald Brittain (Acland 2006). Despite the NFB producing over 10,000 titles, a series of government cuts and shifts in policy prompted Zoe Druick to conclude in her 2007 book that the board is a diminished public institution, no longer a "dynamic part of the process of imagining Canadian society [but] an archive of government in the welfare state" (Druick 2007: 183). At its extensive website, the NFB offers much of its collection gratis to the public via streaming while other titles are available for download rentals or purchases. However, its strategic plan of 2013–2018 calls for the NFB "to create, distribute and engage audiences with innovative and distinctive audiovisual works and immersive experiences that could find their place in classrooms, communities, and cinemas, and on all the platforms where audiences watch, exchange and network around creative content" (NFB 2013).

Making Canadian features: the CFDC and Telefilm

The desire to make Canadian features during the 1960s was not limited to filmmakers at the NFB; various groups representing the industry lobbied government to play a role in financing feature production (Magder 1993: 102, 109–110). The response as stated above was the founding of the CFDC (1967) with an initial 1968 budget of $10 million. State intervention had an immediate impact; within three years, commercial feature production increased by 300 per cent (Dorland 1998: 139). However, the continuing American domination of Canadian exhibition and distribution systems meant that very few Canadians had opportunities to view these films (Magder 1993: 153). Inspired by the blockbuster success of Hollywood's *Jaws* (1975, USA, Steven Spielberg), the 1976 Tompkins Report's solution to these longstanding obstacles to economically viable Canadian features was to sacrifice the cultural specificity of Canadian films such as the CFDC-funded *Goin' Down the Road* (1970, Canada, Donald Shebib), the original "hoser bros" road film about Maritime migrants' journey to Toronto, in favour of Hollywood-like genre projects that could secure international distribution and turn a profit in the US (Magder 1993: 161–164). This policy shift marked the beginning of the so-called "Tax Shelter Boom" whereby US producers were offered attractive tax incentives to make their films in Canada. As Wyndham Wise observes, this policy undermined distinctive Canadian cinemas to produce a "full-blown branch plant industry" (Wise 1999: 24). For all of the shortcomings of the tax-shelter period, it did, as Magder points out, help to develop a cadre of skilled technicians and crews as well as establishing the careers of producers such as Robert Lantos whose Alliance Communications became a major player in production and distribution (Magder 1993: 192). CFDC funding, Capital Cost tax incentives and the government appetite for commercial success contributed to a production climate where such notable Canadian filmmakers as Bob Clark and David Cronenberg enjoyed some success with the horror genre. Although Julian Roffman's 3-D film *The Mask* (1961, Canada) managed to secure some funding from, and international distribution through Warner Brothers (Vatnsdal 2004: 38–42), it was not until the emergence of Clark's and Cronenberg's CFDC-funded titles *Black Christmas* (1979, Canada/USA, Bob Clark) and *Shivers* (1975, Canada, Cronenberg) that a Canadian horror cinema began to become recognisable. After a failed, limited international release in the USA and Canada in 1974, Warner Brothers re-released *Black Christmas*, now recognised as the *ur*-text of slasher films, in the USA (Constanteau 2010), Canada and overseas territories in 1975, where not only did it make a hefty profit in the USA, Asian and European markets, it became the number two film at the Canadian box office, one of very few profitable CFDC-funded titles (Box Office Canada 1975: K-1). Cronenberg shot his body horror film *Shivers* on a budget of $179,000, $75, 000 of which was invested by the CFDC (Vatnsdal 2004: 99). This controversial film received a release in the USA and, like *Black Christmas*, made a healthy return on the CFDC's investment. His next body horror project, *Rabid* (1977, Canada), starring American porn actress Marilyn Chambers as a vampiric woman with a phallic stinger in her armpit, attracted $200, 000 of its $350,000 budget from the CFDC (Vatnsdal 2004: 112); it also returned a substantial profit to the funding body (Melnyk 2004: 150). Cronenberg became recognised as a commercial horror auteur with a unique visual style that he developed in collaboration with *Rabid* production designer Carol Spier over a run of increasingly sophisticated, critical and commercial successes: *The Brood* (1979, Canada), *Scanners* (1981, Canada), *Videodrome* (1983, Canada), *The Fly* (1986, USA/Canada), and *Dead Ringers* (1988, Canada/USA). *Dead Ringers* proved to be a transitional release that, while it contained elements of body horror, saw Cronenberg moving toward the psychological thriller and larger questions about human interrelationships; future works such as the well-received co-productions *A History of Violence* (2005, USA/Germany/Canada), *Eastern Promises* (2007, USA/UK/Canada) and *A Dangerous Method* (2011, UK/Germany/Canada/Switzerland) were removed from the realm of horror. The success of Clark and Cronenberg, the attractive Capital Cost Allowance tax incentives and an increasing global demand for slasher horror, facilitated the production of more of what Vatsndal refers to as "slash for cash" (2004: 121), Canadian horror films starring Americans that were guaranteed international release; some of the more profitable titles are: *Prom Night* (1980, Canada, Paul Lynch), *Happy Birthday to Me* (1981, Canada, J. Lee Thompson) and *My Bloody Valentine* (1981, Canada, George Mihalka).

Of course, the American settings and talent involved in many of the tax shelter films undermined the representation of Canada to Canadians, so much so that by 1980 the Minister for Communications, Francis Fox, adjusted the criteria for what constituted a Canadian film, insisting that the roles of director and screenwriter be filled by Canadians to meet eligibility for Capital Cost Allowance tax deductions (Magder 1993: 198). A handful of films made during this period, such as *Les bons débarras* (Good Riddance, 1980, Canada, Francis Mankiewicz), *Les Plouffe* (The Plouffe Family, 1981, Canada, Gilles Carle) and *The Grey Fox* (1982, Canada, Phillip Borsos) did represent Canada to the Canadians that managed to see them.

Increasingly television, both domestic and overseas, was providing an outlet for Canadian feature films, while the 60 per cent Canadian content regulations governing television broadcasting between 6 pm and midnight established a market and demand for Canadian programming (Magder 1993: 213). The convergence of television and film industries is reflected in the renaming of CFDC as Telefilm Canada in 1984. Telefilm continued to negotiate the thorny issues of distributing and marketing Canadian films to domestic and international audiences by not only increasing money available for production but also funding distribution and promotion of Canadian films at home and abroad (Telefilm 2015: 4). Additionally, the regulatory body rethought using theatrical box office as the only criterion for measuring success, and from 2014 onwards factored in "domestic sales on all platforms" including television and internet streaming, as well as the festival performance of a film (Telefilm 2015: 24).

Branding Canadian cinema(s)

Rules on Canadian content also had to be loosened as Telefilm promotes co-productions such as *The F Word* (2013, Ireland/Canada, Michael Dowse), directed by a Canadian and starring UK national Daniel Radcliffe, and *Room* (2015, Ireland/Canada/UK/USA) directed by Irish national Lenny Abrahamson, adapted for the screen from her novel by Canadian screenwriter Emma Donoghue, and starring American Brie Larson who won a Best Actress Oscar for her performance. Canadian director Deepa Mehta's Telefilm-funded *Midnight's Children* (2012, Canada/UK) adapted from UK writer Salman Rushdie's novel about partition of the Indian subcontinent and its ramifications, set entirely in India and starring many Bollywood actors is another indicator that what was once understood to be Canadian content is not static; in a globalised world transnational filmmakers such as Deepa Mehta are telling stories that speak to and represent the diversity of Canadian identities and histories. Diversity whether it be Srinivas Krishna's *Masala* (1991, Canada), the story of Indo-Canadians negotiating a racialising multiculturalism, Mehta's Indian-set *Elements Trilogy—Fire* (1992, Canada/India), *Earth* (1998, India/Canada) and *Water* (2005, Canada/India)—or the queer cinemas of directors such as John Greyson, best known for the AIDS musical *Zero Patience* (1993, Canada/UK), Bruce La Bruce (*Super 8½* [1994, Canada/Germany/USA]), Lynne Ferney and Aerlyn Weissman (*Forbidden Love: The Unashamed Stories of Lesbian Lives* [1992, Canada]), Léa Pool (*La femme de l'hotel* [A Woman in Transit, 1984, Canada]), Patricia Rozema (*When Night Is Falling* [1996, Canada]), and Chelsea McMullan (*My Prairie Home* [2013, Canada]), has become a part of the Canadian cinemas' brand identity at festivals around the world. The BFI views Canada as a world leader in queer cinema stating that "as the first country to legalize gay marriage [. . .] it comes as no surprise that it has made some of the most exciting queer cinema in the world" (Davidson 2017). The BFI list includes work by Poole, La Bruce, McMullen, and Rozema, cites Greyson as a "hero of Canadian cinema" and includes the first English-language film invited to Cannes, David Secter's student film about same-sex attraction *Winter Kept Us Warm* (1965, Canada), Norman McLaren's balletic queering of the Greek myth *Narcissus* (1983, Canada), as well as more recent queer coming of age titles such as Jean Marc Vallée's *C.R.A.Z.Y.* (2005, Canada), Xavier Dolan's *J'ai tué ma mère* (I Killed My Mother, 2009, Canada) and newcomer Stephen Dunn's *Closet Monster* (2015, Canada). Perhaps one of the more compelling cases for understanding Canadian cinema as "World Cinema" is John Greyson's extension of the exploration of queer subjectivities beyond the limits of a Canadian national field of vision to South Africa in

Proteus (2003, Canada/South Africa, co-directed with Jack Lewis) and *Fig Trees* (2009, Canada), and Sarajevo in *Covered* (2009, Canada).

Queer Indigenous or "Two-spirited" subjects are representing themselves in a recent crop of films programmed for the "Two-Spirit REELness" spotlight of the 2016 Vancouver Queer Film Festival (Dupuis 2016). At the nexus of Queer, Canadian and Indigenous cinemas, fiction features such as Anishinaabe director Adam Garnet Jones' *Fire Song* (2015, Canada) or Métis filmmaker Bretten Hannam's *North Mountain* (2015, Canada) explore the contemporary and historical complexities of First People's sexuality through the lenses of colonisation and decolonisation. Cree artist Kent Monkman travels back to the nineteenth century to revisit the collision of white heteronormative European male sexualities with Indigenous queer sexualities in his classic short *Group of Seven Inches* (2005, Canada, Gisele Gordon and Kent Monkman). Inuit, First Nations and Métis filmmakers play a significant part in the diversity that marks the Canadian cinemas brand globally. Inuit director Zacharias Kunuk's Cannes *Camera d'Or* winner *Atanarjuat* (*Atanarjuat: The Fast Runner* (2001, Canada) and internationally renowned Abenaki documentarian Alanis Obomsawin's *Kanehsatake: 270 Years of Resistance* (1993, Canada) are the two most honoured Indigenous Canadian films. Although the NFB created Studio One as a "Native" Studio for training purposes and the production of documentary works by Canada's First Peoples, fiction feature film funding was withheld from Aboriginal Canada until Zacharias Kunuk's successful battle with Telefilm Canada for completion money for *Atanarjuat*, the first feature-length fiction film written, acted, produced and directed by Inuit in the Inuktitut language (Gittings 2002: 216) (Figure 19.1). The film, an action-adventure story based on a 500-year-old myth exploring good and evil and set before European contact, was a critical and commercial success domestically and internationally; it earned $5 million at the domestic and foreign box office (Box Office Mojo 2003) and is the only Indigenous film to be voted into the number one position of TIFF's *Canada's All Time Top-Ten List* (TIFF 2015) alongside work by Jutra, Atom Egoyan, Brault, Arcand, Cronenberg and Sarah Polley. Obomsawin's life and work bear witness to the colonisation of Canadian First Nations; she has proven a formidable leader in decolonising Indigenous image, culture, territory and peoples through her performances, etchings, recordings, and over thirty films. She has been honoured with invited screenings around the world, including the American Indian Museum in Washington and a retrospective of her work at New York's MOMA in 2008. It was the colonial discourse of white settler documentaries that inspired Obomsawin to pick up a camera and begin the art of decolonising the screen: "I saw how powerful documentaries could be. They were very powerful in terms of putting us in silence, I used it the opposite way" (Obomsawin 2010). *Kanehsatake: 270 Years of Resistance*, her virtuoso POV record of the federal and provincial assault on Mohawk territories at Oka, Québec, dispels the myth of Canada as a nation free from the vestiges of colonialism; Obomsawin embraces difference and human rights by locating the ugly and violent colonial reality of on-going racism and land claims confronting First Nations firmly in the Canadian nation's present. Among the younger generation of First Nations' filmmakers who cite Obomsawin as an influence is fiction feature director and screenwriter Jeff Barnaby, a Listuguj Mi'gmaq from Québec who first encountered Obomsawin when she came to his community to shoot *Incident at Restigouche* (1984, Canada) about the conflict between Mi'gmaq and white settlers over fishing rights (2013 Prospector Films). Barnaby's much lauded debut fiction feature, *Rhymes for Young Ghouls* (2013, Canada), draws on Obomsawin's documentary tradition, Cronenberg's horror genre, *Batman* and *Conan the Barbarian* to project the Residential School experience through the genre codes of horror, action, revenge fantasy and fable. Far from being acculturated or erased as an "other" to American popular culture, a talent such as Barnaby's absorbs and appropriates it, translating it into a decolonising Mi'gMaq cinema that names and shames colonial Canada for its human rights atrocities. Moreover, it was recognition of Barnaby's script from the American industry, in the form of a Tribeca Film Festival Creative Promise Award for Narrative that, according to the film's producer, helped secure production support and distribution at home (Prospector Films 2013). Barnaby prefaces his film with documentary excerpts from the Indian Act that were used to legitimise the torture, sexual assault and murder of Indigenous children in the name of assimilation. What follows is an experiment with genre cinema that represents the lived experience that both Canada's Chief Justice Beverly McLachlin and Truth and Reconciliation Commissioner Murray Sinclair associate with cultural genocide (McLachlin 2015). *Rhymes for Young Ghouls* was listed by TIFF as one of the Top Ten Canadian Films of 2013. In a conversation about the international appeal of *Atanarjuat*, TIFF Bell Lightbox Director of Film Programmes Jesse Wente is very clear on the global branding and cultural identity of Canadian cinemas: "What people outside of Canada view as actual Canadian culture isn't hockey or those sorts of things [. . .] it's actually the culture of the First Nations people—the Inuit and Métis—that they would identify as distinctly Canadian" (Wente in Bergstrom 2015).

Apart from the Tax Shelter years, post 1968 Canadian cinema is characterised, for the most part, by its arthouse auteurs, Claude Jutra, Denys Arcand, Michel Brault, David Cronenberg, Atom Egoyan (*The Sweet Hereafter*,1997, Canada), Patricia Rozema (*I've Heard the Mermaids Singing*, 1987, Canada), Zacharias Kunuk, Guy Maddin (*My Winnipeg*, 2007, Canada) and newer artists like Denis Villeneuve (*Incendies*, 2010, Canada/France), Jean Marc Vallée, Sarah Polley (*Stories We Tell*, 2012, Canada), Xavier Dolan (*Mommy*, 2012, Canada) (Figure 19.2), and Jeff Barnaby. However, industry players such as J. Jolly, the founder of Cinecoup, a filmmaking and marketing incubator, want to disrupt the current system that sees Telefilm fund predominantly arthouse cinema in favour of "pipeline of low-budget, high-performing films" such as creature feature *WolfCop* (2014, Canada, Lowell Dean) funded by $1 million from Clairwood Capital Management and such private investors as Cineplex Entertainment and CANON

Figure 19.1 *Atanarjuat* (Atanarjuat: The Fast Runner, 2001, Canada, Zacharias Kunuk) was the first feature-length fiction film written, acted, produced and directed by Inuit in the Inuktitut language. ©Aboriginal Peoples Television Network/Canada Television and Cable Production Fund License Program (CTCPF)/Canadian Film or Video Production Tax Credit (CPTC)/Canadian Government/Canadian Television (CTV)/Channel 24 Igloolik/Igloolik Isuma Productions Inc./National Film Board of Canada (NFB)/Telefilms Equity Investment Program/Vision Television.

(Beeston 2015). The turn to genre cinema as a balm to heal problems with the distribution and exhibition of Canadian films is not new, as is evidenced by directors in both Anglophone and Francophone cinemas who strive to develop popular cinemas. For example, Paul Gross wants to create a simultaneously popular and populist Canadian cinema to temper what he perceives as a "Canadian film history" that is "peculiarly cerebral" (Kirkland 2009). Gross's populist impulse tends toward essentialist and sentimental "Canadiana" clichéd fare like the curling romcom *Men with Brooms* (2002, Canada) and more recently the war films *Passchendaele* (2008, Canada) and *Hyena Road* (2015, Canada), flag-waving tributes to Canadian military campaigns during World War One and the Afghan War that exploit Hollywood production values and genres to tell Canadian stories with varying degrees of success. Although the critical response to these films was mixed at best, they opened in wide domestic release to deliver a $4.2 million take to *Men with Brooms* (Box Office Mojo 2002) and $4.4 million in receipts to *Passchendaele* (The Numbers 2008), which was also awarded the 2009 Golden Reel for the highest box office gross of any Canadian film that year even though it failed to earn back its $20 million budget. Although *Hyena Road* opened on 184 screens and had an opening weekend of $486,000 in ticket sales, it was expected to close its theatrical run with a gross of only $1.5 million (Houpt 2015). A popular cinema can undergird national cinemas economically and Québec cinema has also experimented with popular genres, perhaps with greater success than Canadian cinemas in English. In Québec Denys Arcand's arthouse film *Le déclin de l'empire américain* (The Decline of the American Empire, 1986, Canada) took the Golden Reel demonstrating the intersection of arthouse fare with a popular audience. Filmmakers and producers in Québec, however, are not immune to tapping popular genres such as the romantic comedy, the police procedural or the hockey film. *La grande séduction* (Seducing Doctor Lewis, 2003, Canada, Jean-François Pouliot), the romantic comedy of a small fishing village whose residents conspire to lure a doctor to their community, was the number one Canadian film at the Québec box office in 2003 taking in $7,285,449 (Ramond 2009). Perhaps the split between the popular and arthouse cinemas is not quite as pronounced in Québec as producers might think; the number two Canadian film that year was Arcand's Academy-Award winning arthouse title *Les invasions barbares* (The Barbarian Invasions, 2003, Canada/France). Louis Saia's *Les boys* (1997, Canada), a comedy/sports film about a group of men who play amateur recreational hockey, has proven the most successful franchise in Canadian film history; the first instalment brought in nearly $5.7 million

Figure 19.2 Xavier Dolan pushes the frame apart (*Mommy*, 2012, Canada, Xavier Dolan). ©Les Films Séville/Metafilms/Sons of Manual.

to the Québec box office (Marshall 2001: 203) while *Les Boys 2* (1992, Canada) and *Les Boys 3* (2001, Canada) grossed $5.9 million and $3.5 million respectively. The success of *Les Boys* undoubtedly influenced the decision to greenlight *Goon* (2011, USA/Canada, Michael Dowse). Co-written by Canadians and Hollywood players Jay Baruchel and Evan Goldberg, *Goon* stars Hollywood actors Sean William Scott and Liev Schreiber as older and younger versions of the hockey enforcer who bring the film to its bloody and tooth-extracting climax when they collide on the ice in front of an arena of braying fans. The $10.5 million made from theatrical and video revenues was enough to spark a Baruchel-directed sequel, *Goon: The Last of the Enforcers* (2017, Canada, Jay Baruchel), while Eric Canuel's bilingual buddy action film cum police procedural *Bon Cop Bad Cop* (2006, Canada) starring Canadian and Hollywood actor Colm Feore made $12.6 million across the country and is the highest grossing domestic release of all time, with a sequel released in March 2017 (Hertz 2016). Diversity is largely absent from these forays into popular genres; arthouse cinema continues to be where we find indigenous, queer, and transnational filmmakers.

Canadian screen futures: digital platforms, crossovers and convergences

Despite TIFF's best promotional efforts on behalf of Canadian cinema—its annual Canadian programming during the festival, its Top Ten lists that do much to promote Canadian films, and its Film Circuit program that brings Canadian titles to communities across the country—Canadian film remains, for the most part, locked out of mainstream distribution and exhibition systems. While there has been limited success in developing popular Anglophone and Francophone cinemas in Canada, distribution and exhibition continue to present challenges to the Canadian industry; in 2015 Canadian films held only a 1.9 per cent market share of the Canadian box office (Government of Canada 2015). As much as Hollywood has enriched the cinemas of the world creatively and been enriched by them, the economic reality of American market saturation cannot be understated. Digital platforms such as the NFB's website and Canada Screens, a VOD site of Canadian titles curated by Canadian talent and filmmakers, are being deployed to circumvent the stranglehold the American majors have on the traditional theatrical distribution and exhibition of Canadian films and ensure Canadian and international viewers have opportunities to experience Canadian cinemas. Canada Screens is an initiative of First Weekend Club, a non-profit started in Vancouver by Anita Adams in 2003 that has supported the release of some 400 Canadian films through its website and special screenings in Canadian cities that include talks with directors, actors and producers. The objective of First Weekend Club, now sponsored by Telefilm, Cineplex Odeon and the Directors Guild of Canada, is similar to that of Canada Screens: making Canadian cinemas accessible to a wider audience. A 2016 study by Telefilm finds that there is a Canadian audience for Canadian films that, for the most part, accesses those films at home through television and streaming. The survey found 61 per cent of Canadians show a "manifest interest" in Canadian movies, but only 48 per cent of those surveyed had watched a Canadian film in the past year (Telefilm 2016: 12). Although the survey found respondents believe Canadian cinema is "unique" and "underappreciated", some audience segments felt Canadian films "looked rushed and thrown together" when juxtaposed to foreign productions shot in Canada with the same crews, such as *X-Men: Apocalypse* (USA, Bryan Singer, 2016) or *Suicide Squad* (USA, David Ayer 2016) (Telefilm 2016: 44).

The lack of Canadian funding to make genre films embraced by larger audiences contributes to a cross-over mode of World Cinema where directors from a variety of national cinemas such as Mexico's Alfonso Cuarón, Alejandro González Iñárritu, Guillermo del Toro, and Canada's Denis Villeneuve bring their transnational visions to bear on American productions. Villeneuve's success with Hollywood genre films *Prisoners* (2013, USA) and *Sicario* (2015, USA) positioned him to direct the science fiction feature *Arrival* (2016, USA) and *Blade Runner 2049* (2017, UK/ Canada/USA). Canadian directors also cross over to make more intimate films with bigger budgets and American stars. One of the most recent Québec auteurs to venture to Hollywood is Xavier Dolan, whose first English-language feature, *The Death and Life of John F. Donovan* (2018, Canada) stars Susan Sarandon, Kathy Bates, Natalie Portman and Thandie Newton. Jean-Marc Vallée's Best Picture-nominated *Dallas Buyers Club* (2013, USA) won Academy Awards for Matthew McConaughey and Jared Leto. The most recent turn in Vallée's career trajectory, directing all seven episodes of the HBO series *Big Little Lies* (2017), speaks to both crossover and convergence; crossover in the migration of Canadian talent to Hollywood, convergence in the further collapsing of the increasingly porous boundaries that separate television and cinema, i.e. the movement of filmmakers and stars who worked exclusively in cinema to television.

Crossover and convergence of screen cultures has been viewed by some as a troubling development for Canadian content; Dolan's, Vallée's and Vielleneuve's recent projects, while contributing to a transnationalisation of the Hollywood industry, are set in American narrative space. The Canadian Radio-television and Telecommunications Commission's (CRTC) recent relaxation of Canadian content regulations has caused concern for the future of Canadian stories on Canadian screens (Wong 2016). However, Sarah Polley's most recent project suggests there might some hope for Canadian content in the age of convergence. Polley adapted and executive produced Canadian novelist Margaret Atwood's *Alias Grace* first as a feature film before reimagining it as a six-hour mini-series co-produced by the CBC and Netflix (Andreeva 2016). Directed by the Canadian Mary Harron, *Alias Grace* (2017, USA/Canada) is the story of accused murderer Grace Marks in nineteenth-century Toronto and will be broadcast in Canada by CBC and streamed globally on Netflix. The future for Canadian cinemas may well be found in this convergence model, or variations on it, where Canadian literary properties may be adapted and co-produced for domestic and international distribution with an international streaming partner like Netflix, Amazon, or Hulu. The success of some of these projects might also go some distance to opening up more spaces for original screenplays. Certainly, the critical and popular success of Toronto's Temple Productions' television series *Orphan Black* (2013–) and its Emmy-winning star Tatiana Maslany are strong indicators of commercially viable Canadian talent and content in a global context. Currently carried by BBC America in North America, the series has also been sold to the UK, Europe, Latin America, Australia, New Zealand and India (2014 Viessing). Maslany is another example of convergence, crossing over from television to Canadian indie film in *The Other Half* (2016, Canada, Joey Klein) and *Two Lovers and A Bear* (2016, Canada, Kim Nguyen). Her popularity in the global markets where *Orphan Black* is available and her high profile Emmy win for the series could bring attention to these small Canadian arthouse productions.

References

Acland, C. (2006) "Imax Systems Corporation", *The Canadian Encyclopedia*, www.thecanadianencyclopedia.ca/en/article/imax-systems-corporation/.

Anderson, E. (1996) *Pirating Feminisms: The Production of Post-War National Identity*. Dissertation AAT 9702776, Minnesota, MN: University of Minnesota of Minnesota, 1996.

Andreeva, N. (2016) "'Alias Grace': Netflix and CBC pick up Sarah Polley Miniseries Based on Margaret Atwood Novel", *Deadline Hollywood*, 16 June, http://deadline.com/2016/06/alias-grace-netflix-cbc-miniseries-margaret-atwood-novel-sarah-polley-1201776121/.

Beeston, L. (2015) "New Production Model for Canadian Filmmaking Seeks Different Future for CanCon", *The Globe and Mail*, 18 June, www.theglobeandmail.com/arts/film/new-production-model-for-canadian-filmmaking-seeks-different-future-for-cancon/article25021685/.

Bergstrom, A. (2015) "The Global Appeal of Atanarjuat: The Fast Runner", *Toronto Film Scene*, 1 November, http://thetfs.ca/article/global-appeal-atanarjuat-fast-runner/.

Bhabha, H. (1983) "The Other Question …", *Screen* 24 (6):18–36.

Box Office Canada (1975) "'Black Christmas' is Canada's No. 2 Film", *Box Office Canada*, K-1.

Box Office Mojo (2002) "Men with Brooms", www.boxofficemojo.com/movies/?id=menwithbrooms.htm.

Box Office Mojo (2003) "The Fast Runner (Atanarjuat)", www.boxofficemojo.com/movies/?id=fastrunneratanarjual.htm

Constantineau, S. (2010) "*Black Christmas*: The Slasher Film Was Made in Canada", *Cineaction* 82: 58–63.

Davidson, A. (2017) "10 Great Canadian Lesbian, Gay and Transgender Films", *BFI*, 7 April, www.bfi.org.uk/news-opinion/news-bfi/lists/10-great-canadian-lgbt-films.

Dorland, M. (1998) *So Close to the State(s). The Emergence of Canadian Feature Film Policy*, Toronto: University of Toronto Press.

—— (2016) Interviewed by David Davidson. *Toronto Film Review*, 6 April, http://torontofilmreview.blogspot.ca/2016/04/interview-with-michael-dorland-so-close.html.

Druick, Z. (2007) *Projecting Canada: Government Policy and Documentary Film at the National Film Board*, Montréal and Kingston: McGill-Queen's University Press.

Dupuis, C. (2016) "These Rising Filmmakers Are Finally Bringing Two-Spirited Stories to the Screen: Indigenous and Queer Identities Intersect at This Year's Vancouver Queer Film Festival", *CBC Arts*, 15 August, www.cbc.ca/beta/arts/these-rising-filmmakers-are-finally-bringing-two-spirited-stories-to-the-screen-1.3721591.

Evans, G. (1984) *John Grierson and the National Film Board: The Politics of Wartime Propaganda*, Toronto: University of Toronto Press.

Gittings, C. (2002) *Canadian National Cinema: Ideology, Difference and Representation*, London and New York: Routledge.

Government of Canada (2015) "Canadian Films' Share of the Box Office Revenues", http://canada.pch.gc.ca/eng/1464190351879.

Grierson, J. ([1944] 1988) "A Film Policy for Canada", in Fetherling, D. (ed.) *Documents in Canadian Film*, Peterborough and Lewiston: Broadview Press, 51–81.

Handling, P. and Véronneau, P. (1980) "Introduction", in Handling, P. and Véronneau, P. (eds) *Self Portrait*, Ottawa: Canadian Film Institute.

Handling, P., Marcel, J and Wise, W. ([2006] 2015) "Canadian Film Animation", *The Canadian Encyclopedia*, www.thecanadianencyclopedia.ca/en/article/canadian-film-animation/.

Hertz, B. (2016) "Colm Feore on Bon Cop, Bad Cop 2: 'It's Our Film, Our Story'", *The Globe and Mail* www.theglobeandmail.com/arts/film/colm-feore-on-bon-cop-bad-cop-2-its-our-film-our-story/article29944288/.

Houpt, S. (2015) "Hyena Road's Battle at the Box Office Brings in $486,000", *The Globe and Mail* 15 October, www.theglobeandmail.com/arts/film/hyena-roads-battle-at-the-box-office-brings-in-486000/article26827049/.

Jessup, L. (1999) "Tin Cans and Machinery", *Visual Anthropology* 12 (1): 49–86.

Jones, D. B. (1981) *Movies and Memoranda: An Interpretative History of the National Film Board of Canada*, Ottawa: Canadian Film Institute.

Kirkland, B. (2009) "Passchendaele DVD recalls WW1 Battle", *Jam! Showbiz*, 2 February, http://jam.canoe.ca/Video/DVD_Column/2009/02/02/8230801-sun.html.

McLachlin, B. Rt. Hon. (2015) "Unity, Diversity and Cultural Genocide: Chief Justice McLachlin's Complete Speech", *Globe and Mail*, 29 May, www.theglobeandmail.com/news/national/unity-diversity-and-cultural-genocide-chief- justice-mclachlins-complete-text/article24698710/.

Magder, T. (1993) *Canada's Hollywood: The Canadian State and Feature Films*, Toronto: University of Toronto Press.

Marshall, B. (2001) *Québec National Cinema*, Montreal and Kingston: McGill-Queen's University Press.

Melnyk, G. (2004) *One Hundred Years of Canadian Cinema*, Toronto: University of Toronto Press.

Morris, P. [1978] (1992) *Embattled Shadows. A History of Canadian Cinema 1895–1939*, Montreal and Kingston: McGill-Queen's University Press.

Obomsawin, A. (2010) Unpublished Interview with Christopher E. Gittings.

ONF/NFB. (2013) "Launch of the 2013–2018 Strategic Plan – *Imagine, Engage, Transform*" *National Film Board of Canada*, 3 April, http://onf-nfb.gc.ca/en/about-the-nfb/organization/mandate/.
Prospector Films. (2013) *Rhymes for Young Ghouls* Press Kit, http://rhymesforyoungghouls.com/RFYG-PRESS-KIT.pdf.
Ramond, C. (2009) "Box office des films québécois de l'année 2003", *Films du Québec*, 18 January, www.filmsquebec.com/box-office-des-films-quebecois-de-lannee-2003/.
Telefilm. (2015) *Talent Without Borders 2014–15 Annual Report*, http://rapport-annuel.telefilm.ca/en/.
Telefilm. (2016) *Understanding and Engaging with Audiences*, https://telefilm.ca/en/studies/understanding-and-engaging-with-audiences.
The Numbers. (2008) "Passchendaele", www.the-numbers.com/movie/Passchendaele#tab=summary.
TIFF. (2015) *Canada's All Time Top Ten List*, http://v1.tiff.net/canadas-all-time-top-ten.
Vatnsdal, C. (2004) *They Came from Within: A History of the Canadian Horror Film*, Winnipeg: Arbeiter Ring Publishing.
Wise, W. (1999) "Canadian Cinema from Boom to Bust: The Tax-Shelter Years", *Take One* 22: 18–24.
Wong, J. (2016) Does Loosening Cancon Rules Hobble Canadian TV Producers?", 22 September, www.cbc.ca/news/entertainment/cancon-crtc-tv-creators-1.3772919.

20

CONVENTIONS, PREVENTIONS AND INTERVENTIONS

Australasian cinema since the 1970s

Jonathan Rayner

Introduction: the case of/for national cinema

The cinemas of both Australia and New Zealand warrant discrete consideration for their specific responses and solutions to key issues of representation, characterisation and thematic differentiation, and the industrial, contextual factors of production, distribution and exhibition historically affecting all national cinemas. Yet they also reward a connective and comparative analysis as parallel cultural phenomena reflecting and articulating similar experiences for filmmakers and audiences at home, and for worldwide critical consumption in a trans- or post-national cinematic era. This chapter explores the development of the cinemas of Australia and New Zealand, considering their enduring national and international, cultural and commercial importance. The histories and critical interpretations of the products of these film industries have been marked by the impact of external and internal, institutional and artistic factors. Textually Australasian films have been made and read as purveyors of highly specific national imagery, ideals and orthodoxies, and as commercial competitors and aesthetic assertions against media imperialism (in the form of British influence before the term was even coined, and American dominance since the end of the Second World War). Contextually, Australasian film production has reflected and reacted to altering patterns of financing and state patronage, which has (depending on perspective) either supported or thwarted the aspirations for sustained, specific, authentic and profitable indigenous cinemas. Historically, Australasian films and filmmakers have assumed responsibilities of cultural representation, and they maintain their distinctiveness, relevance and influential profiles in contemporary international cinema. Both film industries underwent rejuvenations in the 1970s and 1980s, with the proportionally massive increase in feature production heralding and expressing an increased sense of national pride and representation at home and abroad. These revivals or almost unprecedented initiations of national cinematic activity were often facilitated and, at the same time, handicapped by the specific circumstances pertaining to their instigations. Aesthetic ambitions, cultural agendas, local and international audience environments, and ideological as much as industrial contexts, defined these comparatively recent, nascent national cinemas from birth:

> What is typical of the revival period is the intimate interplay of discourses belonging to such varied fields and agencies as policy, production, text, and criticism [...] which became the steady background radiation to the actual products, the films of the revival period.
>
> *(Kuna and Strohmaier 1999: 139)*

Prehistories

The vibrant filmmaking of the silent period in Australia and New Zealand epitomises the distinctiveness, and the distinct challenges, faced by both film cultures. The earliest actualities, either imported from Europe and America or shot by home-grown pioneers, reflected the novelty of the moving image and the connection to local audiences, who may have appeared in the films they watched. Australasian filmmakers were at the forefront of formal developments, in lodging competing claims for the first ever feature-length presentations and productions with *Soldiers of the Cross* (1900, Australia, Herbert Booth) and *The Story of the Kelly Gang* (1906, Australia, Charles Tait) (Pike and Cooper 1980: 5–6; Reade 1983: 88). Subject matter was often closely tied to geography, history and culture, as in narratives making use of unique national landscapes and in the indigenous Australian "bushranger" that resembled but departed from the Hollywood Western in its specific moral bias. However, local innovations were ultimately stymied by external, industrial factors beyond the control of individual producers and directors. The First World War was an international cinematic watershed, after which the fortunes of virtually all film industries, apart from that of the United States, went into decline. Consequently, the connection of Commonwealth films with Britain's protectionist quota systems in the late 1920s, restrictive industrial practices driven by foreign ownership of Australian distribution networks, and increasing production costs with the coming of sound, all had long-lasting, deleterious effects that compounded the difficulties of competing with Hollywood production values (Pike and Cooper 1980: 116; Gaunson, 2015). The careers of a handful of individuals, in some cases stretching from the start of the twentieth century to the 1960s, constituted the highlights of indigenous production. In Australia, Ken G. Hall's and Charles Chauvel's work between the wars and through the 1940s and 1950s attempted to bring commercial and artistic consistency to feature production, and present familiar stories, locations and actors to local audiences (O'Regan 2002: 119). Some international perspectives had been introduced during the Second World War via the production of propaganda films (such as Chauvel's *Forty Thousand Horsemen*, 1940, Australia, *The Rats of Tobruk*, 1944, Australia, and Harry Watt's *The Overlanders*, 1946, Australia, produced by Ealing in the mould of British documentary features), and after the war through British/American co-productions such as *The Sundowners* (Fred Zinnemann, 1960). In New Zealand, Rudall Hayward's output of a few features spread across the 1920s and 1930s, and John O'Shea's handful of films made in the 1950s constituted the bulk of contemporarily recognised and retrospectively revered indigenous production (Roddick, 1985; Conrich and Davy, 1997: 1–2). In both Australia and New Zealand, the revival and renewal of feature film production during the 1970s, and their supporters and practitioners, sought to balance these honourable precedents with contemporary circumstances, demands and expectations of national cinemas, and square the circle of locally relevant and representative films with the need for a commercially viable film industry of international quality and appeal.

Australasian agendas

Calls for increased local production, control and representation in the mass media in Australia and New Zealand during the later 1960s chimed with overt nationalist sentiments, themselves responding to the contemporary political climate calling for separation and distinction from the United States and United Kingdom. These distant, dominant neighbours or cultural exporters were seen as either increasingly irrelevant to, or unduly influential upon, Australasian identities after the disappearance of the British Empire and the debacle of the Vietnam War. In any case, there was an undisputable need for a culturally relevant and representative film and media culture (Weir 1985; Lawson 1985). At the same time, prejudicial circumstances pertained for distribution and exhibition of local films, because of the control of these sectors of the Australian industry by American and British concerns (Thornhill 1985). Government intervention was demanded, and eventually delivered, to provide the funding necessary to nurture local production. The Australian Film Development Corporation, established in 1970 with a A$1 million budget, acted as a new source of direct funding for film and television production, albeit under strict definitions of content, personnel and finance (Dermody and Jacka 1987: 54–55). The lobbying landscape in Australia was complex, reflecting different emphases and interests across television as well as film, the institutional factors of funding and overseas involvement in Australasian media industries, and the concerns of the critical and practitioner communities for a renewed film culture with both commercial sustainability and aesthetic integrity (Dermody and Jacka 1987: 48–50). Such perspectives also epitomised the traditionally different centres of gravity for Australian film (Sydney for the popular entertainment industry, Melbourne for the film festival circuit and more elitist art cinema). Although market-driven decision making gained precedence as direct government funding was reduced during the 1980s, the strategic polarities pertaining to the initial reinstatement of film activity, the "commercial-industrial (mainly initiated by the private sector) and the cultural-interventionist (mainly initiated by the public sector)" (Collins and Davis 2004: 24) continued to abide as the over-arching doctrinal positions for filmmakers and funders.

As suggested by the history of lobbying in Australia, what might be termed the real subject of the Australasian cinemas—national representation—remains a contentious issue even when comparatively large-scale filmmaking is (re)established. Attempts at defining and crafting a national image on screen, as an implicit or explicit agenda linked to cultural capital, prestige and nationhood as much as commercial success and international profile and tied to conditions and criteria of state funding, must negotiate intractable and enduring arguments over who or what is represented, whose culture, image or history has been shown, omitted or purloined (Barclay 2003), and how local and international audiences respond, or are assumed to respond, to such representations (O'Regan, 1996: 304–307). For small film cultures speaking in the immediate to comparatively tiny national audiences that are themselves subdivided along ethnic and/or cultural lines, such problems are acute:

> Obviously, the struggle to find local audiences for local film is not peculiar to New Zealand, especially where there is not a long tradition of film-making or where film-making is regarded as an integral part of state cultural policy. The opportunity to see locally-made films is a fairly recent phenomenon for New Zealanders (even though the novelty has now worn of), and even though structures for government support for New Zealand film-makers remain (primarily through the New Zealand Film Commission), they are also under renewed scrutiny.
>
> *(Leland 2010: 257)*

For such small-scale national industries, the problem of "finding" an audience for "local" films can be fatally compounded by even that potentially economically inadequate imagined community being recognised as several distinctive and incompatible audiences. By comparison, after barely two decades of revived feature film production, both the strategies of "selling out" to Hollywood mimicry with homogenised genre filmmaking and the art cinema option of elitist cultural representation were seen to have failed, prompting a fundamental reappraisal of how Australian films should look as much as how they should be financed (McFarlane and Mayer 1992: 238–242). National imagery and narrative (often retrospective and conservative in both cases) in the Australian films of the 1970s and 1980s were succeeded by more contemporary and eclectic representations in the 1990s. However, national and international critical and commercial successes since 2000, such as *The Dish* (2000, Australia, Rob Sitch,) ironic but celebratory depiction of Australian involvement in the 1969 moon landing and Baz Luhrmann's extravagant self-reflexive spectacle *Moulin Rouge!* (2001, Australia/US), have either revived the conservative, male-oriented comedy emphasis of previous decades or capitalised on specific, recognisable Australian sub-cultures for their popularity:

> In the case of *Moulin Rouge*, Australianness [sic] is effaced only to return as a hybrid, postmodern (distinctively Sydney) sensibility, one that seems entirely at odds with *The Dish*'s tongue-in-cheek style of populist nostalgia for a benignly bucolic Australia. However, both films have been produced as antipodal engagements with New Hollywood in both economic and textual senses.
>
> *(Collins and Davis 2004: 28–29)*

These films' coherent and deliberate engagement with expected Australian "textual" functions (in terms of the representation of national identity and the expression of authorial signature as advantageous commercial characteristics) may appear as assertiveness within or capitulation to the "economic" circumstances of millennial, international cinema. National identities, as recognisable and marketable entities, remain at the top of the agendas despite the gathering momentum of globalisation since the film revivals in Australia and New Zealand.

Principals, pioneers and provocateurs

The provision of funding for renewed film production was received by a community of filmmakers composed of individuals whose creative activity either pre-existed (and therefore anticipated) the mainstream revival or whose first ventures, particularly into the expensive business of feature production, were enabled by it. Bruce Beresford, after training at Sydney's Cinesound and the Australian Broadcasting Corporation and working in Nigeria and at the BFI in the UK, returned to Australia to direct some of the revival's most commercially successful (and in some cases controversial) films (Crowdus and Gupta 1983: 20). Beresford's output epitomised several phases or motifs of Australian production: the ribald and brash Ocker comedies such as *The Adventures of Barry McKenzie* (1972, Australia), adaptations from classic Australian novels such as *The Getting of Wisdom* by Henry Handel Richardson (1977), and sociologically and politically observant dramas such as *Don's Party* (1976, Australia) and *Breaker Morant* (1980, Australia). Other notable directors of this period such as Peter Weir and Fred Schepisi, who had grown up watching American, British and European cinema, began directing features films after apprenticeships in television production, film distribution and advertising (Mathews 1984: 23–30, 76–108). Other key contributors (Philip Noyce, George Miller) were "film buffs" and amateur filmmakers "addicted" to the cinema, who began directing without thought of an industry or a career (Mathews 1984: 231–232).

The works of these directors were in large measure responsible for the establishment of certain narrative types and native Australian genres such as the Ocker comedy, the period film, the Gothic horror film and the male ensemble drama (Dermody and Jacka 1988: 29–74). Other directors such as John Duigan, Paul Cox, Geoffrey Wright, Rolf de Heer and Baz Luhrmann, contemporaries and successors of these initial national figureheads, would extend, affirm and problematise the representativeness and institutionalisation of these narrative formats within the national cinema. Although there were exceptions and challenges to this male-dominated filmmaking community, in the form of producers such as Jan Chapman and internationally acclaimed female directors such as Gillian Armstrong and Jane Campion (Chapman 2002), there were few initial opportunities for indigenous filmmakers despite a growth of Aboriginal media representation and production in the 1980s (Michaels 1984; Langton 1993).

In New Zealand, the emerging generation of filmmakers spanned a very wide aesthetic, generic, ethnic and ideological spectrum. Black and vulgar humour, stunts, action and spectacle on small budgets characterised the early films of Geoff Murphy and Roger Donaldson. These films were innovative in their brash and improvisational feel, their indigenisation of mainstream entertainment genres such as the action thriller (Donaldson's *Sleeping Dogs*, 1977, New Zealand), road movie (Murphy's box office hit *Goodbye Porkpie*, 1981, New Zealand) and the Western (in Murphy's *Utu*, 1983, New Zealand), and the foregrounding and narrativisation of particular aspects of Kiwi masculinity. Where Murphy and Donaldson converged sympathetically in the themes and styles of their films, Peter Jackson and Vincent Ward diverged equally drastically. Jackson explored and exploited the boundaries of taste as much as genre in early examples of horror and science fiction such as *Bad Taste* (1987, New Zealand) and *Braindead* (1992, New Zealand), whereas Ward courted comparisons with European art cinema in pensive portrayals of landscape, history and identity in *Vigil* (1984, New Zealand), *The Navigator: A Medieval Odyssey* (1988, New Zealand/Australia) and *Map of the Human Heart* (1993, Australia/Canada/France/UK) (Grant 1999; Rains 2007).

These successes, and moreover the treatment of Maori characters, narratives and histories in films by white (Pakeha) directors such as Murphy's *Utu* and Ward's *River Queen* (2005, New Zealand/UK) should not detract or distract from a vibrant, highly relevant culture of Maori filmmaking. Barry Barclay's contemplative, realist narrative *Ngati* (1987, New Zealand) represents the first feature film made by a director from an indigenous population. Barclay's career as a director was inseparable from his endeavours as an activist and theorist of indigenous filmmaking (Murray 2007). *Patu!* (1983, New Zealand), a documentary directed by pioneering female Maori filmmaker Merata Mita, delivered an uncompromising portrayal of New Zealand's internal ethnic tensions stirred and reflected by the controversy of a tour by the apartheid-era South African Springboks rugby team. She would later direct *Mauri* (1988, New Zealand), the first feature film made by an indigenous woman (Peters 2007). However, Maori representation both in front and behind the camera was not without controversy. Jane Campion's Palme D'Or winning feature *The Piano* (1993, New Zealand/Australia/France) was greeted with international acclaim for its combination of elements from the Gothic, landscape cinema, art film and feminist filmmaking, but was condemned in equal measure for its patronising, stereotyped representation of indigenous people (Margolis 2000: 2). The impact of *Once Were Warriors* (1994, New Zealand, Lee Tamahori) and its representation of gang culture, socio-economic inequality and domestic violence within an urban Maori community, was praised for its realism and timeliness and criticised for its reinforcement of racial stereotypes (Murray 2011). What such examples underline was that the challenge to use cinematic conventions in innovative, subversive or adaptive ways to suit local conditions also entailed a challenge to wider social conventions.

De-coupling the automatic ways of seeing (politically, ethnically and historically) from the conventionalised ways of showing (culturally, aesthetically and cinematically) would occupy the filmmakers and their critics, audiences and potential funders in both film cultures.

Funding, "types" and genres

Balancing the need for a sustainable industry with the desire for a national cinema has been seen to underpin, and bias, film production and policies for its funding since the 1970s onwards (Formica 2011). At the same time, and arguably as a consequence of the funding policies sequentially introduced by successive governments, Australasian filmmaking has been characterised by and analysed through the emergence of consistent, conventionalised narrative forms. These genres or "types" (Gillard 2007) have formed the basis of critical-historical accounts, interpreting the national cinemas via the regularity of their representations (Ryan 2012). The first commercial successes of the revival, the Ocker films, were:

> greeted with critical hostility, being decried for their sexism and lack of seriousness. However, it was precisely this kind of film which was able to tap audience desire at the time, to overcome diffidence and resistance to Australian cinema.
>
> *(Dermody and Jacka 1987: 170)*

This "tapping" or even creation of a national audience, a factor obscured or disregarded in controversies over nationally representative or culturally appropriate content, can be seen as the genuine achievement of the first revival successes. Under the Whitlam Labour government, the AFDC was succeeded by the Australian Film Commission (AFC), an organisation with a bigger budget, a wider remit for the organisation and manifestation of national film culture and policy, and the support of regional state film boards such as the South Australia Film Corporation (Dermody and Jacka 1987: 59–63). One of the repercussions of this change was a shift from the brash, low-brow Ocker comedies of the early 1970s to the perceived aesthetic refinement and cinematic sophistication of the period film. The basis of many of these films, from *Picnic at Hanging Rock* (1975, Australia, Peter Weir) onwards, in respectable literary adaptation supported by central and state government funding, led to this naturalised heritage cinema being labelled the "AFC genre" (Dermody and Jacka, 1987: 132). The period film can be seen to have cast a long shadow, while offering restricted cultural horizons. Its influence can be seen in conservative representations of Australia's imperial past on film (*Gallipoli*, 1981, Australia, Peter Weir) and in television miniseries (*Anzacs*, 1985, Australia, Nine Network) over more than a decade, at a time when nationally inspired heritage cinema held a similar sway in Europe. Indeed, this international dimension and the perception and reception of Australian cinema overseas, may have been equally instrumental in the support and valuation of certain films:

> The theme of film's role in increasing Australia's international prestige would become an important element in the discourse of politicians and film bureaucrats as the decade continued [...] The (success d'estime) films overseas were, amongst others: *Picnic at Hanging Rock, The Chant of Jimmie Blacksmith, Newsfront, My Brilliant Career, Breaker Morant* and *Gallipoli*. They were praised for their freshness, their innocence, their *distinctiveness*; so, perhaps not surprisingly, it was the *foreign* definition and appreciation of indigenousness that circulated back and created the political climate for further support to similar kinds of films.
>
> *(Dermody and Jacka 1987: 137)*

While it created a visual identity for Australian cinema at home and abroad with pride in (markedly Anglo-Australian) history and culture for national and art cinema purposes, this also coalesced as a "brand name" (Turner 1989: 113–114) with commercial funding implications.

However, a consciousness that the art-versus-industry circle could not be squared led to reconsiderations of the sources and criteria for funding, which in turn precipitated substantial change in the origins, forms and audiences for Australian films. The establishment of supposedly conducive tax incentives (in both Australia and New Zealand), followed by the eventual establishment of a film bank (the Australian Film Finance Corporation, or FFC) and the encouragement of greater investment from private enterprise, sought to engender an environment of industry savviness, based on solid distribution deals and presales, but also facilitated commercial cynicism, and imitative and unimaginative productions:

> Bureaucrats no longer worried about film as public good, but only as public cost. The 1979 report on *The AFC in the 1980s* firmly came down on the idea of putting the house in order commercially. The "policy of bold and adventurous risk taking" in the Film Commission's investment was over, it declared. Now it was time for everybody to "become more business- like, more realistic, more positive" in their policies [...] recommendations like these led directly to the notorious 10BA tax concessions and to the miserable situation the film industry found itself in through most of the eighties.
>
> *(Kuna and Strohmaier 1999: 145)*

Genre films made under this funding pattern, such as the road-movie thriller *Road Games* (1981, Australia, Richard Franklin) which imported its narrative and stars from America, reflected an environment in which the biggest Hollywood companies (MGM/UA, Twentieth Century-Fox, Columbia and Warner Bros) continued to receive as much as 78 per cent of the total Australian box office (Jacka 1986: 20).

Appearing alongside the period film, and perhaps more candid in its commercialism, was the strand of horror and science fiction cinema referred to in both countries as the Gothic. Ironically, a key feature of the Gothic and period films was an emphasis upon the unique antipodean landscape that was crucial to the look and interpretation of both. The Australian "landscape cinema", as a subset of the conservative, nationalistic trend of film narrative, paralleled "the landscape-tradition which, for two hundred years, has been used by white Australians to promote a sense of the significance of European society in 'the Antipodes'" (Gibson 1994: 45). Conversely, Oz and Kiwi Gothic, in examples such as *Long Weekend* (1979, Australia, Colin Eggleston) and *The Scarecrow* (1982, New Zealand, Sam Pillsbury) presented the unique environments of the Southern hemisphere as uncanny, inhospitable and laden with menace embodied by the natural fauna or the unnatural human inhabitants. It was the mobilisation of the natural environment as a cinematic asset and tourist draw (in particular the Kakadu National Park), allied to toned-down Ocker humour and a formulaic romantic adventure narrative, that created the most successful (American-backed) Australian genre film to date: *Crocodile Dundee* (1986, Australia/USA, Peter Faiman) (O'Regan 1989). The penetration of the mainstream American market—unachieved by Australian art cinema successes in Europe such as *Picnic at Hanging Rock* or *Breaker Morant* (1980, Australia, Bruce Beresford) but anticipated by *Mad Max 2* (1981, Australia, George Miller,) and *The Man from Snowy River* (1982, Australia, George Miller)—was realised by writer and star Paul Hogan's film and its sequel (McFarlane 1987: 29–30). A cinematic mobilisation of the New Zealand landscape, in an even more spectacular fashion and to even greater international success, was

Figure 20.1 Peter Jackson's *Lord of the Rings* (2001–2003, New Zealand/USA/Germany) enterprise had long-term benefits for and perhaps disproportionate influence upon the New Zealand film industry. ©WingNut Films.

a central strategy within Peter Jackson's *Lord of the Rings* (2001–2003, New Zealand/USA/ Germany) enterprise (Figure 20.1), with long-term benefits for and perhaps disproportionate influence upon the New Zealand film industry (Bosanquet 2009: 46–47).

Australasian cinema in the 1990s and 2000s

Shifts in funding and representation during the 1990s were in themselves responses to the successes and failures of decision making since the revival. The creation of the Australian Film Finance Corporation altered public finance to a "film bank" footing that encouraged pre-sales and co-production to guarantee markets as much as funding, but that therefore implicitly discouraged the less commercial ventures of documentary, short and experimental filmmaking (Jacka 1993: 191–192). The Film Finance Corporation's *Newsletter* announced in 1993 that "a dozen FFC-backed films with a total budget of around $50 million" were in production, celebrated the screening of five Australian films within the official selections at Cannes and trumpeted the success of Australian features in making a "dent in the once-impenetrable US theatrical market (Rich 1993: 1, 5). It also quoted Jan Chapman, producer of *The Last Days of Chez Nous* (1992, Australia, Gillian Armstrong) and *The Piano* (1993, New Zealand/Australia/ France, Jane Campion) as evidence of the renewed commercial and cultural integrity of the national cinema: "We do seem to be able—and I imagine it is because of the way the FFC exists—to make films that are authentically Australian and aren't subjugating their idiosyncratic or national characteristics to a larger, American-controlled industry" (Rich 1993: 3).

At the same time as the persistence of art cinema and period film precedents were discernible in Chapman's, Armstrong's and Campion's films, a new filmic "brand" appeared to emerge in the form of the "quirky" Australian drama. The outstanding examples (*Strictly Ballroom*, 1992, Australia, Baz Luhrmann; *Muriel's Wedding*, 1994, Australia, P.J. Hogan; *The Adventures of Priscilla, Queen of the Desert*, 1994, Australia, Stephan Elliott,) evinced an instinctively ironic, compulsively eclectic approach to postmodern allusiveness, performance, popular genres, and sub-cultural identities. The utopianism of these films matched their contemporaneity in the acknowledgement of multicultural, urban social realities, but their popularity was also attributable to their dynamic reuse and re-invocation of the commercialism, vulgarity and political incorrectness of the Ocker comedies of the 1970s "dresse[d] up for international consumption" (Barber 1996–1997). Although in some ways these films can be seen to have launched and defined the career of Luhrmann as a significant international film-maker, their representativeness, of the nation or the industry, was debatable:

> *Priscilla*, *Muriel* and the other films of that ilk are the ultimate gesture of revenge against [...] a self-image which, in Australian cultural history, had its origins in the sleepy, self-satisfied, consumerist suburban ethos of the 50s. The "suburban surreal" of *Priscilla* screams that things are happening, that the "tyranny of distance" is easily obliterated by three drag queens on a bus, and that people of every imaginable ethnic and sexual mix can look equally silly to each other.
>
> (Martin 1995: 32)

Other notable successes of the 1990s, such as the melodramatic biopic *Shine* (Scott Hicks, 1996) were seen not so much as manipulating and exploiting an Australian difference for international recognition as achieving a "skilful merchandising of a familiar theme [. . .] placed in an unfamiliar context" (Lapointe 1997: 38). However, a significant and unprecedented increase in the representation of ethnic difference came to characterise Australian cinema over the next ten years. The expansion of Aboriginal representation both within films and within filmmaking itself produced a number of notable and challenging examples that coincided with the "history wars" permeating mainstream society as much as academic debate (Collins and Davis 2004: 133–149). Although, controversially, some of the most high-profile films of this group were directed by non-Aboriginal filmmakers (*Rabbit Proof Fence*, 2002, Australia, Phillip Noyce; *Ten Canoes*, 2006, Australia, Rolf de Heer), their impact reflected the fundamental changes experienced by Australian cinema and society as a whole in the wake of the Mabo land rights case (Collins and Davis 2004: 3–19). The milestone success of the remarkable Aboriginal realist drama *Samson and Delilah* (2009, Australia, Warwick Thornton) marked a substantial shift in the representational potential and aesthetic boundaries of the Australian cinema, as a thought-provoking contemporary medium.

Conclusion: life/support

Within the first decade of the revival, Jan Dawson likened the position of Australian cinema (and that of minor European film industries) in relation to the American cinema to that of "Aboriginals to the mainstream of Australian culture [. . .] an oppressed minority group" (Dawson 1977: 373). The interplay of funding demands, commercial realities, and national and international representational conventions that formed the "background radiation" to the revival still registers consistently in the milieux of production, distribution and consumption for Australasian films since 2000, suggesting that Australasian filmmakers may actually represent an oppressed minority within their own countries. For revival director Tim Burstall, the commercial vigour, authentic observation, and comic-satirical energy of the Ocker film justified its status as the true or truest Australian cinema, which had been stifled by establishment concerns for cultural respectability and representation, not representativeness (Burstall 1985). Reading the combination of low-brow humour and *Candide*-like characterisation that links the commercial hit of the Ocker era, *The Adventures of Barry McKenzie*, the outstanding mainstream success of American collaboration in the 1980s, *Crocodile Dundee,* and the new incarnation of the naive Australian abroad in the new millennium in *Kenny* (2006, Australia, Clayton Jacobson), Benito Cao interprets the recurrent male everyman as the genuine barometer of the Australian cinema:

There are signs that Australian films are repositioning Australia as part of the Global Village, suggesting that Australian national identity might be moving beyond the imperial metaphors of Little America and British Rules [...] The evolution of the relation between Australia and Anglo-Empire symbolized by these three characters suggests we might be entering a post-imperial articulation of Australian-ness.

(Cao 2012: 240)

An example of such rethinking of Australia's economic and political geography and a reflection of the increasing irrelevance of its previous cultural associations with America and Britain is the growth of international co-productions in Asia (Walsh 2012).

Conscious repositioning of the national project has also been undertaken in New Zealand, with reviews of funding, apportionment, representativeness and viability constituting the parameters under which the film industry continues to exist:

According to the New Zealand Film Commission Act (1978), for any production to qualify as "a New Zealand film" it needs to meet criteria of local subject material, locations, creative and acting talent, funding sources, and local ownership of equipment and technical facilities. In 2009, the National Government initiated a review of the NZFC, arguing that the requirements of the 1978 Act no longer reflected the screen-production realities of the twenty-first century. This intervention (not the first since the NZFC was set up) was motivated by continuing complaints that the Commission was failing in respect of the commercial potential of locally-made films, where the great majority of state-subsidized film-making never returns on its costs.

(Leland 2010: 258)

Within this context, the status of Peter Jackson's cinematic and industrial achievements and influence, in establishing the country as a post-production hub as much as an exotic location, are at once a boon and a burden. Gaylene Preston, one of the most respected local filmmakers whose career spans the period since the NZFC's inauguration, has been scathing of the divergence she sees as increasingly evident between the cultural responsibility and commercial expectation of the national filmmaking initiative:

We found out early on that the films that travel are culturally specific. The cultural difference will help the film in the overseas market. There's no use in us trying to make a cheaper version of Hollywood films. [However] The New Zealand Film Commission Act doesn't have the word "culture" in it. From the beginning, unlike in Australia, the NZ Government did not support the film industry in order to get NZ stories told. The overwhelming idea was to attract foreign exchange.

(Bosanquet, 2009: 49)

Despite the cynicism with which government support is frequently viewed, awareness of the inevitability of reliance upon it regulates and limits film production within the national context, and perhaps continues to inspire outstanding Australasian filmmakers to pursue international careers overseas. In interview in 1980 (shortly before his own departure for Hollywood), Peter Weir likened the Australian industry to a "bedridden" critical (or terminal) patient unable to "divorce" itself from government sustenance (Stratton 1980: 293). Director Dean O'Flaherty employed a similar metaphor to describe the film industry in the new millennium (Flanagan 2009). However, the achievements of Australasian cinema under such inauspicious or frankly hostile conditions have been to persist, to represent and broadcast a multiplicity of relevant cultural histories, narratives and identities. Such representation has perhaps been the chief end in itself of film cultures emerging from national cultures in states of constant flux, contestation and introspection. In this regard, the representative national depiction, the international high-profile cinematic success, and the unsuccessful, individual national film, are intrinsic components of a crucial, small cinema responsibility:

> [even] without governmental underwriting, the cinema would still become a vehicle for social problematization, as the social record provides a commercial incentive to follow from and tap public issues. The cinema routinely produces representations which are as much interventions into as they are reflections of social formations.
>
> *(O'Regan 1996: 263)*

References

Barber, S. (1996–1997) "*The Adventures of Priscilla, Queen of the Desert*", *Film Quarterly* 50 (2): 41–45.
Barclay, B. (2003) "An Open Letter to John Barrett from Barry Barclay", *Onfilm* 20 (2): 11–14.
Bosanquet, T. (2009) "From Innocence to Experience: Making Films in New Zealand", *Metro* 160: 46–49.
Burstall, T. (1985) "Twelve Genres of Australian Film", in Moran, A. and O'Regan, T. (eds) *An Australian Film Reader*, Sydney: Currency, 215–222.
Cao, B. (2012) "Beyond Empire: Australian Cinematic Identity in the Twenty-First Century", *Studies in Australasian Cinema* 6 (3): 239–250.
Chapman, J. (2002) "Some Significant Women in Australian Film—A Celebration and a Cautionary Tale", *Senses of Cinema* 22, http://sensesofcinema.com/2002/australian-women/chapman/.
Collins, F. and Davis, T. (2004) *Australian Cinema after Mabo*, Cambridge: Cambridge University Press.
Conrich, I. and Davy, S. (1997) *Views from the Edge of the World*, London: Kakapo.
Crowdus, G. and Gupta, U. (1983) "An Aussie in Hollywood: An Interview with Bruce Beresford", *Cineaste*,12 (4): 20–25.
Dawson, J. (1977) "Australian Film Culture", *Cinema Papers* 12: 373.
Dermody, S. and Jacka, E. (eds) (1987) *The Screening of Australia vol. I: The Anatomy of a Film Industry*, Sydney: Currency.
Dermody, S. and Jacka, E. (1988) *The Screening of Australia vol. II: The Anatomy of a National Cinema*, Sydney: Currency.
Flanagan, E. (2009) "From Business to *Beautiful*: Writer/director Dean O'Flaherty", *Metro* 160: 54–57.
Formica, S. (2011) "When It All Started: Politics and Policies of the Australian Film Industry from the Revival to the International Breakthrough", *Studies in Australasian Cinema* 5 (1): 43-57.
Gaunson, S. (2015) "American Combine: Australasian Films Ltd., and Block Bookings", *Studies in Australasian Cinema* 9 (3): 241–252.
Gibson, R. (1994) "Formative Landscapes", in Murray, S. (ed.) *Australian Cinema*, St Leonards: Allen & Unwin, 44–59.
Gillard, G. (2007) *Ten Types of Australian Film*, Perth: Murdoch University.
Grant, B. K. (1999) *A Cultural Assault: The New Zealand Films of Peter Jackson*, Nottingham: Kakapo.
Jacka, E. (1993) "The Production Process: Film", in Cunningham, S. and Turner, G (eds) *The Media in Australia: Industries, Texts, Audiences*, St Leonards: Allen & Unwin, 1993, 180–192.
Jacka, L. (1986) "The Film Industry in Australia: Trends in the Eighties", *Media Information Australia* 42: 17–21.
Kuna, F. and Strohmaier, P. (1999) "Ecstacies in the Mossy Land", in Verhoeven, D. (ed.) *Twin Peeks: Australian and New Zealand Feature Films*, Melbourne: Damned Publishing, 151–170.
Langton, M. (1993) *Well I Heard It on the Radio and I Saw It on the Television*, Sydney: AFC.
Lapointe, J. (1997) "*Shine*", *Film Quarterly* 51 (1): 36–38.
Lawson, S. (1985) "Australian Film, 1969, *Quadrant* 1969", in Moran, A. and O'Regan, T. (eds) *An Australian Film Reader*, Sydney: Currency, 175–183.
Leland, G. (2010), "Introduction: New Zealand Film in 2009", in Goldsmith, B. and Leland, G. (eds) *Directory of World Cinema: Australia and New Zealand*, Bristol: Intellect, 256–259.

McFarlane, B. (1987) *Australian Cinema 1970–1985*, London: Secker & Warburg.
McFarlane, B. and Mayer, G. (1992) *New Australian Cinema: Sources and Parallels in American and British Film*, Cambridge: Cambridge University Press.
Margolis, H. (2000) "'A Strange Heritage': From Colonization to Transformation", in Margolis, H. (ed.), *Jane Campion's The Piano*, Cambridge: Cambridge University Press, 1–41.
Martin, A. (1995) "More than Muriel", *Sight and Sound* 5 (6): 30–32.
Michaels, E. (1984) "Aboriginal Air Rights", *Media Information Australia*, 34: 51–62.
Murray, S. (2007) "Images of Dignity: The Films of Barry Barclay", in Conrich, I. and Murray, S. (eds) *New Zealand Filmmakers*, Detroit: Wayne State University Press, 88–102.
—— (2011) "*Once Were Warriors*", in Bennett, J. E. and Beirne, R. (eds) *Making Film and Television Histories: Australia and New Zealand*, London: I.B. Tauris, 58–62.
O'Regan, T. (1996) *Australian National Cinema*, London: Routledge.
—— (2002) "Australian Cinema as a National Cinema", in Williams, A. (ed.) *Film and Nationalism*, London: Rutgers University Press, 89–136.
—— (1989) "Fair Dinkum Fillums: The *Crocodile Dundee* Phenomenon", in Dermody, S. and Jacka, E. (eds) *The Screening of Australia vol. II: The Anatomy of a National Cinema*, Sydney: Currency, 155–175.
Peters, G. (2007) "Lives of Their Own: Films by Merata Mita", in Conrich, I. and Murray, S. (eds) *New Zealand Filmmakers*, Detroit: Wayne State University Press, 103–120.
Pike, A. and Cooper, R. (1980) *Australian Cinema 1900–1977: A Guide to Feature Film Production*, Melbourne: Oxford University Press.
Rains, S. (2007) "Making Strange: Journeys Through the Unfamiliar in the Films of Vincent Ward", in Conrich, I. and Murray, S. (eds) *New Zealand Filmmakers*, Detroit, IL: Wayne State University Press, 273–288.
Reade, E. (1983) "Australian Silent Film 1904–1907: The Features Begin", in Fell, J. L. (ed.) *Film Before Griffith*, London: University of California Press, 81–91.
Rich, J. (ed.) (1993) *Newsletter of the Australian Film Finance Corporation*, June/July.
Roddick, N. (1985) "Long White Cloud Cover: New Zealand Film in the Eighties", *Cinema Papers* 3: 24–30.
Ryan, M. D. (2012) "A Silver Bullet for Australian Cinema? Genre Movies and the Audience Debate", *Studies in Australasian Cinema* 6 (2): 141–157.
Stratton, D. (1980) *The Last New Wave: The Australian Film Revival*, London: Angus & Robertson.
Thornhill, M. (1985) "Strategies for an Industry—Government Intervention *Masque* May–June 1968", in Moran, A. and O'Regan, T. (eds) *An Australian Film Reader*, Sydney: Currency, 166–169.
Turner, G. (1989) "Art Directing History: The Period Film", in Moran, A. and O'Regan, T. (eds) *The Australian Screen*, Harmondsworth: Penguin, 99–117.
Walsh, M. (2012) "At the Edge of Asia: The Prospects for Australia–China Film Co-production", *Studies in Australasian Cinema* 6 (3): 301–316.
Weir, T. (1985) "No Daydreams of Our Own: The Film as National Self-Expression, *Nation* 1958", in Moran, A. and O'Regan, T. (eds) *An Australian Film Reader*, Sydney: Currency, 144–149.

PART II

Latitude

21

CINEMAS OF CITIZENS AND CINEMAS OF SENTIMENT

World Cinema in flux

Rob Stone

> Obviously, a rigid, blinkered, absolutist world view is the easiest to keep hold of, whereas the fluid, uncertain, metamorphic picture I've always carried about is rather more vulnerable.
>
> *(Salman Rushdie 1993: 23)*

Arguments over inclusion and exclusion flare when terms such as refugee and migrant hit the headlines and tensions are exacerbated when nation-states change as a result of referenda, elections and conflict. At such times, national identity may freeze when nationalism surges or melt as treaties break boundaries and definitions are diluted. The terms of citizenship are designed to be rigid and inviolate, but shifts in status can impose and withdraw this actually abstract condition, rendering it subject to chimerical criteria. Boxes within boxes make citizenship increasingly opaque—Welsh, British, European; Cuban, Caribbean, Latin American; Hong Kong, Chinese, East Asian—and the consequences for World Cinema are manifold. Beyond the nation-state, between the limitations of national cinemas and before the dispersion of transnational ones, how can the remapping of contemporary World Cinema cope with its ongoing coagulation and dissolution? As Mette Hjort and Scott MacKenzie observe, "many current attempts to articulate the national or nationalist dimensions of cinematic cultures draw on only the most limited corpus of relevant theoretical texts. Indeed, in many cases it is a matter of mobilising Benedict Anderson's modernist conception of the nation as an imagined community" (2000: 2). In this new attempt to facilitate greater recognition of fluidity within considerations of World Cinema, I follow the theorising of the political scientist Georg Sørenson, who looks beyond the nation-state to a world made up of communities of citizens that are defined by an exchange of "political, social and economic rights and obligations" (Sørenson 2004: xiv), and communities of sentiment that are based on an ungovernable flow that extends via empathy to include those along a strata of common or similar cultural, social, linguistic, economic conditions enabling "a historical identity based on literature, myths, symbols, music and art, and so on" (Sørenson 2004: 83). Then, by extrapolating a new theoretical framework of cinemas of citizens and cinemas of sentiment, I apply this to the study of World Cinema in order to ameliorate its submission to what Andrew Higson called "the limiting imagination of national cinema" (2000: 63).

Anderson theorised his imagined communities "as both inherently limited and sovereign" (2006: 6). They were "*imagined* because the members of even the smallest nation will never know most of their fellow-members, meet them, or even hear of them, yet in the minds of each lives the image of their communion" (2006: 6, emphasis in original). This was ideal for Film Studies because the imagined history and membership of a community provided synonyms for both onscreen histories of the nation and the domestic audiences of these films. Anderson's theory of nationhood, which carries nationalism "as if it belonged with 'kinship' and 'religion', rather than with 'liberalism' or 'fascism'" (Anderson 2006: 5), is limited, however, by mapping belonging "on to a carefully demarcated geo-political space" (Higson 2000: 65), one that emphasises its geographical and genetic juxtaposition with other imagined communities, whose differences denote otherness. Scholars of World Cinema focused on these "processes occurring within what is construed as a national communicative space" (Hjort and MacKenzie 2000: 5) as they described the cinemas of Britain (Higson 1989, 1995; Street 1997), Spain (Stone 2001; Triana-Toribio 2003) and Japan (Standish 2006; Philips and Stringer 2007), among others, in deference to the idea that imagined communities belonged to "a world of sovereign states" (Schlesinger 2000: 29). Following Sørenson, however, the Bergsonian notion that World Cinema should be understood as existing in permanent flux, which demands sociological enquiry into the relationships between cinema and identity in a context of political changes and cultural shifts, responds to the demand that the centrality of Anderson's concept be respectfully challenged by "increased awareness, not only of the place of Anderson's concepts and frameworks within the context of larger debates, but of competing accounts" (Hjort and MacKenzie 2000: 2).

One of the bases of Anderson's theory (and revisionist history of the world) was that languages could be barriers on top of borders, but that the visual, performative and creative arts nevertheless managed to communicate commonalities in "a world in which the figuring of imagined reality was overwhelmingly visual and aural" (Anderson 2006: 23). This held true until capitalism reinstated criteria for inclusion and exclusion in relation to states and societies and "not least by its dissemination of print, helped to create popular, vernacular-based nationalisms in Europe" (Anderson 2006: 39). Holding that this "figuring of imagined reality" is an evocative definition of the function of the cinema led to recognition that the advent of silent cinema provided a composite art that truly created an all-inclusive "imagined reality", at least until languages were heard in sound film, causing evolving cinemas to restrain universal visual signifiers in favour of localised linguistic signs. The subsequent categorisation of these cinemas into items of coherent singularity due to their different languages favoured internal stratification within nations that positioned domestic product as a wide range of middlebrow entertainment and pushed anything foreign to the edges via "low-brow" dubbing and "high-brow" subtitling. Distributors grew adept at marketing or dismissing films in terms of their nationhood. Once a profitable export brand for UFA in the 1920s, German expressionist cinema would be rejected as un-American by competitive US distributors in the 1930s, for example, and yet still prove itself an insidious influence on "un-American" film noir. The relation between cinema and nation became the cornerstone of post-war European cinema and the studies that described it; but the recent jump from national to transnational cinemas via globalisation by means of digital technologies in relation to industry, funding and reception (Hjort 2010) has revived the need to understand World Cinema as being formed not only by competing or colluding nation-states but also by ungovernable affinities made visible between communities. Like that of Anderson, Karl W. Deutsch's theorisation of communication and nationalism was centred on the nation-state (1996: 4); but contemporary cinemas no longer have to rely upon the nation-state to be "still the chief political instrument for getting things done" (Deutsch 1996: 188). Indeed, as Deutsch foretold, "the essential aspect of the unity of a people [. . .] is the complementarity or relative efficiency of communication among individuals—something that is in some ways similar to mutual rapport" (1996: 188). Deutsch delves thereafter into the idea of a people forging a nationality that is distinct from nationhood, but I shall argue that this "mutual rapport" must be construed more pointedly as a sentiment that, following Sørenson, is capable of transcending citizenship.

Several scholars have argued the cases for cinemas that oppose national cinemas and have called these accented, migrant, diasporic, small or immigration cinemas (see Naficy 2001; Berghahn and Sternberg 2010; Petrie and Hjort 2007; and Ballesteros 2015, respectively); but a viable framework for recognising and understanding the on-going becoming of all cinemas must include those emerging from filmmaking communities that are both within and beyond as well as aligned with nation-states. The emergence and erasure of representative cinemas that are cognisant of their social, political, economic and aesthetic impact and their implications is a mostly organic occurrence moving through rigidification, dissolution and vaporisation in both directions. At one extreme appear the frozen cores of seemingly rigid, introverted, solipsistic and servile cinemas that are fostered by government funding and in certain regimes may be all a domestic audience gets to see, while at the other extreme flicker inexpensive, untethered audio-visual items adrift on the internet. Both extremes may represent and be received by analytically capable communities, but whereas the latter may be up to the task of constantly rethinking collective and individual identity, the frozen kind may be less keen or able to engage in processes of reinvention. Like ice, water and vapour, these mutable cinemas are essentially the same thing—just films—but we must update our understanding of their condition, context and function because Anderson's assertion that "nation-ness is the most universally legitimate value in the political life of our time" (2006: 3) is simply no longer true. Also faulty therefore is the "linear notion of history that understood the nation-state as the natural, not to say, organic, result of an evolutionary trajectory" (Vitali and Willemen 2006: 3), which follows Deutsch (1953 [1996]) and Ernest Gellner (1983) in being "mainly concerned with how a national culture comes to be created, rather than with how it is maintained and renewed" (Schlesinger 2000: 21).

In his corrective response, Sørenson investigates maintenance and renewal by conceptualising a borderless world beyond the nation-state, one that combines spatial and temporal, real and virtual arenas of communication in which identity is less likely to be withheld, inherited or imposed than, as Anthony Giddens contends, it is to be "discovered, constructed, actively sustained" (Giddens 1994: 82). In *The Transformation of the State: Beyond the Myth of Retreat* (2004), Sørenson assesses the effects of globalisation and concludes that identity is not solely determined by self-serving policies but by generous sentiment too. Thus he argues that modern identity exists in a condition and framework of flux between rigid citizenship and unrestricted sentiment, which I contend is relevant to contemporary World Cinema too. This flux is about more than cinema as an "adjunct of capitalism" (Vitali and Willemen 2006: 7) or movement between "two understandings of cinema: as an industry and as a cluster of cultural strategies" (Vitali and Willemen 2006: 2). When Jürgen Habermas built a theoretical framework that allowed for flux while remaining anchored to nation-states, he described tendencies in the matter of national identity as centripetal and centrifugal forces; that is to say, on the one hand he detected:

> a hardening of national identities as different cultural forms of life come into collision; on the other, the hybrid differentiations that soften native cultures and comparatively homogeneous forms of life in the wake of assimilation into a single material world culture.
>
> *(Habermas 2001: 73)*

Sørenson theorises this as the emergence of a community of citizens on the one hand, and a community of sentiment on the other, but crucially moves beyond the nation-state in order to maintain fluidity and, moreover, posit this as vital to constant renewal. Andrew Higson formulated a similar equation when investigating the limiting imagination of national cinema:

> At times, the experience of an organic, coherent national community, a meaningful national collectivity, will be overwhelming. At other times, the experience of diaspora, dislocation and de-centredness will prevail. It is at times such as these that other allegiances, other senses of belonging besides the national will be more strongly felt.
> *(Higson 2000: 65)*

Higson does not suggest what these "other senses of belonging" are, but their occurrence certainly recalls Deutsch's "mutual rapport" and coincides with the fact that, as Sørenson observes, globalisation and its attendant digital technology mean that in the new millennium "a new system 'beyond' the sovereign state is in the making" (Sørenson 2004: xii). This had already been foretold by James N. Rosenau and Ernst-Otto Czempiel (1993), John Naisbitt (1994) and Kenichi Ohmae (1996), among others, with consensus settling on "a transformation away from governance in the context of national government towards multilevel governance at overlapping national, local and international levels" (Sørenson 2004: xiii). Crucially, however, Sørenson frames his corrective, which is both retrospective *and* prospective, as "a process of transition from modern to what I call postmodern statehood" (Sørenson 2004: xv), in order to contend that the area between the local and the global that was previously dominated by nation-states is now composed of communities of citizens and communities of sentiment that occur within this "new context characterized by the increased salience of globalization and the transnational relations that go with it" (Sørenson 2004: 90). Following Sørenson, I propose that a new framework for understanding World Cinema can be predicated upon the relations between cinemas of citizens and cinemas of sentiment.

Like a community of citizens, a cinema of citizens is one based upon an exchange of "political, social and economic rights and obligations" (Sørenson 2004: xiv). It is in the community of citizens that the provision of healthcare might require payment of taxes, for example, a free or subsidised education may be conditional upon subsequent military service, and clean streets and civil liberties will depend upon the observation of public order. Thus, a cinema of citizens will be one of similarly close links between government and filmmakers that are established and maintained (directly and indirectly) by funding, educational strategies, investment in related infrastructure, policies, quotas, incentives such as tax-breaks, sponsored training and official campaigns that support and exploit the soft power of homegrown films at festivals and awards ceremonies. The rights in such exchanges are, in a sense, rewards that reinforce similarity to other members of the community and a shared experience of its cinema as well as difference from those beyond it. The exchange of rights and obligations is subject to change, of course, but the prevailing criteria for inclusion that they espouse and uphold contribute to the maintenance of a dictated or democratically determined mandate for building or maintaining citizenship and cinema in a place with a shared idea and sense of itself as a subject with a historical, cultural and possibly linguistic identity that is legally binding, verifiable by census and different from those of other communities and cinemas of citizens. Sørenson's communities of citizens are different from Anderson's imagined communities because its members are at least as aware of their economic–legal rights as they are of their cultural–historic obligations. Communities of citizens can coincide with nation-states as they congeal around a consensus of historical criteria for inclusion and exclusion that flows like wet cement to the limits of national borders, although a homogenous ethno-national basis to the community is rarely viable. Correlatively, the cinema of citizens is perceived as having national affiliations and responsibilities although it might not represent the totality of its citizens, many of whom, as we shall see, may claim or pursue membership of cinemas of sentiment instead. If the exchange of rights and obligations is deemed fair, however, then a community and cinema of citizens is generally prone to go along with "banal nationalism"; that is, "a collection of ideological habits (including habits of practice and belief) which reproduce existing nations as nations" in everyday life (Billig 1995: 6).

In comparison, a cinema of sentiment, like a community of sentiment, is more focused on becoming than on being and as such offers "a dynamic picture of a contested identity always being debated" (Sørenson 2004: 85). Sentiment here is defined by awareness, empathy, reflection and acceptance or rejection of elements contributing to or detracting from identity and it is enacted through transactions that are uncontrolled by the state. A community and cinema of sentiment express themselves via a subjectivity that exceeds a legalised or politically circumscribed identity since such "identity formations consist of trying to 'pin us' to a specific, selected sub-set of the many diverse clusters we traverse in our lifetimes" (Willemen 2006: 30–31). This "pinning" negates "flux, the continuity of transition" (Bergson 1992: 16) that allows a cinema of sentiment to represent an analytically competent people engaged in self-reflection. As such, the cinema of sentiment can represent what Manuel Castells calls a "resistance identity", which is one that is generated by those actors that are "in positions/conditions devalued and/or stigmatized by the logic of domination, thus building trenches of resistance and survival on the basis of principles different from, or opposed to, those permeating the institutions of society" (Castells 1998: 8). As Sørenson suggests, whereas the community and cinema of citizens might be said to offer "an offensive, integrating response to globalization and other changes" that hardens the core definition of national identity at a certain moment, the cinema of sentiment offers "a defensive, fragmentary one" (Sørenson 2004: 93) that illustrates and gives voice to regional, ethnic and otherwise marginalised groups seeking a higher degree of autonomy.

The cinema of sentiment is much more fragile than one of citizens. It moves outwards, seeking lifelines thrown by international film festivals, smaller festivals elsewhere based on relevant themes or genres, such as queer cinema or documentary, and new audiences via the internet. The cinema of sentiment can be a response to the weakening, fracture and diffusion of citizenship on the one hand, and to the hardening of criteria for citizenship on the other. Its potential for resistance may be strengthened by international funding and transnational distribution strategies and opportunities that transcend the heterogeneity of localism but may also encourage resistance to the homogeneity of globalization. Here, perhaps, as Hjort suggests, the aim is primarily communication between a number of cultures whose empathy may be "understood in terms of ethnicity, partially overlapping or mutually intelligible languages, and a history of interaction giving rise to shared core values, common practices, and comparable institutions" (Hjort 2010: 17). The sentiment of something shared, which might be regionalism, marginalisation of many kinds, economic sedimentation or much else besides, gives rise to a project of identity construction that suggests and may even realise a collective identity within or above and beyond the communities of citizens from which it emerges. In some cases, such as that in which cinemas of sentiment colluded to invent a nationalist African cinema tradition in the years between 1960 and 1975, such cinemas reveal ambitions to be a synecdoche for an otherwise lacking cinema of citizens in retrospective analysis that "comes on the heels of a moribund national construction discourse, after scores of national governments in Africa failed to provide for their citizenry" (Niang 2014: xii). In other cases, potential cinemas of sentiment, such as those emerging from the White and Black American lower classes in the United States, may fail to cohere because their commonalities are erased in the dominant Hollywood cinema, which is arguably tantamount to a cinema of citizens that caters to aspirational white audiences while often ignoring other ethnic or racial elements of society, as the 2016 uproar over #OscarsSoWhite suggested (Ryan 2016).

Willemen touches on the fact that citizenship is what is currently objectively correct, but sentiment is what is felt to be most relevant, when he notes that "the concern with socio-cultural specificity is different from identity searches and debates" (Willemen 2006: 34). Concern with citizenship tends to look backwards and inwards to a defining core that risks hardening, whereas sentiment tends to look forwards and outwards to possible new configurations and risks dissolution. Flux is evident because sentiment can be patriotic or nationalist too, of course, for an emotional attachment to the nation can be fierce. Indeed, when subscription to the beliefs maintained in a narrow, nationalist selection of "literature, myths, symbols, music and art, and so on" (Sørenson 2004: 83) upholds a socio-cultural criterion for inclusion and exclusion that is inscribed as a legal criterion, then the community of sentiment will become one of citizens. At the same time, cinemas of sentiment may compete with those of citizens by highlighting diversity at home and transnational connections abroad, whereby social media and digital communication also clarify the economic sedimentation of people the world over as a result of globalised neo-liberalism. This means that the horizontal affinities sought by communities of sentiment and manifested in their cinemas will tend to exhibit financially determined similarities in terms of production values, form and aesthetics that currently result from the new digital technologies, multi-platform virtual environment, access to inexpensive filmmaking equipment, online distribution and file-sharing that enable contact between those keen on making and watching certain types of film.

Such affinities are evident in the economic sedimentation of types of film production and the aesthetics of impoverishment shared by the American Mumblecore and the Romanian New Wave, for example. Mumblecore is a contested term that denotes a zero-budget cluster of films that emerged from the American indie scene in the 2000s in order to adequately represent educated but dislocated twenty-somethings, while the Romanian New Wave, which is another contested categorisation, also emerged in the 2000s to describe those filmmakers who responded to the lack of a viable Romanian cinema of citizens by creating one of sentiment. The dissent over categorisation is itself suggestive of flux, because, as Marina Kaceanov explains of Romanian cinema:

> after the troubled years of transformations, socio-economical problems, and constant battles with the bureaucracy of the National Centre for Cinematography, the growing conflict between past and present finally exploded into a cultural revolution. The present requires its own chroniclers, and the younger and more in touch they are with reality, the better. When there is no room, funding or support for younger people, an opposition is born.
>
> *(Kaceanov 2008)*

The limitations of the filmmaking apparatus in both these cinemas of sentiment reveal numerous commonalities; not only the relatively cheap technology employed in their making but the resulting minimalism, long scenes of naturalistic dialogue alternating with patches of silence, the use of subtle camera movement to represent negotiation and power-play between characters, a focus on the personal relationships of young adults that can favour female subjectivity and, ultimately, a tone of lived-in resignation shared by the likes of Marnie (Kate Dollenmayer) in *Funny Ha Ha* (2002, USA, Andrew Bujalski) (Figure 21.1) and Otilia (Anamaria Marinca) in *4 luni, 3 saptamâni si 2 zile* (4 Months, 3 Weeks, 2 Days, 2007, Romania/Belgium, Cristian Mungiu)

Figure 21.1 Marnie (Kate Dollenmayer) (centre) in *Funny Ha Ha* (2002, USA, Andrew Bujalski).

Figure 21.2 Otilia (Anamaria Marinca) (centre) in *4 luni, 3 saptamâni si 2 zile* (4 Months, 3 Weeks, 2 Days, 2007, Romania/Belgium, Cristian Mungiu).

(Figure 21.2). Both Mumblecore and the Romanian New Wave outlived the comparatively brief life expectancy of cinemas of sentiment. Repetition and conformity rendered Mumblecore increasingly redundant and prompted its migration to television in series such as *Girls* (2012–2017, USA, Lena Dunham), *Togetherness* (2015–2016, USA, Jay and Mark Duplass), *Love* (2016–, USA, Judd Apatow) and *Easy* (2016–, USA, Joe Swanberg). And when sustained international festival success for Romanian cinema resembled "less a new wave than a persistent surf-pounding" (Zeitchik 2016), it drew criticism that Romanian filmmakers were second-guessing the sympathies of international juries:

> How much to continue in a style that's served it well but could grow stale, like all styles, is an open question, as is the challenge of keeping on in a nation where even leaders admit they've failed their filmmakers.
>
> *(Zeitchik 2016)*

On the other hand, the persistence of Romanian filmmakers may have prompted their standing as an auteurist elite that so "branded" Romanian cinema it may have obviated a Romanian cinema of citizens and precluded other Romanian cinemas of sentiment from emerging.

Clearly communities and cinemas of citizens and sentiment have the capacity to morph into each other and this is key to the context of flux that they inhabit. A community of citizens that absorbs an unlimited number of immigrants, cedes the provision of rights to a supranational body such as the European Union or subscribes to a doctrine, campaign or manifesto, fragments into regions with claims on autonomy, enters into associations with other territories and/or populations that override internal policy, dilutes the legal criteria for inclusion and invests in cultural partnerships with others that erase differences between them may give rise to a community or communities of sentiment. At the same time, nevertheless, the hardening of criteria for inclusion can lead to exclusions within the community and cinema of citizens as some members are re-classified and lose their rights because of new laws and governments or referenda. The results and ramifications of the UK's 2016 referendum on whether it should leave or remain in the European Union provide a pertinent example of this. Many voters clearly felt that their "British" community of citizens, which was shown to be mainly English, had been superseded by a European community of citizens and so campaigned for a nationalistic "British" community of sentiment that the result of the referendum would convert into a new community of citizens by means of reinstating sovereignty and protectionist immigration policies. Such a community of citizens is potentially transformative, but tends to reassemble as a rigid "historical structure" (Cox 1994) resembling the nation-state when its ambitions are informed by conservatism that exhumes the values of the past. At the same time, however, many other voters felt themselves wrenched from a European community of citizens and alienated from the nationalistic "British" community of sentiment and the community of citizens that it would become, and, following the result, they subsequently clung to and campaigned for membership of a European community of sentiment. In relation to such changes, one might eventually in retrospect be able to recognise cinemas of citizens and of sentiment. A British cinema of citizens will tend towards thematic and generic limitations and favour telling stories that serve soft power policies and repay funding with a flattering view of the community of citizens that watches them, as well as by occasional foreign audiences who enjoy such "English" things as the several timely biopics of Winston Churchill that included *Churchill's Secret* (2016, UK, Charles Sturridge) with Michael Gambon in the role, *Churchill* (2017, UK, Jonathan Teplitzky) with Brian Cox, and *Darkest Hour* (2017, UK, Joe Wright) with Gary Oldman. If, in such situations, filmmakers move away from the traditional themes or genres of a state-centric cinema of citizens they may struggle to obtain funding, which abets ignorance of the "accented cinema" of immigrants and disenfranchised minorities (Naficy 2001) as well as the independent, online and underground films associated with Welsh, Scottish, regional, Black British and queer British cinemas of sentiment and much else besides.

Moreover, although nationhood remains a strong context, cinemas of sentiment may gain strength and also demand rights and changes to the criteria for exclusion and inclusion that determines funding for films, as has happened in Spain, for example, where the Catalan-language cinema of sentiment represents an alternative socio-political context of increasing autonomy for the region of Catalonia and produces what many hope might turn into a Catalan cinema of citizens. Fractures in the close links between citizenship and sentiment are particularly evident when a new system above the national, such as the European Union, provides recognition. In such instances, "with the growth of supranational cooperation, an institutional level 'above' the nation-state [. . .] can become a new partner for the regional movements" (Sørenson 2004: 94). This allows regions within nation-states to appeal legally and emotively to entities beyond them, as with the Basque Country's appeal to Europe during the Francoist dictatorship (Arrieta Alberdi 2015: 77–83), which carried with it the idea that a Basque cinema of sentiment might become part of a European cinema of sentiment or even of citizens—anything but the Spanish cinema of citizens that then enclosed it. Cinemas of sentiment illustrate Yasemin Nuhoglu Soysal's argument that citizenship may be transformed "from a more particularistic one based on nationhood to a more universalistic one based on personhood" (Soysal 1994: 137), which may lessen links between individuals and their communities of citizens by enabling global movements of ethnic, political and social identification and protest too. Individual filmmakers who encounter exclusion in communities and cinemas of citizens for political or religious beliefs, sexuality or ethnicity, for example, may well find inclusion in a community and cinema of sentiment made up of similar and empathetic individuals.

Clearly it is possible to belong to both a community of citizens and a community of sentiment or indeed several at the same time, although the risk of plunging into contradiction and paradox increases. The relationship between cinemas of citizens and sentiment does not have to be conflictive, however. There is often ample space in developed, outward-looking communities of citizens for its centripetal cinema of citizens and various centrifugal cinemas of sentiment to coexist, but if there is competition for resources and the state does not deliver on political, legal and social rights then questions of legitimacy arise and there may even be a switching point at which the revolutionary cinema of sentiment becomes one of citizens and the previous cinema of citizens finds itself redundant or redefined as one of probably resentful sentiment.

Both cinemas of citizens and of sentiment may give rise to a filmmaking elite, although the critical emphasis on auteurism will probably favour the independence of the latter. In addition, governments may maintain funding for an artificially self-sufficient cinema of citizens offering more hagiographic representations of the nation than the multifarious films emerging from cinemas of sentiment. A cinema of citizens may also seek to absorb diversity when intending for this to become a marker of its identity, such as when a potentially oppositional Algerian cinema is "erased by the funding of films 'about' Algeria via the French Centre National de la Cinématographie (CNC)" (Benkhaled 2016: 87–101), or when New Zealand cinema is represented by films about Maori culture such as the realist *Once Were Warriors* (1994, New Zealand, Lee Tamahori) and the mythic *Whale Rider* (2002, New Zealand/Germany, Niki Caro). Then again, if a community of citizens encounters and displays weakness on an economic, political or cultural level, it might not be able to deliver the rights of citizenship, causing fragmentation into potentially ungovernable ethnic, tribal, religious or political loyalties and giving rise to cinemas of sentiment that move beyond ideological centring. And if there is little or no funding for a cinema of citizens within a community of citizens and hardly any domestic or foreign audience for films either, then only fleeting and possibly extremist cinemas of sentiment will be made by ambitious interest groups and individuals.

Crucially, whereas the community of citizens tends to define identity from above and impose it top-down, the community of sentiment creates it from below. The cinema of citizens is introverted when at its most patriotic or nationalistic, but the cinema of sentiment is extrovert by nature, seeking connections with the like-minded and reciprocally empathetic, which means it thrives on the internet and the global network of festivals. Another vital distinction is that the community of citizens is incapable of conceiving of itself as Other, whereas this is an essential trait of the community of sentiment because empathy is how it looks and reaches beyond itself to "discover the reference points of collective identity" (Sørenson 2004: 91). The cinemas of citizens and of sentiment are not mutually exclusive, however, and can twist together like a two-colour spiral when a minority language cinema such as that in Basque or Welsh, for example, is held to be as much of a cinema of citizens as a cinema of sentiment. This spiralling also happens when a cinema that is critical of the community of citizens that birthed it is taken to be representative of it too. The films directed by fifth-generation Chinese filmmakers, such as *Da hong deng long gao gao gua* (Raise the Red Lantern, 1991, China/Hong Kong/Taiwan, Zhang Yimou) and *Ba wang bie ji* (Farewell My Concubine, 1993, China/Hong Kong, Chen Kaige), for example, questioned the totalitarian nationalism of the People's Republic of China although they were officially funded and (mostly) passed by the Chinese censors because they were period films that included characters who espoused Communist dogma and thus formally represented a Chinese cinema of citizens. It was largely the international acclaim that celebrated their visual riches and subtle cultural critiques that revealed them as contradictory, even paradoxical, and therefore evidence of a cinema of sentiment. Similarly, in Spain under Franco (1939–1975), the *cine metafórico* (metaphorical cinema) represented by the likes of *Muerte de un ciclista* (Death of a Cyclist, 1955, Spain/Italy, Juan Antonio Bardem) and *La caza* (The Hunt, 1966, Spain, Carlos Saura) demonstrated dissident, even communist sympathies that smuggled criticism of the dictatorship into international festivals and constituted a cinema of sentiment met by tolerance in Spain. This was partly because the ecclesiastical censor failed to decipher the metaphorical narratives and partly because the regime, seeking foreign investment, could point to such critical films as evidence of a cinema of citizens that represented a tolerant and open society, all the while knowing that these films would be barely distributed in Spain and unpopular with Spanish audiences anyway. The post-Franco removal of censorship prompted the emergence of several cinemas of sentiment from regions with claims on autonomy as well as waves of queer, underground and, in time, immigrant cinema too, with the Basque cinema of sentiment actually becoming a cinema of citizens when the nation-building policies of the newly autonomous Basque government saw 5 per cent of its entire budget dedicated to developing a domestic film industry (Stone and Rodríguez 2015). Similarly, the variety of cinemas that currently represent regions in the Middle East such as the Arabian Peninsula, the Nile Valley, Maghreb, Palestine and the occupied territory of the West Bank as well as cities like Cairo, Beirut and Dubai all make claims to be cinemas of sentiment and may have ambitions to be cinemas of citizens.

Aiming to restore flux to considerations of World Cinema, not simply as moments of change but as an on-going, eternal becoming, this chapter answers Philip Schlesinger's call for "an explanatory grasp of the increasingly evident contradictions between the various levels of culture and identity that are tending to decouple state and nation" (2000: 30). This new framework of cinemas of citizens and cinemas of sentiment thus challenges the long-standing paradigm of eight concepts of national cinemas elaborated by Stephen Crofts (1998), who writes from an occidental view of World Cinema as a collection of "nation-state cinemas" (1998: 390). Crofts thus prioritises "United States cinema" (1998: 390), which retains no such privilege in this new framework. He then proceeds to map World Cinema from a single-point perspective, noting the autonomy of large Indian and Hong Kong cinemas that "can afford to ignore Hollywood" (1998: 390), for example, and ignoring the unruly network of cinemas of sentiment that exist in the shadow of such monoliths as well as the on-going need for the de-Westernization of film theory championed by Ba and Higbee (2012). Furthermore, Crofts takes "Indian" to be synonymous with the Mumbai-based, Hindi-language Bollywood, which means that the Bengali-language Bangladeshi cinema known as Dhallywood is dismissed as an imitation of what is "Indian" cinema, thereby failing to recognise the cinema of sentiment that such apparently imitative but profoundly ambitious practices in Bangladeshi cinema represent. His similar stratifications of "African" cinema spoil the study of what should be approached as a plethora of cinemas of citizens and cinemas of sentiment too. Indeed, describing Australian and Canadian cinemas as "imitations of US cinema" (1998: 390) promotes another hierarchical categorisation that fails to accommodate cinemas of sentiment within both (such as Aboriginal and Canadian French-language cinema) or realise how imitation can shape citizenship and be a vehicle of sentiment too. His description of "totalitarian cinemas" (1998: 390) may correspond to hard-line cinemas of citizens, but his idea of "sub-state cinemas" that are defined "ethnically in terms of suppressed, indigenous, diasporic, or other populations asserting their civil rights and giving expression to a distinctive religion, language or regional culture" (1988: 390) does not allow for the transnational nature of many cinemas of sentiment that may thrive beyond the nation-state. His erroneous categorisation of "Third cinema" as something separate, moreover, does not foresee that such cinemas of sentiment, although oppositional and anti-capitalist, can in time become those of citizens if their values rigidify, thereby inspiring a new cinema of sentiment to rise up and challenge it. This happened in Cuba, for example, where post-revolutionary cinema aspired to be a Third Cinema but became institutionalised, prompting challenges by new filmmakers who operated beyond the control of the Cuban community of citizens thanks to cheap digital equipment and alternative means of dissemination (Stone and Fehimović 2015). Finally, Crofts' broad assertion that "art cinemas vary somewhat in the sourcing of their finances and in their textual characteristics" (1998: 390) lacks a nuanced understanding of how subscription to a collective sentiment or servility to the hegemonic values that define citizenship can determine criteria for funding and be revealed in a film's aesthetics.

Rather than frameworks that cannot keep pace with technological innovation, political change or the movement of people and the networks they inhabit, the concept of cinemas of citizens and cinemas of sentiment embraces the present continuous tense of World Cinema and maps its real-time ongoing evolution. This mutable framework removes the limitations of thinking in terms of national cinemas and, indeed, "a narcissistic, self-reflexive and self-fulfilling view of national cinemas" (Hayward 2000: 92). It also does away with stateless, accented, interstitial and non-cinemas, which are too fixed in their criteria, in favour of flux between cinemas of citizens and cinemas of sentiment. It recognises that a context of increasing rupture between cinema and nation allows for the transfer of social values between the cinema of citizens to a cinema of sentiment and, vice versa, it reacts to new consolidations of citizenship and even nationhood by tracking the evolution of cinemas of sentiment into those of citizens. Unlike strict categorisations of films, filmmakers and cinemas, this framework is defined by its flexibility, which includes and even emphasises overlap and coincidence. The cinema of citizens is intended to strengthen the link between the community and its citizens, whereas the cinema of sentiment may weaken it, while strengthening that between people and *other* people. Taken together, but also separately, cinemas of citizens and cinemas of sentiment illustrate that belonging is both a legal and an emotional quality that may not coincide, but that reveal in their own way how World Cinema is held together and sometimes falls apart.

References

Anderson, B. (2006) *Imagined Communities*, London: Verso.

Arrieta Alberdi, L. (2015) "Vascos en el movimiento Europea (1949–1978)", *Pensamiento y cultura* 4, 77–83.

Ba, S. M. and Higbee, W. (eds) (2012) *De-Westernizing Film Studies*, London and New York: Routledge.

Ballesteros, I. (2015) *Immigration Cinema in the New Europe*, Bristol: Intellect.

Benkhaled, W. (2016) "Algerian Cinema between Commercial and Political Pressures: The Double Distortion", *Journal of African Cinemas* 8 (1): 87–101.

Berghahn, D. and Sternberg, C. (eds) (2010) *European Cinema in Motion: Migrant and Diasporic Film in Contemporary Europe*, London: Palgrave Macmillan.

Bergson, H. (1992) *The Creative Mind: An Introduction to Metaphysics*, New York: Citadel Press.

Billig, M. (1995) *Banal Nationalism*, London: Sage Publications.

Castells, M. (1998) *The Power of Identity*, Oxford: Blackwell.

Cox, R. W. (1994) "Global Restructuring: Making Sense of the Changing International Political Economy", in Stubbs, R. and Underhill, G. R. D. (eds) *Political Economy and the Changing Global Order*, London: Macmillan, 45–60.

Crofts, S. (1998) "Concepts of National Cinema", in Hill, J. and Church Gibson, P. (eds) *The Oxford Guide to Film Studies*, New York: Oxford University Press, 385–394.

Deutsch, K. (1996) *Nationalism and Social Communication: An Inquiry into the Foundations of Nationalism*, Cambridge, MA: MIT Press.

Gellner, E. (1983) *Nations and Nationalism*, Oxford: Blackwell.

Giddens, A. (1994) *Beyond Left and Right: The Future of Radical Politics*, Stanford, CA: Stanford University Press.

Habermas, J. (2001) *The Postnational Constellation: Political Essays*, Cambridge: Polity Press.

Hayward, Susan (2000) "Framing National Cinemas", in. Hjort, M. and Mackenzie, S. (eds) *Cinema & Nation*, London and New York: Routledge, 88–102.

Higson, A. (1989) "The Concept of National Cinema", *Screen* 30 (4): 36–46.

—— (1995) *Waving The Flag: Constructing a National Cinema in Britain*, Oxford: Clarendon Press.

—— (2000) "The Limiting Imagination of National Cinema", in Hjort, M. and Mackenzie, S. (eds) *Cinema & Nation*, London and New York: Routledge, 63–74.

Hjort, M. (2010) "On the Plurality of Cinematic Transnationalism", in Durovicova, N. and Newman, K. (eds) *World Cinemas, Transnational Perspectives*, New York and London: Routledge, 12–33.

Hjort, M. and MacKenzie, S. (eds) (2000) *Cinema & Nation*, London and New York: Routledge.

Kaceanov, M. (2008) "On the New Romanian Cinema", *p.o.v.: A Danish Journal of Film Studies*, 25, http://pov.imv.au.dk/Issue_25/section_3/artc6A.html.

Naficy, H. (2001) *An Accented Cinema: Exilic and Diasporic Filmmaking*, Princeton, NJ: Princeton University Press.

Naisbitt, J. (1994) *The Global Paradox*, New York: Avon.

Niang, S. (2014) *Nationalist African Cinema: Legacy and Transformations*, Plymouth: Lexington Books.
Ohmae, K. (1996) *The End of the Nation-State: The Rise of Regional Economics*, London: Harper Collins.
Petrie, D. and Hjort, M. (eds) (2007) *The Cinema of Small Nations*, Edinburgh: Edinburgh University Press.
Philips, A. and Stringer, J. (eds) (2007) *Japanese Cinema: Texts and Contexts*, London and New York: Routledge.
Rosenau, J. N. and Czempiel, E. (eds) (1993) *Governance without Government: Order and Change in World Politics*, Cambridge: Cambridge University Press.
Rushdie, S. (1993) "One Thousand Days in a Balloon", in S. McDonogh (ed.) *The Rushdie Letters*, Lincoln, NE: University of Nebraska Press, 13–24.
Ryan, P. (2016) "#OscarsSoWhite Controversy: What You Need to Know", *USA Today*, 2 February, www.usatoday.com/story/life/movies/2016/02/02/oscars-academy-award-nominations-diversity/79645542.
Schlesinger, P. (2000) "The Sociological Scope of National Cinema", in Hjort, M. and MacKenzie, S. (eds) *Cinema & Nation*, London and New York: Routledge, 19–31.
Sørenson, G. (2004) *The Transformation of the State: Beyond the Myth of Retreat*, Basingstoke: Palgrave.
Soysal, Y. N. (1994) *Limits of Citizenship: Migrants and Postnational Membership in Europe*, Chicago, IL: University of Chicago Press.
Standish, I. (2006) *A New History of Japanese Cinema: A Century of Narrative Film*, New York and London: Continuum.
Stone, R. (2001) *Spanish Cinema*, Harlow: Longman.
Stone, R. and Fehimović, D. (2014) "Cuba's Cinematic Élan Vital: Cubanidad and Cubanía as Citizenship and Sentiment", *Journal of Latin American Studies: Travesia* 23 (3): 289–303.
Stone, R. and Rodríguez, M. P. (2015) *Basque Cinema: A Cultural and Political History*, London and New York: I.B. Tauris.
Street, S. (1997) *British National Cinema*, London and New York: Routledge.
Triana-Toribio, N. (2003) *Spanish National Cinema*, London: Routledge.
Vitali, V. and Willemen, P. (eds) (2006) *Theorising National Cinema*, London: British Film Institute.
Willemen, P. (2006) "The National Revisited", in Vitali, V. and Willemen, P. (eds) *Theorising National Cinema*, London: British Film Institute, 29–43.
Zeitchik, S. (2016) "Romania Continues an Unlikely Cinematic Domination at Cannes, with a Pair of Rival Directors", *Los Angeles Times*, 25 May, www.latimes.com/entertainment/movies/la-et-mn-cannes-romania-new-wave-movies-mungiu-puiu-20160525-snap-story.html.

22

TRANSWORLD CINEMAS

Film-philosophies for world cinemas' engagement with world history

David Martin-Jones

Introduction

This chapter explores what it might mean to talk about "transworld cinemas". This hybrid term (incorporating the trans of "transnational" and the world of "world cinemas" and situated between the two positions) is designed primarily to provoke new ways of thinking about films. I use this provocation to argue that we should increasingly classify or categorise films much as the field does currently for a national cinema, but with examples from across diverse cinemas. As I will elaborate below, in making this case I am neither original nor unique. However, I argue for it for a specific reason, which is the less usual aspect of my stance. It is my belief that in this way the long-standing historiographical question broached by scholars such as Hayden White, Robert Rosenstone, Marcia Landy, Robert Burgoyne and others—of just how films tell the story of history—can begin to be more rigorously examined in relation to a world of cinemas' engagement with world history. That is, in the sense that the term "world cinemas" (or, as I prefer, "a world of cinemas") is understood in the tradition of scholarship from Ella Shohat and Robert Stam's *Unthinking Eurocentrism* (1994) through to Lucia Nagib's "positive" model of a decentred world of cinemas (2006). There are various ways of proceeding in such an endeavour, and here the film-philosophical is shown to provide some remarkably thought-provoking directions for future exploration.

Reaching beyond the range of more popular philosophers, typically European, who are currently being utilised to explore films (such as Gilles Deleuze, Emmanuel Levinas, Jacques Rancière, Jean-Luc Nancy or Slavoj Žižek), two very contrasting film-philosophical approaches are briefly outlined and suggestions given for how they might be usefully deployed in a larger study. These two approaches are chosen because they can illuminate something of the shared cinematic concerns with world history that are evident across diverse films from around the world.

First, an approach from Latin American philosophy can assist by correlating world cinemas with world systems theory in a way that illuminates a "transmodern" ethics for our globalised world. The example given in this instance is the work of Argentine philosopher Enrique Dussel. His hoped for "transmodernity" speaks to a situation sometimes termed that of "coloniality/ modernity". This is an idea from Latin American Philosophy that looks to address world history through world systems theory. It argues that modernity stems from the conquest of the

Americas in 1492. Modernity's darker side is its coexisting coloniality, a power structure that continues today (albeit transformed to suit a new context), under globalisation (Mignolo 2000; Dussel *et al.* 2008). Second, from political philosophy, contract theory offers many different ways of thinking about new transworld groupings of films, from ecology (the Natural Contract) to gender (the Sexual Contract) to intercultural connections (the Racial Contract) and so on.

As it will be seen, these two seemingly different approaches share much common ground. They are illustrative of a broader engagement evident across a world of cinemas with two things: structural inequality and environmental crisis. As such, they indicate the importance of deploying so far underused philosophical approaches to a world of cinemas if we are to fully grasp the emerging global cinematic engagement with the Anthropocene. This is the term given to the period in global history during which mankind's influence on the planet can be charted, scientifically, by its role in changing geological conditions. Recent definitions of the Anthropocene have, unusually, considered whether it might in fact stem from 1492, thereby making it extremely resonant with concerns such as coloniality/modernity and ideas such as those of the Racial and Natural Contract (Lewis and Maslin 2015). In this sense, to consider cinema transworld means to be open to connections evident in films from around the world, but also to be able to contextualise them in relation to world rather than national history.

We don't need another neologism

What might it mean to talk about transworld cinemas? This is a neologism which sounds rather too much like the name of an airline to be taken very seriously for academic study, and, if truth be told it is not a term I am particularly invested in promoting beyond the confines of this chapter. Rather, I offer it as a term that can encapsulate a way of exploring films that lies somewhere between the study of border-crossing talent and the economics of international co-productions that often characterises explorations of transnational cinema (for example, Mette Hjort's groundbreaking typology of cinematic transnationalisms (2009)) and a world of cinemas, when understood as an inclusive, decentred field without singular origin or dominant history (Nagib 2006). Between these two positions, what a transworld approach to cinema means, I suggest, is to be open to making links across different cinemas of the world, irrespective of whether there are established links between the films discussed (e.g. whether they might be international co-productions), so as to better understand how world cinemas imagine world history.

There are already existing ideas regarding how we might be able to explore cinema in what we might term a transworld fashion. The history of Film Studies contains standout examples of what might be considered transworld taxonomising, even if their emphasis has often been primarily European (and to a degree Eurocentric) in the kinds of films explored. Three of the most famous undoubtedly remain: first, Jean-Luc Comolli and Paul Narboni's "Cinema/Ideology/Criticism" published in *Cahiers du cinéma* in 1969 (and in English translation in *Screen* in 1971), which used conjoined aesthetic and political categories to establish cinematic types; second, the tradition of categorising films as belonging to either first, second or third cinemas, which was initiated in the Latin American manifestos of the 1960s such as those by Glauber Rocha (1965), Fernando Solanas and Octavio Getino (1969), and Julio García Espinosa (1969); and third, French philosopher Gilles Deleuze's *Cinema* books of the 1980s (1983, 1985), which created numerous temporal categories under the broad division of movement-image and time-image. Of the various ways in which transworld taxonomising can be pursued, it is noticeable that these standout examples are all three theoretical/philosophical.

However, there is an important distinction to be drawn between these transworld taxonomies. Comolli and Narboni attempt to create political categories into which various films can be fitted, something which can also be said—perhaps a touch reductively—of the third cinema debate (first, second and third cinemas after all). Deleuze, for his part, was looking to taxonomise around a particular topic: namely that of (movement through) space, and time, across many different cinemas. It is this latter approach, to locating unifying themes and aesthetic practices across diverse movies, which reflects a transworld viewing process. Although, it is joined by the political approach of the former, due to the philosophers chosen and their deployment to assist with world history.

As noted at the start, there have been attempts made to both theorise and undertake such a transworld approach, including several concerned with immigrant flows under globalisation. A pertinent example, influential for the thinking behind the idea of the transworld, is Dina Iordanova's "watching across borders" (2010: 61–64). This practice, she demonstrates, is necessary if we are to adequately address topics such as the movements of diasporas, and immigration in our post-Cold War world, as they emerge across various cinemas globally. Alternatively, cosmopolitanism has proven a fruitful terrain (Eleftheriotis 2016). For instance, Tim Bergfelder demonstrates that cinematic expressions of transnational love (cosmopolitan desire felt for people considered culturally "Other") is suggestive of the potential of an idea like "vernacular cosmopolitanism" (2012: 61) for understanding transnationalism. Bergfelder discusses films as diverse as Douglas Sirk's *La Habanera* (1937, Germany) and Fatih Akin's *Auf der anderen Seite* (The Edge of Heaven, 2007, Germany/Turkey/Italy) to argue that we consider "longer, not always synchronous, discursive as well as cinematic historical continuities" (Ibid.: 79) when exploring how films engage with "attitudes towards the Other in a wider global arena" (Ibid.: 78).

As these standout examples indicate, there is a complex politics involved in a transworld viewing practice. To think of cinemas in a transworld fashion reflects greatly on cinema's global distribution, and the ways in which we tap into it. The links we will make across world cinemas depends on what kinds of films we choose to see, but perhaps more importantly, on what kinds of films are *available* for us to see. The geopolitics of film production and distribution, then, are determining of our ability to make connections transworld, whether we view films in multiplexes, or independent cinemas programming from the festival circuit, on the festival circuit itself, as DVDs, on the internet, or across a variety of such distribution platforms. While we must be aware of this, even so, transworld connections can be productively made. Indeed, it is often films that are co-financed transnationally and are subsequently attempting to reach audiences transnationally (if not worldwide) that offer fertile ground for a transworld approach. While such complexities are an integral part of the negotiation of meaning transworld, this endeavour is nevertheless an important one, as the "transnational turn" in Film Studies moves the field beyond the predominance of the national paradigm, to a much greater consideration of a world of cinemas. In this, how we understand films to express history—whether national, or world—is at stake.

Transworld historiography

The question of how we understand history through film is one that the field has been tackling for many decades. In *Metahistory* (1973), Hayden White draws on a range of case studies from nineteenth-century European historical thought to argue that there are "uniquely *poetic* elements in historiography and philosophy of history in whatever age they are practised" (White 1973: x). Writing about film specifically, he notes the importance of the nineteenth-century historical novel in shaping our expectations of how history is "told" (1996: 18). At the risk of being reductionist with regard to White's extremely sophisticated and in-depth breakdown of historiographical methods, the intervention he makes is to note that history is to a degree always in some way part story. This consideration of the constructed nature of history was taken up later by historians engaging with cinema, who were concerned as to whether films about history were able to do justice to the veracity of history. This includes Robert Rosenstone's championing of the usefulness of films for history in volumes such as *Visions of the Past* (1995). Admittedly, Rosenstone's focus on the kinds of films that might be most adequately suited to engage with history in a meaningful way relies on a binary distinction between more popular and generic (locked into conventions which mitigate against the accurate portraying of history (Ibid.: 29–30)) and more formally experimental films (able to render history in its complexity (Ibid.: 37–41)), which seems a rather elitist one nowadays, after so much work on popular cinemas (e.g. Dyer and Vincendeau 1992; Eleftheriotis 2001). Nevertheless, Rosenstone's exploration of history on film draws on White's position on the constructed nature of all historical explanations, concluding that: "If written history is shaped by the conventions of genre and language, the same will obviously be true of visual history" (Ibid.: 35). White, for his part, responds to Rosenstone's work, re-affirming that: "the historical monograph is no less 'shaped' or constructed than the historical film or historical novel" ([1988] 2009: 56). Films about history are, historically, thus such an anathema to some scholars of history because they raise "the spectre of the 'fictionality' of the historian's own discourse" (Ibid.: 55).

This is not the place to rehearse the development of this debate in depth, as can be found in volumes such as Marnie Hughes-Warrington's comprehensive *Film on History* (2009). What seems most crucial to the earlier works by historians engaging with film—namely, whether it has the ability to construct history with the same degree of accuracy as written historical accounts—now seem rather redundant in the wake of several decades of Film Studies scholarship exploring history on film: not to mention the importance of the "turn to history" within the discipline since the early 1980s. This turn is in itself, although this is rarely recognised as such, inextricably bound up with what we might consider a much broader turn to a world of cinemas (Martin-Jones 2011). Suffice it to say that a series of important scholarly interventions followed, including various works by Rosenstone (1995), Marcia Landy (1996), Robert Burgoyne ([1997] 2010) and others. The majority of these follow White's lead in understanding history as a construction that can be expressed (as it were, "imperfectly") in various different modes, one of which is film. The key point in this entire debate is perhaps the very simple one, implicit in White's initial intervention into historiography, that if history is a construction, to a degree always determined by recognised ways of structuring expression when making meaning, then, just like other media, film can also tell the story, or stories, of history.

With this in mind, what is more important to focus on in this context is that a transworld approach asks us to consider cinema in relation to world, as opposed to national, history. To give an insight into this distinction, we can briefly consider three books by Robert Burgoyne that, taken together, indicate a shift currently taking place in Film Studies that illustrates the growing importance of a transworld approach. Burgoyne's *Film Nation* (1997), in both its original and revised second edition (2010) explores the "undecidable" text of the USA's "national narrative" (2010: ix) as it is expressed in film. Integral to its concern with the construction of national identity (specifically how films express a "counternarrative of nation" [Ibid.: x] that works through various of the established national myths of identity), *Film Nation* examines how national history is constructed in films exploring various pivotal moments in the past—e.g. colonisation in *The*

New World (2005, USA/UK, Terence Mallick), through the civil war in *Glory* (Edward Zwick, 1989, USA) to the Second World War in *Flags of Our Fathers* (Clint Eastwood, 2006, USA) and finally to 9/11 in *World Trade Center* (Oliver Stone, 2006, USA). Again, Burgoyne's *The Hollywood Historical Film* (2008) categorises how Hollywood explores US history (e.g. the war film, epic, biopic, and so on), in what is directly termed a taxonomy (Ibid.: 5). For his corpus, Burgoyne chooses films which re-enact the past, bringing it into dialogue with the present in order to reshape how we understand the past. The methodology with which he explores this form of filmic "historical thinking" (Ibid.: 12) is informed by philosophers Paul Ricouer and Deleuze, but also demonstrates the inheritance of the trajectory previously discussed by White, Rosenstone *et al.* (Ibid.: 7–11).

It is true that Hollywood is not the sum total of the USA's national cinema. Recent research such as that of Toby Miller and others (2001) emphasises Hollywood's global nature—as export product, runaway and coproduction able to tap into global capital—added to which the growth of independent cinema, in its various forms, suggests there is much more to the national in US cinema than solely Hollywood. It is not, in short, a film industry synonymous with the nation per se. Nevertheless, Burgoyne's work clearly and compellingly illustrates how Hollywood constructs not only images of national identity, but also tells the story of the history of the nation.

By contrast, Burgoyne's more recent anthology, *The Epic Film in World Culture* (2011) takes just one category—like all those found in *The Hollywood Historical Film* to reflect upon national history—and explores its different manifestations worldwide. Thus, for Burgoyne, the epic film's "complex array of nested and overlapping production and distribution arrangements" ensures that it "has become the very exemplar of transnational and global modes of film production and reception" (Ibid.: 1–2). It is, in short, a prime example for transworld exploration. This, even if Burgoyne, and his contributors, do not take precisely the same approach as I am taking (exploring shared concerns with global historical events across national cinemas), with several chapters in Burgoyne's anthology remaining focused on national histories. Rather, Burgoyne's intention is to question whether the historical link between "the epic and the imagined community of nation" (Ibid.: 1) remains the genre's defining feature, considering its contemporary "transnational orientation and [. . .] appeal to cross-cultural structures of belonging and identification" (Ibid.: 3), and indeed, its global appeal to communities imagined in ways other than that of the national.

To be clear, then, it is the shift in approach with regard to taxonomising a body of films evident in this most recent publication that recognises a transworld approach to cinema. Its emergence illustrates the movement from a national focus to an investigation of a topic within a context that is globally encompassing. This is necessary because some historical events exist with timescales longer, and borders larger, than places where nations now exist (e.g. the North Atlantic Slave Trade); others have occurred more recently than the emergence of nations in recent centuries, but still with an impact crossing various nations (e.g. the Cold War). To pursue this direction further, I would argue that how such histories are represented in films globally should be explored in terms of historical models beyond that of the nation. For instance, using transnational ideas of history such as those of Patricia Clavin (2005), which provide a different timescale to the historiography of the nation (and can be applied, for instance, to the Cold War), or Immanuel Wallerstein's famous "world systems analysis" (1974) and the various critiques and developments it has spawned (Abu-Lughod, 1989; Chaudhuri 1990; Frank 1998) that help illuminate the North Atlantic Slave Trade, and coloniality/modernity more broadly. Again, we might consider works exploring the intertwined nature of human and planetary history (Chakrabarty 2009; Iriye 2013). While paying due care to the national and transnational realities of filmmaking, looking transworld is to make links in a manner that acknowledges such histories, as they overlap with and exist across and beyond those of the nation.

When we alter our historical contextualising framework from the nation to the world, such historical models suddenly becoming of greater significance. But, just as importantly, a transworld approach requires us to reorient our theoretical (or philosophical) viewpoint towards those ideas which encompass world history. These are often found "beyond" both the (arguably equally Eurocentric) Anglo-American Analytic or Continental philosophical traditions. While the debate on film and history initiated by White, Rosenstone and others, concludes that, yes, films can do history (in as much as any medium can), so too does the debate regarding film and philosophy ultimately reach a similar conclusion: yes, films can do philosophy (Mullarkey 2008; Sinnerbrink 2011). But then the more important question arises, as to how well we are able to interpret this film-philosophising with our chosen philosophers. Put another way, who are the most useful philosophers for our remapping and understanding of a world of cinemas in relation to world history?

Film-philosophy after world cinemas

With this in mind, certain philosophical approaches begin to suggest themselves to the study of films transworld: ethics is a case in point. This might seem a strange example amidst so much discussion of history. After all, an ethics such as that of Levinas, which is currently in vogue in film-philosophical circles, does not seem particularly engaged with history. However, there are other examples to consider from beyond Europe. For example, Dussel offers a post-Levinasian view of ethics which attempts to include all those excluded from the onset of modernity, which he considers to commence with European colonial expansion after 1492. Dussel's approach can be usefully applied to films from various parts of the world to examine issues that reach beyond national borders and into the realm of world history, such as, to give only one example, the increasing movements of immigrants across borders due to globalisation (Martin-Jones 2013).

Dussel is known for his work developing the philosophy of liberation, which stems from Gustavo Gutiérrez's *Theology of Liberation* (1971). His works are increasingly being interpreted, with at least eight major works in English at the time of writing. The potential usefulness of his philosophical approach to ethics—its unique blend of Levinas with a historicised understanding of class derived from Karl Marx, and a Latin American view of history—has slowly begun to be understood in Film Studies since the 2010s (Richards 2011; Martin-Márquez 2011; Martin-Jones 2013). However, as yet these remain but a few scattered examples of works considering how Dussel might illuminate the field. Tellingly, they all deploy Dussel with regard to "peripheral" cinemas, whether their peripheral nature relates to a national, regional or global framework. Yet, I think, there is a much broader application available.

Dussel's usefulness lies in the influence of world systems theory on his ethics. Dussel asks that those peripheral to coloniality/modernity, those excluded from the development of the Eurocentric world system after 1492 (as observed by Wallerstein to be the start of the rise to its current position of global dominance of the Eurocentric world system), be recognised. He believes that a dialogue with this excluded other will enable a transcendence of modernity's structural inequality (trans-modernity). In this respect, Dussel's post-Levinasian position is evident. For Levinas, representative others are the stranger, widow and orphan (1961). For Dussel, the historical other is inclusive of: "The poor, the dominated, the massacred Amerindian, the Black slave, the Asiatic of the opium wars, the Jew of the concentration camps, the woman as sexual object, the child under ideological manipulation" (1996: 80). Dussel's other, then, is that excluded from world history by coloniality/modernity. Thus his work is extremely pertinent for the contemporary world. It resonates with that of various scholars to discuss the inequality of globalisation, such as Félix Guattari ([1989] 2014), Arjun Appadurai (2006) or Michael Hardt and Antonio Negri (2005), amongst others, but with a world historical background underpinning its contemporary relevance.

Dussel describes his transmodern ethics in terms that indicate an imperative to transcend the logic of coloniality/modernity. He argues that it will need more than the kind of overcoming of modernity from within that might be offered by postmodernity, requiring instead:

> The overcoming of cynical management reason (planetary administration), of capitalism (as economic system), of liberalism (as political system), of Eurocentrism (as ideology), of machismo (in erotics), of the reign of the white race (in racism), of the destruction of nature (in ecology), and so on presumes the liberation of diverse types of the oppressed and/or excluded. It is in this sense that the ethics of liberation defines itself as transmodern (because the postmoderns are still Eurocentric).
>
> *(Dussel 1998: 19)*

In this it is noticeable that it is not only humanity that is excluded by the history of coloniality/modernity, but the very world that humanity inhabits, its ecology, or "nature". This inclusion of the ecological indicates the correlation between Dussel's globally historicised ethics (after Wallerstein) and the aforementioned recent views of the Anthropocene that consider it to commence with the arrival of Europeans in the so-called New World. Among other markers recognised by scientists as indicative of the commencement of the Anthropocene (such as crop and animal movements between "Old" and "New" worlds), perhaps most telling is the devastation of the indigenous populations of the Americas by European colonisers. Simon L. Lewis and Mark A. Maslin argue that the sudden absence of over 50 million indigenous Americans—who had previously felled trees in order to farm and cook—led, over the course of around 100 years, to such reforestation that there was a notable decline in atmospheric CO^2 levels. The so-called Little Ice Age that followed, they argue, leaves sufficient geological proof of this era as marking the commencement of the Anthropocene (2015: 175). The Anthropocene, on this view, coincides with coloniality/modernity, one impact of which was that of humanity's many-faceted exploitation of the planet. After all, the extinction of so many humans in such a short time was in part due to enslaved populations being forced to mine the planet's natural resources, including silver for European export to world markets (Frank 1998). Dussel's, then, is a philosophy suited to exploration of humanity's recent world history, that of the exclusion of some by others under coloniality/modernity (including the very planet itself), which continues in a new guise under neoliberal globalisation.

Let us consider some examples of how a Dusselian approach can be used to illuminate precisely the kinds of transnational or world historical events mentioned previously. For instance, how can a transworld viewing of such diverse films about the colonisation of the Americas (as Dussel has it, "the massacred Amerindian, the Black slave") as *Como Era Gostoso o Meu Francês* (*How Tasty Was My Little Frenchman*, 1971, Brazil, Nelson Pereira dos Santos), *Sankofa* (1993, USA/Ghana/Burkina Faso/UK/Germany, Haile Gerima) and *Tambien la Lluvia* (*Even the Rain*, 2010, Spain/Mexico/France, Icíar Bollaín) illustrate the more than 500-year history of the North Atlantic Trade Circuit? How do such different films about globalisation, colonialism and slavery respectively manage to share common aesthetic properties (which appear if they are viewed transworld), and despite being decades apart, each work to triangulate different continental views on this vast swathe of history using similar deployments of the gaze? How might such an idea relate to what Robert Stam and Ella Shohat (2012) refer to as the White, Black and Red Atlantics?

Again, how might *Los rubios* (The Blonds, 2003, Argentina/USA, Albertina Carri), *At the Foot of the White Tree* (2007, Uruguay, Juan Álvarez Neme), *Wo sui si qu* (Though I am Gone, 2006, People's Republic of China, Jie Hu), *S-21, la machine de mort Khmère rouge* (S21: The Khmer Rouge Death Machine, 2003, Cambodia/France, Rithy Panh), *The Act of Killing* (2012, Denmark/Norway/UK, Joshua Oppenheimer), and *L'image manquante* (The Missing Picture, 2013, Cambodia/France, Rithy Panh) demonstrate something of the 60-year history of the Cold War? What can we make of the often striking similarities between the ways these films memorialise lost, forgotten or erased pasts (the results of what, as noted previously, Dussel calls "capitalism [as economic system]", and "liberalism [as political system]")? How are their reconstructions and use of archival footage to explore what Giorgio Agamben calls the "state of exception" (2003), deployed to similarly explore a period characterised by the suspension of the rule of law during which a political opposition is attacked or eradicated? Are such films so aesthetically similar because they are exploring the same world history?

What about the impact on individual bodies of the withdrawal of the state during 40 years (and counting) of neoliberal globalisation? In such films as *Lamerica* (1994, Italy/France/Switzerland, Gianni Amelio), *La Haine* (1995, France, Mathieu Kassovitz), *Lilja 4-Ever* (Lilya 4-Ever, 2002, Sweden/Denmark, Lukas Moodysson), *Dirty Pretty Things* (2002, UK, Stephen Fears), *Chinjeolhan geumjassi* (Lady Vengeance, 2005, South Korea, Chan-wook Park), *Import-eksport* (Import-Export, 2007, Austria/France/Germany, Ulrich Seidl), *Carancho* (Vulture, 2010, Argentina/Chile/France/South Korea, 2010, Pablo Trapero), beaten, broken, drugged, abandoned, kidnapped, incarcerated, tortured and abused bodies are the norm (Dussel again, as above: "the poor, the dominated [. . .] the woman as sexual object, the child under ideological manipulation"). How are these bodies similarly shown, in films worldwide, to be the product of the history of neoliberalism, rendered as physical stores of the recent past through haunted gestures and poses?

Or even, at the opposite extreme, how is the 4.5 billion year history of the earth—or at least, the history of the eco-system which currently supports human life—negotiated in such films as *Sud pralad* (Tropical Malady, 2004, Thailand/France/Germany/Italy, 2004, Apichatpong Weerasethakul), *Nostalgia de la luz* (Nostalgia for the Light, 2010, France/Germany/Chile/Spain/USA, Patricio Guzmán), *Loong Boonmee releuk chat* (Uncle Boonmee Who Can Recall His Past Lives, 2010, Thailand/UK/France/Germany/Spain/Netherlands, Apichatpong Weerasethakul), *Trolljegeren* (Troll Hunter, 2010, Norway, André Øvredal), *The Hunter* (2011, Australia, Daniel Nettheim) and *Beasts of the Southern Wild* (2012, USA, Benh Zeitlin)? What can be understood from the way these films all explore the now extinct or mythical creatures of the past before coloniality/modernity, as it is resurgent in the present, often warning of dire environmental damage from humanity's actions (as Dussel notes, again as above, "the destruction of nature [in ecology]")?

Thus, Dussel's is a philosophy that enables a new type of transworld taxonomy, of the world historical events that exist because of coloniality/modernity. It both encompasses the Anthropocene at its broadest limit—the recent ecological concerns (in fact much older in origin) that have alerted humanity to the planetary destruction implicit in capitalism's search for profit—as well as the gendered, racial and economic inequalities that structure the planet.

In this broad, planetary concern for an ethics that can touch upon so many areas, a Latin American thinker such as Dussel is just the tip of the melting iceberg. Dussel's inclusive transmodern ethics indicates a different but related area of philosophy that is also of value, namely the political philosophy of contract theory. Put a little simplistically, the "cynical management reason" of modernity that Dussel speaks of correlates in its many facets to the various contracts upon which the idea of the Social Contract is predicated. This is the case even if the Social Contract is designed precisely to obscure this very fact. Thus, Michel Serres' *The Natural Contract* (1992) explores precisely Dussel's "the destruction of nature (in ecology)", the origins of which Serres also traces back several centuries to Cartesian thinking (1992: 32). Charles W. Mills' *The Racial Contract* (1997) is Dussel's "the reign of the white race (in racism)", which Mills also traces back to the same origins as those of coloniality/modernity (Ibid.: 20). Carole Pateman's *The Sexual Contract* (1988) evokes "machismo (in erotics)" (albeit this latter description is in need of far greater nuance), and so on.

Such ideas can also be used to consider transworld groupings of films that are equally informed by world historical events. Yet so far only the Racial Contract has received any significant coverage, mainly due to the engagement of philosopher Dan Flory with its possibilities for understanding black film, in *Philosophy, Black Film, Film Noir* (2008) and other works. In this he has been joined by Charles W. Mills himself (2013). While primarily focused on US films, Flory does briefly attempt a transworld use of the Racial Contract, suggesting that in films from the USA, Brazil, South Africa and the UK a "noir Atlantic" (after Paul Gilroy's Black Atlantic) can be identified by a "sensibility about the global connectedness of various oppressions" (2008: 303). Yet there is tremendous scope for further thinking in this respect. Various films from around the world can be said to directly engage with the ramifications of the Racial Contract under globalisation. A productive discussion could be had by examining such generically contrasting films as *La Promesse* (1996, Belgium/France/Luxembourg/Tunisia, Jean-Pierre Dardenne and Luc Dardenne), *La Haine, Nina's Heavenly Delights* (Patibha Parmar, 2006, UK), *Le Havre* (Aki Kaurismäki, 2011, Finland/France/Germany), *Un cuento Chino* (Chinese Take Away, aka. Chinese Take-Out, 2011, Argentina/Spain, Sebastián Borensztein), etc. Similar such transworld groupings can be constructed for the Natural Contract, the Sexual Contract, and so on.

Such philosophical topics that are opened up by a transworld view are indicative of the need to engage more with other disciplines if we are to develop our grasp of a world of cinemas. Most especially, world history/transnational history; coloniality/postcoloniality; and philosophy. In this last category we need to broaden our horizons particularly, so as to go beyond solely the work on time in cinema of a European philosopher such as Deleuze, whose time-image categories still await completion in the myriad cinematic time-images of the world yet to be mapped. To remap a world of cinemas requires a transworld view of films in relation to world historical events, the methodological tools for this new historiography being those of the world's (as opposed to Europe's) philosophies.

References

Abu-Lughod, J. (1989) *Before European Hegemony*, Oxford: Oxford University Press.

Agamben, G. ([2003] 2005) *The State of Exception*, Chicago, IL: University of Chicago Press.

Appadurai, A. (2006) *Fear of Small Numbers*, Durham, NC and London: Duke University Press.

Bergfelder, T. (2012) "Love Beyond the Nation: Cosmopolitanism and Transnational Desire in Cinema", in Passerini, L., Labanyi, J. and Diehl, K. (eds) *Europe and Love in Cinema*, London: Intellect, 59–86.

Burgoyne, R. ([1997] 2010) *Film Nation: Hollywood Looks at US History*, Minneapolis, MN: University of Minnesota Press.

—— (2008) *The Hollywood Historical Film*, Oxford: Blackwell.

—— (ed.) (2011) *The Epic Film in World Culture*, London: Routledge.

Chakrabarty, D. (2009) "The Climate of History: Four Theses", *Critical Inquiry* 35: 197–222.
Chaudhuri, K. N. (1990) *Asia Before Europe*, Cambridge: Cambridge University Press.
Clavin, P. (2005) "Defining Transnationalism", *Contemporary European History* 14 (4): 421–439.
Comolli, J. and Narboni, J. ([1969] 1976) "Cinema/Ideology/Criticism", in Nichols, B. (ed.) *Movies and Methods*, Berkeley, CA: University of California Press, 22–30.
Deleuze, G. ([1983] 2005) *Cinema 1: The Movement-Image*, New York: Continuum.
—— ([1985] 2005) *Cinema 2: The Time-Image*, New York: Continuum.
Dussel, E. (1996) *The Underside of Modernity: Apel, Rorty, Taylor and the Philosophy of Liberation*, Mendieta, E. (trans. and ed.) New York: Humanity Books.
—— (1998) "Beyond Eurocentrism: The World System and the Limits of Modernity", in Jameson, F. and Miyoshi, M. (eds) *The Cultures of Globalization*, Durham, NC and London: Duke University Press, 3–31.
Dussel, E., Moraña, M. and Jáuregui, C. A. (eds) (2008) *Coloniality at Large: Latin America and the Postcolonial Debate*, Durham, NC and London: Duke University Press.
Dyer, R. and Vincendeau, G. (1992) *Popular European Cinema*, London: Routledge.
Eleftheriotis, D. (2001) *Popular Cinemas of Europe*, London: Continuum.
—— (2016) "Cosmopolitanism, Empathy and the Close-up", in Tzioumakis, Y. and Molloy, C. (eds) *Companion to Film and Politics*, London: Routledge, 203–217.
Espinosa, J. G. (1969) "For an Imperfect Cinema", in Martin, M. T. (ed.) (1997) *New Latin American Cinema*, Detroit, MI: Wayne State University Press, 71–82.
Flory, D. (2008) *Philosophy, Black Film, Film Noir*, Pennsylvania: Penn State University Press.
Frank, A. G (1998) *ReORIENT: Global Economy in the Asian Age*, Berkeley, CA: University of California Press.
Guattari, F. ([1989] 2014) *The Three Ecologies*, New York: Bloomsbury.
Gutiérrez, G. ([1971] 1988) *A Theology of Liberation*, New York: Orbis Books.
Hardt, M. and Negri, A. (2005) *Multitude*, London: Penguin.
Hjort, M. (2009) "On the Plurality of Cinematic Transnationalism", in Newman, K. and Durovicová, N. (eds) *World Cinemas, Transnational Perspectives*, London: Routledge/American Film Institute, 12–33.
Hughes-Warrington, M. (ed.) (2009) *The History on Film Reader*, London: Routledge.
Iordanova, D. (2010) "Migration and Cinematic Process in Post-Cold War Europe", in Berghahn, D. and Sternberg, C. (eds), *European Cinema in Motion*, Basingstoke: Palgrave.
Iriye, A. (2013) *Global and Transnational History*, London: Palgrave.
Landy, M. (1996) *Cinematic Uses of the Past*, Minneapolis, MN: University of Minnesota Press.
Levinas, E. ([1961] 1969) *Totality and Infinity: An Essay on Exteriority*, Lingis, A. (trans.) Pittsburgh, PA: Duquesne University Press.
Lewis, S. L and Maslin, M. A. (2015) "Defining the Anthropocene", *Nature* 519: 171–180.
Martin-Jones, D. (2011) "Estudios de cine en el Reino Unido: La mirada hacia los 'cines del mundo'"/"Film Studies in the UK: The Turn to World Cinemas", *33 Cines* 2 (5): 38–47.
—— (2013) "The Dardenne Brothers Encounter Enrique Dussel: Ethics, Eurocentrism and a Philosophy for World Cinemas", in Conceição Monteiro, M., Giucci, G. and Besner, N. (eds), *Além dos limites: ensaios para o século XXI/Beyond the Limits: Essays for the XXI Century*, Rio de Janeiro: State University of Rio de Janeiro Press, 71–105.
Martin-Márquez, S. (2011) "Coloniality and the Trappings of Modernity in *Viridiana* and *The Hand in the Trap*", *Cinema Journal* 51(1): 96–114.
Mignolo, W. D. (2000) *Local Histories/Global Designs*, Princeton, NJ: Princeton University Press.
Miller, T., Govil, N., McMurria, J. and Maxwell, R. (2001) *Global Hollywood*, London: British Film Institute.
Mills, C. W. (1997) *The Racial Contract*, Ithaca, NY: Cornell University Press.
—— (2013) "Race as/ad (Ex)change: Trading Places and the Rise of Neoliberalism", in Flory, D. and Bloodsworth-Lugo, M. K. (eds) *Race, Philosophy, and Film*, London: Routledge, 151–165.
Mullarkey, J. (2008) *Refractions of Reality*, London: Palgrave Macmillan.
Nagib, L. (2006) "Towards a Positive Definition of World Cinema", in Dennison, S. and Lim, S. H. (eds) *Remapping World Cinema*, New York: Columbia University Press, 30–37.
Pateman, C. (1988) *The Sexual Contract*, Cambridge: Polity Press.
Richards, K. N. (2011) "A Shamanic Transmodernity", in Barrios, N. B. (ed.) *Latin American Cinemas*, Calgary: University of Calgary Press, 197–222.

Rocha, G. (1965) "An Esthetic of Hunger", in Martin, M. T. (ed.) (1997) *New Latin American Cinema*, Detroit, MI: Wayne State University Press, 59–61.
Rosenstone, R. A. (1995) *Visions of the Past*, Cambridge, MA: Harvard University Press.
Serres, M. ([1992] 1995) *The Natural Contract*, Ann Arbor, MI: The University of Michigan Press.
Shohat E. and Stam, R. (1994) *Unthinking Eurocentrism*, New York: Routledge.
Sinnerbrink, R. (2011) *New Philosophies of Film*, London: Continuum.
Solanas, F. and Getino, O. (1969) "Towards a Third Cinema", in Martin, M. T. (ed.) (1997) *New Latin American Cinema*, Detroit, MI: Wayne State University Press, 33–58.
Stam, R. and Shohat, E. (2012) *Race in Translation*, New York: New York University Press.
Wallerstein, I. (1974) *The Modern World System*, New York: Academic Press.
White, H. (1973) *Metahistory*, Baltimore, MD: Johns Hopkins University Press.
—— ([1988] 2009) "Historiography and Historiophoty", in Hughes-Warrington, M. (ed.), *The History on Film Reader*, London: Routledge, 53–60.
—— (1996) "The Modernist Event", in Sobchack, V. (ed.) *The Persistence of History*, London: Routledge, 17–38.

23
TRANSNATIONAL CINEMA
Mapping a field of study

Deborah Shaw

Introduction

This chapter examines the development of the concept of transnational cinema in Film Studies, paying particular attention to the ways in which the discipline has responded to developments in the social sciences. It describes the four key areas of focus in the first phase of transnational cinema studies: migration and cinema and exilic and diasporic filmmaking; transnationalising readings of national and regional cinema; historical readings of transnational cinema; and film festival studies. Following this, the chapter discusses approaches to transnational film theory by means of analysis of a selection of key definitional essays on the subject. Finally, the chapter looks towards the second phase of transnational film studies. In so doing, it considers the expanded reach of the transnational to the many fields that make up the discipline of Film Studies and the many approaches to World Cinema in particular.

From transnational studies in the social sciences to transnational cinema studies

A transnational momentum in Film Studies became evident in 2005, with the following years seeing crucial advances made by important conceptual and theoretical essays and edited volumes (Bergfelder 2005; Ezra and Rowden 2006; Durovicová and Newman 2010; Hjort 2010; Higbee and Lim 2010; Berry 2010; Shaw 2013), as well as the founding of the dedicated journal *Transnational Cinemas* in 2010 by Armida de la Garza, Ruth Doughty and Deborah Shaw. That is, of course, not to say that concern with the transnational in Film Studies was unknown before 2005. Hamid Naficy was writing about independent transnational film genre in 1996, holding that it was characterised by exilic "transnational filmmakers as interstitial authors" and highlighting their "configuration of claustrophobic spaces" (1996: 121), while Sheldon Lu's book *Transnational Chinese Cinemas* was published in 1997.

Andrew Higson's "The Limiting Imagination of National Cinema" (Higson 2000: 63–74) was an early attempt to explain and begin to define what is meant by the transnational. Higson refers to multinational casts and crew (67); the international distribution achieved by the most successful films (68); the ways in which the national is harnessed to achieve transnational circulation (69); and diverse forms of reception depending on cultural national contexts (68). This essay, while not promoting the death of the category "national cinema" certainly draws attention to its limitations. Higson notes, "the concept of national cinema is hardly able to do justice either to the internal diversity of contemporary cultural formations, or to the overlaps and interpenetrations between different formations" (2000: 70) and he argues that the "'transnational' may be a subtler means of describing cultural and economic formations that are rarely contained by national boundaries" (64).

The concept of the transnational was clearly transdisciplinary at a time when Film Studies was reacting to the transnational turn in a range of fields from the late 1980s and 1990s in response to technological developments, global flows of finance and people, and resulting social, political and cultural transformations. In his article, "Conceiving and Researching Transnationalism", Steven Vertovec, Director of the British Economic and Social Research's (ESRC) Program on Transnational Communities, provides an overview of the field as it was in 1999: "Transnationalism broadly refers to multiple ties and interactions linking people or institutions across the borders of nation-states" (1999: 447). He identifies clusters or themes as applied in a range of disciplines: "These include transnationalism as a social morphology, as a type of consciousness, as a mode of cultural reproduction, as an avenue of capital, as a site of political engagement, and as a reconstruction of 'place' or locality" (1999: 447). Social morphology refers to transnational social formations and new communities occasioned by ethnic diasporas and transnational networks forged as a result of the technological transformations of the New Information Age (Castells 1996: 449). A type of consciousness references "diaspora consciousness" marked by dual or multiple identifications, and fractured memories and new fluid identities that refuse fixity (Appadurai and Breckenridge 1989; Vertovec 1999: 449–450). In addition, Vertovec maps out the areas of research covered by the ESRC Research Programme initiated in 1997 (1999: 458–459). These include new approaches to migration with a focus on comparative diasporas, refugees and asylum seekers as well as a fresh focus on global economic networks and transnational corporations. Attention is also paid to global political networks, and gender, communities and power, as well as projects concerned with social forms and institutions, such as transnational religious communities. The article therefore demonstrates the turn to the transnational in social, cultural and economic research, and the cross disciplinary influence of critical thinkers writing from the mid-1990s such as Arjun Appadurai, Manuel Castells, Ulrich Beck, Homi Bhabha, Robin Cohen, Rey Chow, Hamid Naficy and Ulf Hannerz, among others. Considered from this perspective, it is clear that the transformation in Film Studies can be located within a larger critical landscape and has been influenced by earlier interventions in social and cultural theory. In fact, as Tim Bergfelder notes (2005: 321), we have arrived late to the transnational table and until now have been slow in applying its key concepts such as "cultural hybridization" and "global Diaspora".

A reason for this may be the fact that Anglophone film studies as an academic discipline is a relatively recent addition to further education courses. It originated not from a sociological base that pioneered debates on the transnational, as seen in the references to the work of Vertovec and others above, but from individual lecturers and their modules from the 1970s on Arts, Literature, Cultural Studies and Modern Languages degree programs (see Grieveson and Wasson 2008). Such courses foregrounded poetics, aesthetics, film movements, narrative theories and concepts of the national, which may explain why a transnational focus only took hold in Film Studies from the mid-2000s, once it became more established in other disciplines. Degree programs in Modern Languages, for instance, are part of the broader discipline of Area Studies for which concepts of the national are central, and, while the national can never be considered without an investigation of transnational relations of power, a national framework is privileged.

Nonetheless, once transnational theory entered the consciousness of Film Studies it took hold and provided a strong conceptual focus for the discipline. Many of the areas identified by Vertovec find their expression in academic work in transnational film studies. For instance, new social transformations and diasporic identities are the subject of *An Accented Cinema: Exilic and Diasporic Filmmaking* (2001) by Hamid Naficy. "Accented Cinema" defines the film texts produced by exilic and diasporic filmmakers whose experiences form their cinematic production, and whose films challenge dominant production modes and constitute a personal counter cinema (Naficy 2001: 6–7). This focus was shared by the research network, *Migrant and Diasporic Cinema in Contemporary Europe*, led by Daniela Berghahn, author of *Far-Flung Families in Film: The Diasporic Family in Cinema* (2003), as well as other scholars, including Yosefa Loshitzky, author of *Screening Strangers: Migration and Diaspora in Contemporary European Cinema* (2010).

In addition to migration and its influence on European cinemas, many scholars since the mid-2000s have applied a transnational framework to their research on regional or national cinemas throughout the world. This includes studies of East Asian cinemas (Hunt and Leung 2008; Morris *et al.* 2006; Berry 2010), Bollywood (Kauer and Sinha 2005; Dudrah 2012), Irish film (McIlroy 2007), Nordic Cinema (Nestingen and Elkington 2005), African cinemas (Krings and Okome 2013), Polish cinema (Mazierska and Goddard 2014), Hispanic Cinema (Dennison 2013) and Asian and Australian cinema (Khoo *et al.* 2013). In addition, several scholars have examined the transnational nature of the film industry from its origins. As Higson notes in a 2010 article in *Transnational Cinemas* entitled "Transnational developments in European cinema in the 1920s", "filmmaking and film exhibition have been transnational since the first public film shows in the 1890s" (2010: 70). Another notable publication that takes a historical and transnational perspective is *Film Architecture and the Transnational Imagination: Set Design in 1930s European Cinema* (Bergfelder, Harris and Street 2007), which documents transnational artistic collaborations in production design with a focus on Britain, France, and Germany.

Another area of increasing interest and importance that is transnational at its core is the study of film festivals, wherein global arts cinema and business intersect. This is an area occupying particular significance in transnational production, exhibition and distribution. As well as providing screening opportunities, festivals are increasingly sites of commerce for "World Cinema" through their markets, such as CineMart, the international co-production market at the International Film Festival Rotterdam, the Marché du film at Cannes, and the Berlinale's European and Co-production markets. This aspect of transnationalism inspired Marijke De Valck's *Film Festivals: From European Geopolitics to Global Cinephilia* (2007) and Dina Iordanova's authorial and editorial work in such volumes as *The Film Festival Reader* (2013) and the film festivals yearbooks published by St. Andrew's University. This transnational research area has also seen the development of a film festival network maintained by Skadi Loist and Marijke de Valck (Film Festival Research) and a vibrant publishing landscape all chronicled in that network's website bibliography ("FFRN bibliography").

To sum up, the first phase of transnational film criticism concerned itself with the foci outlined above, and with setting out terms of reference. This paved the way for the ongoing second phase in which a transnational frame of reference is being applied by a number of scholars to all aspects of Film Studies. The foci and approaches of the first phase continue to inform critical thinking, but the transnational is now being applied to a much wider range of academic interests within the disciplines of Film Studies, as well as Media Studies; but scholars are no longer so concerned with providing definitions for the transnational, rather, as the following case studies demonstrate, they are engaging with specific applications of aspects of the transnational in their analyses.

Conceptual mappings

The transnational in film is clearly not a recent phenomenon. Early cinema benefitted from a coproduction landscape and circulated freely across borders without the linguistic restrictions faced with the introduction of sound (Bean *et al.* 2014). Nonetheless, the field itself is a young one, as the publishing timeline above has demonstrated. In any new area definitional work will dominate the first decade or so of academic engagement and, thus, while the second phase is ongoing, what this chapter seeks to reflect upon and adequately conceptualise is the first phase of transnational film studies. This is essential because the first phase was subject to what Vertovec termed "conceptual muddling" (1999) due to a conflation of discrete areas under its umbrella term (Shaw 2013: 51). The following analysis of three key essays on the essential concepts of transnational cinema—"On the Plurality of Cinematic Transnationalism" (Hjort 2010: 12–33), "Deconstructing and Reconstructing Transnational Cinema" (Shaw 2013: 47–65); and "Concepts of Transnational Cinema: Towards a Critical Transnationalism in Film Studies" (Higbee and Lim 2010: 7–21)—is intended to clarify and effectively map this emergent field in order to lay down firm foundations for scholars intending to work on the transnational. Because the authors of these essays provide different emphases and have diverse views on the value systems ascribed to the transnational, this critical review questions the use of a value system and the notion of degrees of transnationalism, while identifying fruitful approaches to the theorising of the transnational (see also Fisher and Smith 2016).

Hjort's essay was written for the edited volume *World Cinemas, Transnational Perspectives* (Durovicová and Newman 2010) in which Hjort rightly decried the lack of specificity in the usage of the term "transnational" "as a largely self-evident qualifier requiring only minimal conceptual clarification" (2010: 13). Hjort writes: "The term 'transnational' does little to advance our thinking about important issues if it can mean anything and everything that the occasion would appear to demand" (2010: 12). In response, she attempts to apply principles and values to the term, and sketches some categories for its application. Hjort develops the idea of a scale of strong or weak forms of transnationality, depending on the films and their production, distribution and reception. She writes of marked and unmarked transnationality (2010: 13–14), seen in the degree to which filmmakers, through aesthetic and thematic means, direct their audiences to the transnational elements of the film. With regard to the scale of value, Hjort opines that more valuable forms should feature "a resistance to globalization as cultural homogenization; and a commitment to ensuring that certain economic realities associated with filmmaking do not eclipse the pursuit of aesthetic, artistic, social, and political values" (2010: 15). Thus, in this interpretation, stronger and better transnational cinema can be found in what she terms "affinitive and milieu-building transnationalism" (2010: 17–19), which points to collaborations between small nations in order to support filmmaking cultures in the face of Hollywood hegemony. While this is a key intervention in the formation of a new field, and creates some of the definitional blocks that theorists can build on, this attempt to impose a value system on such a broad area of film can result in a reductionist view of the transnational dimensions of more commercial cinema. Nonetheless, this critical mapping of the field seeks to retain the importance that Hjort claims for collaborations that have to be forged to sustain precarious minor cinemas struggling to survive in the shadows of a global cinematic superpower (peopled with characters with superpowers).

Hjort's categories are "epiphanic transnationalism", "affinitive transnationalism", "milieu-building transnationalism", "opportunistic transnationalism", "cosmopolitan transnationalism", "globalizing transnationalism", "auteurist transnationalism", "modernizing transnationalism" and "experimental transnationalism". Hjort provides further explanations of these categories (2010: 15–30) and a selection of these that focus on the key concepts of degrees and values of transnationality will be summarised here. "Epiphanic transnationalism" (2010: 16–17) derives from media articulations that constitute transnational belonging, bringing shared culture to the public beyond a single national border, for which Hjort gives the example of the work of the Nordic Film and TV Fund and its attempts to carve out a cultural space. She then connects this to "affinitive transnationalism" that focuses on bonds created from mutually beneficial cultural collaborations with nations that share values and problems, and she cites Scottish/Danish co-productions as examples that also provide the illustration for "milieu-building transnationalism" (2010: 17–18), which focuses on film cultures in a specific location and ways in which these can be developed through collaborations between countries. For Hjort, then, the concept of the national has a privileged position in her understanding of the transnational, with transnational bonds helping to sustain the cultural productions of small nations. Lower down on the values scale comes "opportunistic transnationalism" (2010: 19–20) for which partnerships are made purely based on financial imperatives, and forging social connections is not a priority (she does acknowledge that the types of transnationalism she outlines can coexist, i.e. that social bonds can be made in opportunistic transactions, and that affinitive networks require an opportunistic approach to finance).

Hjort's is then a theoretical model marked by both a definitional and an ethical approach in which she identifies good and bad, and strong and weak transnationalism. Some forms of cinematic transnationalism are, for Hjort, more worthwhile than others because they promote certain social, political, artistic or aesthetic phenomena (also an achievement of the last of her categories, "experimental transnationalism" (2010: 26–30)). Thus, she celebrates the "community, belonging, and heritage in the case of epiphanic transnationalism; and the social value of solidarity in the case of affinitive and milieu-building transnationalism" (2010: 30). In contrast, she critiques some forms of "auteurist transnationalism" as a weak and unmarked form of transnationalism—she provides the example of the omnibus film *Eros* (2004, USA/Hong Kong/Italy/France/Luxembourg/UK) that includes short films by Michelangelo Antonioni, Steven Soderbergh and Wong Kar-wai (2010: 23).

Notions of strong or weak, marked and unmarked transnationality, valuable and less valuable forms are subject to a form of subjective ethical judgment that can put conceptual limits on audience experience. I would argue that there are diverse forms of transnational film manifestations that can be critically appraised and judged. Like Hjort, in my research for "Deconstructing and Reconstructing Transnational Cinema" (2013), it became apparent that many scholars used the terms in a rather generalised way without specifying what was meant. This necessitated raising and responding to a series of questions:

> Which films can be categorised as transnational and which cannot? Does the term refer to production, distribution and exhibition, themes explored, aesthetics, nationalities of cast and crew, audience reception, or a range of these? Are mainstream Hollywood films transnational as they are distributed throughout the developed world? What about films with smaller budgets made in other national contexts that challenge Hollywood domination and explore the damaging effects of globalisation? Is the term "national" now entirely bankrupt, and if so what does this mean for films that engage with specifically local issues?
>
> *(Shaw 2013: 47–48)*

In response to the above questions, I suggested the following categories while explaining that they are not mutually exclusive and there is overlap between then. These categories are transnational modes of production, distribution and exhibition, transnational modes of narration, cinema of globalisation, films with multiple locations, exilic and diasporic filmmaking, film and cultural exchange, transnational influences, transnational critical approaches, transnational viewing practices, transregional/transcommunity films, transnational stars, transnational directors, the ethics of transnationalism, and transnational collaborative networks. I end with a mention of national films to highlight the fact that while a transnational framework can be applied to most film production across the world in some form (even if we are referring to influences on the filmmakers), there are some predominantly national forms financed by national sources and made for national audiences that escape transnational distribution. The majority of my examples are drawn from Latin American cinema and transnational films made by Latin American directors. These categories were rather descriptive as befits a taxonomical project that set out to establish terms of reference. Nonetheless, they seek to demonstrate the particularities of how the concept can be applied, and in so doing address a risk identified by Higbee and Lim when they ask, "does the focus on a term such as the 'transnational' simply risk becoming a replacement for existing terms such as 'world cinema' as a means of merely describing non-anglophone films?" (2013: 17).

My key aim in writing the chapter was to rescue the term from overgeneralised usage in which it was in danger of losing any meaning. However, in contrast to Hjort, I was not concerned with weak or strong forms and I took a less discriminatory approach while seeking to distinguish between practices and approaches to transnational cinema. To give one example, global Hollywood productions can be argued to be transnational in their modes of production, distribution and exhibition, with multinational agreements and partnerships, foreign ownership of a number of the major studios (McDonald and Wasko 2007: 6) and filmmakers originating from a range of countries. They may also qualify for the term in many other of the categories outlined above. With films of the global reach of *Star Wars: The Force Awakens* (2015, USA, J. J. Abrams), an argument that Hollywood films are less transnational or less valuable than, for instance, a low budget non-English language art film supported by a European funding body and exhibited and distributed through a film festival circuit cannot be sustained. Fan communities and people all over the world are hugely invested in the *Star Wars* franchise and, indeed, a strong case could be made for the advancement of gender and ethnic empowerment in *Rogue One: A Star Wars Story* (2016, USA/UK, Gareth Edwards). They are differently transnational, belonging to separate ends of an economic and artistic scale and performing different functions, but we need to be cognisant of this diversity, and be wary of comparing like with unlike, yet not cast festival art films, or exilic and diasporic filmmaking as uniquely privileged sites of transnational filmmaking. Nonetheless, Hjort's work does necessarily highlight the market dominance of global Hollywood and the transnational cooperation needed to ensure the survival of low budget filmmaking for those who cannot access significant funding.

A way forward is presented by Will Higbee and Song Hwee Lim in their essay advocating a "critical transnationalism" (2010: 7–21). In effect, they produced a "manifesto" for the discipline and argued that central to any analysis should be an exploration of relations of the "postcoloniality, politics and power" (2010: 18) that are at the root of the cross-border activities and transactions that constitute the transnational. They therefore suggest a discursive approach over a prescriptive or descriptive one (2010: 8). Following a review of the field, the authors develop the concept of critical transnationalism in order to "help us interpret more productively the interface between global and local, national and transnational, as well as moving away from a binary approach to national/transnational and from a Eurocentric tendency of how such films might be read" (2010: 10). Higbee and Lim begin by highlighting problems with three previous approaches. First, Higson's notion of the limited national model with a focus on the transnational flows of the business of cinema, which fails to consider "imbalances of power, or thematic concerns of migration and diaspora" (2010: 9). Then, in relation to work that focuses on the regional transnational such as that carried out on films in Chinese or European contexts, they ask why the term is used in place of supranational, regional or pan-European (2010: 9). The third approach that they identify is concerned with diasporic, exilic and postcolonial cinemas, and this has, for Higbee and Lim, a limitation I alluded to above: a tendency to privilege such marginal productions as properly transnational, paradoxically marginalizing mainstream commercial texts from the discussion:

> One of the potential limitations of this third approach [...] is that diasporic or postcolonial 'transnational' cinema is consistently located on the margins of dominant film cultures or the peripheries of industrial practices, making it almost impossible to evaluate the impact such films might have on mainstream or popular cinema within either a national or transnational context.
>
> *(Higbee and Lim 2010: 10)*

They call for a comprehensive approach to a critical transnationalism that should be inclusive of "all forms of cross-border film-making activities" (2010: 18), and they consider the relationship between the marginal and interstitial and the national, and the national and the transnational. They also present a useful warning for Anglophone scholars by asking: "Can transnational film studies be truly transnational if it only speaks in English and engages with English-language scholarship?" (2010: 18). While Transnational Cinema in Anglo-American scholarship is multinational, it is also Anglo-centric and it is therefore vital to add the disclaimer that this critical review of the field is principally limited to English language publications, while sharing the view for the need for more translations from and into English to ensure that the field and any academic work is both multilingual and truly transnational.

The present and future of transnational film studies

Higbee and Lim's article was published in 2010 in the inaugural issue of *Transnational Cinemas* and they note the newness and precariousness of transnational film studies:

> It is, within the *reality* of institutional and disciplinary practices, at best a sub-field with an expanding geography and population, and, at worst, a ghetto whose particular interests would continue to struggle to be perceived—and accepted—as bearing a more general or even universal application and relevance [...] The launch of this journal is a welcome start, but transnational cinema still has some way to go before establishing itself more firmly as a critical concept and as an inclusive field of enquiry within the discipline of film studies.
>
> *(2010: 17)*

We can be optimistic about the vibrancy and future of what we can claim as a field of enquiry that this chapter argues is the second phase of transnational film studies that has seen a shift from definitions to applications, effects and functions. While I am reluctant to provide specific dates to delineate first and second phases, as the concept of phases charts shifts in cultures rather than precise moments in time, perhaps we can identify the development of the Transnational Cinemas Scholarly Interest Group (SIG) in 2013 for the Society for Cinema and Media Studies, run by Austin Fisher and Iain Smith, as a possible starting point for the second phase. While work was clearly being carried out in many areas before this date, the SIG has brought researchers into dialogue with each other, enabling them to trace the breadth of this concept and its application and to chronicle it. Indeed, this phase can be characterised by the enormous expansion of the transnational as a conceptual framework to multiple areas within Film Studies, which also links to my earlier comments cautioning about scales of value and degrees of transnationality as we have moved away from privileging some areas as "proper" objects of study in transnational film studies. A selective overview of panels sponsored by the SIG from 2014 to 2016 testifies to the volume of work carried out in the field. These included: "Positioning Race: Intersectional and Transnational Studies of US Film and Television", "Asian Cinemas in Transnational Contexts", "Film Transnationalism and Colonialism, 1920s–1930s", "Transnationalism, Migration, and Media", "Non-Hollywood Sound: Transnational Approaches, "'Glocal' Perspectives", "Video Essays in Transnational Cinema Studies", "Hollywood Stardom and Transnationalism, 1920–1960", "Towards a Transnational Fan Studies", and "Marketing Globalization, Globalizing Markets: Big and Small Worlds". In the three years to date of the Scholarly Interest Group's existence, the range of workshops and panels demonstrates that there were few areas within Film Studies on which transnational cinema had not left its imprint, and that it is not simply confined to the expected work on migration, diasporic and (post)colonial cinemas, although of course, these remain important areas of scholarship. Transnational frameworks are now applied to pedagogy, early cinema, star studies, remakes/adaptations, feminist film theory, fan studies, exploitation cinema, genre studies including horror film, queer film studies, film and the environment, experimental film, the growing area of audiovisual essays, sound studies, readings of race, regional/national studies, the business/economics of film, and audience studies, among others.

The health of the field is also revealed in the number of academic courses dedicated to, or incorporating, transnational cinema. In a 2015 study by the Society for Cinema and Media Studies "The State of the Field of Film and Media Studies", in the US, produced by Aviva Dove-Vieban with SCMS executive director Jill Simpson, 179 departments/programs selected "global or transnational cinema and/or television" in response to the instruction, "please select the categories that represent the specialties of film, television, and media/new media faculty in your department/program" (Dove-Vieban 2015). This study was limited to the US, but a more global study would be likely to yield similar results. The period has also seen a boom in publishing in this area, and the number of conferences and panels has proliferated in recent years. Developments in the field thus reveal Higbee and Lim's fears that transnational cinema could constitute "a ghetto whose particular interests would continue to struggle to be perceived" (2010: 17) to be entirely unfounded.

References

Appadurai, A. and Breckenridge, C. (1989) "On Moving Targets", *Public Culture*, 2: i–iv.

Bean, J. M., Kapse, A. and Horak, L. (eds) (2014) *Silent Cinema and the Politics of Space*, Bloomington, IN: Indiana University Press.

Bergfelder, T. (2005) "National, Transnational or Supranational Cinema?: Rethinking European Film Studies", *Media, Culture & Society* 27 (3): 315–331.

Bergfelder, T., Harris, S. and Street, S. (2007) *Film Architecture and the Transnational Imagination: Set Design in 1930s European Cinema*, Amsterdam: Amsterdam University Press.

Berghahn, D. (2003) *Far-Flung Families in Film: The Diasporic Family in Cinema*, Edinburgh: Edinburgh University Press.

Berry, C. (2010) "What Is Transnational Cinema? Thinking from the Chinese Situation", *Transnational Cinemas* 1 (2): 111–127.

Castells, M. (1996) *The Rise of the Network Society* (*The Information Age: Economy, Society and Culture, Volume 1*), Malden, MA: Blackwell Publishers.

Dennison, S. (ed.) (2013) *Contemporary Hispanic Cinema: Interrogating Transnationalism in Spanish and Latin American Film*, Woodbridge: Tamesis.

De Valck, M. (2007) *Film Festivals: From European Geopolitics to Global Cinephilia*, Amsterdam: Amsterdam University Press.

Dove-Vieban, A. (2015) "The State of Film and Media Studies", http://c.ymcdn.com/sites/www.cmstudies.org/resource/resmgr/SCMS_StateoftheField2015.pdf, 1–16.
Durovicová, N. and Newman K. (eds) (2010) *World Cinemas, Transnational Perspectives*, London: Routledge/American Film Institute Reader.
Dudrah, R. (2012) *Bollywood Travels: Culture, Diaspora and Border Crossings in Popular Hindi Cinema*, Contemporary South Asia Series, London: Routledge.
Ezra, E. and Rowden, T. (eds) (2006) *Transnational Cinema: The Film Reader*, London: Routledge.
"FFRN bibliography" (2016) www.filmfestivalresearch.org/index.php/ffrn-bibliography/.
"Film Festival Research" (2016) www.filmfestivalresearch.org.
"Film Festival Research: Film Festival Theory and Methodology" (2016) www.filmfestivalresearch.org/index.php/ffrn-bibliography/1-film-festivals-the-long-view/1-1-film-festival-studies/1-1-a-film-festival-theory.
Fisher, A. and Smith, I. R. (2016) (eds) "Transnational Cinemas: A Critical Roundtable", *Frames Cinema Journal*, 9, http://linkis.com/framescinemajournal.com/umQIn.
Grieveson, L. and Wasson, H. (eds) (2008) *Inventing Film Studies*, Durham, NC: Duke University Press.
Higbee, W. and Lim S. H. (2010) "Concepts of Transnational Cinema: Towards a Critical Transnationalism in Film Studies", *Transnational Cinemas* 1 (1): 7–21.
Higson, A. (2000) "The Limiting Imagination of National Cinema", in Hjort, M. and MacKenzie, S. (eds) *Cinema and Nation*, London and New York: Routledge, 63–74.
Higson, A. (2010) "Transnational Developments in European Cinema in the 1920s", *Transnational Cinemas* 1 (1): 69–82.
Hjort, M. (2010), "On the Plurality of Cinematic Transnationalism," in Durovicová, N. and Newman, K. (eds), *World Cinemas, Transnational Perspectives*, London: Routledge/American Film Institute Reader, 12–33.
Hjort, M. and MacKenzie, S. (eds) (2000) *Cinema & Nation*, London and New York: Routledge.
Hunt, L. and Leung, W. (eds) (2008) *East Asian Cinemas: Exploring Transnational Connections on Film*, London and New York: I.B. Tauris.
Iordanova D. (ed.) (2013) *The Film Festivals Reader*, St Andrews: St Andrews Film Studies.
Kaur, R. and Sinha, A. J. (eds) (2005) *Bollyworld: Popular Indian Cinema through a Transnational Lens*, New Delhi: Sage.
Khoo, O., Smaill, B. and Yue, A. (2013) *Transnational Australian Cinema: Ethics in the Asian Diasporas*, Lanham, MD: Lexington Books.
Krings, M. and Okome, O. (2013) *Global Nollywood: The Transnational Dimensions of an African Video Film Industry*, Bloomington, IN: Indiana University Press.
Loshitzky, Y. (2010) *Screening Strangers: Migration and Diaspora in Contemporary European Cinema*, Bloomington, IN: Indiana University Press.
Lu, S. (ed.) (1997) *Transnational Chinese Cinemas: Identity, Nationhood, Gender*, Honolulu: University of Hawai'i Press.
McDonald, P. and Wasko, J. (2007) (eds) *The Contemporary Hollywood Film Industry*, Malden, MA: Blackwell.
McIlroy, B. (ed.) (2007) *Genre and Cinema: Ireland and Transnationalism*, London and New York: Routledge.
Mazierska, E. and Goddard M. (2014) (eds) *Beyond the Border: Polish Cinema in a Transnational Context*, New York: Rochester University Press.
Morris, M., Leung Li, S. and Chan Ching-kiu, S. (2006) (eds) *Hong Kong Connections: Transnational Imagination in Action Cinema*, Durham, NC: Duke University Press.
Naficy, H. (1996) "Phobic Spaces and Liminal Panics: Independent Transnational Film Genre", in Wilson, R. and Dissanayake, W. (eds) *Global-Local: Cultural Production and the Transnational Imaginary*, Durham, NC and London: Duke University Press, 119–144.
Naficy, H. (2001) *An Accented Cinema: Exilic and Diasporic Filmmaking*, Princeton, NJ: Princeton University Press.
Nestingen, A. and Elkington, T. (eds) (2005) *Transnational Cinema in a Global North: Nordic Cinema in Transition*, Detroit, IL: Wayne State University Press.
Shaw, D. (2013) "Deconstructing and Reconstructing 'Transnational Cinema'", in Dennison, S. (ed.) *Contemporary Hispanic Cinema: Interrogating Transnationalism in Spanish and Latin American Film*, Woodbridge: Tamesis, 47–65.
Vertovec, S. (1999) "Conceiving and Researching Transnationalism", *Ethnic and Racial Studies* 22 (2): 447–462.

24

"SOFT POWER" AND SHIFTING PATTERNS OF INFLUENCE IN GLOBAL FILM CULTURE

Paul Cooke

Introduction: the changing global film market

Writing in the *Financial Times* in 2013, Andrew Edgecliffe-Johnson argued that the BRICS group of emerging nations (Brazil, Russia, India, China and South Africa) had now reached a point in their development where they had effectively "'flipped' the film market, focusing US filmmakers and distributors on international opportunities and creating a bigger US market for foreign films" (Edgecliffe-Johnson 2013). The main focus for Edgecliffe-Johnson, as well as several other commentators at the time, was in actual fact the rapid growth of the Chinese market, which in 2012 became the second largest film market after the USA, and which some commentators predicted it would overtake as soon as 2018 (Plowright 2015). For all Edgecliffe-Johnson's suggestion that this development might open up the world's cinema to more international US co-productions that could increase Hollywood's appetite for the production of non-English-language films for international markets, the main opportunity in the sights of the Hollywood majors at the time was, without doubt, the chance to sell their mainstream, English-language, product into the Chinese market, a market that, moreover, seemed immune to the overall slowdown in the Chinese economy. This offered proof—it was needed—as Peter Shiao observes, CEO of Orb Media Group and Chair of the annual US-China Film Summit, that "if history is any indicator when there is stress in the social fabric of society people rely on movies even more" (quoted in Carroll and Phillips 2015).

The growing importance of the Chinese market for Hollywood, as well as the broader shifts in the global geopolitical landscape signalled by the rise of the wider BRICS grouping, has had a range of knock-on effects for global film culture. Remaining for the moment with China, this has led, as Chris Homewood has noted, to the growing incorporation of Chinese elements into Hollywood blockbusters in order to win one of the coveted thirty-four places allocated a year to non-domestic productions (Homewood 2014). For example, it is noticeable the extent to which China has been presented as a *deus ex machina* in recent Hollywood films, the country's apparently boundless resources and technological ingenuity being used to save the likes of John Cusack and Matt Damon from calamity in a host of epic blockbusters, be it via new-age "arks" in the environmental disaster movie *2012* (2009, USA, Roland Emmerich), or the Chinese rocket booster deployed to help save a stranded astronaut in *The Martian* (2015, USA/UK, Ridley Scott). That said, how necessary, or even helpful, these elements really are is disputed by commentators. As Yuxing Zhou observes, while the Chinese censor might at times seem to use the accusation of an unfavourable depiction of China and Chinese culture as a way of preventing, or at least delaying, the release of a Hollywood film—*Mission: Impossible III* (2006, USA/Germany/China, J.J. Abrams), for example was ostensibly refused a screening permit due to the inclusion of a scene depicting laundry hanging on bamboo poles in a Shanghai street—the real reason for such decisions is far more likely to be economic rather than political. Such decisions invariable involve films looking for a release during the summer, China's most popular film-going season, which the authorities tend to want to protect for domestic productions (Zhou 2015: 6). What is less in doubt is the importance of the increasing number of English-language US–Chinese co-productions facilitated by the China Film Co-Production Corporation (CFCC). CFCC productions such as *Transformers: Age of Extinction* (2014, USA/China, Michael Bay) and *Fast & Furious* 7 (2015, USA/Japan, James Wan) not only count as "domestic" releases and so stand outside the 34-film non-domestic quota, they also allow the Hollywood partner to keep a larger percentage of the box-office receipts (Homewood 2014). It is this that has driven the major growth in Hollywood's engagement with China.

For Hollywood, the motivation for this engagement is straightforwardly financial. However, more complex, and for some Western commentators at least more controversial, has been China's motivation. The year 2012 also saw a series of events in the US domestic market that, on the one hand, seemed to complement developments in China but, on the other, appeared to some intent upon challenging Hollywood's cultural hegemony at home. In July of that year, China's Dalian Wanda Group acquired AMC, the second largest movie theatre chain in the US. This was the beginning of a series of moves by Wanda that led in 2015 to its takeover of production and finance company Legendary Entertainment for $3.5 billion, the largest deal of its kind by a Chinese company. Wanda moreover made it clear that the company still had a long way to go, its ultimate ambition being to become a major player in the global film industry, growing the number of culturally Chinese, internationally focused productions made in the country (Fritz and Burkitt 2016). At the same time, President Xi Jinping had been engaging in high level talks with several of the Hollywood majors aimed at further strengthening China's relationship with the US film industry. These developments provoked a good deal of attention among industry commentators, being seen by many as a worrying example of China's strategic focus on its global "soft power", with the Chinese authorities ostensibly using the country's economic might to buy its way into the Hollywood "Dream Factory" and in so doing gain the kind of cultural influence American governments have long sought to achieve via this particular industry (Nunns 2012; Homewood 2014). "China buys soft power with hard cash in Hollywood", declared the French Associated Press in 2016, warning readers that "there is no such thing as a free lunch" and that China's growing influence will have significant consequences for the industry (AFP 2016).

Soft power and culture

The term "soft power" was coined by the political analyst Joseph Nye in the 1990s to describe what he saw as the increasing emphasis put on the "power of attraction" in international foreign relations rather than the "hard power" of "coercion or payments", focusing in particular on the role of America, at the time the world's only superpower (Nye 2004: ix). Since then, "soft power" has been much discussed, migrating, as Nye has more recently noted, from being "an academic concept [. . .] to the front pages of newspapers" and finally to the speeches of "top leaders" around the world (Nye 2011: 81). There are any number of examples of the term's usage by political elites to characterise their approach to international relations and, in particular, the role of culture as a soft power vehicle for public diplomacy. Xi Jinping might certainly agree with the commentators cited above that China's engagement with Hollywood is indeed part of the state's self-conscious aim to generate soft power through its cultural policy, if not with the concerns they share (*The China Post* 2014). Fellow BRICS' premier Vladimir Putin also emphasises the role of cultural soft power as part of Russia's "comprehensive toolkit for achieving foreign policy objectives", while simultaneously decrying what his government defines as the "unlawful use of 'soft power' and human rights concepts to exert political pressure on sovereign states" (Putin 2013). Similarly, in the UK one might mention the 2014 House of Lords select committee report on "Soft Power and the UK's Influence", which explored the way the country's cultural assets should be leveraged to promote and protect the nation's economic and wider political interests globally (House of Lords 2014). Or one could point to the centrality of culture in the EU's "Preparatory Action" report *Culture in EU External Relations* that puts forward a series of suggestions for the ways in which member states' collective "cultural power can [. . .] be *transformed* into soft power" through the more effective coordination of resources in order to support the circulation of cultural products (via, for example, European film festivals). Crucially the report highlights what it perceives to be the attractiveness of "the European 'narrative'", which it defines as a celebration of the fundamentally "European" values of "cultural diversity" and "freedom of expression" (Isar *et al.* 2014: 7–20, italics in original).

From this snapshot of some of the ways in which the soft power of culture has been instrumentalised by political elites, it is clear that soft power is a complex term. Indeed, for some commentators, Nye included, the increasingly varied contexts in which it is being used can run the danger of making the term so elastic as to be of little analytical use (Nye 2011: 81). Nonetheless, the manner in which it is used around the world highlights the variety of ways national governments understand the role of national and transnational "narratives"—to return to the EU report for a moment—in helping to shape global interactions, and the role that culture generally, and film and media in particular, has to play in this context. For China, the country's enormous financial resources have supported a whole host of cultural initiatives, from the Confucius Institutes it has set up around the world in order to promote Chinese culture and the learning of the Chinese language to the expansion of China Central Television (CCTV) into a global media network and, of course, its ever closer engagement with Hollywood. In the UK, the relationship between economics and soft power assets works in the opposite direction, the nation's cultural capital (its language, the global recognition of certain British cultural brands, from the Premier League to the BBC) being leveraged to support economic growth. With regard to film, here one might mention film director Danny Boyle's opening ceremony for the 2012 Olympics, which was frequently cited as a key reason for the UK topping the soft-power league table that year and a significant contributing factor to the £9.9bn boost to the economy the games ostensibly generated (Gillespie and O'Loughlin 2015: 388–389). Similarly, the British film industry was an important partner in VisitBritain's 2014 campaign, which featured British film treasures such as James Bond, and Wallace and Gromit, that was timed to coincide with the release of a new Paddington Bear movie. The "Paddington is GREAT Britain" campaign is said to have generated over £1.2bn in extra tourism, trade and investment (Sweney 2015). In Putin's foreign policy statement, soft power is conflated with questions of propaganda and the way governments have sought to (mis)represent Russia's national mission through its culture.

Film, once again, provides a useful way to illustrate this. The nomination of Andrey Zvyagintsev's 2014 film *Leviafan* (Leviathan, 2014, Russia) for the foreign-language Oscar was hugely controversial. The nomination of a film that offered a critical image of contemporary Russian institutions outraged the Kremlin, which saw this as a deliberately provocative act by the American Academy of Motion Picture Arts and Sciences. Although, as Vlad Strukov argues, the film has a far more ambivalent relationship with the state than the headlines about the Oscar nomination suggest. The production of the film was in fact supported financially by the state and, Strukov suggests, the debate it generated was ultimately instrumentalised by the government to increase the international visibility of Russian culture, for all its criticism of the film's content (Strukov 2017). At the same time, Putin's statement challenges the fundamental principle of soft power as a means of gaining influence precisely *not* through exerting pressure but by highlighting the attractiveness of a country's culture in order to suggest the attractiveness of its wider value system.

It is this principle that is at the centre of the EU's conceptualisation of the role of soft power in its external relations, suggesting a model of interaction—however utopian this might appear—of mutuality and shared responsibility between nations in order to promote a collective understanding of "*global cultural citizenship* that recognizes shared cultural rights as well as shared responsibilities" (Isar *et al.* 2014: 8, emphasis in original). Of course, as the UK's vote for Brexit in 2016 showed, this is far easier said than done, since it ultimately involves ceding control of the "national narrative", allowing it to be co-created in partnership with others. This process of co-creation becomes both more complicated still, and more necessary, in the digital age, when it is increasingly difficult for an individual, or even a government, to control the way any single source of information will be distributed and interpreted by end users on the internet. Now more than ever, as Nye suggests, "global politics involves 'verbal fighting' among competing narratives" (Nye 2011: 87). And, as we can see from our discussion of China above, it is a contest where the role of the traditionally dominant "combatants", not least the US, is increasingly challenged.

Hollywood, soft power and national narratives

At least since Griffiths, film has, of course, been recognised as an important medium for the communication of a nation's values to the rest of the world. And again, at least since Griffiths, the terms of engagement with this form of communication have largely been dictated by Hollywood. This is most clearly evidenced in the continued economic dominance of Hollywood films that consistently achieve the biggest worldwide grosses (Cooke 2007: 1–2). The dominance of Hollywood in much of the world is attributable to a wide variety of factors, not least to the consistent efforts US Governments have put into gaining global dominance in the areas of distribution and exhibition. It is Hollywood that largely controls which films audiences get to see wherever they may be. With most cinema screens in large parts of the world showing Hollywood product, it is with such films that spectators are most familiar. It is often very difficult for non-Hollywood films to gain international distribution, particularly in the US. Even films from outside North America that do well at the major film festivals such as Venice, Berlin or Cannes generally remain confined to the periphery, unable to gain the screen space that would allow them to secure a bigger share of the audience. Little wonder, then, that it is by Hollywood's standards that we define what we mean by "mainstream" filmmaking in much of the world. The US is also fiercely protective of its distribution dominance, lobbying for increasing global deregulation during the GATT and subsequent World Trade Organization talks so that it could further increase its market share in parts of the world that continue to protect domestic film production and distribution (Miller *et al.* 2004). Having said that, one cannot deny the extraordinary pull of Hollywood, even in some places where its films are harder to find. As Geoffrey Nowell-Smith puts it:

> Sometimes the banal truth are the valuable ones and the fact is that the much-mouthed banalities about Hollywood as dream factory are not only true but important. [...] Hollywood is the biggest fabricator of fantasy, and that is its enormous unchallenged strength.
>
> *(Nowell-Smith 1998: 12)*

Look, for example, at the failure of *Kong Zi* (Confucius, 2010, China, Mei Hu), a large-budget Chinese historical biopic that was the product of a Chinese cultural policy intended to showcase to the world the potential of the Chinese film industry. The film famously flopped, even at home, being unable to compete with global hit *Avatar* (2009, USA/UK, James Cameron), despite the Hollywood film receiving only very limited distribution in China. *Avatar* grossed $4.8 million on the first day of its release, while *Confucius* only $1.8 million during its entire first week, and this despite a much wider release (AFP 2010).

Hollywood has long been a key US soft power asset, regularly deployed by the government to support its drive to communicate the benefits of its value system, of democracy and the potential of the "American Dream". Here one might mention the post 9/11 discussions between the White House and Bryce Zabel, then chairman of the Academy of Television Arts and Sciences, about how Hollywood "could help the government formulate its message to the rest of the world about who Americans are, and what they believe" (Miller and Rampton 2001). The rationale behind this was that if more (specifically the Muslim part) of the world understood the benefits of American democracy it would help protect the country against further terrorist attacks. This is an approach that also recalls US cultural policy towards Germany post-World War Two, when Hollywood was similarly seen as a tool for spreading democracy. As Jennifer Fay has shown, however, the power of Hollywood to present a universally understandable message of democracy was challenged in the specific reading of its films by audiences in Germany at the time. The success of soft power is always rooted in a process of co-creation. Far from seeing Hollywood movies as straightforward depictions of the "American Dream", Fay highlights how they were often taken to parallel the spectacle of Nazi cinema, and in so doing seemed to reveal, for many in Germany, the racist foundations of the American nation. This was particularly common in the reception of the Westerns that were a staple of the films supplied by the US occupation force at the time, their depiction of native Americans as violent savages who must be controlled by the white settlers being read as reminiscent of the Nazi presentation of Jews (Fay 2008: 81).

More successful was West Germany's own form of cultural diplomacy in the 1970s, when it promoted the self-critical films of the New German Cinema abroad via its cultural organisation the Goethe Institute. Produced by a generation of filmmakers who were accusing the nation of not having come to terms with its culpability for the crimes of National Socialism, the state's active promotion of films by Rainer Werner Fassbinder, Margarethe von Trotta, Volker Schlöndorff and others conversely showed to the world that the nation was indeed attempting to face its past and that its democratic structures were strong enough to engage in dialogue with its detractors (Knight 2004: 28–30).

That said, for all its critics, Hollywood remains very attractive to audiences around the world and, as is evidenced in both the much cited annual *Monocle* soft power survey as well as Ernst &Young's "Soft Power Index", it continues to function as a key plank in the on-going success of America as one of the world's leading exponents of soft power, despite the role the nation played in generating the global financial crisis in 2008 as well as in the destabilisation of Middle Eastern states in the wake of George W. Bush's "War on Terror" (Ernst & Young 2012;

Bloomfield 2013). Nonetheless, as suggested in Edgecliffe-Johnson's article for the *FT*, things would appear to be shifting. Or at least it would seem that other parts of the world are seeking either to emulate—or indeed, as in the case of China, to co-opt—Hollywood to support their soft-power strategy.

Film, the BRICS and cultural policy

This strategy is particularly visible in India. The Hindi film industry, known around the world as Bollywood, produces around 1,000 feature films annually, attracting in excess of a billion spectators at home and across the Indian diaspora. This diasporic audience is hugely significant not only for the success of the film industry but for the entire Indian economy, "Non Resident Indians" (NRI) invest around $70 billion annually (4 per cent of India's GDP) in the country (Bellman 2015). The growing importance of NRI has had a particularly noticeable impact on the image of the Indian migrant in Bollywood. As Ingrid Therwath puts it: "Once unloved and portrayed as the epitome of moral corruption, [the NRI has become] the embodiment of the national ethos as well as of a triumphant capitalism" (Therwath 2010: 4). Since the 1990s, the NRI has frequently been presented as a "Brand Ambassador" for India, reflecting a cosmopolitan version of modernity that embraces global capitalism while preserving traditional Indian (patriarchal) values (Therwath 2010: 4). *Ek Tha Tiger* (Once There Was a Tiger, 2012, India, Kabir Khan), for example, a musical spy adventure partially set in Dublin, presents its protagonists as cosmopolitan travellers, comfortable in the most exotic of settings—specifically in this case a "Bollywoodised" version of the Irish capital, replete with leprechaun hats and a Bhangra-dancing Hurling team (Figure 24.1). This is the Ireland of the "Celtic Tiger" that is distinct from, but sits comfortably with, the Indian "Tiger", the film's eponymous hero (Barton 2016: 176–178).

There is no official compulsion in India for filmmakers to support a government-driven soft power strategy. The Indian industry is notoriously unregulated and receives very little in the way of financial state support that might incentivise its official collaboration with

Figure 24.1 Salman Khan and Katrina Kaif bring Bollywood to Dublin, *Ek Tha Tiger* (Once There Was a Tiger, 2012, India, Kabir Khan). ©Fantastic Films/Prime Focus/Yash Raj Films.

governmental initiatives. The use of Dublin as a location was due to Ireland's generous tax-credit system for film productions. However, within the Indian industry there is also support for the country's overall aim of using its soft power assets to present the nation favourably to the NRI community. The producer and director Yash Chopra, for example, insists that the industry has a "moral responsibility [to] depict India at its best. We're the historians of India [. . .]. The Indian Diaspora must maintain its identity, its roots" (quoted in Therwath 2010: 9). And, this has been strongly welcomed by the government, as the former Prime Minister Manmohan Singh made clear in 2008:

> the soft power of India in some ways can be a very important instrument of foreign policy. Cultural relations, India's film industry—Bollywood—I find wherever I go in the Middle-East, in Africa—people talk about Indian films. So that is a new way of influencing the world about the growing importance of India.
>
> *(Quoted in Therwath 2010: 10)*

Bollywood is a key component of "Brand India", its increasingly globally recognised stars such as Shah Rukh Khan and Deepika Padukone helping to drive the international visibility of the nation. The Indian film industry, as well as the size of the global audience that wishes to see the films produced, is hugely significant for the nation's soft power appeal. And, as we have seen above, although the Chinese film industry does not consistently achieve the level of success attained by Indian films, there is, to a degree, a similar dynamic at work within China. Since 2000 there have been a number of internationally successful Chinese films, such as *Ying xiong* (Hero, 2002, China/Hong Kong, Yimou Zhang) and *Shi mian mai fu* (House of Flying Daggers, 2004, China/Hong Kong, Yimou Zhang) that suggest the potential global appeal of the nation's cinema. With the growth of Wanda, one might imagine that this potential could gradually be realised.

While what is often termed "Chindia" by commentators is a case apart from the rest of the BRICS, the role of the Brazilian, Russian and South African film industries, along with the economic pull of their markets, also plays an important role in these nations' soft power strategies, not least as they individually seek to present the BRICS as a coherent political bloc. Chinese commentators, for example, point to the need for the BRICS to work more effectively together in order to use the media in a coordinated way to realise the group's potential as a representative body for the whole of the Global South. Reporting on the 2014 BRICS summit held in Brazil, timed to coincide with the start of the Football World Cup, Li Congju argued that while the economic power of the group was (at the time at least) growing, its collective voice, along with that of the rest of the developing world continues to be "drowned out by the much louder media of the West" (Congju 2014). However, as already noted, this is changing. China (CCTV), Russia (RT) and Brazil (Rede Globo) all support media organisations with an international reach. This is part of a global trend that, Jeremy Tunstall notes, has in fact been visible at least since the late 1980s, pointing to the fact that the US has now become "a large-scale media importer", suggesting that while the US mass media is still dominant, its influence is declining (Tunstall 2008: xiv). Yet more importantly in terms of the overall argument of this chapter, it begs the question Daya Kishan Thussu and Kaarle Nordenstreng ask: "Does the impressive growth of media in the BRICS countries and their greater visibility across the globe indicate the end of globalization as Westernization?" (Thussu and Nordenstreng 2015: 13). There is little evidence that the likes of RT and Globo will heed Li Congj's call to coordinate their efforts. It is difficult to see how CCTV could engage with Brazil's hugely successful *telenovela* industry, for example, one of the country's key cultural exports. However, with

Figure 24.2 The first BRICS film festival, signalling a new phase in international cooperation across the group?

regard to film production specifically, there is an appetite for greater cooperation between BRICS member states. The year 2016 saw the launch of a BRICS film festival in India, for example, designed to coincide with that year's BRICS summit and to emphasise the potential of BRICS as a cultural, as well as an economic, collaboration (ANI 2016) (Figure 24.2).

More significantly, one sees an increasing number of international co-production deals being signed across the group, allowing mutual access to this huge global market that already outstrips the US and is continuing to grow. In the process, member states are given the opportunity to generate, and leverage the potential of, cultural soft power through mutual cultural exchange (Pham 2012).

That said, the ability of these nations to take advantage of this opportunity remains contingent of their relative economic position within what is still a very diverse group, as well as the particular strength of their film industry and the economic model that shapes it. Russia and South Africa, for example, are in very different positions, in terms of their film economies, to India or China. Nonetheless they, like all the BRICS, are concerned to utilise the potential of soft power and to present the value of their national "narrative" to the world. In South Africa, successive cultural ministers have emphasised the role of film as way of telling the South African "story", as former Minister Paul Mashatile for example puts it, "a story of a people that have overcome adversity and are now working together towards a shared and prosperous future" (Mashatile 2013). Or, as Elizabeth Sidiropoulos suggests:

> On the continent, setting aside external actors, South Africa is probably the country with the best claim to the exercise of soft power, as defined by Nye: through its culture, its political values, and the legacy of its foreign policy. Nigeria may have Nollywood (cultural reach through its film industry), and its economy may have overtaken South Africa's as the largest in Africa, after the April 2014 rebasing of its gross domestic product calculations; however, Nigeria still has some way to go in rivaling the South African story.
>
> *(Sidiropoulos 2014: 197)*

The comparison with Nigeria is particularly illuminating in terms of South Africa's soft power aims. While South Africa has seen huge investment in its film industry and may well have a "better" story to tell, however this might be defined, it has struggled to realise the soft-power potential of its film industry. Domestic film has seen huge growth since 2000, even gaining the Foreign-language Oscar for *Tsotsi* (Thug, 2005, UK/South Africa, Gavin Hood), a much coveted accolade for a national film industry. However, this growth has largely been as a service industry for Hollywood runaway productions. Thus, unlike Nollywood, where the technical infrastructure of the industry has grown in tandem with its creative expertise, there is little space in the South African industry to develop local talent and to tell authentically South African stories (Barnard and Tuomi 2008: 665).

Conclusion

Across the BRICS, the group's success in increasing its global profile ultimately remains contingent not only on the economic power of each of its constituent nations, but also on their ability to embrace the need for the "co-creation" of soft power, as identified by the EU, that is, the need for political elites to cede authority in the generation of the "national narrative" to others. If we return to China, while the country and its growing media industry wishes to increase the number and success of culturally Chinese films internationally, as indicated in its "Go Abroad" strategy, the government's repeated efforts to control the types of films that are shown internationally and at home is stifling the creativity of the industry. At home, there is, it should be noted, some space for experimental, even critical, low-budget film production, generally distributed straight to DVD. However, these films do not tend to find their way to the big screen, a far more rigidly controlled medium of exhibition (Zhou 2015: 240). Thus, they have limited impact on the mainstream industry and certainly do little to support the generation of the type of soft power we saw, for example, in the West German government's support for the socially critical New German Cinema of the 1970s. As Lauren Rivers writes in her analysis of the 2013 *Monocle* soft power rankings:

> does all this monetary investment matter, when the global public needs to accept your values and legitimacy? In the case of China, many argue that the crackdown on modern and radical expressions of Chinese art and free speech, muddled with the inability for countries to trust their values with communist overtones are posing serious obstacles to their influence, no matter how much they spend.
>
> *(Rivers 2014)*

Nonetheless, as we have seen, the influence of China *is* increasing, as is its impact on global film culture. And while in the West, and on the pages of *Monocle*, there is often discussion of the need for China to address human rights issues, in other parts of the world, particularly Africa, China has a great deal of influence, with the public's view of the country frequently aligning with the version of China found in recent Hollywood films. The nation's ability to support the development of the world's technical infrastructure is frequently seen to be collective good (Cooke 2009). Of course, only time will tell whether, or how long, the BRICS will remain a significant political grouping, given the ever-more fragile status of the economies of Russia, Brazil and South Africa, the slowdown in the growth of China as well as the political turmoil provoked by charges of corruption at the highest level in Brazil and South Africa. Nonetheless, however global geopolitics continues to develop, and indeed however consumption patterns of audio-visual culture continue to shift as the technologies of distribution and exhibition develop in the digital age, film culture, for the moment, remains a key asset as national governments and transnational groups vie for visibility and influence on the global stage.

References

AFP (2010) "*Confucius'* Struggles against *Avatar*", *Taipei Times*, 5 February, www.taipeitimes.com/News/feat/archives/2010/02/05/2003465224.

—— (2016) "China Buys Soft Power with Hard Cash in Hollywood", 15 March, www.scmp.com/news/china/society/article/1925692/china-buys-soft-power-hard-cash-hollywood.

ANI (2016) "BRICS Film Festival to Kick-off on Friday", *The Indian Express*, 2 September, http://indianexpress.com/article/india/india-news-india/brics-film-festival-to-kick-off-on-friday-3009286/.

Barnard, H. and Tuomi, K. (2008) "How Demand Sophistication (De)limits Economic Upgrading: Comparing the Film Industries of South Africa and Nigeria (Nollywood)", *Industry and Innovation* 15: 647–668.

Barton, R. (2016) "The Ironic Gaze: Roots Tourism and Irish Heritage Cinema", in Cooke, P. and Stone, R. (eds) *Screening European Heritage: Creating and Consuming History on Film*, Basingstoke: Palgrave, 163–179.

Bellman, E. (2015) "India Wins the Remittance Race Again", *The Wall Street Journal*, 15 April.

Bloomfield, S. (2013) "The Soft Parade", *Monocle* 69: 67–82.

Carroll, R. and Phillips, T. (2015) "Why Hollywood Isn't Panicking about China's Economic Crisis", *The Guardian*, 28 August, www.theguardian.com/film/2015/aug/28/china-hollywood-makes-hay-in-land-of-eastern-promise.

China Post, The (2014) "Xi Jinping Stresses Core Socialist Values", 4 March, www.chinapost.com.tw/china/national-news/2014/03/04/401981/Xi-Jinping.htm.

Congju, L. (2014) "BRICS News Organizations Can Play a Bigger Role in International Communication", *China Daily USA*, 14 July, http://usa.chinadaily.com.cn/world/2014-07/14/content_17756276.htm.

Cooke, J. (2009) "Chinese Soft Power and Its Implications for the United States", in McGiffert, C. (ed.), *Chinese Soft Power and Its Implications for the United State: Competition and Cooperation in the Developing World, a report of the CSIS smart power initiative*, Washington DC: Centre for Strategic and International Studies, 27–44.

Cooke, P. (2007) "Introduction", in Cooke, P. (ed.), *World Cinema's "Dialogues" with Hollywood*, Basingstoke: Palgrave, 1–16.

Edgecliffe-Johnson, A. (2013) "BRICS Turn Film Market on Its Head: Box Office Growth Leads Distributors to Cater to Foreign Tastes", *Financial Times*, 3 April, www.ft.com/content/66b2ae96-9c76-11e2-9a4b-00144feabdc0.

Ernst & Young (2012) *Rapid-growth Markets Soft Power Index*, May, http://emergingmarkets.ey.com/wp-content/uploads/downloads/2012/05/TBF-606-Emerging-markets-soft-power-index-2012_LR.pdf.

Fay, J. (2008) *Theaters of Occupation: Hollywood and the Reeducation of Postwar Germany*, Minneapolism MN: University of Minnesota Press.

Fritz, B. and Burkitt, L. (2016) "China's Dalian Wanda Buys Legendary Entertainment for $3.5 Billion", *The Wall Street Journal*, 12 January, www.wsj.com/articles/chinas-dalian-wanda-buys-legendary-entertainment-for-3-5-billion-1452567251.

Gillespie, M. and O'Loughlin, B. (2015) "International News, Social Media and Soft Power: The London and Sochi Olympics as Global Media Events", *Participations* 12: 388–412.

Homewood, C. (2014) "Transformers 4: China Is Using Hollywood to Take on the World", *The Conversation*, http://theconversation.com/transformers-4-china-is-using-hollywood-to-take-on-the-world-28817.

House of Lords (2014) *Persuasion and Power in the Modern World: Select Committee on Soft Power and the UK's Influence*, London: The House of Lords.

Isar, Y., Fisher, R., Figueira, C. and Helly, D. (2014) *Culture in EU External Relations, Engaging the World: Towards Global Cultural Citizenship*, 10 June, http://cultureinexternalrelations.eu/report-publication/.

Knight, J. (2004) *New German Cinema: The Images of a Generation*, New York, Wallflower Press.

Mashatile, P. (2013) "Address by the Minister Paul on the Occasion of the 4th Film Indaba, Emperors Palace", 14 November, www.gov.za.

Miller, L. and Rampton, S. (2001) "The Pentagon's Information Warrior: Rendon to the Rescue", *PR Watch*, 4.8: 11–12.
Miller, T., Govil, N., McMurria, J. and Maxwell, R. (2004) *Global Hollywood 2*, London: BFI.
Nowell-Smith, G. (1998) "Introduction", in Nowell-Smith, G. (ed.), *Hollywood and Europe: Economics, Culture and National Identity 1945–1995*, London: BFI, 1–16.
Nunns, C. (2012) "Hollywood Bows to China Soft Power", *The Diplomat*, 16 February, http://thediplomat.com/2012/02/hollywood-bows-to-china-soft-power/.
Nye, J. S. (2004) *Soft Power: The Means to Success in World Politics*, New York: Public Affairs.
—— (2011) *The Future of Power*, New York: Public Affairs.
Pham, A. (2012) *BRIC Report*, www.ndpculture.org/media/W1siZiIsIjIwMTQvMDcvMzAvNGMyen l5YWNual9icmljLnBkZiJdXQ?sha=8b7f423d7b8c3c7b.
Plowright, M. (2015) "Furious Competition in China's Fast-Growing Film Industry", *Financial Times*, 1 June (Reprinted in *Chinese Portal*, 2 June, http://chineseportal.net/news/article/furious-competition-in-china-s-fast-growing-film-industry).
Putin, V. (2013) "Concept of the Foreign Policy of the Russian Federation Approved by President of the Russian Federation V. Putin on 12 February 2013", *Ministry of Foreign Affairs of the RussianFederation*, 13 February, www.mid.ru/brp_4.nsf/0/76389FEC168189ED44257B2E0039B16D.
Rivers, L. (2014) "Time for a Softer Approach? Engaging with the 2013 Annual Soft Power Rankings", *Future Foreign Policy*, 21 January, www.futureforeignpolicy.com/time-for-a-softer-approach-engaging-with-the-2013-annual-soft-power-rankings/.
Sidiropoulos, E. (2014) "South Africa's Emerging Soft Power", *Current History*, 113: 197–202.
Strukov, V. (2017), "Russian 'Manipulative Soft Power': Film Industry, Zviagintsev's Oscar Nomination and Contradictions of the Globalised World", *New Cinemas* 14 (1): 31–49.
Sweney, M. (2015) "Global Ad Campaign to Promote the UK Brings in £1.2bn", *The Guardian*, 5 June, www.theguardian.com/media/2015/jun/05/global-ad-campaign-to-promote-the-uk-brings-in-12bn.
Therwath, I. (2010) "'Shining Indians': Diaspora and Exemplarity in Bollywood', *South Asia Multidisciplinary Academic Journal* 4: 1–19.
Thussu, D. and Nordenstreng, K. (2015) "Introduction: Contextualising the BRICS Media", in Thussu, D. and Nordenstreng, K. (eds), *Mapping BRICS Media*, London: Routledge, 1–22.
Tunstall, J. (2008) *The Media Were American: U.S. Mass Media in Decline*, Oxford: Oxford University Press.
Zhou, Y. (2015) "Pursuing Soft Power through Cinema: Censorship and Double Standards in Mainland China", *Journal of Chinese Cinemas*, 9, 239–252.

25

REALIST CINEMA AS WORLD CINEMA[1]

Lúcia Nagib

The idea that "realism" is the common denominator across the vast range of productions normally labelled as "World Cinema" is widespread and seemingly uncontroversial. Thus, it is not surprising that Thomas Elsaesser should start his insightful essay on "World Cinema: Realism, Evidence, Presence" by declaring: "European art/auteur cinema (and by extension, world cinema) has always defined itself against Hollywood on the basis of its greater realism" (2009: 3). It is easy to infer the whole story behind this formula: World Cinema started in Europe, more precisely with Italian neorealism in the 1940s, which, on the basis of a documentary approach to the real, offered fertile ground for the development of art and auteur cinema. Turning its back on Hollywood fantasy and standing on the grave of the Nazi-fascist propaganda machine, this new realist cinema unveiled on screen the gritty reality of a poverty-stricken, devastated Europe in the aftermath of the Second World War. As we know, the raw aesthetics and revelatory power of this foundational movement inspired a flurry of subsequent (social-)realist schools in the world, such as Indian independent cinema in the 1950s, Brazilian Cinema Novo in the 1960s, African post-independence cinemas in the 1970s, the New Iranian Cinema in the 1980s, Danish Dogme 95 in the 1990s and many other new waves and new cinemas, remaining influential up to today. Neorealism was moreover the touchstone of André Bazin's concept of cinematic realism, the world's most revolutionary and enduring film theory ever written, albeit in the form of short magazine articles. As is well known, the film medium, for Bazin (1967a), is intrinsically realist thanks to the "ontology of the photographic image", that is, the medium's recording property that establishes a material bond with its referent in the objective world, a process later equated by Peter Wollen (1998: 86) to "indexicality" as defined by Charles Sanders Pierce's semiotic theory. Bazin was moreover, and most importantly to my own approach, the first to locate realism *at the point of production*, by extolling about neorealism (Rossellini, Visconti, De Sica) the regular use of real locations, non-professional actors (as well as actors stripped of their acting personas) and the combination of long takes and long shots that preserve the space–time integrity of the profilmic event.

But Elsaesser's synthetic formula also contains some incendiary material. Should we take for granted that Europe is the centre of "world cinema" and that theory about it must consequently be Eurocentric, or at least Europe-centred? Does all "world cinema" depend on its artistic and auteurist pedigree? And is "world cinema" forever condemned to be the other of Hollywood—or Bollywood, or Nollywood, or any popular cinema? These questions were at the heart of world cinema theorising at the beginning of the new millennium, as an increasingly globalised world made it imperative to look at different cinemas through their transnational relations. I too have attempted to define "world cinema" positively, as a set of active expressions of local histories and cultures, rather than mere reactions against commercially and/or ideologically hegemonic cinemas (see Nagib 2006; Nagib *et al.* 2012). In this chapter, however, I shall propose to leave the Euro- and Hollywood-centric as well as the art/auteur vs commercial dilemma behind and move a step further by replacing the rather vague, and often unhelpful, "world cinema" appellation with the more substantive "realist cinema", which is defined by an ethics of the real that has bound world films together across history and geography at cinema's most creative peaks.

In order to do so, it is first necessary to ask: where does realism actually lie? Why is it so easy to define as "realist" a film such as *Boyhood* (2014, USA, Richard Linklater), made at the gravitational centre of mainstream cinema, the United States, by Richard Linklater who Rob Stone (2015: 67) refers to as "one of the most important filmmakers in world cinema?" It is certainly not for its reasonably conventional "illusionist" mode of storytelling, nor its relative commercial success, and not at all for any overwhelming sensory experience it might afford the spectator, but most certainly for its realist *mode of production*, that is, because the film crew went through the trouble of spending twelve years filming a boy as he grew up from six to eighteen years of age so as to achieve a complete fusion between the actor and the character. As much as the Deleuzian time-image and the sensory-motor relation it establishes with the spectator have become the all-time champions of world-cinema theorising, not least thanks to the rise of what became known as "slow cinema", it is now time to turn the gaze to *how* these images and sounds are produced and captured, and the tremendous effort a number of film crews and casts from all over the world put into *producing* as well as reproducing reality. It is necessary to ask: why did a filmmaker such as Joshua Oppenheimer need to remain for eight years in close contact with utterly dangerous and powerful criminals in Indonesia, and to learn Indonesian in the process, in order to make *The Act of Killing* (2012, UK/Denmark/Norway), an instant landmark in documentary making? Why do some filmmakers have their cast perform real sex for the camera, as in Nagisa Ôshima's erotic masterpiece *Ai no korīda* (In the Realm of the Senses, 1976, Japan/France), when others are perfectly happy with simulating it? Why does Werner Herzog have to travel to the remotest corners of the world, exposing his cast and crew to the rigours and perils of the Amazon jungle or the Sahara Desert when he could stage these acts in a studio?

In order to address these questions, this chapter will veer away from the recent trend of focusing on the materiality of the spectatorial body and the sensuous reception of films, locating instead cinematic realism in the way films are made. I will argue that film crews and casts who choose to produce rather than just reproduce reality and to commit themselves to unpredictable events are moved by an ethics that Alain Badiou has defined as "an active fidelity to the event of truth" (2006: xiii; see also Nagib 2011: 1ff. in this respect). Three facts speak in favour of this model. First, realism at the point of production is clearly identifiable and measurable, as opposed to the "reality effect" at the point of reception, which varies widely from one individual to another, remaining inevitably restricted to the speculative realm. Second, realism can be achieved at the point of production regardless of the technology utilised for the capturing of images and sounds, whether it is the now obsolete celluloid strip or digital equipment. And third, realism is timeless, as the recurrent emergence of realist trends at certain historical junctures demonstrates, and is consequently not the result of the "evolution of the language of cinema" or tributary to a supposed postwar modernity, as Bazin (1967b) would have had it.

In order to substantiate these contentions, I will start, unavoidably, by revisiting Bazin's realist theory, as well as its recent revival, defined by Elsaesser (2009: 11) as "ontology mark two".

I will then proceed to laying out a possible taxonomy of cinematic realism according to modes of production, address, exhibition and reception. This will be followed by a look at sub-modalities of the realist mode of production in the light of representative film examples, from the negation of cinema that changes it into a way of living and interfering politically with the world phenomena; to the intermedial procedure that turns other art forms within films into a channel to the real; and finally to the utopian "myth of total cinema" that Bazin defined as the human desire for "integral realism".

Reality between modernity and the digital age

Bazin is central to this chapter because most of what he said about realism in the late 1940s and 1950s would apply to what is understood under "world cinema" nowadays. This being a term originated in the Anglophone world, untranslatable in most other film cultures and unavailable in Bazin's time, he chose to give to the new realism of his time the name of "modern cinema".

As I have discussed at length elsewhere (Nagib 2016a: 25ff.), this choice was coherent insofar as it represented the culmination of Bazin's evolutionist approach, according to which the best films ever made could not but be located in his own time. "Modern cinema" thus starts with Italian neorealism in the late 1940s, excluding from its ranks not only what Bazin (1967b) calls the "classical" Hollywood cinema, but pre-war modernist cinema itself, as represented by Eisenstein and Soviet cinema, German Expressionism and the European avant-gardes in general, due to their allegiance to montage. Though circumstantial and transient at origin, the concept of "modern cinema" has prevailed in film studies ever since, having been lavishly applied to signify almost any narrative films produced outside the Hollywood system from World War II onwards. However, beyond the questionable opposition between modernity and modernism, this model is further flawed by the fact that many realist filmmakers of Bazin's own pantheon, including Renoir, Stroheim, Murnau and Dreyer, were active much before World War II and were already resorting to the techniques he deemed both realist and modern. Conversely, neorealist filmmakers were not necessarily averse to montage, if one considers the quick-fire editing in *Germania anno zero* (Germany Year Zero, 1948, Italy/France/German, Roberto Rossellini), a neorealist milestone that is more akin to the urban velocity featured in a modernist film such as *Berlin: Die Sinfonie der Grosstadt* (Berlin: Symphony of a Great City, 1927, Germany, Walter Ruttmann) than to the contemplative attitude associated with the Bergsonian *durée* at the base of Bazin's definition of modern cinema. These contradictions have not stopped Bazin's evolutionist model from continuing to be widely adopted in film scholarship, not least thanks to the endorsement it received from Deleuze (2013), the most influential film philosopher of all time, who adopted World War II as the dividing line between classical and modern cinema, these being respectively characterised by the "movement-image" and the "time-image", which disregard chronology even more frontally than Bazin.

While paying due respect to these seminal theories, my proposal is to think about realism and "world cinema" away from evolutionist models that fail to cohere even with the schemes in which they originated, and that inevitably place Europe as the gravitational centre of world/modern cinema and in irrevocable opposition to Hollywood and all other so-called classical/commercial cinemas. As David Martin-Jones (2011: 7) rightly suggests, keeping away from Eurocentric and "othering" mechanisms can reinvigorate these thinkers' ideas and broaden their scope for future usage. Thinking in terms of modes of production would do precisely that without excluding works pre- or post-World War II, along the lines, for example, of Siegfried Kracauer, whose book *Theory of Film: The Redemption of Physical Reality* describes cinema as dominated from the outset by "realistic" and "formative" tendencies, represented respectively by Lumière's documentaries and Méliès' fantasy films (1997: 30ff.).

My proposal of a timeless view of realism has nonetheless to overcome a serious historical hurdle that is the advent of digital technology. Both Bazin and Kracauer were theorising on the basis of photographic recording, or, in Bazin's terms, the "ontology of the photographic image", through which the object is directly imprinted on the film emulsion without the mediation of the human being, as in the case of the death mask or the Holy Shroud (Bazin 1967a: 14). However, digital technology changed the process of recording in radical ways that disrupted film's fundamental link with the objective real, as Miriam Hansen was quick to note in her introduction to the 1997 edition of Kracauer's book:

> Digital technologies such as computer enhancement, imaging, and editing have shifted the balance increasingly toward the postproduction phase. Not only can "mistakes" made during shooting be "corrected" and recorded effects be maximized, but on the very level of production live-action images and sounds can be generated independently of any referent in the outside world.
>
> *(Hansen 1997: viii)*

This argument was later expanded upon by new-media herald Lev Manovich, who observes:

> Cinema traditionally involved arranging physical reality to be filmed through the use of sets, models, art direction, cinematography, etc. Occasional manipulation of recorded film (for instance, through optical printing) was negligible compared to the extensive manipulation of reality in front of a camera. In digital filmmaking, shot footage is no longer the final point but just raw material to be manipulated in a computer where the real construction of a scene will take place. In short, the production becomes just the first stage of post-production.
>
> *(2016: 29)*

While perfectly valid in principle, this argument obscures the fact that many filmmakers continue to valorise production above post-production, even when using digital technology. Indeed, one of the most remarkable consequences of the digital revolution was to enable filmmakers from the most disparate areas of the globe to embark on otherwise unthinkable realist ventures. An example is the first ever Inuit feature-length film, *Atanarjuat* (Atanarjuat: The Fast Runner, 2001, Canada, Zacharias Kunuk), which could only come to life thanks to the light-weight, versatile digital equipment that allowed for shooting in sub-zero temperatures and in remote areas of the Arctic circle inaccessible to motor vehicles. No tricks and effects added in post-production could ever efface the indexical power of this film, in which, for the first time, an entirely Inuit cast re-enacts their mythology in their own territory, language and costumes, climaxing with actor Natar Ungalaak running stark naked and barefoot on the glacial landscape during more than seven minutes of edited stock. Probably because the evidentiary power of digital filming could be brought into question, some footage from the filmmaking process was added to the final credits, in which we see Ungalaak being followed by the camera mounted on a sledge pushed by other crew members, and later wrapped in a blanket to keep warm between shots.

Having sparked an avalanche of scholarship and ushered in a "post-cinematic" era, as announced in the excellent newly launched collection *Post-Cinema: Theorizing 21st Century Film* (Denson and Leyda 2016), the digital revolution is also at the core of Elsaesser's aforementioned essay, which defines realism in the post-photographic era as an "ontology mark two" (Elsaesser 2009: 6).

It is, however, intriguing that Elsaesser should produce evidence for his thesis through the analysis of a film such as *Bin-jip* (3-Iron, 2004, South Korea/Japan, Kim Ki-duk). Granted, in this film humans share agency with objects and spaces, the animate and inanimate swap roles, and characters become visible and invisible at will. The real and its representation are thus brought into question, but only as a *mode of address*, that is, as fictional subjects in a plot akin to postmodernism and the horror genre. As a result, "ontology mark two" avers itself as a mere exercise in style.

Whatever the case, Elsaesser's film example is useful as it highlights the blind spot still in need to be clarified: the phases and modes in which cinematic realism may (or may not) be produced. In order to clarify this point, I will now proceed to laying out a tentative taxonomy of cinematic realism covering the film process in its various phases, from production to reception.

Towards a possible taxonomy of cinematic realism

Bearing in mind the limitations and artificiality of all schemes, and that the modes below never come isolatedly, but are entwined and mutually dependent, I will attempt to establish the possible locations of realism in cinema as shown in Figure 25.1 below.

In recent times, most theories on cinematic realism have been concerned with the last category, that is, with realism as a *mode of reception*. This has a history that I have addressed in detail in two books, *World Cinema and the Ethics of Realism* (2011) and *Realism and the Audiovisual Media* (2009), and are briefly summarised here. The emphasis on spectatorial reception emerged as a reaction against Cartesian traditions of body–mind dualism as seen in psychoanalytic approaches to film in the 1970s, in particular in French semiology and the *Screen* criticism, that famously

Modes of Production	Modes of Address	Modes of Exhibition	Modes of Reception
Physical engagement on the part of crew and cast with the profilmic event	Narrative realism as obtained by the "cinematographic apparatus"	Films that include live performance, such as in expanded cinema experiments	Audiences' and market behaviour
Identity between casts and their roles	The production of an "impression of reality"	Or the opposite, films aiming at extreme illusionism: 3D and Imax environments, and 4D Virtual Reality works	The way films affect the "mind" or "mental structures"
Real location shooting	The "reality effect" derived from graphic or sensational representations		Realism as affect involving the body and the senses
Emphasis on the index			Interactive behaviours as enabled by the Internet, DVDs, games, etc.
The inclusion of artworks in progress within the film			

Figure 25.1 Taxonomy of cinematic realism.

defined the film spectator as a passive subject regressed to the Lacanian mirror-stage infancy. Most notably, cinematic realism was debunked as a "bourgeois genre" by critics such as Colin MacCabe, who compared it with the nineteenth-century realist novel on the basis of a narrative discourse that "allows reality to appear and denies its own status as articulation" (1974: 9). MacCabe then proceeded to place neorealism on an equal footing to Hollywood so as to reject both ([1976] 1986: 180). Because of his defence of the former, Bazin was accused by MacCabe of rendering a "characterization of realism [. . .] centrally concerned with a transparency of form which is reduplicated within Hollywood filmic practice" ([1976] 1986: 180).

Most contentiously within the *Screen* criticism, but bearing uniquely foundational insights, Laura Mulvey's essay "Visual Pleasure and Narrative Cinema" ([1975] 2009) condemned spectatorial pleasure as elicited by Hollywood cinema as narcissistic, scopophilic and ideologically charged. The reaction to these accusations came in the 1980s, when David Bordwell (1997), drawing on Constructivism, formulated theories around "mental structures" to explain the universal popularity of American mainstream cinema, while cognitivists such as Noël Carroll (1988) and Murray Smith (1996) rejected the Brecht-inspired opposition between illusionistic absorption and critical spectatorship. In the early 1990s, Deleuze's emphasis on sensory-motor modes of communication motivated critics such as Steven Shaviro (2006) to add the body to this equation, with a view to reinstating pleasure as constitutive of spectatorial experience. This was followed by the celebration of the "embodied spectator" in the 2000s, as most notably represented by Vivian Sobchack. Drawing on Merleau-Ponty's phenomenology, Sobchack proposed "embodiment" as "a radically material condition of the human being that necessarily entails both the body and consciousness, objectivity and subjectivity, in an *irreducible ensemble*" (2004: 4; emphasis in original). Along the same lines, Laura Marks put forward the concept of "haptic criticism" as a kind of physical fusion between film and viewer (2002: xiii–xv).

As can be seen, the common thread across these views is the focus on realism as a *reality effect* on the human body and senses, hence on realism at the point of reception. It is indeed a fact that, regardless of their recording processes or modes of storytelling, audiovisual media can affect spectators by means of graphic representations able to cause physical and emotional impact even when there is no representational realism at play, for example, when the physical impact on the spectator derives from animation or computer-generated images and sounds (Black 2002). Traditional 2D screenings of action films are perfectly capable of producing reality effects, but particular *modes of exhibition*, such as 3D projections, Imax environments and the more recent 4D Virtual Reality devices, have been specifically designed to enhance them. With all of them, however, reality effects can only be effects and not actual reality, given the interdiction of spectatorial participation. Even Virtual Reality devices, though allowing the viewer to move their head freely and choose what to look at or listen to within a 360° spectrum, are unable to provide any kind of actual interaction. As Christian Metz was the first to note (1982: 61–65), there is an unbridgeable fracture between seeing and being seen in audiovisual media due to the temporal gap that separates the moment of shooting from that of viewing, and this is why, for Metz, the spectator's position at any film projection is necessarily scopophilic.

Reality effects are moreover subordinate to the varying subjective susceptibilities, hence impossible to measure by universal standards. There is also the fact that, as technology evolves and tricks are cracked, reality effects tend to wane with time and lose the battle against the human brain, which opposes a natural resistance to illusionism. A historical example is that of the audience members who purportedly fainted or ran away when first exposed to Lumière's *L'arrivée d'un train en gare de La Ciotat* (Arrival of a Train at La Ciotat, 1895, France), a film that has become perfectly innocuous to current-day spectators. As Oliver Grau aptly explains:

> When a new medium of illusion is introduced, it opens a gap between the power of the image's effect and conscious/reflected distancing in the observer. This gap narrows again with increasing exposure and there is a reversion to conscious appraisal. Habituation chips away at the illusion, and soon it no longer has the power to captivate. It becomes stale, and the audience are hardened to its attempts at illusion. At this stage, the observers are receptive to content and artistic media competence, until finally a new medium with even greater appeal to the senses and greater suggestive power comes along and casts a spell of illusion over the audience again.
>
> *(2003: 152)*

There is, however, one case in which objective realism can be found at the exhibition stage: when the film projection involves live performance. Expanded cinema experiments are the ultimate expression of this category, insofar as they preserve the auratic *Einmaligkeit* (or uniqueness) held by Benjamin as the very definition of an artwork. However, for this same reason, they also have to relent on the recording and replicating properties of the film medium aimed at reaching the masses—the "public" without which, as Bazin claims (1967c: 75), there is no cinema—as well as to the possibility of being preserved for posterity. Film studies tools alone are therefore insufficient to address such phenomena.

As for *modes of address*, realism must forcibly be associated with the impression of reality elicited by what Baudry (1986) famously defined as the basic cinematographic apparatus (*l'appareil de base*), including the projector, the flat screen and the dark, collective auditorium. Despite film's vertiginous technological development since its invention and the multiplication of its uses, supports and platforms, the basic cinematographic apparatus as provided by the cinema auditorium has demonstrated extraordinary resilience, remaining for over a century the standard outlet for filmic experience. This endurance, I believe, is due to the comfort zone it affords the spectator between the reality effect and the natural brain resistance to total illusionism. It is moreover a space capable of accommodating a range of cinematic genres and styles, from classical narrative cinema of closure, devoted to eliciting an impression of reality, to mixed-genre productions endowed with disruptive devices that draw attention to the reality of the medium. Moreover, as Arnheim (1957: 3) had already noted, human 3D perception of reality is itself an illusion, given that the human retina is as flat as the traditional cinema screen. The three-dimensional impression we have of objective reality is only produced thanks to our stereoscopic vision that promotes the fusion of two slightly different images resulting from the distance between our eyes.

This brings us back to the hypothesis announced at the beginning that the only clearly identifiable and measurable cinematic realism derives from the first category, that is, from *modes of production*, relying heavily on: the physical engagement on the part of crew and cast with the profilmic event; the near identity between the cast and their roles; real location shooting; the audiovisual medium's inherent indexical property; and the engagement with works of art in progress within the film. In films resulting from this mode of production, the illusionistic fictional thread (if existing) interweaves with documentary footage and/or approach, as well as with crew and cast's direct interference with the historical world, aimed not only at highlighting the reality of the medium but also at producing, as well as reproducing, social and historical reality. Needless to say, none of the modes above exist per se, a film relying on physical engagement at production point being only thus conceived for the specific reality effect it is expected to have on the spectator. Modes of production are however, I wish to argue, the only *objective* way of proofing and proving a film's intention, given the countless variables inflecting the ways in which films are subjectively perceived by each individual.

Realism from non-cinema to the myth of total cinema

My first case study of realism as mode of production refers to a filmmaker who systematically refuses to abide by the rules of cinema in the name of a politics of the real: Jafar Panahi (see also Nagib 2016b in this respect). Any of Panahi's films could illustrate this hypothesis, but I will focus on *In film nist* (This Is Not a Film, 2011, Iran), a title that already reflects an aversion to representational strategies. Confrontational and self-reflexive to the core, the film was made in defiance of the Iranian authorities, who had prohibited the director from making films and placed him under house arrest. With the complicity of assistant Mojtaba Mirtahmasb behind the camera, Panahi undertakes to secretly stage, inside his house, the difficulties of his current situation. But he dislikes the result and at a certain point decides to "remove his cast". The reference is to the nine-year-old Mina, the lead of one of his early films, *Ayneh* (The Mirror, 1997, Iran), who suddenly decides to abandon the shoot. She throws away the cast from around her arm, which was part of her character, changes into her normal clothes and sets out to find her way back home by herself on foot. The film then cuts to the section of *The Mirror* where this happens, which is shown on Panahi's TV set, after which the director confesses to his feeling that he had been pretending and lying in his own staging at home. Addressing Mirtahmasb behind the camera, he wonders whether this is a problem faced by all filmmakers, to which Mirtahmasb confirms that he is currently involved in a film entitled *Behind the Scenes of Iranian Filmmakers Not Making Films*, turning the self-denying effect of *The Mirror* into a specular mise-en-abyme (Figure 25.2).

The film *The Mirror* itself, made when Panahi was still relatively free as a filmmaker, demonstrates how his method had always been solidly anchored on a Real that clashes against and ruins the possibility of a conventional film. For him, losing a character does not mean losing an actor, and accordingly he orders the crew to continue to shoot, profiting from the fact that Mina still has a functioning mic attached to her clothes. With the bus in which the team had been shooting they follow her as she braves Tehran's chaotic traffic in a similar way her character would probably have done in the fictional story. In pursuit of the girl on their bus, the crew often lose

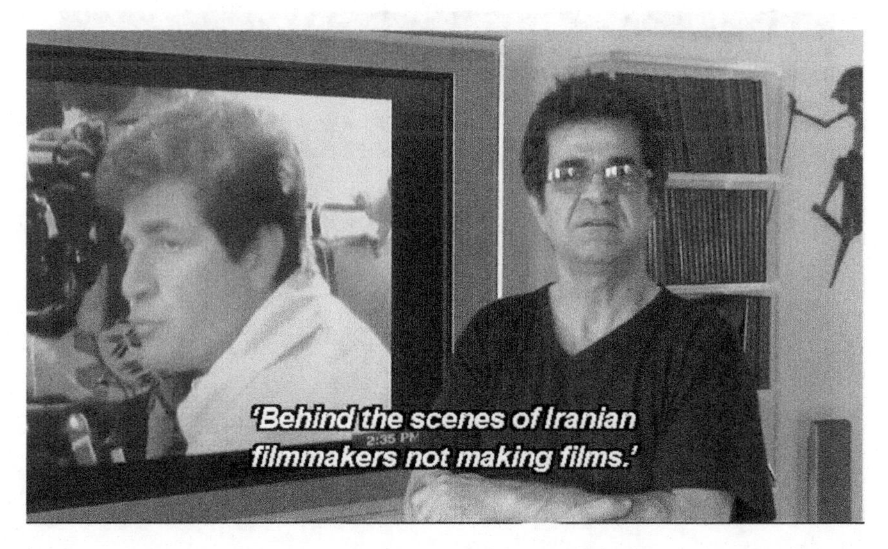

Figure 25.2 Cinematic self-negation mise-en-abyme: Jafar Panahi attempts to turn his film into real life. *In film nist* (This Is Not a Film, 2011, Iran, Jafar Panahi and Mojtaba Mirtahmasb). ©Jafar Panahi Film Productions.

sight of her and, at times, also the signal of her mic. As a result, the film is a collection of "what is fortuitous, dirty, confused, unsteady, unclear, poorly framed, overexposed", as Lyotard had defined "acinema" (1986: 349), and the pure expression of the crew's fidelity to the unpredictable event of truth, in Badiou's definition of ethics. As for *This Is Not a Film*, now part of a trilogy including *Pardé* (Closed Curtain, 2013, Iran) and the Berlin Golden-Bear-winner *Taxi* (Taxi Tehran, 2015, Iran), all made in contravention of the filming ban imposed on Panahi, it ends literally with the "pyrotechnics" that Lyotard (1986: 351), citing Adorno, describes as the "only truly great art", as the director observes the fireworks celebrating the New Year from behind the gate of his building that he and his film cannot trespass. A self-consuming film is thus brought to light whose burning energy momentarily prevails over an oppressive regime.

My second case study provides material evidence to Bazin's (1967c) argument that realist is not only the cinema that straddles real life but also the one that merges with the other arts. The Brazilian film *Crime Delicado* (Delicate Crime, 2006, Brazil, Beto Brant) is a literary adaptation that changes consecutively into theatre and painting, without recognising frontiers between these different mediums. One of the film's narrative strands focuses on Inês, a young woman who has a disability both in the film and in real life: she lacks a leg. Inês models for a painter, José Torres Campana, played by Mexican diplomat Felipe Ehrenberg, who is also a painter in real life. At a certain point, Inês is shown posing for the film's key work, called "Pas de deux". Painter and model are naked and engaged in different embraces during which he draws the sketches which are subsequently transferred to the canvas. Both processes (the drawing of the sketches and the actual painting) are shot while in progress, that is, Ehrenberg produced this painting during the actual shooting of the film. Thus, what we see in this scene is the actors leaping out of representation and into a presentational regime in which the production of an artwork is concomitant with its reproduction (Figure 25.3).

Indeed, the most startling aspect of the scene of the painting of "Pas de deux" is that a real painter and a real model agreed to create an artwork in real life while simultaneously playing fictional characters in a film. The fact that this involved full nudity and physical intimacy between

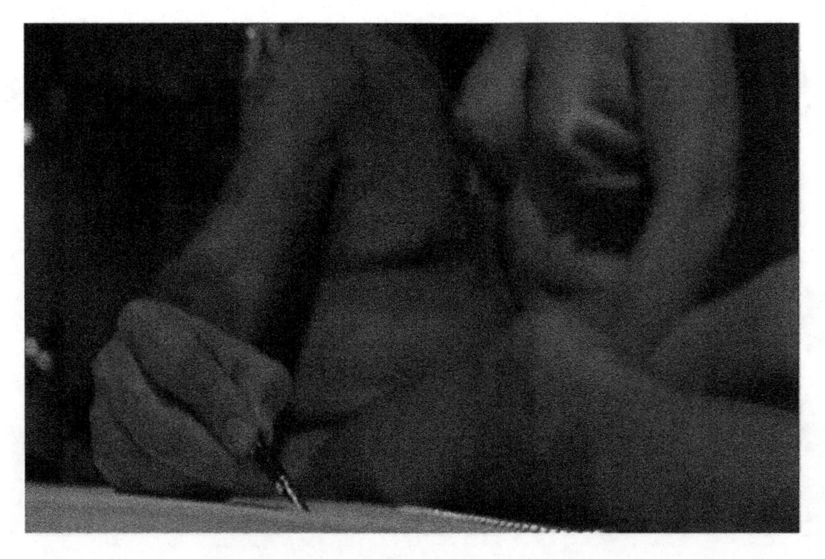

Figure 25.3 Sexual embraces turn into drawing and painting, establishing an indelible link between living and representing reality: *Crime Delicado* (Delicate Crime, 2005, Brazil, Beto Brant). ©Drama Filmes/Lumière/MG Ricca/MegaColor.

both, and that, to that end, the model, who is disabled in real life, had to remove her prosthetic leg before the camera, indicates the transformative effect the film necessarily had on the actors' actual lives (as became known, the actress Lilian Taublib never wore her prosthetic leg again after the film). The resulting picture has in its centre an erect penis placed next to a dilated vulva, implying that if the painting was real, so was also the sexual arousal between painter and model. Suggestively, the male organ appears as substitute for the missing leg, filling in the representational gap that allows for art (and sex) to become reality.

To complete my analysis, I will now address an impulse pointing in the opposite direction to non-cinema, which is total cinema. In lieu of a cinema that, in order to acquire the status of art and political power, dissolves itself into real life or the other arts, total cinema is the one that aspires to change life itself into film. Our world is becoming increasingly captive to the power of speed and the cut, as represented by the typical Facebook super-short films, made for the minuscule screens of mobile phones or even wristwatches. However, the films I am addressing here under the name of "total cinema" place all their bets on duration and the giant screen, as an unflinching commitment to the film medium as we used to know it. Instead of the constant distraction of the Internet, this cinema proposes immersion in the traditional sense of the "basic cinematographic apparatus", according to Braudry's famous formula, which includes the collective audience, the dark room, the projector and the large screen, as well as the long duration, which together produce an illusion of reality analogous to that produced in Plato's cave. In formulating his concept of "total cinema", Bazin (1967d) was most certainly inspired by René Barjavel, whose futuristic book-length essay *Cinéma total: essai sur les formes futures du Cinéma*, written in 1944, has only recently returned to the debate. Barjavel's enormously insightful take on cinema's relentless search for realism through technological development predicted the collapsing of all arts into cinema in the following terms: "Total cinema will not replace the traditional arts. It will give them a new vigour, feeding them with the blood donated by the masses" (1944: 39). Such an assertion curiously chimes with Jens Schröter (2010: 113), who ascribes the yearning for the fusion between art and life to the same "genealogical line" of Wagner's total work of art. For Bazin, however, total cinema is a "myth" insofar as its unattainable utopia is "integral realism", that is, the perfect identity between cinema and real life (1967d: 21). As a result, and in tune with his aversion to illusionism as produced by montage cinema, spectatorial engagement in total cinema would be the act of actually and materially inhabiting it. Bazin goes even further by describing, a propos of total cinema, a desire to achieve a "complete imitation of nature" (1967d: 21), and indeed the notion of "nature" is key to the films in question here, whose totalising endeavour expresses itself in the form of monumental landscapes and the emphasis on the long shot, as opposed to the fragmentation of the close-up.

An important section of "world cinema" over the last decade has been prone to the landscape film, more specifically as regards threatened landscapes. Examples abound from all over the world, with the likes of Carlos Reygadas in Mexico, Lisandro Alonso in Argentina, Jia Zhangke in China, Lav Diaz in the Philippines, Andrey Zvyagintsev in Russia, Nuri Bilge Çeylan in Turkey, Abderrahmane Sissako in Mali and many others. Although all of them make full use of digital technology, their films are marked by an obsessive preoccupation with production rather than post-production, that is, with capturing objects within a wider whole, with an indexicality that establishes a material link between the film and its historical and geographical context. These films stand therefore in direct opposition to mobile-phone super-short film fragments, which are an endless exercise in decontextualization.

Paradoxically, however, it is the unavoidable human figure, behind and before the camera, that is the greatest threat to this cinema. Simon Schama states that "nature may exist without us [. . .] it doesn't need us, whereas landscape requires some degree of human presence and affect" (cited in Lefebvre 2011: 70). Thus, the first obstacle to the realisation of total cinema is that its images are not anymore the "nature" that Bazin refers to, but simply landscapes, framed and limited by the human eye. The second obstacle refers to cinema's own temporality which, in contrast to static arts such as photography and painting, necessarily adds to any landscape an evanescent character. Take, for example, the opening of *Leviafan* (Leviathan, 2014, Russia, Andrey Zvyagintsev). A series of shots of monumental cliffs on the seashore slowly unveils the human presence, indicated by electric towers, winding roads and derelict fishing boats at the port. Eventually, a house and one of its inhabitants are presented to the camera, now duly contextualised within the landscape and in conflict with it, for it changes it into a suburban setting carrying the sign of death (the end of an autonomous fishing tradition replaced by industrial mass fishing and processing). Total cinema here is defined as the mutual exclusion between human being and nature resulting in the evanescent landscape and hinting at the excessive character of the object total cinema craves for without ever managing to capture in its entirety.

Kant (1960) distinguishes between the "beautiful" and the "sublime", noting that the former refers to the object's form and is limited, whereas the latter derives from a formless, unlimited object. For Kant, human sensibility and imagination are insufficient to fully comprehend phenomena happening in the realm of the sublime. This assessment curiously resonates with Bazin's total-cinema idea as read by Tom Gunning, who states that "a myth always exceeds a concept, and Bazin's essay examines one of the traditional tasks of myth, a tale of origin" (2011: 120). Indeed, there is a clear supra-rational and inexplicable element in the cinematic landscapes in question here, signalling not at a divine or supernatural presence but simply at the materiality of death, as in the magnificent image, in *Leviathan*, where a whale's gigantic skeleton confronts a child criminal, its disproportionate dimensions in comparison with the minute human subject still insufficient to prevail over the latter's destructive will and power (Figure 25.4).

The films I am referring to as adept of the "myth of total cinema" are actually political in the strongest sense, animated as they are by questions such as tourism invasion, in Nuri Bilge Çeylan's *Kis uykusu* (Winter Sleep, 2014, Turkey/Germany/France), the spread of fundamentalist terrorism as represented by Al Qaeda and the Islamic State in Abderrahmane Sissako's *Timbuktu* (2014, Mauritania/France), property expansion in *Leviathan*, or the flooding of millions of homes for the construction of the Three Gorges Dam in Zhangke Jia's *Sanxia haoren* (Still Life, 2006, China/Hong Kong). In the latter film, as Cecília Mello (2014) has beautifully analysed, the Three Gorges landscape, printed as a national symbol on a 10 Yuan bill, is reduced

Figure 25.4 The human presence presents a death threat to real landscapes, shattering the myth of "integral realism": *Leviafan* (Leviathan, 2014, Russia, Andrey Zvyagintsev). ©Non-Stop Productions.

to a miniature of itself when framed by the monetary power symbolically held by the hand of a construction worker who unwittingly contributes to its end.

In his neo-realist manifesto, "Cinema Antropomorfico" (Anthropomorphic Cinema), Luchino Visconti ([1943] 1996: 102) states: "I could make a film of a wall, if I knew how to retrieve the traces of true humanity of the men standing in front of this bare prop: retrieve them and retell them." This humanity Visconti is referring to is what makes total cinema at once necessary and impossible, restricted as it is by its own humanist realism. But it is here, in the face of the human limits imposed on integral realism, that total cinema meets non-cinema, and world cinema becomes simply realist cinema: a mode of production and a way of life.

Note

1 This chapter is an output of the AHRC/FAPESP-funded IntermIdia project, www.reading.ac.uk/intermidia/.

References

Arnheim, R. (1957) *Film as Art*, Berkeley/Los Angeles, CA and London: University of California Press.
Badiou, A. (2006) *Being and Event*, trans. by Feltham O., London and New York: Continuum.
Barjavel, R. (1944) *Cinéma total: essai sur les formes futures du Cinéma*, Paris: Denoël.
Baudry, J-L. (1986) "Ideological Effects of the Basic Cinematographic Apparatus", in Rosen, P. (ed.) *Narrative, Apparatus, Ideology*, New York: Columbia University Press, 286–298.
Bazin, A. (1967a) "The Ontology of the Photographic Image", in *What Is Cinema?* Vol. 1, essays selected and trans by Gray, H., Berkeley/Los Angeles, CA and London: University of California Press, 9–16.
—— (1967b) "The Evolution of the Language of Cinema", in *What Is Cinema?* Vol. 1, essays selected and trans. by Gray, Berkeley/Los Angeles, CA and London: University of California Press, 23–40.
—— (1967c) "In Defence of Mixed Cinema", in *What Is Cinema?* Vol. 1, essays selected and trans. by Gray, Berkeley/Los Angeles, CA and London: University of California Press, 53–75.
—— (1967d) "The Myth of Total Cinema", in *What Is Cinema?* Vol. 1, essays selected and trans by Gray, Berkeley/Los Angeles, CA and London: University of California Press, 17–22.
Black, J. (2002) *The Reality Effect: Film Culture and the Graphic Imperative*, New York: Routledge.
Bordwell, D. (1997) *Narration in the Fiction Film*, London: Routledge.
Carroll, N. (1988) *Interpreting the Moving Image*, Cambridge: University of Cambridge Press.
Deleuze, G. (2013) *Cinema II: The Time-Image*, trans. by Tomlinson, H. and Galeta, R., London/New Delhi/New York/Sydney: Bloomsbury.
Denson, S. and Leyda, J. (eds) (2016) *Post-Cinema: Theorizing 21st-Century Film*, REFRAME Books: http://reframe.sussex.ac.uk/post-cinema.
Elsaesser, T. (2009) "World Cinema: Realism, Evidence, Presence", in Nagib, L. and Mello, C (eds) *Realism and the Audiovisual Media*, Basingstoke: Palgrave, 3–19.
Gunning, T. (2011) "The World in Its Own Image: The Myth of Total Cinema", in Andrew, D. and Joubert-Laurencin, H. (eds) *Opening Bazin: Postwar Film Theory & Its Afterlife*, Oxford/New York: Oxford University Press, 119–126.
Grau, O. (2003) *Virtual Art: From Illusion to Immersion*, Cambridge, MA/London: MIT Press.
Hansen, M.B. (1997) "Introduction", in Kracauer, S. (1997) *Theory of Film: The Redemption of Physical Reality*, Princeton, NJ: Princeton University Press, vii–xlv.
Kant, I. (1960) *Observations on the Feeling of the Beautiful and Sublime*, trans. by Goldthwait, J. T., Berkeley/Los Angeles, CA and London: University of California Press.
Kracauer, S. (1997) *Theory of Film: The Redemption of Physical Reality*, Princeton, NJ: Princeton University Press.
Lyotard, J. F. (1986) "Acinema", in Rosen, P. (ed.) *Narrative, Apparatus, Ideology*, New York: Columbia University Press, 349–359.
Lefebvre, M. (2011) "On Landscape in Narrative Cinema", *Canadian Journal of Film Studies* 20 (1): 6178.
MacCabe, C. (1974) "Realism and the Cinema: Notes on Some Brechtian Theses", *Screen* 15 (2): 7–27.
—— ([1976] 1986) "Theory and Film: Principles of Realism and Pleasure", in Rosen, P. (ed.) *Narrative, Apparatus, Ideology*, New York: Columbia University Press, 179–197.

Manovich, L. (2016) "What Is Digital Cinema?", in Denson, S. and Leyda, J. (2016) (eds) *Post-Cinema: Theorizing 21st-Century Film,* REFRAME Books: http://reframe.sussex.ac.uk/post-cinema, 20–50.
Marks, L. U. (2002) *Touch: Sensuous Theory and Multisensory Media*, Minneapolis, MN and London: University of Minnesota Press.
Martin-Jones, D. (2011) *Deleuze and World Cinemas*, London and New York: Continuum.
Mello, C. (2014) "Space and Intermediality in Jia Zhang-ke's *Still Life*", *Aniki* 1 (2): 274–291.
Metz, C. (1982) *The Imaginary Signifier: Psychoanalysis and the Cinema,* trans by Britton, C. Williams, A., Brewster, B and Guzzetti, A., Bloomington and Indianapolis, IN: Indiana University Press.
Mulvey, L. ([1975] 2009) "Visual Pleasure and Narrative Cinema", in *Visual and Other Pleasures*, 2nd edn, Basingstoke: Palgrave, 14–30.
Nagib, L. (2006) "Towards a Positive Definition of World Cinema", in Dennison, S. and Lim, S. H. (eds) *Remapping World Cinema: Identity, Culture and Politics in Film*, London: Wallflower Press, 30–37.
—— (2011) *World Cinema and the Ethics of Realism*, New York and London: Continuum.
—— (2016a) "The Politics of Slowness and the Traps of Modernity", in De Luca, T. and Barradas Jorge, N. (eds) *Slow Cinema*, Edinburgh: Edinburgh University Press, 25–46.
—— (2016b) "Non-cinema, or the Location of Politics in Film", *Film-Philosophy* 20 (1): 131–148.
Nagib, L. and Mello, C. (eds) (2009) *Realism and the Audiovisual Media*, Basingstoke: Palgrave.
Nagib, L., Perriam, C. and Dudrah, R. (eds) (2012) *Theorizing World Cinema*, London/New York: I.B. Tauris.
Schröter, J. (2010) "The Politics of Intermediality", *Film and Media Studies*, 2: 107–124.
Shaviro, S. (2006) *The Cinematic Body,* Minneapolis, MN and London: University of Minnesota Press.
Smith, M. (1996) "The Logic and Legacy of Brechtianism", in Bordwell, D. and Carroll, N. (eds) *Post-Theory: Reconstructing Film Studies.* Madison, WI: University of Wisconsin Press.
Sobchack, V. (2004) *Carnal Thoughts: Embodiment and Moving Image Culture,* Berkeley/Los Angeles, CA and London: University of California Press.
Stone, R. (2015) "About Time: Before Boyhood", *Film Quarterly* 68 (3): 67–72.
Visconti, L. ([1943] 1996) "Cinema Antropomorfico", in Micciché, L. *Luchino Visconti: Un profilo critico.* Venice: Marsilio, pp. 100–102. Originally published in *Cinema*, VIII, n. 173–4, 25/09–25/10/1943, 108–109.
Wollen, P. (1998) *Signs and Meaning in the Cinema*, London: BFI.

26
REGIONAL CINEMA
Micro-mapping and glocalisation

Alex Marlow-Mann

Vantage points: the national, the transnational and the regional

At the 2002 BAFTA award ceremony, Alan Parker, who was then chairman of the UK Film Council, made a speech in which he suggested that:

> We need to abandon forever the 'little England' vision of a UK industry comprised of small British film companies delivering parochial British films [...] It's time for a reality check. That 'British' film industry never existed, and in the brutal age of global capitalism, it never will.

He went on to say that the UK needed to "compete in the world marketplace" by redefining what we mean by a British film (Parker, quoted in Cox 2004: 113). Shortly afterwards filmmaker Alex Cox issued a public response in an address to the "Film Parliament". He claimed that Parker's suggestions would have meant abandoning any idea of British cinema and instead handing taxpayer money over to support American blockbusters, a proposal he described as "outrageous" and "based on imaginary premises" (Ibid.). Instead, Cox suggested that the government should concentrate on supporting filmmaking *throughout* Britain. Arguing that both the British government and London-based film producers have their eyes firmly set on the other side of the Atlantic, Cox argued that, "the greatest indigenous British features have always been made up North [. . .] it is impossible for me to understand how the Film Council can get away with having no regional remit at all" (Ibid.: 115).

Alan Parker is, of course, a London-born director with a significant career in the Hollywood mainstream who at the time of this speech had just finished shooting his latest film, *The Life of David Gale* (2003, USA). Alex Cox, on the other hand, was born in Bebington, just South of Liverpool, educated at UCLA, had a film career outside the mainstream in the US and Mexico and had recently returned to Liverpool to shoot *Revenger's Tragedy* (2002, UK) as a low-budget indie. This partly explains their difference of opinion, but the implications of their debate transcend individual biographies and career trajectories and instead point towards two contrasting visions of the world of cinema: one that "zooms out" in order to view films as the product of global or transnational processes, and the other that "zooms in" to emphasise the cultural and industrial specificities of localised and differentiated film cultures. The ramifications of these contrasting visions are crucial to an understanding of the contemporary cinematic landscape.

Since the start of the new Millennium, the notion of "transnationalism" has become increasingly prevalent within the discipline of film studies—largely in response to the accelerating process of globalisation—and has to a large extent displaced previous discourses around "national cinema" (see Chapter 23). Some scholars working on national cinemas now even feel the need to defend their choice of methodology (see Iordanova 2016); yet, as Dina Iordanova rightly points out, it is not a matter of mutually exclusive positions, but rather of differing perspectives:

> this whole issue is about what you want to see and the respective selection of a vantage point. If you anchor yourself within one nation—which is a valid position—you see one type of things; if you anchor yourself supranationally, you see different things—that is all.
>
> *(Ibid.)*

The "transnational turn" in film studies has undoubtedly served an important function, complicating the simplistic and uncritical ways that the concept of national cinema has sometimes been employed. However, its current ubiquity also entails significant risks in terms of the erasure of cultural specificities and the homogenisation of disparate film cultures: zooming out allows one to see certain things, but it also obscures others. Yet this risk is neither new nor unique to transnationalism. Indeed, one of the critiques of national cinema is that it tends to reduce a complex film culture to a monolithic single identity. As Cox's polemical claims for the superiority of filmmaking in the North suggests, however, filmmaking is not always confined solely to the capital, and films made elsewhere may present substantive or qualitative differences from the national model. Perhaps there is a need, then, to zoom in further and examine variations in films and film culture within individual nations?

This essay will argue, therefore, that film studies is in need of a "regional turn" to counterbalance the "transnational turn" of recent years. Such an approach would involve a "micro-mapping" of production contexts and distribution and exhibition strategies, but also of locally specific manifestations of larger cinematic modes, genres and styles that would complement the comparative and macro-perspectives of transnational studies. The term "micro-mapping" derives from cartography, where it describes the mapping of small-scale features, such as individual buildings or objects in public spaces, or small maps representing details of a larger whole, and has subsequently been employed in a wide-range of scientific contexts. Drawing on the concept of "glocalisation", this essay will argue that such an approach should not simply posit the regional in opposition to the national or transnational, but rather recognise that all three are merely stages along a continuum, constantly in tension and dialogue with one another. Films may be oriented towards a particular point along this continuum, but few (if any) films are simply and unequivocally "regional", "national" or "transnational". The adoption of multiple or flexible perspectives is thus required if we are to form a complete and rounded understanding of a particular film or film culture. *Revenger's Tragedy* may have been shot in Merseyside by a director from the region through his purpose-built Liverpool-based company Revengers Ltd, but it also drew on finance from sources both national (including the UK Film Council, via its New Cinema Fund) and international (Pathé International) and circulated through the international film-festival circuit, with screenings in Locarno, Tokyo and Tromsø, while in Hong Kong it was implicitly equated with the national cinema when it screened as part of the UK Film Festival. Equally, *The Life of David Gale* may suggest a clear instance of a transnational film given that it is a US/UK/German co-production, with scenes shot in both the US and Spain, making use of both English and some

Spanish-language dialogue, directed by a British filmmaker and with American and British leads, but it is also set and principally shot in Texas and deals with the question of capital punishment, which is a highly state-specific piece of legislation. While I would not want to suggest that it constitutes an example of a Texan regional cinema (see Lev 1986 and Stone 2013), it would nonetheless be a mistake to overlook its regional aspects.

Defining regional cinema: location, voice and authenticity

The question of terminology is a thorny one. To term cinemas operating below the national level as "regional" risks confusion with the use of the term to describe broader transnational categories such as Scandinavian, Balkan or Latin American cinema. However, the most obvious alternatives, such as "local cinema" smack of parochialism, reinforcing traditional hierarchical structures and hegemonies that it would be better to avoid (see below). Moreover, the term "region" is a recognised administrative term within many nations, and as such is employed to describe the apparatus for stimulating such cinemas employed by a number of governments, such as the UK's former Regional Screen Agencies. For this reason, I propose retaining the term "regional cinema" and distinguishing between the "sub-national" and the "supra-national" where necessary. For the remainder of this essay the term "regional cinema" will be used to refer to the sub-national context. A second, but related point concerns at what level one demarcates a particular regional cinema. Should it be based around a city, a county, a province, a region? There is no single answer to this, but rather the definition will vary from case to case, because nations vary greatly in size and are sub-divided differently—from the federal States of the US, to the counties of England, the "regioni" (regions) and "provincie" (provinces) of Italy, and the "comunidades autónomas" (autonomous communities) of Spain—and because individual regional cinemas may differ in terms of size and locus. Thus, Peter Lev (writing about the US) is correct to suggest that "the major cinematic regions should be identified according to which categories [. . .] are most determinative and definitive of cultural experience" (Lev 1986: 61). A third and final point remains to be made about the distinction between regional and national cinema. It could be argued that, since a film has to be made somewhere, all films are in a sense regional. However, in most nations the film industry tends to be centred around one place, the "cinematic capital", which may also be the national capital (e.g. London in the case of British cinema), or may not (e.g. Los Angeles in the case of American cinema). I propose, therefore, that the term "regional cinema" should be reserved for filmmaking that takes place at "regional" level but at a remove from the cinematic capital.

A purely geographical definition of regional cinema is insufficient, however, as the example of *The Life of David Gale* suggests. In his discussion of the cinema of Texas, Peter Lev claims that, "the fundamental characteristics of regional cinema include: presentation of a specifically regional theme; historical and cultural accuracy; and visual accuracy [. . .] geographical setting is not in itself enough to indicate regionalism" (Lev 1986: 61). For Lev, it is not sufficient for a film to be made or set in a particular place for it to be considered regional. Rather, it is the cultural specificity and authenticity that distinguishes the regional film from the national mainstream, or indeed from other independent films that may happen to have been shot in the region. For Lev, Parker's *The Life of David Gale* would not constitute a Texan film. But where does this authenticity originate? Brian Jacobson goes further than Lev to argue that:

> While it is not uncommon for fictional films in general to build stories around actual places or persons, the regional film is distinguished by its ability to speak from a position of closeness or identification with the people and place it represents. It is not simply

> about, but comes from the region. That is to say the regional voice(s) is somehow articulated in the text, whether directly by the filmmaker who comes from the area, or through the agency of an actor or people portraying themselves as fictional characters or social actors.
>
> *(Jacobson 1991: 20)*

Adopting a linguistic model, Jacobson goes on to argue that regional films constitute an alternative/oppositional discourse to the mainstream, arguing that such films are "double voiced" in that they articulate the perspective of both the filmmakers and the regional community (Ibid.: 22). A good example would be the participatory methodology employed by Ermanno Olmi to narrate the disappearing peasant culture of Bergamo in *L'albero degli zoccoli* (The Tree of Wooden Clogs, 1978, Italy). This double voicing is a delicate balancing act, however, as Marijke De Valck observes in the case of the representation of the Pacific Yakel tribe by Australian filmmakers Martin Butler and Bentley Dean in *Tanna* (2015, Australia/Vanuatu), which results in a "staged authenticity" (see Chapter 32).

The ideal regional film is not, I would argue therefore, "double-voiced" but single-voiced. It does not "speak from a position of closeness or identification with the people and place it represents", rather it speaks from that very same position. The truly regional film would therefore be written and directed by a local filmmaker, produced by a local company, draw on local/regional finance and employ a predominantly local cast and crew; it would be filmed and set in the region and utilise the local language/dialect/accent; it would feature characters from that region, address themes relevant to the region and draw on locally specific cultural references; and it would appeal specifically to local audiences, utilising limited or targeted distribution strategies and/or attracting larger or more appreciative audiences in the region. Such a film would constitute the direct expression of local voices addressing their peers about shared issues, without mediating factors of outside influences. The examples of such a pure regional cinema are, however, few and far between. The logistical demands of financing, producing and distributing a film means that it is difficult to achieve and may even be undesirable, since the resulting film may be too solipsistic and of limited appeal. Instead, we should identify various "degrees of regionality" in a broader range of films fulfilling some, but not all, of these characteristics—and thus sitting at varying points along the regional–national–transnational continuum—and employing various strategies in order to articulate a regional voice. To see more clearly how this operates in practice, let us consider four films from Naples, in the South of Italy.

Cient'anne (1999, Italy, Ninì Grassia) is a low-budget film set in Naples. It was independently produced in the city, directed by a Neapolitan director and starred two Neapolitan singers extremely popular in the South of Italy. Basing a narrative centred around the titular song, it mimicked a traditional form of Neapolitan theatre (the *sceneggiata*) which also had a long tradition in the cinema. It premiered in Naples, but was never shown theatrically outside the local region of Campania. Subsequently it was distributed on home video by the local firm Quality Sound Video, particularly through street markets and other unofficial outlets. *I vesuviani* (1997, Italy, Pappi Corsicato, Antonietta De Lillo, Antonio Capuano, Stefano Incerti and Mario Martone), on the other hand, is a co-production between the Neapolitan company Megaris and the Rome-based Mikado and supported by funding from the State and national television; it was written and directed by five Neapolitan directors and entirely set in the city. It premiered at the Venice Film Festival and had a wide national release but its international circulation, either in festivals or theatrically, was extremely limited. *Gomorra* (Gomorrah, 2008, Italy, Matteo Garrone) is the adaptation of a non-fiction book by a Neapolitan journalist dealing with the impact of the Camorra (Neapolitan Mafia) which became an international bestseller. It was directed by a Roman-born filmmaker and produced by one of Italy's leading production companies, the

Rome-based Fandango, with funding from state and satellite TV and the support of the Italian State and European Union. But it uses several Neapolitan personnel in its crew, an exclusively Neapolitan cast, is shot in thick dialect necessitating partial subtitles for its Italian release, takes place in the specific sub-culture of the "ghetto" of Scampia on the edge of the Naples and relies entirely on local Neapolitan music for its diegetic soundtrack. It (arguably) provides a highly authentic representation of a specific sub-culture based on the author's journalistic research. The film won the Grand Prix ex-acqueo at Cannes, and was widely distributed internationally, theatrically, on home video and on television. Finally, *Gomorra—La serie* (*Gomorrah*, 2014–, Stefano Sollima *et al.*) is a TV spin-off that relies on Saviano's source material only for its sociological context and as inspiration for a few narrative moments, substituting his interlocking narratives with a more generic tale of infighting within a crime family. The series was again shot locally using local actors and dialect, but employed a more standard, national crew and was produced by national film and TV production companies (Cattleya, Fandango and Sky Italia). It was broadcast widely both nationally and internationally to critical acclaim and commercial success.

Each of these titles can be considered examples of a "regional cinema" and can be usefully studied via a regional perspective; yet each occupies a slightly different position along the regional–national–international continuum: *Cient'anne* is exclusively regional, in terms of its production, distribution and, to a large extent, content; *I vesuviani* straddles the regional and the national; and *Gomorrah* (in particular in its TV variant) encompasses regional, national and international components. While the first two titles are likely to be unknown to most readers of this volume, the *Gomorrah* adaptations may well be more familiar. Despite its generic framework and reliance on melodramatic artifice, *Cient'anne* can be seen as an authentic expression of a Neapolitan voice in the sense that its conventions express a particular Neapolitan "world-view" (see Marlow-Mann 2011: 41–69). *The Vesuvians* and the "New Neapolitan Cinema" of which it is a member have also been interpreted as offering a more authentic representation of (contemporary) Neapolitan culture (Marlow-Mann: 2011). While on a global stage, the film of *Gomorrah* has also been celebrated for its realism and rejection of gangster film cliché (or "authenticity"; see for example, Covino 2009 and Radovic 2009), which arguably derive in-large part from its origins in journalistic research and its attempt to represent the mindset of a particular sub-culture.

Glocalisation: theorising regional cinema

The "degrees of regionality" definition proposed above requires a new, and more nuanced, understanding of the relationship between regional cinema, the national and the global. Traditionally, regional cinema has been defined primarily in relation to the national. Typical, in this sense, is Carole Sklan, who builds on Steve McIntyre's idea of the opposition between "core" and "peripheral" industries (McIntyre 1985) to argue that regional cultures are defined and co-opted by the national cinema:

> 1 The centre defines what is "excellent", "innovative", "competent", "relevant", "commercially appealing", etc.
> 2 Its power requires the internalization of these beliefs by those in the peripheries, who seek to ape these values and preferences.
> 3 The centre then under-develops the peripheries by siphoning off the "productive" possibilities that emerge there, claiming them as their own, as evidence of their correctness. They can then point to what has been denied, excluded, devalued and suppressed in the periphery and say "They are just not good enough, they haven't got what it takes." (Sklan 1996: 237)

Sklan's argument suggests a hegemonic relationship in which the national dominates and subsumes the regional. It could explain the dismissal of *Cient'anne* as a failure to correspond to the values of the centre, and also the evolution across the various iterations of *Gomorrah* as the gradual siphoning off of "productive possibilities" into more easily consumed mainstream forms. This dualism also characterises the other approaches to regional cinema discussed thus far, with Jacobson arguing that "the regional does not designate a fixed geographical, social, or political reality, but rather describes a relationship of marginality to the mainstream or centralizing influence of the metropolis" (1991: 19) and with Lev positing the regional as preferable (more "authentic") to the national.

This dichotomy requires rethinking, however. Cinema has always been a global art form and its global (and transnational) dimension has only accelerated in recent decades. It has been argued that globalisation involves a flattening out, or decentralisation. If this is the case, then the centre diminishes in importance and the peripheral begins to acquire newfound significance. Indeed, this is, arguably, the subtext behind Cox's response to Parker. Parker uses the "brutal age of global capitalism" to justify subsidising a transnational UK film industry, to which Cox counters with a call to support and emphasise the kind of cultural specificity found in (peripheral) Northern filmmaking. The resurgence in regional filmmaking in recent years described above is therefore better understood not in relation to the national, but to the process of globalisation underway during this period.

First coined in Japan in relation to marketing, the notion "glocalisation" has subsequently been taken up by the fields of economics, political science and sociology to describe the role played by the local in the process of globalisation (Robertson 1992: 173–174). It maintains that globalisation does not simply entail an erasure of the local, but rather implies a complex (and sometimes contradictory) interplay between global and local forces. Examples of glocalisation would include on the one hand the way global brands are tailored to specific local realities (as in the subtly different menu and products offered by McDonald's in France, memorably debated by John Travolta in the famous "Royale with Cheese" speech in *Pulp Fiction*, 1994, USA, Quentin Tarantino), and on the other, the way small, local products such as ethnic jewellery are marketed internationally (sometimes in diluted or inauthentic forms). Both of these phenomena concern global processes but also attest to a continued significance of the local. Applied to the cinema, we could interpret glocalisation in two ways. First, when global blockbusters are adapted to locally specific cultures: through dubbing/subtitling, retitling, alternative marketing strategies, re-editing, or the insertion of locally specific elements. In certain cases, this may even impinge on production, with filmmakers adapting their vision to fit the demands of specific and lucrative foreign markets, through the adjusting of plot elements or the addition of a foreign star or location, a process that is likely to increasingly affect Hollywood films as the importance of the Asian market grows (see Lubin 2016). It may even involve adapting films and franchises from one culture to a different national and cultural context, as when Hollywood blockbuster franchises such as *Spiderman*, *Batman*, *Star Trek* and *James Bond* are regularly (and unofficially) remade and adapted for markets such as Turkey, India and the Philippines (see Smith 2017). The second example of glocalisation would be when regionally specific films are marketed to a global audience, either through remaking or reworking. Francis Veber's comedy *The Dinner Game* (1998, France) was not only remade for the English-language and US market as *Dinner for Schmucks* (2010, USA, Jay Roach), but also for the Indian market as *Bheja Fry* (2007, India, Sagar Ballary); similarly, Miramax is infamous for acquiring prestige foreign titles and then tailoring them to the US market through re-editing.

The above examples consider the process of glocalisation at the level of the national–global, but it applies equally at the sub-national level. *Gomorrah* provides a clear example

Figure 26.1 A kitsch mansion-cum-fortress within the ghetto of Scampia on the outskirts of Naples in *Gomorrah—La serie* (2014–, Italy, Stefano Sollima *et al.*). ©Cattleya/Fandango/Sky.

of this. Drawing on its non-fiction source's observations about how Hollywood films constitute a key cultural reference point for local criminals and gangsters, the film version contains several scenes in which petty criminals Ciro and Marco adopt the persona of Al Pacino's Tony Montana in *Scarface* (1983, USA, Brian De Palma) while moving through a derelict replica of his villa (a real location, reconstructed by a mob-boss from the filmic model and subsequently confiscated and abandoned after his arrest). Such a scene represents the first type of glocalisation, invoking a global cultural icon to help explain the appeal and persistence of a particular criminal mentality in the specific world of the Neapolitan ghetto around which the film revolves. In *Gomorrah—La serie* we also see a similar location in the form of crime boss Pietro Savastano's kitsch mansion-cum-fortress (this time neither derelict nor explicitly modelled on a filmic reference) (Figure 26.1). Here the operation is the opposite, and embodies the second form of glocalisation: a culturally specific trope (deriving from Saviano's non-fiction description of the homes of real life mob bosses, and thus "authentic") is invoked but inserted within the more recognisable and universal generic template of the gangster film.

We could therefore interpret the various iterations of *Gomorrah* in contrasting ways: either as the siphoning off and cultural dilution of an "authentic" expression of a regional culture for a globalised mainstream or, alternatively, as the injection of regionally specific cultural elements into a globalised art form in order to produce an interesting, exciting (and possibly more authentic) new variant on an existing template. Once again, it all depends on one's perspective: someone approaching *Gomorrah* with a regional perspective (such as a scholar of Neapolitan culture) might see the former, while someone concerned with a global perspective (such as a scholar of genre cinema) might see the latter. But both positions are valid and, if we are to form a rounded understanding of such a film, both must be embraced. An approach based around a "micro-mapping" of cultural and cinematic form would therefore involve either/or: 1) the tracing of the way various global genres, narrative forms, stylistic tropes or iconography are adapted (glocalised) to a specific regional context; 2) the identification of regionally inflected genres, narrative forms, stylistic tropes or iconography and the tracing of their movement through a variety of regional, national and global cinematic contexts.

Push and pull: factors influencing regional cinema

If films can orient themselves towards various positions along the regional–national–continuum, this raises the question of why some choose to position themselves at the regional end. Why might a film such as *Cient'anne* only be distributed locally? Is it because its concerns and approach would only be of interest to local audiences? And if so, why would a filmmaker choose such a resolutely local mode of production and address topics that have such localised appeal? In short, what factors might encourage a regional filmmaking practice?

The reasons can be divided, broadly, into industrial and cultural factors, both of which are responses to the need to carve out filmmaking opportunities within a highly competitive environment. In terms of the former, regional cinemas tend to flourish where production infrastructure, significant agglomerations of artistic or technical personnel or sources of funding emerge in locations beyond the "cinematic capital". Central government funds designed to incentivise businesses to relocate to economically underdeveloped or declining areas (either through tax breaks or other financial incentives) can stimulate local production infrastructure, as can arts funding streamed through regional bodies or local government to stimulate regional film culture. For example, Anne Jäckel describes how a Canadian regional cinema was stimulated in the Atlantic provinces through the establishment of branches of Telefilm Canada with a regional remit in both Halifax and Vancouver, together with a range of film agencies "responsible for developing film policies and providing financial and other support for developing film production locally" (Jäckel 2007: 25). (See also the discussion of the former "Regional Screen Agencies" in the UK in Newsinger 2009 and Olof Hedling's discussion of the role of regional film funds in Sweden in Chapter 11.) Film commissions may also play a role. Their remit is primarily to attract producers from the national industry or abroad to a region with a view to the benefits they bring to the local economy: generating business for local firms, bringing wealth to the economy, creating jobs and raising the region's profile, thus favouring future investment and tourism. Sometimes they provide financial incentives to attract producers, in other cases they merely provide logistical assistance and facilitate production. However, their actions can also stimulate local production, encouraging the development of a local skills-base that in turn facilitates regional production. Turin, in Northern Italy, is one example of a particularly successful confluence between an active film commission and funding via the regional government (see Cuoco 2013 and Ferrero-Regis 2009).

The presence of film and arts institutions, including film festivals, also plays a key role. The Sundance Film Festival began as the Utah/US Film Festival with an explicit regional remit (see Jacobson 1991: 18), but even in its later incarnation it played a key role by giving space and prominence to American Indies—including regional films. Smaller local festivals often provide a window for locally shot films that might not be widely seen theatrically otherwise. Film festivals also stimulate local film culture, which can in turn encourage local production. While South Korea's national and cinematic capital remains Seoul, the seaside town of Busan's role as the site of East Asia's most significant film festival, together with its state of the art film centre, has stimulated local film culture and raised the film's profile, which in turn has arguably contributed to its newfound prominence on cinema screens: 24 films were shot in the town in 2014 (Lee 2013) (Figure 26.2). Similarly, film schools or universities offering practical film courses do not solely feed the national industry, but also provide a hub to nurture filmmaking outside the capital.

Sometimes, the success of an individual filmmaker who has chosen to shoot in his home region for personal (as much as for business) reasons is sufficient to stimulate the regional scene. The success of Shane Meadows (*Once Upon a Time in the Midlands*, 2002, UK; *Dead Man's Shoes*, 2004, UK; *This Is England*, 2006, UK) was instrumental in the growth of a North (of)

Figure 26.2 The Busan Cinema Center, site of Asia's premier film festival, the Busan International Film Festival, has stimulated film culture in the seaside town. ©Alex Marlow-Mann.

Midlands regional cinema, helping to launch the production company Warp Films (http://warpfilms.com/), as well as facilitating actor Paddy Considine's move behind the camera to make the Leeds-set *Tyrannosaur* (2011, UK), also produced by Warp (see Spicer and Presence 2016). Similar examples in other geographical contexts include Richard Linklater, who has had a significant impact on the film scene in Austin, Texas (see Stone 2013) and Peter Jackson, whose phenomenal success with the *Lord of the Rings* films and whose production company, WingNut Films, and special effects company, Weta Digital, have contributed to the development of a significant skill base and production infrastructure in Wellington, New Zealand, away from the greater metropolis of Auckland.

In terms of cultural factors, distinct regional cinemas tend to arise in areas that have a strong cultural identity that is markedly distinct from that of the nation as a whole. This identity may be due to differences in language, religion or ethnicity, or to historical or political factors. Perhaps the most dramatic example of such culturally driven regional cinemas in the world can be found in India, and this is due to the size of the nation, the multiplicity of languages spoken, the religious and cultural differences, and historical–political factors, coupled with the fact that this is probably the largest film industry in the world, producing 700–1000 films annually (Benei 2008: 84). Not only are there numerous, large-scale regional industries in India, but many of these have clear regional identities and distinct aesthetics. Best known, of course, is Bollywood—Hindi-language cinema produced primarily in Mumbai; this is arguably the closest thing to an Indian national cinema. This cinema is very distinct from "Tollywood", the Bengali-language filmmaking centred around Kolkata, best known for the "parallel cinema" art films of filmmakers such as Satyajit Ray and Ritwik Ghatak. Internationally this is probably the second most recognisable form of "Indian" cinema. However, the region responsible for the largest number of films after Mumbai—as well as the site of the largest studios—is centred around Hyderabad, producing films in the Telugu language. Then there is "Kollywood", produced in the state of Tamil Nadu, primarily (but not solely) in the Tamil language; "Chandanavana" or "Sandalwood", based in

Bengalaru in the state of Karnataka; and many, many more (for a general overview of Indian regional cinemas, see Saran 2012).

The regional complexities of Indian cinema are even greater than this brief overview suggests, however. In Chapter 17, Madhuja Mukherjee explains how Hindi-language cinema was not limited solely to Mumbai, but rather straddled regions and was affected by historical and political factors such as the ascendancy of the Bengali bourgeoisie and the post-Independence partition of the nation. Thus it is clear that historical and political factors also play a key role in determining the existence of certain regional cinema. A good example here is that of Basque cinema. The granting of regional autonomy in 1979 during the period of transition that followed the death of Franco led the Comunidad Autónoma del País Vasco [later Euskadi] to implement supportive and protectionist measures to stimulate a Basque cinema, filling a gap left by the Miró Law governing national production in Spain (Stone and Rodríguez 2015: 4–6). However, the existence of a "Basque cinema" depends less on government decrees and institutional initiatives than it does on a sense of Basque identity, an inherently political "sentiment" of belonging, of being Basque rather than (or in addition to) being Spanish, that unites both filmmakers and audiences (see Stone and Rodríguez 2015 and Chapter 21). Sometimes the political nature of this regional impulse can be sufficient to lead regional filmmakers into direct conflict with State censorship and the national cinema, as in the case of the persecution of Georgian/Ukrainian filmmaker Sergei Parajanov in the Soviet Union and the censorship of his "Ukrainian" film *Tini zabutykh predki* (Shadows of Forgotten Ancestors, 1965, USSR) and "Armenian" film *Sayat Nova* (The Color of Pomegranates, 1969, USSR) (Figure 26.3).

Thus, regional cinemas can be the result not only of a "push" (stimuli from governments, funding bodies and institutions) but also a "pull" (the desire to express—or see expressed—a regional identity deriving from linguistic, cultural or political differences). Regional cinemas are

Figure 26.3 The depiction of Armenian culture in *Sayat Nova* (*The Color of Pomegranates*, 1969, USSR) brought director Sergei Parajanov into conflict with the Soviet authorities. ©Armenfilm.

most likely to form where there is a confluence of these factors. In the case of Naples, we can see how the flourishing of a regional cinema was influenced by a variety of factors. The collaborative anthology *I vesuviani* was the product of an agglomeration of creative personnel that developed around the creative hub of Teatri Uniti, a theatrical collective that achieved prominence in the previous decade. However, it was also an indirect product of government subsidies stimulating investment in the less economically developed South, given that the producers had relocated to their native Naples from the cinematic capital of Rome in order to take advantage of such streams. Historical, cultural and political factors are also significant. Naples has a strong and distinct cultural identity that results from the fact that Italy was only unified a century and a half ago and that, prior to that, Naples was the capital of an independent nation and home to a monarchy. A strong sense of Neapolitan identity and a certain degree of alienation from the national body politic have favoured the evolution of distinct and readily identifiable cultural traditions (particularly in music and theatre), and this undoubtedly drove the production of *Cient'anne*. Similarly, Saviano's documentation of a particular, distinctive and oppositional subculture in the Neapolitan periphery provided the impetus behind *Gomorrah*.

From regional to national and back again: historicising regional cinema

Regional cinemas, then, are the product of a confluence of "push" and "pull" factors that are necessarily historically contingent and therefore emerge in particular places at particular times. It is difficult to historicise the evolution of regional cinema in global terms since there are enormous variations in the cultural and political factors affecting different regions. One of the central claims of this essay is the need for a "regional turn" that pays attention to these variations and employs regionally specialist knowledge in order to "micro-map" such specificities, including their historical evolution. I will therefore limit myself to a number of general observations regarding large-scale technological and industrial shifts that have influenced the fortunes of regional cinemas at different period. I will also limit myself to Britain and the US as (not-necessarily typical) case studies.

The "pre-industrial" cinema of the late nineteenth/early twentieth century was, to all intents and purposes, regional: produced at local level by inventors and entrepreneurs. In Britain we can find early pioneers in cities such as Brighton and Sheffield. The documentary film *Holmfirth Hollywood* (2006, UK, Steve Webb), for example, charts how a small village in Yorkshire for a short while became a significant centre of film production thanks to the filmmaker James Bamforth and camera manufacturers the Riley Brothers, based in nearby Bradford. It is only when filmmaking began to adopt production-line processes and evolved into an industry that true "cinematic capitals" begin to emerge. In the case of the US this occurred when filmmakers headed West in an effort to escape the stranglehold over patents held by New York-based firms and the unpredictable East Coast weather, in so doing establishing the cinematic capital of Hollywood. Significantly this process of industrialisation also resulted in the emergence of the concept of "national cinema", as America began to establish its global dominance and European film industries (in particular) attempted to create distinctive identities in order to compete. Thus, the transition from dispersed regional cinemas to concentrated national cinemas resulted from both economic imperatives (standardisation of production; agglomeration) and political and cultural ones (the promotion of national identity). The dominance of the national cinema model was then reinforced by the coming of sound, introducing the problematic question of language for the first time.

In the US, the resurgence in regional cinemas was a result of the break-up of the studio system and the end of the classical era. John Cassavetes' *Shadows* (1959, USA) was shot in

Figure 26.4 John Cassavetes' New York-based *Shadows* (1959, USA) differed markedly from the national cinema model produced in Hollywood. ©Lion International.

New York by a native New Yorker (albeit one who had relocated to Los Angeles), offering a strong air of cultural specificity and authenticity and an aesthetic markedly different from that of the national cinema produced in the cinematic capital of Hollywood (Figure 26.4). It heralded not only a revitalisation of American amateur filmmaking but also the possibilities for the subsequent emergence of an alternative, independent regional cinema. Similarly, in the UK the alternative aesthetics promoted by the London-based "Free Cinema" filmmakers led them to head North to film a series of social realist dramas such as *Saturday Night and Sunday Morning* (1960, UK, Karel Reisz) and *This Sporting Life* (1963, UK, Lindsay Anderson), inaugurating the tradition to which Cox alluded in his speech. Although these films were essentially "runaway productions" of the cinematic capital, their attempt to escape the artifice of the studio-bound, mainstream (national) model in favour of a greater authenticity also implicated a rediscovery of (regional) cultural specificity. But it was not only the search for authenticity and the desire for independence that drove the resurgence in regional filmmaking, but also commercial opportunism. In the US, the possibilities for turning a quick buck via the drive-in circuit, the particularities of regional booking and exhibition practices such as "four walling" (the hiring of venues by filmmakers to screen their own films) allowed regional filmmakers working in the exploitation ghetto to flourish: from David Friedman and Herschell Gordon Lewis (in Chicago first then Miami) to George A. Romero (in Pittsburgh) (for a more detailed look at American regional filmmaking in the exploitation sector, see Thrower 2008). At the same time, the development of smaller and lighter cameras and faster film stocks requiring less light also began the process of liberating potential filmmakers from the technical and industrial demands of the commercial industry and thus also facilitating production away from the cinematic capital. In the 1980s, the arrival of video (as both a production and exhibition medium) created new possibilities for regional filmmaking and distribution. This process accelerated dramatically in the 2000s with the development of affordable, high definition digital technology, on the one hand, and the alternative distribution and marketing possibilities offered by Web 2.0, on the other. A dramatic expansion of regional cinema is now undoubtedly underway, even if much of this lies beyond the traditional definition of "cinema" (feature length, theatrically distributed feature films).

New technologies have thus allowed filmmakers to make films much more cheaply and to a large extent freed them from the reliance on the expensive and cumbersome infrastructure of the traditional mainstream filmmaking process—making the "pull" less dependent on the "push". It is now much easier for someone to simply begin making "films" in their home town—and making them available to global audiences—than it was throughout the twentieth century, and the explosion of film festivals and the emergence of university filmmaking courses during the same period has only facilitated this further. Writing in the mid-1980s about filmmaking in Texas, Peter Lev expressed reservations that "independent regional production is in some ways a utopian dream" (Lev 1986: 60). Two decades later, technological developments seem to have rendered these concerns obsolete.

Micromapping: studying regional cinemas

New technologies and globalisation have thus diminished the dominance of "core" national industries (partially) decentralising and flattening out the filmmaking map and reorienting it towards the isolated pockets of production found in cinema's early years. Clearly this is not an absolute process but rather one that exists in a fragile dialectic with the concurrent homogenisation of an increasingly placeless global mainstream. Film Studies needs to respond to both of these processes, adopting both a transnational, macro-perspective and a glocalised, micro-one. What, then, are the possibilities for a glocalisation of film studies and what is the current state of scholarship?

As with national cinema, we can approach the regional from a variety of perspectives: economic, text-based, exhibition-led and criticism-led (Higson 1989). Thus far, exhibition-led approaches are the most prevalent examples of glocalised film studies, as in the numerous (small scale) studies of local film culture, exhibition and audiences, often carried out by committed amateurs or local (film) historians and/or produced or supported by local bodies (see, for example, the "Cinema St. Andrews" project, http://cinemastandrews.org.uk/). A particularly interesting and sophisticated example of exhibition-led, glocalised scholarship would be the AHRC-funded research project headed by John Caughie that utilises geo-databases to chart the circulation of early cinema within and across Scotland (see Vélez-Serna and Caughie: 2015). This work was published as part of a special issue of the *International Journal of Humanities and Arts Computing* dedicated to "Exploring Geocultural Space: New Horizons in Digital Humanities Research" which also features Christian B. Long's regional mapping of the trajectories of French mainstream hits using ArcGIS technology (Long 2015). Both of these constitute clear examples of a "micro-mapping" of distribution and exhibition practice. As far as studies of individual regional cinemas are concerned, the book series "Luci sulla città" [City Lights] edited by Marsilio on the cinemas of individual Italian cities provides a good example of the combination of a primarily economic and exhibition-based approach, examining the films produced and the film exhibition that takes place in a particular city. The aforementioned works on Neapolitan and Basque cinema by Marlow-Mann (2011) and Stone and Rodríguez (2015), respectively, attempt a more holistic approach, examining the economic production context and the circulation of films but devoting particular attention to the thematic and stylistic peculiarities of their individual cinemas and the processes by which a "regional cinema" is constructed.

The above is not an exhaustive list of glocalised film studies (and nor does it intend to be), but rather an indication of possible approaches. Nevertheless, the study of individual regional cinemas remains at this time a seriously underdeveloped field and this makes the subject potentially one of the most productive areas for future study. Just as the transnational perspective has in recent years provided both a useful corrective to the previously dominant national cinema tradition and a fruitful new avenue of scholarship, so the regional approach may offer new areas and lines of enquiry in the future.

References

Benei, V. (2008) "Globalization and Regional(ist) Cinema in Western India: Public Culture, Private Media, and the Reproduction of a Hindu National(ist) Hero, 1930s–2000s", *South Asian Popular Culture* 7 (2): 83–108.

Covino, M. (2009) "La malavita: *Gomorrah* and Naples", in *Film Quarterly* 62 (4): 72–75.

Cox, A. (2004) "A Call to Arms: Alex Cox Addresses the Film Parliament", *The Journal of British Cinema and Television* 1: 112–119.

Cuoco, M. (2013) "The State to the Regions: The Devolution of Italian Cinema", *Journal of Italian Cinema and Media Studies* 1 (3): 263–277.

Ferrero-Regis, T. (2009) *Recent Italian Cinema: Spaces, Contexts, Experiences*, Leicester: Troubadour.

Higson, A. (1989) "The Concept of National Cinema", *Screen* 30 (4): 36–46.

Iordanova D. (2016) "Choosing the Transnational", *Frames Cinema Journal*, 9 April, http://framescinema journal.com/article/choosing-the-transnational/.

Jäckel, A. (2007) "Film Policy and Practice in Canadian Regional Cinema: The Case of the Atlantic Provinces", *British Journal of Canadian Studies* 20 (1): 25–50.

Jacobson, B. (1991) "Regional Film: A Strategic Discourse in the Global Marketplace", *Journal of Film and Video* 43 (4): 18–32.

Lee, E. (2013) "24 Feature Films Shot on Location in Busan in 2012", *Korean Film News*, 8 January, http://m.koreanfilm.or.kr/mobile4/jsp/News/KoreanFilmsNewsView.jsp?blbdComCd=601006&seq=2151.

Lev, P. (1986) "Regional Cinema and the Films of Texas", *Journal of Film and Video* 38 (1): 60–65.

Long, C. (2015) "Where Is French Cinema, 1976–2013?" *International Journal of Humanities and Arts Computing* 9 (2): 180–195.

Lubin, G. (2016) "18 Hollywood Movies That Pandered to China's Giant Box Office", *Business Insider UK*, 14 October, http://uk.businessinsider.com/hollywood-movies-in-china-2016-10?op=1&r=US&IR=T/ - marvels-doctor-strange-changed-the-ancient-one-from-tibetan-in-the-comics-to-celtic-if-you-acknowledge-that-tibet-is-a-place-and-that-hes-tibetan-you-risk-alienating-o.

McIntyre, S. (1985) "National Film Cultures: Politics and Peripheries", *Screen* 26 (1): 66–78.

Marlow-Mann, A. (2011) *The New Neapolitan Cinema*, Edinburgh: Edinburgh University Press.

Radovic, R. (2009) "McMafia Rising", *Film International* 7 (1): 6–11.

Robertson, R. (1992) *Globalization: Social Theory and Global Culture*, London/Thousand Oaks/New Delhi: Sage Publications.

Saran, R. (2012) *History of Indian Cinema*, New Delhi: Diamond Books.

Sklan, C. (1996) "Peripheral Visions: Regionalism, Nationalism, Internationalism", in *Film Policy: International, National and Regional Perspectives*, London and New York: Routledge.

Smith, I. R. (2017) *The Hollywood Meme: Transnational Adaptations in World Cinema*, Edinburgh: Edinburgh University Press.

Spicer, A. and Presence, S. (2016) "Autonomy and Dependency in Two Successful UK Film and Television Companies: An Analysis of RED Production Company and Warp Films", *Film Studies* 14, Spring: 5–31.

Stone, R. (2013) "Locating Linklater", in *Walk Don't Run: The Cinema of Richard Linklater*, London and New York: Wallflower Press, 7–38.

Stone, R. and Rodríguez, M. P. (2015) *Basque Cinema: A Cultural and Political History*, London and New York: I.B. Tauris.

Thrower, S. (2008) *Nightmare USA: The Untold Story of the Exploitation Independents*, Goldalming: FAB Press.

Vélez-Serna, M.A. and Caughie, J. (2015) "Remote Locations: Early Scottish Scenic Films and Geo-databases", *International Journal of Humanities and Arts Computing* 9 (2): 164–179.

27

GLOBAL WOMEN'S CINEMA

Kate Ince

In the twenty-first century, a literature suggesting that women's cinema be considered as (a) world cinema has begun to emerge. Both of these terms—"women's cinema" and "world cinema"—are contested labels with multiple possible meanings, which makes an introductory summary of debates about their usage advisable, but before offering even this, a quotation from feminist film scholar Kathleen McHugh's article "The World and the Soup: Historicizing Media Feminisms in Transnational Contexts" (McHugh 2009) will show how what she calls the "problem of the world" has been engaged with afresh in twenty-first-century feminist film studies:

> In the past decade, feminist film scholars have employed a number of strategies to engage this "problem of the world" and the distinct, often paradoxical *transnational* cultural specificities of women's and feminist film production. They have recovered and remobilised the concept of "women's cinema," first popularised by Anglophone scholars such as Claire Johnston, and submitted it to the politics of location, charting its instantiation across and through different cultural contexts and modes of production. In monographs, articles, and special issues of journals, their work advances transnational conceptual frameworks such as "minor cinema" or "women's cinema as world cinema" to apprehend women's creative, diverse, and transnational contributions to cinema systematically, beyond encyclopaedic reference and national or regional formats.
>
> *(McHugh 2009: 118)*

Here McHugh refers first to Ella Shohat's essay "Post-Third-Worldist Culture: Gender, Nation and the Cinema", then (along with Claire Johnston's discussion of women's cinema in her 1973 essay "Women's Cinema as Counter-Cinema") to Adrienne Rich's coinage of the concept of "the politics of location" in an essay included in Rich's *Blood, Bread, and Poetry: Selected Prose 1979–1985*. The "transnational conceptual frameworks" of "minor cinema" and "women's cinema and world cinema" she alludes to next were offered in Alison Butler's book *Women's Cinema: The Contested Screen* (2002), and by Patricia White, first in the *Global Cartographies of Cine-Feminisms* programme for a conference held in April 2008 at Ewha Woman's University, Seoul, South Korea (McHugh 2009: 144n18) and more recently in *Women's Cinema, World Cinema: Projecting Contemporary Feminisms*. Another recent book-length study that advances discussion of women's cinema as a global phenomenon is Sophie Mayer's *Political Animals: The New Feminist Cinema* (2016), an energetic manifesto for women's filmmaking that ranges from the "world-beating cultural phenomenon" (Mayer 2016: 1) that is the 2013 Disney production *Frozen* (written and co-directed by Jennifer Lee) to a considerable number of films directed by Mexican, African and Chinese women. The subject of both *Women's Cinema, World Cinema* and *Political Animals* is twenty-first century film: White confirms that her book's primary focus "is on directors who made their first features after 2000" (White 2015: 7) after explaining how "the contours of women's cinema [were] redrawn by shifts in global production, circulation, and evaluation of films as well as by changing perceptions and practices of feminism" (White 2015: 6) in the first decade of the 2000s. Mayer, after citing White's attention to "'the worlding of women's cinema' and 'the gendering of world cinema' as twenty-first-century effects", insists that what is new about the "new feminist cinema" of the twenty-first century is "its negotiation of a transgenerational feminist film history of four decades within a reflexive awareness of the interruption and re-vision of feminisms, and interconnectedly of film cultures, in the new millennium" (Mayer 2016: 5–6).

Butler's *Women's Cinema: the Contested Screen* (2002) has perhaps come closer than any other to tracing a genealogy of its titular concept, the early popularisation of which is linked by McHugh to Claire Johnston's work of the first half of the 1970s. Its contestatory character is explained by Butler as follows:

> Women's cinema is not "at home" in any of the host of cinematic or national discourses it inhabits, but [...] is always an inflected mode, incorporating, reworking and contesting the conventions of established traditions [...] The distinctiveness of women's filmmaking is therefore not based on an essentialist understanding of gendered subjectivity, but on the position—or positions—of women in contemporary culture [...]: neither included within nor excluded from cultural traditions, lacking a cohesive collective identity but yet not absolutely differentiated from each other.
>
> *(Butler 2002: 22)*

Citing exactly these two sentences approvingly, White expresses her matching sense "of the anti-essentialist and essential project of connecting up all kinds of women's interventions in the medium of cinema with each other" (White 2015: 13). Butler ended her book with a discussion of Deepa Mehta's *Fire* (1996, Canada/India) that summed the film up as "an imperfect women's film, which rises to some of the challenges of transnationalism but fails to negotiate others" (Butler 2002: 123), thus signalling a connection between her own idea of women's cinema as minor cinema and the transnationalism explored in much greater depth by critics such as White. White, who mentions that "some might find the term [women's cinema] dated to the analogue era of second-wave feminism" but firmly counters this tendency by stating that "the discursive terrain referenced by women's cinema is still very much at stake" (White 2015: 3), observes that questions of gender have yet to be "significantly" brought together with the remappings of World Cinema currently being undertaken by scholars of film, postcolonial studies and transnational studies in many countries worldwide (White 2015: 6). Her own book and Mayer's *Political Animals* have decisively advanced this *rapprochement* of fields, and this is to my mind partly because both authors do not run away from the cries of "essentialism!" and "ghettoisation!" that the concept of women's cinema has often inspired, electing instead to view it positively and with an open mind. The project of "connecting up all kinds of women's interventions in the medium of cinema with each other" (White 2015: 13) requires a drive towards inclusivity and a resolve to bring together not just practitioners working in locations far removed from one another, but critical and theoretical perspectives and literatures not often enough considered in the same frame. The survey of twenty-first-century women's filmmaking worldwide around which this essay is organised will emphasise connection and inclusivity over fragmentation and exclusion, and my intention in supplying it is to imitate White's strategy in *Women's Cinema, World Cinema*, where she contributes to making women's cinema a worldwide phenomenon by discussing it in those terms.

As Saër Maty Bâ and Will Higbee note in the introduction to their co-edited volume *De-westernizing Film Studies*, contemporary moving image culture "is more globalized and diversified than at any time in its history" (Bâ and Higbee 2012: 1). The fragmentation and disconnection that the forces of twenty-first-century global capitalism threaten would seem to make the work of "connecting up" all the more important, and Bâ and Higbee, like White and Mayer, mention its importance to their project:

> *De-Westernizing Film Studies* complicates and/or rethinks how local, national, and regional film cultures "connect" globally, seeking polycentric, multi-directional, non-essentialised alternatives to Eurocentric theoretical and historical perspectives found in film as both an artistic medium and an academic field of study.
>
> *(Bâ and Higbee 2012: 1)*

The above description seems entirely pertinent to the approach White takes to women's cinema as a field in *Women's Cinema, World Cinema*, and I shall for this reason be guided by it too when setting out the understanding of women's cinema as (a) world cinema that I formulate in the rest of this chapter. In entitling their book *De-Westernizing Film Studies*, Bâ and Higbee are forging, by means of novel terminology, a path that overlaps with twenty-first-century debates about World Cinema while remaining distinct from them. The "polycentric, multi-directional, non-essentialized alternatives to Eurocentric theoretical and historical perspectives" (Bâ and Higbee 2012: 1) that they say they are seeking have also been sought in much of the work on World Cinema drawn on by contributors to their volume, and I shall comment briefly on this set of debates before looking more closely at the geopolitics of contemporary women's filmmaking.

Polycentric multiculturalism versus uncentred inclusivity: World Cinema in the twenty-first century

In "Situating world cinema as a theoretical problem", the introduction to their edited collection *Remapping World Cinema* (2006), Stephanie Dennison and Song Hwee Lim note that World Cinema shares with world literature "an investment in the Third World and the postcolonial" (Dennison and Lim 2006: 2). An emergent field of study that film studies was grappling with as Dennison and Lim prepared their volume and that is younger than either postcolonial studies and Third World Studies is transnational studies, which must now be added to the list of interdisciplinary areas essential to any mode or medium of culture qualified by "world". Since Third Worldism and postcolonial studies predate scholarship on the transnational, however, feminists engaged with them earlier, leading to key publications in feminist postcolonialism such as Ella Shohat's "Post-Third-Worldist Culture: Gender, Nation and the Cinema" (1997). Appearing shortly after *Unthinking Eurocentrism* (Shohat and Stam 1994), the volume of postcolonial criticism Shohat co-wrote with Robert Stam, Shohat's essay discusses a range of feminist film and video works produced between the 1970s and the mid-1990s, declaring that she means this "as a simultaneous critique both of Third-Worldist anticolonial nationalism and of First-World Eurocentric feminism" (Shohat 1997: 184). The Eurocentrism—or at least, thoroughgoing Western-ness—of feminist film theory of the 1970s and 1980s is undeniable, and Shohat's critique pinpoints how the "generally monocultural agenda" (Shohat 1997: 184) it pursued inhibited the located, material politics espoused by multicultural feminists:

> Prestigious feminist film journals have too often ignored the scholarly and cultural feminist work performed in relation to particular Third-Worldist national and racial media contexts; feminist work to empower women within the boundaries of their Third-World communities was dismissed as merely nationalist, not "quite yet" feminist. Universalizing the parameters for feminism and using such ahistorical psychoanalytical categories as "desire", "fetishism", and "castration" led to a discussion of "the female body" and "the female spectator" that was ungrounded in the many different—even opposing—women's experiences, agendas, and political visions.
>
> *(Shohat 1997: 185)*

Offering a list of eleven "Third-Worldist" women filmmakers from Guadeloupe, Colombia, Lebanon, Cuba, Senegal, India, Sri Lanka, Brazil, Egypt, Tunisia and Puerto Rico, Shohat asks rhetorically whether their prominence at Third-World "rather than feminist film programs and conferences" (Shohat 1997: 185) can be a coincidence. That Third-Worldist anticolonial nationalism as well as this First-World Eurocentric feminism is the target of her critique is assured by Shohat's principal focus on later generations of female filmmakers than the eleven Third-Worldist women she lists initially, and by her illustration of how the revolutionary paradigm they adopted was anchored in "the resistance work these women have performed within their communities and nations" (Shohat 1997: 186), always part of a local and specific struggle, and always multicultural rather than monocultural. What she is attempting to do in "Post-Third-Worldist Culture: Gender, Nation and the Cinema" is "to forge a 'beginning' of a post-Third-Worldist narrative for recent film and video work by diverse Third-World, multicultural, diasporic feminists" (Shohat 1997: 187), and this entails situating the work in question "between gender/sexuality and nation/race" (Shohat 1997: 187), after the narratives of women's liberation and anticolonial revolution yet before the post-postmodern and post-decolonialising stage of globalisation that began at around the turn of the new millennium. By 1997 the term "Third World" itself had begun to be viewed "as an inconvenient relic of a more militant period" (Shohat 1997: 188), and the Three-worlds theory and accompanying Three-cinema theory in which "First Cinema is cinema made in Hollywood, Second Cinema is the *auteur* cinema of the *nouvelle vague* or Cinema Novo, and Third Cinema is a cinema of liberation films "that the System cannot assimilate and which are foreign to its needs, or [. . .] film that directly and explicitly sets out to fight the system" (Dennison and Lim 2006: 5) had come to seem simplistic and homogenising, limiting in its genderedness in comparison to the work of feminist critics such as the Egyptian Nawal El-Saadawi, the Indian Vinz Mazumdar, the Sri Lankan Kumari Jayawardena, the Moroccan Fatima Mernissi and the Brazilian Lelia Gonzales (Shohat 1997: 188).

Dudley Andrew's chapter in Dennison and Lim's collection drew attention to the importance of Shohat and Stam's *Unthinking Eurocentrism* as "a first and crucial 'World Cinema' textbook" (Dennison and Lim 2006: 5). *Unthinking Eurocentrism* had included a call for polycentric filmmaking intended to directly challenge the "Hollywood and the rest" thinking that dominated early contributions to debates about world cinema, such as Wimal Dissanayake's chapter "Issues in World Cinema" for *The Oxford Guide to Film Studies* (1998) and John Hill and Pamela Church Gibson's *World Cinema: Critical Approaches* (2000). The notion of polycentrism is decisively taken up by Lucia Nagib in her essay for *Remapping World Cinema*, "Towards a positive definition of World Cinema", which she begins by stating the indisputable truth that to define "world cinema" as "non-Hollywood cinema" is a "restrictive" and "negative" (Nagib 2006: 30) approach to the phenomenon at issue. The Three-worlds and Three-cinema theory whose insufficiency for a post-national and diasporic world Shohat had sought to update in "Post-Third-Worldist Cinema" also fails to satisfy Nagib, at least in the manner it is drawn on in two books that appeared in 2003, Guneratne and Dissanayake's *Rethinking Third Cinema* and James Chapman's *Cinemas of the World*, which is divided into three sections entitled "Hollywood Cinema", "European Cinemas" and "World Cinemas" respectively. "The result of viewing world cinema as 'alternative' and 'different' is that the American paradigm continues to prevail as a tool for its evaluation", Nagib warns (Nagib 2006: 31). Despite approving of the awareness of and concern about "the reduction and simplification entailed by the binary approach" shown by Andrew in "An Atlas of World Cinema" (Andrew 2006), Nagib still finds echoes of the binary opposition between Hollywood and the rest of the world in his vocabulary (Nagib 2006: 33). Insisting that "[a] truly encompassing and democratic approach has to get rid of the binary system as a whole", the only fellow critics Nagib wholeheartedly endorses are Shohat and Stam, who "dismiss as unnecessary and ultimately wrong the world division between 'us' and the 'other', 'centre and periphery', 'the West and the Rest'" (Nagib 2006: 34).

It is no surprise, given the preference for Shohat and Stam's approach to world cinema(s) Nagib states in "Towards a Positive definition of World Cinema", that agreement with their concept of "polycentric multiculturalism" recurs in the 2012 collection she co-edited with Chris Perriam and Rajinder Dudrah, *Theorizing World Cinema* (Nagib *et al.* 2012). To what extent this volume actually does any theorising is questionable, however, as the editors state in their introduction that their understanding of "theory" "follows David Bordwell and Noël Carroll's suggestion [in *Post-Theory: Reconstructing Film Studies* in 1996] of in-depth research on representative cases" (Nagib *et al.* 2012: xxii). The last sentence of their introduction refers to "the polycentric method" to studying World Cinema, and this elision of theory and method picks up on some corresponding grey areas in the concluding paragraphs of "Towards a Positive Definition of World Cinema". Here, Nagib states her view that "the belief in a centre is as mythic as the quest for origins" (Nagib 2006: 34), and her preference for "a method in which Hollywood and the West would cease to be the centre of film history". In the new tripartite definition of World Cinema that opens the conclusion to her essay, Nagib says that World Cinema "has no centre" (Nagib 2006: 35). It is no small quibble to point out the contradiction between polycentrism and uncentredness, and I would maintain that it is on account of not thinking through this contradiction that other statements in Nagib's conclusion—that World Cinema "is a global process" and "is circulation"—fail to convince. In the conclusion's second bullet point, she suggests that "[w]orld cinema is not a discipline, but a method" (Nagib 2006: 35), a formulation that ignores Dennison and Lim's highly persuasive argument in "Situating World Cinema as a Theoretical Problem" (Dennison and Lim 2006: 6–9) for thinking of World Cinema as a discipline *as well* as a methodology and a perspective. The definition of "World Cinema" that the title of Nagib's essay identifies as the ultimate objective of her thinking is at its *most* positive when she says "I propose, following Shohat and Stam's suggestion, the inclusive method of a world made of interconnected cinemas" (Nagib 2006: 34)—but polycentrism does not figure in this formulation. I shall return to these points about centredness, disciplinarity and method(ology) in the conclusion to this essay, but turn now to its *raison d'être*, the survey of twenty-first-century worldwide women's filmmaking.

Women's cinema goes global

In Kathleen McHugh's *Camera Obscura* article from which I quoted at the start of this essay, McHugh refers to the many monographs, articles and special journal issues through which the *systematic* apprehension of women's "creative, diverse and transnational contributions to cinema" has now begun, following calls such as Pam Cook's in 1998 for a *positive* recognition of "the historical contribution of women to cinema across the board" (Cook 1998: 244). Cook went on:

> This involves a shift in perception—away from counting the relatively small numbers of female directors towards a more historical and contextual analysis of different points of entry into the industry by women, in what is, after all, a collaborative medium. The influence of female audiences, and the considerable impact of feminism—or should I say feminisms—across the full range of production have scarcely begun to be addressed.
> *(Cook 1998: 244)*

At present, such positive evaluation of women's contributions to the world's film industries is indisputably underway, but far more developed in the West—the collaborative project that launched the UK's Women's Film and Television History Network between 2009 and 2011 is a prime example—than in the countries and regions without a documented tradition of women's filmmaking. A rapid survey of the countries and regions for which a twenty-first-century breakthrough into visibility by female directors (for their films and themselves) can be claimed is a near-impossible task, but I shall attempt to construct one nonetheless, by drawing on material from White's *Women's Cinema, World Cinema* and Mayer's *Political Animals*, where possible observing trends in this "worlding of women's cinema" (White 2015: 8–14) as I do so.

The two "continents" whose novelty as "producers" of female film directors is most obvious in White's and Mayer's books are East Asia—China, Taiwan, Korea and Japan—and Central and Latin America, particularly Argentina and Peru. There is also a history of women's filmmaking in Latin America in the twentieth century, of course, but a director such as Lucrecia Martel, who shot one feature-length film alongside a number of shorts in the 1990s but only found success in the 2000s with *La ciénaga* (The Swamp, 2001, Argentina/France/Spain/Japan), *La niña santa* (The Holy Girl, 2004, Argentina/Italy/Netherlands/Spain) and *La mujer sin cabeza* (The Headless Woman, 2008, Argentina/France/Italy/Spain), has contributed significantly to the renewed global profile of Argentine filmmaking, along with compatriot Lucía Puenzo, whose *XXY* (2007, Argentina/Spain/France), *El niño pez* (The Fish Child, 2009, Argentina/France/Spain) and *Wakolda* (The German Doctor, 2013, Argentina/Spain/Norway/France) have garnered considerable acclaim. Another Latin American director closely considered by White is Peruvian Claudia Llosa, of whose work White says "[it] inhabits the spaces of contemporary world cinema in a way that is emblematic for this book" (White 2015: 187). Women's filmmaking in China, spearheaded by directors such as Ning Ying, Guo Xiaolu, Li Yu and Liu Jiayin has already been written about as a transnational cinema by Lingzhen Wang in *Chinese Women's Cinema: Transnational Perspectives*, from which White quotes a sentence in the introduction to *Women's Cinema, World Cinema* that is entirely supportive of the theme of her book as well as my argument in this essay: "Feminist film studies must step outside the restrictive framework of the nation-state and critically resituate gender and cinema in a transnational feminist configuration that enables examination of relations and power and knowledge among and within cultures" (White 2015: 12). Over half of White's chapter on Asian Women Directors (the only area-based chapter of five) is devoted to Taiwanese director Zero Chou, whose film *Ci qinq*

(Spider Lilies, 2007, Taiwan) won Best Feature at the Berlin International Film Festival even before going on general release in Taiwan and across Asia, and was followed in 2008 by *Piao lang qinq chun* (Drifting Flowers, 2008, Taiwan), which travelled the international film festival circuit almost as much as *Spider Lilies*. Chou's status as an out lesbian as well as her thematisation of lesbianism and gay male sexualities has considerably expanded the profile of Asian queer cinema, to which Hong Kong-based directors Yau Ching (*Ho yuk* [Let's Love Hong Kong, 2001, Hong Kong]) and Ann Hui (*Duk haan chau faan* [All About Love, 2010, Hong Kong]) also drew attention in the 2000s.

A double parallel between fifth-generation Chinese film directors and recent sub-Saharan African cinema is drawn by White in the introduction to *Women's Cinema, World Cinema* when she notes that "strong central female characters are signature features" of these films and that "women directors working in these movements are much less well known internationally and receive less support at home" (White 2015: 6). The paucity of sub-Saharan African female filmmakers with an international reputation has long been noted by feminist film critics: where are the women *auteurs* to stand alongside Abderrahmane Sissako and Souleymane Cissé? White offers little commentary on African women's filmmaking, somewhat more of which is provided by Mayer in *Political Animals*, who picks out a "singular" feature film of the 2000s directed by Fante Régina Nacro, *La nuit de la verité* (The Night of Truth, 2004, Burkina Faso/France), "a rare example of a feature by an African female filmmaker to receive international distribution" (Mayer 2016: 65). *The Night of Truth* resembles Claire Denis' third Africa-based feature *White Material* (2009, France/Cameroon) in its setting in a fictional African nation, unnamed in *White Material* though named as Bonandé and Nayak in *The Night of Truth*. A further transnationally funded and exhibited African film discussed by Mayer in the chapter of *Political Animals* entitled, "Water Rites: Ecocinema's New Earth Mothers", is Kenyan Wanuri Kahiu's short film *Pumzi* (2009, South Africa/Kenya), which "premiered at Sundance in 2010 and screened at festivals around the world" (Mayer 2016: 45), trading off its novelty as the first-ever Kenyan science fiction film to be set in a world without water.

The importance of diasporic women's filmmaking to the "worlding" of women's cinema is obvious from the second chapter of *Women's Cinema, World Cinema*, which focuses on Indian-born émigré to Canada Deepa Mehta, and in particular *Water* (2005, Canada/India), the third in her "elements" trilogy after *Fire* (1996, India/Canada) and *Earth* (1998, India/Canada), and then on Iranian diasporan directors Mariane Satrapi and Shirin Neshat. By telling an autobiographical story of post-revolutionary Iran from a young woman's point of view, Satrapi's co-adaptation (with Vincent Paronnaud) of her own highly successful graphic novels into *Persepolis* (2007, France/USA) also drew attention to the careers of fellow Iranian women, although Mayer suggests that the success of Samira Makhmalbaf's *Sib* (The Apple, 1998, Iran/France) had already "opened a door to distribution for subsequent Muslim-world girlhood films by adult filmmakers", such as *Persepolis* and *Wadjda* (2012, Saudi Arabia/Netherlands/Germany/Jordan/United Arab emirates/USA, Haifaa Al-Mansour), the first film directed by a woman ever to emerge from Saudi Arabia. Samira Makhmalbaf's younger sister Hana made her first short film at the age of eight, and her first feature at a similar age to Samira: *Buda as sharm foru rikht* (Buddha Collapsed Out of Shame, 2007, Iran/France), which is set in war-torn Afghanistan and won the Berlin film festival's Crystal Bear in 2008, is described by Mayer as "the precise and perfect example of global feminist cinema's riposte to US international politics under George W. Bush" (Mayer 2016: 63). Along with directors such as Tahmineh Milani, the title of whose *Nimeh-ye penham* (The Hidden Half, 2001, Iran) draws attention to women as "the hidden half" of Iran's population, and Marzieh Meshkini, the mother of Hana Makhmalbaf and co-writer of *Buddha Collapsed Out of Shame*, Iran boasts a contribution to global women's cinema that outstrips most other Middle Eastern nations, not including the countries of the Maghreb (usually said to include Morocco, Algeria, Tunisia, Libya and Mauritania), although such a nation-focused view obviously excludes important exilic voices such as the Beirut-born Mona Hatoum, based in Britain since the 1970s, as well as Palestinian Annemarie Jacir, director of the first full-length feature by a Palestinian woman *Milh Hadha al-Bahr* (The Salt of This Sea, 2008, Palestine/Belgium/France/Spain/Switzerland), which she followed with *Lamma shoftak* (*When I Saw You*, 2012, Palestine/Jordan/Greece/United Arab Emirates). Close attention to women's roles in the historic decolonising struggles of Algeria and Morocco—as seen through women's eyes in the case of Moufida Tlatli's acclaimed *Samt el qusur* (The Silence of the Palace, 1994, Tunisia/France)—is paid by Ella Shohat in "Post-Third-Worldist: Gender, Nation and the Cinema", and as White comments in relation to the internationally successful Lebanese director Nadine Labaki, "[f]inancing deals, filmmaker labs, and festival showcases have benefited Labaki and other young women filmmakers from North Africa and the Middle East" (White 2015: 223n25).

North American films feature more in Mayer's *Political Animals* than in White's *Women's Cinema, World Cinema*, and Mayer underlines the importance of ecocinema and films about war as modes of filmmaking (if not fully fledged genres) that US women directors have favoured in the new millennium. Kelly Reichardt seemed to pause between releasing her first feature *River of Grass* (1994, USA) and her second, *Old Joy* (2006, USA), but has since 2006 made five features in a decade by following *Old Joy* with *Wendy and Lucy* (2008, USA), *Meek's Cutoff* (2010, USA), *Night Moves* (2012, USA) and *Certain Women* (2016, USA), and in her "Water Rites" chapter on women's ecocinema, Mayer also dwells briefly on "the intersection of eco- and sexual diversity" to be found in Beth Stephens' *Goodbye Gauley Mountain: An Ecosexual Love Story* (2013, USA), a project Stephens co-directed and produced with her partner Annie Sprinkle, the artist and pro-pornography feminist. The most acclaimed US woman filmmaker of the last thirty years, Kathryn Bigelow, has led the recent trend in female-directed films about war with her Oscar-winning *The Hurt Locker* (2008, USA) and *Zero Dark Thirty* (2012, USA), about the war in Iraq and the killing of Osama bin Laden respectively, but Mayer also draws attention to Meg McLagan and Daria Sommers's *Lioness* (2008, USA), about "the traumatic experiences of the first US women soldiers sent into direct ground combat, in contravention of official policy, due to a shortage of active combat troops caused by the US' dual illegal invasions of Afghanistan and Iraq" (Mayer 2016: 66) and Beth Freeman's *Sisters in Arms* (2010, Canada), *Lioness*'s "Canadian equivalent" (Mayer 2016: 67). A further film of the 2000s critical of the US military's policy was *Stop-Loss* (2008, USA), the first film in almost a decade from Kimberley Peirce, director of the acclaimed *Boys Don't Cry* (1999, USA).

Other chapters of Mayer's *Political Animals* to focus on Anglophone films include "I Have No Country: British Cinema as a Runaway Girl", and Great Britain and Ireland, like France, Germany and Spain, are of course regions of Europe where some tradition in women's filmmaking can be traced and has already been researched. This is less true of smaller nations such as Denmark, where the name of Susanne Bier is picked out by both Mayer and White as a director whose "back seat" (White 2015: 6) in the Dogme 95 movement did not prevent her winning the Oscar for Best Foreign Language Film in 2011, for *Hæven* (In a Better World, 2010, Denmark/Sweden). In Greece, Athena Rachel Tsangari's *Attenberg* (2010, Greece) has been "hailed as part of the 'weird wave of Greek cinema'" (Mayer 2016: 36) headed by Yorgos Lanthimos, whose 2009 hit *Kynodontas* (Dogtooth, 2009, Greece) Tsangari produced. And two younger directors from the relatively new nation of Bosnia picked out by White are Jasmila Žbanic and Aida Begié: Žbanic's film *Grbavica* (Esma's Secret—Grbavica, 2006, Bosnia and Herzegovina/Croatia/Austria/Germany) is described by White (2015: 26) as the "legacy of the siege of Sarajevo"; it is treated as the key case study for Balkan cinema in her chapter "Is the Whole World Watching? Fictions of Women's Human Rights", and is also discussed by Mayer in her chapter "Home Front: Women at War, Women against War" (Mayer 2016: 73).

Conclusion

The necessarily condensed survey of global women's filmmaking in the twenty-first century offered above illustrates the geographical range achieved by recent studies of the topic: the "specific articulation of gender, geopolitics, and cinema" (White 2015: 2) identified at the very start of *Women's Cinema, World Cinema* is now indisputably a discourse with which Film Studies has to contend. Among the critical concepts that have emerged from this essay's survey of how women's cinema functions as (a) world cinema in the twenty-first century, authorship and transnationalism are at the top of the list: these two concepts overlap with the two historiographic strategies adopted by McHugh in "The World and the Soup: Historicizing Media Feminisms in Transnational Contexts"; "*follow the filmmaker*, indicative of feminisms' inescapably transnational character, and *follow the money*, indicative of its material force" (McHugh 2009: 122). McHugh's strategic historicisation of women's filmmaking in the transnational contexts of the contemporary globalised world can be contrasted with—though can also complement—the project of transnationalising women's film history set out by Christine Gledhill in her introduction to the dossier devoted to the topic in *Framework: The Journal of Cinema and Media* (Gledhill 2010), while the plan for a virtual archive for women's cinema proposed in Rosanna Maule's article for the same dossier (Maule 2010) offers an exciting (if possibly utopian) way round the barriers women filmmakers still often face within transnational distribution networks.

In her Afterword to *Women's Cinema, World Cinema*, White lists a number of crucial changes to the articulation of gender, geopolitics and cinema that had taken place by *c.*2010:

> Training opportunities expanded; transnational financing for art cinema reached more women directors in more countries: costs of feature film production decreased with digital technologies; festival economies—of taste as well as sales—proliferated; and cinephilic criticism and digital streaming exploded on the Internet.
>
> *(White 2015: 199)*

If sustained, these may prove to be the kind of changes that will allow additional areas of the world to be added to the global map of women's cinema now in existence. The positive evaluation of women's contributions to the world's film industries and cultures for which Pam Cook called in 1998 is sufficiently advanced for White to be able to state that "women's cinema today cannot be defined in terms of Western texts and theories" (White 2015: 201), and as I have suggested, the de-Westernising of film as a medium and film studies as a discipline set out by Bâ, Higbee and their contributors in *De-westernizing Film Studies* is particularly pertinent to the juncture at which women's cinema finds itself. The same type of global forces that divide and fragment film-viewing societies everywhere in the 2010s—flows of capital and ever more complex economic and political relations—also enfold new possibilities of connection, in the shape of transnational finance and digital communications, and women's cinema has already shown itself more than capable of taking advantage of these. Whether such a cinema is polycentric or uncentred is debatable, and my personal view is that it makes more sense to describe Women's Cinema (like World Cinema) as a disciplinary field rather than as a method or methodology, but whichever terms are chosen, the conjunction of Women's Cinema and World Cinema is now established and growing. The final sentence of White's "Afterword" to *Women's Cinema, World Cinema* is both cautious and hopeful, not the kind of rallying-call employed by Mayer as the title of her introduction to *Political Animals*, "Girls to the Front", but an assessment of the status quo and an optimistic look to the future: "Contemporary cinema studies must now contend with a critical mass of films by women directors; doing so could change the world" (White 2015: 201).

References

Andrew, D. (2006), "An Atlas of World Cinema", in Dennison, S. and Lim, S. H. (eds) *Remapping World Cinema*, London: Wallflower Press, 19–29.

Bâ, S. M. and Higbee, W. (eds) (2012) *De-Westernizing Film Studies*, London: Routledge.

Butler, A. (2002) *Women's Cinema: The Contested Screen*, London: Wallflower Press.

Chapman, J. (2003) *Cinemas of the World: Film and Society from 1895 to the Present*, London: Reaktion.

Cook, P. (1998) "No Fixed Address: The Women's Picture from *Outrage* to *Blue Steel*", in Neale, S. and Smith, M. (eds) *Contemporary Hollywood Cinema*, London: Routledge, 229–246.

Dennison, S. and Lim, S. H. (eds) (2006) *Remapping World Cinema: Identity, Culture and Politics in Film*, London: Wallflower Press.

Gledhill, C. (2010) "Introduction: Transnationalizing Women's Film History", *Framework: The Journal of Cinema and Media* 51 (2): 275–282.

Guneratne, A. R. and Dissanayake, W. (eds) (2003) *Rethinking Third Cinema*, New York and London: Routledge.

Hill, J. and Church Gibson, P. (2000) *World Cinema: Critical Approaches*, Oxford: Oxford University Press.

Mayer, S. (2016) *Political Animals: The New Feminist Cinema*, London and New York: I.B. Tauris.

Maule, R. (2010) "Women Filmmakers and Postfeminism in the Age of Multimedia Reproduction: A Virtual Archive for Women's Cinema", in *Framework: The Journal of Cinema and Media* 51 (2): 350–353.

McHugh, K. (2009) "The World and the Soup: Historicizing Media Feminisms in Transnational Contexts", *Camera Obscura* 72: 110–151.

Nagib, L. (2006) "Towards a Positive Definition of World Cinema", in Dennison, S. and Lim, S. H. (eds) *Remapping World Cinema*, London: Wallflower Press, 30–37.

Nagib, L., Perriam, C. and Dudrah, R. K. (eds) (2012) *Theorizing World Cinema*, London: I.B.Tauris.

Shohat, E. (1997) "Post-Third-Worldist Culture: Gender, Nation and the Cinema", in Jacqui Alexander, M. J. and Talpade Mohanty, C. (eds) *Feminist Genealogies, Colonial Legacies, Democratic Futures*, New York and London: Routledge, 183–209.

Shohat, E. and Stam, R. (1994) *Unthinking Eurocentrism: Multiculturalism and the Media*, London and New York: Routledge.

White, P. (2015) *Women's Cinema, World Cinema. Projecting Contemporary Feminisms*, Durham, NC: Duke University Press.

28

PROVINCIALISING HETEROSEXUALITY

Queer style, World Cinema

Rosalind Galt and Karl Schoonover

Introduction

Queer theory has always asked what counts as a queer text. Is a queer film one made by a filmmaker who is queer, or featuring queer characters, or does queerness rather inhere in a film's political commitment or its affective registers? Is queerness a matter of form? Ten years after the Museum of Modern Art in New York curated an exhibition of LGBT films from around the world, confidently entitling it "Another Wave: Global Queer Cinema", can something like a coherent queer global style be identified? Queer cinema speaks to world politics, whether in relation to globalisation efforts by governments, corporations and NGOs, or in human rights debates, conflicts around national and regional sovereignty, anti-homophobia grassroots organising, or fostering cultures of resistance. Where Western-centric understandings of both film history and queer experience have often viewed Euro-American practices as a norm against which the rest of the world could be compared (and with which it has to catch up), our work begins from an assumption that queerness—in whatever form or style it takes—shapes and always has shaped the world. In contrast to narrow definitions of queer cinema that focus only on Western forms and LGBT identities, we insist that all non-normative modes of being and the texts that register them contribute to queer cinema and its global life. To think queer cinema in the world, we must shift our perspective towards our understanding of film history and of the place of sexuality and gender within it.

In one of queer theory's famous early revisionist gestures, Eve Kosofsky Sedgwick brilliantly exposes the heterosexist and ethnocentric unconscious of canon formation. In discussing the question of minority artists, she asks the following:

> From the keepers of a dead canon we hear a rhetorical question—that is to say, a question posed with the arrogant intent of maintaining ignorance. Is there, as Saul Bellow put it, a Tolstoi of the Zulus? Has there been, ask the defenders of a monocultural curriculum, not intending to stay for an answer, has there ever yet been a Socrates of the Orient, an African-American Proust, a female Shakespeare?

Moving from the colonialist geopolitics of the traditional literary canon to the question of sexuality, she continues:

> From the point of view of this relatively new and inchoate academic presence, the gay studies movement, what distinctive soundings are to be reaching by posing the question our way—and staying for an answer? Let's see how it sounds.
> Has there ever been a gay Socrates?
> Has there ever been a gay Shakespeare?
> Has there ever been a gay Proust?
> Does the Pope wear a dress?
>
> *(Sedgwick 1990: 51–52)*

Of course, these figures are already gay and even the most canonical literary history, Sedgwick demonstrates, was already queer. We can make the exact same move with regard to film history:

> Has there ever been a gay Eisenstein?
> Has there ever been a gay Murnau?
> Has there ever been a lesbian Arzner?
> Are cinemas not theatres of deviant desire?

Even working from Western film history, these examples reveal an ideological process that blinds us to the canon's queerness. Queerness animates major trajectories of film form and style. International film histories are already queer and queer experience has always influenced the aesthetics and politics of cinema worldwide.

In this chapter, then, we aim to provincialise heterosexuality. Dipesh Chakrabarty's influential work of postcolonial theory *Provincializing Europe* demonstrated the need to understand modernity without reference to Europe as a centre, and in a similar way, we aim to reframe World Cinema *both* without installing Europe and America as the source of film style upon which all other iterations of film style are based *and* without assuming heterosexuality (its desires, its orientations, its priorities) as the necessary precondition and determinant of the cinematic experience (Chakrabarty 2000). Existing histories of film style are replete with queer film-makers (Lino Brocka, Chantal Akerman, the Wachowskis) and with queerly-oriented films (*Iskanderija. . . lih?* [Alexandria, Why?, 1979, Egypt/Algeria, Youssef Chahine], *Yeogo goedam II* [Memento Mori, 1999, South Korea, Kim Tae-yong and Min Kyu-dong], for instance, or *El lugar sin límites* [The Place without Limits, 1978, Mexico, Arturo Ripstein]), and any account of contemporary world cinema would include the queer films of Lucrecia Martel, Apichatpong Weerasethakul and Tsai Ming-liang. To understand World Cinema, we argue, it is necessary to take account of its queerness.

Including queer global film and film theory

But if cinema has always been queer, its Eurocentrism and heteronormativity has worked to minimise and exclude queer global film. How would film history change if it was forced to accommodate films such as *Fukujusô* (Pheasant Eyes, 1935, Japan, Jirô Kawate), a Japanese silent film about a same-sex attraction that develops between two sisters-in-law? *Pheasant Eyes* was based on a story written by Yoshiya Nobuko. Nobuko lived with her female partner, but her relatives continue to control her work, recently refusing its reprinting in a queer anthology. Rarely screened today and not available on DVD, the film is not well known, though copies exist in the National Film Centre in Tokyo. When it has been screened at film festivals in Japan and in Europe, *Pheasant Eyes* makes queer history visible both textually and extra-textually.

However, the visibility of this film (and potentially many more lost or forgotten films) remains constricted by the homophobia and heterosexism of various institutions (family, the marketplace, film historiography).

A similar blindspot can be found occurring at a theoretical level, when, to take as an example Jean-Luc Comolli and Jean Narboni's influential polemic, "Cinema / Ideology / Criticism", sexual dissidence is oddly separated from radical politics. Discussing militant cinema, Comolli and Narboni raise "the problem of deciding whether 'underground' films should be included in the category, on the pretext that their relationship to drugs and sex, their preoccupation with form, might possibly establish new relationships between film and audience" (Comolli and Narboni 1977: 30n.7). This article has been foundational to debates in film theory about what constitutes the political in cinema, and how dominant ideologies can be destabilised. It has enabled feminist and queer arguments about the political value of film form, yet it finds problematic a category that in 1969 would certainly have included the films of Andy Warhol, Jack Smith, Jean Genet and Kenneth Anger. Indeed, the article was first published in *Cahiers du cinéma* in the same month that Toshio Matsumoto's queer underground classic *Bara no sôretsu* (Funeral Parade of Roses, 1969, Japan) was released. Sex, drugs and a preoccupation with cinematic form describe Matsumoto's film precisely, and it explicitly ties these qualities to militant politics and a queer resistance to capitalism's globalising violence. Such queer films present a form of militancy that postclassical film theory has trouble including.

Funeral Parade of Roses also explicitly reflects on underground cinema and in particular Jonas Mekas, whose name is mentioned several times in the film. Interestingly, Mekas had by this point already dismissed queer desire as a distraction in the work of American experimental filmmakers. Discussing Anger, Smith, and others, and under the heading "The Conspiracy of Homosexuality", Mekas wrote: "The perversion of sex seems to be accepted by these film poets (in their films) as a natural way of life" (Mekas 1955). An otherwise praising review by well-known San Francisco critic Albert Johnson pathologises the film's setting as the "night town of unnatural Toyko" and dismisses the moments of the film dominated by transgender and gender-queer homo men as humorous, satirical and/or a kind of fashion-magazine extravagance (Johnson 1970). When *Funeral Parade of Roses* was released in the US, *New York Times* critic Vincent Canby said of the film that it "keeps up a brave but quite frankly fake front" (Canby 1973). These critical responses echo Comolli and Narboni's ambivalence about the inclusion of sexual politics in the project of political modernist filmmaking, demonstrating the stakes of their comments for a wider film culture.

As if undoing these dismissals, recent film historians have retraced the transnational aesthetic and political allegiances of underground cinema. Juan Suárez insists on the value of transnational and queer structures of influence (Suárez 2014). He links the American filmmaker Jack Smith to Brazilian Tropicalismo (a fusion of 1960s popular and avant-garde culture in Brazil), finding points of contact between apparently disparate nodes of queer visual culture. Queer film histories open up unexpected points of contact, influence and exchange across continents. *Funeral Parade of Roses* rewrites the Oedipus story, transforming and queering the European narrative par excellence into a saga critiquing the economic and social redevelopment of Tokyo. The Greek film *Strella* (A Woman's Way, 2009, Greece, Panos H. Koutras) makes a similar appropriation, except this time from within the heart of European classical culture. Both films feature a couple who have sex without knowing that one partner is the father of the other: in *Funeral Parade of Roses* the child is a gay drag performer and in *A Woman's Way* she is a transgender woman for whom the protagonist has long searched, thinking he was looking for his son. Judith Butler has written of *A Woman's Way* as:

> perhaps the most important cultural contribution in recent years to thinking about oedipalisation within queer kinship, as well as about contemporary challenges to understandings of sexuality and kinship, all through a meditation on very contemporary modes of living and loving that nevertheless draw on ancient norms.
>
> *(Quoted in Butler and Athanasiou 2013: 59)*

Employing the frame of queer world cinema, then, demonstrates not only how queers have historically challenged traditional shapes of living but also how desire remains a crucial ground for contestatory politics. Queer film aesthetics create contiguities and affinities across geographic and historical distances, and these aesthetics demand different modes of viewing, attention and critique. Through cinematic means, the shapes of a world remade in queer terms can become known and felt.

Queer film style

Teresa de Lauretis has influentially defined queer textuality as that which destabilises the signifier (de Lauretis 2011). In other words she argues for the necessity of style to the production of queer culture. Her claim seems compelling, both in the sense of a poststructuralist account of the radical potential of form and language, and in the more everyday sense that queerness has often been associated with swag, panache, fierceness, saunter or exuberant expressiveness. But what is queer film style? Can it be described with critical precision? What pitfalls occur when a concept of queer style is rendered on a global scale? At a 2013 roundtable discussion at the London Lesbian and Gay Film Festival, none of the participants thought that a global queer style was desirable (Capó *et al.* 2013). For filmmaker Jim Hubbard and festival programmer Kam Wai Kui, any globalised vision of queer cinematic style conjured ideas of a prescriptive set of formal codes, a calcifying of creativity that would negate the power of queerness to overthrow conventional ways of thinking and being. We share this anxiety about the potentially homogenising role of film festival culture and film funding institutions. A recognisable style can be stifling as often as it liberates.

Recent work by Nick Davis illustrates the productive potential of thinking queerness filmically. Queer desire cannot be narrowed into a particular universal stylistic idiom, but it can be found in the "desiring-image", Davis's neo-Deleuzian term. Precisely because the cinematic image—at its very core—refuses to reify desire into bodies, identities, dualistic genders, it has a potentially radical visuality able to attend to queer being. Davis writes, "desire does not settle into any one arrangement but concerns flows and frictions across *and* with them all [. . .] passing through or forcing changes with subjects rather than belonging to them as static, innate, or identitarian fixtures" (Davis 2013: 20; emphasis in original). Davis's project depends largely on New Queer Cinema for case studies, but as with Suárez's transits of influence, Davis is careful not to fasten one particular style to a queer politics. As he writes:

> I do not believe that the excitingly collective, eccentrically political, impressively deterritorializing impetus behind New Queer Cinema or behind *any* contemporary queer cinema ever went away [...] To urge those desires and energies toward new frontiers [...] is not to bury but to praise the deterritorializing impulses that constitute a desiring-image in the first place, forcing new productions and responding to the world in its innumerable, changing facets.
>
> *(Davis 2013: 247; emphasis in original)*

Just as queerness promises to articulate dissident ways of being in the world, Davis prompts us to understand the desiring-image of cinema to be a complex assemblage of collective aspirations, longings and orientations that emerge across subjectivities while never confining itself to a single subject. So, while the desiring-image cannot be pinned down to a single technique or even a collection of formal devices that add up to a coherent style, queerness becomes visible and experiential through film form. Davis's desiring-image complicates notions of style in ways not unlike a perverse adaptation of Miriam Hansen's "vernacular modernism" (Hansen 1999). As an expression of dissident ways of being, style enables us to think queer cinema's worldliness in terms of what Raymond Williams called a "structure of feeling" (see, for example, Love 2009: 11–12; Muñoz 2009: 41).

For Williams, a "structure of feeling" names precisely the type of experience that is not sedimented in ideology or cultural form, and indeed is experienced by the individual in tension with dominant modes of art and life. In *Marxism and Literature*, he writes that this "tension is as often an unease, a stress, a displacement, a latency: the moment of conscious comparison not yet come, often not even coming". This concept, so well-worn in cultural studies, still has the capacity to offer fresh insight, and we find in it a suggestive description of contemporary queer cinematic style. Style, first of all, defines "a particular quality of social experience and relationship" (Williams 1977: 130). Williams does not call for the recuperation of formalism; rather he privileges style as a function of social relations. Style provides a critical access to, and perspective on, "structures of feeling", experiences that confound standard means of registration or representation. And the social relations Williams describes are peculiarly apt to queer experiences: he was writing primarily about the tension between working-class life and official culture in the UK, but the experiences of stress and displacement, of temporal lags and latencies, also speak evocatively to the disjunctive temporalities of queer subjectivity in many parts of the world. Instead of a homogenous official queer style, a structure of feeling rather describes the process by which "affective elements of consciousness and relationships"—feelings that are often thought of as private and subjective—can be analysed in social and historical terms. A queer cinematic structure of feeling would thus locate the "emergent, connecting and dominant characteristics" in queer world cinema, tracing the formal elements that are not immediately apparent to view and yet that articulate the shifting potentialities of queerness in the world (Williams 1977: 132).

Williams memorably describes a structure of feeling as "social experiences in solution, as distinct from other social semantic formations which have been precipitated and are more evidently and immediately available" (Williams 1977: 132–134). For Williams, a different orientation to the social requires careful attention to those experiences that are just coming in to being, those experiences that have not yet been "properly" named, or that exist in the pre-discursive and are yet to be co-opted. Experiences, sensations, modes of living and bonding that have not been fixed or reified by mainstream culture remain "in solution". Such experiences do not grant resolution or assurance: rather, they form a vital force that resists calcification and might lead to a cogent critique of the world system. Our theorisation of queer film style extends from Williams' faith in *style* as a means of accessing these precarious modes of experience.

As a structure of feeling, queer cinematic style could be seen as dispersed and diasporic, apparently always diluted by the overwhelming straightness of canonical film histories and always threatened by co-optation or censure. Yet in its temporal and geographical displacements, in its tension with dominant forms and historiographies, queer style articulates a relationship between what can be felt and what can be said. It establishes form as a problem of being in the world. Williams describes "the peculiar location of a structure of feeling", as "the endless comparison that must occur in the process of consciousness between the articulated and the lived" (Williams 2015: 168).

In many queer films, that tension between the experiential and the figurable renders dissident forms of intimacy precisely as problems of cinematic style. The radical shifts in LGBT lives wrought by the forces of globalisation, modernisation and their various resistances have prompted a new structure of feeling, in which emergent modes of relationality can be glimpsed in the visual and affective forms of queer cinema. To assert a queer structure of feeling is thus to valorise non-linear models of influence, to nourish discursively unstable categories of being, to allow that which is "in solution" to matter, and to resist efforts to banish the more dynamic and disruptive modes of experience as "incomprehensible", "over styled" or "decadent. Williams's unstable temporality—which is really rather queer—pushes us to understand queer film style as a complex terrain capable of figuring shifting social relations and of rendering new modes of relationality.

Queering the international film festival film

Perhaps the style most feared by Hubbard and Kam Wai Kui at the London roundtable was what we might think of as the international film festival film. Often the type of art film that travels globally via the film festival circuit is criticised for ignoring the forms and concerns of its home culture in favour of courting cosmopolitan arthouse audiences (Farahmand 2010). Such films can be viewed as elitist, as selling out, and as flattening genuine cultural difference into easily-digestible arthouse style. But what might it mean to look, in these festival films, not for the smoothness of dominant forms but for traces of queer transnational influence and registrations of queer attachments within globalised capitalism? The mixture of realism and melodrama in the British film *Weekend* (2011, UK, Andrew Haigh), for example, resonates with the Indonesian *Lovely Man* (2011, Indonesia, Teddy Soeriaatmadja) and with the Brazilian *Hoje Eu Quero Voltar Sozinho* (The Way He Looks, 2014, Brazil, Daniel Ribeiro). Each film registers the flowering of romantic or familial bonds through sentimental twists of connectivity that are in tension with their naturalistic formal strategies. Urban settings (in Nottingham, Jakarta and São Paulo) embed the difficulties of making and maintaining queer bonds in the normative social spaces of the housing estate, the school, the roadside, and the café. As much as these films speak of what queer lives share, they also articulate the perils and pleasures of a specific place.

This tension can be clearly seen in *Baek-ya* (White Night, 2012, South Korea, Leesong Hee-il), a South Korean drama about a gay flight attendant who returns to his homeland after years away (Figure 28.1). In many ways, the film exhibits formal techniques typical of contemporary international art cinema: it uses extensive shallow focus to isolate characters from their environments, and through unfocused and refracted lights, it effects aesthetic intensities of loneliness and dystopic relationships in late capitalism. It represents urban spaces as both alienated and glamorous, juxtaposing neon cityscapes in long shot with tawdry locations under a highway bridge. However, in its shifts in register, the film intervenes in the politics of desire in a manner similar to that of other queer world filmmaking practices. Moving from restrained art cinematic drama to violent noir and back to melodrama, *White Night* articulates the proximity of homophobic violence to tender romance in the social spaces of many queer people. Maintaining a smoothly consistent tone is impossible in queer life worlds and generic mixing expresses emotional and physical fractures. Moreover, the film formalises a tension between belonging and exclusion, a means by which many queer films since Wong Kar-wai's *Chun gwong cha sit* (Happy Together, Hong Kong/Japan/South Korea, 1997) imbricate queer relationality and globalised spaces of living.

White Night proposes travel and diasporic life as at once freedom and exile for queers. The film juxtaposes Won-Gyu, who left and who has been scarred by this self-imposed exclusion from family and friends, with Tae-Jun, who stayed with his homophobic family and made

Figure 28.1 *Baek-Ya* (White Night, 2012, South Korea, Leesong Hee-il) creates a tension between belonging and exclusion in globalised space. © Cinema Dal.

compromises to maintain a community-based life. Won-Gyu's career as a flight attendant enables a certain kind of mobility but his status as a diasporic queer forecloses on any simple return home. And although Tae-Jun has stayed in Seoul, his job as a courier is equally tied to international circulation. Globalisation organises both their lives, and their romantic communications are mediated through courier company notepads and airline IDs. *White Night* uses the discourses of travel found in many films that adopt a "world cinema" idiom, but how it formalises spaces as affective zones of longing, detachment and desire makes it queer. This vision of the world, like Tsai's oddly disjointed and multinodal correspondences in *Ni na bian ji dian* (What Time Is It There?, 2001, Taiwan/France, Tsai Ming-liang), insists that the difficulties of mobility and belonging are queer dilemmas, or more accurately, that the disorientating experience of untethering belonging from sharing the same place and time is a queer experience.

In one scene, the film uses a shot that has become a stylistic marker of art films depicting gay sex—a high-angle shot, looking down on the couple from above and behind. This penetrative angle shot is followed by a cutaway to a window, out of which we see the night sky and the Seoul cityscape. In this sequence, we discern a queer structure of feeling that locates intimacy not in shared space but in sharing the same distant view at different times. These distances come together in the space of the film; cinema makes otherwise impossibly opposite vectors of space run side by side. Through Won-Gyu's desire, queerness is closely linked to concepts of home, exile and return, and those places are seen as only semi-accessible to queers. Both the threat of violence and the promise of intimacy are articulated in the film's narration of national, transnational and bodily spaces. The cityscape seen from the window registers at once Won-Gyu's desire for homecoming, a memory of past belonging, and his present disjunctive separation from home. (We can see a similarity to *Happy Together*, a film which through its gorgeous attention to the texture and feel of spaces—overly filled and cramped, or empty and abandoned—draws the viewer into the messy dynamics of gay desire cut through by dislocation, migrancy and homesickness.)

Queerness, here, is felt in the draw of home and relationality constructed as a point of impossibility, melodramatic loss and desire tethered to an uncertain place in the world. The scene deploys the high-angle shot to place the spectator at once close to the position of the penetrating partner, in a prosthetic subjectivity of active desire, but also above the lovers, pulled back so that we can see the site of a queer sex act, located in this room, in Seoul, with the city just outside the window. *White Night* could easily look like just another festival film, emulating a world cinema style to get noticed in the transnational marketplaces of art cinema. However, when we try to map how the film visualises desire itself and find that desire is so complexly interwoven with the politics of being in a globalised world, we begin to find something specifically queer. Looking for a queer structure of feeling in contemporary world cinema leads us to discern in cinematic styles the condensation of queer experiences that form resistant modes of being and indeed propose different worlds.

The institutional distortion of patriarchy

If a queer structure of feeling is necessarily dispersed, fragmentary, and often hard to discern, part of what renders it invisible is the institutional distortion of patriarchy. Patricia White has pointed out how few women are seen as stylists of cinema and, moreover, how world cinema as a category is often gendered as male. The politics of film style are not neutral and female directors are less often accorded the status of auteur. For White, lesbian filmmakers such as Zero Chou are given less weight than their male counterparts and style is used as a tool of patriarchy, to dismiss their work as insufficiently artistic (White 2015). We can certainly trace the institutional challenges of viewing lesbian cinema: women find it harder to access film education, production funding, distribution deals and these disadvantages are multiplied when they are queer, of colour, working class, or from the Global South. Queer film festivals disproportionately programme gay male films, in large part because there are fewer lesbian-oriented films being made. Gender is a pressing concern for many queer film festival programmers. And yet, a queer structure of feeling is equally visible in films made by women about female same-sex desire and queer gender identities.

Take, for example, the work of Argentinian filmmaker Lucía Puenzo. Her film *XXY* (2007, Argentina/Spain/France) deploys some aspects of art cinematic realism but its attenuated narration operates more with conceptual affinities than with naturalism. Intersex protagonist Alex's journey toward self-discovery takes place alongside a tension between the city and the country, and through Alex's travels in the woods, the beach, and submerged in water, the film considers how bodily and gendered identities can be articulated within an environment that is at once local and worldly. *XXY* is set in rural Uruguay, and Alex's bourgeois family use the country house as a retreat from discrimination in Argentina. Whereas Alex's parents want Alex to undergo surgery to be assigned as female, Alex resists these forces of normativity, insisting by the end of the film that there is no choice to be made. Alex's father is a marine biologist, and his relationships with the local fishermen and the injured turtle he treats propose biology, ecology and transnational capitalism as closely interlinked. Puenzo's next film, *El niño pez* (The Fish Child, 2009, Argentina/France/Spain), develops her close attention to place and class, this time focusing on a sexual relationship between a wealthy young woman in Buenos Aires and her family's Paraguayan maid. The films are generically quite different—*The Fish Child* shifts registers between art film, noir, and melodrama—but both climax in an assertion of place-ness that allows Puenzo to draw out the intersections of class, ethnicity and desire in a decidedly queer fashion. *The Fish Child* develops Puenzo's mixture of realism and expressionism: where the turtle in *XXY* offered a non-human figure who might (or might not) have affinities with Alex, *The Fish Child* creates a magical realist realm underwater, where a drowned baby might become the mythic fish child. In both films, men threaten bodily harm and queer desire has the potential not only to cross national and class boundaries, but also to escape patriarchal violence.

This intersectional impulse is recurrent in female-authored queer films. *Mosquita y Mari* (2012, USA, Aurora Guerrero) is an American film that was very popular on the queer film festival circuit. Set in a Chicana community in Los Angeles, its lesbian romance plot is as interested in the challenges facing immigrant families as it is in sexuality. Focusing on the pressures of young women with heavy responsibilities for their families' future, it articulates same-sex desire with the complex intersections of economic precarity, gender, class, ethnicity and citizenship status. In a very different cultural context, Filipina director Sigrid Bernardo's 2013 film *Ang huling cha-cha ni Anita* (Anita's Last Cha-Cha, 2013, Philippines) is equally adept at joining the intimate messiness of young love with the pressures of community. The film is a coming-of-age story about a twelve-year-old butch girl who falls for mysterious newcomer in town Pilar. The film addresses themes of lesbian identity, queer childhood and female masculinities alongside those of sexism and religion in rural communities. Bernardo worked extensively with non-professional child actors, and this neo-realist-influenced mode of production can be seen also in the films of French filmmaker Céline Sciamma, who is equally invested in the emerging gender and sexual identities of young women. Her three films *Naissance des pieuvres* (Water Lilies, 2007, France), *Tomboy* (2011, France) and *Bande des filles* (Girlhood, 2014, France) all think through queer adolescence, exploring the multiple pressures of gender and sexual dissidence in girlhood. All three films emphasise the weight of gender norms through the resistances the protagonists experience to moving freely in socially constrained spaces. The deftness of Sciamma's approach—its effective use of realism to lend a leadenness to the mise-en-scène to bespeak how people with non-normative sex/gender orientations can feel abandoned and dislocated right at home, in the places where they were raised—is also its queerness.

A "storing house for those 'clandestine countermemories'"?

Olivia Khoo has argued that the category queer in art cinema tends to exclude Asian woman directors. She writes that "[q]ueer cinema constitutes a more political international dimension of contemporary Asian cinema", and yet, "the contributions to queer Asian cinema of women filmmakers [. . .] have not been as visible as those of their male counterparts", largely because much of their work is not feature-length (Khoo 2014: 34). As Gayatri Gopinath insists, how we constitute an archive matters. Global queer lives, she proposes, leave "traces that resist textualization" and locating queer cinema outside of the wealthy centres of cultural production demands that we "rethink what constitutes a viable archive" (Gopinath 2005: 21). To return to Sedgwick, canon-formation matters and imagining a global queer corpus of films is a political project. For Gopinath, a queer archive can be a "storing house for those 'clandestine countermemories'" (Gopinath 2005: 21). In queer cinema studies, to ignore short films and genres outside of art cinema is often to exclude the practices of queer women and of filmmakers in the Global South.

Khoo focuses on Asian films, drawing on White's concept of lesbian minor cinema. But as Gopinath's concern for the queer global archive suggests, Khoo's larger questions are productive beyond the specifics of her argument. Deleuze and Guattari's concept of minor literature has been productive for thinking about queer textuality and equally for considering cinematic practices outside the major languages of world cinema (whether we understand languages here in terms of film genre, mode of production, or dominant spoken language) (Deleuze and Guattari 1986). Queer film festivals screen a multitude of short-form work that often also circulates online. For example, *t sigo (es p rando)* (w8ing 4 u, 2008, Puerto Rico, Mairym Llorens), is a Puerto Rican short drama shot on a mobile phone that creates a queerly disjointed temporality out of texting and lo-fi images. Two women have arranged to meet at the same time, on the same beach, every year, but the desired meeting does not take place. Memories of the past mix with a future of 2038 in which the lover has still not arrived. The poverty of Puerto Rico's film industry nourishes such small-scale works, in which the precariousness of queer connections is mediated by equally precarious technologies.[1]

Attending to such marginal practices offers one way to counter the corporate and often neo-colonial brand of globalism that has become so dominant in LGBT culture. As one of the world's biggest and oldest queer film festivals, San Francisco's Frameline has found itself at the centre of these debates over the shape and ownership of queer visual culture. The festival has been at the forefront of programming and circulating international queer cinema, but its relationship to the politics of queer activism has been fraught. In 1996, it took part in an effort to found the first queer film festival in Siberia, which Julie Dorf of the International Gay and Lesbian Human Rights Commission characterised as "the perfect way to use art as an organizing tool" (Quoted in Taller 1996). That Western acknowledgement of a region through a film festival might lead to protection of queer human rights is a common impetus for a certain kind of liberal LGBT globalism. Beginning in 2007, though, Frameline suffered a series of protests, after it accepted funds from the Israeli government and was boycotted by pro-Palestinian groups for its apparently knowing participation in so-called "pinkwashing" campaigns orchestrated by the Israeli embassy and pro-Israeli lobbying organisations. Following a similar logic, many governments have supplied key funds to film festivals beyond their own national borders. These events do not simply serve to promote the funding nation's queer culture. Instead, the liberal logic of the queer film festival serves an implicit need to deem the funding nation as a homophobic space that requires intervention from the West. Festival scholars Skadi Loist and Ger Zielinski describe how the Saint Petersburg festival depended upon the safe spaces of "local foreign culture venues, such as the Goethe Institute, the British Council and Dutch, Swedish and Norwegian agencies", and these diplomatic venues are also used by festivals in locations such as Kolkata, Beijing, Hanoi and Nairobi (Loist and Zielinski 2012).

But queer cinema has a long history of critical globalism. For example, across the 1960s and early 1970s, Pier Paolo Pasolini was at once an arthouse auteur and a radical political activist. In an essay reflecting on Pasolini's infamous sympathies with the police rather than the wealthy students during the protests of 1968, queer Canadian filmmaker and media activist John Greyson contemplates how Pasolini might react if faced with contemporary anti-globalisation protests and their violent policing methods:

> From Eisenstein onwards, the desiring gaze of the committed avant-garde has often come to rest on the bodies of its heroes and foes [...] The questions raised by such gazes are many. Does eroticizing activism run the risk of romanticizing it? Does critique soften when it's mediated by a crush? Is focus undermined when it's distracted by a crotch?
>
> *(Greyson 2013: 292)*

Greyson goes on to remind us that unruly desires are not, as Narboni and Comolli might conclude, identitarian distractions from politics proper but rather the generative material of radical cinema.

Richard Fung points out that as much as issues of sexuality, Greyson's work is "devoted to theorizing and enacting cross-border affiliation and solidarity" (Fung 2013: 102). This solidarity prompts a very overt question of what it means to be a queer filmmaker in the world, exemplified in his stance against pinkwashing. Fung links Greyson's films to his activism in support of Boycott, Divestment and Sanctions (BDS) of Israel. He has made activist films about the politics of BDS (e.g. *BDS Bieber*, 2011, which urged the pop star not to play in Israel), pulled his own film out of the Toronto International Film Festival in 2009 in protest of the festival's participation in what he saw as pinkwashing, and travelled to Palestine to report on an international medical effort, during which he was arrested and jailed in Egypt for over a month. International issues of social justice are queer issues in this context. Greyson's queer style inheres in resistance to presiding notions of global sexual citizenship, and many contemporary queer films insist that sexual and gender identities cannot be imagined or lived without at once imaginatively reconstituting the world.

Such films do not have to be explicitly transnational: the Bolivian feminist collective Mujeres Creando stage interventions and make activist documentaries such as *Mamá no me lo dijo* (Mom Did Not Tell Me, 2003), which connect the effects of patriarchy, homophobia, neo-imperialism and capitalism in Bolivia to an internationalist resistance to globalisation. Such queer practices imagine the world from a grounded location and a rich political tradition. Often, though, a critique of dominant postcolonial modes of transnational mobility is foregrounded. In Abdellah Taïa's *L'armée du salut* (Salvation Army, 2013, France/Morocco/Switzerland), for instance, a gay Moroccan man trades the claustrophobia of homosexual encounters at home for the racism he experiences as a white man's exotic boyfriend in Europe. Or, to take an institutional example, the Lesbian and Gay Film Festival in Hamburg in 2012 organised a workshop to create short films in solidarity with queers in St Petersburg, together with young people from Russia invited to the festival. Queer film festivals can offer alternative modes of worlding and can turn their globalised status toward forms of solidarity and affiliation that work against globalisation's more pernicious initiatives (precarity, casualisation, etc.).

Conclusion

As our examples suggest, much of contemporary queer cinema makes a structure of feeling discernible in its spaces of dislocation. As aesthetic endeavours, these films intervene simultaneously in our experience (i.e., our sense of the existing world) and in our political imagination (i.e., our sense of what is possible for this world). In doing so they send ripples through the politics of queer globalism, queering (disrupting) the impulse of both racialised globalisation and LGBT progress narratives. The work of these films to deterritorialise desire via the image also represents an intervention in the rendering of the world, renegotiating the terms of its scale (its proximities and distances) in ways that not only make queer modes of living recognisable and sustainable but also make those modes matter to the world and its history. In other words, bringing a critical attention to particularly queer structures of feeling helps to provincialise heterosexuality. By attending to the disjunctions and tensions—but also the political and carnal exuberances—of queer world cinema, we hope not only to offer a more variegated and complex reckoning of how form works in queer cinema, but also to argue for a queerer account of the film image.

Note

1 We appreciate Vilma Castaneda for bringing this film to our attention.

References

Butler, J. and Athanasiou, A. (2013) *Dispossession: The Performative in the Political*, Cambridge: Polity Press.

Canby, V. (1973) "Oedipus Myth Is Theme of 'Parade of Roses'", *New York Times*, 8 June, 47.

Capó, S., Wai Kui, K., Hubbard, J., Robinson, B., Galt, R. and Schoonover, K. (2013) "Global Queer Cinematic Spaces: Roundtable Discussion with Suzy Capó, Kam Wai Kui, Jim Hubbard, Brian Robinson, Rosalind Galt, and Karl Schoonover", London Lesbian and Gay Film Festival, London, 19 March.

Chakrabarty, D. (2000) *Provincializing Europe: Postcolonial Thought and Historical Difference*, Princeton, NJ: Princeton University Press.

Comolli, J. and Narboni, J. (1977) "Cinema / Ideology / Criticism", in Nichols, B. (ed.) *Movies and Methods: An Anthology, Vol. 1*, Berkeley, CA and Harmondsworth: University of California Press, Penguin, 22–30.

Davis, N. (2013) *The Desiring-Image: Gilles Deleuze and Contemporary Queer Cinema*, New York: Oxford University Press.

de Lauretis, T. (2011) "Queer Texts, Bad Habits, and the Issue of a Future", *GLQ: A Journal of Lesbian and Gay Studies* 17 (2–3): 243–263.

Deleuze, G. and Guattari, F. (1986) *Kafka: Toward a Minor Literature*, Polan, D. (trans.), Minneapolis, MN: University of Minnesota Press.

Farahmand, A. (2010) "Disentangling the International Festival Circuit: Genre and Iranian Cinema", in Galt, R. and Schoonover, K. (eds) *Global Art Cinema: New Theories and Histories*, Oxford: Oxford University Press, 263–281.

Fung, R. (2013) "John Greyson's Queer Internationalism", in Longfellow, B., MacKenzie, S. and Waugh, T. (eds) *The Perils of Pedagogy: The Works of John Greyson*, Montreal: McGill Queens University Press, 101–112.

Gopinath, G. (2005) *Impossible Desires: Queer Diasporas and South Asian Public Cultures*, Durham, NC and London: Duke University Press.

Greyson, J. (2013) "Something Always Seems to Go Wrong Somewhere: Eisenstein at the Barricades, Pasolini at the Baths", in Longfellow, B., MacKenzie, S. and Waugh, T. (eds) *The Perils of Pedagogy: The Works of John Greyson*, Montreal: McGill Queens University Press, 283–293.

Hansen, M. (1999) "The Mass Production of the Senses: Classical Cinema as Vernacular Modernism", *Modernism/modernity* 6 (2): 59–77.

Johnson, A. (1970) "Funeral Parade of Roses", San Francisco Film Festival programme: 37.

Khoo, O. (2014) "The Minor Transnationalism of Queer Asian Cinema: Female Authorship and the Short Film Format", *Camera Obscura* 85 (29/1): 32–57.

Loist, S. and Zielinski, G. (2012) "On the Development of Queer Film Festivals and Their Media Activism", in Iordanova, D. and Torchin, L. (eds) *Film Festivals and Activism: Film Festival Yearbook 4*, St Andrews: St Andrews University Press, 57, 49–62.

Love, H. (2009) *Feeling Backward: Loss and the Politics of Queer History*, Cambridge, MA: Harvard University Press.

Mekas, J. (1955) "The Experimental Film in America", *Film Culture* 3, 15–20.

Muñoz, J. E. (2009) *Cruising Utopia: The Then and There of Queer Futurity*, New York: New York University Press.

Sedgwick, E. K. (1990) *Epistemology of the Closet*, Berkeley, CA: University of California Press.

Suárez, J. A. (2014) "Jack Smith, Hélio Oiticica, Tropicalism", *Criticism* 56 (2): 295–328.

Taller, D. (1996) "Gay Film Festival Comes to Siberia / U.S. Organizers Hope to Build Up Activism", *SFGate*, www.sfgate.com/entertainment/article/Gay-Film-Festival-Comes-to-Siberia-U-S-2970557.php, 15 August.

White, P. (2015) *Women's Cinema, World Cinema: Projecting Contemporary Feminisms*, Durham, NC: Duke University Press.

Williams, R. (1977) *Marxism and Literature*, Oxford: Oxford University Press.

—— (2015) *Politics and Letters: Interviews with New Left Review*, London: Verso.

29
STARS ACROSS BORDERS
The vexed question of stars' exportability

Ginette Vincendeau

Introduction

The star-system began, in the silent era, as a worldwide phenomenon with stars such as Max Linder, Lillian Gish, Sessue Hayakawa, Pola Negri and Rudolph Valentino reaching the four corners of the globe, unhindered by language. Soon, however, the development of the American studio system and the coming of sound erected linguistic barriers for non-Anglophone actors, while reinforcing the hegemony of Hollywood stars. Performers from outside north America continued to be attracted to Hollywood, either "lured" there by studios or producers, or following their own desire for the glamour, economic might and promise of global fame afforded by US cinema. As a result, for many viewers and scholars alike, "stardom" and "the star-system" have long been synonymous with Hollywood, a fact largely underlined by foundational work within star studies (Morin 1960; Dyer 1979).

The increased globalization of film and media in the twenty-first century accelerated the mobility of actors without displacing Hollywood's hegemony over global audiences while the export of non-Anglophone stars across the globe remains a hit-and-miss affair (actors from English-speaking countries outside the US clearly have privileged access to Hollywood cinema and thus are excluded from this study). This chapter explores the imbalance in the ability of stars to achieve an international or transnational level of fame, focusing on France as a country with a thriving film industry and indigenous star system and yet a poor record in the export of its stars.

Film historiography traditionally places the birth of the star-system in Hollywood with the emergence of Florence Lawrence the "Biograph Girl" in 1910 (DeCordova 1990). Revisionist history sees a more international picture, with, among others, the French Max Linder altering the received periodisation to France in 1908 (Vincendeau 2000) and research on the Japanese Sessue Hayakawa showing how, from the point of view of stars, cinema "has been a transnational cultural form from the early period of its history" (Miyao 2007: 8). However, as Sabrina Yu points out, the term transnational "is often used within critical discourse as a self-evident term" (Yu 2012: 1) and is applied interchangeably with international. In my discussion I will follow Yu's distinction between international, meaning "a star who achieves international recognition and fame, even if he or she never makes a film outside his or her own country" and transnational, as referring to stars who "physically transfer from one film industry to another to make films, often in a different language from his or her own"

(Yu 2012: 1-2). I will add a third, intermediate category, that of the cross-regional star, a performer who travels within a region (e.g. Europe or Asia), but does not make the further step to the international level in a sustained way.

International, cross-regional and transnational stardom

The movement of actors across the globe has long been a subject of fascination in journalistic and scholarly writing on stars. An important current within studies of Hollywood focuses on its import of foreign stars, notably European actors, as a result of industrial patterns or political exile, or both (Russell-Taylor 1983; Heilbut 1993; Vasey 1997; Phillips and Vincendeau 2006). Other works focus on "ethnic" or non-white performers to examine their deployment of "exotic" images (see for example Dyer 1987 on Paul Robeson; Bergfelder 2004 on Anna May Wong; Shaw 2013 on Carmen Miranda) and Diane Negra analyses the subtle racial nuancing affecting film stars, in what she calls "off-white Hollywood" (Negra 2001). These scholars examine the actors' personal journeys, their projection of foreign and/or ethnic identities on screen frequently through stereotyping, their struggle to adapt to different performance norms, and their success or failure in sustaining careers within the Hollywood, and hence, international star system. A leitmotiv is the frequent discrepancy between major stardom on domestic film markets and disappointing careers in English-speaking productions. In the case of Europe, alongside the glittering fame of Maurice Chevalier, Charles Boyer, Greta Garbo, Marlene Dietrich and Ingrid Bergman, there were many lacklustre or calamitous trajectories (among others Alain Delon, Jean Gabin, Hildegard Knef, Anna Magnani, Marcello Mastroianni, Isa Miranda, Romy Schneider and Ivan Mosjoukine). In the immediate post-war period, this one-way pattern was modified to some extent by star movements within particular regions. In the 1950s and 1960s for instance, European actors such as Schneider, Sophia Loren, Gina Lollobrigida, Brigitte Bardot, Fernandel, Curt Jurgens and Louis de Funès became pan-European stars. Similar cross-regional permeability can be found in other areas of the globe. There are prominent examples of pan-Asian stars, including the Chinese Jet Li (Yu 2012), the Taiwanese–Japanese Kaneshiro Takeshi (Tsai 2005) and many others such as South Korean Jun Ji-hyun and the Hong-Kong star Chow Yun-fat. But in both Europe and Asia, these cross-regional movements rarely translated into international or transnational stardom—exceptions include Hong Kong martial arts stars Jackie Chan (Holmlund 2010; Marchetti 2012), Jet Li (Yu 2012) and Bruce Lee (Yu 2015), and from Europe Bardot (Vincendeau 2013). As the studio era drew to a close, Hollywood diversified and increased its overseas productions (especially in Europe). European actors started working on international projects on a more fluid and temporary basis, appearing in English-language films largely financed by Hollywood but shot around the world (the so-called "runaway productions"). In the new millennium, an even more fluid global film industry, in terms of sources of finance and outlets, and patterns of global migration, exile and diaspora, diversified further circuits for stardom. Refracted through the Internet and social media, film stardom is now subsumed under the wider celebrity culture (Marshall 2006; Holmes and Redmond 2006; Holmes and Negra 2011) and with the easier availability of films on DVD, tablets or streaming, stars can more readily reach specific audiences around the globe. Indian stars are a case in point, given the size of the Indian diaspora (Raminder and Sinha 2005; Athique 2011).

The more atomised nature of the film industry, star system and audiences sketched out above has led to convincing arguments to "shift the primary focus of Star studies from Hollywood to the multiple centres of stardom across five of the world's continents" (Bandhauer and Royer 2015: 1), and displace the Hollywood vs. the rest of the world binary, in favour of a polycentric approach (Nagib *et al.* 2012). However, we may theorise audiences as "a postnational community of moviegoers" (Halle 2008: 44) and agree that it is increasingly impossible to understand "stardom within the singular scale of the nation" (Meeuf and Raphael 2013: 1), the film industry nevertheless still "relies on English as a medium of communication to win over greater audiences" (Halle 2008: 43). As a result, whether we like it or not, the hold of (mostly white) English-speaking Hollywood stars on worldwide audiences continues apace. The site *Vulture* names as the 2015 top ten stars: Jennifer Lawrence, Robert Downey Jr., Leonardo DiCaprio, Bradley Cooper, Dwayne Johnson, Tom Cruise, Hugh Jackman, Sandra Bullock, Channing Tatum and Scarlett Johansson (*Vulture* 2015); the complete list of 100 names includes not a single star from non-English speaking film. The same year, the *Mail Online* top 100 stars' list adopts a more historical (though entirely male) approach with its top ten as Al Pacino, Robert de Niro, Tom Hanks, Kevin Spacey, Harrison Ford, Jack Nicholson, Anthony Hopkins, Sean Connery, Ewan McGregor and Cary Grant. The first non-English speaking stars appear at number 88 (Juliette Binoche), number 90 (Gérard Depardieu) and number 92 (Amitabh Bachchan) (*Mail Online* 2015). The *Vulture* list shows explicitly the results as linked to the appeal of blockbusters (the *Star Wars*, *The Matrix*, *Iron Man* and *Hunger Games* franchises among others), but also implicitly to the domination of the English language. As Corey Creekmur sums up in a discussion of transnational stardom, while the "flows of transnational stardom, [the] movements across borders" are possible to a degree never attained before, the crossover for non-Anglophone stars "hasn't happened" (Meeuf and Raphael 2013: 21). Creekmur's pessimistic conclusion relates to Indian stars, but the point is equally valid for European actors whose capacity to achieve international and transnational stardom has actually diminished since the end of the studio system. White and "off-white" European actors are less subject to the racism that bars Asian, Latino and African American performers from Hollywood/transnational stardom (see Bogle 2006; Chow 2016) but their path is blocked by other factors.

Lacking the capacity to produce international blockbusters, notably within action film genres, Europe offers a clear example of the difficulties domestic stars—however major at home—experience in trying to penetrate foreign markets, starting with other countries within the continent. As a result, while scholarship on individual film producing nations in Europe recognises national star systems (see among others Babington 2001 on British cinema; Vincendeau 2000 and Austin 2003 on French cinema; Landy 2008 on Italian cinema), scholars have a much more pessimistic view about the viability or even existence of a European star system (Hedling 1996, 2015; Finney 2016). Nevertheless a few European actors do achieve international, and sometimes transnational, fame, and below I examine the ways in which European stars today transcend the limitations of national stardom, before moving on to a comparative study of four French actors—Jean Dujardin, Omar Sy, Audrey Tautou and Marion Cotillard—to illustrate in finer detail how some succeed or fail at exporting themselves.

The traditional route for European stars to make an impact on the world stage is through their connection to art cinema, via an association with a film movement or an *auteur*. Thus, Emil Jannings and Conrad Veidt were the stars of German expressionism, Jean Gabin the star of French poetic realism, and Anna Magnani of Italian neo-realism. Historically, European stars have benefitted from the prestige of working with well-known directors, and as a result occasionally received invitations to work in Hollywood (for instance Greta Garbo and Mauritz Stiller, Giulietta Masina and Federico Fellini, Hanna Schygulla and R.W. Fassbinder). In her book on Schygulla, Ulrike Sieglohr shows how such a pairing was a touchstone in the critical reception of the actress, and argues, "It is unlikely that Schygulla would have become an international star if Fassbinder had not re-established contact in 1978, offering her [. . .] the starring role in *Die ehe der Maria Braun* [The Marriage of Maria Braun, 1979, West Germany, Rainer Werner Fassbinder]" (Sieglohr 2014: 37). In the post-classical era, such a trajectory rarely moves the stars in question beyond the rarefied circuits of festivals and art cinema venues. (A major contemporary exception can be found in Spanish stars Penélope Cruz, Javier Bardem and Antonio Banderas, in large part because their Hispanic identity enables them to play "emblems of Latin-ness" [Sanchez-Biosca 2006: 133] and thus address the vast Latino market.) But for most European stars, other strategies are necessary, which can be summed up as learning English properly and making an impact on global celebrity culture.

The linguistic ability of French stars when it comes to speaking English has long been a sore point. The careers of Maurice Chevalier and Charles Boyer are evidence that in the 1930s a French accent was considered a charming selling point within specific popular genres: the musical, romantic comedy, the woman's film. The failure of others, such as Gabin in the 1940s and Delon in the 1960s points to lesser tolerance in realist drama or action film for French male stars (Vincendeau 2006, 2014), while French female stars in the 1940s found it difficult to translate their particular brand of gendered national identity to Hollywood (Sellier 2002). In contemporary cinema, a slight French accent may lead to picturesque small parts (such as Mathieu Amalric as the villain in *Quantum of Solace* (2008, UK/USA, Marc Forster) but for lead roles near-perfection is expected. However narratively justified, an accent must be "understood by the American middle-class and three quarters of the planet" (Vignoli 2014: 72). The need to shift to this higher linguistic level is attested by the rise of the language coach as a key adjunct to the French star system. Now a recognised necessity, professional language coaches work with stars such as Marion Cotillard, Léa Seydoux and Juliette Binoche (Vignoli 2014), with evident results in terms of eradicating accents for both onscreen comprehension and off-screen networking. Besides language proficiency, other factors determine the ability for French stars to sustain a career outside France. To examine this, I will turn, not to Binoche, Catherine Deneuve or Gérard Depardieu, whose careers are well charted (Vincendeau 2000, 2014; Downing and Harris 2011). Here I wish to shift the emphasis to four younger stars: Jean Dujardin, Omar Sy, Audrey Tautou and Marion Cotillard. Instead of relying on *auteur* cinema as a stepping stone to international fame, as many European stars—including Binoche, Deneuve and Depardieu—have traditionally done, these four actors were thrown into the limelight thanks to a *popular*

Figure 29.1 Audrey Tautou was thrown into the limelight thanks to the international success of *Le fabuleux destin d'Amélie Poulain* (Amélie, 2001, France/Germany, Jean-Pierre Jeunet. ©Claudie Ossard Productions/Union Générale Cinématographique (UGC)/Victoires Productions/Tapioca Films/France 3 Cinéma/MMC Independent.

French film that met with international success: *Le fabuleux destin d'Amélie Poulain* (Amélie, 2001, France/Germany, Jean-Pierre Jeunet, 2001) for Tautou (Figure 29.1), *La môme* (La Vie en Rose, 2007, France/UK/Czech Republic, Olivier Dahan) for Cotillard, *The Artist* (2011, France/USA/Belgium, Michel Hazanavicius) for Dujardin and *Intouchables* (The Untouchables, 2011, France, Olivier Nakache and Eric Toledano) for Sy. Besides their similarities in profile and age (all four were born in the 1970s), and their featuring in celebrity culture and advertising, interesting differences appear between Dujardin and Sy on the one hand and Cotillard and Tautou on the other, that point to the complex way in which gender intersects with international celebrity culture and national identity.

Exporting French stars

After the worldwide success of *The Artist,* and winning an Oscar as Best Actor and a host of other prizes including a Golden Globe, Jean Dujardin expected to pursue a Hollywood career. He appeared in two major Hollywood films, Martin Scorsese's *The Wolf of Wall Street* (2013, USA) and George Clooney's *The Monuments Men* (2014, USA/Germany), though in minor parts. In parallel, he projected an image that showed him as belonging to a circle of suave Hollywood male stars, with an ad for Nespresso coffee alongside Clooney. The bulk of his career, however, has remained on the French side, where, alongside the thriller-biopic *La French* (The Connection, 2014, France/Belgium, Cédric Jimenez) and Claude Lelouch's melodrama *Un + Une* (2015, France), he reprised his familiar comic persona in television sketches and films such as *9 mois ferme* (9-Month Stretch, 2013, France, Albert Dupontel) and especially *Brice 3* (2016, France, James Huth), a typically "inexportable" French comedy. Thus, if *The Artist* and its aftermath gave Dujardin access to international exposure and higher prestige at home, a transnational career failed to materialise. In interviews he presents the situation as positively opting for France and French cinema, and rejecting the massive commitment required of actors in promoting their work in the USA: "I don't want to become my own mouthpiece, it bores me" (in the same piece, he acknowledges his less-than-perfect English [*Le Parisien Magazine* 2015]). Yet in December 2013 Dujardin took part in a revealing Canal+ television spoof series. In *Le Débarquement 2: Jean Dujardin is Mr Propre*, Ben Stiller, wearing a smart suit and tie, makes him do the washing-up in a garishly decorated kitchen; Dujardin, decked up in apron and rubber gloves, scours a plate while muttering "They're a pain, those Yanks, I won't even be in the trailer". The short parody ends with a bottle of washing-up liquid with a smiling Dujardin on the label, and the caption, "In Hollywood it's French actors who do the washing-up". While the short film is part of a comic series in which Dujardin regularly appears, there is no mistaking the undertone of bitterness under the wry self-parody, which pinpoints the national pecking order in US cinema.

A similar pattern characterises Omar Sy's trajectory, to some extent complicated by racial issues. A relatively well-known television comic, Sy, a Frenchman of West African parentage, shot to fame with the unexpected triumph of *The Untouchables* in 2011—in which a black working-class man (Sy) cares for a paralyzed white aristocrat. *The Untouchables* became the most successful French film of all times at the French box-office and the highest grossing French-language film internationally (except in the UK), despite critical disparagement on account of its stereotypically racist depiction of blacks (Figure 29.2). Much fanfare accompanied Sy's decision to relocate with his family to L.A., perfect his English and pursue a career in Hollywood, ostensibly to escape celebrity and the burden of racial identity: "over there I am a Frenchman, not black [. . .] the colour of my skin does not matter" (Guichard 2016: 10)—a remark that in view of debates concerning racial representation in Hollywood cinema seems

Figure 29.2 The popular TV comic Omar Sy, a Frenchman of West African parentage, shot to fame with the unexpected success of *Intouchables* (The Untouchables, 2011, France, Olivier Nakache and Eric Toledano). ©Quad Productions.

at best optimistic. In the intervening years, Sy appeared in blockbusters (*Jurassic World* [2015, USA, Colin Trevorrow], *X-Men: Days of Future Past* [2014, USA/UK/Canada, Bryan Singer] and *Inferno* [2016, Hungary/USA, Ron Howard]); however, like Dujardin, he features only in small parts. And with the exception of *Inferno*, Dujardin's caustic remark about not appearing in the trailer applies. Sy's lead roles since *The Untouchables* have all been in French films: the social drama *Samba* (2014, France, Olivier Nakache and Eric Toledano), Roschdy Zem's *Chocolat* (2016, France), the biopic of real-life black clown Rafael Padilla and Hugo Gélin's hit comedy *Demain tout commence* (Two Is a Family, 2016, France/UK). Despite relocating to LA, he remains a national star, and not just on screen: since 2011, he has consistently figured in the top three most popular men in France in the influential annual poll by Sunday newspaper *Le Journal du dimanche* (he was number one in 2013 and again in 2016). His off-screen media exposure has also been much more prominent in the French press than in international media—appearing for instance on the cover of the French *Vanity Fair* in June 2014 and the French *GQ* in December 2014. The two male stars thus seem unable to convert the massive exposure generated by one hit film into sustained international or transnational fame. Tautou and Cotillard illustrate two very different configurations.

Audrey Tautou first appeared in the bittersweet comedy *Vénus beauté (institut)* (Venus Beauty, 1999, France, Tonie Marshall), which secured her persona as a demure Lolita. According to legend, director Jean-Pierre Jeunet spotted her on a poster for that film and cast her in *Amélie* (2001). Despite critical controversies—the film was accused of presenting a "whitewashed" and postcard vision of Paris—*Amélie* was a global hit, seen by 30 million spectators worldwide (a score unparalleled for a French language film until *The Untouchables*) and it turned Tautou into "the world's most bankable French star" (Henley 2008) as well as the best-paid actress at home, though not the most popular, for instance compared to her rom-com rival Sophie Marceau who regularly comes first in popularity polls as "France's favourite star", but whose elevated status on the domestic market is not matched abroad. Conversely, what Tautou lacks in home popularity she makes up in international status. In April 2002, *Time* magazine featured her on the cover of an issue on the theme of "Why France is Different", with the subtitle: "Actress Audrey Tautou whose *Amélie* proved the French can make movies the world wants to see."

Her romantic persona, petite stature and big brown eyes project an image of the cute Parisian waif that proved exportable, and endowed her with the magic power of international appeal. In the trailer for Alain Resnais' *Pas sur la bouche* (Not on the Lips, 2003, Switzerland/France), André Dussolier, who provided the voice-over in *Amélie*, says in mock-confidential tones: "With Audrey Tautou, the American market opens up." As a result, her French films are better distributed outside France: for instance her rom-com *Hors de prix* (Priceless, 2006, Pierre Salvadori, France) was sold to thirty-three countries, whereas Marceau's *LOL* (2008, France, Liza Azuelos), a much bigger domestic success, was sold to only fifteen countries; instead *LOL* was remade by Azuelos in Hollywood as *LOL* (2012, English/French/Ukrainian) with Demi Moore in the Marceau role—a different form of export for French cinema but not one favourable to stars who rarely play their own part in the English-language version; one rare exception is Gérard Depardieu in *Mon père ce héros* (My Father the Hero, 1991, France, Gérard Lauzier) and its remake *My Father the Hero* (1994, France/USA, Steve Miner).

Tautou's international fame did not, however, translate into a lasting transnational one. Despite appearing in significant roles in *The Da Vinci Code* (2006, USA/Malta/France/UK, Ron Howard) with Tom Hanks and in Stephen Frears' *Dirty, Pretty Things* (2002, UK), Tautou has remained a star of French film. Like Dujardin and Sy, she is on record as presenting this as her own preference (Mueller 2014), but, judging from films and screen interviews, it is noticeable that her English, while fluent, remains distinctly accented. It is likely that leading parts in American films have not materialised for that reason. Yet, unlike Dujardin and Sy, Tautou has retained greater international visibility, long after the "*Amélie* effect" wore off, through her association with fashion and cosmetics, in particular Chanel. The biopic *Coco avant Chanel* (Coco Before Chanel, 2009, France/Belgium, Anne Fontaine), in which she plays the young Chanel, came out in France on 22 April 2009. Two weeks later, a lavish Chanel N°5 perfume commercial directed by Jeunet was released on the internet. The 2'25" film, set on the Orient-Express and in Istanbul insistently recalls *Amélie* with its saturated retro colours and multiple references to the film's narrative. Between *Amélie* and *Coco Before Chanel*, Tautou's role in *Priceless* also associated her with high-end French fashion, jewellery and perfume brands and cosmopolitan locations such as the Côte d'Azur. The Chanel N°5 commercial—and assorted photo campaigns—had arguably as much, if not more influence internationally on the star's visibility as *Coco Before Chanel*.

If Sophie Marceau offers a useful contrast with Tautou in terms of domestic vs. international fame, Marion Cotillard provides the best point of comparison for a distinction between international and transnational stardom. Cotillard featured in over 30 films, including many comedies, before her breakthrough *La vie en rose* (2007). The success of the film, a biopic of the singer Edith Piaf for which she won an Oscar, shifted her performance register firmly towards drama, while it provided a passport to Hollywood. Between 2007 and 2016 Cotillard appeared in twelve English-speaking and seven French-speaking films in leading roles, working with critically acclaimed directors such as Christopher Nolan, James Gray, Woody Allen, Steven Soderbergh in English-language films and Jacques Audiard, Nicole Garcia, the Dardenne brothers and Xavier Dolan in French-language productions. A significant number of her international films met with box-office success and she became the "most bankable French actress" (Maad 2014), with Tautou coming second. Cotillard's ability to navigate between France and Hollywood is arguably facilitated by her melodramatic range, more exportable than Tautou's quirky, more comic register (Figure 29.3). Cotillard's linguistic proficiency is clearly crucial too, with near-perfect English in spoken dialogue and song. Building on these factors, her transnational success rests also on the convergence of film and advertising, which places her within the realm of "commodity stardom" (Cook 2012: 63–64).

Figure 29.3 Marion Cotillard's ability to navigate between France and Hollywood is arguably facilitated by her melodramatic range. *De rouille et d'os* (Rust and Bone, 2012, France, Jacques Audiard). ©Why Not Productions/Page 114/France 2 Cinéma/Les Films du Fleuve/ Radio Télévision Belge Francophone (RTBF)/Lumière/Lunanime.

Cotillard's slim physique, oval-shaped face and striking large blue eyes (frequently filled with tears in films) construct a romantic onscreen persona. Off-screen, her glamorous allure has been deployed in advertising. In addition to innumerable magazine covers and fashion shoots, Cotillard has featured as "ambassador" for Dior in a much-discussed series of short films that deliberately blur the boundaries between advertising and fiction filmmaking. The series, designed to advertise the "Lady Dior" handbag, features Cotillard as "Lady Noire", a mysterious femme fatale devised by Dior designer John Galliano; it consists of *The Lady Noire Affair* (2008, Olivier Dahan), *Lady Rouge: The Eyes of Mars* (2010, Jonas Akerlund), *Lady Blue Shanghai* (2010, David Lynch); *Lady Grey London* (2011, John Cameron Mitchell) and *L.A. by Dior* (2011, John Cameron Mitchell). The massive financial investment by the French fashion brand is evident in the choice of directors, the length and quality of the films, which range from six to sixteen minutes, and their duality which among other things "reflects the two feature film markets to which Cotillard's presence is seen to appeal: the selective art house set, and the more mainstream crowd" (Berra 2012: 242). Of course there has always been a close relationship between film stars and fashion (Moseley 2005), but the new millennium has seen a sharp increase in the involvement of stars and celebrities with fashion and cosmetics (Church Gibson 2011; Munich 2011). Given that the sector is strongly marked as feminine and French, with giant French companies such as LVMH (owner of Dior), L'Oréal and Kering dominating the market, the convergence can be seen to work especially in favour of female French stars such as Tautou and Cotillard, able to channel a version of French identity that has worldwide recognition thanks to its synergy with globally exportable brands.

Conclusion

The trajectories examined above illustrate the many shades of success (and failure) in terms of the exportability of French stars. Although such trajectories are embedded within the French film industry and French culture, they point to conditions that are echoed around the globe. These include major success at home, the skills to perform convincingly in the host language, and the ability for the star to practice the "international vocabulary" that characterises the contemporary star-system within the global culture of commodities (Benhamou 2002: 424). The transnational star also walks a tightrope in terms of national anchorage. Too much embedding within national identity curtails the possibilities of export, too little may provoke rejection at home. Indeed, transnational success in French stars always meets with an ambivalent mixture of pride and resentment in the domestic media. While she is recognised as the most successful French film star export of her generation, Cotillard (along with her partner, the actor and filmmaker Guillaume Canet) has been in equal measure admired and lauded, and mercilessly mocked and criticised (Guichard 2013), pointing to the complex role stars play as carriers of national identity.

References

Athique, A. (2011) "Diasporic Audiences and Non-Resident Media: The Case of Indian Films", *Participations*, 8 (2). www.participations.org/Volume8/Issue2/1aAthique.pdf.

Austin, G. (2003) *Stars in Modern French Film*, London: Arnold.

Babington, B. (2001) *British Stars and Stardom: From Alma Taylor to Sean Connery*, Manchester: Manchester University Press.

Bandhauer, A. and Royer, M. (eds) (2015) *Stars in World Cinema*, London: I. B. Tauris

Benhamou, F. (2002) *L'Economie du star-système*, Paris: Odile Jacob.

Bergfelder, T. (2004) "Negotiating Exoticism: Hollywood, Film Europe and the Cultural Reception of Anna May Wong", in Fisher, L. and Landy, M. (eds) *Stars: The Film Reader*, London and New York: Routledge, 59–75.

Berra, J. (2012) "*Lady Blue Shanghai*: The Strange Case of David Lynch and Dior", *Film, Fashion & Consumption* 1 (3): 233–250.

Bogle, D. (2006) *Mulattoes, Mammies, & Bucks, An Interpretive History of Blacks in American Films*, 4th edn, New York: Continuum.

Chow, K. (2016) "Why Won't Hollywood Cast Asian Actors?", *The New York Times*, 22 April, www.nytimes.com/2016/04/23/opinion/why-wont-hollywood-cast-asian-actors.html?_r=0.

Church Gibson, P. (2011) *Fashion and Celebrity Culture*, London: Berg Publishers.

Cook, P. (2012) *Nicole Kidman*, London: BFI/Palgrave Macmillan.

DeCordova, R. (1990) *The Emergence of the Star System in America*, Urbana, IL: University of Illinois Press.

Downing, L. and Harris, S. (eds.) (2011) *From Perversion to Purity: The Stardom of Catherine Deneuve*, Manchester: Manchester University Press.

Dyer, R. (1979) *Stars*, London: British Film Institute.

—— (1987) *Heavenly Bodies: Film Stars and Society*, London: BFI/Macmillan.

Finney, A. (2016) *The State of European Cinema, A New Dose of Reality*, London: Cassell.

Guichard, L. (2013) "En vedettes américaines", *Télérama* 3305, 15 March, 34–36.

—— (2016) "Omar Sy", *Télérama* 3446, 27 January, 6–10.

Halle, R. (2008) *German Film After Germany: Toward a Transnational Aesthetic*, Champaign, IL: University of Illinois Press.

Hedling, O. (1996/2009) "Possibilities of Stardom in European Cinema Culture", in Soila, T. (ed.) *Stellar Encounters: Stardom in Popular European Cinema*, London: John Libbey Publishing, 254–264.

—— (2015) "The Trouble with Stars: Vernacular versus Global Stardom in Two Forms of European Popular Culture", in Harrod, M., Liz, M. and Timoshkina, A. (eds) *The Europeanness of European Cinema: Identity, Meaning, Globalisation*, London and New York: I.B. Tauris, 109–124.

Heilbut, A. (1993) *Exiled in Paradise*, Berkeley, CA: University of California Press.

Henley, J. (2008) "It Doesn't Take Much to Catch a Man", *The Guardian*, 13 June, www.theguardian.com/film/2008/jun/13/filmandmusic1.filmandmusic4.

Holmes, S. and Redmond, S. (eds) (2006) *Framing Celebrity: New Directions in Celebrity Culture*, New York: Routledge.

Holmes, S. and Negra, D. (eds) (2011) *In the Limelight and Under the Microscope: Forms and Functions of Female Celebrity*, New York: Continuum.

Holmlund, C. (2010) "Celebrity, Ageing and Jackie Chan: Middle-aged Asian in Transnational Action", *Celebrity Studies*, 1 (1): 96–112.
Landy, M. (2008) *Stardom, Italian Style: Screen Performance and Personality in Italian Cinema*, Bloomington, IN: Indiana University Press.
Le Parisien (2015) "Jean Dujardin: Bye, Bye, Hollywood!", 10 December 2015, www.leparisien.fr/magazine/grand-angle/jean-dujardin-bye-bye-hollywood-10-12-2015-5358385.php.
Maad, A. (2014) "Marion Cotillard, reine du box-office français", *Le Figaro.fr Madame*, 22 April, www.madame.lefigaro.fr/celebrites/marion-cotillard-reine-box-office-francais-220414-850808.
Mail Online (2015) "The Top 100 Film Stars", www.dailymail.co.uk/tvshowbiz/article-179643/The-100-film-stars.html.
Marchetti, G. (2012) *The Chinese Diaspora on American Screens*, Philadelphia, PA: Temple University Press.
Marshall, P. D. (ed.) (2006) *The Celebrity Culture Reader*, London and New York: Routledge.
Meeuf, R. and Raphael, R. (2013) *Transnational Stardom: International Celebrity in Film and Popular Culture*, London: Palgrave Macmillan.
Miyao, D. (2007) *Sessue Hayakawa: Silent Cinema and Transnational Stardom*, Durham, NC: Duke University Press.
Morin, E. (1960) *The Stars*, New York: Grove Press.
Moseley, R. (ed.) (2005) *Fashioning Film Stars: Dress, Culture, Identity*, London: British Film Institute.
Mueller, M. (2014) "Audrey Tautou Interview: 'I Haven't Refused America—I Just Feel Very French", *The Independent*, 5 June, www.independent.co.uk/arts-entertainment/films/features/audrey-tautou-interview-i-haven-t-refused-america-i-just-feel-very-french-9492203.html.
Munich, A. (ed.) (2011) *Fashion in Film*, Bloomington, IN: Indiana University Press.
Negra, D. (2001) *Off-white Hollywood: American Culture and Ethnic Female Stardom*, London: Routledge.
Nagib, L., Perriam, C. and Dudrah, R. (2012) *Theorizing World Cinema*, London: I. B. Tauris.
Phillips, A. and G. Vincendeau (eds) (2006) *Journeys of Desire: European Actors in Hollywood, A Critical Companion*, London: BFI.
Raminder, K. and Sinha, A. J. (eds) (2005) *Bollyworld, Popular Indian Cinema through a Transnational Lens*, New Delhi, London: Sage Publications.
Russell-Taylor, J. (1983) *Strangers in Paradise: The Hollywood Emigrés 1933–1950*, London: Faber & Faber.
Sanchez-Biosca, V. (2006) "The Latin Masquerade: The Spanish in Disguise in Hollywood", in Phillips, A. and Vincendeau, G. (eds) *Journeys of Desire: European Actors in Hollywood, A Critical Companion*, London: BFI, 133–139.
Sellier, G. (2002) "Danielle Darrieux, Michèle Morgan and Micheline Presle in Hollywood: The Threat to French Identity", *Screen* 43 (2): 201–214.
Shaw, L. (2013) *Carmen Miranda*, London: Palgrave.
Sieglohr, U. (2014) *Hanna Schygulla*, London: BFI/Palgrave Macmillan.
Tsai, E. (2005) "Taneshiro Takeshi: Transnational Stardom and the Media and Culture Industries in Asia's Global/Postcolonial Age", *Modern Chinese Literature and Culture* 17 (1): 100–132.
Vasey, R. (1997) *The World According to Hollywood*, Exeter: Exeter University Press.
Vignoli, L. (2014) "Hollywood Lesson 1". *Le Magazine du Monde*, 17 May: 71–72.
Vincendeau, G. (2000) *Stars and Stardom in French Cinema*, London: Continuum.
—— (2006) "Not for Export: Jean Gabin in Hollywood", in Phillips, A. and Vincendeau, G. (eds) *Journeys of Desire: European Actors in Hollywood, A Critical Companion*, London: British Film Institute, 115–123.
—— (2014) "The Perils of Trans-national Stardom: Alain Delon in Hollywood Cinema", *Mise au point*, http://map.revues.org/1800.
—— (2015) "Juliette Binoche: The Perfect European Star", in Harrod, M., Liz, M. and Timoshkina, A. (eds) *The Europeanness of European Cinema: Identity, Meaning, Globalisation*, London and New York: I. B. Tauris, 131–144.
Vulture (2015) "Vulture's Most Valuable Stars of 2015", www.vulture.com/2015/11/vultures-most-valuable-stars-of-2015.html.
Yu, S. Q. (2012) *Jet Li and Transnational Kung Fu Stardom*, Edinburgh: Edinburgh University Press.
—— (2015) "Dancing with Hollywood: Redefining Transnational Chinese Stardom", in Bandhauer, A. and Royer, M. (eds) *Stars in World Cinema*, London and New York: I. B. Tauris, 104–116.

30

FILM FUSIONS

The cult film in World Cinema

Mark Goodall

Introduction

As this collection makes abundantly clear, the concept of "World Cinema" can be hard to define. To further establish a sensible definition of what "*cult* world cinema" might be is to stretch, contort and confuse understanding even further. Scholars have made bold attempts at defining what "cult cinema" might be that range from the "informal" to the "intertextual" by way of the "subcultural". For instance, Karl and Philip French's notion of cult as an "intense personal interest and devotion to a person, idea or activity" sought to access the devotional, sacramental aspect of engagement with cinema (French and French 1999: 6). A study by Jancovich and colleagues argued that it is the reception of films and their distinction from, and opposition to, the "mainstream" that defines films as "cult" (Janovich *et al.* 2003: 2). Mathijs and Sexton (2011) later promoted a rich, intertextual sense of what cult cinema might be, while admitting that because the numerous attempts at defining cult cinema approach the subject from the perspective of the vernacular—"highlighting elements that cannot be caught in a description"—any definition of cult cinema must be tantalisingly "intangible" and "intersubjective" (Mathijs and Sexton 2011: 6).

Cult cinema, I suggest in this chapter, is both culturally specific and yet transglobal. Institutional practices central to the specific geographical location play a part, whether these are related to production (the making of the films) or reception of films (critical reaction); at the same time, practices developed beyond a specific geographical territory are also key. In terms of the film works themselves, we can see that they also grow and develop out of complex, transglobal relationships, understandings and interpretations. Consequently, I follow other chapters in this volume that reject a notion of World Cinema as an esoteric "other" to mainstream (Hollywood) film culture, just as I seek to problematise the role of "the other" in definitions of "cult". Instead, I posit that film operates through a complex system of frequently transglobal interconnections. Thus, World Cinema must, to some degree at least, be conceptualised straightforwardly as "the cinema of the world" (Cooke 2007: 8), while also acknowledging that the term often brings with it a specific set of values and expectations, just as the word "cult" does with regard to film.

Most canonical texts on cult cinema emerged from the Anglo-Saxon academic sphere and so interpretations and readings of the cult films tend to be coloured by the biases, prejudices and tastes of the writers schooled in this tradition. My work, it should be mentioned, also draws on this tradition, but clearly there is space for other approaches. One way of challenging the dominance of the Anglo-Saxon sphere might be to provide an overarching gloss of as diverse a range of cult world films as possible in order to decentre a Western-centric view of cult film. However, such "lists" tend to be intellectually unhelpful and emotionally unstimulating. I instead wish to identify key examples of cult cinema from around the world and address these in some detail as exemplars of what has been made and what is possible in the future. The world, and World Cinema, is vast, and totalising endeavours often fail to bring understanding any closer. Nonetheless, while recognising the difficulties of defining cult cinema, it is also worth looking to extend the definition of what might constitute cult film in the twenty-first century, especially in relation to World Cinema. In addition to the sociological, reception-based, textual and aesthetic analyses proposed by Mathijs and Sexton (2011) (and the amalgam and departure from these methods that they ultimately advocate), we can also utilise a "multi-plane" technique to discuss cult world films. Such an approach has emerged from the field of experimental film studies (Ulmer 1994; Ray 2001) and media archaeology, where a Foucauldian, experimental, radical, playful and anti-linear approach to media has been developed, coming at the subject via a simultaneous range of historical, technical and anecdotal perspectives, what Mathijs and Sexton define as the aesthetic "phenomenal experience of the spectator" (Mathijs and Sexton 2011: 17). It is impossible for scholars to know everything about films inside or outside of their specific cultural codes, and yet this does not prevent them from enjoying the affect of World Cinema and cult film, in the process leading to "some pure insight into a profound form of truth" (Mathijs and Mendik 2011: 1). By exploring the specific art of any film, returning to the cinematic effect/affect, "considering the movies themselves" (Ibid.), we can reveal something about its status as a cult object.

What can we expect from world cult cinema that is not evident in mainstream or arthouse films? Cult films offer "transgression, abjection, freakery, utopia, exotica, badness, intertextuality and irony [. . .] each of these concepts upsets notions or normality of taste" (Mathijs and Mendik 2011: 1). As Cline and Weiner (2010) have argued, cult films can operate at the vector of arthouse and grindhouse, high and low forms of cinematic art collapsing and merging. The perversion of many cult films can be sexist and debasing but it can also be liberating (and on rare occasions both at the same time—see discussion of *Baise Moi* [Rape Me, 2000, France, Virigine Despentes, Coralie Trinh Thi] below). The specific cultural mores of a particular geographical location feed into the cult film and interpret the politics and poetics of transgression in unique ways. The process is complementary: for every cult attribute adopted by a form of national cinema, the special characteristics of that cinema are absorbed back into the cult canon: a form of transgressive cultural feedback. That said, I am not interested in the more recent and deliberate marketing and creation of "cult films", nor in any labelled "genre" of cult cinema, but more in individual works of world film art that can be interpreted as, and have organically become, through a variety of chance and random processes, "cult". In other words, I am interested in the ways in which "cult" emerges out of the combination of a contradictory attitude on the part of the filmmaker and "unexpected audience engagements" by the consumers of such films (Mathijs and Sexton 2011: 8). The link between cult films and exploitation cinema has been made since the earliest theorising on the genre. The surrealists, back in the early 1960s, praised "bad films" ahead of quality studio productions (Kyrou 2000: 68; see also Sconce's discussion of "paracinema" as "less a distinct group of films than a particular reading protocol, a counter-aesthetic turned subcultural sensibility devoted to all manner of cultural detritus" 1995: 372). As already noted, in much of the scholarship on cult cinema, the focus has been on Anglo-American films and what we might call "world cult cinema" remains elusive. Thus, it is crucial to discuss here films

Figure 30.1 *Mondo Cane* (1962, Italy, Paolo Cavara, Gualtiero Jacopetti and Franco Prosperi). ©Cineriz.

outside of the Anglo-American sphere, in order that we might aim for a transnational, transgressive perspective, even if the cult world films under analysis often draw their inspiration from the European and American avant-garde.

Historicising cult World Cinema

I now wish to define three aspects of how cult films relate to world cinema and thereby highlight how our understanding of cult film must also be inflected historically. The first dimension of cult world cinema can be termed *colonial* cult cinema. Here we see Western filmmakers projecting, and exploiting, dubious ideas about the "other" onto cinema screens. A key example of this is *Mondo Cane* (1962, Italy, Paolo Cavara, Gualtiero Jacopetti and Franco E. Prosperi) (Figure 30.1). Exoticism was, of course, evident in cinema before the 1960s, but at this point it reached a new height. *Mondo Cane* is a Technicolor tour of unusual rituals and practices—determined unusual by the directorial team that is. These generally fall into two categories: so-called "primitive rites", such as Melanesian Cargo Cults, and "civilised wrongs" such as the results of European Atomic Bomb tests in the pacific. The huge success of *Mondo Cane* at the box office led to multiple copies of the film, where the pattern of shifting rapidly from one location to the next, jumbling up cultures and practices and throwing every cinematic trick from crash zooms to syrupy soundtracks into the edit was repeated *ad infinitum*. The film presented a problematic interpretation of global culture, but at the same time it critiqued such representations with scenes depicting what they saw as the degeneration of Western culture. Indeed, the early wave of mondo films was admired by J. G. Ballard for reflecting the "horrors of peace" back to its audience (Goodall 2006: 14). Mondo films at times invoked revolutionary reaction (see for example Getino and Solanas's manifesto "Towards a Third Cinema" [1971: 25] where they labelled Jacopetti and his cinema "fascist"), at times parody (see, for example, *The Gods*

Must be Crazy [Botswana/South Africa, 1980, Jamie Uys], where a Kalahari tribe, insulated from the rest of the world, is corrupted when a Coca-Cola bottle dropped from a passing aeroplane lands in their territory, causing envy, anger and violence). The parody of the so-called "Cargo Cult" belief system and its simplistic representation of native peoples echoes the worst excesses of the mondo film). In a more complex way *Mondo Cane* inspired cult films such as Alejandro Jodorowsky's *El Topo* (1970, Mexico) and Haskell Wexler's *Medium Cool* (1969, USA), where a news cameraman, played by Robert Forster, has a picture of Belmondo from *À bout de souffle* (Breathless, 1960, France, Jean-Luc Godard) on his wall but carries out his work in the manner of a merciless and cynical mondo practitioner.

In terms of world cinema, the subject of *Mondo Cane* was the world and the film world responded by producing its own "mondo movies". These include *La femme spectacle* (Night Women, 1964, France, Claude Lelouch), *Australia After Dark* (1975, Australia, John D. Lamond), *Des morts* (Of the Dead, 1979, Belgium, Jean-Pol Ferbus, Dominique Garny and Thierry Zéno) and *Mondo New York* (1988, USA, Harvey Keith) and portraits of specific nations by non-native directors such as Sweden (*Svezia inferno e paradiso* [Sweden: Heaven and Hell, 1968, Italy, Luigi Scattini]), and continents such as the far East (*Shocking Asia* [1976, Hong Kong/West Germany, Rolf Olsen]). The mondo aesthetic also rears up in more contemporary Western films such as *The Killing of America* (1981, USA, Sheldon Renan and Leonard Schrader) and *Baraka* (1992, USA, Ron Fricke). Like the western or gangster genres, the mondo film became a global film style. In addition, the mondo aesthetic is evident in exemplars of more arthouse fare. The "paternalistic" tendency of the mondo film, both in terms of shaping the subjects of the film is evident, as Richards (2006) points out, in the work of Werner Herzog (*Aguirre, der Zorn Gottes* [Aguirre, Wrath of God, 1972, West Germany] and *Fitzcarraldo* [1982, West Germany/ Peru]) and Dennis Hopper (*The Last Movie*[1971, USA]) who both produced cult films where problematic relations exist between the film director and the subjects and landscapes of their works, forged to a greater or lesser extent out of "neo-colonial precepts" (Richards 2006: 56). In the extreme version of this cinema, according to one famous critique of *Africa Addio* (Farewell Africa, 1966, Italy, Gualterio Jacopetti and Franco Prosperi), "Man is turned into an extra who dies so Jacopetti can comfortably film his execution" (Getino and Solanas 1971: 25).

Exploitation movies

Exploitation films have been defined by Eric Schaefer as "any low budget movie with a topical bent" (Schaefer 1999: 4). Initially, discussion of such films tended to focus on the methods exploited by the film producers, later this focused more on the subjects being exploited. In the 1960s and 1970s such exploitation films typically incorporated a range of subjects including sexuality (sexploitation) and race (blaxploitation). In Australia, an indigenous exploitation industry developed, capitalising on the colonial impulse. At the same time as national film industries were beginning to use Australia as a backdrop for adventure films (*Ned Kelly* [1970, Australia/ UK, Tony Richardson], *Walkabout* [1971, UK/Australia, Nicolas Roeg], etc.) a smaller group of indigenous filmmakers were creating a parallel industry of cult films. One of the greatest successes of this era was *The Adventures of Barry McKenzie* (1972, Australia, Bruce Beresford) and the sequel *Barry McKenzie Holds His Own* (1974, Australia, Bruce Beresford). These were followed by a series of *Alvin* films, directed by Tim Burgess, sexploitation works that functioned as a kind of *Alfie* (1966, UK, Lewis Gilbert) in reverse where the principal character, in supposedly comic fashion, tries to *escape* from the women who lust after him. Horror films such as *Night of Fear* (1972, Australia, Terry Bourke), *Patrick* (1978, Australia, Richard Franklin) and *Long Weekend* (1978, Australia, Colin Eggleston) also contributed to a dissident sense of excess to be found across these films. Hence the story of the Australian film industry, in addition to incorporating acclaimed arthouse films such as those of Peter Weir, has to include a wide variety of genre and cult film practices (action films, martial arts films, car chase films, and so on). This 'Ozploitation' cinema is traceable up to *Mad Max* (1979, Australia, George Miller), the point at which the Ozploitation film arguably goes mainstream, with a resurrection of sorts in 2004 with Greg McLean's *Wolf Creek* (2005, Australia, Greg McLean). *Australia After Dark* (1975, Australia, John D. Lamond) was the nation's own *Mondo Cane*, which purported to reveal the "truth" about Australian culture and attitudes. The film took the *Mondo Cane*-style approach of a tour around the oddities of behaviour "down-under", including sexploitation vignettes concerning body painting, bondage clubs, transvestites and obviously fake satanic rituals. There were also more serious sequences on alcoholism and the poverty of the native Australian population. Lamond also directed the clever and beautifully shot *The ABC of Love and Sex* (The ABC of Love and Sex: Australia Style, 1978, Australia, John D. Lamond), a tongue-in-cheek and mildly informative discourse on modern attitudes to sexuality. Much like the mondo film, the "sexy" documentary grew into a significant genre resulting in series such as the infamous and hugely popular *Schoolgirl Report* (Schulmädchen-Report, 1970–1980, West Germany, Ernst Hofbauer) series; more than seven million Germans watched the first film. The cult film is often derivative and the above examples demonstrate how the Australian cult film copied neo-colonial impulses, was built on, and even relished, the stereotypical colonial image of itself.

"Excessive" sexuality plays a key role in the chauvinism of cult film, where women in particular are exploited for commercial gain. In cult world cinema, one vivid example of this occurs in the films of Armando Bo, who based his trashy films around the figure of actress Isabel Sarli, a former Miss Argentina and subsequently Bo's wife. While the "serious" Argentinian cinema of The Liberation Film Group in the 1960s is known and respected, the exploitation cinema of the time is less so. Bo's films, for example, are almost completely lost. By exploiting the voluptuous figure of Sarli, Bo created Argentina's first sex symbol and in some respects the duo's frank and brazen construction of sexuality in the face of censorship "changed Argentinian cinema forever" (Tombs 1997: 130). Sarli's character is always either the nymphomaniac, unable to control her volcanic desires, or the "good woman who in spite of herself stirs up a whirlpool of passion, sex and violence" (Ibid.). *Fuego* (Fire, 1969, Argentina, Armando Bo) is a classic example of this aesthetic containing, despite the sexual shenanigans, a surprisingly downbeat and tragic finale. Another Sarli film, this time directed by Leopoldo Torre Nilsson, *Setenta veces siete* (The Female, 1962, Argentina), despite being clearly exploitative, utilises experimental, New Wave techniques and monochrome photography. The Bo/Sarli films have developed a following among cult film fans keen on sexual kitsch. John Waters, for example, has expressed his admiration for *Fuego*, describing it as "a hetero film for gay people to marvel at" (*Dangerous Minds* 2015) and these films can be viewed as a South American companion to the cinema of American sexploitation director Russ Meyer.

Transglobal cult film

In response to this neo-colonial form of cinema, a second phase of cult film emerged, the *transglobal*, where cinemas from the non-Western tradition undergoing processes of decolonisation begin to absorb and instrumentalise, sometimes radically, avant-garde and exploitation practices. The central notion here is of the "New Wave", associated primarily in Anglo-Saxon criticism with the French, German and British variants but evident in a wide range of global cinematic practices, including those of South America, Africa and Eastern Europe. South American New Waves took a very different form from their Northern European variants. Cult cinema here tended to emerge out of more "serious" cinematic production. *La battaglia di Algeri* (The Battle of Algiers, 1966, Italy/Algeria, Gillo Pontecorvo), for example, although directed by an Italian attempted to project the decolonisation struggle with depth and empathy, with dialogue from the Algiers Kasbah, delivered in Arabic, mixing moral questioning and sympathetic, nuanced portraits of both the oppressed and the oppressors. The "compassionate humanism" (Vogel 1974: 123) and gritty docu-verité style of the film, which utilised a powerful original musical score, would become a useful blueprint for revolutionary cinema across the globe that was to target power elites, whatever their hue. Vogel (1974) argued that subversion in the twentieth century derived from art movements such as surrealism, dada and expressionism, and in transglobal cult films we glimpse how they were adapted and put to good use when blended with indigenous aesthetic practices and cultural mores of a more anarchic spirit. The complex politics and aesthetic of films such as *The Battle of Algiers* would be subsequently adapted into much more exploitative versions of cinema. Such exchanges and borrowings between "high" and "low" film cultures reflect the "conceptual inclusiveness" theory offered by David Andrews for "folding into one flexible category all the art cinemas that people used to call 'art cinema'" (Andrews 2013: xi) with the other categorisations of "art cinemas that few critics have ever called 'art cinema'"—in other words cult films.

The development of the cult film in India makes for an interesting case study. Indian industrial cinema (Bollywood), the auteur films of Satyajit Ray, Ritwik Ghatak and Mrinal Sen and the "Parallel Cinema" movement, films that were in the words of Muzaffar Ali "non compromising without being non-commercial" (Robinson 1981: 393) are highly regarded and important contributions to the history of World Cinema in a variety of ways. While there is some truth in the argument that "Indian cinema is so successful at satisfying the own needs of its own audience that it rarely bothers with the world outside" (Tombs 1997: 77), there have been some instances of re-working other cinemas to powerful effect. As Geetha, Rao and Dhakshna (2007) argue, the driving force of much Indian commercial cinema is an aesthetic process derived from the *Natyashastra*, a second-century Indian text on art and performance, where different emotions are blended to create a rich spectacle. This "aesthetic alchemy" (Ibid: 74) is evident in cult films where the violent, ambiguous anti-hero—the epitome of *Raudhra* concept—thrives in a deeply cynical world.

Films such as *Sholay* (1975, India, Ramesh Sippy) were successful in capitalising on the genre traditions of the West, in this case the Italian or "Spaghetti" Western, turning them into commercial successes, a formula developing "star value" and "mainstream-ising existing generic formats" (Vitali 2008: 193) by mediating existing genres into specific Asian contexts. *Sholay* was a big-budget film, India's first 70mm spectacle, and typical of the kinds of film "capable of incorporating generic elements associated with foreign films and re-proposing them to the Indian mainstream domestic market" (Ibid.: 224). Yet as with other films operating within the studio realm, box-office failure resulted in a cult audience discovering the film on home video formats and promoting the perceived cult attributes of the films via alternative networks. *Shalimar* (1978, India/USA, Kishan Shah) was a commercial failure when it was released but is now one of the finest examples of Indian cult cinema. The film's cult status lies in its exhilarating blend of traditional Bollywood elements (songs, dances, panoramic scenery) with new European techniques such as abstract collision editing and a strong generic crime premise similar to Italian and French films of the same era. This postmodern fusion is evident from the opening of the film: a dance routine to the music of R.D. Burman that is a fusion of psychedelic pop and Indian instrumentation; a reworking of the "cha cha cha" via a filter of late 1960s' grooviness. The modernism of European genre film is also present; skyscrapers and pop art interiors litter the film. The latest video technologies (some created in London post-production houses) are used to create special effects and hallucinogenic CCTV scenes. The traditional Indian studio film trope of the elaborate dance routine is rendered as an exotic surreal snake god ritual, and thus could be straight out of a mondo film. *Shalimar* also manages to incorporate a Spaghetti Western-style chase on horseback at the climax and even an anti-colonial message when the natives murder the British arch-criminal (played by Rex Harrison). The critical indifference *Shalimar* first provoked is still evident today (it is ignored in almost all existing studies of Indian cinema). Yet the film slowly developed a cult status through the DVD-video circuit and it continues to be debated online with the "so bad it's good" argument raging (see Ghosh 2013; Big Indian Picture 2014). This reading as "minority resistance and niche celebration" (Mathijs and Sexton 2011: 8) makes *Shalimar* a global cult film *par excellence*.

The traditional cult/exploitation tropes of sex and horror were utilised in Indian cinema as far back as the 1930s, in films such as *Hunterwali* (The Princess and the Hunter, 1935, India, Homi Wadia) and more recently in titles such as *Avalude Ravukal* (1978, India, I. V. Sasi) and *Naag Nagin* (1989, India, Ramkumar Bohra). "It is in popular cinema that we see most vividly the 'Indianness' of Indian cinema" (Gokulsing and Dissanayake 1998: 23) and it is in Indian cult cinema that we see the outer fringes of this "Indianness".

Beyond the neo-colonial

Finally, one finds examples of non-Western cinema that exist entirely independently of neo-colonial traditions. Brazil's Cinema Novo movement produced its share of exemplary new films concerned with promoting a progressive nationalism and an "indigenous, socially relevant cinema" (Vogel 1974: 159). When dealing with cult films, on the other hand, Espinosa states in his famous essay "Towards an Imperfect Cinema" that "Imperfect cinema is no longer interested in a specific taste, let alone 'good taste'" (Espinosa 1971: 67), advocating a new form of challenging cinema at least partly aligned with the definition of cult cinema. I am arguing here that the energy of these new cinemas also led to the creation of critically less favoured cult films, but films nonetheless connected, however thinly, to the emergence of independent locally specific forms of cinema and experimental new practices of art.

Poet Oswald de Andrade's *Cannibalist Manifesto* of 1928 promoted an experimental modernism where Brazilian writers, artists and filmmakers could extend the boundaries of taste, meaning and aesthetics. The use of the cannibal metaphor "permits the Brazilian subject to forge his specular colonial identity into an autonomous and original (as opposed to dependent, derivative) national culture" (Barry 1991: 35). European culture is "devoured" to create an entirely new work. We can see this acted upon in many films of 1960s Brazilian cinema. *Macunaíma* (1969, Brazil, Joaquim Pedro de Andrade), for example, is a cult film existing outside of the more serious Brazilian national cinemas, a film that appears to have taken de Andrade's (no relation to the film's director) manifesto deeply to heart and that can be aligned more closely with the soft-core aesthetic of the subsequent *pornochanchada* genre (Figure 30.2). One of the features of the cult film is that it is often tasteless and gross in subject matter and style and *Macunaíma* achieves that effect with aplomb, combining elements such as humour, innuendo and the "clash between the archaic and the modern in society" (Shaw and Dennison 2007: 91) later exploited in the *pornochanchada*. Filmed with tremendous energy (hand-held shots; filming on boats and on water; swift editing), the film pushes the boundaries of taste in comparison to the more serious offering of the period. The "hero" character of Macunaíma, who shape-shifts from black to white, exists as a comedic composite of the Brazilian character. The jokes and puns in the *Cannibalist Manifesto* are echoed in de Andrade's film, a series of outrageous adventures and incidents. In place of the bleak and barren lives portrayed in the films of Rocha and others,

Figure 30.2 *Macunaíma* (Jungle Freaks, 1969, Brazil, Joaquim Pedro de Andrade). ©Condor Filmes/ Filmes do Serro/Grupo Filmes/Instituto Nacional de Cinema (INC).

the rural landscape of Brazil becomes a comedic backdrop for a series of farcical, grotesque and fantastical happenings, a terrain filled with spurting hillocks and boiling puddles. Although the film resembles at times the "panic" aesthetic of Arrabal and Jodorowsky, it has a crazed, truly original and indigenous "cannibalistic" (Technicolor) style. With its deranged, outrageous and offensive manner *Macunaíma* perfectly expresses the surrealism of de Andrade's textual language: "Down with all importers of canned consciousness [. . .] Down with the reversible world" (Barry 1991: 39).

A further instance of Brazilian invention in the cult realm, where the magic, mysticism and ritual of South America is abused to exploit an audience's baser instincts, are the horror films of José Mojica Marins. The character of Zé do Caixão (translated as Coffin Joe)—an evil black-suited, top-hatted undertaker with a cape and grotesquely long, curled fingernails—appears in many of Marins' films and is, according to screenwriter Rubens Luchetti, a "horror character that is purely Brazilian". The first Coffin Joe film *À meia noite levarei sua alma* (At Midnight I'll Take Your Soul, 1964, Brazil, José Mojica Marins) was Brazil's first horror film. It is a sensational and cruel début. The opening scene features Coffin Joe (played by José Mojica Marins) speaking the following words direct to the camera:

> What is Life?
> It's the beginning of death.
> What is death?
> It is the end of life.
> What is existence?
> It is the continuity of blood.
> What is blood?
> It is the reason to exist!

This is followed by an address by a witch who warns the viewer "not to watch the following film". *O estranho mundo de Zé do Caixão* (The Strange World of Coffin Joe, 1968, Brazil, José Mojica Marins), an anthology film of the sort once popular in cult horror and sci-fi genres, features the character only fleetingly. The film begins with a fierce boiling sky and Coffin Joe emerging slowly and menacingly intoning solemnly and philosophically about courage and fear and the "terror of ghosts". Three short episodes of terror ensue including, first, the story of a doll-maker who uses real human eyes to make his creations; second, a tale of obsession and necrophilia and finally the vile experiments of a cannibalistic professor (played by Marins) who appears to have taken the *Cannibalist Manifesto* and de Andrade's attack on reason all too literally. Marins' films are like a bizarre and freakish distortion of the "Third Cinema" aesthetic, mixing harsh black and white stills of violence and "the masses" with collision editing, jump-cuts, sexploitation tricks, pop culture signifiers and sadistic trash effects. *The Strange World of Coffin Joe* is a classic example of the cult film provoking questions of voyeurism, scopophilia and visual perception (both real and imagined) through the medium of the trash/shock aesthetic. Marin's films, like many cult films, "transgress common notions of good and bad taste [. . .] and challenge genre conventions and coherent storytelling" (Mathijs and Mendik 2008: 11). The politics and revolution of "Third Cinema" is almost completely lacking; in place is a cheap cinema of sensation and exploitation, albeit of an original and indigenous type. The sexist cruelty, nihilism and sacrilegious violence of the Coffin Joe films—Marins' scorn for the living and mockery of the dead—were too much for the Department of Public Security in Brazil. Despite Coffin Joe's tortured demise on the Day of the Dead at the hands of the spirits of the dead he had mocked, the films still today make troubling viewing. "Mojica was doing something different from American and European cinema", critic Rubens F. Luchetti observes, and this makes his films, despite their poor reception, original and significant (Barcinski and Finotti 2009). A revival of Marins' films courtesy of the American exploitation video company Something Weird in the 1990s created a body of work suited to a cult consumption and reception.

Another of the most strikingly original instances of cult cinema occurs in the realm of modern Japanese cinema. Sexuality, one of the most "pronounced motifs of cult movies" (Grant 2000: 21), is key. In fact, sex and death are the two key tropes of this cinema, with the two realms often interacting and overlapping. A year before *Ai no korīda* (In the Realm of the Senses, 1976, Japan/France, Nagisa Ôshima), Noburu Tanaka made *Jitsuroko Abe Sada* (A Woman Called Abe Sada, 1975, Japan), based on the same true story of the woman who in May 1936 erotically strangled her lover, cut off his genitals and carried them around with her as love trophies. If Ôshima's lush Franco-Japanese production created controversy among the arthouse audience, Tanaka's more modest but still effectively-made feature can be considered a lost cult classic, only recently reissued as part of a resurgence of interested in Japanese *pinku eiga* ("Pink") cinema to which it is loosely affiliated.

The recurring theme of exploring lost time and space can be found in cult films of this era. *Môjû* (Blind Beast, 1969, Japan, Yasuzô Masamura) is a lurid but haunting narrative concerning a blind sculptor who kidnaps a young model as the inspiration for his final artistic masterpiece. The couple eventually descend into an intense and disturbing sadomasochistic pattern resulting in mutilation and suicide. What is striking and original about these films is the lush imagery (grotesque Kabuki aesthetics; mutilated flesh; falling snow), frank approach to sexuality and violence, varied techniques, poetic structure and evocative use of music (the song "I Killed Him Because I Love Him" recurs throughout *A Woman Called Abe Sada*). It is no surprise that these films have influenced twenty-first-century cult film directors such as Quentin Tarantino. The inherent unique surrealism of the Japanese film technique is found in great measure in cult films. There are links that can be found between this aesthetic and European cult directors such as Buñuel and Franju, yet the Japanese style is of its own and survives without recourse to the history of Western cinema.

Animation and the influence of manga

Another cult work is the obscure feature animation *Kanashimi no Beradonna* (Belladonna of Sadness, 1973, Japan, Eiichi Yamamoto) from the Mushi studio (Figure 30.3). The studio had pioneered "Animerama", a trilogy of adult animé feature films made at Mushi in the late 1960s to early 1970s and visually linked to radical European animators such as Rene Laloux and Walerian Borowcyzk. *Belladonna of Sadness* is the story of a young woman possessed by Satan. The graphically intense tableaux, based on artists such as Klimt and Cocteau as well as Beardsley and Rops' pornographic drawings, is matched with psychedelic patterns and a groovy jazz-infused soundtrack. The elliptical scenarios are based on Jules Michelet's cult 1862 work *La sorcière* (The Sorceress), a serious study of witchcraft emphasising the role of women in the story of possession and resistance. Indeed, for all its sexually explicit and erotic surreal imagery, the film ends with a statement on the "revolutionary power of women" over images of the 1789 French revolution, including Delacroix's famous painting "La Liberté guidant le people" (Liberty Leading the People, 1830), itself a conflation of freedom, violence and sex. Yamamoto's film thus echoes Michelet's text in emphasising the sorceress as a potentially powerful figure, a "living reality" as opposed to an "empty conception" of the devil (Michelet 1965: 230).

A more recent exemplar of this highly original style of cult cinema, where sex and death reign supreme, is *Ôdishon* (Audition, 2001, Japan, Takashi Miike), a horror film from the "margins of genre cinema" (Hantke 2005: 55). The film has become a cult film because in addition to its extreme imagery and narrative it has managed in reception terms to "cross social and national boundaries" (Ibid.). *Audition* and *Ringu* (Ring, 1998, Japan, Hideo Nakata) have progressed the

Figure 30.3 *Kanashimi no Belladonna* (Belladonna of Sadness, 1973, Japan, Eiichi Yamamoto). ©Mushi/Nippon Herald Films.

representation of women in cult Japanese cinema from objects of abuse and veneration to powerful figures exacting revenge on such a corrupt system of signs. The Japanese phenomenon of the manga comic book title has also influenced original Japanese cult cinema. One of the best examples of this is *Uzumaki* (Spiral, 2000, Japan, Higuchinsky), which, in addition to drawing in manga aesthetics, reworks the Japanese fascination with technology and videotape culture. One of the victims of the occult spirals that take over an anonymous town in the film manically records all kinds of spirals, including his own suicide inside a washing machine.

A particular and somewhat neglected field in debates about cult film is in the field of animation, where such films, denied mainstream distribution, have been left languishing in the realm of specialist clubs and private connoisseurs. Like the revolutionary manifestos of "Third Cinema", the art of animation developed its own cult status through seditious form and challenging subject matter with provocative mission statements. The MOUVART manifesto, signed by Fred Wolf, Yoji Kuri and Walerian Borowcyzk advocated animation as a "total art form" (MOUVART 1968: 15) outside of the studio conventions. Borowczyk (Polish but working mostly in France) and Santiago Álvarez in Chile made cultish animations still held in high regard by the underground. Borowczyk produced films using some form of artistic alchemy mixing the detritus of medieval and classical art and culture (books and maps, photographs, etchings, lithographs) with the obsessions of modern life (space exploration, experimental electronic music). Borowczyk fetishised mechanical objects and women, often combining the two obsessions in his uncanny short animations and erotic feature films. Critics often accused the director of being a pornographer; however, Borwczyk's regular cinematographer Nöel Very argues that Borowczyk's work was in fact a "revolutionary form of eroticism" (Bird 2014). With works ranging from the early collaborations with Jan Lenica and Chris Marker to directing *Emmanuelle 5* (1987, France/USA), Borowczyk is an exemplary cult filmmaker. Álvarez's short documentary *LBJ* (1968, Cuba) is a wild and sardonic critique of American imperialism. The film is made from a collage of still images lifted from magazines such as *Life* and *Playboy*, snatches from American gangster and cowboy films, adverts, comic strips and pulp rock and roll songs such as "Surfin' Bird" cut with Carl Orff and Nina Simone.

La planète sauvage (Fantastic Planet, 1973, France/Czechoslovakia, René Laloux) is a science-fiction feature animation that has retained cult status largely through its use of the disturbing drawings of Roland Topor (the third member of Jodrowsky and Arrabal's *Mouvement panique*) and the soundtrack by Alain Goraguer. Laloux went on to bridge the gap between the surreal animation of the 1960s and 1970s with the introduction of CGI films, working notably with Jean Giraud (AKA Mœbius) to create *Les maîtres du temps* (Time Masters, 1982, France/Switzerland/West Germany/UK/Hungary, René Laloux).

Women in cult films

As we have observed, representations of women in cult films are generally problematic. Female characterisation and narrative experiences are often related from a warped male perspective. Women in cult films usually appear as sex objects, objects of abuse or sexualised monsters. Cult cinema does, however, contain some rare instances where a more dynamic and three-dimensional female perspective is found. Two cult films in particular, *Jeanne Dielman 23, quai du Commerce, 1080 Bruxelles* (Jeanne Dielman, 23 Commerce Quay, 1080 Brussels, 1975, Belgium/France) directed by Belgian auteur Chantal Akerman, and *Baise Moi* (Rape Me, 2000, France, Virginie Despentes and Coralie Trinh Thi) are worth highlighting. The films, while vastly different, share certain concerns, exploring as they do issues around prostitution, murder and empowerment and have both been hailed as feminist texts, albeit for differing reasons.

Jeanne Dielman is a 201-minute narrative about a widow who lives with her teenage son in a Brussells apartment block. The everyday routine of Jeanne—cooking, cleaning, shopping, etc.—is reproduced in almost real time. Domestic chores are combined with the visits of male clients for sex. The soothing repetition of the routine is unravelled leading to a shocking climax. It is the quiet rituals of this routine shattered by the seismic effects of a single orgasm that offer an unusual feminist perspective on the act of prostitution. As the actor who plays Jeanne Delphine Seyrig observed, "when subjects like prostitution are handled by women I think it will be from a totally new angle" (Frey 1975). The film was made by a crew that was 80 per cent female and is regarded as an arthouse classic. Its extraordinary length and measured pacing have resulted in few screenings and cemented its status as a cult film.

Baise Moi, by contrast, offers an extremely violent and pornographic take on female self-determination. Shot like a gritty and cheap sex film, by and about women, the film has gained cult status due to the graphic nature of the sex and violence it depicts (it was temporarily banned in its native France and other countries when it was released) and the blank, nihilistic nature of the killing spree the two female characters embark upon. Most of the violence on the film is meted out to male characters, who are almost universally unpleasant. The hatred towards these male characters may reflect the abusive treatment the directors and the principle actors faced daily working in the hardcore sex film industry. Cult cinema offers many examples of rampaging murderous male figures; here, women are the deranged and wild instigators of chaos and rupture. The cult status of the film, and the ambiguity of cult film politics, where the politics of gender is complex and "oppositionality often works to reaffirm rather than challenge bourgeois tastes and masculine dispositions" makes *Baise Moi* problematic (Jancovich *et al.* 2003: 2). Film scholars have noted that for cult fans "the feminist perspective is an added bonus; the core meaning is the nihilistic rampage and revenge itself" (Mathijs and Mendik 2011: 19).

Conclusion

Cult cinema is now established as a serious area for study and debate, "a key part of film criticism and media/cultural studies theory" (Mathijs and Mendik 2011: 1). Films that were once seen as peripheral trash or failed experiment can now be reviewed alongside established classics. The contribution made by cult films to World Cinema is, at times, still questioned. Charles Kilgore once (somewhat crudely) defined the mondo film as "the ugly bastard child of the documentary and the peepshow" (Staples 1995: 111). Thinking about the established world cinema canon, one could view cult films as the "unruly child" of the European arthouse movement and the "serious" national cinemas of the post-war global film epoch. Nevertheless, it is clear that the critical aspects that make cult cinema what it is—transgressive, disruptive and carnivalesque—are worth examining and enrich the cinematic output of a particular geographical space. The marginal, violent and tasteless films of world film culture deserve to be addressed as important signifiers of nations' psyche and socio-cultural landscape. As Glauber Rocha noted back in the 1970s, "cinema is a means of expression that opens up new avenues to knowledge" (Rocha 1971: 77). The "knowledge" that cult film offers may be problematic but it can, on occasion, be priceless.

References

Andrews, D. (2013) *Theorizing Art Cinemas: Foreign, Cult, Avant-Garde and Beyond*, Austin, TX: University of Texas Press.

Barcinski, A. and Finotti, I. (2009) *Coffin Joe: The Strange World of José Mojica Marins*. DVD: Anchor Bay.

Barry, L. (1991) "Oswald de Andrade's 'Cannibalist Manifesto'", *Latin American Literary Review* 19 (38): 38–47.

Big Indian Picture (2014) http://thebigindianpicture.com/2014/11/back-to-the-shalimar-i-ii, November.
Bird, D (2004) "Film Is Not a Sausage" (film) in *Walerian Borowczyk: Short Films and Animation* (DVD), Arrow Films.
Cline, J. and Weiner, R. (eds.) (2010) *From the Arthouse to the Grindhouse: Highbrow and Lowbrow Transgression in Cinema's First Century*, Lanham, MD: Scarecrow Press.
Cooke, P. (2007) "Introduction", in Cooke, P. (ed.) *World Cinema's "Dialogues" with Hollywood*, Basingstoke: Palgrave, 1–16.
Dangerous Minds (2015) "A hetero film for gay people to marvel at", http://dangerousminds.net/comments/john_waters_calls_fuego_a_hetero_film_for_gay_people
Espinosa, J. G. (1971) "For an Imperfect Cinema", *Afterimage* 3: 55–67.
French, K. and French, P. (1999) *Cult Movies*, London: Pavilion.
Frey, S. (1975) *Autour de Jeanne Dielman*, DVD: Criterion.
Geetha, V. Rao, S. and Dhakshna, S. (2007) *The 9 Emotions of Indian Cinema Hordings*, London: Tara Publishing.
Getino, O. and Solanas, F. (1971) "Towards a Third Cinema", *Afterimage* 3: 16–35.
Ghosh, A. (2013) "Shalimar's director Krishna Shah was a trailblazer", *Times of India*, 18 October, http://blogs.timesofindia.indiatimes.com/Addictions/shalimar-s-director-krishna-shah-was-a-trailblazer.
Gokulsing, K.M., Dissanayake, W. (1998) *Indian Popular Cinema: A Narrative of Cultural Change*, Stoke on Trent: Trentham Books.
Goodall, M. (2006) *Sweet and Savage: The World, Through the Documentary Film Lens*, London: Headpress.
Grant, B. K. (2000) "Second Thoughts on Double Features: revisiting the Cult Film", in Mendik, X. and Harper, G. (eds) *Unruly Pleasures: The Cult Film and its Critics*, Guildford: Fab Press, 14–27.
Hantke, S. (2005) "Japanese Horror Under Western Eyes: Social Class and Global Culture in Miike Takashi's *Audition*", in McRoy, J. (ed.) *Japanese Horror Cinema*, Edinburgh: Edinburgh University Press, 54–65.
Jancovich, M., Reboll, A. L., Stringer, J. and Willis, A. (eds) (2003) *Defining Cult Movies: The Cultural Politics of Oppositional Taste*, Manchester: Manchester University Press.
Kyrou, A. (2000) "The Marvellous Is Popular", in Hammond, P (ed.) *The Shadow and Its Shadow: Surrealist Writings on the Cinema*, San Francisco, CA: City Lights, 39–41.
Mathijs, E. and Mendik, X. (eds) (2008) *The Cult Film Reader*, Maidenhead: McGraw-Hill.
—— (eds) (2011) *100 Cult Films*, London: BFI.
Mathijs, E. and Sexton, J. (2011) *Cult Cinema*, Chichester: Wiley-Blackwell.
Richards, K. (2006) "Export Mythology: Primitivism and Paternalism in Pasolini, Hopper and Herzog", in Dennison, S. and Hwee Lim, S. (eds) *Remapping World Cinema: Identity, Culture and Politics in Film*. London: Wallflower Press, 55–64.
Michelet, J. (1965) *Satanism and Witchcraft: A Study in Medieval Superstition*, London: Tandem.
MOUVART (1968) "Manifesto", *Platinum*, Essex: University of Essex Film Society, 15.
Ray, R. (2001) *How a Film Theory Got Lost and Other Mysteries in Cultural Studies*, Bloomington, IN: Indiana University Press.
Robinson, D. (1981) *World Cinema 1895–1980*, London: Eyre Methuen.
Rocha, G. (1971) "Cabezas Cortadas", *Afterimage* 3, 68–77.
Schaefer, E. (1999) *Bold! Daring! Shocking! True!: A History of Exploitation Films, 1919–1959*, Durham, NC: Duke University Press.
Sconce, J. (1995) "'Trashing' the Academy: Taste, Excess, and an Emerging Politics of Cinematic Style", *Screen* 36 (4): 371–393.
Shaw, L. and Dennison, S. (2007) *Brazilian National Cinema*. London: Routledge.
Staples, A. J. (1995) "An Interview with Doctor Mondo", *American Anthropologist* 97 (1): 110–125.
Tombs, P. (1997) *Mondo Macabro: Weird and Wonderful Cinema Around the World*. London: Titan Books.
Ulmer, G. (1994) *Heuretics: The Logic of Invention*, Baltimore, MD: Johns Hopkins University Press.
Vitali, V. (2008) *Hindi Action Cinema: Industries, Narratives, Bodies*, New Delhi: Oxford University Press.
Vogel, A. (1974) *Film as a Subversive Art*, New York: Random House.

31

PERPETUAL MOTION PICTURES

Sisyphean burden and the global screen franchise

James Walters

Introduction

Somewhere in the world, Batman fastens his utility belt. Somewhere in the world, James Bond loads a Walther PPK. Elsewhere in the world, different individuals watch the same actions performed by Batmen and Bonds that have different faces, different attitudes, and belong to different eras. The pattern can repeat and repeat, as global audiences experience characters that span years and years of screen time, creating perpetual chains of continuity and variation. Given that these repetitions extend beyond a few shared gestures involving belts and guns, we are entitled to speculate upon the wider resonances of the global screen franchise. Moving beyond more familiar considerations of commercial imperatives and audience responses, this chapter seeks to find some ways of discussing the global screen franchise in relation to questions of value and meaning. More specifically, I am interested in how a series of screen texts that involve a fundamental structure of Sisyphean repetition (and perhaps, as a consequence, risk a perceived lack of invention or originality) might achieve meaningfulness precisely as a result of themes and ideas being continually revived and revisited.

Each Hollywood franchise shares the core ambition of attracting a substantial global audience. Following its success in the domestic United States box office ratings, for example, *Star Wars: The Force Awakens* (2015, USA, J. J. Abrams) was almost immediately scrutinised in terms of its performance in the equivalent territories of China, India and Japan, not to mention Central Europe (Frater 2016). In this particular instance, the international box office success of *Star Wars: The Force Awakens* could be seen to provide an indication of the long-term performance of a franchise recently acquired by the Walt Disney Company in its 2012 purchase of Lucasfilm for $4.05 billion, and consequently an early vindication of the media conglomerate's capital investment (Krantz *et al.* 2012). Of course, the commercial value of the Star Wars franchise extends well beyond box office receipts to incorporate a vast plethora of merchandise including toys, video games and apparel. Nevertheless, the success of *Star Wars: The Force Awakens* in cinemas was a central facet in refreshing the screen brand following the somewhat difficult prequel releases of 1999, 2002 and 2005. With Disney further committing to a series of forthcoming Star Wars film titles over a number of years, including *Rogue One: A Star Wars Story* (2016, USA, Gareth Edwards) and a *Han Solo* prequel (2018, USA, Ron Howard), the global impact of the first release in a newly configured franchise carried considerable weight, hence the acute interest in its box office performance.

In many respects, Disney's acquisition of Lucasfilm replicated its 2009 $4 billion buyout of Marvel Entertainment, with both deals leading to a long-term schedule of film releases that underpin and extend the worldwide commercial reach of the brands and their concomitant titles (Clark 2009). There can be little doubt that Disney's strategy for the Star Wars and Marvel franchises represents an especially large-scale attempt to capitalise upon the extensive global marketing potential offered by each. It is difficult not to be struck by the breadth of ambition inherent in a scheduled list of releases that extends well into the future and seeks to dramatically expand the "cinematic universes" of each franchise respectively (Shepherd 2016). In addition, as icons such as James Bond and Batman have each endured and, to a significant extent, matured as film and television franchises, we might reflect that their respective legacies have always placed an emphasis on their status as marketable commodities. And, increasingly, these titles have exploited their potential to reach extensive global markets: the twenty-third Bond title *Skyfall* (2012, UK/USA, Sam Mendes) was the first to generate $1 billion in box office sales, of which 72.5 per cent are attributed to foreign territories (Hough 2012), and even the more recent critical disappointment *Batman v Superman: Dawn of Justice* (2016, USA, Zack Snyder) managed $872 million in box office returns based on 62 per cent of foreign sales (Box Office Mojo 2016). It seems uncontroversial to surmise that a significant factor in the longevity of these franchises is their ability to capitalise upon their global opportunities as screen events and as merchandisable properties.

The simple relaying of these kinds of statistics and, indeed, the broader emphasis placed upon commercial imperatives raises questions about the ways in which we might usefully approach global screen franchises. It is difficult not to get drawn into discussions surrounding box office sales and merchandising as, in a certain context, these might constitute legitimate markers of success and achievement: how much of something is sold and to whom. We are entitled to ask, therefore, whether global screen franchises can *only* have value and meaning in relation to their financial performance and, as a consequence, whether any discussion of worth is irretrievably tied to matters of material accumulation: capital worth. It is certainly true that this emphasis on the commercial profiles of global film franchises represents a move away from the material detail of the films themselves. Engagement with the onscreen text is filtered through forms of collected data that record the ways in which individuals engage with those texts as both consumers and viewers. As a result, evaluative judgements about the film are dependent upon the thoughts and actions of others: whether, why and to what extent they "bought into" a particular franchise. Missing from that data is an independent critical perspective on the films themselves: simply, an opinion as to whether they possess critical value.

Approaching global film franchises

That "move away" from the films might be seen to continue a more general trend in criticism whereby the products of global franchises do not always invite the same levels of analysis and evaluation devoted to other types of filmmaking. Indeed, we may be encouraged to look in a different direction, towards ostensibly more subtle or self-consciously thoughtful releases, and away from the perhaps more obvious attractions of the large-scale, bombastic global blockbuster. In a 2002 essay, Jeffrey Sconce draws attention to this potential as he identifies a group of American films from the turn of the century that display, in his terms, a "smart" sensibility (Sconce gives a broad range of examples including the work of directors such as Wes Anderson, Todd Solondz, Alexander Payne and Paul Thomas Anderson). He explains that:

> Taken together, these admittedly disparate yet often ideologically sympathetic films suggest an interesting shift in the strategies of contemporary "art cinema," here defined as movies marketed in specific counterdistinction to mainstream Hollywood fare as "smarter," "artier," and more independent (however questionable and manufactured such distinctions might actually be).
>
> *(Sconce 2002: 350)*

In describing this group of American indie (or perhaps faux-indie in some cases, given their big studio financial backing) titles as "smarter" or "artier" than mainstream Hollywood cinema, Sconce references implicitly the familiar suggestion that films in the latter category embody the oppositional qualities of dim-wittedness and artlessness. Indeed, he provides specific reference to this notion as he continues:

> While these films vary greatly in terms of conditions of production and financing, they are almost invariably placed by marketers, critics and audiences in symbolic opposition to the imaginary mass-cult monster of mainstream, commercial, Hollywood cinema (perhaps best epitomised by the "dumb" films of Jerry Bruckheimer, Michael Bay and James Cameron).
>
> *(Sconce 2002: 351)*

It is worth noting the care Sconce takes in establishing "smart" cinema as a marketed concept, thus conforming to a particular commercial strategy that is often less forcefully asserted, and is perhaps left intentionally indistinct, when compared to the more obvious and blatant profit hunger of mainstream Hollywood cinema. We might also observe an equivalent level of care in the choice of directors' names that, even by 2002, had become synonymous with a kind of cinema that is often perceived to be laden with empty spectacle and bereft of meaningful narrative: "dumb" films. That Bruckheimer, Bay and Cameron can so readily conjure such vivid distinctions suggests a kind of *negative* recognition that, in some critical circles at least, works against the traditional notion of an identifiable film author existing as an indicator of quality and achievement.

Bruckheimer, Bay and (to an arguably lesser degree) Cameron have each contributed to the swell of lucrative film franchises, most notably with titles such as the *Pirates of the Caribbean* (2003–, USA), *Transformers* (2007–, USA) and the (planned) *Avatar* series (2009–, USA). It might well be argued that each of these franchises possesses a distinctive aesthetic tone and design, yet such features are certainly not regarded as equivalent to the work of other directors, such as Wes Anderson or Todd Solondz, whose films also possess a discernible style and characteristic traits. In critical accounts of Bruckheimer and Bay's work, particularly, artistic design is often seen to involve complexity without sophistication, cramming the screen with exhausting visual spectacle that, while precisely choreographed, lacks meaningful execution. It is also the case, particularly with the *Pirates of the Caribbean* and *Transformers* franchises, that each new instalment introduces a further level of aesthetic redundancy as individual films within the series become almost indistinguishable from each other and, instead, extend a process of hollow repetition. The metonymic association between the names of certain directors and a kind of mass-appeal "dumb" film product was, however, beginning to shift at the time Sconce first formulated his distinctions. Indeed, we might regard the involvement of 'indie' directors such as Christopher Nolan (*Batman*), Peter Jackson (*Lord of the Rings*), Michel Gondry (*Green Hornet*), Bryan Singer (*X-Men*) and Ang Lee (*Hulk*) in franchise titles as a deliberate strategy on the part of the studios to raise the level of creative credibility and, in turn, perhaps the critical respectability of these films. And yet, it might equally be argued that the reputations of these directors still remain distinct from the critical standing of the film franchise so that, in the cases of Nolan or Jackson, they are seen to elevate otherwise functional material and, in the cases of Gondry and Lee, are actually incongruous elements within the production of mass entertainment titles.

When Sconce draws attention to the work of Wes Anderson or Todd Solondz at the expense of Michael Bay or Jerry Bruckheimer, he fulfils implicitly a traditional role of the critic in highlighting the achievement of artists who may otherwise not receive sustained public attention. The potential for academic discourse to shift that public focus is relatively limited but, nevertheless, it supports and sometimes leads the more widespread effort represented in mainstream film publications, broadsheet arts columns and independent awards ceremonies that champion works that might otherwise be lost or underappreciated. The difficulty with global screen franchises is that, although we might recognise a public familiarity with and a certain critical apathy towards them, it is not necessarily the case that their achievements have been *overlooked*. Indeed, they are perhaps too familiar. We are left to question legitimately whether there is anything further to appreciate in these works. This question is not made less awkward if we reflect for a moment upon the fact that these films risk inviting predictable critical judgements, precisely because their cyclical, perpetual structures of ongoing sequels, prequels and reboots involve unusually strong elements of predictability. What, then, is left to say about them?

"The Myth of Sisyphus"

A possible way forward, and one I shall pursue for the remainder of this essay, is to engage directly with the repetitiveness and relative predictability of the global screen franchise as a meaningful thematic structure. Such a course will require us to take these texts seriously and, in turn, to suppose that they have something serious to say. My approach will furthermore oblige us to take seriously another work of fiction: "The Myth of Sisyphus." The myth is relatively familiar. Having cheated death twice and having, at one stage, put an end to death itself, Sisyphus is condemned by the Gods to forever push a rock to the top of a summit, only to see it roll down again and begin the effort once more. Sisyphus' act is endlessly cyclical, and hence the word "Sisyphean" has become a kind of metonym in contemporary culture for an apparently ever-repeating task. The term is often related to the hardships of monotonous everyday duties such as housework or the Sisyphean attempts made to reduce the contents of an ever-growing email inbox. Indeed, the ubiquity and straightforwardness of the term may create an obstacle to the myth of Sisyphus being considered in any great detail: it has a general relevance to a relatable condition and, as a consequence, we may feel that we already understand and appreciate any significance it holds. Certainly, the myth of Sisyphus has not inspired the same complex range of references that the myths of Odysseus or Heracles have, for example. There may be good reasons for this. Unlike those myths, there is no quest, no end, and no obvious heroism to Sisyphus' story. As a narrative, it is especially limited and presents a challenge to anyone seeking meaningful resolution. It is perhaps these qualities that lead Richard Taylor to suggest that, in the myth:

> We have the picture of meaninglessness, pointless toil, of a meaningless existence that is absolutely *never* redeemed. It is not even redeemed by a death that, if it were to accomplish nothing more, would at least bring this idiotic cycle to a close [...] Nothing comes of it, nothing at all.
>
> *(Taylor 2000: 320, emphasis in original)*

It follows that these notions of meaninglessness can be applied to global screen franchises if we accept, for the moment, Taylor's characterisation of the Sisyphean myth. When cycles of seemingly endless repetition increasingly become a defining hallmark of these film series, so we are entitled to question what dramatic consequences their narratives can offer. As Disney/Marvel extend the titles in their "cinematic universe", for example, the protagonists in the series are never able to see an end to their efforts or the culmination of their endeavours—nor even, as Taylor points out, the permanent release through death. How are we to accept the various deadly threats made to characters such as Thor, Iron Man or Captain America, for example, when at the same time we are fully aware that each of these heroes is certain to appear again in already-planned future instalments of the Avengers franchise? In this sense, Taylor's notion of "pointless toil" does not seem so removed from the scenario we are presented with here.

It is also the case that, even when included within these Sisyphean cycles of repetition offered by screen franchises, death itself can lose its finality. For example, the dramatic impact of Han Solo's (Harrison Ford) death in *Star Wars: The Force Awakens* might be brief and somewhat diminished as a result of our awareness that the character is due a return to the screen a mere three years later, albeit as an earlier incarnation, in a planned prequel movie. We can recognise without too much difficulty the commercial logic in not allowing a highly marketable character such as Han Solo to simply fade from the franchise. Nevertheless, it is entirely in keeping with the Sisyphean form of the film franchise that this individual should be kept "alive" on screen through a process that returns us to an earlier period of his life: recapitulating the narrative and suspending the kind of progress or resolution that might evoke the finality of death with indelible force.

It is apparent, then, that applying Taylor's reading of the Sisyphus myth to the structures of global screen franchises has the potential to create a somewhat sceptical assessment of their potential value. Indeed, that central characteristic of perpetual return becomes, in itself, an act devoid of meaningful purpose and, thus, cannot achieve meaningful worth. The discussion might end there (providing the kind of resolution a Sisyphean narrative cannot) if we did not attend to Albert Camus' alternative reading of Sisyphus, which counters implicitly some of the claims Taylor wishes to make and, as a consequence, provides us with a possible means of finding value in the repetitive structures of global screen franchises. Camus' consideration of the myth occurs as part of a famous wider meditation on the philosophical concept of the absurd. Camus sees Sisyphus as the archetype of the absurd hero, a man who is conscious of his plight, of his misery and of his tragedy and yet continues without appeal to unseen Gods, and without the release of death. In achieving this aim, Camus attempts to see Sisyphus not simply as a straightforwardly symbolic mythical figure but as a physical and psychological reality. He begins with the physical:

> As for this myth, one sees merely the whole effort of a body straining to raise the huge stone, to roll it and push it up a slope a hundred times over; one sees the face screwed up, the cheek tight against the stone, the shoulder bracing the clay-covered mass, the foot wedging it, the fresh start with arms outstretched, the wholly human security of two earth-clotted hands.
>
> *(Camus 2005: 116)*

What should strike us immediately from this passage is the way in which Camus engages sincerely with the act that Sisyphus finds himself performing again and again. Where most accounts of Sisyphus' life quite understandably *end* with his eternal punishment (his fate), Camus takes this as a starting point, imagining what that punishment might look like and, crucially, how it might feel.

And, rather than seeing Sisyphus' existence as only the epitome of meaninglessness, Camus goes on to consider what meaning could be found in such an existence. As a way of approaching those questions, he concerns himself with the moment at which the rock has rolled back yet again, and Sisyphus must descend to retrieve it. Camus says that:

> It is during that return, that pause, that Sisyphus interests me. A face that toils so close to stones is already stone itself! I see that man going back with a heavy yet measured step towards the torment of which he will never know the end. That hour like a breathing-space which returns as surely as his suffering, that is the hour of consciousness. At each of those moments when he leaves the heights and gradually sinks towards the lairs of the gods, he is superior to his fate. He is stronger than his rock.
>
> *(Camus 2005: 117)*

Camus finds an unlikely nobility and honour in the myth of Sisyphus that Taylor's account can never accommodate. For Camus, it is the moment of descent once the stone has rolled back down that provides the greatest emphasis of Sisyphus' strength and resolve. Taylor interprets this moment as Sisyphus' life at its most meaningless yet, in Camus' account, that same character finds his peak of moral determination at the very point when he makes yet another physical descent. If this introduces a more optimistic and even heroic interpretation of Sisyphus' fate, it is also true that Camus regards the myth as tragic precisely because the hero is *conscious* of his burden. Indeed, the "hour of consciousness" provides Sisyphus with arguably his greatest test, when the hopeless repetition of his labour stretches out before him. We can recognise more abstract forms of that kind of consciousness in various examples of screen franchises. Indeed, a great majority of titles make self-conscious reference to the fact that certain scenarios occur in a pattern of repetition. Allusions of this kind can be delivered with brevity and even levity: the repeated use of the phrase "I've got a bad feeling about this" by various characters in different Star Wars films, although perhaps somewhat overused now, does at least provide the clear indication that a character's current predicament—and the moment in which they speak the line—can resonate strongly with a series of very similar occurrences that have happened and will continue to happen within the same franchise.

"Rebooting" the franchise

In other instances, franchises can display more complex levels of self-consciousness in relation to their cycles of perpetual repetition. *Casino Royale* (2006, UK/USA/Czech Republic/Germany/Italy, Martin Campbell) (Figure 31.1) is generally considered to be a "reboot" of a James Bond series that was regarded as having reached a creative lull with *Die Another Day* (2002, UK/USA, Lee Tamahori), released four years earlier. In a discussion of overarching Sisyphean structures, the manner in which this reboot is introduced becomes a matter of interest. The film begins in black and white, with even the MGM lion and Columbia Pictures torch-bearer tinted in monochrome. We then track the progress of a man as he enters and moves through an office building in Prague (a location revealed in an onscreen credit as the film opens). The movements of the man are captured in a series of pronounced high and low angle shots that, combined with the use of black and white, loosely evoke a *film noir* style of a much earlier period. On entering his office, the man sees that the door to his safe is open and, turning around, finds another man sitting directly behind him. Any viewer with even a faint awareness of the promotional material for *Casino Royale* would recognise this other man to be James Bond, played by Daniel Craig. Bond's opening lines establish the relationship between these two men: "M really doesn't't mind you earning a little money on the side, Dryden. She'd just prefer it if it wasn't selling secrets." They are both secret agents and one of them is corrupt. A discussion ensues and it is disclosed that Bond has yet to achieve his 00 status, which requires him to kill twice before it is awarded. In a series of flashbacks that intersect the conversation, it is revealed that Bond has in fact killed one man—Dryden's informer—already and he concludes his present encounter by killing Dryden himself, thus achieving 00 status. We then return to the scene with Bond and Dryden's informer as he recovers from Bond's attempts to drown him, only to be shot dead by Bond in an iconic point-of-view shot that begins the film's title sequence. Bond's struggle with Dryden's informer is represented in a manner that accentuates the visceral physicality of combat. Set in a public toilet, the two men clumsily throw each other around the space, losing and regaining their hold, landing brutal kicks and punches as they inadvertently shatter sinks, mirrors and urinals. A clear attempt is made, then, to progress the Bond franchise from a kind of fantasy, consequence-free violence that had become a hallmark during the Pierce Brosnan era towards a more realistic portrayal of physical aggression. Some aspects of that old style are retained, however. As Dryden reflects dryly on his informer's demise by saying "You needn't worry, the second is—" he is interrupted by Bond firing a single bullet into his head. Surveying his work, Bond quips sardonically: "Yes, considerably", recalling the type of witty one-liners that have defined the eras of every previous Bond incarnation.

The opening moments of *Casino Royale*, therefore, are caught between a move to establish a new aesthetic realism in the Bond series, and so mark out a fresh direction, and a need to reference and return to certain traits that are hallmarks of the franchise. The use of black and white becomes a key indicator of the film's internal conflict. On the one hand, it provides a kind of documentary grittiness that brings Bond in line with equivalent titles such as the Bourne series of films. At the same time, however, it is an unavoidably retrograde step that returns us to an era when black and white film was far more prevalent: the 1960s, when the Bond franchise began. Even the attempt at a more realistic depiction of violence contains a reference to a previous era, recalling a fighting style found in the early Sean Connery releases before the more overtly choreographed sequences of the Roger Moore years. The opening may be a reboot, but it is

Figure 31.1 *Casino Royale* (2006, UK/USA/Czech Republic/Germany/Italy, Martin Campbell) displays a more complex level of self-consciousness in relation to the James Bond films' cycles of perpetual repetition. ©Columbia Pictures/Eon Productions/Casino Royale Productions/Stillking Films/Studio Babelsberg/Danjaq/United Artists.

also a recapitulation. We can certainly appreciate the commercial need to retain certain aspects of the franchise in order to retain its market definition. However, in looking both backwards and forwards, to the past and the future of the franchise, *Casino Royale* also emphasises its hero's particular timelessness and his endlessness. The film makes the explicit point that scenarios of this kind have been played out before and will be played out again. Whether or not the aesthetic depiction of them is altered, there is an unbreakable line of continuity that stretches across the whole Bond series. And, furthermore, *Casino Royale* centres that cycle of return and repetition upon violence and, specifically, killing. The endless task—the *Sisyphean* duty—that Bond must perform is murder. So the film begins with acts of killing, and it emphasises the endlessness of Bond's endeavours by introducing the narrative condition that he kills these men in order to earn a licence to kill: his 00 credentials. Consequently, acts of murder achieve nothing more than providing an opportunity to commit yet further acts of murder. While Bond's fictional existence cannot be characterised as entirely pointless, as might be suggested by Taylor's reading of the Sisyphus myth, it certainly lacks satisfactory resolution when we consider the franchise as a whole. Indeed, as *Casino Royale* states explicitly, no amount of killings can provide an end and, rather, each killing leads only to a further opportunity to kill. The film approaches this fact in an especially self-conscious way by acknowledging directly that chain of recapitulation, stating overtly that we have been here before, and we will go here again.

It follows that, in these perpetual cycles of repetition that screen franchises create, the very notion of an ending becomes difficult. *The Dark Knight Rises* (2012, USA/UK) marks the end of a trilogy of Batman films by director Christopher Nolan (Figure 31.2). And, indeed, in its final moments the film finds a tone of sombre finality that complements such a conclusion. In an act of self-sacrifice, Batman (Christian Bale) has elected to fly an atomic bomb out across the ocean, away from Gotham City, thus saving the lives of its residents but ending his own. Having framed Batman's triumphant flight from the city, the film turns back to one if

Figure 31.2 In the perpetual cycles of repetition that screen franchises create, the very notion of an ending becomes difficult. *The Dark Knight* (2008, USA/UK, Christopher Nolan). ©Warner Bros./Legendary Entertainment/Syncopy/DC Comics.

its citizens, police officer Blake (Joseph Gordon-Levitt) as he watches the hero depart. At this point, the mood changes from active to reflective. We approach Blake's face in slower motion, the strident orchestral score subsides into a softer melody featuring a single female soprano, and the preceding crazy-logic forward momentum of events is consumed by a newly mournful disposition. This style of representation continues as we cut back to a close-up of Batman's face, then to a shot of his vehicle disappearing against the horizon, then to the bomb's countdown timer ticking down its last second. The pace of events is slowed and saddened to such a degree that, when the bomb does explode in a faraway mushroom cloud and Gotham's joyful citizens emerge in montage, the emotional release contrasts uncomfortably with the more predominant themes of sorrow and loss. In case we have failed to register the tragedy that a whole city has been saved by an unknown hero, the soundtrack incorporates the voice of Commissioner Gordon (Gary Oldman) reading the final speech of Sydney Carton, that emblematic figure of heroic self-sacrifice in Charles Dickens's *A Tale of Two Cities*, as images of Gotham's saved souls continue to fill the screen. From here, the atmosphere of grief becomes yet more palpable as we join Gordon's eulogy at the graveside of Bruce Wayne (Batman's alter-ego), followed by Alfred's (Michael Caine) tearful apology made to the graves of Wayne's parents, followed by Blake describing the injustice of Gotham citizens not knowing their real saviour, followed by the unveiling of a statue in Batman's honour, followed by a reading of Wayne's will that donates his estate to the city's orphans, all accompanied by a heavy, elegiac string arrangement. And then the momentum picks up again. The music begins to return to a rhythmic, driving pace as Blake follows the instructions in Wayne's will to find the Batcave, Fox (Morgan Freeman) finds that the autopilot on Batman's flying machine had been fixed before its last journey, Commissioner Gordon finds the previously-destroyed Bat-Signal repaired, and Alfred makes his way through an Italian café. Seated, having finished the drink he ordered, Alfred looks up from his open wallet and performs a second-glance that he sustains as he recognises someone across the space. He half-smiles, nods, and a reverse-shot reveals the recipient of these gestures to be Bruce Wayne, now alive and well. Wayne returns the half-smile as he nods and raises his own glass to greet an old friend.

In one sense, we might regard this legitimately as an end. If the Nolan trilogy is seen as a discrete narrative world in its own right, then this is a real departure and withdrawal for its central character. And yet, if we take into account the legacy of the Batman character and the historical spread of the franchise, we can view Bruce Wayne's acknowledgement of his old friend as a recognition that stretches out beyond this one isolated moment. Batman is an enduring character that exists outside of any contained storyline and so, as he raises his glass to Alfred, this Bruce Wayne acknowledges the multitude of Bruce Waynes that have gone before and all that will come after. The perpetual screen franchise creates large-scale macro-narratives that span decades and generations, binding each incarnation together in an ever-expanding character arc. In this moment, then, Bruce Wayne has become Sisyphus at the bottom of the mountain, in the "breathing space" to which Camus refers, conscious of the burden that will never be lifted.

In the context of the Sisyphean cycles that screen franchises create, Bruce Wayne's half-smile in the final moments of *The Dark Knight Rises* can therefore be seen to possess a greater significance. Within the plot of this film, it is clearly a subdued acknowledgement to Alfred that all is well: he has survived. Taken outside of that one film and viewed within the framework of a much broader, much longer line of struggle that the Batman character endures, the half-smile denotes a moment of ease with the burden that all generations have borne and will be asked to bear again. The small expression resonates with this wider portrait of the Batman, declaring not only an attitude towards his survival in this instance but also an acceptance of the fact that he will *always* survive, that release through death is not available to the Sisyphean hero. Wayne's ease, read in this wider framework, echoes the wry humour of Bond's "Yes, considerably" as he completed his double killing. As with Wayne, the fractional moment of lightness reveals the character's attitude to their burden, the extent to which he embraces the particular confines of his existence. In Camus' terms, he is "stronger than his fate". But Camus goes further to consider the sensibility of the Sisyphean figure as he concludes:

> I leave Sisyphus at the foot of the mountain! One always finds one's burden again. But Sisyphus teaches the higher fidelity that negates the gods and raises rocks. He, too, concludes that all is well. This universe henceforth without such a master seems to him neither sterile nor futile. Each atom of that stone, each mineral flake of that night-filled mountain, in itself forms a world. The struggle itself towards the heights is enough to fill a man's heart. One must imagine Sisyphus happy.
>
> *(Camus 2005: 119)*

The happiness that Camus describes is particular, given that it is dependent upon perpetual toil and struggle. And yet, this is the condition of the Sisyphean hero found in global screen franchises. The commercial (and creative) imperative to revisit and recapitulate certain characters and scenarios has given rise to extended timelines of constant labour. The hero's burden is not only to continue with that work but, as Camus suggests, to recognise it as fulfilling rather than futile—and to carry on. As various Bonds and Batmen embrace their fate again and again, they embody a form of Sisyphean happiness.

Conclusion

By centring our thoughts upon these screen franchises' various investments in notions of the Sisyphean hero, we can begin to suggest ways in which they might function as meaningful or even useful texts. For example, given that our lives contain any number of apparently Sisyphean tasks, these films offer, through their protagonists, a means of embracing those burdens and, indeed, of being happy. The need to perform repetitive and repeating tasks is a universal feature of human existence and, in this sense, the texts I draw attention to provide a response to the weight of that existence in their dramatic narratives. Attending to the universality of this human condition also helps to re-emphasise and re-examine the relationship of the screen franchise to notions of the global. Defining the global in terms of the commercial performance of screen franchises in different national territories is a secure but relatively limited enterprise. In contrast, reflecting upon the ways in which these texts address certain facets of human life is less assured but also offers a range of further possibilities for discussion and analysis. Whereas we might be tempted to say that global screen franchises function only as the blandest form of mass entertainment because they aim for such a wide audience reach, we might instead begin to understand the ways in which they offer complex and, at times, reassuring responses to global human experience of being alive. And so, even as these texts reach ever-wider audiences, they may in fact smarten up rather than dumb down.

It might conceivably be concluded that reading global screen franchises through the filter of Camus or the myth of Sisyphus imposes an interpretative context for which they were never intended. Perhaps, although we might suggest Camus does exactly that with his reading of Sisyphus; we would be wrong to regard global storytelling as a new phenomenon. Moreover, it can equally be contended that these franchises offer a means of extending Camus' work, of appreciating it in new and challenging contexts. They animate the myth of Sisyphus and extend it across an ever-expanding range of worlds and heroes. In this way, we may want to make the case for these texts being philosophical essays, too. Certainly, they provide the opportunity to reconsider a further feature of the myth of Sisyphus: the rock itself. As a final thought, we can ask what becomes of that stone when the story is taken up by these screen franchises. What weight are the protagonists of these texts made to bear? We need only look at who is being saved in almost every one of these narratives to discover the answer: the human race. Powerless and purposeless, it is we that require constantly the help of these Sisyphean heroes and, as a consequence, unwittingly extend the duration of their task again and again. We are the rock. We are the burden. And so, somewhat disconcertingly, while these franchises may offer useful potentials for how to approach our personal Sisyphean existences, they remain especially sceptical about our capacity for active empowerment on a broader scale.

References

Box Office Mojo (2016) www.boxofficemojo.com/movies/?id=superman2015.htm.

Camus, A. (2005) *The Myth of Sisyphus*, London: Penguin Books.

Clark, A. (2009) "Disney Buys Marvel Entertainment", *The Guardian*, 31 August.

Frater, P. (2016) "*Star Wars: The Force Awakens* Scores in China, But What About Other Asian Markets?" *Variety*, 19 January.

Hough, A. (2012) "Skyfall: 'Most Successful' James Bond Film Tops $1bn at Global Box Office", *The Telegraph*, 30 December.

Krantz, M., Snyder, M., Della Cava, M. and Alexander, B. (2012) "Disney Buys Lucasfilm for $4 Billion", *USA Today*, 13 October.

Sconce, J. (2002) "Irony, Nihilism and the New American 'Smart' Film'", *Screen* 43 (4): 349–369.

Shepherd, J. (2016) "Star Wars and the Marvel Cinematic Universe Will 'Go on Forever,' Says Disney CEO Bob Iger", *Independent*, 26 January.

Taylor, R. (2000) *Good and Evil*, New York: Prometheus Books.

32

SCREENING WORLD CINEMA AT FILM FESTIVALS

Festivalisation and (staged) authenticity

Marijke de Valck

Introduction

> Individual films gain value both for their regional distinctiveness and for their universal appeal.
>
> *(Nichols 1994b: 17)*

> [Authenticity] is the respectable child of old-fashioned exoticism. It demands that sources, forms, style, language and symbol all derive from a supposedly homogeneous and unbroken tradition.
>
> *(Rushdie 1991: 67, quoted in Taylor 2001: 7)*

In the South Pacific Ocean lies Tanna, one of the larger islands of Vanuatu, an archipelago with British–French colonial history that has been independent since 1980. The island's tropical forests and working volcano on Mount Yasur offer a stunning backdrop to a Romeo and Juliet love story played by indigenous amateur actors in the Australian film *Tanna* (2015, Australia, Bentley Dean and Martin Butler). In the film a young woman—Wawa—and a young man—Dain—fall in love. The camera captures their budding romance with breathtaking cinematography, depicting secret forest rendezvous and lush riverside relaxation away from village duties and tribal surveillance. As island custom is based on arranged marriages the destiny of the young lovers is ill-fated. When Wawa is married off to appease relations with a neighbouring tribe, the couple decides to resist the traditional ways and run away. They enjoy precious moments of happiness—frolicking at the beach, delighting in each other—but ultimately realise their tribe faces retaliatory actions and someone will have to pay a prize for their rebellion. Cinematographically, the roaring volcano echoes Wawa and Dain's despair. Gazing at lava splatter and hot gas fumes the young lovers see no future; together they swallow poisonous fungi on the volcanic crater edge to prevent the unleashing of tribal war on their village and secure their unity in death.

Tanna premiered at the 72nd Venice International Film Festival in 2015 as part of the International Critics Week, where it collected a prize for Best Cinematography and the Audience Award. Subsequently it travelled the festival circuit, picking up more nominations and awards during its run, most notably in Australia where it was selected in August 2016 as the Australian entry for the Best Foreign Language Competition of the 89th Academy Awards. On 19 December 2016 *Tanna* made the shortlist. The film offers a striking case to discuss the intricate relations between film festivals and World Cinema. Film festivals screen a variety of content, including at times Hollywood productions that will enjoy a (wide) theatrical release later on. More importantly, however, festivals program films that are less easily found in cinema theatres, such as documentary, animation, shorts and foreign-language films. Festival circulation has developed in the second half of the twentieth century as one of the main ways of bringing these pictures to global audiences. Driving the global festival economy is an investment—mostly with the currencies of attention, love and prestige—in cinematic excellence, critical voices, cultural diversity and idiosyncratic styles. The belief that there is more to cinema than the latest star vehicle, sequel/prequel to a box office hit, or seasonal blockbuster carries this phenomenon and bridges professional and general publics, however diverse they may be. *Tanna* constitutes a good example of festivals' muscle against cultural homogenisation, enchanting audiences worldwide with a glimpse into the world, customs and beliefs of the indigenous people living in and around the small tribal village of Yakel in Tanna. A reading of the film and its framing for festival circulation, however, will necessarily also call attention to certain disenchantments of globalisation, in particular a vexed engagement with the notion of authenticity that seems to be inherent to festivals' formula for success.

Cosmopolitanism and commerce

Before examining the case of *Tanna*, I want to trace in some detail the trajectories film festivals followed to arrive at this juncture. Looking back, it seems clear that although the ambition to contribute to a diverse and cosmopolitan film culture was at the heart of festivals' origins, festival programming has not been sheltered from political or economic currents at any point in history. Rather, the sustainability of festivals as a cultural force has been dependent on festivals' ability to adapt, adjust and appropriate broader societal transformations, and work with diverging stakeholder needs (Dayan 2000; De Valck 2007; Rhyne 2009). Through this process of adaptation, film festivals gradually came to embrace World Cinema.

The first festival to take place on a regular basis was the Mostra Internazionale d'Arte Cinematografica della Biennale di Venezia, also known as the Venice International Film Festival, which was founded in 1932 as part of the Biennale, a large-scale cultural event dedicated to the exhibition of contemporary art. It was the period following the introduction of sound cinema, and the subsequent American push for control over global film markets. In the face of Hollywood tightening its grip in European territories, schemes were envisioned to maintain visibility of the various national cinemas in Europe, and the Italians were among the first to introduce the idea of a film festival. The festival took place on the Lido island, first biannually and from 1935 onwards annually. A competition component was introduced for the second edition in 1934, and took the form of an international showcase; the festival invited countries to participate, submit one or more films and send representatives to the screenings in Venice. Nineteen countries were present in 1934. The festival received critical acclaim and attracted hundreds of journalists that wrote favourably about the cosmopolitan rendezvous of film cultures in Venice. In the run-up to the Second World War, however, Fascist influence was felt all over Italy, and the festival was no exception. Being absorbed by the newly founded Ministry of Propaganda the Mostra morphed from cosmopolitan cinematic celebration towards public display at the service of the Rome–Berlin axis. When in 1938 the American favourite,

Disney's first animation feature *Snow White and the Seven Dwarfs* (1937, USA, David Hand), was denied the Mussolini Cup—the grand prize—and the award for Best Foreign Film instead went to *Olympia* (1938, Germany, Leni Riefenstahl), dissatisfaction reached a climax. It gave occasion to contemplate the foundation of a new festival, one that would honour the adjective "international" and restore the original cosmopolitan aspirations of the Venice event. This idea for a counter festival would culminate in the Cannes Film Festival, the world's most famous and most important film festival to date.

The first edition of the Cannes Film Festival was scheduled to take place in September 1939, but due to the German invasion of Poland and the outbreak of the Second World War the festival's first edition did not commence until the 20 September 1946. There was a backlog of American productions that had not made it across the Atlantic during the war, and the American submission—eight films in total—was screened to eager audiences on the Riviera alongside submissions from ten European nations, Mexico, India and Egypt. In the years to come Cannes set itself on the map with a seductive mix of cinematic masterpieces, stars and frivolity. Images of Brigitte Bardot, parading in front of the paparazzi in a bikini, travelled the world, as did reports about exuberant parties. With glamour and glitz taking centre stage in the 1950s, the post-war ideal of cinema as a tool to promote peace and international understanding was side-lined (Ostrowska 2016). Moreover, festivals had been discovered as suitable sites to do business, and in addition to the unofficial meetings taking place in hotels, restaurants, bars and other venues, soon proper markets were organised. Money, stars, gossip, business—one could easily forget how film festivals had originally taken up the challenge to diversify film culture and establish cinema as the seventh art, a medium with its own language, rich in expressive powers and in itself worthy of the world's attention. It was again in Cannes that the development of film festivals would take a decisive turn. In 1968 Jean-Luc Godard, François Truffaut and followers travelled to the festival to express their solidarity with labour and student strikers in France. The protesters demanded the festival be closed, at first because what happened on the barricades in Paris could not be ignored on the beach in the South. Soon however, the festival itself was called upon to reform. Cinema, it was proclaimed, ought to be restored to the centre of the festival's efforts, and room had to be made for original voices, unheard stories and new waves, such as the French New Wave to which many of the protesters belonged.

Discoveries and New Waves

The late 1960s and the 1970s witnessed an important change in film festivals' orientation. From showcases of national cinemas, film festivals transformed into independently programmed events. Instead of inviting countries to participate, festival directors and programmers ventured out into the world to look for new cinematic cultures. There was a vested interest in selecting films from all over the world, identifying new trends, acting as a harbinger of new film styles and participating in public debates, in particular in relation to political and activist causes (De Valck 2007: 174–177). In retrospect, there was a thin line between genuine interest in foreign cultures, openness to unfamiliar aesthetics and support for indigenous struggles on the one hand, and—one could argue neocolonial—ambitions to map, frame and "discover" those cultures on the other (De Valck 2007: 71). Adapting the original idea of festivals as a kind of Olympics of Film to the focus on authorship, artistic achievement and political relevance led to a practice of labelling something a "New Wave" if there were sufficient filmmakers with interesting work, preferably but not necessarily sharing some characteristics, and coming from the same country or region. James Tweedie writes:

> From France to Finland, from Germany to Japan, this fascination with newness rejuvenated World Cinema in the 1960s and 1970s, and both domestic and foreign observers were quick to encapsulate these widely dispersed movements in a rhetoric of commonality whose preferred term of art was "New Wave".
>
> *(2013: 2)*

Festivals played a key role in generating new waves. Often the national cinemas being discovered under the umbrella term of "wave" had been overlooked at home, either because they failed to appeal to popular taste or because of issues with censorship. Festivals in these cases offered international recognition that could lead to art house circulation. In the 1980s, for example, China's so-called fifth generation, filmmakers working outside the academy system controlled by the Chinese state, were embraced in the West. Directors such as Chen Kaige and Zhang Yimou received acclaim and won awards in Berlin, Cannes and Venice. While their films screened at international film festivals and in Western arthouses, they remained, however, largely unknown in mainland China (Wong 2011: 17).

Festivalisation and authenticity

Two significant developments unfolded in the 1990s. The first concerned a revival of festivals' support of the industry. The second comprised a more explicit orientation towards festival audiences, and included the professionalisation of outreach and, arguably in its wake, the popularisation of festival visits. It was in the 1990s that film festivals really caught on with the general public. Audience numbers for big international film festivals were overall on the rise, while new specialised initiatives reached niche audiences. This can be placed in the larger trend of the "festivalisation" of culture (Bennett *et al.* 2014) in which festivals not only allow audiences to articulate (alternative) identities, but also accommodate a diverse range of (commodified) lifestyles.

The proliferation of film festivals furthermore spurred competition between festival events. Contemporary film festivals compete with each other over attention from the industry and public as well as over films, trying to secure world premieres that attest to the value of their events on the circuit (Stringer 2001). There are at least 6,000 film festivals worldwide according to *Filmfestivals.com.* This sprawling and globalised festival circuit consists of hierarchies and sub-networks, for example dedicated to LQBT cinema, Human Rights film or documentary (Loist 2016). There is wide diversity; festivals may be big or small, border on the mainstream or stay strictly niche, lean toward the industry or be community-driven, and take place in traditional cinema venues, outdoor locations or online. Clearly not all events are equally important. Mark Peranson distinguishes between business and audience festivals (2008). The real power, he points out, is concentrated in the hands of business fests, the events that host markets and cater to the industry with targeted services. While these festivals ultimately only make up a small fraction of the annual festival calendar, they are the occasions that set things in motion on the circuit. Nowadays it is at the film markets, co-production markets, producer corners, video booths, festival funds, training initiatives, and so on, that many of the new film projects are hatched and filmmaking talent scouted (Iordanova 2015). What does it mean that these films become available through global flows in which festivals play a crucial role? How far does the influence of festival funds and markets reach? What role do festivals play in our understanding of World Cinema? Questions like these have gained prominence within film festival studies since 2010.

Substantial critical scholarly attention has been devoted to film festivals' involvements with World Cinema through funds, co-production markets and training. Dorota Ostrowska, for example, writes how "there appears to be a correlation between the debates around 'World Cinema' and the projects enabled by festival funds", pointing specifically to "the role of the festivals in actively fostering non-Western arthouse filmmaking" (2010: 145). Well-known festival funds include the Hubert Bals Fund of the International Film Festival Rotterdam, the World Cinema Fund affiliated with the Berlinale, Cine en Construcción (San Sebastion/Toulouse), the Global Film Initiative in the USA, Fonds Sud in France and the Doha Film Fund, Qatar. The Hubert Bals Fund was the first of its kind to offer monetary support to filmmakers from developing countries to realise projects for which no funding would be available in their home countries. The fund has supported filmmakers from Latin America, Asia and Africa since the late 1980s, and selects projects from filmmakers working in developing countries on "artistic qualities" as well as authenticity (De Valck 2014: 52–53). The criticism that is levelled towards the work of this and other funds often stems from the uncomfortable and unequal dependency of filmmakers from the so-called Global South on Western entities. Miriam Ross, for example, evokes concern about the international climate in which the festival funds operate, specifically the taste for "poverty porn" among distributors, and concludes "that it is hard to escape the view that third-world countries are producing cultural artefacts for their first-world benefactors" (2011: 267). This concern essentially comprises two key critiques. First, that Western tastes, in particular the preference for art cinema aesthetics, dictate which projects get funded by festivals (see also Falicov 2010: 5). Second, that filmmakers are forced to produce authentic imagery and narratives, in spite of the transnational production circumstances that may apply, and thus to exploit their "exoticism" for Western audiences (Shaw 2014: 128; Falicov 2016: 218). I will touch upon these critiques in my reading of *Tanna*.

Scholarly concern about festivals' impact on World Cinema is apparent in the recurrent framing of their role as "producers"—despite acknowledgement that the money received by the beneficiaries of these funds is typically modest. While the influence of festivals in the pre-production phase has unmistakably increased since the 1990s, it has been on the level of circulation, rather than production, that festivals contributed to the success of the notion of World Cinema, particularly in relation to non-Western cinema. Since the 1960s labels such as *auteur* and new wave have been used as rhetorical tools to flag quality and topicality while claiming distinction from mainstream cinema. What changed with the advent of globalisation and the increasing commodification of culture in the 1990s is that festival discourse progressively doubled as a branding tool. Media companies developed niche marketing strategies that heavily relied on festival exposure and hark back to the familiar rhetoric from the 1960s to appeal to global audiences. The logic of film festivals, moreover, feeds into this dynamics. Film festivals not only screen World Cinema, they select, intervene and frame. The most powerful business festivals act as "sites of passage" (De Valck 2007: 30) through which the flows of World Cinema move in search for cultural legitimisation (see Elsaesser 2005; De Valck 2016). Festival discourse is thus utilised for multiple ends: consecration, cultural translation, criticism, activism, marketing, branding, as well as confirmation of festivals' key role in bringing quality, topicality and discovery into the limelight.

The case of *Tanna* lends itself very well to scrutinising how World Cinema—and non-Western cinema in particular—is framed for festival circulation. To properly understand the particular dynamics of this film and its success on the circuit, it is crucial to start at the stage of production, as the story of the film's making is arguably an integral part of the film's success. *Tanna* was *not* hatched on the festival circuit. It was not pitched at a forum or written on a talent campus, but started off without any funding as the personal project of two Australian filmmakers.

Authenticity

In interviews and festival Q&A's *Tanna*'s co-directors Bentley Dean and Martin Butler talk at length about the production process and their motivation in making the film. The filmmakers had previously collaborated in co-directing *Contact* (2009, Australia), a documentary built around historical footage of a group of Martu people coming into first contact with modern Australia, and *First Footprints* (2013, Australia), a four-part documentary series about Aboriginal history. *Tanna* is their first feature film and continues their interest in regional indigenous cultures. The Pacific island of Tanna was chosen as a location because of its stunning volcano as well as for personal reasons. Dean wanted to give his children "an experience before school age in Melbourne" (Van Zanten 2015). He lived seven months with his young family as part of the Yakel tribe, one of the last indigenous communities in the South Pacific that live according to traditional rules. Before the filmmakers set foot in the village in 2013, its people had never seen a movie. They screened *Ten Canoes* (Rolf de Heer, 2006, Australia)—which they praise for its collaboration with indigenous people—to give the community a sense of what they had in mind for their film. The aim was not to make a film about these people, but with them.

Two elements of the film's production are foregrounded by Bentley and Dean in their accounts in press and person. First, they stress that the story of Wawa and Dain was not only performed by villagers, but also *chosen* by them. The story is taken from recent Yakel history, based on true events that took place in 1987 when the tragic death of two lovers challenged the custom of arranged marriage. Second, an almost anthropological approach to the tribe emerges from their account of the production process. They recount spending two months familiarising themselves with daily life in Yakel and the laws and beliefs of the tribe before starting to discuss a storyline. Dean immersed himself in village life—the chief is reported to have given his own hut to Dean and his family—and Butler undertook several short stays, flying in from Sydney. Crucial for their communication with the villagers was Jimmy Joseph Nako—aka JJ—the only member of the tribe who spoke English. JJ acted as translator and helped with the production. His efforts guaranteed that the film was faithful to indigenous culture. JJ is quoted in Australia's largest national newspaper *The Australian* saying that "to us it was not acting, it was doing what was real. There was nothing difficult at all because we were performing what we were used to in our daily life" (Narayan 2015). Such blurring of reality and performance is enforced, moreover, by the decision to let the cast perform under their given names (Marie Wawa is Wawa, Mungua Dain is Dain), and the anecdote about writing the role of the little sister, the most enduring and photogenic character in the film, into the script. As the daughter of Dean's host family in Yakel, she captured his eye with her rascal ways, and they decided early on she had to be part of the film, playing herself.

This story of the film's making revolves around the idea of authenticity. The term authenticity has a long history of scholarly use, in particular in museum and tourism studies, but is not very stable as a concept (Reisinger and Steiner 2006: 299–300). Authenticity connotes the ideas of tradition and originality, which is typically located in other cultures or in the past. In the literature on tourism the validity of this conventional concept of authenticity and its usefulness to explain tourist experiences have been widely examined (Wang 1999). Dean MacCannell's notion of "staged authenticity" (1973) in particular, spurred numerous critical studies on the production of authenticity for tourist consumption (see the overview in Hughes 1995). However, MacCannell (1976) argues that the tourist's desire for an authentic experience is genuine and stems from the alienation between self and society in modern society (see also Cohen 1988: 373–374). Tourists travel to other (primitive or pre-modern) places to find the authenticity that is absent from their own modern lives (MacCannell 1976: 160). Writing on the circulation of new cinemas at film festivals, Bill Nichols draws on MacCannell's work to argue that festival audiences are interested in discovering what he terms "back region" knowledge (Nichols 1994a: 19). Film festivals provide a form of mediated access to local cultures and traditions that is linked to the real and genuine desire for the authentic that is also at the heart of certain forms of tourism and museum exhibitions.

Thus, *Tanna*'s successful circulation on the festival circuit originates in modern man's desire to experience a sense of authenticity. At the heart is the premise of a secluded island with a tribe living according to traditional rules. The directors, however, are outsiders—Australians—and this complicates the film's claim to authenticity and may raise concerns about the neocolonial appropriation of indigenous culture (Battiste 2011) and exoticisation, which are addressed below. Bentley and Dean seem well aware of this looming criticism and emphasise close collaboration with the tribe. Since the mid-1980s indigenous people have been using film and video for "self-determination and resistance to cultural dominance" (Ginsburg 1995: 256). However, viewers are informed that the Yakel tribe had never seen a film before. The suggestion seems to be that making the film together with the Australian directors *creates* a form of self-representation and offers them a chance to document tribal life. Dean and Butler shun away from taking explicit ownership of the film, giving credit to the villagers, and JJ specifically. On the film's Facebook page, JJ is referred to as Cultural Director of the film, and he frequently accompanies Butler or Dean to festival screenings, becoming the voice of the Yakel people abroad. On one of these occasions JJ is quoted saying: "In all the decision-making with the story, we all discussed and consulted together, which is our normal way of making decisions" (Narayan 2015). In this way *Tanna* is constructed as a product of authentic tribal culture.

Festival strategy

Tanna premiered in Venice on 9 September 2015. For the occasion, four members of the cast, JJ and members of the crew were flown to the Lido island. The world premiere was accompanied by the usual mix of festival exposure and additional PR, both of which aimed to generate buzz and create global coverage. The Venice Film Festival belongs to a top tier of what Peranson (2008) calls business festivals, which implies that films in competition come with distribution strategies already in place. In this context, the story of the film's making, as told by Butler and Dean in press conferences and interviews, becomes part of the film's marketing strategy. It proves to be a convincing account: virtually no critical reviews appear in the media and press after the Venice premiere. Buzzwords that circulate widely and inform the film's festival discourse are "traditional", "unique culture", "true story" and "every-day life."

Looking back on the launch, it is surprising that some parts of the PR did not generate criticism, in particular the role played by the actors, who made promotional appearances at the festival dressed in traditional clothes, not only posing for the cameras but also performing local dances. Images of the semi-nude villagers wearing nothing but grass shirts and penis sheaths dominated the film's world coverage. Wawa and Dain are captured striking poses on the Venetian canals and in a gondola, as if they were really in love. Lacking context, these images are misplaced, triggering an orientalist gaze that eclipses indigenous self-determination. Writing on tourism in New Zealand, John Taylor problematises the equation of authentic and "true" Maori culture with a pre-modern past, before the "discovery" of New Zealand by Europeans. He writes:

The significance of Maori culture in such narratives does not, therefore, appear on its own terms. It is instead a means of reconstituting the Christian eschatological narratives of sin, sacrifice, and redemption. "They" become the lost sacredness of Western culture, they become its Other, and they are ascribed a spiritual and physical authenticity which the "materialist" West has somehow lost.

(Taylor 2001: 10)

In a similar way Vanuatan culture—symbolised by the actors' traditional dress and dance—is appropriated for global image consumption (Nicholls 1994b), gratifying a nostalgic desire for authenticity. In the strategy for the Venice premiere the exotic is instrumentalised as attraction (Berghahn 2016). Indigenous culture, moreover, is overtly juxtaposed with Western civilisation. Reports and videos featuring the casts' encounter with the modern world were made available as part of the film's PR. For Marie Wawa, Mungua Dain, Marceline Rofit (Selin, the little sister) and Lingai Kowai (Selin's father) it was the first time they set foot outside Vanuata, and reportedly also the first time outside their village. Their visit to Australia, where they spent a couple of days with Butler before onward travel to Venice, was recorded on video. Australian *ABC News* reported:

Their first day in Australia is filled with other firsts. They get in their first elevator, use their first seat belt, experience their first tunnel and are impressed by the first tall buildings they have ever seen. Selin, 8, and her father Lingai are amazed at how the traffic lights direct cars through the city and out to Butler's home at Bondi Beach.

(Sherden 2015)

The contrast with the tribal life depicted in *Tanna* is immense. But is the modern world really that far removed from Vanuata?

Staged authenticity

Professor of Anthropology Lamont Linstrom, who has studied local communities on Tanna since 1978, notes how "[a]part from romantic love, the filmmakers have meticulously scrubbed away other signs of global modernity" (Lindstrom 2015). While it is true that the villagers choose to live in ancestral ways, they are familiar with the modern lifestyles that exist a few kilometres away and travel to larger towns such as Lenakel to do shopping. Most people own mobile phones. Yakel, he explains, is a popular tourist destination, and tourism a main source of income that can be traced back to the 1970s:

A freelance photojournalist in the early 1970s convinced people from this community to take off their clothes to boost the appeal of his photographs. Ever since, men here (especially when paying tourists come around) sport traditional penis wrappers, and women wear bark skirts.

(Lindstrom 2015)

With tourism as its main source of income, Vanuata and the island of Tanna will receive a further boost from the film and the coverage it has generated. Moreover, Butler and Dean are not the first Westerners to film in Tanna. Dean visited the island before as a participant of the ABC TV documentary series *Race Around the World* (1997, Australia, Stephen Jones) and to report on the Christian John Frum movement in 2003. In 2004 the ninth season of *Survivor* (2000–,

USA, Charlie Parsons) was shot on the Vanuatan islands. In 2007 JJ and other villagers starred in the British real-life documentary series *Meets the Natives* (2007, UK, Gavin Searle) which was broadcast in the UK, Australia and France. This context is conspicuously absent from the marketing campaign and the larger festival discourse. Moreover, when one investigates further, additional details emerge that complicate the two central claims in the story of the film's making. Notably, few details were disclosed about John Collee, a seasoned scriptwriter with films such as *Happy Feet* (2006, USA/ Australia, George Miller, Warren Coleman and Judy Morris) and *Master and Commander: The Far Side of the World* (2003, USA, Peter Weir), who worked together with Dean, Butler and the villagers on the script. Interestingly, although the "people of Yakel" are credited as co-writers on the website of funder *Screen Australia*, on IMDB only the names of Bentley, Collee and Dean appear. Similarly, the emphasis on ethnographic fidelity is contradicted by other details of the production that were not widely shared. For example, when asked about the most difficult aspect of working with amateur actors, the directors replied that it was hard for Wawa and Dain to display affection, because men and women do not interact let alone touch each other in public on Tanna. Such a revelation raises the question of why "authentic behaviour" was not prioritised for this crucial plotline. The desire for the film to speak to global audiences through the use of a universal, ill-fated love story would seem to be the most likely explanation.

MacCannell is sceptical about tourists' ability to have an authentic experience. He writes: "It is always possible that what is taken to be entry into a back region is really entry into a front region that has been totally set up in advance for touristic visitation" (1973: 597). His concept of staged authenticity is closely linked to commodification. More recently, scholars such as Reisinger and Steiner have pointed out that "the rise of relativism, postmodernism, poststructuralism and constructivism has convinced many that there is no actual, true, genuine, objective reality that can be the standard against which to assess authenticity" (Steiner and Reisinger 2006: 69). The appropriation of the idea of authenticity for marketing purposes, however, is widespread, and globalisation appears only to have fuelled (post-)modern man's longing to escape the cultural homogeneity of corporate production. Paradoxically, this differentiation from standardisation is itself subject to commodification.

In film festival studies these issues are addressed in the literature on festival funds, co-production markets and training. At a time of festivalisation and globalisation, distribution strategies are crucial for success. Films are *framed* for their festival launch and subsequent global image consumption. *Tanna* boasts the right combination of "regional distinctiveness" and "universal appeal" (Nicholls 1994b: 17). It aggressively reached out to global audiences with a marketing campaign linked to the Venice premiere, but also explicitly addressed key issues such as cultural ownership and authenticity that might otherwise have evoked fierce criticism in the press and thwarted further festival circulation. Promotional imagery and narratives play different roles in this process: the forthright exoticism of images and videos that circulated was softened by ideas about collaboration and an ethnographic approach which were articulated as part of a convincing story of the film's making.

In this story, as in the film, life in the Yakel tribe is distilled to a pure essence, untouched by modern influences. For MacCannell, staged authenticity is "insidious and dangerous" (1973: 599). Others have questioned his strict position. Tourism has, for example, been re-framed as "situated within zones of contact" that become part of local reality (Taylor 2001: 14). Despite commodification, Cohen (1988: 382) argues, this may create new opportunities for cultural self-representation. Is it possible, therefore, that the Yakel people willingly contributed to the circulation of an idealised version of tribal life, to its staged authenticity? One reason to believe so is put forward by JJ in *Island Life*, "the South Pacific only general interest magazine" when he explains:

> We are proud of our kastom … [and] … want to keep our kastom alive and we would like to share it with the world. This is why we think this film is good, because it allows us to share our kastom and will help make it stronger.
>
> *(JJ quoted in Gil Garcia 2016)*

If we take JJ at his word, collaboration with the Australian filmmakers is not only a form of self-presentation, but also a significant contribution to the preservation of cultural traditions. The making of *Tanna* then, becomes valuable for converting a way of life into heritage, and can be seen as "a new mode of cultural production in the present that has recourse to the past" (Kirshenblatt-Gimblett 1998: 149).

Conclusion

The case of *Tanna* confirms that there is a close and complex inter-relationship between film festivals and World Cinema. While the notion of authenticity is fundamental for our understanding of their dynamics, its conceptual strength is dependent on a critical reading of the different articulations of the idea of authenticity and the ends to which these are used. It is important, moreover, to underline that the present-day engagement with authenticity is not a novel bond that connects festivals to World Cinema. In the cosmopolitan, early decades of their existence, film festivals carved out a space for an international film world, particularly to resist the cultural homogenisation that loomed with Hollywood's encroaching hegemony. Instead, the films screened at festivals offered a window on the world. In the decades that followed that view was increasingly opened up to accommodate a wider variety of film production from around the world. As the festival network continues to proliferate and extends online, spaces available for screening of World Cinema multiply and flourish. Festivals' future is therefore tied up with a sustainable commitment to cultural diversity and a willingness to attend to its complexities. These include tensions between universalism and particular needs, weighing international or cosmopolitanism tendencies against national or local interest, consideration of the role of place as well as space, and an understanding of the way key notions—such as authenticity—are instrumentalised in the engagement with cinema in all its diversity.

References

Battiste, M. (2011) *Reclaiming Indigenous Voice and Vision*, Vancouver: University of British Columbia Press.
Bennett, A. J. Taylor and Woodward, I. (2014) *The Festivalization of Culture*, London: Routledge.
Berghahn, D. (2016), "The Cosmopolitan Exotic on the Film Festival Circuit", NECS Conference, Potsdam, 29 July.
Cohen, E. (1988) "Authenticity and Commodification in Tourism", *Annals of Tourism Research* 15: 371–386.
Dayan, D. (2000) "Looking for Sundance: The Social Construction of a Film Festival", in Bondebjerg, I. (ed.) *Moving Images, Culture and the Mind*, Luton: University of Luton Press, 43–52.
De Valck, M. (2007) *Film Festivals: From European Geopolitics to Global Cinephilia*, Amsterdam: Amsterdam University Press.
—— (2014) "Supporting Art Cinema at a Time of Commercialization: Principles and Practices, the Case of the International Film Festival Rotterdam", *Poetics* 42: 40–59.
—— (2016) "Fostering Art, Adding Value, Cultivating Taste: Film Festivals as Sites of Cultural Legitimization", in de Valck, M., Kredell, B. and Loist, S. (eds) *Film Festivals: History, Theory, Method, Practice*, London: Routledge, 2016, 100–116.
Elsaesser, T. (2005) *European Cinema: Face to Face with Hollywood*, Amsterdam: Amsterdam University.
Falicov, T. (2010) "Migrating South to North: The Role of Film Festivals in Shaping and Funding Global South Video", in Elmer, G., Davis, C. H., Marchessault, J. and McCullough, J. (eds) *Locating Migrating Media*, Lanham, MD: Lexington Books, 3–21.

—— (2016) "The 'Festival Film': Film Festival Funds as Cultural Intermediaries", in de Valck, M., Kredell, B. and Loist, S. (eds) *Film Festivals: History, Theory, Method, Practice*, London: Routledge, 2016, 209–229.

Gil Garcia, P. (2016) "The Making of Tanna—The Story Behind the Film That Stole Our Hearts", *Island Life*, 4 March, www.islandlifemag.com/island-life-magazine/tanna_movie/.

Ginsburg, F. (1995) "Mediating Culture: Indigenous Media, Ethnographic Film, and the Production of Identity", in Devereau, L. and Hillman, R. (eds) *Fields of Vision: Essays in Film Studies, Visual Anthropology and Photography*, Berkeley, CA: University of California Press, 210–235.

Hughes, G. (1995) "Authenticity in Tourism", *Annals of Tourism Research* 22 (4): 781–803.

Iordanova, D. (2015) "The Film Festival as an Industry Node", *Media Industries* 1 (3): 7–11.

Kirshenblatt-Gimblett, B. (1998) *Destination Culture: Tourism, Museum, and Heritage*, Berkeley, CA: University of California Press.

Lindstrom, L. (2015) "Award-winning Film Tanna Sets Romeo and Juliet in South Pacific", *The Conversation*, https://theconversation.com/award-winning-film-tanna-sets-romeo-and-juliet-in-the-south-pacific-49874.

Loist, S. (2016) "The Film Festival Circuit: Networks, Hierarchies, and Circulation", in de Valck, M., Kredell, B. and Loist, S. (eds) *Film Festivals: History, Theory, Method, Practice*, London and New York: Routledge, 49–64.

MacCannell, D. (1973) "Staged Authenticity: Arrangements of Social Space in Tourist Settings", *American Journal of Sociology*, 79 (3): 589–603.

—— (1976) *The Tourist: A New Theory of the Leisure Class*, New York: Shocken.

Narayan, R. (2015) "Vanuatu Tribe Finds International Success with Film 'Tanna'", *The Australian*, 5 November, www.loopvanuatu.com/content/vanuatu-tribe-finds-international-success-film-'tanna'.

Nichols, B. (1994a) "Discovering Form, Inferring Meaning: New Cinemas and the Film Festival Circuit", *Film Quarterly* 47 (3): 16–30.

—— (1994b) "Global Image Consumption in the Age of Late Capitalism", *East–West Film Journal* 8 (1): 68–85.

Ostrowska, D. (2010) "International Film Festivals as Producers of World Cinema", *Cinéma & Cie: International Film Studies Journal* 10 (14–15): 145–150.

—— (2016) "Making Film History at the Cannes Film Festival", in de Valck, M., Kredell, B. and Loist, S. (eds) *Film Festivals: History, Theory, Method, Practice*, London and New York: Routledge, 18–33.

Peranson, M. (2008) "First You Get the Power, Then You Get the Money: Two Models of Film Festivals", *Cineaste* 33 (3): 37–43.

Reisinger, Y. and Steiner, C. J. (2006) "Understanding Existential Authenticity", *Annals of Tourism Research* 33 (2): 299–318.

Rhyne, R. (2009) "Film Festival Circuits and Stakeholders", in Iordanova, D. and Rhyne, R. (eds) *Film Festival Yearbook 1: The Festival Circuit*, St. Andrews: St. Andrews Film Studies, 9–39.

Ross, M. (2011) "The Film Festival as Producer: Latin American Films and Rotterdam's Hubert Bals Fund", *Screen* 52 (2): 261–267.

Shaw, D. (2014) "Fonds de financement européens et cinéma latino-américain: Altérisation et cinéphilie bourgeoise dans *La teta asustada* de Claudia Llosa", *Diogène* 245: 125–141.

Sherden, A. (2015) "Vanuatu to Venice: First-time Tanna Actors Arrive in Sydney Ahead of Debut at Film Festival", ABC News, 8 September, www.abc.net.au/news/2015-09-08/tanna-actors-debut-in-venice/6757810.

Steiner, C. J. and Reisinger, Y. (2006) "Reconceptualizing Object Authenticity", *Annals of Tourism Research* 33 (1): 65–86.

Stringer, J. (2001) "Global Cities and International Film Festival Economy", in Shiel, M. and Fitzmaurice, T. (eds) *Cinema and the City: Film and Urban Societies in a Global Context*, Oxford: Blackwell, 134–144.

Taylor, J. P. (2001) "Authenticity and Sincerity in Tourism", *Annals of Tourism Research*, 28 (1): 7–26.

Tweedie, J. (2013) *The Age of New Waves: Art Cinema and the Staging of Globalization*, New York: Oxford University Press.

Van Zanten, C. (2015) "Interview Martin Butler and Bentley Dean on Tanna", *Roffa Mon Amour*, www.roffamonamour.com/blog/interview-directors-martin-butler-and-tanna/.

Wang, N. (1999) "Rethinking Authenticity in Tourism Studies", *Annals of Tourism Research* 26 (2): 349–370.

Wong, C. (2011) *Film Festivals: Culture, People, and Power on the Global Screen*, New Brunswick, NJ: Rutgers University Press.

33
CINEPHILIA GOES GLOBAL
Loving cinema in the post-cinematic age

Belén Vidal

Introduction

Cinephilia is both straightforward and elusive. The word alludes to the bonding desire for cinema, but also to the practices and cultures that this desire has inspired and brought to life. In this respect, cinephilia can be said to spring from two foundational moments: the rituals practised by the early twentieth-century avant-garde artists fascinated by the possibilities of the cinematograph, and the culture of viewing, talking and writing about film animating the various cosmopolitan centres in the post-World War II period, most notably Paris. The journal *Cahiers du cinéma*, founded by André Bazin and home to the well-known group of film critics, later *cineastes* of the New Wave, is credited with the invention of the auteur and the valorisation of classic Hollywood cinema as art. These two by-products of the era's intense cinephilia smoothed the path towards cinema's consideration as a worthy object of academic study. Yet, paradoxically, cinephilia would be later sidelined by a nascent discipline—Film Studies—in search of academic legitimation (Elsaesser 2005; Sperb and Balcerzak 2009; Baumbach 2012). The break of 1968 and the era of counter-culture were the turning point for successive waves of specialist debates that shaped Film Studies in the second half of the twentieth-century. Film theory rejected cinephilia's perceived amateurism and disarming sincerity in pursuit of more rigorously scientific methods, under the pressure of new political priorities (Andrew 2000).

The first decades of the twenty-first century have seen, however, a new host of viewing and writing practices that have invoked the spirit of cinephilia on both sides of the divide between scholarly analysis and film criticism (Bordwell 2011), a cinephilia that has real-world meeting places and communities (notably the worldwide boom of film festivals) as well as virtual ones. The moving image is consumed on a variety of platforms, while film-related content floods social media, including blogs and video streaming channels, where it enjoys unprecedented speed of access and dissemination. The birth of digital film cultures has seen the rebirth of cinephilia on a truly global scale: variously called "New Cinephilia", "cinephilia 2.0", or "digital cinephilia" (Jullier and Leveratto 2012; Shambu 2014), in the twentieth-first century the love for cinema has mutated into true *cinephagia*. This indiscriminate desire for film has transformed viewing practices, while new tools of analysis have reinvigorated cinephilic writing: with objects such as the supercut (fan-made video that compiles similar moments from diverse films) and the audiovisual essay, which tends to combine text and image in a transmediation of the essay form, the cinephile of the digital era records her fascination with specific fragments, or pursues an idea through the image itself. These forms of thinking through film and writing *with* film address intersecting communities of cinephiles, whether amateur or specialist. Endowed with a new lease of life by the digital turn, cinephilia has become firmly embedded in the discourse of the post-theory era.

Cinephilia, then, bookends the evolution of Film Studies, yet it has equally been disavowed on account of its excessive, unruly nature or, worse, dismissed as a solipsistic tendency to subjectivity and ahistoricism. In their discussion of contemporary cinephilia, Marijke de Valck and Malte Hagener highlight its ambiguity and multiplicity, approaching it as "an umbrella term for a number of different affective engagements with the moving image" (2005: 14). In this spirit, I want to explore further the persistence of the attachment to the cinematic in the post-cinematic age, and the kinds of knowledges that such attachment may yield. After Susan Sontag, writing at the end of the twentieth-century, declared cinephilia dead (1996), its rebirth in millennial film debates, and its potential as a form of historiography continue to warrant investigation.

A matter of time: cinephilia's generational thinking

Antoine de Baecque defined cinephilia as the "invention of a gaze": a particular way of "watching films, of discussing them, of spreading this discourse" but also, he adds, "the true way of considering cinema in its context"—therefore, as a historical object (2003: 11). In his reconstruction of this watershed moment in post-war French culture, de Baecque refers to the "holy trinity" of introduction, screening and discussion at the cine-club sessions where Bazin conducted this ritual "like others would hold mass" (2003: 40, my translation). Brimming with quasi-religious connotations, cinephilia is born out of what Hagener calls a "paradoxical structure of feeling, a specific disposition that is both radically subjective, but strives for communication and understanding" (2014). The dialectic between the spectator's intimate relationship with the film, manifesting in the practices of cinema-going and cinema-sharing, and the lasting print legacy left by this generation of self-avowed film lovers is what makes cinephilia historically legible.

Thomas Elsaesser has established a fundamental distinction between this particular moment—which he calls cinephilia "take 1"—as opposed to contemporary cinephilia: cinephilia "take 2". Cinephilia take 1 speaks of a state of synchronicity between the films and cinephiles, in which cinephilia is lived in the present tense, rooted in the urban culture of the cinemas of Paris in the 1950s and in the fleeting visibility of the films whose arrival had been delayed by the war, and that now flooded the city's screens. This picture has been both mythologised and deconstructed in subsequent iterations of cinephilia, acquiring the trappings of a generational phenomenon. Elsaesser refers to the delays and deferrals that facilitated the "oedipal time" of cinephilia: the young cinephiles at *Cahiers* would be able to discover the work of Hollywood and European filmmakers and reinvent themselves as the children of Alfred Hitchcock, Howard Hawks or Roberto Rossellini, while rejecting the mainstream French cinema made by established names of the older generation, which they dismissed as the *cinéma de papa* (2005: 31). Elsaesser extends this generational struggle to the film culture of 1970s London, where competing discourses in film magazines such as *Sight & Sound* and *Movie* were upstaged by the first breakthroughs of film theory of semiotic and psychoanalytical inspiration. Yet, as Laura Mulvey wrote in 2009, her call to arms for the political rejection of pleasure in her key intervention "Visual Pleasure and Narrative Cinema" (1975) was less a rejection of Hollywood than an admission of her and her generation's fascination with it, finding in the American genre cinema of the previous decades—and especially in the excessiveness of melodrama—an appealing alternative to the conservatism of mainstream high culture in Britain, and to a certain "tiredness with the traditions of English realism" (Mulvey 2009: xii).

Generational dissent was a fixture of early cinephilic cultures, but subsequent iterations have seen this reactive aspect give way to a sense of desired legacies. In the preface to a Spanish translation of a selection of film criticism from *Cahiers du cinéma*, Cristina Pujol identifies a new university-educated cinephile in Spain, bred on both contemporary Hollywood, as well as an abundant dose of (mostly) European and American classics watched on television. This generation, she argues, is "happy to live on the borrowed cinephilia of their teachers" (Fecé and Pujol 2005: 23, my translation), teachers who, in turn, struggled to reconcile their own imported cinephilia with the urgency of their political militancy in the 1970s. By the 1990s cinephilia had lost its synchronicity with its object of love, yet the ensuing sense of self-conscious belatedness and cultural displacement only increases the rippling intensity of the feeling: an undercurrent of nostalgia not only for cinema, but also for cinephilia, feeds the post-2000 return to this particular lost moment, from myriad different places.

Between contemporary cinephilia and past generational histories stands, however, a seismic shift provoked by medium (r)evolution. Access to film progressively became the province of television and more crucially, home video. The introduction of the first domestic VCR machines in 1975 radically altered the cinephile's habits and rituals: as Barbara Klinger notes, the conditions permitting cinephilia would be thereafter "relocated and rearticulated within the complex interactions among media industries, commodity culture, and the private sphere" (2006: 55). The spread of home video transformed a culture based on scarcity—the cinema as a "series of phantoms that the cinephile was trying to capture at out-of-the-way venues, at odd hours or at distant festivals" (Vernet 1999: 93)—to a culture of abundance, supported by ease of access outside metropolitan centres, and the democratisation of film collecting. The transition to this domesticated "new cinephilia" created new rituals and forms of compulsive love, but not without frictions and resistances since, as Nico Baumbach points out, "cinephilia is necessarily allied with some idea of medium specificity even if it tends to define the essence of the medium as undefinable" (2012: 52). Videophile Charles Shiro Tashiro speaks of the labour involved in the physical interaction and segmentation of the film experience enjoyed on video, claiming that it makes possible positive forms of connoisseurship that the theatrical experience discourages (1991: 16); in his discussion of cinephilia after videophilia, Lucas Hildebrand, however, concludes: "I am more likely to experience distanced aesthetic appreciation in a theatre but more emotional openness at home" (2009: 216–217).

As early as 1978, the symptoms of what Elsaesser would call cinephilia's disenchantment were already evident in the very same places where cinephilia had been most ardently nurtured. An example of this is Louis Skorecki's lengthy tirade published in *Cahiers du cinéma* that year (with some delay due to editorial disagreements) in which he dissects the excesses of classic cinephilia (such as the overvaluing of Hollywood cinema regardless of the films' political content) and criticises the new cinephilia's readiness to uphold auteurism as a prerogative of the market (1978: 33–35, 50–52). Skorecki's combative scepticism with regard to past and present forms of cinephilia foreshadows fundamental changes. First, the new(est) cinephilia shuns the gatekeeping of taste of classical cinephilia, now perceived as elitist, and champions instead the egalitarian fan competences of "popular cinephilia" (Jullier 2009: 203). Second, this cinephilia prefers "ubiquity over purity", jettisoning aesthetic concerns in favour of immediate access (Quandt 2009: 208).

Cinema as an institution and an experience seems to have lost pride of place in the social imaginary (Gaudreault and Marion 2015: 14–15), but its resilience as an object of love has deepened with its imbrication with other media, notably television and the digital.

Contemporary cinephilia or, cinephilia "take 2" (in Elsaesser's words) arises from a culture of continuous recycling, remaking and remixing: "The need to always be conscious of several temporalities [. . .] has become a generalised cultural condition" (Elsaesser 2005: 40). As a result, cinephilia is caught in the nostalgia for the medium while thriving on the anachronisms prompted by the consumption of past cinema histories on new digital platforms: the new cinephile may have the entirety of the canon at her disposal, but risks losing her way down the rabbit hole of the seemingly limitless archive without the compass provided by the experience of classical (pre-video) cinephilia. The concern with the fading of historicity is in evidence in the work by scholars poised between the two moments of cinephilia (Elsaesser, but also Willemen 1994: 227–230, Keathley 2006: 23–25). Jenna Ng, a theorist of digital cinephilia, puts it differently: she asks to what extent "contemporary cinephilia" is an oxymoron, since "one cannot have contemporariness in a project located specifically in the past" (Ng 2005: 66). The answer to this pressing question lies in the technological remediation of cinephilia on a global scale, as we will see in the next section.

Global online cultures: technology, consumption and world cinephilia

Any attempt at defining contemporary cinephilia needs to take into account the twin factors of unprecedented technological development, and the diversity of cross-cultural film experience that it has enabled (Ng 2005: 69)—factors that challenge the Eurocentric underpinnings of cinephilia's narrative in the twenty-first century. The intertwining of the technological and the sociological is in evidence in Jullier and Leveratto's three categories of cinephilia, which they link to three different stages in practices of film consumption: classical cinephilia and the cinema experience up to the mid-twentieth century; modern cinephilia and the privatisation of experience through home-viewing (1950–1980), and postmodern cinephilia (1980–2010) in relation to the relocation of the cinematic experience and the proliferation of user-controlled screens (2012: 153–154). The rhetoric about the death of cinema has become part of the genealogy of the medium's historical development (as noted by Tom Gunning and Paolo Cherchi Usai, cited by Gaudreault and Marion 2015: 16–18). Likewise, though thriving on technological change, the social practices of cinephilia exist in almost contradictory relationship to a reactive discourse that sees the same technological evolution as a symptom of cinephilia's unavoidable decline. In a perceptive account of this double dynamic, Sarah Keller goes as far as stating that there is no cinephilia without *cinephobia*—in other words, it is the shifting relationship between love and fear that defines the cinematic experience in a climate of constant technological change. From the literary to the visual, from silent to sound, from analogue to digital film, Keller traces cinephobia in the spectator's epistemological relationship with a medium in constant change, and the social anxieties this relationship generates, including the fear of the loss of the medium itself. In this respect, cinephobia is the flip side to cinephilia's nostalgic desire for an about-to-be-forgotten cinematic past (Keller 2014). Francesco Casetti's choice of deliberately archaic metaphors is telling in this regard: Casetti discusses the spectator's relationship with cinema after cinema's digital relocation in terms of "relics" and "icons". The former encompasses the film watched on DVD or on a lovingly restored print; these objects keep a metonymical relationship with the larger body of cinema, which is invested with the aura of its sacred remains. In contrast, the new settings in which film may be consumed (the digital home theatre) are icons, copies designed to replicate the original viewing conditions that produced the first wave of cinephilia, and thus to add an extra layer of authenticity to the watching experience (Casetti 2015: 63–66). We are back in the transcendent language of first-wave cinephilia, remediated into the digital era, yet such terms belie the everyday nature of the diverse practices feeding digital cinephilia (Hildebrand 2009: 217).

Postmodern cinephilia spells out the ending of the cinema experience as a social event, displaced by isolated acts of consumption. In contrast, the production of cinephilic discourse has become increasingly visible through the digital public sphere and related forms of networked labour. The forms of sociability facilitated by the Internet have given a new reach to the notion of the cinephilic community; intersubjectivity and connectivity are the two essential features of cinephilia in its new, global stage (de Valck and Hagener 2005: 14). In 2003, the influential volume *Movie Mutations: The Changing Face of World Cinephilia* (edited by Jonathan Rosenbaum *et al.*) produced a possible mapping of the global paths of cinephilia through a traditional literary format. The volume is made up of short essays and a series of public letters by a select group of consolidated film critics, festival programmers and film academics across the world, most of them born around 1960. The epistolary exchanges in *Movie Mutations* are proof of the self-reflective quality of a cinephilia cultivated mainly in film festivals, and attentive to the flows of global auteur cinema. The often passionate conversation is presented as a form of group writing driven by a desire to reconfigure the borders of classic cinephilia through an internationalist outlook. For example, looking at Howard Hawks through the prism of his reception in Japan, and putting him in relation to neglected Japanese director Yasuzo Masumura brings to the fore what veteran U.S. critic Rosenbaum calls "global synchronicity" or "the simultaneous appearance of the same apparent tastes, styles and/or themes in separate parts of the world" in the course of his dialogue with Japanese academic and author Shigehiko Hasumi (Rosenbaum and Hasumi 2003: 61).

Such instances of global synchronicity offer new opportunities for a latitudinal re-mapping of cinephilia built on the input of an ever-widening circle of participants, beyond hegemonic centres of discourse production (notably Western Europe and the US) (Shambu and Campbell 2009: 55). In a dossier about Indian cinema's global reach, Dina Iordanova makes a passionate plea for the individual testimony and the memory anecdote as tools for filling in the gaps in a potential historiography of international cinematic exchanges; according to the personal experience of the discussants involved, Indian popular cinema would emerge as a dominant presence in the markets of Eastern Europe, the Middle East and Africa at roughly the same time, challenging standard accounts of Hollywood domination in the industrial and the social imaginary (Iordanova *et al.* 2006: 113–117). The consideration of the worldwide presence of Indian cinema as the seed of a parallel cinephilia is but an example of the specificity of local cultures and the potential for a popular cinephilia to inform alternative historiographies (also see the exchange between Catherine Benamou and Lucia Saks on the transnational circulation of films *of* and *in* countries of the Global South in *Movie Mutations*, 2003: 150–165).

While reclaiming the cinephilic roots of Film Studies, *Movie Mutations* also demonstrates that it is not only cinema that has mutated, but also cinephilia, losing something of its original amateur impulse in favour of a specialised discourse. Against the persistent negative stereotype of the cinephile as an elitist snob with a passion for the obscure and the difficult, Nico Baumbach (borrowing from Jacques Rancière) predicates the "New Cinephilia" on *la politique de l'amateur*, which may bring the "breaking down [of] the strict divisions that separate filmmakers, critics, theorists, and cinephiles" (2012: 53). In this respect, the interpersonal practices of Internet film bloggers are perhaps the most prominent mode of writing through which twenty-first-century cinephilia may become legible. References in this field are Girish Shambu's film blog *girish* (Shambu 2004), running since September 2004, and his subsequent book-length essay *The New Cinephilia* (2014). In the latter, Shambu highlights the Internet's inverting of the relationship between a reduced number of active writers and a large number of passive readers that defined the era of classical cinephilia (2014: 20). In other words, contemporary cinephilia is de-centred and more democratic, spawning a multi stranded dialogue through an increasingly large number of social networking platforms (Shambu 2014: 4). *The New Cinephilia* fully inhabits the forms and modes of interaction afforded by the "horizontal terrain of Internet cinephilia" (Shambu 2014: 44). The essay is also a spirited polemic that proposes an unabashedly utopian vision of digital cinephilia as a social force with the potential to give rise to communities that buck the dominant trend towards the compartmentalisation and specialisation of knowledge predicated by present-day "realist capitalism" (Mark Fisher 2009, cited in Shambu 2014: 45). Thus, cinephilia emerges as an idiom that may be shared by specialists and amateurs through the unregulated spaces of the Internet: "learning communities" made up of different constituencies with unique perspectives (Shambu 2009: 219) that were, in the best of cases, imagined, now become tangible in the virtual arena.

Digital cinephilia may have turned into yet another expression of participatory culture (Jenkins 1992), but its opportunities come not without challenges, such as the friction between different interest groups (e.g. fans versus cinephiles, Sperb and Balcerzak 2009: 22) and the suspicion felt by many a professional film critic that blogging and the Twittersphere may be encroaching upon the domain of professional film criticism in ways that ultimately allow the logic of neoliberalism to erode the spaces for paid intellectual labour (Frey 2015: 10–12; James 2015). If horizontal Internet cinephilia has the potential to distil some of Film Scholarship's most durable ideas into everyday criticism (Shambu 2014: 31), it has also helped Film Studies reclaim a space for the intuitive and the subjective that seems to have been ruled out of academic writing. This question is at the centre of the next section.

Writing cinephilic histories

Blogging and film-related image-sharing make for a treasure trove of online micro-criticism that organises film-related thinking (observations, unexpected connections, personal philias and phobias) into heterogeneous forms of exchange (Shambu 2014: 21–29). These instances of micro-criticism may seem random, dead-end forms of cinephilic expression. However, the fixation with the small segment, the fragment and the isolated image that criss-crosses the everyday creative practices of fans (as in the YouTube genre of the supercut) has also effected a shift in the ways scholars, now in possession of a set of digital tools for moving-image writing (DVD, video files, user-friendly editing software) have put the fragment at the centre of their theoretical thinking around cinephilia.

After the watershed of "grand" screen theory and the urgency of the (unresolved) battles around film and cultural politics, the return of cinephilia in Film Studies marked a return to the textual flesh and bones of film. Scholars practising formal analysis through a cinephilic prism both acknowledge and disavow the structural thinking behind the paradigm wars of the 1970s and 1980s (semiotics, psychoanalysis, and later the schemata of neo-formalism and cognitivism), as well as the consideration of cinema as a machine for the production of narrative competences and psycho-social identities. Instead, the theorists of the new cinephilia have staked their territory in earlier and peripheral moments of film theory. For example, Cardinal refers to the leftfield readings of the image by artists and critics close to Surrealism as a sort of "errant dream-criticism" (1986: 114) fed by an eye wandering off after the apparently meaningless detail in the edges of the frame, and by moments that seemed to transcend a film's explicit subject matter. With Roland Barthes, this attention to the incidental begets an elaborate taxonomy (the *obtuse* meaning; the 'third meaning'; the *punctum*). Thus, Barthes turns to the elusive qualities of the photographic image in a series of essays that intersperse a personal unveiling within the wider remit of cultural criticism (see Cardinal 1986; Burgin 2004; Keathley 2006). Other scholars of cinephilia have turned to Jean Epstein's fascination with the disruptive qualities of the close-up, and to his reflection on the image as enigma, in his work on *photogénie* (Willemen 1994; Keller 2012). These scholars seek to explore aspects of spectatorship that may complicate the regulated relationship between the viewer and the film object.

Instead, cinephilia leads into more unpredictable attachments. The fragment and the "peripheral" detail (Cardinal 1986) enable epiphanic moments; Paul Willemen uses this phrase to single out particular moments pregnant with affective power, within and beyond the elements that belong to the conventional and highly coded forms of narrative film. The *cinephiliac* moment arises "in excess of the film's register of performance, as potentially undesigned, unprogrammed" (Willemen 1994: 239). Willemen's choice of adjective deliberately echoes the necrophiliac, for both modes carry the fascination with former life becoming *alive* in front of our eyes: Georges Méliès's remark about the rustling of leaves in the background of the film by the Lumière Brothers *Le repas de bébé* (Baby's Dinner, 1895, France) is a reaction to a moment that, as historian Georges Sadoul was prompted to note, would barely register today. However, this often-reproduced anecdote informs how we think of cinema as a form able to absorb the contingent and the spontaneous in ways that seemed radically new (Vaughan 1990: 65). Likewise, it lays the ground for future milestones of film criticism during the period of classical cinephilia, such as Bazin's thinking about cinema form in relation to the world framed. Thus, on the one hand, the cinephiliac moment throws light upon the particular relationships between film and burgeoning moments in film culture. Willemen retrospectively reads the writing of the Young Turks at *Cahiers du cinéma* in this vein, as a series of responses to "moments which, when encountered in a film, spark something which then produces the energy and the desire to write, to find formulations to convey something about the intensity of that spark" (1994: 235). From consumption to production, the *cinephiliac* moment (perhaps more so than the variant "cinephilic") alludes to the *history* of cinephilia as a "serialisation of moments of revelation" (1994: 233), thus embedding it into history. On the other, the foregrounding of different temporalities is what gives cinephilia its value as a historiographic tool; this aspect has been explored by several important monographs that return to Hollywood cinema, and to the scene of classic cinephilia, as key sites for the formation of contemporary Film Studies.

In *Cinephilia and History, or The Wind in the Trees* (2006) Christian Keathley returns to pivotal moments in classic film theory and looks at modes of watching cinema repressed by historical discourse. Whether conjuring up the cinephile's active "panoramic perception" (2006: 29–53) in alignment with other tropes of technological modernity, or tracing the Surrealist taste for the uncanny and the arbitrary association in the thinking of Bazin, Keathley goes back to well-established histories through attention to the fragment, the marginal detail and the personal anecdote. This practice opens alternative routes that may alter our sense of the archive, introducing the contingent, the sensuous, and the subjective experience as paths into historical thinking. The potential of this approach is further explored by Rashna Wadia Richards's study of classical Hollywood cinema as a collection of open-ended, cinephilic moments. Inspired by Walter Benjamin's materialist, non-linear historiography, Richards approaches classical Hollywood's closed system through a network of cinephilic "flashes", moments that, rather than corroborating standard accounts of Hollywood history, perform as "fleeting images from the past [that] rupture the tedious narration of timeless truths" (2013: 20). The interruptions, incongruities and anomalies repressed by the classical narrative system yet intermittently visible in the body of the film make for a "network of uncanny coincidences" that reads transitional moments in Hollywood history (such as the passage from silent to sound) as open to contingency and variation.

Laura Mulvey's *Death 24 x a Second: Stillness and the Moving Image* (2006) is perhaps the most decisive contribution in terms of a potential cinephilic historiography. Mulvey's notion of "delaying cinema" captures the continuum between the scholar's and the cinephile's attachment to the film as a material object, and between the fugitive image of classical cinephilia and the full availability (and manipulability) of the digital image in postmodern cinephilia. The desire to slow down or "freeze" the film in order to apprehend a particular moment is a typical form of fetishistic possession, most notably in relation to the iconic images of film stars. But this form of delaying cinema also allows the cinephilic gaze to look for clues of what cinema represses. In both cases, the material basis of the medium (be it the film strip, or the frame capture apprehended through the freeze-frame function on video or DVD) enables the "shifts of consciousness between temporalities" (2006: 184): the deferral of narrative movement makes the indexical trace of pro-filmic time emerge, with the attendant uncanny effects. Thus, Mulvey's close look at the frame in an early scene in *Imitation of Life* (1959, USA, Douglas Sirk) makes an anonymous African American actress in a walk-in role become visible for a second on the edge of the frame, in the periphery of the action centred on the (white) stars, Lana Turner and John Gavin. In this sequence, a brusque yet choreographed gesture by Turner accidentally spoils the snapshot of the anonymous black woman, occluding her presence in the mise-en-scène. This gesture is narratively unremarkable yet, when seen today, is tantalising with displaced meaning with regard to the off-screen context of racial segregation as well as the themes of racial relations and invisible black labour espoused by the film. Mulvey's illustration of the process of stopping the image, and putting it back in narrative context with a surplus of deferred meaning (2006: 151) is a powerful example of the affective import of the cinephiliac moment. Through the delaying of cinema, the alertness to the peripheral detail reveals an altogether visible *yet* dormant archive that yields unexpected returns through the filter of historical distance and the re-reading of favourite films.

Mulvey's emphasis on the material basis of cinema is richly informed by her own practice as an avant-garde filmmaker as well as a scholar (as noted in Grant 2013). Whereas Raymond Bellour (writing in 1975, just prior to the advent of video) calls cinema "the unattainable text", forever slipping through the fingers of the analyst, in 2003 Nicole Brenez states that "nothing clarifies an image like another image, nothing analyses a film better than another film" (2003: 23). This is what the increasingly consolidated field of the audiovisual essay, or "videographic criticism", sets up to do (Keathley and Mittell 2016).[1] A performative mode of writing about film *through film*, the audiovisual essay allows the cinephile simultaneously to "play with a source text as a way to think about it, and about her interaction with it, and to signal its value to her" (Grant and Keathley 2014), taking a step further towards the integration of cinephilic consumption and production. The audiovisual essay remediates both the historical undercurrent of film criticism drawn to the fragment and the peripheral detail, and the formal strategies of delay in cinema, inscribing the author's fascination with a particular film moment through a set of critical questions. By incorporating the object itself through different forms of reframing (slowing down a gesture, or re-cutting or captioning a particular scene to elaborate on a point of style or performance) the audiovisual essay is by its very nature an experimental, open-ended form that draws on both explanatory and poetic modes of exegesis (Keathley 2011: 180–182), ultimately approaching the (*readerly*) film object in the spirit of Barthes's *writerly* text (self-reflective, inconclusive and open-ended). To extend the Barthesian analogy further, we could argue with Grant (2013) that the experimental practice of videographic criticism productively incorporates the subjectivity and pleasure (*jouissance*) historically repressed with the turn from cinephilia to politics, *while* reclaiming *both* cinephilia *and* politics in our encounters with the film object.

The rise of videographic Film Studies echoes contemporary art's use of film. Installation pieces such as Douglas Gordon's *24-Hour Psycho* (1993) or Christian Marclay's *The Clock* (2010) play on the tension between the fragment and the work, the medium and the institution, popular and avant-garde film: *24-Hour Psycho*—remarked by Mulvey as a creative instance of delaying cinema—"stretches" Hitchcock's *Psycho* (1960) to a twenty-four hour projection by slowing down the electronic image, whereas *The Clock* puts together hundreds of film clips displaying ticking clocks into a single supercut that lasts twenty-four hours. Represented time and screening time become (almost) perfectly aligned: a complete day is required for one viewing of the entire piece. The incorporation of film in contemporary installations fetishises and commemorates cinema while deconstructing the illusion of presence and plenitude connoted by the original work (Balsom 2013: 30). Contemporary art thus performs as another form of cinephilic production, setting up a dialogue with remembered films that accentuates the import of time in the spectator's cinephilic experiences and attachments.

Conclusion

In the context of a globalised film culture and the transition to the digital medium, cinephilia has resurfaced with a renewed urgency arising from a certain nostalgia for the materiality of cinema and the rituals of film love. Films themselves are also actively joining in the process of memorialisation and historicism, as the cinema of the twenty-first century embarks on the retelling of its twentieth-century history. Mainstream fictions such as *Hugo* (2011, USA, Martin Scorsese), *The Artist* (2011, France, Michel Hazanavicius) or *Blancanieves* (Snow White, 2012, Spain, Pablo Berger) lovingly recreate a film historical imaginary (Gorfinkel 2005), to different effects: celebrating the technological aspects of cinema put at the service of the imagination, dramatising the crises and rebirths of the medium, or fusing iconographies and styles. These cinephilic films are not so much concerned with the trappings of history, as with a specific spectatorial experience belonging to film history—experience that they re-inflect through a contemporary film-literate language (Sperb 2016: 52–70). Films, as Lalitha Gopalan puts it with regard to the self-reflexive plots in popular Indian cinema, can "'read' our desire as much as we can marshal our critical machinery to read their creations" (2002: 2). Films can be the subject, as well as the object, of cinephilia.

This chapter has looked at the various facets of world cinephilia: as an attachment to film mediated by temporal displacement and technological change, as a social practice bringing together ever widening communities, within and outside the traditional centres of film culture, and as a discourse that shifts the boundaries between specialised and amateur practice, and produces a set of tools for rethinking cinema's past and future. The persistence of cinephilia spells its truly global reach as an ongoing dialogue across generations of cinema lovers.

Note

1 There already exist a number of curated academic spaces dedicated to the audiovisual essay, the most prominent of which is the *Cinema Journal*-endorsed online journal *[in]Transition* (http://mediacommons.futureofthebook.org/intransition).

References

Andrew, D. (2000) "The 'Three Ages' of Cinema Studies and the Age to Come", *PMLA* 115 (3): 341–351.
Balsom, E. (2013) *Exhibiting Cinema in Contemporary Art*, Amsterdam: Amsterdam University Press.
Baumbach, N. (2012) "All That Heaven Allows: What Is, or Was, Cinephilia? An Inquiry into the Love That Dare Not Speak Its Name, Except When It Does", *Film Comment* 48 (20): 47–53.
Bellour, R. (1975) "The Unattainable Text", *Screen* 16 (3): 19–28.

Benamou, C. and Saks, L. (2003) "Circumatlantic Media Migrations", in Rosenbaum, J. and Martin, A. (eds) *Movie Mutations: The Changing Face of World Cinephilia*, London: British Film Institute, 150–165.

Bordwell, D. (2011) "Academics vs. Critics. Never the Twain Shall Meet: Why Can't Cinephiles and Academics Just Get Along?" *Film Comment*, May–June, www.filmcomment.com/article/never-the-twain-shall-meet/.

Burgin, V. (2004) *The Remembered Film*, London: Reaktion.

Cardinal, R. (1986) "Pausing over Peripheral Detail", *Framework* 30–31: 112–130.

Casetti, F. (2015) *The Lumière Galaxy: Seven Key Words for the Cinema to Come*, New York: Columbia University Press.

De Baeque, A. (2003) *La cinéphilie: Invention d'un regard, histoire d'une culture 1944–1968*, Paris: Fayard.

De Valck, M. and Hagener, M. (2005) "Introduction. Down with Cinephilia? Long Live Cinephilia? And Other Videonsyncratic Pleasures", in de Valck, M. and Hagener, M. (eds) *Cinephilia. Movies, Love and Memory*, Amsterdam: Amsterdam University Press, 11–24.

Elsaesser, T. (2005) "Cinephilia or the Uses of Disenchantment", in de Valck, M. and Hagener, M. (eds) *Cinephilia. Movies, Love and Memory*, Amsterdam: Amsterdam University Press, 27–43.

Fecé, J. L. and Pujol, C. (2005) "Prólogo: a propósito del amor", in Fecé, J. L., de Baecque, A. (eds) *Teoría y crítica del cine. Avatares de una cinefilia*, Barcelona: Paidós.

Frey, M. (2015) "Introduction: Critical Questions", in Frey, M. and Sayad, C. (eds) *Film Criticism in the Digital Age*, New Brunswick, NJ: Rutgers University Press.

Gaudreault, A. and Marion, P. (2015) *The End of Cinema?: A Medium in Crisis in the Digital Age*, Barnard, T. (trans), New York: Columbia University Press.

Gopalan, L. (2002) *Cinema of Interruptions: Action Genres in Contemporary Indian Cinemas*, London: British Film Institute.

Gorfinkel, E. (2005) "The Future of Anachronism: Todd Haynes and the Magnificent Andersons", in de Valck, M. and Hagener, M. (eds) *Cinephilia. Movies, Love and Memory*, Amsterdam: Amsterdam University Press, 154–167.

Grant, C. (2013) "How Long Is a Piece of String? On the Practice, Scope and Value of Videographic Film Studies and Criticism", *The Audiovisual Essay. Practice and Theory of Videographic Film and Moving Image Studies*, http://reframe.sussex.ac.uk/audiovisualessay/frankfurt-papers/catherine-grant/

Grant, C. and Keathley, C. (2014) "The Use of an Illusion: Childhood Cinephilia, Object Relations, and Videographic Film Studies", *Photogénie*, June, www.photogenie.be/photogenie_blog/article/use-illusion.

Hagener, M. (2014) "Cinephilia in the Age of the Post-Cinematographic", *Photogénie*, June, www.photogenie.be/photogenie_blog/article/cinephilia-age-post-cinematographic.

Hildebrand, L. (2009) "Cinematic Promiscuity: Cinephilia after Videophilia", *Framework* 50 (1–2): 214–217.

Iordanova, D. with contributions from Goytisolo, J., Singh, K. G., Šešić, R., Suner, A., Shafik, V. and Skantze, P. A. (2006) "Indian Cinema's Global Reach. Historiography through Testimonies", *South Asian Popular Culture*, 4 (2): 113–140.

James, N. (2015) "Who Needs Critics?" (2008), in Frey, M. and Sayad, C (eds) *Film Criticism in the Digital Age*, New Brunswick, NJ: Rutgers University Press, 225–229.

Jenkins, H. (1992) *Textual Poachers: Television Fans & Participatory Culture*, New York: Routledge.

Jullier, L. (2009) "Philistines and Cinephiles: The New Deal", *Framework* 50 (1–2): 202–205.

Jullier, L. and Leveratto, J-M. (2012) "Cinephilia in the Digital Age", in Christie, I. (ed.) *Audiences, Defining and Researching: Screen Entertainment Reception*, Amsterdam: Amsterdam University Press.

Keathley, C. (2006) *Cinephilia and History, or The Wind in the Trees*, Bloomington, IN: Indiana University Press.

—— (2011) "La caméra-stylo. Notes on Videocriticism and Cinephilia", in Clayton, A. and Klevan, A. (eds) *The Language and Style of Film Criticism*, Abingdon: Routledge, 176–191.

Keathley, C. and Mittell, J. (eds.) (2016) *The Videographic Essay: Criticism in Sound and Image*. Montreal: Caboose.

Keller, S. (2012) "Jean Epstein's Documentary Cinephilia", *Studies in French Cinema* 12 (2): 91–105.

—— (2014) "Cinephobia. To Wonder, To Worry", *Lola* 5, www.lolajournal.com/5/cinephobia.html

Klinger, Barbara (2006) *Beyond the Multiplex: Cinema, New Technologies, and the Home*, Berkeley, CA: University of California Press.

Mulvey, L. (1975) "Visual Pleasure and Narrative Cinema", *Screen* 16 (3): 6–18,

—— (2006). *Death 24x a Second: Stillness and the Moving Image*. London: Reaktion.

—— (2009) "Introduction", in *Visual and Other Pleasures*, 2nd edn, London: Palgrave, ix–xvi.

Ng, J. (2005) "Love in the Time of Transcultural Fusion Cinephilia, Homage and *Kill Bill*", in de Valck, M. and Hagener, M. (eds) *Cinephilia. Movies, Love and Memory*, Amsterdam: Amsterdam University Press, 65–79.

Quandt, J. (2009) "Everyone I Know Is Stayin' Home: The New Cinephilia", *Framework* 50 (1–2): 206–209.
Richards, Rashna Wadia (2013) *Cinematic Flashes: Cinephilia and Classical Hollywood*, Bloomington, IN: Indiana University Press.
Rosenbaum, J. and Hasumi, S. (2003) "Two Auteurs: Masumura and Hawks", in Rosenbaum, J. and Martin, A. (eds) *Movie Mutations: The Changing Face of World Cinephilia*, London: British Film Institute, 61–93.
Rosenbaum, J., Martin, A., Jones, K., Horwath, A., Brenez, N. and Bellour, R. (2003) "Movie Mutations: Letters from (and to) Some Children of 1960", in Rosenbaum, J. and Martin, A. (eds) *Movie Mutations: The Changing Face of World Cinephilia*, London: British Film Institute, 1–34.
Shambu, G. (2009) "What Is Being Fought for by Today's Cinephilia(s)?", *Framework* 50 (1–2): 218–220.
—— (2014) *The New Cinephilia*, Montreal: Caboose.
—— (2004–) *girish*, http://girishshambu.blogspot.co.uk.
Shambu, G. and Campbell, Z. (eds), with Darr, B., Sallitt, D. and Horbal, A. (2009) "The Digital Cine-Club: Letter on Blogging, Cinephilia and the Internet", in Balcerzak, S. and Sperb, J. (eds) *Cinephilia in the Age of Digital Reproduction: Film, Pleasure and Digital Culture*, London: Wallflower Press, Vol. 1, 54–67.
Skorecki, L. (1978) "Contre la nouvelle cinéphilie, *Cahiers du cinéma* 293: 31–51.
Sontag, S. (1996) "The Decay of Cinema", *New York Times Magazine*, February 25, www3.nytimes.com/books/00/03/12/specials/sontag-cinema.html.
Sperb, J. (2016) *Flickers of Film: Nostalgia in the Time of Digital Cinema*, New Brunswick, NJ: Rutgers University Press.
Sperb, J. and Balzerzak, S. (2009) "Introduction: Presence of Pleasure", in Balcerzak, S. and Sperb, J. (eds) *Cinephilia in the Age of Digital Reproduction: Film, Pleasure and Digital Culture*, London: Wallflower Press, Vol. 1, 7–29.
Tashiro, C. S (1991) "Videophilia: What Happens When You Wait for It on Video", *Film Quarterly* 45 (1): 7–17.
Vaughan, Dai (1990) "Let There Be Lumière" (1981), in Elsaesser, T. with Barker, A. (eds) *Early Cinema: Space, Frame, Narrative*, London: British Film Institute, 63–67.
Vernet, M. (1999) "The Fetish in the Theory and the History of the Cinema", in Bergstrom, J. (ed.) *Endless Night: Cinema and Psychoanalysis, Parallel Histories*, Berkeley, CA: University of California Press.
Willemen, P. (1994) *Looks and Frictions: Essays in Cultural Studies and Film Theory*, London: British Film Institute.

34
ANOTHER (HI)STORY?
Reinvestigating the relationship between cinema and history

Vito Zagarrio

Introduction

> If history exists, only cinema can reveal it. All you have to do is watch. There is no need to write it, because you are written by it. Cinema is the only trace, the only witness.
> *(Jean-Luc Godard quoted in Farassino 1996: 13, author's translation)*

Godard's provocative comments provide a suitable entry point into this essay's investigation into the relationship between film and history. The intention is to retrace a long debate that began at the end of the last century, to suggest different methodological approaches and case studies, and also to try to understand the evolution of this relationship at a time when the terms themselves are in flux. "Cinema" has been transformed by the digital revolution, converging with other media and arts to create an "expanded cinema"; but "history", too, is an evolving concept that both refers to the study of the past and intersects with contemporary political and ideological debates and questions of national and cultural identity.

Film, history and ideology: symptoms of the European debate

Scholars began addressing the interrelationship between cinema and history in the late 1970s in Europe, above all in France. This was a moment when history had lost its past certainties, along with any hope of definitively interpreting man's past and positively directing his imminent future; it had been overwhelmed by the crisis of ideology and the consequent breakdown of ethical and theoretical postulates. Instead it began to display a belated interdisciplinary interest in psychoanalysis, anthropology, sociology, mass psychology, cultural phenomena and language. In short, between the end of the 1970s and the beginning of the 1980s, the necessity of relating history to other disciplines and equipping it with new instruments became increasingly evident. The central role played by the mass media in cultural life made it a crucial topic for historical analysis, and as the dominant art of the twentieth century the cinema assumed a role of particular significance. It was to be studied as a mixed and multiple discipline, both as a document and a testimony of the collective imaginary of the past and, simultaneously, as a producer of a contemporary imaginary, a form and ideology, a language and image.

Marc Ferro's *Cinéma et Histoire* (1977) played a pivotal role in this belated disciplinary shift; although it was made up of essays already known to film researchers and those interested in pure history, it constituted the first synergetic attempt to reflect and critique the cinema from the point of view of history. However, the difficulty of locating and defining the terms of this relationship, which is evident in the varied contributions to this volume, betrayed the fact that the debate was still in its infancy. Was cinema to be defined as historic "agent", and thus a medium capable of participating in the developments (and/or contradictions) of society, or only as a "document" bound to a certain era and particular social organisation? Should the survey be limited to either documentary or archival films or should historical and costume films be taken into account? Should it concern itself with "history", the chronicling of daily life, as in the pioneering "micro-histories" of French historians; or should it limit itself to "History" with a capital "H", events that shaped and transformed communities and ways of thinking? Should the study focus on films that explicitly address historical themes, or also those where history takes place off-stage? Do historical films provide audiences with new interpretations of a society, or do they merely reflect the specific historical period that produced them? Should such studies confine themselves to a single "historical" genre or address all genres in the light of history? Is cinema itself, in one way or another, history? Ferro's volume addressed such questions, explicitly or implicitly, and the issues it raised remain relevant today.

Ferro believed the task was to compare history to the imaginary that it helps create; to carry out textual analysis without losing the focus on the historical context. For a historian such as Ferro, the "imaginaire" is history as much as history itself. However, his choice of films was questionable, being limited to "classical", ideological and political genres—from the early Soviet cinema to French cinema of the popular front and from *Chapaev* (1934, USSR, Georgi Vasilyev and Sergey Vasilyev) to *La Marseillaise* (1938, France, Jean Renoir). It was an ideological approach led by the idea of a "militant" cinema capable of "reflecting" society (in the sense intended by Lukács), but also of changing it. Ferro also suggested a use of historiography (strengthened by psychoanalytical and anthropological tools) and applied to cinema to support a determined (if not predetermined) ideological thesis. In this way, separate analyses of individual films such as *Jud Süß* (Süss the Jew, 1940, Germany, Veit Harlan) and the aforementioned *Chapaev* and *La Grande Illusion* inevitably led to ideological anti-Nazi, anti-Stalinist and anti-bourgeoisie conclusions.

Let us consider the most representative titles in Ferro's survey, the most famous of which is undoubtedly *Süss the Jew*. The point is to understand whether or not it constitutes (either explicitly or implicitly) a Nazi film given the fact that, when put on trial at the end of the war, the director managed to convince the judges that his honest authorial purpose was overruled by those in charge of Nazi cultural politics. According to Ferro, there is a hidden element in the film that betrays Harlan, in the form of four crossfades in which his "guilt" emerges: the dissolve between a ducal emblem and the Jewish ghetto symbol shows a dangerous transfer of power from Arians to the Jewish; the dissolves used to speed up the transformation of Süss's face from beardless to bearded that impart a ridiculous and evil quality to the features of the Jewish race; and finally a dissolve from golden coins to desirable ballerinas that mirrors the perversion for money and vice. Veit Harlan was betrayed by his own art. Ferro thus proceeds with an unusual methodology, combining a structuralist dissection with a re-proposition of ideology that turns to moralism. Another example would be his analyses of Soviet cinema, a macroscopic case of the intervention of the State in the control of image media. According to Ferro, it is a cinema strictly connected to history in that it is functional either to a propagandistic aim or to the elaboration and exportation of a national image. Films such as *Aleksandr Nevsky* (1938, USSR, Sergei M. Eisenstein) and *Andrej Rublëv* (1996, USSR,

Andrei Tarkovsky) serve a common foreign policy purpose, respectively anti-German and anti-Chinese. Ferro considers *Dura Lex* (1926, USSR, Lev Kulešov), on the other hand, as anti-Stalinist text: Jack London's story is suited to the ideological and expressive needs of the director and the Canadian Klondike becomes a metaphor for Stalinist Russia during the period of the trials. Here too, a "slip" betrays the author: the accurate recreation of American scenery is compromised by the inclusion of a Russian-style lunch. Is this a directorial mistake, an authorial mannerism or the sub-textual invocation of Stalinist despotism? The aforementioned *Chapaev*, on the other hand, is associated with the prototypes of Soviet propagandistic cinema: the story of the legendary folk hero Chapaev and of his encounter/conflict with the Bolshevik Furmanov contains all the theoretical postulates of Russian society during the strengthening of the Soviet party and State: heroes die and the party remains, spontaneity dies and organisation is born, the peasants form an alliance with the urban working class, the values of Russian tradition persist and are absorbed into the new state institutions. To counterbalance these Soviet examples, Ferro mentions two Western films: *The Third Man* (1949, UK, Carol Reed), which he compares to Graham Greene's original story and thus interprets as a truly anti-Communist film; and *La Grande Illusion*, of which he provides an ambivalent double-reading, as either a libertarian/internationalist work or a conservative/collaborationist one.

Regardless of their ultimate interpretation, Ferro believed that moving images represented a unique patrimony, an archive of collective memories that we were only beginning to reclaim now that the moving image had ceased to be an "orphan" and had achieved its own theoretical foundations. For Ferro, then, cinema leads both to social and cultural awareness. Thus he posited the idea of a sort of cinematic library, based around Super 8 and the Hachette-Pathé video products of the period, in so doing prefiguring the kind of research on digital archives proposed in the 2000s.

Roughly contemporaneous to Ferro, and also operating in France (although now resident in Italy), is Pierre Sorlin, who applied sociological and ideological criteria to cinema and was arguably responsible for establishing the value of film as a source in historical research (Sorlin 2015). Sorlin's research has always focused on the relationship between cinema and history, both theorising and practising the use of audiovisual documents as a means of surveying the history of the twentieth century and investigating the production and use of images in modern society. His research has its origins in the use of audiovisual documents as evidence in the context of social history. In this context, the study of the cinematic image assumed a central position, as demonstrated by the various stages of his academic career: professor of sociology of film at Paris VIII-Vincennes from the late 1970s and aesthetics of cinema at Paris III-Sorbonne Nouvelle since the late 1990s and then co-director of the historical Institute Parri in Bologna, Italy, since 1987. The first substantial result of this research agenda was the monograph *Sociologie du cinéma* (1977), in which he developed the central notion of the "visible" and applied it in particular to Italian cinema after World War II. A similar approach was also evident in the essays he wrote in collaboration with Marie-Claire Ropars-Wuilleumier and Michèle Lagny, on the topic of revolution in Eisenstein (1979) and the popular French films of the 1930s (1987). Given that he was resident in Italy, Sorlin's work also significantly influenced the Italian debate, for example the work of Pasquale Iaccio (1998), who became a specialist on the topic, and Pietro Pintus (1980), who analysed the commedia all'italiana ("comedy Italian style") from this perspective.

Postmodern history and the loss of the real

However, the ideological/sociological approach pioneered by Sorlin is not the only way of rethinking the question of film and history. Shortly after, in the early 1980s, Jean Baudrillard also addressed the question, but from a philosophical perspective. According to the philosopher, during the tumultuous years between the two World Wars and during the Cold War, myth was exiled from reality by the violence of history and instead took refuge in the cinema. In a similar fashion, history also invaded the cinema (Baudrillard 1981). After influencing the contemporary world through its myths, history was thus exorcised, banned from our lives, transformed into a myth and resurrected on the screen. It became our lost referent, that is to say our myth, and as such, it took the place of myth on screen. History is a *scenario retro*, it is a "corpse" that can be placed on the screen, it is a "fossil" that can be represented and "simulated". For Baudrillard, then, history entered cinema with a late triumph. However, this re-apparition does not stand for an acknowledgment, but, instead, for the nostalgia of a lost reference point. Baudrillard's line of reasoning was perfectly consistent with the Vietnam war film of the period, and especially with *Apocalypse Now* (1979, USA, Francis Ford Coppola) in which Kurtz's body, symbolically slaughtered by Willard could correspond to the "corpse" of history.

By the 1990s, the imaginary was changing as the Vietnam years gave way to the Post-Communist era. History was now manipulated through electronic processes, with the media full of images of the daily bombardments in Serbia, refugees from Kosovo or Albanian, Kurdish illegal immigrants, destroyed bridges, crashed trains and targets hit from above as if in a computer game. All these images only served to remind us of the imaginary power of audio-visual media. The point is brought home by the way in which the American military intervention in the conflict, in the wake of the Clinton–Lewinsky scandal, seems to re-enact the plot of Barry Levinsons's paradoxical and parodic film *Wag the Dog* (1997, USA), in which an American president "invents" a war in Albania in order to distract public opinion from his own sexual indiscretion. In Levinson's film, Robert De Niro's spin doctor and Dustin Hoffman's film producer successfully conspire to artificially construct a "war" through a computer, producing a false image of a desperate woman, apparently escaping from a village burned to the ground using a virtual set and a computer generated kitten (Figure. 34.1 and 34.2). This ironic film recalls the paradox of Baudrillard's slogan, issued immediately after the first war in Iraq, that "the Gulf War never existed" (Baudrillard 1991).

During this period Sorlin also turned his attention to the world of the media (especially television, which, like cinema, helps "construct" reality) and to the theme of the "historical" film. In a book first published in Italian, *L'immagine e l'evento* (1999), Sorlin pointed out how a film about the past essentially reorganises the present; but he also pushed this argument further and—echoing Baudrillard—suggested a priority of the representation over the event itself. According to Sorlin, the twentieth century is the century of the moving image, and thus trying to construct a history of it without constant reference to cinema and TV is pointless. Not only

Figure 34.1 and 34.2 Virtual technology for a virtual war: fake history in *Wag the Dog* (1997, USA, Barry Levinson).

does our information and knowledge of events both near and distant derive largely from what is shown on screen, but our whole imagination is built on film models. Images represent the world and sometimes affect circumstances or suggest ways to interpret events. They elaborate on the evolution of events, turning the unfolding of everyday events into history, which is just as significant as the official histories written by historians. In this book, Sorlin reinvestigates the history of the twentieth century as a history of the media and, specifically, of audio-visual media. He addresses the theoretical problem of history in cinema by relating it to the idea of cinema as a storytelling apparatus that uses identification and mechanisms for triggering desire, arguing that the image is intrinsically attractive and that pleasure is an integral part of our relationship with audio-visual media.

The (un-)representability of history

In the 1990s the question of the "representability" of history became more pressing, particularly in relation to the cinema. At the same time, the debate over the relationship between cinema and history became a more complex patchwork, intersecting with the disciplines of sociology, anthropology, psychoanalysis, feminism and cultural studies. The general feeling was that it was becoming increasingly difficult to identify history.

Thus, in this period many theoretical books dealing with the definition of the "historic" event (and often adopting feminist, postmodernist or poststructuralist approaches) appeared in the US. For example, Vivian Sobchack dedicates an entire book to the identification of this object:

> What is both poignant and heartening about this novel form of historical consciousness is that it has no determinate 'object'. In great part, the effects of our new technologies of representation put us at a loss to fix that 'thing' we used to think of a history or to create clearly delineated categorical temporal and spatial frames around what we used to think of as the 'historical event'.
>
> *(Sobchack 1996: 5)*

The third part of Sobchack's book in particular proposes the theory of an "end" (or multiple "ends") to history, or at least of the dead end posed by the traditional way of carrying out historiography:

> As Robert Rosenstone puts it, there is now a pervasive sense 'that traditional history has in this century run up against the limits of representation.' But this sense of ending brings with it the constructive task of creating a new kind of history and forging a usable past that speaks both to the present and of a future.
>
> *(Sobchack 1996: 11–12)*

Rosenstone's thesis, in his essay in Sobchack's volume, is that:

> among theorists of and apologists for postmodernism (the two categories overlap), there are a few who take time to discuss a new kind of historical writing—a postmodern history which, apparently, brings the way we know or think of the past into line with the post-structuralist critique of current historical practice.
>
> *(Rosenstone 1996: 201)*

Meanwhile, Hayden White observed how the events of the twentieth century threatened the coherence of the traditional historiographic narrative; quoting Gertrude Stein, he claimed that, in the age of television, camcorders and digital manipulation, everyone can be taken, filmed, interviewed or "digitalised" inside a "historic" scene or significant event (Sobchack, 1996: 4 and 17; White 1996: 17). The effects of new technologies of representation lead to the loss of a "fixed" object of study, of a clear spatial/temporal framing that could define historic events. This helps explain why the American publications addressed so many different topics; everything, in the end, can constitute history, as can be seen in the wide variety of topics and methodologies, not only in Sobchack (1996) and Rosenstone (1995), but also Kaes (1989) and Rollins (1983).

At the same time, two writers approached the topic of the complex relationship between film and history through a common strategy: Carlo Ginzburg and Natalie Zemon Davis, writing in Italy and America respectively. Carlo Ginzburg, one of the promoters of "micro-history" since the 1970s (Ginzburg, 1979, 1983, 2015), argues that history is above all *narration*. He expounds on this idea in an afterword to Natalie Zemon Davis' *The Return of Martin Guerre* (1983), which reconstructs a remarkable sixteenth-century case in which a French peasant returned after several years of absence to discover that his role has been assumed by a lookalike: for Ginzburg, the word invention is intentionally provocative. Davis's research and narration are not built on the opposition between "true" and "invented" but on the integration of "realities" and "possibilities" (Ginzburg in Zemon Davis 1984: 302–310). All history books, Ginzburg says, have an intrinsically narrative component; an idea that had already been widely discussed by philosophers and methodologists, but not sufficiently by historians themselves (although it is also addressed by Hayden White and Robert Rosenstone). This dimension walks hand in hand with relativistic attitudes that tend to erase any distinction between fiction and history. Both historian and novelists represent and illustrate the past. Zemon Davis's book demonstrates how subtle the distinction can be between narrating history and writing novels. "Both the historian and the novelist have the task of representing and illustrating the past and human beings' actions" (Ginzburg in Zemon Davis 1984: 314; author's translation). Ginzburg quotes Henry James, and says that Zemon Davis demonstrated that an historian can also write men and women "stories", like those of Bertrande and Pansette in *Martin Guerre.*

The author herself claims to have thought that this was a story for a film when she first discovered the case of Martin Guerre (Zemon Davis 1984) so it isn't surprising that this Pirandello-like story became the plot for several films. Indeed, Zemon Davis herself co-wrote the script of *Le retour de Martin Guerre* (The Return of Martin Guerre,1993, France, Daniel Vigne), which was adapted from Janet Lewis' novel on the case, while this was in turn later remade in an English language version by Jon Amiel as *Sommersby* (1993, France/USA).

Cinema-history in the new millennium

As the new century dawned, 11 September 2001 changed all the cards on the table. The tragedy of the Twin Towers and the television images and videos uninterruptedly reproducing this nightmare drove history into daily life. In an essay originally published in *Le Monde,* Baudrillard reconfirmed the crucial role he played in contemporary cultural debate (Baudrillard 2002, 2003) claiming that the World Trade Centre and Pentagon attacks were the main event, the one from which all the rest followed, the perfect event that contains all those that never happened. 11 September was a new kind of terrorism that changed the rules of the game, turning the strengths of a leading world power against itself; the terrorists had used the planes, computers and media of Western society in order to stage a terrorist attack that seemed to have been borrowed from Hollywood movies. The 9/11 attack, inspired by disaster movies, exceeded its reality and with the obsessive re-proposal and re-editing of the Twin Towers fall, the media world (television, video, digital cameras) became accomplices of the historic disaster. According to Baudrillard

(2002), 9/11 represented the fight of globalisation against itself and inaugurated a fourth world war: the first defeated the European supremacy, the second Nazism, the third Communism, the fourth, which we are experiencing today, is the most complex and global of them all.

Following the turning point of 9/11, and in the light of the problems of representation posed by the postmodern digital age, an evolution took place in cinema's relationship with history. The relationship in question was now between history and a sort of hybrid and expanded cinema, including borderline and "non-orthodox" media such as television, video-art, videogames and the web. This led to new ways of thinking, such as: the representation of history as a *myth* (Rosen 2001); its representation as "counter-history", that is, as a counterbalancing hypothesis or "virtual history" ("What if?"); its representation as "anti-history", adopting a sceptical attitude to the present and the future; history based on an anachronism, as in Georges Didi-Huberman's "heretical" look at the connections between images and history (Didi-Huberman 2000). Perspectives such as these highlight, on the one hand, the need to expand cinema's horizon to encompass a wider field of visual culture and, on the other, the "exuberance" and "complexity", of images themselves, necessitating a rethinking of the dichotomy between cinema and history and the process of memory building. Cinema comes to be seen as a "place" of either individual or collective memory, often overwhelmed with nostalgia—that assumes a conservative, negative or problematic meaning (Boym 2002)—freeing the past from a strict literalism, humanising and constantly changing history itself. This yielded a range of new approaches and topics, such as: the digital imaginary between memory and history (Burgoyne 2003); the feminist or gender-filtered reconsideration of stories, methods and knowledge; the legacy of Foucaultian genealogic thought in feminist theories; the intersecting paths of technologic, social, cultural, sexual systems, etc.

In this period, scholars sought to overcome traditional cinema histories, moving from "official history" to "popular history", from a focus on "ideologically committed" cinema to a "cinema of entertainment", reconsidering those works that, in an attempt to create a coherent historical narrative, were previously excluded from the category of "historical film" (Landy and Bové 1994; O'Leary 2014). The idea of cinema as history was now employed as a method to investigate a wide range of film categories: films related to a remote or recent past; but also, and above all, films set in the present that exhibited a problematic, dialectical approach to the past (in particular in relation to issues of national, cultural, gender and political identity) and exerted an influence on the imaginary and mentality of their time, becoming active historical agents/entities in their own right; and, finally, films that represent the material habits and traditions of their age and thus constitute precious resources for research into contemporary reality.

Images of war from the past and from the present

All of the above is readily evident in the way that Hollywood blockbusters think about history—especially after 9/11—balancing realism with fantasy. See for example *Olympus Has Fallen* (2013, USA, Antoine Fuqua) and its sequel *London Has Fallen* (2016, USA/UK/Bulgaria, Babak Najafi). It is interesting to note that the latter, a hyper-American, anti-Islamic film, is directed by a Swedish director with Iranian roots. Both films mirror the Western fear of homeward terrorism: the first describes an attack on the White House, whereas the second shows an attack in London, where the world's most powerful people are attending a state funeral. The plots are poor and predictable, but the films' interest lies in the use of linguistic codes taken from videogames and the constant—if naïve—focus on contemporary iconography (drones, surveillance, Skype, etc.); there can be no doubt that contemporary history dominates these films. The destruction of the Twin Towers, the decapitations, the nightmare of ISIS—all enter the cinematic imaginary without the need for filters or the passage of time.

Such a focus on contemporary history can produce effects bordering on the comic, as in the re-visitation of American national history through the representational codes of computer games in Peter Berg's *Battleship* (2012, USA), a mainstream American film based on a computer game, which itself draws on a much older analogue game. What is most interesting about the film is its ideological position and the historical revisionism. The film is set in Pearl Harbour on board the famous Missouri ship that survived the Japanese attack. While the Americans and Japanese simultaneously play international sports games, aliens arrive. So, the two old enemies find themselves united in a common fight against the extra-terrestrial invader, with an unavoidable sort of sweet final rhetoric in which the aliens come to symbolise other new "aliens", be they Islamic terrorists or the immigrants from anywhere in the world. The "old" American national history, based on the still unhealed wound of Pearl Harbour, is married to a "new", post-9/11 history of global terrorism.

The even more bizarre example of Timur Bekmambetov's *Abraham Lincoln: Vampire Hunter* (2012, USA) transforms the American civil war into a clash between vampires and humans. Though undoubtedly in the splatter-movie genre and aimed at an adolescent audience, it offers a chance to analyse the way in which the cornerstones of history are represented in postmodern cinema. There are parallels with the mocking narrative style of director Quentin Tarantino in *The Hateful Eight* (2015, USA) in which a fake letter by Lincoln constitutes a key plot point in a film that blends diverse genres—western, horror/splatter, mystery, but also the historical film—and faces up to the myths underpinning the social and political pacts of the American Nation. It is clear that Hollywood cinema of the new millennium rethinks history by mixing genres (action, fantasy, western, science fiction), epochs (the civil war, the search for a new frontier, the era of terrorism, a forthcoming future), and mythologies (the West, the President as hero, the arrival of aliens).

In an era dominated by the wars in Afghanistan and Iraq, ISIS videos and decapitations, history invades the collective imaginary immediately without the need for time or critic distance. Baudrillard's view, expressed in *Simulacra and Simulation* (1981), is even more pertinent in the contemporary context: the myth, banned from reality, from history's violence, finds shelter in cinema. It is in the same scenario that history invades cinema today. This much is clear when one considers Clint Eastwood's *American Sniper* (2015, USA), which narrates the "heroic" story of Iraq war marksman Chris Kyle, is based on an autobiography and ends with footage of his actual funeral in order to commemorate an American patriot and war hero. Or Brian De Palma's *Redacted* (2007, USA/Canada), in which the Iraq war constitutes a pretext for a metalinguistic interpretation of cinema itself in the digital and global communication era. The Middle East (and Iraq in particular) now seems to have replaced Vietnam as a wonderful film set that plays host to multiple narrative variations and experiments with language and technology. A whole series of films from the 2000s seem to confirm this observation: Kathryn Bigelow's *The Hurt Locker* (2008, USA; set in Iraq) and *Zero Dark Thirty* (2013, USA; in Iraq and Pakistan), Sam Mendes's *Jarhead* (2005, USA/Germany; on the war in Kuwait), David O. Russell's *Three Kings* (1999, USA; set during the Gulf War), Paul Haggis' *In the Valley of Elah* (2007, USA; in Iraq) Paul Greengrass' *Green Zone* (2010, USA/UK/France/Spain; in Iraq), Peter Berg's *The Kingdom* (2007, USA/Germany; set in Saudi Arabia), Ridley Scott's *Body of Lies* (2008, USA/UK; set in the Middle East). The list could even be expanded to other geographic areas: Ridley Scott's *Black Hawk Down* (2001, USA/UK; set in Somalia) or Mike McCoy and Scott Waugh's *Act of Valor* (2012, USA; set between the Philippines and Costa Rica). These titles suggest the global dimension of the "American war" and imply that all settings and scenarios are valid grounds for experimenting with film genres and language.

Most of these films derive from autobiographies or novels inspired by true stories, presenting an intersection between private stories and history with a capital H. Emblematic in this regard, and therefore worthy of further analysis, is *American Sniper*, Clint Eastwood's adaptation of the autobiography of Chris Kyle, a Navy Seal sniper with the distinction of having accumulated the highest number of enemy kills. The book's tagline advertises "the true story that inspired the movie", drawing attention to the film's purported fidelity and simultaneously revealing the existence of a separate "true history" behind it (although serious challenges to its truthfulness have subsequently emerged). A Texan cowboy and—by family tradition—hunter, Kyle joins the Seals and is sent to Iraq immediately after the start of the 2003 war. He takes part in many missions as a frontline member and soon becomes a legend thanks to his courage and ability with a rifle. When he finally retires to spend time with his family, a veteran suffering from post-traumatic stress ironically kills him. After his death, Kyle receives the honour of a state funeral, thousands of people greet his coffin in the streets and his autobiography becomes a belated testament, a diary of our times. In his autobiography, Kyle expresses no doubts, and divides the world clearly into good and bad; the Iraqis are presented as "savages", just like the American Indians in Westerns, or "Charlie" in Vietnam movies. The book can thus be defined as "reactionary": "If I had to make a list of priorities, their order would be God, Homeland and Family" (Kyle *et al.* 2012: 13). Eastwood adapts the book fairly faithfully and would therefore seem to endorse its perspective. So, is the film equally "reactionary"? At first glance, the answer would seem to be "yes". Although he proclaims himself politically conservative, Eastwood's films frequently deal with delicate themes for contemporary America: as in *Gran Torino* (2009, USA/Germany) or *A Perfect World* (1993, USA). While his two World War Two historical films, *Flags of Our Fathers* (2006 USA) and *Letters from Iwo Jima* (2007, USA) show compassion towards the Japanese enemy, in *American Sniper* they are mere shadows, as in John Ford's *Stagecoach* (1939, USA). But the film translates Kyle's autobiography into pure cinema through its use of special effects and the videogame aesthetic characteristic of millennial cinema—the "fireworks" of the postmodern cinema experience described by Laurent Jullier (1997)—and through its aura of hyperrealism (Figure 34.3). *American Sniper* is a great genre movie: a war film set in Iraq that repeatedly and explicitly echoes the Vietnam movie tradition. The film replicates the aesthetic of a videogame, with targets who move like "zombies", always unrealistically falling down at the first shot, and "game levels" gradually becoming more and more difficult as the film progresses. *American Sniper* is full of dichotomies: documentary and fiction; truth and falsehood; the glorification of the American war and its critique. Although its politics are (at least apparently) reactionary, it is one of the most intense Hollywood war films of the post-9/11, post-traumatic cinema.

Figure 34.3 The recent history of the war in Iraq is filtered through a videogame aesthetic in *American Sniper* (2015, USA, Clint Eastwood).

Writing about 11 September and *24* (2001–2010, USA, Joel Surnow and Robert Cochran), Slavoj Žižek, observes that not only had the communication media already harassed us about the threat of terrorism, but this threat had also already been loaded with a "libidinal investment" (Žižek 2002). Consequently, America obtained exactly what at first was the object of its fantasy, and this was the biggest surprise. It was not "reality" that was to enter our image, but, instead the image entered and subverted our reality (Žižek 2006). In this essay on *24,* the philosopher stands against the legitimation of violence and the fact that violence has been turned into something ordinary, something already "declared"; to make his case, he cites the scenes in which the hero, Jack Bauer (Kiefer Sutherland) is willing to use all kinds of tortures on his enemies to protect his homeland and family.

Hollywood cinema has always shown itself to be capable not only of representing conflicts (be they social contrasts or wars) as they happened, but also of anticipating processes that were yet to take place. But this is even truer in today's American TV series than ever before: aside from representing the most advanced trends of cinematic language, they capture events reflecting the political and sociological "zeitgeist". *House of Cards* (2013–, USA, Beau Willimon), a cult series dealing with political intrigues inside the White House, is a clear example: set in modern Washington DC, the episodes tell the events surrounding Frank Underwood (Kevin Spacey), a democratically elected member of the fifth congressional district and leader of a majority in the Chamber. After being deprived of the role of Secretary of State that he had been promised by the new President, Frank employs a variety of tricks in an effort to reach the highest political office. Almost all of the most stylistically experimental series of recent years have something to do with history, be it the remote past, recent past, or current reality.

There are also numerous contemporary productions (in both cinema and TV) that employ a successful contamination of the genres of history and fantasy: *The Lord of the Rings* (2001–2003, New Zealand/USA/Germany, Peter Jackson), to which Kristin Thompson (Thompson 2007) dedicated a book; cult TV series *Game of Thrones* (2011–, USA, David Benioff and D. B. Weiss); the numerous series set in the Middle Ages/Renaissance, such as *The Borgias* (2011–2013, USA, Neil Jordan), *The Tudors* (2007–2010, UK/Ireland/Canada, Michael Hirst) and *Da Vinci's Demons* (2013–2015, USA/UK, David S. Goyer); the many films mixing history with fantasy genres, such as *The Outlander* (2009, USA/Germany/France, Howard McCain), in which an alien crash lands and finds himself in a Viking territory, becoming a hero of the time, *Beowulf* (2007, USA, Robert Zemeckis), or even the recent cycle of films dedicated to superhero Thor (e.g. *Thor,* 2011, USA, Kenneth Branagh, *Thor: The Dark World,* Alan Taylor, 2013, USA).

Conclusion

The relationship between cinema and history is in flux. Both terms require new definitions: "film" is now digital and "cinema" has been hybridised with other media (TV, internet, etc.); history, on the other hand, has become increasingly intertwined with contemporary politics and the unfolding of current events, moving away from the "macro" of big events to the "micro" of individual lives. The pioneering work of Ferro and Sorlin now appears somewhat naïve and simplistically ideological, while the impact of postmodernism has necessarily imposed new approaches to the interpretation of an increasingly complex society. Thus, the question has shifted from being the identification and (ideologically driven) analysis of "the historical film" to using the concept of film as history as a method to analyse a wide range of films and genres. These dramatic changes have not lessened the importance and relevance of the debate, however. Rather, in less than forty years since film was first taken seriously as an object for historical study, the question of cinema's engagement with history has now become one of the central questions in the study of world cinema.

References

Baudrillard, J. (1981) *Simulacra and Simulation*, Ann Arbor, MI: University of Michigan Press.

—— (1991) *The Gulf War Did Not Take Place*, Bloomington, IN: Indiana University Press.

—— (2002) *Power Inferno*, Paris: Galilée.

—— (2003) *The Spirit of Terrorism and Other Essays*, London: Verso.

Boym, S. (2002) *The Future of Nostalgia*, New York: Basic Books.

Burgoyne, R. (2003) "Memory, History and Digital Imagery in Contemporary Film", in Grainge, P. (ed.) *Memory and Popular Film*, Manchester: Manchester University Press, 220–236.

Didi-Huberman, G. (2000) *Devant le temps. Histoire de l'art et anachronisme des images*, Paris: Éditions de minuit.

Farassino, A. (1996) *Jean-Luc Godard*, Milan: Il Castoro cinema.

Ferro, M. (1977) *Cinéma et Histoire. Le cinema, agent et source de l'histoire*, Paris: Éditions Denoël/Gonthier.

Ginzburg, C. (1979) "Spie. Radici di un paradigma indiziario", in Gargani, A. (ed.) *Crisi della ragione*, Turin: Einaudi; reprinted in C. Ginzburg (1986), *Miti emblemi spie. Morfologia e storia*, Turin: Einaudi.

—— (1983) "Di tutti i doni che porto a Kaisàre: leggere il film, scrivere la storia", in *Storie e storia: quaderni dell'Istituto storico della resistenza e della guerra di liberazione del circondario di Rimini*, 5 (9): 6–17.

—— (2015 [2006]) *Il filo e le tracce. Vero falso finto*, Milano: Feltrinelli.

Iaccio, P. (1998) *Cinema e Storia. Percorsi immagini testimonianze*, Napoli: Liguori.

Jullier, L. (1997) *L'écran post-moderne: un cinéma de l'allusion et du feu d'artifice*, Paris: L'Harmattan.

Kaes, A. (1989) *From Hitler to Heimat: The Return of History as Film*, Cambridge, MA: Harvard University Press.

Kyle, C. with McEwen, S. and DeFelice, J. (2012) *American Sniper: The Autobiography of the Most Lethal Sniper in U.S. Military History*, New York: W. Morrow.

Lagny, M., Ropars, M. C. and Sorlin, P. with the collaboration of Nesterenko, G. (1987) "Générique des années 30", in *Vingtième Siècle: révue d'histoire*, 16 (1): 160–161.

Lagny M., Ropars, M. C. and Sorlin, P. (1979) *Octobre: La révolution figure*, Paris: Éditions Albatros.

Landy, M. and Bové, P. (1994) *Cinematic Uses of the Past*, Minneapolis, MN: University of Minnesota Press.

O'Leary, A. (2014) "Towards an Ecology of Cinema and History", in *The Italianist*, 34 (2): 250–252.

Pintus, P. (1980) *Storia e film. Trent'anni di cinema italiano (1945–1975)*, Rome: Bulzoni.

Rollins, P. C. (ed.) (1983) *Hollywood as Historian: American Film in a Cultural Context*, Lexington, KY: University Press of Kentucky.

Rosen P. (2001) *Change Mummified: Cinema, Historicity, Theory*, Minneapolis, MN: University of Minnesota Press.

Rosenstone, R. (1995) *Visions of the Past: The Challenge of Film to Our Idea of History*, Cambridge, MA/London: Harvard University Press.

—— (1996) "The Future of the Past: Film and the Beginning of Postmodern History", in Sobchack, V. (ed.) *The Persistence of History: Cinema, Television, and the Modern Event*, London: Routledge.

Sobchack, V. (ed.) (1996) *The Persistence of History: Cinema, Television, and the Modern Event*, London: Routledge.

Sorlin, P. (1977) *Sociologie du cinéma*, Paris: Aubier Montaigne

—— (1999) *L'immagine e l'evento L'uso storico delle fonti audiovisive*, Turin: Paravia.

—— (2015) *Introduction à une sociologie du cinéma*, Paris: Klincksieck.

Thompson, K. (2007) *The Frodo Franchise: The Lord of the Rings and Modern Hollywood*, London: Penguin Books.

White, H. (1996) "The Modernist Event", in Sobchack, V. (ed.) *The Persistence of History: Cinema, Television, and the Modern Event*, London: Routledge.

Zemon Davis, N. (1983) *The Return of Martin Guerre*, Cambridge, MA: Harvard University Press.

—— (1984) *Il ritorno di Martin Guerre. Un caso di doppia identità nella Francia del Cinquecento*, Turin: Einaudi. Italian translation with an introduction by Carlo Ginzburg.

Žižek, S. (2002) *Welcome to the Desert of the Real*, London: Verso.

—— (2006) *Jack Bauer and the Ethics of Urgency*, *Lacan.com*, www.lacan.com/zizbauer.htm.

35
ARCHIVAL CINEMA

Paolo Cherchi Usai

Introduction

Michelangelo's frescoes at the Sistine Chapel in Rome are not called "archival paintings", and the Ishtar gate at the Pergamon Museum in Berlin is not "museum architecture", but Georges Méliès *Le Voyage dans la Lune* (A Trip to the Moon, 1902, France) is generally regarded as an "archival film". The roots of this blatant disparity are to be found in the cultural dictionary of the moving image, characterised by an inherent tension between professional and non-specialised language. The occurrence is all the more remarkable in that film professionals do not have control over the terminology pertaining to their own field of expertise once their work is translated into mainstream jargon. This gap between conceptual accuracy and convention is particularly manifest in the discussions about the reuse of cinematic images. "When I fixed upon this subject I was somewhat taken aback by the fact that there was no name for it", wrote Jay Leyda in a book that is still regarded as a key reference work on the topic; "the proper term would have to indicate that the work begins on the cutting table, with already existing film shots." By his own admission, the focus of his work could only "be referred to [. . .] in various inconsistent ways" (Leyda 1964: 9).

Not surprisingly, Leyda's unsuccessful attempts to pinpoint an adequate term for his theme include words no longer used in the scholarly idiom, such as "library films"; some of them are a blend of timelessness and obsolescence ("chronicle montage films"); others, such as "stock shot films" and "documentary archive films", still resonate in both connoisseur and journalistic lingo. Leyda was particularly unhappy with "compilation film" ("what an awkward, incomprehensible and unacceptable term for this form!"), but could not suggest better alternatives. In its clumsy combination of adjective and noun, "Archival film" (Leyda preferred to use a dual noun, "archive film") is the outcome of the same schizophrenic pattern lamented by the eminent film historian in the mid-1960s. "Archival cinema" signifies different things to different constituencies; to further complicate matters, its purported meaning is also dependent upon the geographic and idiomatic context where the definition is conveyed. In chronological terms, the emergence of "archival cinema" as a descriptive formula coincides with the rise of "digital cinema", but its semantic roots are much deeper, and deserve to be explained. As we shall see, each translation reveals a set of conflicting views on how moving images created in the past should be summoned to a contemporary viewer.

Idiomatic definitions

Film scholarship has produced a plethora of studies about specific "archival films" and their makers, but no authoritative synthesis since Leyda paved the way to the entrance of this taxonomic labyrinth; one of the few exceptions is Roland Cosandey's provocatively forthright solution to Leyda's dilemma through the adoption of the term "images antérieures" ("former images") as the most impartial way to indicate the subject (Cosandey 2016). This seemingly drastic approach is justified on the grounds of some basic empirical considerations. At face value, the most prevalent definition of "archival cinema" embraces all the cinematic images of the past utilised as building materials for another object, not necessarily cinematic in nature. In its apparent neutrality, the coupling of the two words is riddled with value judgements and opacities. To begin with, "cinema" is presented here both as a tool and its outcome: it is tacitly assumed that the source images have been transmitted to us in analogue form, that is, as motion picture stock of various formats (8mm, Super8, 16mm, 35mm, and so on), but the entity resulting from their use may well be non-cinematic and yet be characterised as an "archival film". In other words, the "archival film" may or may not exist on celluloid, but necessitates the borrowing of film stock in order to be defined as such. Should the source material be in electronic or digital form, the newly created work would then have to be called otherwise. Still, the question remains of when does cinema (or the post-analogue moving image in general) become "archival" in order to be treated as a distinct category of scholarly inquiry.

It should be noted that the above definition makes no mention of originality, let alone novelty. A copy of a 1918 newsreel projected in its entirety, regardless of the medium in which it is exhibited, is indicated as an "archival film"; an assemblage of excerpts from the same newsreel, whether or not combined with other cinematic images, is an "archival film" as well. Together, they rightly belong to the family of "archival cinema." The same label can be therefore attached to what is totally new and what isn't, as long as its content is drawn from the cinema heritage. The corollaries to this axiom are not as obvious as they may appear at first sight. The first is that the carrier that makes "archival cinema" possible ought to bear a relationship of some sort with the photochemical process. So far, there is no significant evidence of a public perception that moving images made in electronic or digital form should be included in this realm.

Moreover, it is taken for granted that the images of an "archival film" should be easily recognised by the viewer as being chronologically remote, both because of the way they look and in light of the events they depict; hence the word "archival", referred to something that was retrieved from a collecting entity, either individual or institutional. The relative indifference to the physical location of the source is embedded in the choice of this term as opposed to other plausible options: in the common parlance, there is no such thing as a "museum film". The source material is deemed relevant because it was preserved per se, rather than by virtue of its cultural status. The value attached to it derives from the fact that it is available for viewing and that it can be used for this purpose, irrespective of the rationale behind its survival. In its raw state, the "archival film" is seen as a mute, pliable witness of history; it is primarily a document rather than a conveyor of meaning. Its equivalent in the lexicon of digital culture is "content", a fashionable term in the early twenty-first century.

The contradictions embedded in the term "archival cinema" are revealed in all their depth through a cursory survey of its correspondent in other languages. The most common French equivalent, "images d'archives", alludes to the practice of recycling the institutional relics of cinema's past into a new entity called "film de montage": this is the "compilation film" that Jay Leyda refers to in his discussion of Esfir Shub's *Padenie dinastii Romanovyh* (The Fall of the Romanov Dynasty, 1927, USSR), celebrating the tenth anniversary of the Bolshevik revolution through an assemblage of previously made newsreels. A parallel variation in French, "film de compilation", is derived from music, where a "compilation" or "compile" indicates the juxtaposition of excerpts from existing scores. A trendy alternative—"film de found footage"—emerging at the dawn of the twenty-first century highlights the difference between a museum's collection and all moving images retrieved from unofficial sources, from flea markets to the dumpsters of film laboratories, or from the wholesale of 16mm reels disposed by television networks and primary schools.

Similarly, the German language draws a distinction between "Kompilationsfilm" (bits and pieces of archival footage) and "Archivfilm" (the "archival film" as a self-contained entity). The latter seems to be used with increasing frequency, with the occasional appearance of the all-encompassing "Archiv-Kompilationsfilm". "Archival footage" is most commonly translated as "Archivmaterial", as seen in the end credits of films or television programs where films from archives are featured, but also in the informal talk among filmmakers and editors. By and large, however, scholarly German language adapts to English, with "Found-Footage-Film" as the most widely used label for works made by authors with an avant-garde background (Bruce Conner, Joseph Cornell, Ken Jacobs, Gustav Deutsch, Peter Forgacs, Bill Morrison, Peter Tscherkassky). The habit finds its origins in the late 1980s and early 1990s, when operations of this type constituted a self-contained strand in the experimental and independent film world.

The English influence is even more strongly felt in other languages. As a film genre, ファウンド•フッテージ (faundo futtēji) is the phonetic transliteration in katakana of "found footage." There is no proper Japanese term for "archival footage", thus leaving another transliteration, アーカイバル•フッテージ (aakaibaru futtēji), as the preferred option. An accurate but rather inelegant alternative is offered by 挿入映像 (sonyu eizo), which could be rendered as "inserted moving image" or "inserted film footage." There is no Swedish term for "archival film" as a genre; "archival footage" is most often labelled as "arkivbilder." Nor is there one in Russian, where монтажный фильм (montazhnyi film) is the only widely known descriptive term, pioneered by Lilia and Otsep Brik during the golden age of Soviet constructivism. Esfir Shub's 1927 tribute to the Bolshevik revolution, referred to earlier, is broadly indicated as "montazhnyi film"; students and filmmakers were also familiar with учебный фильм (uchebnye filmy), "study films", made for educational purposes under the aegis of the Soviet Union filmmakers' school, VGIK.

Other variations to the theme are to be found in Latin languages. In Italian, alongside "film di repertorio" (archival footage) and "film d'archivio", two other terms—"film di famiglia" and "film amatoriale"—are employed as synonyms, a virtual merger of "home movie" with "amateur film". In Spanish, "material de archivo" stands for "archival footage", but "archival film" and "found footage films" as a genre are generally indicated as "cine de apropiación". The poignancy of "appropriation" as a qualifier for images retrieved from the past for the benefit of present-time viewers brings the lexicon of archival cinema to a startling watershed: it is an "amateur" product, thus implying a superiority of the viewer over images made by nameless predecessors; it is also a statement of possessiveness, as it endorses the viewer's right to manipulate and redefine the meaning of images created by someone else by simply calling them "home movies". Belittling the ancestors of the moving image while taking ownership of their creativity is a troubling and yet crucial ingredient of the derivative body of work currently known as "archival cinema".

Provenance, authentication, falsification

The only common denominator of "archival films" in the above mentioned languages is their perceived status as photochemical images belonging to an abstract "yesterday", which puts the burden of proof on the eye of the beholder and, to a lesser extent, on the attitude of the presenter. The relevance of both criteria is illustrated by one of the earliest known examples of archival film, in which the creator and the viewer are involved, respectively, in the presentation and consumption of cinematic images created in the past but displayed as if they were new. Evidence drawn from the comparative analysis of extant prints has revealed that in the mid-1910s the Triangle Film Corporation was recycling elements from its own productions in order to create entirely different films. *The Trouble Hunter* (1920, USA, Jess Robbins) cannibalised an earlier Triangle feature, *The Americano* (1916, USA, John Emerson), whose images had been reshuffled—with the aid of new intertitles—as building blocks of a separate narrative; a similar fate was bestowed upon *The Matrimaniac* (1916, USA, Paul Powell), reissued in 1917 as *The Missing Millionaire* with a radically altered storyline.

Another film by Triangle, *The Iced Bullet* (1917, USA, Reginald Barker), is an extreme instance of the same practice. Its prologue shows a struggling writer (William Desmond) haplessly trying to sell a scenario to the Thomas H. Ince studios in Culver City; having fallen asleep on a couch in the office of an executive, he dreams a plot—also shown in the pages of an actual script—of a murdered banker and a detective (Desmond himself) solving the case. The flagrant disconnect between the frame story and the main body of the film suggests either the borrowing of material from of a previous production, or the outright reprocessing of an aborted project, whose footage was salvaged with the creation of a completely new film. If this is indeed the case—as it certainly is with *The Trouble Hunter* and *The Missing Millionaire*—the audience of 1917 was the witness of an "archival film" without knowing it. The same applies to *Trail of the Pink Panther* (1982, USA, Blake Edwards), made with unused footage from *The Pink Panther Strikes Again* (1976, USA, Blake Edwards), together with scenes from other instalments of the Pink Panther series.

The case of the Blake Edwards film adds a further twist to our story. The audience of *Trail of the Pink Panther* may have been aware that its protagonist, Peter Sellers, had passed away two years before the film's release, but pretended to ignore this, which amounts to saying that an "archival film" had been publicly released as an act of overt complicity between the producers and their customers. *It Happened Here* (1965, UK, Kevin Brownlow and Andrew Mollo) takes this approach to further ends in a blunt reversal of roles between "archival film" and the present. *It Happened Here* is an imaginary rendition of the final years in World War II, in which the United Kingdom is invaded by Nazi troops (Brownlow 2007). Set around 1945 and shot in grainy black and white, the film presents its vision of a dystopian past with the look and feel of a newsreel, an archival film in dramatised fashion. In an astonishing feat of historical simulation, Brownlow and Mollo present their narrative as a visual time capsule, seamlessly bridging the gap between 1965 and 1945.

No less astounding is the stratagem adopted by Brownlow and Mollo in order to overcome the financial limitations of their project, which was completed on a shoestring budget. A few images of the film—notably, the shot of a steam engine train—were taken from an actual newsreel from the period, and mixed with the new footage in such a way that it is virtually impossible to distinguish them from the rest. The same goal was attempted by D. W. Griffith during the production of *Hearts of the World* (1918, USA), when the director recruited the film unit of the French army for some location shooting on the European front, a landmark instance of "archival cinema" on demand. Since then, archival film has been a staple of narrative cinema to such an extent that its exploitation is barely noticed by the casual viewer. There is "archival cinema" in Orson Welles' *Citizen Kane* (1941, USA), presented as complement to the biography of an imaginary character, and in *Casablanca* (1942, USA, Michael Curtiz), as background information to the film's dramatic framework. Countless examples of the same treatment are to be found in commercial cinema, mostly unacknowledged and unidentifiable by default.

The anonymity of archival cinema was not only thought of as unavoidable; it was also desirable, inasmuch as its nameless truth would serve the purpose of blending the objectivity of History with the imaginary story portrayed in the film.

The 8mm Kodachrome II roll of safety stock used by Abraham Zapruder on a Bell & Howell camera for the amateur reel showing the assassination of John F. Kennedy on November 22, 1963 has been the object of the fiercest debate ever bestowed upon an archival film (Wrone 2003), but also of the most audacious manipulation of archival images ever attempted in a commercial feature. The strategy adopted in Oliver Stone's *JFK* (1991, USA) is to some extent the opposite of what Brownlow and Mollo applied to *It Happened Here*. In addition to images from the actual Zapruder film, *JFK* displays a plethora of original, imitative, or plainly fictional images, all presented as "archival footage". As a result, the viewer becomes immersed in a visual hall of mirrors where it eventually becomes impossible to clearly distinguish the historic document from its recreation. By achieving this vertigo effect, Oliver Stone's film highlights the duality of the "archival film" as a material object requiring the voice of an interpreter in order to be confirmed as such.

So far, our attention has been focused on "archival cinema" as a relic, either treated as an autonomous entity or as a component of a separate creative work. Before examining its other incarnations, it is important to tackle the question of how the viewer is made aware of the film's "archival" identity, that is, its status of material evidence, a question pertinently addressed by Laurent Véray (2011) as a polemical response to Claude Lanzmann's refusal to utilise archival footage in his monumental documentary on the Holocaust, *Shoah* (1985, France/UK). The answer is as predictable as it is deceptively simple: one recognises archival cinema by the fact that its images look "old". What "old" stands for in this context is the product of a two-layered belief. First, it is assumed that the viewer will easily perceive the temporal remoteness of its subject matter; from this standpoint, the degree of authenticity of archival cinema is directly proportional to the shared perception that the events portrayed in the film occurred a long time ago. Second, it is expected that the spectator will easily recognise the older footage by the way it looks, as opposed to newly-made moving images.

The latter axiom, largely undisputed until the dawn of the post-analogue era, was supported by expressive codes presented in the form of visual indicators that referred to the material condition of the carrier: scratches, speckles of dirt, and other blemishes on the film stock. At a deeper level, the archival status of the film was—and, to a large extent, still is—confirmed by the inferior photographic quality of the image, resulting either from a flawed reproduction process of the original into a copy, or from the conviction that the original photographic image had always been of inferior quality because of the unrefined technology that made it exist. Translated into the crude honesty of non-specialist language, this means that archival film must have a "primitive" aura, enhanced by the precarious state of its physical carrier. These two variables, combined with the "vintage" look of the people and the places observed in the film, determine a cumulative feeling of psychological distance between archival cinema and the public of the present time.

The effect is notoriously compounded by projecting films from the silent era at a higher speed than normal, but this is only one of the many ways in which the identity of archival cinema is artificially 'improved' through deliberate or involuntary falsification. As the video compilation *Guidelines dealing with Misuse and Use of Film and Archive Material* (1998, International Federation of Television Archives) amply demonstrates, manipulation is a favourite instrument in the harvesting of archival films for public consumption, a practice inaugurated in the early 1930s when silent films were reissued with a synchronised soundtrack consisting of music, sound effects, and a voiceover commentary (a common practice in Europe during the transition from silent to sound cinema). These cinematic hybrids represent a watershed between "archival cinema" and modernity; they are recognised as historic artefacts in their own right insofar as the circumstances of their creation and dissemination are clearly explained to a contemporary audience. An "archival film" that looks too new to be true is allegedly a contradiction in terms, as it would defy the purpose of deploying archival film as a messenger of things past.

In defiance of this logic, those who use archival film as part of contemporary fictional or documentary works are often inclined to work in the opposite direction by adjusting vintage cinema to the expectations of the modern viewer. A typical expression of this attitude is the insertion of diegetic sound to an otherwise silent film, such as the whistle of a locomotive or the noise of marching troops in a programme on World War I. With the introduction of digital technology, the ideology of archival cinema takes an even more aggressive stance by embracing image enhancement as an expressive tool: a documentary produced by the BBC, *Psychedelic Britannia* (2015, UK, Sam Bridger), exhibits archival footage of live rock concerts showing a crisp contrast and polished, saturated colour, smoothly integrated to the grading of present-time interviews. Scratches and dust are thereby matched by their exact opposite, with the extra option of using dedicated software in order to apply scratches and speckles where there are none. Colour and sound are the key additives in the trade of archival cinema as a commodity in the digital marketplace.

Film history on celluloid

Archive cinema became an independent form of expression at the end of the silent era. One of its earliest manifestations as a self-contained creative endeavour—that is, without any ancillary purpose—is a feature-length "autobiography of motion pictures" in fourteen reels, first called *Early History and Growth of the Motion Picture Industry* (1925), then *Thirty Years of Motion Pictures* (1927), and eventually *The March of the Movies*. It was made exclusively of excerpts from notable films, mainly produced in the United States, assembled from actual clips of 35mm release prints (Case 2015); a re-edited version in ten reels was curated by a film historian, Terry Ramsaye, who had recently published his landmark book *A Million and One Nights* (Ramsaye 1926). Despite its very limited circulation (mainly in trade conventions and educational institutions), the film's influence spread like wildfire, prompting the creation of a vast repertory of archival films produced with the same purpose of documenting the cinematic legacy. Anthony Slide's book *Films on Film History* (Slide 1979) lists over six hundred features, shorts, documentaries and compilations. Despite its claim, it is far from being complete, and it is almost exclusively focused on films distributed in North America; nevertheless, the breadth and scope of this filmography highlights the vast influence of this genre in public culture, soon extended to television productions.

At the end of his overview, Slide pays tribute to the figure of Robert Youngson (1917–1974), presented as the "father of the compilation film on the history of cinema" (Slide 1979: 199) and credited for a number of anthologies, mostly on the golden age of silent cinema. Youngson is also remembered as the author of the first archival films produced on a significant budget, released through Twentieth Century-Fox and Metro-Goldwyn-Mayer. *When Comedy Was King* (1960) was reportedly completed with a US$100,000 budget and grossed more than twice at the box office in the first months of its release. Youngson's feature compilation for MGM, *Big Parade of Comedy* (1964, USA, Robert Youngson), is considered the direct ancestor of the most profitable archival film ever made, *That's Entertainment!* (1974, USA, Jack Haley, Jr). Produced to celebrate the fifty years of MGM with a budget of a little over 3 million dollars, it earned over 19 million on the first year of distribution, thus spurring two sequels and a third film of related nature, *That's Entertainment, Part II* (1976, USA, Gene Kelly), *That's Dancing!* (1985, USA, Jack Haley, Jr.), and *That's Entertainment! III* (1994, USA, Bud Friedgen and Michael J. Sheridan), all from MGM.

In the meanwhile, archives and museums had begun creating archival films of their own. Their main goal was to provide audiences with a digest of their most treasured holdings, mostly presented in the form of a compendium of national cinema in their respective countries. No comprehensive filmography of these films is known to exist, but the example of *Antologia del cinema italiano. Capitolo I: Il film muto* (1956, Italy, Antonio Petrucci) serves as an emblematic example of their structure and purpose. The film is a chronological survey of Italian cinema during the silent period, with early and short films presented in their entirety, and key sequences from canonical feature films. When this and similar films were produced, well before the age of electronic media, access to collecting institutions was often difficult, and projection prints hard to obtain. The "archival compilation film" was a relatively simple and practical way to provide students, teachers, and the audiences of film societies with a manageable and authoritative summary of the history of cinema. For this reason, copies of films such as Petrucci's would be exchanged with other archives and museums, or deposited with embassies and cultural missions outside the films' country of origin.

Archival film as artwork

One of these films, *Lyrisch nitraat* (Lyrical Nitrate, 1991, Netherlands, Peter Delpeut), was the catalyst of a turning point in the evolution of archival cinema. It was, albeit indirectly, the tangible expression of the work of a film archive: at the time, Delpeut was an employee of the Nederlands Filmmuseum (re-baptised as Eye Nederlands Filminstituut in 2011). *Lyrical Nitrate* was, by all means, an "archival film", as it was presented as a collage of excerpts from films held by the Dutch institution, notably from the collection of Jean Desmet, a film distributor in the early years of cinema. It was not, however, a compendium of film history in the conventional sense of the term. Its content could be labelled as "early cinema", but it was drawn from films of various countries, and presented with an intention that was markedly different from whatever the pioneers of cinema had in mind. To the extent of their abilities, collecting institutions were attempting to showcase archival films without any intervention other than the excision of parts of the original works; Delpeut tried instead to present them through the lens of his personal interpretation of the past.

Delpeut juxtaposed fragments and sequences from films unrelated to each other, slowing down their projection speed, and emphasising image details—a far cry from the orderly string of clips presented so far by archives in their compilation films. His strategy was not new: *Tom, Tom, the Piper's Son* (1969, USA, Ken Jacobs) had taken the same approach in a more uncompromising manner by expanding a brief segment from a 1905 film with the same title (shot by G. W. "Billy" Bitzer for the American Mutoscope & Biograph Company) into a 115-minute experimental film. Contrary to Jacobs' meditation on the deconstruction of the moving image, however, Delpeut's *Lyrical Nitrate* is firmly rooted in the archival nature of the films borrowed for his work, to the point that the fragility of the medium and the decay of the image carrier is displayed with poetic intentions, not without a hint of nostalgia. The "archival film" emerges here as an auteurist statement, the conscious expression of a viewpoint on the identity of the cinematic artefact as a museum object.

By the time Delpeut completed a second film of the same kind (*Diva Dolorosa*, 1999, Netherlands), the very definition of "archival film" had dramatically changed, as seen in other experiments at the borderline between documentary and "art cinema" such as *Moeder*

Dao—de schildpadgelijkende (Mother Dao, the Turtlelike, 1995, Netherlands, Vincent Monnikenda). Ken Jacobs had not been alone in the use of archival footage for the creation of entirely new works of fiction: Standish Lawder's *Intolerance (Abridged)* (1972, USA) double printed every twenty-six frames of the three-hour silent epic *Intolerance* (1916, USA, D.W. Griffith), turning it into an impressive 12-minute synthesis between structuralism and psychedelic cinema. With *Lyrical Nitrate*, though, the archival identity of the moving image was firmly set at the centre of the artist's preoccupations. Others followed Delpeut's path, from Gustav Deutsch in the *Film ist* (Film is) series (*Film is. 1–6*, 1998, Austria; *Film is. 7–12*, 2002, Austria; *Film is. A Girl & a Gun*, 2009, Austria/Germany) to Bill Morrison, whose *Decasia* (2002, USA) amplifies the intuition of the finale in Delpeut's film into a visual leitmotiv of chemically decomposed and undecipherable images. What these directors have in common is a two-tiered relationship with the archival image; the provenance of their expressive tool is declared with the utmost transparency; by the same token, the borrower redefines and reshapes its meaning well beyond the intentions of their makers.

The artists involved in this kind of creative work are inspired by archival cinema in general (Flaig and Groo 2016); they also find their inspiration by copying archival films in the public domain, or by ignoring (either blissfully or provocatively) that their legal or intellectual ownership belongs to someone else. Cinematic images of the past were a favourite playground of experimental filmmakers (Bordwell 1997: 102–105): Hollis Frampton (*Public Domain*, 1972, USA), Malcolm LeGrice (*After Lumière—L'arroseur arrosé*, 1974, UK), Al Razutis (*Méliès Catalog*, 1973, Canada), Ernie Gehr (*Eureka*, 1974, USA), and many others, ranging from the avowedly academic (Noël Burch, *Correction, Please or How We Got Into Pictures*, 1979, UK) to the realm of visual poetry (in the works of Yervant Gianikian and Angela Ricci Lucchi, from *Dal Polo all'Equatore*, 1997, Italy, to *Oh! uomo*, 2004, Italy). Despite the profound differences in their respective approaches, the modus operandi of these filmmakers highlights a fundamental question, so far unanswered. When does a film become an archival film? *Rose Hobart* (1939, USA, Joseph Cornell) makes extensive use of footage from *East of Borneo* (1931, USA, George Melford), a Universal Pictures production. It is a landmark experimental work by a famous artist, represented in the collections of major fine arts museums; in this sense, *Rose Hobart* is in itself an archival film that makes use of archival footage. Should a 35mm reel of *Avatar* (2009, USA, James Cameron) become the object of a similar operation, how and when would this qualify as an archival film, and isn't *Avatar* itself an archival film, to the extent that a collecting institution has it in its custody?

It may be argued that Christian Marclay's *The Clock* (2010, UK), a 24-long assemblage of clips from hundreds of narrative films, is not an example of archival cinema: first, because it is not cinema, despite the fact that its components were taken from extant cinematic works; second, because it is not archival, in the sense that there is no obvious connection between the images shown in the film and their origin as collection artefacts. The dividing line between what is or isn't "archival" undeniably stems from a qualitative judgement, and is not immune from subjectivity. Any print of a film, however, is bound to acquire an archival citizenship of sorts whenever it becomes part of an institution. Our 35mm reel of *Avatar* saved from the dumpster hardly qualifies as "found footage" if the rescuer has identified it and wishes to give it a home. The requisites for comparing the reel to a foundling include the material status of the object as abandoned property and the legal vacuum surrounding it as an orphan of intellectual ownership, but also the absence of an orphanage protecting it. The reel is no longer "found footage" when a collecting body decides it should be preserved for posterity.

Panorama Ephemera (2004, USA, Rick Prelinger) provides the most straightforward discussion of this point with the admirable clarity of its treatment. The work includes dozens of excerpts from educational, industrial, amateur and advertising films, and doesn't make any explicit claim about aesthetic or cultural value. The sequences are assembled in a coherent fashion, but the author's intentions do not overshadow the fact that each segment had a life of its own; in the absence of an off-screen narrator, the compiled images are allowed to speak for themselves, enabling the viewer to establish meaningful and often surprising connections between them. Jan Šikl's film cycle *Soukromé Století* (Private Century, 2006, Czech Republic) emphasises the ethical implications of the same approach by presenting family films with the direct contribution of their owners, their descendants, or with the accompanying evidence of written documents. The voiceover of *Private Century* recites the text of letters, diaries and transcripts of oral history interviews with members of the families in which the home movies were made, often to poignant effect. In the same vein, Czech filmmaker Petr Skala brings to the sublime the archival nature of "found footage" with his cinema as an object of purely visual expression based on light, colour, and the materiality of film stock. In the early 1970s, at a time when Czechoslovakia was plagued by political and intellectual repression, Skala created abstract films at home with discarded blank or exposed 16mm and 35mm footage, a magnifying glass, crude engraving tools such as needles and manicure sets, and basic materials such as dishwashing liquid, sand, egg white, cigarette lighter fluid, acetone, sugar and honey. This looks like making art from the relics of a post-apocalyptic world; it is, in fact, the product of a vision that found its shape in a society where vision itself was a forbidden word. Petr Skala's films are tiny miracles of "archival film" as craftsmanship achieving visual ecstasy, like sunlight coming through stained glass of an imaginary church.

Is there a "digital archival film"?

In a very brief but highly influential essay, Eileen Bowser formulated the most compelling answer to the ultimate question surrounding the multifaceted identity of archival cinema. In describing the objectives of film preservation, she pointed out that archives and museum do so, among other things, in order to foster creativity and encourage the creation of new works (Bowser 1990: 173). Bowser's visionary assessment of the rationale behind the safeguard of the cinematic image brings us to the yet uncharted territory of digital-born moving images as part of archival collections. Alain Resnais' *Nuit et brouillard* (Night and Fog, 1955, France), a short film about Nazi concentration camps, has long been regarded as the quintessential case study of "archival cinema" where historic footage becomes part of a new artwork (Raskin 1987). Both the film and its sources originated on photochemical stock. Another short film, *Steps* (1987, USA/UK, Zbigniew Rybczyński), is an avant-garde exercise in electronic manipulation of footage from a silent film by Sergei Eisenstein. If there is no reason not to include this in the realm of archival cinema, the same argument could be made for *Der Riese* (The Giant, 1983, West Germany, Michael Klier), entirely made with images captured by video surveillance cameras but pervaded by an exquisite cinematic sensibility. So far, archival cinema has been treated within the parameters of analogue technology and aesthetics. Its digital avatar—both as a collection item and as an artwork—awaits proper consideration.

References

Bordwell, D. (1997) *On the History of Film Style*, Cambridge, MA: Harvard University Press.

Bowser, E. (1990) "Some Principles of Film Restoration", *Griffithiana*, 13 (38–39): 170–173.

Brownlow, K. (2007) *How It Happened Here*, London-Amsterdam-Shizuoka: UKA Press.

Case, J. (2015) "*Thirty Years of Motion Pictures*", in *Le Giornate del Cinema Muto. Official Catalogue of the 34th Pordenone Silent Film Festival*, Pordenone: Le Giornate del Cinema Muto, 200–202.

Cosandey, R. (2016) "Les images antérieures. Notes pour une approche possible des usages filmiques de l'archive", Lausanne: Cinémathèque Suisse, www.cinematheque.ch/f/documents-de-cinema/complement-de-programme/les-images-anterieures.

Flaig, P. and Groo, K. (eds) (2016) *New Silent Cinema*, New York: Routledge.

Leyda, J. (1964) *Films Beget Films*, London: George Allen & Unwin.

Ramsaye, T. (1926) *A Million and One Nights: A History of the Motion Picture Through 1925*, New York: Simon & Schuster.

Raskin, R. (1987) *Nuit et Brouillard: On the Making, Reception and Functions of a Major Documentary*, Aarhus: Aarhus University Press.

Slide, A. (1979) *Films on Film History*, Metuchen, NJ: The Scarecrow Press.

Véray, L. (2011) *Les images d'archives face à l'histoire. De la conservation à la création*, Chasseneuil-du-Poitou/ Paris: Éditions SCÉRÉN, CNDP-CRDP (Collection Patrimoine).

Wrone, D.R. (2003) *The Zapruder Film: Reframing JFK's Assassination*, Lawrence, KS: University Press of Kansas.

36
DIGITAL CINEMAS

Sean Cubitt

Introduction

All contemporary cinema is digital. Analogue cinema still lives on in archives, specialist theatres and collections showing celluloid or nitrate film, but otherwise we make and view cinema digitally in the twenty-first century. Financing, production management and accounting, sound and image generation, recording and post-production, distribution, marketing, audience intelligence and critical response all use digital tools. In this sense, cinema is digital from conception to delivery. However, in many instances, digital tools make little difference: accountancy software is only a more efficient update of double-entry book-keeping. Meanwhile, some things have not changed at all. There is no such thing, for example, as a digital lens: glass technology and lens housings remain more or less as they have been since the late 1940s. The art and craft of filmmaking still demands real people to do real things in real places. Stunts still require stunt artists; animals still require wranglers; even synthespians (digital actors such as Gollum in *The Lord of the Rings,* 2001–2003, New Zealand/USA/Germany, Peter Jackson: see King 2011; Prince 2012: 112–157) rely on specialist performances by live actors. Animations still require voice artists (though the music industry has employed synthetic modulations and overlays as effects since the arrival of analogue electronics in the 1960s, no studio or effects house lays claim to viable voice synthesis, making any claim to "totally digital cinema" to that degree incorrect). A script hammered out on a typewriter is not distinguishable from one crafted in Movie Magic. Props, make up, locations, sets, cranes, dollies, transport, catering, crew and actors remain obdurately physical. The machinery inside edit suites has changed but the architecture remains, as do executive offices and auditoria. Nothing has changed, and yet everything has.

The political economy of World Cinema

One of the ways everything changes concerns the political economy of world cinema. One aspect of digitisation is that once circulated as files, transmitted or on DVD, movies can also circulate in pirate forms, leading to an escalating war between pirates and studios to create or break miscellaneous digital rights management (DRM) software. The same struggle has led to increasing use of streaming rather than download as a way of protecting intellectual property rights in films, as well as new forms of licensing through industry-dominating online services such as Amazon, Netflix and Apple's iTunes. Here, as well as in the theatrical and sell-through markets, contactless and mobile payment are the retail end of a massive movement from physical to electronic money. Since cinema is a business, the dematerialisation of money has significant implications. It increases the speed of financial flows and introduces new challenges for monitoring expenditure and revenue. Pre-production now routinely uses digital tools to integrate the translation of scripts into workflows, shoot planning, crew management, post-production tasks and timetables, and, at every stage, integration into budgets. Grant-aided and crowd-funded producers have new machineries of Paypal and electronic banking to learn and work with. New opportunities to syphon off cash arise when the dark arts of studio accountants meet those of "black hat" hackers. Digital financing and revenues are now integral to the global film industry, placing it squarely inside the new economics of financialisation. Similarly, labour in the film industry shares the new configurations of flexibility, precarity, offshoring and outsourcing as sub-contracting cascades from major to minor specialist suppliers, for example, of effects and code services, where bitter competition reduces profit margins and wages drastically (Turnock 2014). Even if we disregard the decades-old tradition of self-exploitation among creatives committed to making their work and getting it seen with little or no pay for their efforts, we can observe that digital cinema is as deeply involved in the global economy, and as deeply implicated in the speeds of transaction and vulnerability of self-employment as any other business.

Like digital money, new technologies also enable a radical globalisation of cinema production. Network media allow transnational productions to synchronise shoots, effects and post-production across time-zones. Compositors match location dailies from one city with effects footage from another and send results back to producers in a third, often using differences in time-zones to create a 24-hour production process. Specialist software allows directors and producers to synchronise sound and visual edits conducted hemispheres apart. Rapid broadband network communication erases the temporal distinction between shoot and edit: postproduction is no longer necessarily "post" but concurrent with production. In one of the most significant changes, whether shot digitally or analogue, the laboratory processing and grading over which directors and editors had little control is now undertaken in digital intermediates (Belton 2008). Where films used to pass out of the direct control of creative staff into the hands of expert chemists, creative staff are in control, although that control also permits the intervention of producers and financiers. While cheaper equipment democratises production and opens the cinema to smaller, even individual projects, at the same time digitisation encourages participation and collaboration, but not necessarily in democratic mode: the hierarchy that places financiers at the pinnacle of decision making, with craft and talent often far lower down, is if anything strengthened by digital means of production and distribution. It is equally notable that, with the partial exception of arthouse and festival films, global distribution is remarkably dominated by English-language, especially Hollywood exports, while English-speaking markets are equally remarkably impervious to popular cinemas from the rest of the world. Ease of circulation and diminishing transaction costs seem not to have encouraged genuinely open circulation of non-Hollywood product. Indeed, this seems to have coincided with a closing of the market to such films.

Digital data in production

On set, digital tools are now ubiquitous. Aaton, ARRI and Panavision stopped making film cameras in 2011, and although Kodak continue to manufacture motion film stock, Fujifilm abandoned production in 2012. In their place are cameras based on CMOS and CCD chips boasting 4K and higher resolution, with light and colour responses equal to 35mm film. Microphones record using a variety of techniques, including some still based in the analogue carbon mic, but many now use lasers in optic fibre mics, while MEMS (Micro Electrical-Mechanical System) microphones, in which the pressure-sensitive diaphragm is built directly into a chip that encodes directly to digital, are increasingly the industry norm. Lighting rigs now use digital dimmers extensively, and traditional lamps have been exchanged for LED arrays that give directors of photography fine control over colour as well as brightness. Digital motion sensors track and record camera moves for matching with computer-generated or managed assets for compositing. Lidar (light-based radar) was already in use in films such as *Déjà Vu* (2006, USA, Tony Scott) to record the spatial data of a set, rather than its visual appearance. The mass of data gathered in production is now the centre of a new profession, that of data management, whose goal is to minimise the unavoidable loss of data consequent on its passage from recording device to storage media, editing software and final product. Production data—including not only sound and vision recordings but light, acoustic and spatial readings from locations and motion capture data from performers—could potentially be completely integrated, in the way CGI characters, buildings and landscapes already are, as libraries from which new combinations, new movies, can be made. Digitisation of archive footage also creates a resource for new films. Pre-digital movies such as *Dead Men Don't Wear Plaid* (1982, USA, Carl Reiner) were precursors of wholly digital films recycling pre-digital footage, from *Tarnation* (2003, USA, Jonathan Caouette) to *Decasia* (2002, USA, Bill Morrison), the latter especially a reminder that a good deal of the work of film archives now involves digital restoration (Fossati, 2009).

Not only archival restoration but the circulation of historic films originally made on celluloid depends on digital media. The formats in which they circulate—optical media, broadcasts, online repositories—share in a radically normative group of technical standards. From the biggest theatres to the most personal screens, and from blockbusters to home video, video transmission and display requires codecs (compression-decompression algorithms used to transport audiovisual content with the greatest possible efficiency). The market in codecs is dominated by MPEG, a standard established through a combination of international engineering bodies and corporate interests (there are minor contenders, embroiled in what promise to be decade-long lawsuits over patents, but they work on the same basic principles). Codecs manage audiovisual data by reducing non-essential elements, using software to reinstate the most likely details otherwise lost in transmission. Even so-called 'lossless' formats such as RAW files lose data, where necessary replacing it with what in a human would be called intelligent best guesses as to what has been mislaid en route. These processes fit to the now standard form of the pixel grids, rectilinear arrays of standard red, green and blue picture elements. Whether projected or backlit, all screens are scanned from top left to bottom right, in rigid lines and numerically placed points to which arithmetic colour and luminance (brightness) values can be ascribed. In many respects scanning—which dates back to the earliest electronic images—and the grid are the most ubiquitous features of digital imaging that distinguish it from its analogue predecessors. It could be argued that the greatest distinction between analogue and digital film is the disciplining of the random scatter of photochemicals into the rigid lines of digital screens, and the fact that electronic images, being scanned, are never complete in the way that a single frame of celluloid is, when, as Garrett Stewart (2007: 53) has it, motion "is located not in the photogram's continual disappearance across the frame of the aperture but in an internal remaking of the digital frame itself".

The distinction between analogue and digital imaging dominated the critical literature on digital cinema in the late 2000s. However, the central debate concerned the term "indexicality", deriving from the philosopher C. S. Peirce's description of a particular kind of sign, the index that, like the index finger, points at something (a "referent") in the real world. Smoke, for Peirce, is an index of fire: it "means" fire, but is also directly caused by it. For a tradition in film criticism extending back to André Bazin (1967) and Siegfried Kracauer (1960), photography and cinematography have an indexical relation to reality: a photograph or film frame is caused by events occurring in front of the lens. Thus, unlike language and painting which describe the world using something different from the world—words and paint—photographs have an indexical relation to reality that more recent critiques, notably D. N. Rodowick (2007) and Mary-Anne Doane (2007), claim that digital media do not. Analogue film, they argue, being made of random scatterings of light-sensitive silver salts, catches the real light reflected into the lens and holds it faithfully, through all the processing that ensues on its way to projection on screen. There are technical reasons to doubt that this is significantly different to the way digital cameras work. Both use lenses to control the activity of light before it is recorded. Both rely on the physical properties of a light-sensitive material—analogue film undergoes a chemical change, electronic cameras react to light by releasing electrons. Both require amplification—chemical "fixing" in analogue, conversion from charge to voltage in digital cameras. Both use filters—tripack film in analogue, Bayer masks in digital—to control colour responses. Most of all, both are open to the same critiques concerning the choices made of what to shoot, how to shoot it, and what to leave out, topics addressed by ideological, feminist and postcolonial criticism. Doane and Rodowick assert, however, that the arithmetic processing of digital data removes it from the direct account of the real that analogue film was capable of.

In reply it might be said that such a broad description inadvertently throws entire sections of world cinema out of the realm of realism, for example the Nigerian video feature film industry colloquially known as Nollywood. It is also the case that digital recording is, if anything, more accurate in its account of the world than analogue, as its extensive use in scientific instruments indicates. The key difference, as far as indexicality is concerned, can also be mapped onto the history of scientific instruments. As Peter Galison (1997) observes, these come in two types, picturing and counting. One, like the images associated with the discovery of the Higgs' Boson, gives complex coverage of a single and possibly unique event; the other gives a numerical overview of many events. The unexpected feature of these two traditions in instrumentation is that they are regularly combined in contemporary scientific practice. In analogue cinema, films such as *Pyaasa* (Thirsty, 1957, India, Guru Dutt) and *Greed* (1927, USA, Eric von Stroheim) are as capable of addressing universals at the same time as particulars as are digital films such as Jia Zhangke's *Sanxia haoren* (Still Life, 2006, China). The Tamil action comedy *Naduvula Konjam Pakkatha Kaanom* (A Few Pages Are Missing in Between, 2012, Balaji Tharaneetharan) is no less faithful to its locations for being shot on DSLR, if less meticulously observational, than Frederick Wiseman's *Belfast, Maine* (1999), shot on similarly domestic format 16mm film. At the same time, as Kristen Whissel (2014) argues, digital visual effects allow for a heightened from of allegory she dubs "effects emblems", in which major and often highly complex thematic content is distilled into spectacular scenes of massed crowds or scenes of flight or falling. The compression of themes mirrors the composition of cinematic elements into composite shots, a radical intensification of the semantic carrying capacity of the frame, even as the frame itself becomes subject to the new micro-temporality, and radical incompletion, of scanning.

Digital cinema and the posthuman condition

Where digital tools are content to record any quality of the world, whether humanly perceptible or not, the canon of realist cinema embraced by critics such as Doane and Rodowick is concerned with reproducing, not the world as it is, but as it appears or would appear to a human observer. In this sense, we might then argue, with another group of critics (Brown 2013; Pick and Narraway 2013; Hauskeller *et al.* 2015), that an increasingly digital cinema corresponds to an increasingly posthuman condition, a term that, since its development by Cary Wolfe (2009), has been increasingly reflected in cultural and Film Studies (Shaviro 2010; Braidotti 2013). The term has a double edge. On the one hand, it speaks of a philosophy that comes after the humanism that lay at the heart of the European Enlightenment and the subsequent Romantic and Modernist periods; on the other it suggests that human beings are in some way no longer or no longer only "human", and that our increasingly complex and dense physical involvement and emotional investment in machines and networks has led us to a point where we are free of, or cast adrift from, anything we might look back on as human nature. The idea of digital cinema as posthuman chimes with the numerous films produced in the twenty-first century concerned with enhanced humans or human-machine hybrids (Short 2005), predominantly in the English-speaking world, but with important examples in European (*Renaissance*, Paris 2054: Renaissance, 2006, France, Christian Volckman; *The Thirteenth Floor*, 1999, USA/Germany, Josef Bosma) and East Asian cinema (*The One*, 2001, USA, James Wong; *Tetsuo*, Tetsuo: The Iron Man, 1989, Japan, Shinya Tsukamoto; *Naechureol siti*, Natural City, 2003, South Korea, Min Byung Chow). At the same time, however, as Michele Pierson (2002) recounts, a significant amount of effort has been spent in creating visual effects that emulate what a human observer might have seen, for example at the maiden voyage dockside in *Titanic* (1997, USA, James Cameron). Ubiquitous use of digital post-production to remove unwanted elements from cinematography, such as anachronistic location features or the wires used in stunt work, often comes under this general heading of creating verisimilitude, rather than impossible or fantastic spectacles: the mundane, often unavailable for filming, is itself then open to digital recreation. However, Lisa Purse is at pains to point out that in many instances the same shot might have been achieved by analogue means, requiring careful analysis to understand whether the tools employed are relevant to the audience's work of interpretation (Purse 2013: 15).

The banal and the everyday form a central value in the critical work of André Bazin, the doyen of realist film critics, as evidence that cinema confronts the uncontrolled and uncontrollable contingency of the real world. Comparisons between, for example, the massed extras forming battle ranks in a film such as *Cleopatra* (1963, USA, Joseph L. Mankiewicz) and the synthetic armies of *The Mummy* (1999, USA, Stephen Sommers) show the effects of randomness—of wind and weather conditions, or aberrations from set actions—in the former, while even programmed multiplication of possible behaviours in synthespians leaves a sense that the visual world is under control of its makers. This level of control echoes the rigidity of the pixel grid, and communicates far more than even the total cinema of wide-screen epics from the late classical period in Hollywood the appetite of cinema for a baroque command over the emotional and intellectual responses of audiences (Ndalianis 2004; Klein 2004). The everyday captured in long takes, deep focus and staging in depth that Bazin set such store by has instead become a feature of fantastic settings in the diegesis and cinematography of spectacular effects movies, blending elaborate set dressing with digital set extensions carefully matched to Steadicam and crane moves. As Purse points out in the case of the closing shots in Alfonso Cuarón's 2006 *Children of Men*, where physical and digitally enhanced fog shrouds the vessel that might or might not rescue our protagonists, both individual frames and editing imply "that the ship is both 'here' and 'not here'" (Purse 2013: 16).

This complex relation to ontology of the referent, of the apparatus and potentially of the viewing relationship is in many respects at the heart of a digital aesthetics. In one way, it might be argued that digital cinema expresses an advanced moment in the development of the "integrated spectacle" (Debord 1990), in which community, dialogue and logic have all been lost in a condition where absolute knowledge is ascribed to a computational Other, even by our rulers. In the same vein, digital cinema partakes in Baudrillard's "perfect crime", the murder of reality, perfect because in the end there was no victim (Baudrillard 1996). To stigmatise spectacular effects films as vacuous would then simply be to say that they express, with the perfection of ideological clockwork, the vacuity of late capitalism. If, however, we must also acknowledge the capacity of digital recordings to capture sound and light in motion with exquisite detail, in the realist mode of Dick Pope's cinematography for *Mr Turner* (2014, UK/France/Germany, Mike Leigh), but also in the capture of landscapes for compositing in fantastic landscapes, as in Peter Jackson's *Lord of the Rings* trilogy, then we must recognise at the least digital cinematography's ability to emulate analogue film. The contrary directions of faithfulness to perception, the hallmark of cinematic realism, and the fantastic create a deep ambiguity in representation that critics generally see as a major task of cinema. Critics of the 1970s were adamant that all cinema, insofar as it was representational, was also therefore ideological. In this sense, therefore, we might understand digital cinema as a cinema that embraces its own ideological formation in the form of a significant ambiguity about its truth status.

Moreover, while the music industry has used autotuning and vocoders extensively to generate artificial voices, cinema sound has largely been very conservative in its use not only of actors' own voices but in its approach to electronic musical scores, even when both are recorded digitally. The enhancement of theatrical and domestic sound through stereophony, noise cancellation and Dolby and other surround sound systems has in general sought verisimilitude, with the exception of sounds made by imaginary objects such as flying saucers. However, Foley and generated sound effects have a long history, and the practice of overdubbing equally so, notably in the Italian post-war cinema and in the profession of Indian playback singers. Though Renoir (1974: 106) believed that "Dubbing is equivalent to a belief in the duality of the soul", the practice is old enough to have been satirised in *Singin' in the Rain* (1952, USA, Gene Kelly and Stanley Donen). Anchoring a voice to a character other than the one producing the voice, or even dubbing a retake of the same actor's voice over the original performance at a later date, would already constitute the kind of witchcraft Renoir refused in direct sound films of the Popular Front era. Yet few directors subsequently would have had any compunctions in re-recording or re-voicing where a performance failed to live up to expectations. Indeed, in many digital animations, the same actor that voices a character is employed for motion-capture to create gestures, movements and facial expressions for their character, for example Tom Hanks in the *Toy Story* franchise (1995–, USA), or Johnny Depp in *Rango* (2011, USA, Gore Verbinski). This simultaneous matching and displacement of voice and actor parallels the ontological uncertainty of the digital frame that composites imagery gathered from the coincidences of location filming with the controlled environment of computer-generated imagery.

In motion capture, the contingencies of human action are extrapolated in order to be re-performed by synthespians, specifically in order to retain elements that escape control. In composite performances such as that of Shah Rukh Khan in *Ra.One* (2011, India, Anubhav Sinha), the star is retained not only as box office draw but in order to provide precisely those details of performance, including unconscious effects such as the movement of hair, that digital procedures cannot produce adequately. The flood of improvements in animation technique have not altered the inhumanity of pure synthespians, such as those featured in *Final Fantasy: The Spirits Within* (2001, USA, Hironobu Sakaguchi and Moto Sakakibara), even with the benefit of a decade and a half of work. If anything, the extreme apparent proximity required for 3D presentations, as in the case of *Ra.One*, make even greater claims on versimilitude in performances. At the same time, such doubling of human and digital performers creates an uncanny hint of duplicity that needs to be either explained or healed through narrative, as in the storyline explaining the doubling of the lead characters in *Avatar* (2009, USA, James Cameron).

From *Kōkaku Kidōtai Gōsuto In Za Sheru* (*Ghost in the Shell*, 1995, Japan, Mamoru Oshii) and *Mononoke-hime* (Princess Mononoke, 1997, Japan, Hayao Miyazaki), which employed Canadian firm Softimage's Toonshader filter to make CG animations look like cels, to *Uchū Kaizoku Kyaputen Hārokku* (Space Pirate Captain Harlock, 2013, Japan, Shinji Aramaki), which rejoices in its computer-generated sheen, animated film has been at the forefront of digital cinema. Intriguingly, Japanese animation has been outsourced increasingly to offshore drawing and computer-aided illustration labs throughout Southeast Asia to provide the labour required to produce the hours of animation demanded by TV, and now also film outlets. The globalisation of animation production echoes that of the effects houses engaged in live-action effects movies. Animation has the benefit of being less anchored in the specifics of its home culture, and therefore more open to the scale of export that cinema has not really known otherwise since the days of silent stars such as Charlie Chaplin. The US market for Japanese anime is now well over 2 billion dollars a year; while US animations also have particularly successful mass markets in China and Japan. At the same time, it is worth reiterating that even the open field of internet distribution and streaming services is not enough to break down the hegemony of Hollywood product in the English-speaking world and well beyond it, or to overcome the traditional lack of interest in Indian, Chinese and Japanese cinema, as well as popular cinemas of the rest of the world. This despite the fact that, for example, major international company Gaumont invested heavily in *Bakemono no Ko* (The Boy and The Beast, Japan), Mamoru Hosoda's 2016 anime, with a view to breaking the international market (Hosoda is widely seen as the heir to the globally successful Miyazaki, with whom he trained). A feature of these films is that they deal with characters who discover or have revealed to them a truth about the world, or hidden within them, effectively learning that they have been living double lives, or that the world has a hidden double. The is trope carried over into recent Hollywood animations such as Pixar's *Inside Out* (2015, USA, Pete Docter), which within a saccharine tale reveals the schizophrenic structure of the contemporary psyche.

This multiplication of identities also holds of films themselves in the digital era. Although theatrical release still provides the trigger for a mass of pre- and post-release marketing, the film itself appears as trailers and teasers for weeks, sometimes months ahead of release; backed with leaked material to fan sites in the case of major franchises such as *Harry Potter* (2001–2011, UK/USA), *The Hobbit* (2012, 2013, 2014, New Zealand/USA) and *Star Wars* (1977–, USA). Subsequent releases in multiple formats engage audiences in multiple experiences (Klinger 2006), from the physical (theme parks, toys, clothing, pioneered by *Star Wars* marketing in the late 1970s) to the digital (apps, games, social media). Such extensive and intensive marketing creates (apparent?) communities of interest and (actual?) extremely individual fantasy investment in the narratives and storyworlds of favoured films. Here too the mass circulation combines with intensely personalised experience and cultural capital so as to create a curiously contradictory intersection of individual and mass in the digital consumption of films.

Conclusion

There is, then, a trajectory in the analysis and interpretation of cinema that sees it as tending towards increasing control over perception and dissemination of moving image media, stretching from codecs to digital rights management. In certain respects, this continues the trajectory of mechanical media, whose standard aspect ratios, frame rates and lenses still underpin digital media, but take the principle of control to a new level by offering producers far greater control over the contingent features of reality. Control extends to the sub-perceptual scales of temporal order in scanning and algorithmic processing of images and sounds, and appears in the distance between digital representations and the natural appearance of the world to an ordinary human observer. To take one more example, digital colour is organised around a psychological model of a standard observer first formulated in 1931.

At the same time, the vulnerability of encoded audiovisual data to manipulation by producers also means that it is open to remaking by end-users, as in the cultures of mash-ups, revoicings and crash editing of scenes, even whole movies; the culture of parody of features documented by Klinger (2006: 191ff.), and the emergent culture of mobile phone movie making, with its own festival and distribution circuits. The reduction of picture elements to enumerable points of colour and luminance arrayed in geometric order in digital displays, dominated by bitmap or raster technology, is at odds with the major form of digital image generation that uses the vector principle (Smith 2014). The construction of coherent space, one of the major goals of compositing, is constantly undermined by 3D display technologies that emphasise their planar discontinuities. And while the foregoing survey emphasises uncanny and unstable elements of screen and audio presentations, other scholars note their implications for spectators. Sobchack (2000) and Bukatman (2012) tend toward the control end of the spectrum when analysing morphing technologies through which the spectacle of characters turning into something other than themselves can be shown on screen. At the other end, while sympathetic to such claims, Brown (2013: 74) suggests that morphs "do not so much make all 'objects' (or other people) 'subjective' (or 'the same') as challenge the very distinction between subject and object", noting in particular the positive implications such uncertainty has for the imposition of gender identities. There is, then, a genuine dialectic between control and democratisation, between commodification and liberation, and between identity as imposition and as community building both enabled and represented by digital media. It may indeed be that digital cinema has difficulty picturing the real as it appeared in the twentieth century, but if so it is because, as Dudley Andrew (2011: Ch. 3) argues in his major contribution to this debate, "cinema must press forward into the new century, by taking into itself the subject matter that surrounds it, increasingly a new media culture".

References

Andrew, D. (2011) *What Cinema Is!*, London: Blackwell-Wiley.

Baudrillard, J. (1996) *The Perfect Crime*, Turner, T. (trans.) London: Verso.

Bazin, A. (1967) "Ontology of the Photographic Image", in *What Is Cinema?*, Vol. 1. Gray, H. (trans.) Berkeley, CA: University of California Press, 9–16.

Belton, J. (2008) "Painting by the Numbers: The Digital Intermediate", *Film Quarterly* 61 (3): 58–65.

Braidotti, R. (2013) *The Posthuman*, Cambridge: Polity.

Brown, W. (2013) *Supercinema: Film Philosophy for the Digital Age*, London: Berghahn.

Bukatman, S. (2012) *The Poetics of Slumberland: Animated Spirits and the Animating Spirit*, Berkeley, CA: University of California Press.

Debord, G. (1990) *Comments on the Society of the Spectacle*, Imrie, M. (trans.), London: Verso.

Doane, M. A. (2007) "The Indexical and the Concept of Medium Specificity", *differences: A Journal of Feminist Cultural Studies* 18 (1): 128–152.

Fossati, G. (2009) *From Grain to Pixel: The Archival Life of Film*, Amsterdam: Amsterdam University Press.

Galison, P. (1997) *Image and Logic: A Material Culture of Microphysics*, Chicago, IL: University of Chicago Press.

Hauskeller, M., Philbeck, T. D. and Carbonell, C. D. (eds) (2015) *The Palgrave Handbook of Posthumanism in Film and Television*, London: Palgrave.

King, B. (2011) "Articulating Digital Stardom", *Celebrity Studies* 2 (3): 247–262.

Klein, N. M. (2004) *The Vatican to Vegas: A History of Special Effects*, New York: The New Press.

Klinger, B. (2006) *Beyond the Multiplex: Cinema, New Technologies and the Home*, Berkeley, CA: University of California Press.

Kracauer, S. (1960) *Theory of Film: The Redemption of Physical Reality*, New York: Oxford University Press.

Ndalianis, A. (2004) *Neo-Baroque Aesthetics and Contemporary Entertainment*, Cambridge, MA: MIT Press.

Pick, A. and Narraway, G. (eds) (2013) *Screening Nature: Cinema beyond the Human*, Oxford: Berghahn.
Pierson, M. (2002) *Special Effects: Still in Search of Wonder*, New York: Columbia University Press.
Prince, S. (2012) *Digital Visual Effects in Cinema: The Seduction of Reality*, New Brunswick, NJ: Rutgers University Press.
Purse, L. (2013) *Digital Imaging in Popular Cinema*, Edinburgh: Edinburgh University Press.
Renoir, J. (1974) *My Life and My Films*. Denny, N. (trans.), London: Collins.
Rodowick, D. N. (2007) *The Virtual Life of Film*, Cambridge, MA: Harvard University Press.
Shaviro, S. (2010) *Post Cinematic Affect*, Alresford: Zero Books.
Short, S. (2005) *Cyborg Cinema and Contemporary Subjectivity,* London: Palgrave.
Smith, A. R. (2015) "A Taxonomy and Genealogy of Digital Light-Based Technologies", in Cubitt, S., Palmer, D., Tkacz, N. and Walkling, L. (eds) *Digital Light*, London: Open Humanities Press, 48–69.
Sobchack, V. (2000) "'At the Still Point of the Turning World': Metamorphing and Meta-Stasis", in Sobchack, V. (ed.) *Meta-morphing: Visual Transformation and the Culture of Quick-Change*, Minneapolis, MN: University of Minnesota Press, 131–158.
Stewart, G. (2007) *Framed Time: Toward a Postfilmic Cinema*, Chicago, IL: University of Chicago Press.
Turnock, J. A. (2014) *Plastic Reality: Special Effects, Technology, and the Emergence of 1970s Blockbuster Aesthetics*, New York: Columbia University Press.
Whissel, K. (2014) *Spectacular Digital Effects: CGI and Contemporary Cinema*, Durham, NC: Duke University Press.
Wolfe, C. (2009) *What Is Posthumanism?*, Minneapolis, MN: University of Minnesota Press.

37

ACCESS AND POWER

Film distribution, re-intermediation and piracy

Virginia Crisp

World Cinema *is* circulation

In the introduction to their 2006 edited collection *Remapping World Cinema* Dennison and Lim urged scholars to think about World Cinema as a discipline, methodology and a perspective. Such a suggestion was posited in response to the fact that the term "World Cinema" had, at that time, "given origin to a highly questionable, though enduringly popular, opposition between the American mainstream and the rest of the world" (Nagib *et al.* 2012: xviii). In one of the chapters in the *Remapping World Cinema* collection, Lúcia Nagib summarises the issue thus:

> Despite its all-encompassing, democratic vocation, it [World Cinema] is not usually employed to mean cinema worldwide. On the contrary, the usual way of defining it is restrictive and negative as "non-Hollywood cinema" [... in doing so] it unwittingly sanctions the American way of looking at the world, according to which Hollywood is the centre and all other cinemas are the periphery.
>
> *(2006: 30)*

This framing of Hollywood as the pre-eminent player on the global film industry stage has the unfortunate consequence of positioning US filmmaking as the benchmark by which other filmmakers and industries are measured. Not only is such positioning highly questionable on ideological grounds, it also fails to recognise the realities of "film production, distribution, and consumption [which] have long been a global affair" (Roberts 1998: 62). While the tendency to consider World Cinema through a Western or American lens is "deeply-engrained" (Nagib 2006: 31), such an impetus is being eroded as "distinctions between dichotomies such as Western and non-Western, self and other, [. . .] are beginning to dissolve" (Dennison and Lim 2006: 4).

Employing World Cinema as a perspective as Dennison and Lim suggest enables a consideration of film that embraces concepts such as "hybridity" and "border crossing" (2006: 6). Such an approach also serves to highlight why a World Cinema perspective necessarily has questions of media distribution at its core. This reasoning is elucidated in a definition of World Cinema from Nagib where she argues: "World Cinema is simply the cinema of the world. It has no centre.

It is not the other, but it is us. It has no beginning and no end. World Cinema, as the world itself, is circulation" (Nagib 2006: 35). So, if World Cinema *is* circulation then considerations of distribution practices are necessarily at the heart of any such discussion. As such, this chapter's aim, to consider how power is shifting between traditional and new media gatekeepers, is pertinent to all discussions of World Cinema because distribution is often the key to dictating which films are able to circulate around the globe and which are not.

Distribution and power

While distribution has until recently been largely overlooked within all but a few academic studies of the media industries, within such research it has long been acknowledged as the route to power within the global film industry (Wasko 2002, 2003; Miller *et al.* 2004; Balio 2013). As Dudley Andrew states: "the real film wars have been waged less over production than over competition for audiences (i.e. distribution)" (2004: 11). Furthermore, while trying to avoid reasserting the dominance of Hollywood on the global stage and thus reproducing the tendency to consider the film industry from a centre vs. periphery perspective, it is important to consider how control over channels and mechanisms of distribution is so often a site of struggle that reveals complex power relations. As Ezra and Rowden suggest, "the vast majority of the world's film producing countries rarely find audiences (that is, audiences rarely find them) outside their own borders" (2006: 5). Furthermore, this is not an accident of happenstance but rather points to the fact that "because of their higher production values and access to more extensive distribution networks and marketing campaigns, the more heavily financed films tend to cross national borders with greater ease" (Ezra and Rowden 2006: 5).

While acknowledging that the "fact" of Hollywood's dominance of the global film industry is hotly debated, nonetheless, the permanence of that supposed dominance is invariably questioned whenever technological developments such as TV, VHS and the Internet have proposed new modes of media production, distribution and consumption. In recent years, as traditional forms of film and media distribution are arguably being "disrupted" by new piracy practices and Video on Demand (VoD) services enabled through the Internet, the term "disintermediation"—that is where "the intermediary in a supply chain [is said to become] obsolete" (Iordanova 2012: 3)—has become *de rigueur* in many discussions of media dissemination.

This chapter seeks to problematise such assumptions by asserting that, while the media landscape has undoubtedly changed and there are many new methods and means of media distribution, the process of disintermediation is not as pervasive as we might imagine—especially when considered from a global perspective. In such a context the term "re-intermediation" might be better employed to describe the current media distribution landscape, that is, one where power can be seen to shift between cultural gatekeepers rather than away from them.

I would argue that such terminological wrangling is necessary in much the same way that it was important to revise the discussions of the deregulation of the US/UK media industries in the 1980s and 1990s so as to consider the changes that took place at the time as a matter of re-regulation rather than deregulation. Such an updating of terms more accurately reflected that legislation and regulations were not removed entirely during this period; they were simply replaced with "new legislation and regulation, much of which favoured [. . .] the interests of large private corporations and their shareholders" (Hesmondhalgh 2013: 127). Of course, it is not the same multinational corporations that are necessarily reaping the benefits of the current re-intermediation process because new global giants such as Amazon and Netflix are vying for control in a complex media landscape. However, I would also maintain that the more traditional intermediaries, while facing threats to their dominance on multiple fronts, have not seen their influence diminish entirely, nor has their role as cultural gatekeepers completely shifted into the hands of others.

Disintermediated distribution?

Those who govern the channels of media distribution are able to shape popular experiences of media cultures(s) by selecting which films and TV shows are available to audiences and which are not. That is not to say that other tastemakers such as film critics, journalists, historians, academics, fans and audiences more generally have no role in shaping what we understand as our media culture(s). However, those judgements on the quality and worth of certain films and TV shows are ultimately restricted by what has been made, and what content has been lucky enough to enjoy wide distribution and substantial marketing budgets. Furthermore, where the film industry is concerned, this control over distribution is far from unintentional. The vertical integration of the Hollywood system (where all film production, distribution and exhibition is handled in house by a set of multinational corporations) is an organisational structure that the US majors have created in an effort to dominate the global film and TV industries. However, these attempts are arguably being undermined by new intermediaries such as Hulu, Netflix, iTunes and Amazon Instant providing Pay Per View (PPV) and Subscription Video on Demand (SVoD) services, not to mention the increased prominence of free at the point of access streaming platforms such as YouTube or Vimeo.

Furthermore, there are other avenues for the dissemination of film and TV media that are not officially sanctioned by copyright holders who are also posing a challenge to the existing distribution oligopoly held by the Hollywood studios. Within this category we might include both physical piracy of DVDs, VHS tapes and in some instances VCDs, and also the dissemination of films online as media files. Such channels have been dubbed "informal" by theorist Roman Lobato (2012) who, in his book *Shadow Economies of Cinema: Mapping Informal Film Distribution*, designates the distinction between formal and informal distribution by suggesting that "formality refers to the degree to which industries are regulated, measured, and governed by state and corporate institutions. Informal distributors are those which operate outside this sphere, or in partial articulation with it" (Lobato 2012: 4). Lobato takes great pains to suggest that all of these informal manners of dissemination should be included within the definition of media distribution and should be understood not as marginal practices but as central drivers of the global distribution of film (2012: 3). Indeed, while informal distribution exists as a counterpoint to the formal distribution of films in cinemas, on television and on various home video formats, it is important to note that the informal and formal realms are not necessarily separated by rigid and straightforward boundaries (Lobato 2012; Cunningham 2012). Indeed, as Tristan Mattelart (2012: 739) points out, the informal economy is often "closely intertwined" with the official economy and so too are the informal and formal modes of media distribution that exist within and alongside these formal and informal economies.

However, while formal and informal forms of distribution undoubtedly intersect and overlap with one another (and I would definitely support the claim that informal methods of distribution require more scrutiny in terms of the role that they have to play in access to content) it does not necessarily follow that power is distributed equally in both formal and informal settings. As Cunningham points out, while the informal and formal might in many instances influence one another, it is not necessarily always the case that power is equally distributed among the players on both sides (2012: 416). Indeed, the power dynamics between formal and informal distribution channels is very complex and will be touched upon again later in this chapter.

Everything right here, right now: the panacea of piracy?

While it is certainly not always the case, many informal distribution practices involve an element of copyright infringement. Whether one is ripping a CD from a friend, downloading files from sites such as the *Pirate Bay*, exchanging cracked software through direct download links, buying a counterfeit DVD on eBay or engaging in the mass producing of VCDs for sale in physical street markets, one is doing so in contravention of the intellectual property laws that protect against the unauthorised use and distribution of copyright protected content. Indeed, the means of disseminating media content en masse is no longer the preserve of the organised criminal gangs but has become a ubiquitous everyday activity. The supposed exponential growth of everyday pirate practices across the globe has caused the creative industries to loudly bemoan the risks posed to their bottom line, the security of those working in these industries and even the future of creativity itself. Such rhetoric has been heavily scrutinised (see Denegri-Knott 2004; Yar 2005) and again serves to reinforce the fact that control over distribution is of utmost importance to media companies.

Amid such concerns there have also been positive claims that informal mechanisms and modes of distribution are capable of transgressing traditional power formations and as such can be seen as part of the process of disintermediation that is removing ultimate power and influence from the hands of the media distributors (see Li 2012; Meng 2012; Vandresen 2012). This has been particularly emphasised when considering how Hollywood's perceived dominance might be challenged around the globe.

For instance, Li's work on D-buff communities in China points to a pirate market that does not just distribute content but also functions as a training ground for new indigenous talent (2012: 543). In such a context, "the viral infrastructure of piracy, with the density, ubiquity, and flexibility of its "long tails", has proven a suitable channel for distributing alternative cinemas that target only a niche audience" (Li 2012: 556). Thus, in such circumstances these D-buff groups enable the distribution of Chinese films that have been produced outside of the shackles of state control and thus such activities might even be considered "subversive" in the Chinese context (Li 2012: 542–543).

Another example of informal distribution networks challenging the formal can be found in Brazilian production of fan-made subtitles. In her work in this area, Vandresen argues that the practice of the fansubbers "defies the current model of content distribution" (2012: 629). She goes on to suggest that the activities of these fansubbers "challenge[s] power levels, compressing hierarchies through as-yet-unimagined forms of participation" (Vandresen 2012: 628).

Consequently, it might seem sensible to suggest that the power of traditional distributors is being eroded and thus the disintermediation argument would seem to hold some weight. However, in the rest of the chapter I will argue that this is not in fact the case, because first, while old gatekeepers might be withering, new intermediaries with considerable levels of influence (in both formal and informal settings) are gaining in prominence. Second, while further research is needed in this area, existing evidence would seem to suggest that the sort of content circulated within pirate networks tends to mirror the slant towards the mainstream within formal distribution channels. Finally, this mirroring would imply that while distribution channels have become more varied and dispersed, formal distributors are still able to exert considerable influence as they do, for the time being at least, still have considerable sway over how both production and marketing functions within the global film business.

While informal distributors might be enjoying unprecedented levels of freedom at present, brought about by the ease of duplicating and distributing films, music, games and software as files online or as cheap discs for sale, such technological shifts do not mean that intermediaries have been removed altogether. Indeed, do these informal distributors themselves not act as gatekeepers to media content? While Mattelart makes the observation that "the merchants of the informal sector are able to adapt themselves more efficiently to the specific needs of their customers" (2012: 740), such a comment assumes that a customer/seller and demand/supply scenario is unquestionably present. To imagine that the black market seller of DVDs is any more mindful of their customer's best interests than the formal distribution company is somewhat naïve. While I would agree that they are certainly more capable of adapting, there are other factors at play that shape the demand of audiences that are not within the control of these new gatekeepers. Furthermore, when a distributor is acting from motivations other than supplying the customer with what they supposedly 'demand' then a much more complex picture of gatekeeping practices emerges.

As I have noted in my previous work (2013; 2015), within filesharing communities there are often specific gatekeepers who exert a disproportionate amount of power within the community and thus effectively decide what is released and what is not. I am not alone in suggesting that a few influential community members exert a disproportionate amount of control over what content is shared within P2P networks. Bodó and Lakatos have made similar observations in their work on Hungarian P2P networks where they suggest that these "releasers and site administrators [. . .] perform the same function in P2P piracy as publishing does in the book industry" (2012: 430). Furthermore, the official channels of film distribution are able to influence the decisions of these gatekeepers in a number of ways through their control over what films are produced and how they are marketed. Ultimately, the professional film distribution sector is able to influence what films are released, which "cut" of the film is released in certain territories, the technical quality of that released version and often which films get produced in the first place. They are thus also able to exert a considerable influence on what content circulates within filesharing networks.

This is because when sharing film and TV files online, even if users are sharing what they download, they invariably are not actually increasing the range of films available online. Indeed, they are merely sharing those files already being shared by others. In order for this sharing to take place someone must source the original copy and then convert it into a format that others can download. As Bodó and Lakatos point out "Just as one can only buy a book that has been published, one can only download a film that has been transformed into a digital copy and made available to the P2P community" (2012: 430).

It is easy to look around and conclude that we are experiencing an epoch of unprecedented access to films, books, TV shows and games from across the globe. This era is enabled by the fact that we have digital content that can be streamed or downloaded at the touch of a button. However, there are a number of convincing reasons why one should counsel caution when subscribing to this theorem.

First, it is possible to assert that this era of plenty actually brings with it an era of overflow. As De Meulenaere, Van den Broeck and Lievens suggest "extensive choice and availability of content on various platforms can potentially create an information and sensory overload for the viewer" (2012: 306). In such a scenario it becomes difficult for the individual to make choices from the plethora available, leading them to rely on fewer sources when making decisions about what to watch and stick to seeking out content that they are already familiar with. Thus, we could claim that an era of limitless content, rather than putting the power in the hands of the consumer, it returns power squarely to the gatekeepers.

Now it might be possible to claim that with the growth of social media we listen to the recommendations of friends rather than the claims of advertisers. For example, Cunningham suggests that in the era of social media the choices of other people become particularly influential

(2012: 416). However, Bodó and Lakatos (2012) have observed in P2P networks in Hungary that films that are popular within filesharing networks are not necessarily made popular by "word-of-mouth" or based on perceived "quality", but by the marketing that is associated with the official release of the film. So, remembering that there are the aforementioned gatekeepers operating within these spheres as well, Bodó and Lakatos conclude that "sales effort has a bigger relative influence on what is shared by P2P gatekeepers than on what ordinary network users are actually looking for" (2012: 432).

Indeed, as has previously been discussed, within many pirate networks US TV and film content is dominant. Such content is backed by incredibly expensive and, significantly, global marketing campaigns. Thus, while these films and TV shows are promoted internationally, only a small proportion of the worldwide population can afford to experience these cultural goods through official means. Thus, as Mattelart claims, "Pirated products are then, for many consumers of the countries of the South or the East, a privileged means to access, despite their limited resources, these shows promoted by global marketing campaigns" (Mattelart 2012: 740). Such a global perspective, then, also highlights another flaw with the "era of plenty" argument, that is that this age of abundance is not being experienced unilaterally around the globe.

Third in the list of criticisms against the argument that film and TV content is more accessible than before is linked to the continued role of distributors (and hence marketing) in the process of film and TV production. Indeed, the influence of marketing can only be measured in relation to films that have been produced in the first place. Thus, an issue that cannot be ignored is the role that distributors have to play in film financing. Indeed, according to the Film Distributor's Association (2011) it is often considered preferable for a distribution deal to be arranged even before a film goes into production, because this makes it easier to secure funding to cover production costs. As guarantees of distribution deals are so important to the initial financing of a film production, the role that professional distributors play in dictating which films get produced in the first place cannot be underestimated. Thus, by influencing what films are made and officially released on DVD/BluRay, film distributors exert considerable sway over the films that circulate within filesharing networks. Therefore, even though such networks represent "alternative" channels of distribution, traditional intermediaries in the form of professional distributors still have a considerable level of influence over the films that audiences are able to enjoy.

Such influence is evident in the scholarship that attests that far from damaging their profits, piracy "primes a proto-licit market for Hollywood [and] arguably, is in Hollywood's longer-term interest" (Cunningham 2012: 417). Cunningham is not alone in his assessment as Mattelart makes the point that in the countries surveyed as part of his own collaborative research project on piracy, that is, Tunisia, Algeria, Morocco, the Ivory Coast, South Korea, Colombia, Bulgaria and Russia, while some content is available from places such as India, Hong Kong, Egypt and Nigeria, US content is undoubtedly dominant (Mattelart 2012: 740). Mattelart further suggests that piracy actually increases the presence of Hollywood's products in markets they would otherwise not dominate and as such could be seen as "preparing [. . .] the ground for future legal exports" (Mattelart 2012: 747). Meng similarly argues that the work of fansubbers in Chinese communities such as Zimuzu ultimately increases the audience for the American content that is subtitled by its members (Meng 2012: 475). While we might celebrate "alternative" forms of distribution on the one hand, we have to consider whether these alternatives are actually circulating diverse content and/or serving niche audiences, on the other.

A similar tendency can be observed when looking at TV sharing. Here, Newman has made the claim that it is prime time US television that circulates more widely within pirate networks than other TV content (2012: 466). He points to the work of Ernesto who suggests that "During one week in 2009, more than 1.7 million people accessed the latest episodes of *Heroes* and *Lost* using BitTorrent. Other heavily shared shows included *24*, *The Big Bang Theory*, and *Battlestar Galactica*" (cited in Newman 2012: 466). Such big-budget high-profile shows are the major texts circulating within such networks. Furthermore, Newman goes on to claim that global audiences actually feel "a sense of entitlement to American content" (2012: 468) and that they see US TV as forming the bedrock of a "common global popular culture", a culture that they have restricted access to due to "legal, political, and economic structures that slow or forbid transmission of American shows to viewers in other countries" (2012: 468). Mattelart supports this assertion by noting that accessing pirated materials allows the poorer members of society to feel as if they can in some way participate in the global "information society" from which they are so often excluded (2009: 319).

In particular, we must be careful not to assume that potentially subversive piratical practices that are enacted within countries that have strict censorship laws are comparable to filesharing and downloading practices where little censorship exists to circumvent. As Mattelart suggests, black/grey market distribution channels are inextricably linked to the authoritarian regimes and policies in the host country (2012: 737–738). As such, we have to consider the authoritarian context that stimulates forms of "subversive" piracy like those observed by Li in China (Li 2012: 552) and in doing so we must ask whether informal distribution elsewhere is enabling access to a more diverse range of content than hitherto, and encouraging new and vibrant filmmaking practice. In other words, with little overt censorship to circumvent, is Western piracy as "vibrant" and "subversive" as the D-buff culture in China or the fansubbing practices in Brazil described by Li and Vandresen respectively?

Disruptive innovators

It is also imperative to note that filesharing networks are not the only new kids on the block. There are new intermediaries in the form of online subscription VoD services such as Netflix. Cunningham calls these new players in the game (Amazon, Google, Apple and Netflix) "disruptive innovators" who are "challenging the premium content–premium pricing–mass media model" (2012: 417). The disruptive innovators control platforms that represent a form of media convergence. Thus, sites such as Hulu and Netflix offer both TV and film content and furthermore they allow viewers to be freed from the shackles of television scheduling and film programming. Bodó and Lakatos suggest this "enables content to resurface and circulate in contexts defined by viewers and not by the producers or professional middlemen responsible for contextualizing and programming traditional content flows" (2012: 415). Within such a context the audience is able to engage with content in times and spaces of their own choosing. Again, this would seem to suggest that power has shifted away from middlemen and into the hands of consumers.

However, there are a number of issues with this suggestion. First, as mentioned briefly before, these platforms are not available to everyone on a global scale due to practices such as geoblocking which mean that VoD sites such as Netflix are only available in certain territories (Newman 2012: 477). Consequently, before heralding the dawn of a new era of unprecedented choice, we must consider that not everyone has access to the same services, in the same way, and under the same conditions.

If we look at the US we see a variety of options available, for example, Netflix, Hulu, Red Box and Ultraviolet to name but a few. The UK has mainstream film and TV streaming services such as Netflix and Amazon Instant but other mainstream competitors such as Hulu and Red Box are not available. Indeed, Netflix launched their online VoD service in the US in 2008 but only launched in the UK in 2012 and their push into the rest of the world only followed in 2016. There have also been questions raised about the quality of Netflix in these new territories as connection speeds are variable and catalogues of available titles are limited when compared to the US (Torre 2016).

In addition to such vagaries of access to services and the catalogue of TV and films on offer, there are also still release windows that mean that films and TV shows are released in different countries at different times and are available on different platforms at different times. The structure and length of release window again varies from country to country. So, even if one can legally access services such as Netflix and Amazon Instant it does not automatically follow that these services will allow the viewer access to recent films and TV shows.

Furthermore, even if access is possible, our ability to timeshift and watch where we like represents only limited freedom over the films and TV shows that we engage with. As Newman points out, "in general, the availability, accessibility, and desirability of legal online downloads or streaming is appealing, but not in every instance. The terms are never entirely the audience's own preferred options" (2012: 477). For instance, if we pay to download a film or TV show through iTunes, our ownership of that content is limited by the Digital Rights Management (DRM) encoded into the file. Such DRM limits the type and amount of devices upon which we can play the file. Such content also has no resale value because there is no physical copy of the film on DVD or BluRay that can be traded in or sold. We might stream content but this gives us even more limited access and importantly, means we have no ability to personally archive the content we have paid for. Such restrictions have led Newman to make the rather bold claim that "In some sense, Hulu and other legitimate forms of access appeal to the audience most of all by being legal rather than being more useful or convenient than illegal downloading" (Newman 2012: 477).

Finally, when considering these gatekeeping practices it is important to consider how audiences react to this unprecedented access to seemingly unlimited choice of films and TV shows to stream. In their work on TV consumption in Belgium, De Meulenaere, Van den Broeck and Lievens note that among their focus group participants, even though the more techno literate had access to a greater range of content through online channels, they often chose to watch the same video content as those with access to less variety (De Meulenaere *et al.* 2012: 319). We might ask why people with access to a broad range of content choose to watch exactly the same things as people whose choice is much more limited. This question is too broad to be adequately considered here and is an area that requires further investigation but one response to this question might relate to the way that sites such as Netflix are structured.

Netflix is not just a transparent portal that allows users access to content. The structure of the website and the various applications that allow access to the content through one's iPad, iPhone, Xbox or Smart TV, shape the viewing experience. These sites might act as wonderfully convenient portals to online content but they also heavily regulate our experience of films and TV. We may have the ability to shift film and TV consumption in time and space but the promise of complete control is an illusion. On one level, sites such as Netflix give the feeling of limitless content by presenting you with rows upon rows of potential films and TV series to peruse. On another level, the first thing that greets a user when they log on to the service is a page that offers "Netflix selections for you" or the "most popular" films/TV on Netflix. What is particularly interesting about presenting the recently arrived Netflix subscriber with a list of the "most popular" programmes is that it actively encourages the user to engage with this content. Thus, being in the "most popular" category creates a feedback loop whereby a film or TV show becomes more popular because it is already popular. The use of the "most popular" moniker then also furthers the illusion that this is a platform that is viewer-centred.

Netflix's user interface presents the illusion that it is the viewer who decides what is or is not "popular", as though the algorithm that produces the selection is necessarily impartial.

These websites ask us to contribute to the constant creation of metadata by asking us to rate watched titles. In the creation of a "Top 10 for Virginia", this allows the metadata to exert "technocratic control" over the circulation and consumption of the content. As Morris states, "[m]etadata are a key technology for tracking and surveying the flow and use of digital objects, and unlike TiVo or ratings, users contribute metadata knowingly in the hopes of making digital commodities more useable" (2012: 858). In such a way the website then predicts our future preferences and, I would argue, in doing so it also has the potential to influence them. This, in turn has the potential to create a feedback loop whereby popular titles become more popular and the less well-known titles languish in obscurity. Cleverly, all of this is done while presenting the audience with an interface that increases their sense of control over the content that they have access to.

Conclusion

By approaching World Cinema as a "perspective", as Dennison and Lim advise, there is more scope to see the overlap and intersections between cinemas rather than a tendency to resort to dichotomous thinking about the USA and their imagined resistant other. Distribution is at the centre of any such consideration because it enables us to consider the flows of media texts and in doing so their associations with geographies, politics and cultures become more visible as these traits are used for promoting such texts to non-domestic audiences. In such a context there are structures, cultures, institutions (and their associated power dynamics) that dictate the success of the individual and their associated works. Furthermore, while we are witnessing the growth of new intermediaries who are able to shape our access to culture, they are doing so in conjunction with the old intermediaries and have not deposed them completely. However, the choices of these gatekeepers are themselves ultimately restricted by what films have been made and officially distributed, and how those films are marketed. These are decisions that all reside in the hands of traditional film distributors. Thus, rather than these distributors losing power, as the disintermediation argument would suggest, their influence is still significant.

Furthermore, although it seems tempting to suggest that the new subscription VoD services have the power to disrupt the current media monopolies, the extent of their influence has yet to be established. So while mediation and curation are no longer the sole preserve of the media industry elite, their gate-keeping power has not been removed entirely but has become dispersed through informal as well as formal contexts in quite complex ways. Thus, the process of re-intermediation (rather than disintermediation) needs to be examined in far more detail.

References

Andrew, D. (2004) "An Atlas of World Cinema", *Framework: The Journal of Cinema and Media* 45 (2): 9–23.

Balio, T. (2013) *Hollywood in the New Millennium*, London: Palgrave.

Bodó, B. and Lakatos, Z. (2012) "Theatrical Distribution and P2P Movie Piracy: A Survey of P2P Networks in Hungary Using Transactional Data", *International Journal of Communication* 6: 413–445.

Crisp, V. (2013) "The Piratical Is Political", *Soundings* 55 (55): 72–81.

—— (2015) *Pirates and Professionals: Film Distribution in the Digital Age*, London: Palgrave.

Cunningham, S. (2012) "Emergent Innovation through the Coevolution of Informal and Formal Media Economies", *Television & New Media* 13 (5): 415–430.

De Meulenaere, J., Van den Broeck, W. and Lievens, B. (2012) "From Era of Plenty to Era of Overflow: What Shall I Watch?" *Journal of Communication Enquiry* 36 (4): 305–321.

Denegri-Knott, J. (2004) "Sinking the Online Music Pirates: Foucault, Power and Deviance on the Web", *Journal of Computer-Mediated Communication*, 9 (4), http://jcmc.indiana.edu/vol9/issue4/denegri_knott.html.

Dennison, S. and Lim, S. H. (2006) "Situating World Cinema as a Theoretical Problem", in Dennison, S. and Lim, S. H. (eds) *Remapping World Cinema: Identity Culture and Politics in Film*, London and New York: Wallflower Press, 1–18.

Ezra, E. and Rowden, T. (2006) "General Introduction: What Is Transnational Cinema", in Ezra, E. and Rowden, T. (eds) *Transnational Cinema: The Film Reader*, London and New York: Routledge, 1–12.

Film Distributor's Association Website (2011) www.launchingfilms.tv/acquisition.php.

Hesmondhalgh, D. (2013) *The Cultural Industries*, Los Angeles, London, New Delhi, Singapore, Washington DC: Sage.

Iordanova, D. (2012) "Digital Disruption: Technological Innovation and Global Film Circulation", in Iordanova, D. and Cunningham, S. (eds) *Digital Disruption: Cinema Moves Online*, St Andrews: University of St Andrews Press, 1–31.

Li, J. (2012) "From the D-Buffs to the D-Generation, Piracy, Cinema and an Alternative Public Sphere in Urban China", *International Journal of Communication* 6: 542–563.

Lobato, R. (2012) *Shadow Economies of Cinema: Mapping Informal Film Distribution*, London: BFI.

Mattelart, T. (2009) "Audio-visual Piracy: Towards a Study of the Underground Networks of Cultural Globalization", *Global Media and Communication* 5 (3): 308–326.

—— (2012) "Audiovisual Piracy, Informal Economy, and Cultural Globalization", *International Journal of Communication* 6: 735–750.

Meng, B. (2012) "Undetermined Globalization: Media Consumption via P2P Networks", *International Journal of Communication* 6: 467–483.

Miller, T., Govil, N., Mcmurria, J., Maxwell, R. and Wang, T. (2004) *Global Hollywood: No. 2*, London: BFI.

Morris, J. W. (2012) "Making Music Behave: Metadata and the Digital Music Commodity", *New Media Society* 14 (5): 850–866.

Nagib, L. (2006) "Towards a Positive Definition of World Cinema", in Dennison, S. and Lim, S. H. (eds) *Remapping World Cinema: Identity Culture and Politics in Film*, London: Wallflower Press, 30–37.

Nagib, L., Perriam, C. and Dudrah, R. (2012) "Introduction", in Nagib, L., Perriam, C. and Dudrah, R. (eds) *Theorising World Cinema*, London: I. B. Tauris, xvii–xxxii.

Newman, M. Z. (2012) "Free TV: File-Sharing and the Value of Television", *Television and New Media* 13 (6): 463–479.

Roberts. M. (1998) "'Baraka': World Cinema and the Global Culture Industry", *Cinema Journal* 37 (3): 62–82.

Torre, P. (2016) "Global Streaming: Netflix Expands into New Territories", paper presented at the *Society for Cinema and Media Studies* Conference, Atlanta GA, 30 March–3 April 2016.

Vandresen, M. (2012) "Free Culture Lost in Translation", *International Journal of Communication* 6: 626–642.

Wasko, J. (2002) "The Future of Film Distribution and Exhibition", in Harris, D. (ed.) *The New Media Book*, London: BFI.

—— (2003) *How Hollywood Works*, London: Sage.

Yar, M. (2005) "The Global 'Epidemic' of Movie 'Piracy': Crime-wave or Social Construction?" *Media, Culture and Society* 27 (5): 677–696.

38

THE EMERGING GLOBAL SCREEN ECOLOGY OF SOCIAL MEDIA ENTERTAINMENT

Stuart Cunningham and David Craig

Introduction

The emerging shape of screen industries in the twenty-first century encapsulates deep changes in consumer habit and expectation and content production related "to a larger trend across the media industries to integrate digital technology and socially networked communication with traditional screen media practices" (Holt and Sanson 2013: 1). This emerging new screen ecology has given rise not only to major challenges to established media, but is being shaped by a set of newly prominent online screen entertainment platforms, most prominently Apple, Amazon and Netflix, but also and pre-eminently Alphabet/Google/YouTube. Cunningham and Silver (2013) have previously examined the broad contours of this phenomenon. Arguably one of the most challenging and innovative elements of the evolving screen ecology is a very low-budget tier of mostly advertising-supported online channels driven mainly by the professionalisation and monetisation of previously amateur content creation. We call this "social media entertainment" (SME) and distinguish it from the professionally generated content (PGC) strategies of Netflix, Amazon and others, that constitute the other part of the new screen ecology.

In this chapter, we advance and critically examine claims for the distinctiveness of this new screen ecology as compared to earlier and other, dominant mainstream contemporary screen industry formations. We identify the following key elements that may lay claim to distinctiveness:

1 The political economy of online distribution: for arguably the first time in the history of the dominant US screen formation, challengers to this dominance are appreciably larger firms, with much deeper pockets than the incumbents.
2 Social media and the end of media scarcity: online video platforms have converted media scarcity into content abundance while beginning to attract both experienced and new advertisers and brands, the critical underpinning of the traditional screen ecology.
3 Social media entertainment and the online creator: the professionalisation and monetisation of online creators has contributed to the rise of a new twenty-first-century media-meets-communication industry.
4 Content innovation and the vlogger effect: social media entertainment features content that is a radical break from the professional norms of cinema and most television, reverse engineering legacy media programming.

5 Technological affordances of social media entertainment: this new screen ecology occupies a fundamentally convergent space between social media communication and entertainment content and is structured by a level of networked interactivity and viewer- and audience-centricity arguably without parallel in screen history.
6 Qualitatively different global reach, Intellectual Property dynamics and monetisation strategy: previous points of distinction come together to explain why this form of content is being produced and distributed globally in ways that radically depart from principles and practices of territorial rights and indeed of traditional IP control.

This chapter draws on our larger programme of research into the new screen ecology of social media entertainment, mapping the platforms and affordances, content innovation and creative labour, monetisation and management, new forms of media globalisation, and critical cultural concerns raised by this nascent media industry. In 2015, about 100 interviews with creators, platform and intermediary executives and managers, talent agents, technology integrators, and policy makers have formed part of the programme, some of which are drawn on in the chapter.

The political economy of online distribution

Analyses of the rate of change of the membership of the Fortune 500 (the largest US companies) show clearly that the velocity of turnover has increased as time has passed (Strangler and Arbesman 2012). In contrast, there has been remarkable stability in business dominance in the screen industry. Of the original eight companies that dominated film (Paramount, MGM, Fox, Warner Brothers, RKO, Universal, Columbia and UA) during the first half of the twentieth century, only RKO fell from grace, replaced within the oligopoly by Disney during the 1950s. MGM-UA slipped from the annual list of top ten studio-distributors during the 2000s. The oligopoly in broadcast television, while somewhat shorter-lived, is even tighter. CBS, NBC and ABC have dominated the TV landscape for almost seventy years, with Fox the only addition as a major network.

The Majors have adapted to waves of significant change in regulatory structure, technology and taste across more than a century, reforming into corporate structures that now have re-established a form of de-facto vertical integration through their parent conglomerates: NBC-Universal; Viacom-Paramount-CBS; Time-Warner; Disney-ABC and Fox. However, they are now confronted by arguably unprecedented challenges. The fragmentation of once-stable viewership means that TV's splintering-but-still-big audience remains valuable to advertisers, but industry analysts predict that digital advertising revenue will beat out traditional television advertising revenue globally by the year 2017 and by 2016 in the US (Brouwer 2015). The core North American cinema box office is kept high by increasing ticket prices to offset stagnant attendance, and the cable TV industry, faced with escalating cord-cutting, responds with subscription increases that only contribute to further rates of exit.

The fundamental differences between the new platforms—Apple, Amazon, Google, Facebook, Yahoo!, Netflix—and media incumbents are that they are Internet "pure-play" businesses that have large online customer or user populations, generating extensive data on search behaviour and purchasing; they share an overriding focus on technical innovation; and they have years of experience marketing directly to their customer base targeting those most likely to be interested in a particular genre or programme based on each individual's past behaviour. They are working around content blocking tactics of the Majors by commissioning new content, facilitating substantial change in the presentation, distribution, and types of content, and lead in controlling the platforms that deliver content to burgeoning audiences across multiple screens. In the US, Netflix

Figure 38.1 Google's Venice, California, headquarters. ©Stuart Cunningham and David Craig.

and YouTube now account for over 50 per cent of prime time Internet traffic. People around the globe upload more than 400 hours of video to YouTube every minute. Netflix already refers to itself as the "world's leading Internet TV network". The 2013 revenues of the Majors (with their parent conglomerates) were 77.5 per cent of those of the new players (Apple, Amazon, Google, Facebook, Yahoo!, Netflix, Microsoft, Intel)—US$249.69 billion versus US$322.1 billion (Cunningham *et al.* 2015: 141).

Challenges to media incumbents are, of course, not new. The rise of television in the 1950s threatened the incumbency of film studios, turning cinema audiences into home-bound viewers. Within a decade, however, television co-evolved and converged with Hollywood. The film studios became as co-dependent on TV for syndication revenue, particularly a newly launched subscription channel called Home Box Office (HBO), as TV had upon the content generation and talent management skills of Hollywood. The new screen ecology of home video helped sustain an independent cinema industry throughout the 1980s and 1990s.

Similarly, the challenge of cable distribution represented a similar pattern of co-evolution over time, especially in programming. For example, with full distribution across the cable universe, most ad-based networks shifted their programming strategies to embrace Hollywood storytelling in order to secure larger audiences and higher advertising returns. The former Arts and Entertainment network evolved into A&E, and went from British co-productions to reality programming, while AMC has shifted from American Movie Classics to classy American series (*Mad Men*, 2007–2015, USA and *Breaking Bad*, 2008–2013, USA).

As we have seen, the new digital platforms together constitute a corporate challenge unprecedented in scale and scope. Netflix has rapidly evolved, from vanquishing the likes of Blockbuster home video to competing with, if not surpassing, the HBO/SHOWTIME premium incumbency that has dominated for nearly four decades. With 60 million subscribers in 130 countries, and growing rapidly, industry pundits suggest that "the traditional TV industry should be in panic mode" (McNab 2016). Amazon seeks to compete in the same category, launching premium, award-winning programming such as *Transparent* (2014–) and *Mozart in the Jungle* (2014–). Amazon and Netflix have emerged as platforms of destination for what was the former independent film market (Siegel 2016), and Apple is also planning to launch original content (Gutelle 2016). But these PGC strategies are essentially old wine in new bottles.

Moreover, a crucial distinction lies in the underlying value proposition of these platforms. Amazon's programs function as promotion, to sell memberships for its far more profitable e-commerce business. Similarly, Apple's iTunes, which is limited to transactional and syndicated distribution while avoiding the messiness of content promotion, fuels their core business of iProducts. In some respects, this is as it ever was. NBC was to RCA television sets as Disney has been to plush toys and theme parks, as Philco and Texaco was to broadcast, ad-supported television, and movie theatres are to popcorn and soft drinks. In the PGC part of the new screen ecology, media content and distribution operates as a means to an end for other higher margin industries interested in selling products to consumers more than storytelling for audiences.

Social media and the new scarcity

Social media entertainment is a fast-growing, global phenomenon based around advertising-supported online channels on video platforms coupled with social network affordances. No platform has secured greater global scale than YouTube, which is only a decade old, and now features over 1 billion users. Its competition is an ever-increasing proliferation of diverse platforms, including Vine, Instagram, Snapchat, Vimeo, Periscope and Vessel, rapidly securing global audiences in the millions. Combined, these platforms have challenged a century's worth of media scarcity, allowing users, distributed globally, access to not only watch but also upload virtually unlimited content. In fairness, historical scarcity was only ever artificial, namely through regulatory restraint and spectrum management by organisations such as the Federal Communications Commission (FCC) in the US, as outlined by Streeter (1996).

Despite this disruption within and proliferation of media distribution, the debate continues whether distribution or content operates as the primary driver of this new screen ecology. This tension can be seen in the rapidly evolving business strategies of the major platforms as they seek to disrupt traditional media incumbents. The premiere example is YouTube. To avoid crippling battles over intellectual property and piracy, YouTube instigated a state-of-the-art content management system that new players such as Facebook Video have been forced to emulate. To optimise their own income streams, YouTube introduced ad sales programmatics, an automated sales platform that was designed to circumvent media buyers and sales agents, offering advertisers direct access to highly coveted and precision-targeted audiences through the analytics of the platform.

As a consequence, YouTube alone generated ad sales revenue of nearly $9 billion in 2015, which is comparable to what all the US broadcasters generated in upfront revenue the same year, and 30 per cent more than Netflix generated through subscriptions (Ingham 2016). Nearly 40 per cent of YouTube's audience is watching music videos on channels and networks like record-label-owned Vevo, arguably developing as much programmatic co-dependency for the music industry as television has with film over the last century (Ingham 2016). Similarly, Facebook's video play, combined with Instagram and mobile advertising, helped to generate $5 billion in revenue in 2015, a leap of 50 per cent from the previous year (Kiss 2016). The industry last witnessed a similar feat when Google launched advertising in 2006. While media scarcity may have been eclipsed, premium advertising has its limits and these tech upstarts have co-opted the mainstream advertising industry as rapidly as they have Hollywood audiences.

Less well understood is that a significant portion of YouTube's revenue—typically 55/45 in favour of the partner—is also split with their 1 million "partners", including the professionalising-amateur creators who launched the nascent SME industry and who engage in content innovation that barely resembles Hollywood storytelling. We will now look more closely at these creators.

Social media entertainment and the online creator

The data that usually headline the scope of YouTube are well known: it has more than 1 billion users, 4 billion videos are watched per day, there are uploads of 400 hours per minute and 2.7M videos watched per minute, viewing now comes 50 per cent from mobile (Gutelle 2014; Relseo 2015; YouTube 2016). What is perhaps less well known is that more than 1 million YouTube creators now receive some level of remuneration from their uploaded content. 1500 YouTube channels have at least a million subscribers (to say nothing of the rest, as many of the most influential, breakout channels do not have a million subscribers and sometimes much less). And these creators are spread widely, albeit predominantly in the West.

These creators are professionalising, previously amateur, content creators using new entertainment and communicative formats, including vlogging, gameplay, how-to, sketch comedy and webisodic micronarrative, to develop significant followings that can extend across multiple platforms. The infrastructure of SME is comprised of diverse and competing platforms featuring online video players with social networking affordances, including YouTube, Facebook, Vine, Instagram, Snapchat, Vimeo and Vessel. These platforms have generated iterating business models that entrepreneurial content creators have harnessed to engage in content innovation that represents a radical break from the professional norms of cinema, broadcast television and even most cable television. This nascent media industry has emerged rapidly over the past few years to compete with and co-evolve alongside traditional media industries.

Based on our research, we know that the first wave of creator entrepreneurs almost all started out as hobbyists with little intention of developing any form of income, let alone a sustainable career. Each was simply filming their hobby or passion and uploading to YouTube (like YouTube's very first video, each now sees their first work as a terrible early version of their craft) "just for fun" or "to see what happened". All were surprised to note audience growth and engagement, and, inspired by this initial success, started to steadily increase their output. All tell the story of how, as their channels grew, their workloads grew and—through trial and error—their production quality and professionalisation improved, with incremental expansions to include better quality cameras, microphones, studio lighting, advanced editing programmes, more capable computers, and in one instance some professional training, and a work ethic that sees maintaining a community of engagement through various social media as an integral component of their "job".

The quite radical difference offered by the new screen ecology's provision of potential career opportunity, even celebrity status, through amateur hobbyism and personal expression cannot be gainsaid. This category of previously amateur, full-time professionalising content creators reverses the normative route through which media talent is filtered. YouTubers must be seen as a class of content creators who are able to exercise a higher level of control over their career prospects than any previous models of professionalising talent. The head of the digital division of a leading Hollywood talent agency commented in interview:

> A traditional film or television artist—a writer, a director, a performer—has spent a certain amount of their life preparing to be ready for when opportunity knocks [...] The mentality of a digital creator is the exact opposite. They're not preparing for an opportunity; they're creating it themselves.
>
> *(Weinstein 2015)*

The typical YouTube creator has had no or little specific training and few qualifications, but enters the YouTube revenue-sharing system with some degree of success already established and seemingly abundant clarity about their relationship with their "fan base". Assumptions about talent management services intent on moving clients from the "farm to the big league" are fraught with complication and viable for only a small subset of content creators. Traditional media has less value for these on-screen performers, who have never cultivated the core Hollywood skills of acting, screenwriting or directing. Only a small percentage of content creators recognise the value in working in Hollywood, whether for lack of adequate remuneration, control or time. For the more successful content creators, some of whom are earning six or seven figure sums from multiple revenue streams, traditional film and television fees can be uncompetitive. Other content creators are less willing to give up the virtually absolute control they have over their own work. Meanwhile, the time required to write or perform in traditional media, including protracted periods of development or simply waiting around on set for the lighting to change, can cost the creators valuable time spent creating their own proprietary content and fostering further engagement with their fans.

The rise of amateur content creators on new media platforms is not in itself new. Early amateur and non-profit radio operators emerged out of the basements of American households. The development of home movie cameras launched a generation of filmmakers in their backyards. Garage bands and punk rockers began their careers in small venues, playing to friends and family. But the analogy ends there. In the US, the amateur broadcasters were "brushed aside" by a federally imposed commercial system (Streeter 1996: 251). To guarantee audiences, the filmmakers were forced to enter the film festival circuit or the studio system to secure distribution. The musicians were inevitably forced to sign with record labels that controlled not only their distribution but also their destinies.

There is simply no comparison with these online creators—across multiple variables, not least of which is access to unlimited distribution across multiple platforms. In addition, the means of digital production affords not only low budget production but virtually no division of labour except at the top most tier of the ecology. The creator has replaced the writer, producer, director, actor above the line, as well as the editor, location scout, composer and visual effects supervisor below. In addition, through the entrepreneurial agency afforded by these platforms, a content creator can operate as their own ad sales representatives, securing partnerships with the platforms for split revenue.

More notably, creators can field direct inquiries from advertisers extending influencer marketing deals at significant CPMs. Gone in this ecology are the ad sales divisions of the television networks and the creative agencies and media buyers who crafted the thirty-second spots and bought the airtime. Ingrid Nilsen is a "glambassador" for cosmetics brand Covergirl, although she describes this partnership as providing a service to the brand that aligns with her own. In fact, as she noted in our interview, "I turn down brands all the time. I'm either not interested in the product or it doesn't fit with what I'm doing or I worked with them before and it didn't work out" (Nilsen 2015). And the agency and entrepreneurism extends well beyond the platforms and the content. Michele Phan parlayed her DIY makeup expertise from her YouTube channels into a lifestyles empire, including her Ipsy makeup subscription service valued at $84 million (Bowles 2014).

With personal agency unlike anything in traditional media labour, these entrepreneurs leave their day jobs, or in some instances, never held one, although admittedly for jobs that require operation around the clock. Ingrid Nilsen, who incubated her YouTube career in the bathroom of her Berkeley university dorm, mentioned, "Had I gone the traditional 9-to-5 route, I would have sat there with regrets. By then, I was already making more money than I would at an entry-level job" (Nilsen 2015). Contrast Nilsen's account with the average aspirant in Hollywood, an industry notorious for requiring years of underpaid dues-paying and apprenticeship in toxic and demanding positions.

Content innovation and the vlogger effect

Furthermore, these creator entrepreneurs are engaging in forms of content innovation that barely resemble that of legacy media. Prominent YouTube genres include game play, DIY/how-to videos, including subgenres such as "unboxing", and, most remarkably, the personality vlogger. This content reflects the networked affordances of social media that allow for intense fan engagement and participation. PewDiePie's game play featuring his crude and off-colour commentaries may reflect a cross between ESPN's Sports Centre and Daniel Tosh's US comedy show *Tosh.0* (2009–), but are equally grounded in the logics of interactive videogames. HGTV, Cooking, and the DIY Channel offer linear accounts of house hunting, food prep, and home renovation, but still require the production skills of a trained team of videographers, editors, makeup artists, and producers, not to mention the means of distribution afforded by cable. In contrast, the DIY subgenre of "unboxing" often features, in some instances, a pair of hands, or a voiceover performer, coupled with a musical score, while audiences in the billions watch as toys and electronics are opened and assembled. "Assembly required" has become as simple as a click and play.

The hard-to-define personality vlogger operates at the business and cultural centre of this new screen ecology. Perhaps there is a resemblance to the reality show persona, the talk show guest, or *America's Funniest Home Videos* (1990–). But this genre (or format) exhibits far closer affinity with online communication staples such as the blog and feature personalities sharing their quotidian experiences who now "own the world of YouTube" (Samuelson 2014). In contrast to the content creators in legacy media, these vloggers excel neither in storytelling nor what we have come to define as media "talent." As Barry Blumberg, a veteran Hollywood executive and Chief Content Officer for Defy Media who manages the Smosh comedy duo, noted, "there's a good mix of people who don't have talent but were there at the beginning of a platform" (Blumberg 2015). Furthermore, the opportunities for these vloggers in traditional media are limited, whether in casting as actors playing roles other than themselves, or writer–directors crafting and producing complex media narratives.

But the mistake in evaluating the content innovation with this new industry would be to limit the success of these creators in this genre to mere timing, luck or opportunism or define their talent solely against norms of traditional entertainment storytelling, production or performance. Rather, these creators have built a media brand on the basis of their personalities and through the mediated discourses of authenticity that vlogging provides. According to Byron Austin Ashley, talent manager for Big Frame:

> By human nature, people are interested about other people. That's why vlogging is as big as it is. I want to know: What is it like to have a brain tumour? What is it like to be gay? What is it like to be beautiful and review makeup? People will always be interested in other people if it's authentic.
>
> *(Ashley 2015)*

The mediated authenticity of online vlogging, the appeals to the "real", may be comparable to the rise of reality television were it not for the lack of mediators. No camera crews off screen and story editors in post contriving storylines only loosely inspired by the lives of the people on screen. This is commercialised, mediatised, agentic impression management (Goffman 1959). For these vloggers, YouTube is a stage, but they are more than mere performers. They sell the tickets.

Arguably, the capital backing of these new media platforms, coupled with the rise of creator talent engaging in content innovation, should share similar trajectories to other media platforms. Television programming has introduced audiences to unique formats and storytellers, from sitcoms to police procedurals, Rod Serling to Shonda Rhymes. Content innovation occurs regularly in mainstream media, especially with digital technologies, whether it be reality talent competitions or docusoaps. But one last element of this new screen ecology offers one more vital distinction from what audiences have witnessed before or rather, as Jay Rosen (2006) termed them, "the people formerly known as the audience".

The technological affordances of social media entertainment

This new screen ecology occupies a fundamentally convergent space between social media communication and entertainment content and is structured by a level of interactivity and viewer- and audience-centricity arguably without parallel in screen history. The history of the screen audience is one of higher and higher order claims about the industry's responsiveness to viewer behaviours, needs and wants. From William Goldman's "nobody knows anything" (Goldman 1983), to movie test focus groups, to TV viewing diaries, to ratings. Fully fledged academic communication theories have been given over to studying viewer "uses and gratifications". More recently these concerns have come under the aegis of audience and fan studies, stressing audience agency in decoding and using media messages and the deep commitments and creative engagements of fans in their co-creation of meaning with media producers (e.g. Jenkins 1992). Mainstream audience engagement has been preoccupied with creating the "water cooler effect" or "must watch TV" (the antecedents to "binge viewing"). In the present, the PGC component of the new screen ecology (streaming services Netflix, and its numerous national imitators, Amazon and premium brands such as HBO decoupled from cable packages) has tended to attract greater attention than the SME component because of its appeal to mainstream viewer demographics, essentially replacing linear broadcast mainstream entertainment options with à la carte options. Much has been made of the streaming services' new affordances for "binge viewing" and hyper targeting micro demographics (e.g. Anderson 2006). However, busting the tyranny of the linear schedule started decades ago with box sets, and the degree to which the newly dominant streaming services use big data to hyper-target viewer segments but engage in very little interactivity has given rise to critical concern over the power of the algorithm in contemporary entertainment (Hallinan and Striphas 2016).

In contrast, the SME business is a radical hybrid of entertainment and community development and maintenance: it is "communitainment." Subscriber/fan engagement is not only critical; it is what triggers the revenue-sharing business model that replaces IP control (we turn to this in the next section). We know from detailed interviews with numerous YouTube creators that managing YouTube feedback commentary and other social media accounts takes up the largest portion of the working week. Managing interaction across several social media accounts—vital for maintaining authenticity and maximising promotion—significantly extends their workload. As one fashion and lifestyle vlogger said:

> Having your followers and being on social media is something that is still there for the majority of every single day. I would say that there is probably 2 to 3 hours a day, apart from sleeping, when we are not actually on social media. And that's a good day.
> *(Anderson 2015)*

The social networking practice of community-building represents far more than the development of fandom and celebrity that legacy media has perfected over the past century. The direct interaction between creator and community is precedential. Beyond the fan selfie on the red carpet, when is the last time a Hollywood star engaged directly with their audience? These mediated interactions ought to be distinguished from traditional media fandom or media consumers. Baym (2010) alludes to these distinctions as "networked communities" or "networked individualism" and insists that we must understand these "capabilities" if we are to understand the consequences. The monetisation of these fan engagement practices contributes one further challenge for screen studies scholarship.

Qualitatively different global reach, IP dynamics and monetisation strategy

YouTube's scale and scope, as we have seen, are impressive. Additionally, it is notable that 80 per cent of YouTube traffic comes from outside the US, and 60 per cent of creators' views come from outside their home country (YouTube Creator Blog 2015; YouTube 2016). YouTube operates a corporate presence in eighty-five countries and in seventy-six languages, but it is accessed for uploading and viewing in most of the world, even while it is blocked in China and North Korea, and often blocked in many countries of the Middle East.

Media globalisation has been an enduring topic in film and media studies. Frequently centred on questions of US "cultural imperialism" through widespread dissemination and popularity of its film and television output, debates of long-established vintage have been staged, for example, around whether global television traffic is a "one-way street" (Nordenstreng and Varis 1974) or a "patchwork quilt" (Tracey 1988). However, it is possible to posit a qualitatively new wave of media globalisation based on the global availability and uptake of YouTube that is relatively frictionless compared to national broadcasting, systems of film and DVD release and licensing by "windowed" territory (Cunningham 2015). And compared to film and television, there is very little imposed content regulation (apart from substantial self-regulation) on major platforms such as Google/YouTube and Facebook, some of the world's largest information and communication companies, as their use as content distributors proliferates globally.

For the major PGC streaming services such as Netflix, aggressive global expansion (having reached 130 countries to 2015) requires it to negotiate with pre-existing rights holders in each new territory and often requires it to close down informal means of accessing its popular content such as VPN workarounds in such territories. While, longer term, the streaming giants may well drive territorial licensing to the wall, SME content is largely "born global". This is because this massively growing content industry, in stark contrast to content industries in general and Hollywood and broadcast television in particular, is not primarily based on IP control. YouTube elected to avoid the messy and legally cumbersome traditional media model of owned or shared IP. YouTube also avoided paying fees for content as well as offering backend residual or profit participation. Rather, YouTube entered into "partnership agreements" with their content creators based on a split of advertising revenue from first dollar. This strategy has proven effective. In the eight years since the partner plan launched, YouTube has secured over 1 million YouTube partners worldwide.

Figure 38.2 The Millennials' Mills of Mumbai. Once the centre of India's cotton trade, factories in the old industrial district have been turned into spaces for digital content production. ©Stuart Cunningham and David Craig.

YouTube talks of being primarily a facilitator of creator and content in the many international markets in which it operates. The key difference between traditional media operating multinationally and YouTube is that the former produces, owns or licences content for distribution, exhibition or sale in multiple territories, while the latter seeks (for clear reasons we come to momentarily) to avoid the conflation of YouTubers as the IP creators with YouTube as "platform" and "middleman" operating to facilitate linking of brands and advertisers with YouTube creators and multi-channel networks.

There are significant reasons for YouTube not taking an IP ownership position, which have to do with its continued status as a platform or online service provider rather than a content company. The US Digital Millennium Copyright Act 1998, in addition to criminalising circumvention measures and heightening the penalties for copyright infringement on the Internet, created "safe harbour" provisions for online service providers (OSPs, including ISPs) against copyright infringement liability, provided they responsively block access to alleged infringing material on receipt of infringement claims from a rights holder.

YouTube's lack of conventional IP control has not inhibited its monetisation strategies. YouTube's (and increasingly other platforms') monetisation strategies have exposed the faltering co-dependency between media and advertising, reflecting the inefficiencies of traditional media advertising while highlighting the affordances and targeted efficacy of online analytics. Social media platforms, including YouTube and Facebook, are leaders in the use of programmatic advertising—the automation of ad buying and placement through the deployment of big data analytics. This enables them to generate great efficiencies in matching advertising to digital content as content travels virtually seamlessly across borders and regions.

Looking forward

Peering into the future, how might this emerging global screen ecology of social media entertainment consolidate? There is nothing unitary about the challenge to established screen industries of the new digital platforms. These platforms are competing as much against each other as they are posing challenges to established screen media industries. There are clear dividing lines between platforms committed to professional content and competing directly against cable and broadcast (Netflix, Amazon) and those that, though iterating content strategies and monetising through advertising, remain firmly on the social media side of social media entertainment (Facebook, Vine, Snapchat, Instagram). YouTube sits somewhere in the middle. More intense competition with diverging business models among these platforms may see a destructive fragmentation of the new screen ecology.

There are historical precedents and some impetus for the gradual assimilation of this new screen ecology into mainstream protocol and practice, but there is more evidence to suggest it may grow in parallel with, and as a continuing challenge to, the more traditional, established modes of professional screen industrial practice. With the proliferation of new screen platforms capable of luring away traditional media advertising, there is less incentive for the new screen players to transition to the mainstream. Rather, having carved out their own media brands, through unique audience-centric practices and content innovation, the social media creator is a wizard of a parallel screen ecology. We're not in Hollywood anymore, Dorothy.

References

Anderson, C. (2006) *The Long Tail: Why the Future of Business Is Selling Less of More*, New York: Hyperion.

Anderson, R. (Rachellea, www.youtube.com/user/justsugarandspice) (2015) Interview by Stuart Cunningham, February.

Ashley, B. A. (Senior Talent Manager, Big Frame) (2015) Interview by David Craig, 11 June.

Baym, N. (2010) *Personal Connections in the Digital Age*, London: Polity Press.

Blumberg, B. (Chief Content Officer, Defy Media) (2015) Interview by Stuart Cunningham and David Craig, 13 May.

Bowles, N. (2014) "Michelle Phan: From YouTube Star to $84 Million Startup Founder", *Recode.net*, 27 October, http://recode.net/2014/10/27/michelle-phan-youtube-star-to-startup-founder/.

Brouwer, B. (2015) "Digital Advertising Will Overtake TV Ad Spend Globally by 2017, In the U.S. by 2016", *Tubefilter*, www.tubefilter.com/2015/12/07/digital-advertising-will-take-over-tv-ad-spend-globally-by-2017-in-the-u-s-by-2016/.

Cunningham, S. (2015) "The New Screen Ecology: A New Wave of Media Globalisation?" *Communication Research and Practice*, 1 (3): 275–282.

Cunningham, S. and Silver, J. (2013) *Screen Distribution and the New King Kongs of the Online World*, Basingstoke: Palgrave.

Cunningham, S., Flew, T. and Swift, A. (2015) *Media Economics*, London: Palgrave.

Goffman, E. (1959) *The Presentation of Self in Everyday Life*, New York: Anchor.

Goldman, W. (1983) *Adventures in the Screen Trade*, New York: Warner Books.

Gutelle, S. (2014) "YouTube Reportedly Brings in $10,654 Per Minute", *Tubefilter*, 2 July, www.tubefilter.com/2014/07/02/infographic-youtube-minute-downloader-blog/.

—— (2016) "Apple Could Launch Original Content in Tandem With iPhone 7", *Tubefilter*, 29 January, www.tubefilter.com/2016/01/29/apple-original-content-iphone7/.

Hallinan, B. and Striphas, T. (2016) "The Netflix Prize and the Production of Algorithmic Culture", *New Media & Society* 18 (1): 117–137.

Holt, J. and Sanson, K. (eds) (2013) *Connected Viewing: Selling, Streaming, & Sharing Media in the Digital Era*, New York and London: Routledge.

Ingham, T. (2016) "YouTube Earnt $9bn in Revenue Last Year, Towering over Spotify", *MusicBusinessWorldWorldwide.com*, 5 January, www.musicbusinessworldwide.com/youtube-will-earn-9bn-in-revenue-this-year-towering-over-spotify/.

Jenkins, H. (1992) *Textual Poachers: Television Fans & Participatory Culture: Studies in Culture and Communication*, New York: Routledge.

Kiss, J. (2016) "Facebook's Quarterly Earnings Surpass $5b for the First Time Thanks to Ad Sales", *The Guardian*, 27 January, www.theguardian.com/technology/2016/jan/27/facebook-fourth-quarter-earnings-ad-revenue.

McNab, J. (2016) "Netflix Is on F***ing Fire", *Medium*, 3 January, https://medium.com/swlh/netflix-is-on-f-ing-fire-1675d47e722-.eqq0xp250.

Nilsen, I. (missglamorazzi: www.youtube.com/user/missglamorazzi) (2015) Interview by David Craig, 22 September.

Nordenstreng, K. and Varis, T. (1974) "Television Traffic: a One-way Street", *UNESCO Reports and Papers on Mass Communication No. 70*, UNESCO, Paris.

Relseo (2015) "500 Hours of Video Uploaded to YouTube Every Minute", www.reelseo.com/hours-minute-uploaded-youtube/.

Rosen, J. (2006) "The People Formerly Known as the Audience", *Press Think*, 27 June, http://archive.pressthink.org/2006/06/27/ppl_frmr.html.

Samuelson, K. (2014) "25 Vloggers under 25 Who Are Owning YouTube", *Huffington Post*, 26 October, www.huffingtonpost.co.uk/2014/12/17/25-vloggers-under-25-who-are-owning-the-world-of-youtube_n_6340280.html.

Siegel, T. (2016) "Sundance: How Amazon, Netflix Turned the Market on Its Head", *The Hollywood Reporter*, 27 January, www.hollywoodreporter.com/news/sundance-how-amazon-netflix-turned-859372.

Strangler, D. and Arbesman, S. (2012) "What Does Fortune 500 Turnover Mean?" *Ewing Marion Kauffman Foundation*, June, www.kauffman.org/what-we-do/research/2012/06/what-does-fortune-500-turnover-mean.

Streeter, T. (1996) *Selling the Air: A Critique of the Policy of Commercial Broadcasting in the United States*, Chicago, IL: University of Chicago Press.

Tracey, M. (1988) "Popular Culture and the Economics of Global Television", *Intermedia*, 16 (2): 19–25.

Weinstein, B. (Head of Digital Media, United Talent Agency) (2015) Interview by Stuart Cunningham and David Craig, 13 May.

YouTube (2016) "Statistics", www.youtube.com/yt/press/statistics.html.

YouTube Creator Blog (2015) "Found in Translation: Language Tools for Building a Global Audience", http://youtubecreator.blogspot.com.au/2015/11/found-in-translation-language-tools-for.html.

39

REMAPPING WORLD CINEMA THROUGH AUDIENCE RESEARCH[1]

Huw D. Jones

Introduction

This chapter explores how audience research can enhance our understanding of World Cinema. It focuses in particular on the insights that can be drawn from box-office figures, audience surveys and focus groups. I will use these methods to examine how contemporary European audiences engage with films from around the world, though the methods can of course be applied to other contexts. The research itself comes out of the *Mediating Cultural Encounters through European Screens* (MeCETES) project, a three-year collaborative research project that examined the funding, production, distribution, reception and policy circumstances that enable European films and television dramas to be made and to circulate within contemporary Europe (www.mecetes.co.uk/).

The term "World Cinema" traditionally refers to "non-Hollywood cinema". However, as Nagib suggests (2006: 30), "[this] unwittingly sanctions the American way of looking at the world, according to which Hollywood is the centre and all other cinemas are the periphery". "The result", Nagib (2006: 31) argues, "is that other cinemas of the world are of interest insofar as they adopt 'a different aesthetic model of filmmaking from Hollywood'". As a way of "escaping the binary" between Hollywood and non-Hollywood film, Nagib (2006: 35) redefines World Cinema as "circulation" and suggests we should map the "interconnections" between filmmakers and cinematic movements operating in different parts of the globe. As an example, she notes how the New German Cinema of the 1960s and 1970s "re-elaborated elements of the Brazilian *cinema novo*" (Nagib 2011: 2).

Despite this shift in the way World Cinema is defined, much research in the field remains focused on the critical analysis of film texts and the contexts in which they are produced. Attention may have shifted to the transnational interconnections between films and their makers (e.g. Dennison and Lim 2006; Cooke 2013; Nagib *et al.* 2012), but few have considered how audiences engage with the global circulation of films.

This chapter addresses this gap. Drawing on box-office figures, audience surveys and focus groups, I examine how many Europeans actually watch films from other parts of the world, who these films appeal to and why, and how they are interpreted by audiences in different European countries. Because of the context in which the research was conducted, I pay particular attention to how audiences engage with "non-national European films"—that is to say, films primarily produced in one European country but consumed in another. However, I also touch on the audiences for films from other parts of the world, including the US.

Audience research is by no means new. While more developed in the field of television studies, a growing body of literature on film audiences has nevertheless emerged since the 1980s (see Gripsrud 2000). Research has particularly focused on the history of exhibition spaces, practices of cinema-going, and the social composition of audiences during the early period of cinema (from the 1890s to the 1960s), drawing on archival material and oral histories (e.g. Stokes and Maltby 1999; Biltereyst, Maltby and Meers 2012). However, as Gripsrud notes, "Present-day, actual film audiences get very little attention" (2000: 206). There is a notable lack of comparative research on how audiences in different countries engage with contemporary films, although Mathijs and Barker's 2008 international survey on the cross-national reception of *The Lord of the Rings* (2001–3, Peter Jackson, New Zealand/USA/Germany) is an important exception. Moreover, few film researchers have got to grips with the tools (e.g. web-scraping or data mining) for collecting and analysing the huge amount of audience data becoming available online. This chapter goes some way to addressing these concerns. As well as examining how contemporary Europeans engage with films from around the world, I discuss key sources of audience data and what these can reveal. I also note some of the limitations of this data. Audience research can certainly enhance our understanding of World Cinema, but like all approaches to film analysis, evidence still needs to be read with a critical eye.

Box-office figures: how many people watch World Cinema?

Admissions or box-office figures provide an indication of how many people actually watch a particular film or type of film (e.g. genre or nationality) in the cinema based on ticket sales. Commercial firms such as comScore (formerly Rentrak) produce very detailed box-office figures, but these can be expensive to obtain. Nevertheless, there is a considerable amount of open data available online. Trade papers such as *Variety* and *Screen International* publish weekly headline figures (e.g. Top 20 films in the UK), while websites such as Box Office Mojo (www.boxofficemojo.com) and The Numbers (www.the-numbers.com) provide extensive box-office data for particular titles and territories, albeit in terms of box-office revenue rather than admissions. Most national film agencies also annually publish headline figures for their territory. The British Film Institute's (BFI) *Statistical Yearbook*, for example, lists the Top 20 films in the UK, the Top 20 British films, the Top 20 UK independent films and the Top 10 non-English-language films, along with a wealth of other useful admissions data (http://www.bfi.org.uk/education-research/film-industry-statistics-research/statistical-yearbook). The Motion Picture Association of American's (MPAA) *Theatrical Market Statistics* and European Audiovisual Observatory's *Focus: World Film Market Trends* provide similar data for the US and European markets respectively.

A particularly useful open source of primary data is the European Audiovisual Observatory's LUMIERE database (www.lumiere.obs.coe.int/web/search/). This provides cinema admissions figures for films released in Europe since 1996, including their total EU ticket sales and audience numbers within thirty-six European countries and the US. The Observatory has also recently launched LUMIERE PRO, which for a fee (€1,500 for European territories and €3,000 for selected territories worldwide), allows non-profit research organisations to download cinema admissions for particular countries, so they can produce their own analysis of admissions trends.

The MeCETES project has used LUMIERE PRO admissions figures, combined with data (e.g. the film's language(s), genre(s) and location(s) of production) harvested via "web scraping" from sources such as the Internet Movie Database (IMDb), to examine how films from particular countries or regions of the globe perform in European cinemas. Although somewhat reductive in the sense that each film is assigned a single nationality based on the country that "provided the majority financial investment in the production" (European Audiovisual Observatory 2006), this nevertheless allows us to map in general terms in the transnational circulation and reception of films in contemporary Europe.

Analysis of the period 2004–2014 shows that just under 1 billion cinema tickets are sold in Europe (defined as EU and EFTA member states) each year—meaning the average European visits the cinema about twice per year. Icelanders are the most frequent cinemagoers (with 4.9 cinema visits per year), followed by the Irish (3.7 visits), the French (3.1 visits) and the British (2.7 visits). Romanians (0.3 visits), Bulgarians (0.5 visits) and Slovakians (0.6 visits) are the least frequent cinemagoers. Richer countries in Western Europe tend to have higher cinema admissions per head of population than the poorer countries of Central and Eastern Europe.

On average, two-thirds (65 per cent) of the films seen by European cinemagoers are primarily American in origin. National films (e.g. a French film consumed in France) account for one fifth (21 per cent) of admissions, while non-national European films (e.g. a French films consumed in Germany) represent just over a tenth (12 per cent) of admissions. Films from the Rest of the World (i.e. films primarily produced in Africa, Asia, Australasia and Latin America) account for only 2 per cent of admissions.

These market shares vary from country-to-country (Figure 39.1). Admissions for US films tends to be highest in small countries with a weak national film industry (e.g. Romania, Iceland, Bulgaria) and lowest in large countries where the domestic film industry is strong (e.g. France, Italy, Poland). Admissions for non-national European film are highest in small countries that not only have a weak national film industry, but also share a common language with a larger neighbour. For example, French films account for a large proportion of the non-national European films seen in Belgium, Luxembourg and Switzerland. The countries with the highest admissions for films from the Rest of the World also tend to be small producing nations with close cultural ties to a larger neighbour. The Baltic states, for example, consume a high proportion of Russian films due to their large numbers of Russian speakers. With the exception of heavily-marketed American and US-studio backed films, audiences are generally drawn to films from countries to which they share a close "cultural proximity" (Straubhaar 1991).

Most of the cinema tickets sold in Europe are concentrated on a small number of films. In 2012, for example, there were 2,001 films released in Europe, but the top 100 titles (5 per cent of film releases) accounted for 78 per cent of European cinema admissions. Of these top titles, 64 per cent were American (in most cases produced by major Hollywood studios), 14 per cent were French, 9 per cent were British and 11 per cent came from other European countries. These include a number of European titles that were only successful in their own domestic market (e.g. Italy's *Benvenuti al Sud* [Welcome to the South, 2010, Luca Miniero]; or Spain's *Tengo ganas de ti* [I Want You, 2012, Fernando González Molina]). Only two titles—the Canadian/Spanish horror *Mama* (2013, Andrés Muschietti) and the South African children's animation *Zambezia* (2012, Wayne Thornley)—came from the Rest of the World. However, at least twelve of the top 100 titles (e.g. *The Impossible*, 2012, Spain/USA, J. A. Bayona; *Argo*, 2012, USA, Ben Affleck) were filmed outside Europe and North American (even though such films tend to view these places through Western eyes). Eighty-one per cent of the top 100 titles were primarily shot in English (though not necessarily screened in English—France, Germany, Italy and Spain tend to dub foreign-language films). These include not only American and British films, but also some German (e.g. *Cloud Atlas*, 2012, USA/Germany, Lana Wachowski, Tom Tykwer, Lilly Wachowski), French (e.g. *Taken 2*, 2012, France, Olivier Megaton) and Spanish productions (e.g. *The Impossible*). Only two of the top 100 titles were primarily produced in a non-hegemonic European language: the Danish-language thriller *Jagten* (The Hunt, Thomas

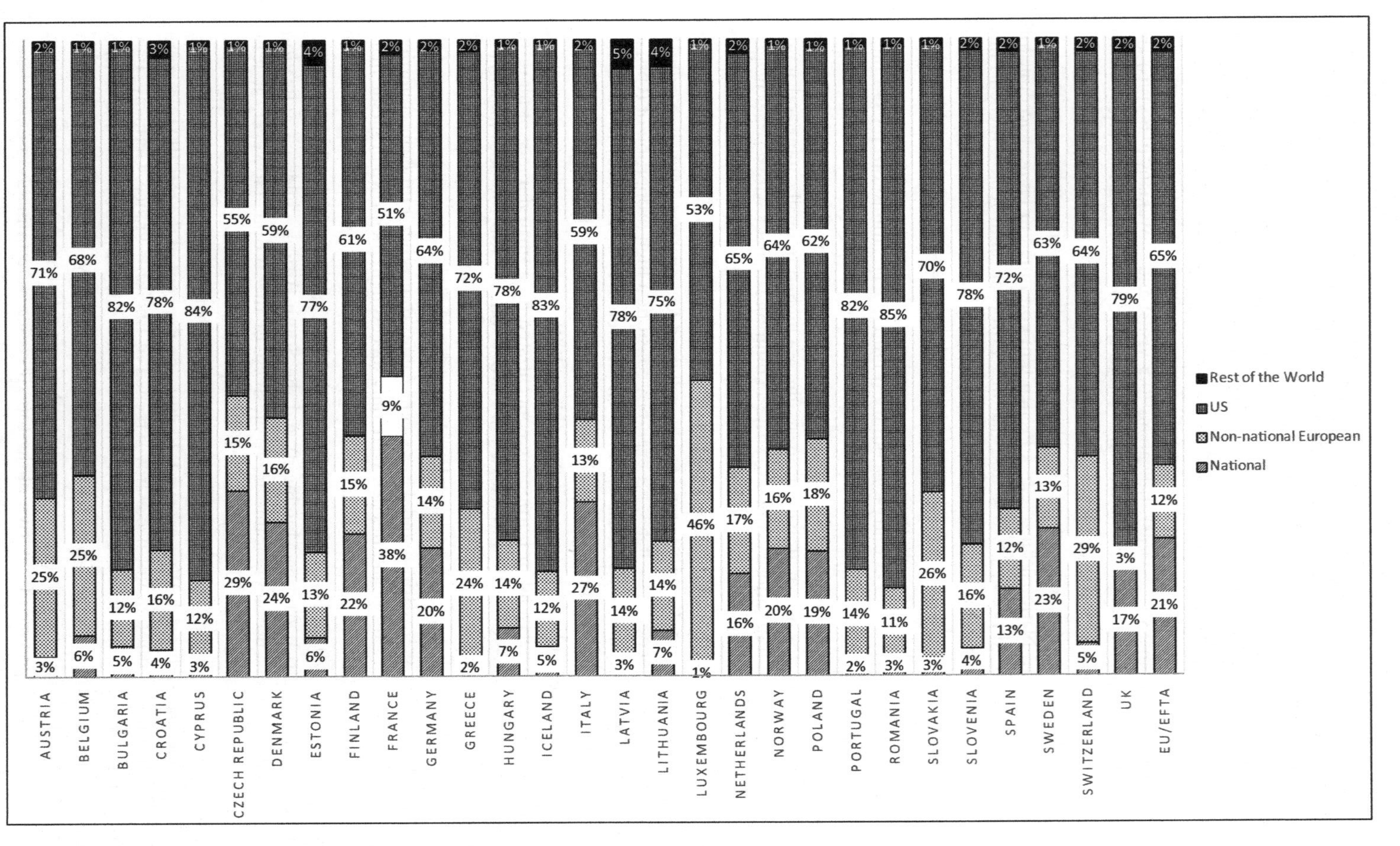

Figure 39.1 Box office market shares by film's country-of-origin, 2004–2014.

Source: MeCETES/LUMIERE Pro.

Vinterberg, 2012) and the Finnish children's animation *Nikko 2* (2012, Finland/Denmark/Germany/Ireland, Kari Juusonen, Jorgen Lerdam). Nevertheless, two-thirds of the top 100 titles feature more than one language, including elements of Arabic (*Zero Dark Thirty*, 2013, USA, Kathryn Bigelow), Japanese (*Life of Pi*, 2012, USA, Ang Lee), Hindi (*The Best Exotic Marigold Hotel*, 2012, UK/USA/United Arab Emirates, John Madden), Thai (*The Impossible*), Swahili (*Un plan parfait* [A Perfect Plan, 2012, France, Pascal Chaumeil]) and Scottish Gaelic (*Prometheus*, 2012, USA/UK, Ridley Scott).

In terms of genre, about a third of the top 100 titles of 2012 were action-adventure blockbusters (e.g. *Skyfall*, 2012, UK/USA, Sam Mendes; *The Dark Knight Rises*, 2012, UK/USA, Christopher Nolan). Just over a quarter were comedies (e.g. *Ted*, 2012, USA, Seth MacFarlane; *The Dictator*, 2012, USA, Larry Charles), a fifth were dramas of various types including crime, history and biography (e.g. *The Impossible; Lincoln*, 2012, USA, India, Steven Spielberg) and just under a fifth were family films and animations (e.g. *Brave*, 2012, USA, Mark Andrews, Brenda Chapman; *Wreck-It Ralph*, 2012, USA, Rich Moore). A small number of horror films (e.g. *Mama; Sinister*, 2012, USA/UK, Scott Derrickson) make up the remainder. None of the top 100 titles were documentaries. The cultural range of films actually consumed by European cinemagoers is therefore quite limited. Most Europeans watch American movies or, to a lesser extent, films from their own country. While some popular US or European titles do feature cultural elements from other parts of the world, there is little engagement with films that actually originate from Asia, Africa, Latin America or even other parts of Europe. At the same time, the audience for non-Hollywood film is not insignificant. Even though, for example, only 2 per cent of cinema admissions in Europe are for films from the Rest of the World, this still represents about 20 million cinemagoers per year.

Furthermore, LUMIERE admissions data says nothing about the audience for films outside the cinema. Most Europeans watch films on television, and an increasing number are also viewing films via video-on-demand (VOD) platforms, such as Netflix or Amazon Video, or through illegal streaming or torrent websites. Such platforms potentially make it easier for audiences to access films from any part of the world. Obtaining audience data for TV, DVD and VOD is difficult. Commercial firms such as the French-based market research company Mediametrie do collect television viewing figures for films broadcast in Europe, but these data are expensive to obtain, and strict licensing agreements mean the results cannot always be shared. Viewing figures for VOD platforms or illegal streaming sites are even more inaccessible. Because sites such as Netflix are paid for by subscription rather than commercials, they are under no pressure to publish viewing figures to attract advertisers.

Some headline figures for films broadcast on television are available in certain territories. The BFI's *Statistical Reports*, for example, publishes the year's Top 10 films broadcast on UK television. Analysis of these data further underlines the dominance of US films in the UK. In 2015, for example, the most-watched film screening on terrestrial television was the Disney animation *Brave* with 6.1 million viewers (BFI 2016: 3). The top independent UK film was *Quartet* (2012, UK, Dustin Hoffman) with 2.7 million viewers, while the top non-English-language title was the French-language biopic *La Vie en Rose* (2007, France/UK/Czech Republic, Olivier Dahan) with only 179,300 viewers. Over the past decade, only five non-English-language films—*Der Untergang* (Downfall, 2004, Germany/Austria/Italy, Oliver Hirschbiegel) *Shi mian mai fu* (House of Flying Daggers, 2004, China/Hong Kong, Yimou Zhang), *El laberinto del fauno* (Pan's Labyrinth, 2006, Spain/Mexico/USA, Guillermo del Toro), *Hung fan kui* (Rumble in the Bronx, 1995, Hong Kong, Stanley Tong) and *Män som hatar kvinnor* (The Girl with the Dragon Tattoo, 2009, Sweden/Denmark/Germany/Norway, Niels Arden Oplev)—have secured more than one million viewers on UK television.

There are also some reports on the range of films available on television and online in Europe. The European Audiovisual Observatory's *Fiction on European TV channels 2006–13* report, for example, notes that in terms of airtime, 9 per cent of the feature films broadcast on television in Europe in 2013 were national in origin, 30 per cent were non-national European and 62 per cent were from the US and the Rest of the World (Lange 2014). This suggests that non-national European films (particularly co-productions) are regularly broadcast on television in Europe. However, there is no data on how many viewers actually watch these films.

The Observatory's *Origin of Films in VOD Catalogues in the EU* report for the European Audiovisual Observatory likewise provides an indication of the range of films available online (Ene and Grece 2015). Based on the analysis of 75 VOD catalogues, it found that 27 per cent of films offered on VOD in the EU are (national and non-national) European productions, compared with 59 per cent for US films and 14 per cent for the Rest of the World. This indicates that on-demand services in Europe do provide a diverse range of films from around the world, though again, it remains to be seen how many Europeans actually watch films from foreign countries other than the US.

Audience surveys: who does World Cinema appeal to and why?

Another way of identifying what films audiences actually watch is through audience surveys. Although expensive and challenging to conduct from scratch, there is a substantial amount of primary and secondary data openly available online for researchers to make use of. Perhaps the most relevant in a European context is the European Commission's *Profile of Current and Future Audiovisual Audiences* (2014), which polled almost 5,000 Europeans in ten EU countries. The survey found that, across all media platforms, 58 per cent had seen "many" US films in the last year (Figure 39.2). By comparison, 20 per cent had seen "many" national films, while 14 per cent had seen "many" non-national European titles. Only 5 per cent had seen "many" films from the Rest of the World. The survey also found that "Blockbuster films with star cast, big budget [and] visual effects" were the most popular type of film (38 per cent had seen "many" in the last year), while "Foreign language films excluding US films" (11 per cent) and "Independent or 'indie' films, typically made with smaller budgets" (5 per cent) were the least popular types of film.

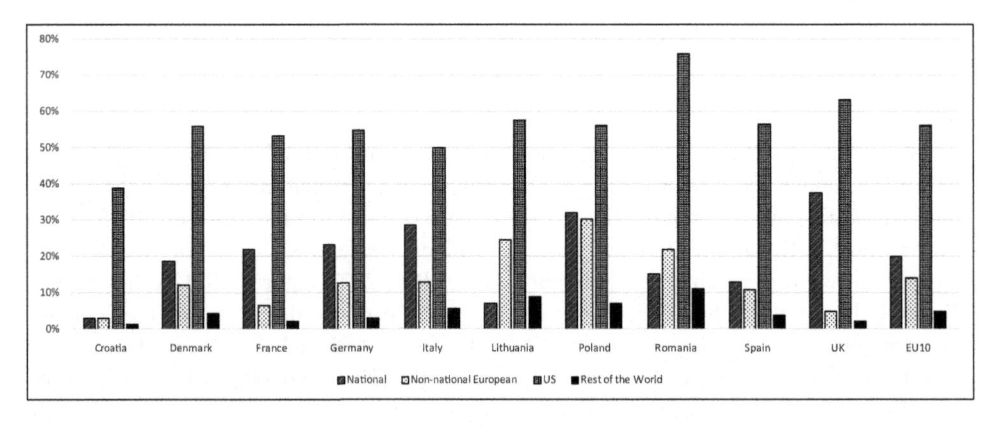

Figure 39.2 Film consumers who say they have seen "many" films in the last few months on any platform by films' country-of-origin.

Source: European Commission 2014.

Such findings should be treated with caution. The terms "European film" and "many" are open to interpretation. Some respondents may perceive a French-language auteur drama such as *Amour* (2012, Austria/France/Germany, Michael Haneke) to be a "European" film, but not necessarily an English-language Hollywood-style blockbuster such as the French-made *Taken 2*. For some, "many" might mean watching two or three titles, while for others it might mean five or more. Nevertheless, the report confirms the dominance of US blockbusters in Europe and the fact that only a minority of Europeans engage with films from other European countries and the Rest of the World. The report also provides some concrete figures for the films that Europeans have actually seen, like or are aware of. The US film titles tested in the survey were typically seen by 30–50 per cent of respondents, with extremely high awareness for big franchises such as *The Hobbit* (2012–2014, USA/New Zealand, Peter Jackson: 90 per cent awareness) or *The Twilight Saga* (2009–, USA: 91 per cent awareness). By comparison, the European films included were typically seen by 10–15 per cent of respondents. Nevertheless, some European films were very well known; 76 per cent of Europeans polled, for example, were aware of the French comedy-drama *Intouchables* (The Intouchables, 2011, France, Olivier Nakache, Eric Toledano); 38 per cent said they had seen this film and 36 per cent said they liked it. If we assume these figures are representative of the EU population, then potentially 386 million Europeans are aware of *The Intouchables*, while 194 million have seen it across all media platforms (including 44 million at the cinema).

Audiences surveys not only provide an indication of how many people actually watch films from around the world, but also who these films appeal to and why. The aforementioned European Commission report, for example, found that the 14 per cent of Europeans who have seen "many" non-national European films in the last few months "tend to be younger, more often women living in medium cities, with low revenue, high education, good [media] equipment, heavy media viewing and easier access to theatres" (European Commission 2014: 109). These so-called "Europhiles" were also found to be heavier film consumers than the population as a whole and more likely to define themselves as "film fans".

Like most film consumers, Europhiles primarily watch films "for entertainment and to have fun", but they are also more likely than others to watch films to "discover and learn about people and cultures" or to "experience strong feelings and emotions" (European Commission 2014: 117). Their criteria for choosing films is primarily determined by the film's story (theme, plot, character, setting) or genre (comedy, drama, etc.) and less by the film's nationality or the awards it has won (Figure 39.3). However, in comparison to mainstream film consumers, they tend to prefer more "serious" types of films, such as drama, documentary, current affairs and history, and watch fewer films with strong visual effects, such as action, adventure and fantasy (European Commission 2014: 117–118).

The report suggests the main reason why non-national European films are less popular than US films in Europe is due to distribution and promotion. Only a third of Europeans, for example, agree that non-national European films are "well promoted" or "sufficiently available in my area" (European Commission 2014: 163). However, these films also have perceived flaws in terms of their content. While many agreed non-national European films can be "original and thought-provoking" and "less stereotypical than US films", they also see them as "too dark", "slowed-paced" and "too focused on social issues", without "clear plots, [that are] easy to follow" (European Commission 2014: 163). Such views were found to be broadly similar across all the EU countries surveyed.

However, it is important to keep in mind that "non-national European film" covers a diversity of genres, nationalities and subject matters that may appeal to different audiences for very different reasons. As such, it is also important to consider the audience for particular film titles.

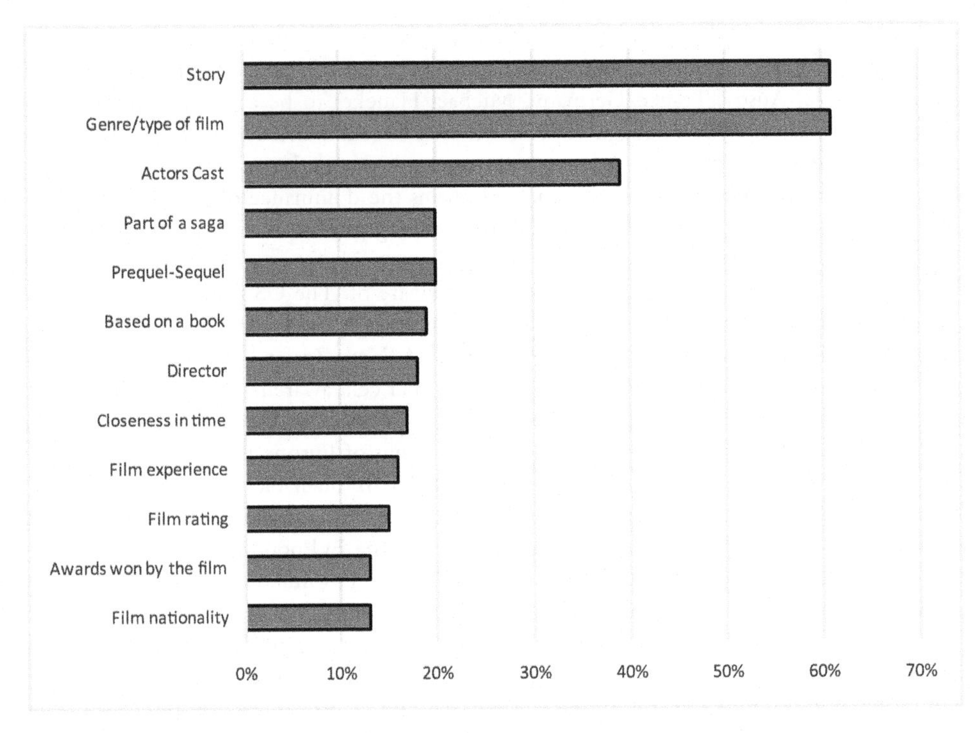

Figure 39.3 Criteria which Europhiles say is "very important" when choosing films.
Source: European Commission 2014.

Although survey data of this kind is harder to come by, some useful sources are available online. The BFI website, for example, contains cinema exit polls for over 170 "specialised" films (i.e. UK independent, foreign-language, arthouse, documentary and classics) released in the UK with BFI support since 2004. The amount of social demographic data is fairly basic (age and gender only) and not always consistent (some polls, for example ask if respondents are aged 35 or over while others if they are 25 or over), but they do provide some indication of film preference by age and gender. Analysis of these data suggests the non-national European film most likely to appeal to female audiences was *Coco avant Chanel* (Coco Before Chanel, 2009, France/Belgium, Anne Fontaine), following by *Coco Chanel & Igor Stravinsky* (2009, France/Japan/Switzerland, Jan Kounen) and *En kongelig affære* (A Royal Affair, 2012, Denmark/Sweden/Czech Republic/Germany, Nikolaj Arcel) (all notably romantic costume dramas with strong female leads), while the one most likely to appeal to male audiences was the crime thriller *Pusher* (2012, UK, Luis Prieto), followed by the war drama *Days of Glory* (2006, Algeria/France/Morocco/Belgium, Rachid Bouchareb) and the fantasy horror *Trolljegeren* (Trollhunter, Norway, André Øvredal, 2010) (all films with very macho, violent or scary subject matter).

The polls also reveal what attracted audiences to the film (the so-called "bait to attendance"). Analysis confirms that the most common bait to attendance for non-national European films is "the story", followed by "genre/type or film" and "reviews", while the least common is for the film to be "shown at a festival" or "nominated/received an award". However, there are some exceptions. In the case of films directed by Pedro Almodóvar (e.g. *Volver*, Spain, 2006; *Los abrazos rotos* [Broken Embraces, 2009, Spain]; *La piel que habito* [The Skin I Live In, Spain, 2011]) or

Lars Von Tier (*Nymphomaniac*, 2013, Denmark/Belgium/France/Germany), "the director" is the main bait to attendance. Similarly, for films based on best-selling books (e.g. *The Girl with the Dragon Tattoo*) or that focus on lives of well-known historical figures or events (e.g. *Coco Before Chanel*) "source material" and "subject matter" respectively are the main baits to attendance.

The website YouGov Profiles (www.yougov.co.uk/profileslite#/) provides some more detailed demographic data for film audiences in Germany, the US and the UK. Analysis of the British consumer profiles for twenty-one recent non-national European films confirms these films tend to appeal to an audience that is relatively young (25–39), metropolitan (London), professional middle-class (social grade AB) and liberal or left-wing in terms of political outlook. But again there are some exceptions. Pedro Almodovar's *Volver* and *Girl with the Dragon Tattoo*, for example, appealed to a much older audience, while the horror films *Låt den rätte komma in* (Let the Right One In, 2008, Sweden, Tomas Alfredson) and *Troll Hunter* appealed to a more working-class (C3DE) non-metropolitan audience. For certain well-known films (e.g. *Skyfall*) it is possible to compare the British demographic profiles with those in Germany and the US. However, data on more specialised titles are limited, and the samples are often too small to draw any firm conclusions.

Focus groups: what do audiences think about World Cinema?

While audience surveys can be used to identify broad trends among a representative sample of the population, they do not go into detail about what audiences actually think about specific films. Surveys normally only allow respondents to choose from a limited number of answers, and they do not give much scope for adding their own thoughts and opinions. Nor do they allow researchers to ask follow-up questions to clarify or expand upon responses. Focus groups are one way of obtaining more detailed responses from audiences. They typically involve between four and seven participants and may be socially mixed (to represent a range of different views and backgrounds) or more homogenous (to focus on a specific social group). One of the advantages of focus groups is that they allow researchers to gather a range of different perspectives in a relatively short period of time. However, there is a danger the discussion becomes dominated by one individual or goes off topic (making it hard to compare findings across focus groups). They can also be difficult to arrange, particularly in terms of recruiting participants.

The MeCETES project conducted twenty focus groups (involving a total of 120 participants) in Germany, Italy, Bulgaria and the UK in order to find out more about people's views on European film. Participants were recruited within locations where members of the research team had existing links. Most responded to an online "screener" questionnaire that was posted on various websites and social networking sites (e.g. Facebook, Twitter, Streetlife). Others responded to recruitment posters that were published in local newspapers or posted on community noticeboards. Respondents were encouraged to share the online questionnaire and invite their friends and family to participate in the study, leading to the recruitment of further participants. This "snowballing" method is useful for accessing hard-to-reach groups, but can skew the sample population towards people who share similar views and backgrounds. Thus, although different ages, genders, ethnicities, social and educational backgrounds were recruited, the groups were not necessarily representative of the countries where they took place. However, they may be seen as fairly typical of the audience for European film. Most participants, for example, had seen at least two or three European film titles from the list of twenty included in the screener questionnaire.

Each group was shown trailers for six recent European films, representing a range of genres and nationalities. After each trailer, participants were asked whether they liked the film and what elements (e.g. story, actors, nationality) particularly appealed to them. They were also asked whether they knew where the film was set and whether this challenged or reinforced their perception of the country or place. The discussion was recorded (with the participants' consent), transcribed and translated into English (where necessary), and then coded and analysed using Nvivo, a programme for qualitative data analysis.

Analysis of the focus group transcripts reveals that the most popular non-national European film shown was *The Intouchables*, followed by *Das Leben der Anderen* (The Lives of Others, 2006, Germany, Florian Henckel von Donnersmarck) and *The Hunt* (Figure 39.4). These films were typically popular because they were seen as true-to-life stories with a strong plot and characters with which audiences could empathise. The least popular film was *Taken 2*, followed by *A Royal Affair* and *El orfanat* (The Orphanage, 2007, Spain, J.A. Bayona). *Taken 2* was seen as too violent, predictable and exaggerated, while *A Royal Affair* and *The Orphanage* represented niche genres (costume dramas and horror respectively). In general, the most popular films were ones with less of the perceived flaws associated with non-national European films (i.e. "too slow", "too dark" and "without a clear plot, which is easy to follow") or Hollywood productions (i.e. exaggerated, stereotypical, predictable).

Most of the films were liked because of their "story" or "premise"—something that mirrors the audience surveys discussed above. This is of course one of the main draws of Hollywood films as well. However, the focus group participants generally perceived non-national European films to be less stereotypical than mainstream Hollywood blockbusters. Subject-matter was also seen as another important element, particularly in the case of historical dramas (e.g. *Coco Before*

	All participants	**Italy**	**UK**	**Bulgaria**	**Germany**	**18-34**	**35+**	**Male**	**Female**	**No degree**	**Degree**	**Key elements**
The Intouchables	1	3	1	1	2	1	2	3	1	2	2	Story
The Lives of Others	2	1	1	4		3	1	1	4	1	3	Subject-matter
The Hunt	3	2	4	3	1	2	3	2	2	3	1	Story, nationality
Volver	4	8	5	2		4	4	4	3	4	4	Director
Girlhood	5	4	9		12	7	8	9	6	8	6	Subject-matter
Blue Is The Warmest Colour	6		3		8	16	5	12	5	6	11	Subject-matter, nationality
Love Is All You Need	7	6	13		3	14	9	11	10	10	8	Actors, genre
Ida	8	9	7		7	8	11	6	13	9	10	Cinematrography, story
Coco Before Channel	9	7	12			6	12	14	8	5	11	Subject-matter, actors
The Great Beauty	10		8		8	14	5	6	11	15	5	Cinematrography, nationality
Let the Right One In	11	12	6	5		5	13	5	14	14	8	Genre
Two Days One Night	12	5	9		8	13	10	16	9	13	6	Actors, subject matter
Skyfall	13	10		6	8	17	7	6	17	12	14	Genre, actors
The Orphanage	14		15		4	10	13	14	12	6	16	Genre
A Royal Affair	15	13	11		5	11	17	17	6	11	16	Genre
Taken 2	16	11	16		6	12	15	10	15	16	15	Genre, actors
Gomorrah	17		13			9	16	12	16	17	13	Subject-matter

Figure 39.4 Films shown in focus group ranked by order of preference.

Chanel; The Lives of Others) and films that focused on particular social issues (e.g. *La Vie d'Adèle* [Blue Is the Warmest Color, 2013, France/Belgium/Spain, Abdellatif Kechiche]); *Bande de filles* [Girlhood, 2014, France, Céline Sciamma]; *Deux jours, une nuit* [Two Days, One Night, 2014, Belgium/France/Italy, Jean-Pierre Dardenne, Luc Dardenne]). Many participants said they liked watching historical dramas for the opportunity to learn about particular periods or events in history. Accordingly, they thought it was very important that the film was historically accurate—which was seen as more likely to be the case with non-national European films than Hollywood movies. Similarly, part of the appeal of non-national European films was that they dealt with social issues and topics (e.g. race, sexuality, labour rights) that were ignored by mainstream Hollywood productions.

Genre was another key element that determined people's opinion of non-national European film, particularly in the case of films they had never seen before. Many, for example, said they would not see *Let the Right One In* because it is a horror film, even though few had actually seen the film itself. (Those who had, tended to point out that it was not straightforwardly a horror film but more of a socially committed romantic drama). Rather stereotypically, horror and action films tended to be most popular with men, while costume dramas, romantic comedies and films with strong female leads tended to be most popular with women.

Given the emphasis that distributors often place on director, reviews, festivals and awards when marketing European films, it is interesting to note that few respondents said they were drawn to these elements. As with the BFI's exit polls, the director was an important pull only in the case of Pedro Almodóvar's *Volver*, although even he was only well known among the Italian respondents. The only actors with significant appeal were the Danish actor Mads Mikkleson, who stars in *The Hunt* and *A Royal Affair*, and the French actress Marion Cotillard, star of *Two Days One Night*. Likewise, few were drawn to any of the films because of the country or place they portrayed. As one German participant put it, "I am just about the story. I wouldn't like a film better just because it is from a certain country." However, some expressed a preference for films produced in France and Denmark, which were seen as countries with distinctive cinematic styles and strong filmmaking traditions.

Participants generally had a good idea about where films were set through being able to identify the language or the landscape that appeared on screen. Yet most suggested these images confirmed rather than challenged or modified their perception of the country or place. One notable exception was Ken Loach's *The Angel's Share* (2012, UK/France/Belgium/Italy) which as one Italian participant put it, "challenges the stereotype of the UK as a rich, happy place". Most participants agreed that watching non-national European films helped them to understand other European cultures and perhaps see some of the traits they held in common. However, few thought this made them feel more European. As one Italian respondent put it, "I am European, but it's not related to films".

A couple of the films screened were much better received in some countries than others. However, this probably had more to do with the social make-up of the groups than deeper national differences in terms of taste. *Let the Right One In*, for example, was more popular in Bulgaria and the UK than in Italy. Yet this can be partly explained by the fact that two Italian groups shown the film were almost entirely made up of older women (who as we have seen are less likely to prefer horror films than younger men). Its unpopularity can be better explained by age and gender than nationality. Indeed, closer reading of the focus group transcripts reveals some striking similarities in terms of how participants in Germany, Italy, Bulgaria and the UK responded to the same films. The same kind of phrases and discourses were even heard in different countries.

This can be illustrated by focusing in more detail on the responses to *The Intouchables*, a French comedy-drama about the unlikely friendship between a rich white aristocrat who has been paralysed and his black streetwise carer. As noted above, *The Intouchables* is one of the most successful European films of recent years. It was seen by 44 million in the cinema across Europe (including 23 million outside its native France), and it has potentially been seen by 194 million Europeans once other platforms are taken into account. The film performed particularly well at the German and Italian box office (9.5 million and 2.8 million respectively), but was less well received in Bulgaria (10,890) and the UK (319,855). When it was released in 2012 some British (and American) film critics were exceedingly snooty about the film. *The Independent*, for example, called it "a third-rate buddy movie that hardly understands its own condescension" (Quinn 2012), while *The Financial Times* said the film "conforms to classist and racist clichés" (Andrews 2012). However, the audience focus group participants in all four countries were extremely positive about the film, often saying it was their favourite of the six films they were shown. Two key elements were highlighted in particular. The first was the fact that the film was based on a true story. For participants in all four countries, this made the unlikely friendship seem more credible and thus more enjoyable:

> The strength of this kind of films is that it's *based on a true story*. You appreciate it more [...] knowing that these kind of stories do happen in real life is somehow reassuring, makes you feel better.
>
> *(Male 45–54, Italy)*

> It impresses me a lot that the film is *based on a true story*.
>
> *(Female 45–54, Germany)*

> [I liked the fact that] *it's based on a true story*"
>
> *(Female 18–24, Bulgaria)*

> I wasn't quite sure how to take it in the start, but when it said that it is *based on a true story* that was what switched it for me.
>
> *(Female 25–34, UK)*

The second key element had to do with the way the film combines comedy with more serious social issues to do with disability, race and class, so inviting a range of feelings and emotions:

> The film is not only funny, it's also very moving, because it's able to make you laugh about a serious issue such as disability. When a film is able to do such thing, *to make you laugh about serious themes, it means that it's well done.*
>
> *(Female 25–34, Italy)*

> I liked it. *It is a really tragic story but they made it as a comedy* and that's just incredible.
>
> *(Female 55–64, Germany)*

> *It is funny and life-affirming* and just re-watching the trailer now I have a smile on my face. I really enjoyed it.
>
> *(Female 25–34, UK)*

> *It touches on a lot of things*: racism, class separation, educated–uneducated, rich–poor, the film shows this. And it shows that [different people] can live together. *It's also a comedy*. There are also a lot of real moments.
>
> *(Male, aged 25–34, Bulgaria)*

One might even argue that the approval of the film's message about the common humanity of people from very different social and ethnic backgrounds is evidence of a shared liberal and cosmopolitan outlook among European film audiences.

At the same time, some responses were very specific to the country where the discussion took place. In the Italian focus groups, for example, there was a strong feeling that France had become particularly good at producing these kinds of serious-but-funny comedy-dramas in recent years. Other examples cited included *Bienvenue Chez les Ch'tis* (Welcome to the Sticks, 2008, France, Dany Boon) and *Le prénom* (What's in a Name, 2008, France/Belgium, Alexandre de La Patellière, Matthieu Delaporte). This led to a discussion about how French comedies compared with Italian comedies, with many suggesting that Italian comedies were less sophisticated and exportable, because they were based on crude, local stereotypes that were deemed unintelligible outside Italy. As one Italian respondent put it:

> The French film *Bienvenue Chez les Ch'tis* [Welcome to the Sticks], once it was remade into the Italian version *Benvenuti al Sud* [Welcome to the South], lost something. It has been charged with the typical patterns we use to make [us] laugh. But those patterns are not understandable outside Italy. The French version was light-hearted and elegant, the Italian version is worse—and so is the sequel *Benvenuti al Nord* [Welcome to the North]. So I'm a big fan of French comedy, especially of these last years.
>
> *(Male 45–54, Italy)*

These sentiments partly reflect the particularities of contemporary Italian cinema, with its high output of domestic comedies that dominate the national box office, yet perform poorly abroad. They also illustrate the fact that—despite the transnational nature of contemporary filmmaking—audiences still think of themselves and the films they watch in national terms.

Conclusion

At the start of this chapter it was noted that the traditional definition of World Cinema as non-Hollywood cinema "unwittingly sanctions the American way of looking at the world, according to which Hollywood is the centre and all other cinemas are the periphery" (Nagib 2006: 30). Within the European context, there are certainly examples of filmmakers drawing on influences outside Hollywood (e.g. the influence of Brazilian Cinema Novo on New German Cinema). However, from an audience perspective, Hollywood is still very much at the centre of European film culture. As this chapter has shown, the majority of films which European audiences have seen, or are aware of, are US films (mostly Hollywood productions).

Nevertheless, a minority of Europeans do engage with films from other countries. Each year, about 12 per cent of cinema admissions in Europe are for non-national European films, while a further 3 per cent are for films from the Rest of the World. Meanwhile, TV, DVD and VOD are opening up further opportunities to engage with the cinema of the world. As a result, some non-national European films (e.g. *The Intouchables*) have become extremely well known across Europe. However, as the evidence presented in this chapter shows, what draws audiences to these films is not necessarily the film's nationality or the opportunity to observe a specific culture or place, but rather the fact that these films offer an alternative to mainstream Hollywood productions. For example, their stories are seen as less predictable and stereotypical and more likely to deal with social issues that Hollywood ignores.

Even so, Hollywood remains the key reference point around which European cinematic tastes are defined.

The focus groups also revealed striking similarities in the way audiences in different European countries respond to the same films. The case of *The Intouchables*, for example, illustrates how certain films have strong transnational appeal and are even interpreted in broadly similar ways regardless of national context (notwithstanding the culturally specific comments made by Italian focus-group participants). If there are differences of opinion, these often have more to do with age and gender than nationality. One reason why there is such uniformity among Europhiles in different countries might be because non-national European films tend to appeal to a particular social demographic—the university-educated, liberal metropolitan middle classes. At the same time, few felt that watching non-national European films made them feel more European, even if it gave them a better understanding of other European cultures.

Of course, these findings need to be treated with caution. Admissions figures for non-theatrical platforms are scarce; audience survey questions can be reductive and misunderstood; and focus groups are open to biases and different interpretations, particularly when discussions are translated from another language and the transcription only captures verbal communication. Nevertheless, combining evidence from a variety of qualitative and quantitative sources does allow us to build up a fairly robust picture of how contemporary European audiences engage with films from around the world. This can certainly enhance our understanding of World Cinema. But clearly there are audiences in other global contexts (e.g. Africa, Asia and Latin America) that still need to be explored.

Note

1 This work comes out of the *Mediating Cultural Encounters through European Screens* (MeCETES) project. MeCETES has received funding from the Humanities in the European Research Area (HERA) Joint Research Programme (www.heranet.info) under grant agreement number 291827. HERA is co-funded by AHRC, AKA, BMBF via PT-DLR, DASTI, ETAG, FCT, FNR, FNRS, FWF, FWO, HAZU, IRC, LMT, MHEST, NWO, NCN, RANNÍS, RCN, VR and The European Community FP7 2007–2013, under the Socio-economic Sciences and Humanities programme. The author would like to acknowledge the support of Jessica Van Roye, Martina Lovascio and Maya Nedyalkova for their invaluable assistance with the focus groups in Germany, Italy and Bulgaria respectively.

References

Andrews, N. (2012) "Just Another Bloody Day in the Underworld", *The Financial Times*, 20 September, www.ft.com/content/c9f40b44-0306-11e2-a484-00144feabdc0.

BFI (2016) *Film on UK Television*, London: BFI.

Biltereyst, D., Maltby, R. and Meers, P. (eds) (2012) *Cinema, Audiences and Modernity: New Perspectives on European Cinema History*, London: Routledge.

Cooke, P. (ed.) (2013) *World Cinema's "Dialogues" with Hollywood*, Basingstoke: Palgrave.

Dennison, S. and Lim, S. H. (eds) (2006) *Remapping World Cinema: Identity, Culture and Politics in Film*, London: Wallflower Press.

Ene, L. and Grece, C. (2015) *Note 4: Origin of Films in VOD Catalogues in the EU*, Strasbourg: European Audiovisual Observatory.

European Audiovisual Observatory (2006) "Identification of Films in the LUMIERE Database", 11 August, http://lumiere.obs.coe.int/web/sources/astuces.html.

European Commission (2014) *A Profile of Current and Future Audiovisual Audiences*, Luxembourg: Publications Office of the European Union.

Gripsrud, G. (2000) "Film Audiences", in Hill, J. and Church Gibson, P. (eds) *Film Studies: Critical Approaches*, Oxford: Oxford University Press, 200–209.

Lange, A. (ed.) (2014) *Fiction on European TV Channels 2006–13,* Strasbourg: European Audiovisual Observatory.

Mathijs, E. and Barker, M. (2008) *Watching The Lord of the Rings*, Bern: Peter Lang.

Nagib, L (2006) "Towards a Positive Definition of World Cinema", in Dennison, S. and Lim, S. H. (eds) *Remapping World Cinema: Identity, Culture and Politics in Film*, London and New York: Wallflower Press, 30–37.

—— (2011) *World Cinema and the Ethics of Realism*, London: Continuum.

Nagib, L., Perriam, C. and Dudrah, R. (eds) (2012) *Theorising World Cinema*, London: I. B. Tauris.

Quinn, A. (2012) "Untouchables (15)", *The Independent,* 21 September, www.independent.co.uk/arts-entertainment/films/reviews/untouchable-15-8160904.html.

Stokes, M. and Maltby, R. (eds) (1999) *Identifying Hollywood's Audiences: Cultural Identity and the Movies*, London: BFI.

Straubhaar, J. (1991) "Beyond Media Imperialism: Asymmetrical Interdependence and Cultural Proximity", *Critical Studies in Mass Communication* 8: 39–59.

40

EYES ON THE FUTURE

World Cinema and transnational capacity building

Mette Hjort

Introduction

"World Cinema", Dudley Andrew remarks, is now "permanently with us" (Andrew 2004: 9).[1] The term's current centrality in Film Studies signals a substantial shift in thinking: a previously influential "foreign art film" category is no longer seen as adequate to the task of doing justice to moving images produced in a host of sites around the globe; once the object of survey-style discussions undertaken from afar, these images now prompt a deeper and more systematic engagement with the cultures from which they arise. Indeed, as Andrew sees it, the role of the World Cinema scholar is to "zero in" on specific "cinema sites", to provide "coordinates for navigating" the "world of World Cinema" (Andrew 2004: 9). Consistent with Andrew's proposal is Lúcia Nagib's positive definition of "World Cinema" as "cinema worldwide", as compared with "non-Hollywood" cinema. Advocating a polycentric approach that is at once democratic and inclusive, Nagib foregrounds the need to give due attention to "peaks of creation in different times and periods" throughout the world (Nagib 2006: 30). In this equalizing model, Hollywood becomes one centre among others, ceasing thereby to be the standard against which varieties of moving image production elsewhere must be measured.

The idea of a diminished role for Hollywood is an appealing one, as is the invitation to seek a deep understanding of specific "cinema sites". A comparative focus on the cinematic contributions of small nations, one aimed at establishing or further developing supportive networks among relevant practitioners, offers a fruitful way of implementing an inclusive approach to World Cinema. This transnational approach to small-nation Cinema Studies requires a broad conception of small nationhood that recognises the implications not only of geographic scale and population size, but also of limited resources (measured in GDP) and histories of diminished political autonomy (especially colonial ones) (Hjort and Petrie 2007: 3–78). As for the call for site-based explorations, case studies are promising in this regard, especially if they give due attention to what I call "practitioner's agency" (Hjort 2010a: 40–99). The process of coming to understand the aspirations, practices, and intentions of practitioners—of festival organisers, film commissioners, film educators and filmmakers—brings to light the institutional, professional and personal networks, many of them transnational, that are operative within a given site. Consideration of practitioner's agency also helps to reveal the constraints and opportunities by which the relevant context is defined, thereby providing a basis for assessing the nature of the contributions made by different instances of cinematic expression.

The aim in this chapter is to trace collaborative links between sites of cinematic activity in the Global North and Global South. More specifically, it seeks to explore a range of film-related projects involving film practitioners, production companies, government and non-profit organisations in five sites that are variously shaped by one or more of the defining elements of small nationhood: Denmark, Burkina Faso, Mali, Kenya, and Uganda. Film-based collaboration between the Nordic country and the West African and East African countries in question is structured through bilateral agreements that are government-supported, development-oriented, and generally attuned to the promise of regional synergies. The programme names and funding periods are as follows:

- Mali–Denmark: Cultural Co-Operation Programme (2008–2012; 2012–2016)
- DANFASO—Culture and Development Programme for Burkina Faso (2011–2013, extended through 2014; 2015–2017)
- Uganda Youth Cultures Project (2010–2013; 2014–2016)
- Kenya Culture and Development Programme (2014–2017)

These collaborative North/South programmes are all instances of what I have called "milieu-building transnationalism" (Hjort 2010b), for at the heart of each of them is a "resource partnership" (Ministry of Foreign Affairs 2013: 4) that is intended to facilitate knowledge exchange and capacity building in some film-related area (ranging from production skills through to audience development). Special attention will be given to the Uganda Youth Cultures Project, which has been especially fruitful. Due to limited space, the other projects will be discussed in a summary way.

The motivation for examining the values, challenges and achievements of different examples of policy-based milieu-building transnationalism on a North/South basis is threefold. First, the intent is further to expand the scope of World Cinema Studies. The claim throughout is that it is of crucial importance to look beyond the "peaks of cinematic creation" (Nagib 2006: 30) to the ground where the conditions for different types of film-related success are being prepared. The study of World Cinema, that is, must also be about the rich varieties of film-focused initiatives that are fuelled by the *aspiration* to develop creative milieus to the point where talk of "peaks" becomes possible. Questions having to do with the quality and quantity of film productions are relevant here, but so are issues related to the appropriateness of types of capacity building, to audience development, to the need to nurture a local voice and perspective, and to governments' policies regarding broadcasters' commitment to local content. The drive fuelling milieu-building aspirations can often be traced to a gifted filmmaker who, in spite of having achieved recognition both nationally and internationally, is operating in relative isolation and under conditions that make regular filmmaking difficult, if not impossible. World Cinema Studies cannot afford to ignore such figures, whether they are emerging or established talents. In many cases these figures' milieu-building initiatives are as important as their films. Typically, their interventions in specific sites are based on deeply held convictions about the public value of moving images, or, in other words, about their capacity to contribute to the creation of sustainable "good" societies. By taking efforts to develop a creative milieu seriously, even in the absence of a significant number of high quality films, a capacious approach to World Cinema helps to answer a crucial question to which many films emerging from the affluent and well-established sectors of the Global North suggest a poor answer: why make films in the first place?

A second reason for drawing attention to examples of Nordic/African partnerships has to do with tendencies in small-nation Cinema Studies. Certain small nations, some of them in the Nordic region, have managed to overcome many of the recurring obstacles associated with small nationhood and have built thriving film milieus. In the context of small-nation Cinema Studies, attempts, for example, to explain Denmark's success with film since the late 1980s have emphasised film policy on a national, Nordic and European level, as well as institution building within the country itself (Hjort 2005; Bondebjerg 2016). Thus, the National Film School of Denmark, an elite conservatoire-style film school, is seen as playing a critically important role (Philipsen 2004; Novrup Redvall 2010) within a larger and quite variegated film training landscape that itself affords diverse opportunities for the enhancement of skills and pathways into filmmaking. Case studies have documented the National Film School's commitment to developing independent documentary filmmaking in the Middle East and North Africa (Hjort 2013), as well as CPH:DOX's (Copenhagen International Documentary Festival) "twinning" of European and non-European filmmakers through DOX:LAB (later renamed CPH:LAB), a capacity-building programme for a small number of selected filmmakers (Hjort 2016). Collaboration between the National Film School and the Danish Film Institute on the one hand and a variety of stakeholders in Bhutan, on the other, has also been the object of cogent analysis (Grøn 2016). What has yet to be properly captured, however, is the full extent to which practitioners in the Danish filmmaking milieu have looked beyond not only the Nordic region, but Europe and the Western coast of the United States too, to forge productive relationships with filmmakers in the Global South, often with the support of government-funded organisations and through the implementation of official development strategies. Denmark's longer-term, partner-based engagement with film beyond the Global North extends to the Middle East and Asia, as well as to West Africa and East Africa.

The third reason for examining the partnerships in question concerns the role of human rights thinking in the context of North/South collaborations with a focus on film. The transnational partnerships that are considered here are implemented through the Danish Ministry of Foreign Affairs' development strategy, and this, as we shall see, is explicitly framed in terms of support for human rights beyond Danish borders. As Michael Ignatieff points out in a critical vein, "human rights is increasingly seen as the language of a moral imperialism just as ruthless and just as self-deceived as the colonial hubris of yesteryear" (2001: 19–20). Titles evoking the scepticism to which Ignatieff seeks an alternative include *The End of Human Rights* (Douzinas 2000), *The Last Utopia* (Moyn 2010), and *The Endtimes of Human Rights* (Hopgood 2013). Of interest, then, are questions regarding the ways in which the Danish government's overarching rights-based framework for development work contributes to or hinders the establishing of productive, reciprocally rewarding relationships among film practitioners on a transnational, North/South, as well as South/South basis.

The analysis presented below is based on a mix of methods. Policy documents, government strategies, grant applications, country reports, and interim as well as final reports on specific partnership programmes have been scrutinised carefully. Films produced by practitioners associated with the partnerships, or through the partnerships themselves, have been studied with an eye to identifying thematic and stylistic features, as well as issues having to do with local culture. In the case of Burkina Faso, non-participant observation was possible, as I assisted with training programmes at Gaston Kaboré's film school, IMAGINE, during FESPACO in 2011 and 2013; in 2013, at the same time as a Danish trainer was conducting a workshop at the school. A great deal of weight has been given to practitioner interviews and site visits. In addition to field trips to Burkina Faso, a research trip to Kenya was undertaken in the Spring of 2016. Practitioner interviews, either face-to-face or through Skype, have been conducted with, among others: current and former employees at the Centre for Culture and Development (CKU, under the Danish Ministry of Foreign Affairs; Vibeke Munk Petersen [2015]; Louise Friis Pedersen [2015]; Elizabeth Maina [2016], based in Nairobi, Kenya); the Head of the continuing education arm of the National Film School of Denmark (Tina Sørensen [2013]); film trainers at the Danish film school for children and young people, Station Next (Claus Michaelsen [2014]); a film trainer (Frederick Kigozi [2014]) and project coordinator (Denis Pato [2014]) associated with Mira Nair's Maisha in Uganda; filmmakers in Kenya (Judy Kibinge [2016]) and Burkina Faso (Gaston Kaboré [2011; 2013); the Head of the Danish Film Institute's (DFI) Film Archive (Jacob Trock [2014]); the Head of the Children and Youth Department at the DFI (Charlotte Giese [2008]); and a key trainer in the Mali programme (Anne Juul [2015], previously with Zentropa and currently production manager at Metronome). Analysis of the values, challenges and achievements of the transnational programmes makes reference, not only to central film-makers but also to cinematic works, however short or long, that have been developed through them. In some cases, selective reference is also made to films that provided a rationale for the establishing of specific transnational partnerships in West and East Africa.

Development strategies: the role of the Danish Centre for Culture and Development (CKU)

The programmes in Mali, Burkina Faso, Uganda and Kenya were developed by CKU and it is thus necessary to clarify the mandate and mode of operation of this body. Established in 1998 as a self-governing institution under the auspices of the Danish Ministry of Foreign Affairs, CKU is guided in its work by two fundamental goals: the strengthening of art and culture in developing countries; and the enhancement of Danish audiences' knowledge and apprecia-tion of these countries' artistic and cultural contributions. In the Danish context, this second goal has been pursued through the IMAGES festival, an Arts Fund that supports collaborative artistic projects, and the youth programme known as World Images in Motion. The mobility of artists is a clear emphasis here, for the festival and fund enable cultural practitioners to travel to Denmark for the purposes of artistic collaboration, performances and a direct engagement with Danish audiences.

CKU has, since 2013, been charged with implementing Denmark's Strategy for Culture and Development, "The Right to Art and Culture" (Danida 2013). This cultural strategy is itself encompassed by Denmark's overarching "strategy for development cooperation", "The Right to a Better Life" (Danish Government 2012). The latter strategy identifies two objec-tives, poverty reduction and the promotion of human rights, and encourages their pursuit through activities in four priority areas (human rights and democracy; stability and protec-tion; green growth; and social progress). "The Right to Art and Culture" is designed to bring about "positive change" through art and culture, recognising that "a rich artistic and cultural life [also] has value in itself". Describing Denmark's "strong cultural policy traditions" as a resource on "the global stage", Christian Friis Bach, then Minister for Development Cooperation, foregrounds an aspiration to "create equal and strong cultural partnerships, including in new dynamic emerging economies with a cultural and religious identity that is distinctly different from ours" (Danida 2013: 3). The implementation of "The Right to Art and Culture" is to be effected through five priority areas: "empowering people through active participation in art and cultural activities"; "ensuring freedom of expression for artists and cultural actors"; "enhancing economic growth through creative industries"; "strengthening peace and reconciliation in post-conflict areas through art and cultural activities" and "promoting intercultural dialogue and intercultural collaboration" (Danida 2013: 6). Inasmuch as the government's strategy for development cooperation, including development through art and culture, rests on a rights-based approach, CKU's design of programmes since 2013 has made reference to different categories of rights:

> a) Cultural rights, e.g. [the right to] partake in culture, freedom of artistic expression and creativity, [the] promotion of cultural diversity, [the] protection of tangible and intangible cultural heritage, etc.
> b) Other human rights treaties and articles that have a *specific relevance* for artists and culture operators, e.g. intellectual property rights, copyright, freedom of movement, freedom of assembly, etc.
> c) Areas where art and culture initiatives can make a *positive contribution* to the realisation of rights—e.g. civil and political rights, social and economic rights, [the] right to development, [the] rights of indigenous people, [the] rights of women, [the] rights of children etc.
>
> *(CKU 2014: 9)*

Programmes (in Mali, Uganda and Burkina Faso) that predate the "Right to Art and Culture" strategy are broadly consistent with the abovementioned priorities, although less strategically focused. However, assessment of the effectiveness of these programmes has typically made reference to the strategy in question. Thus, programmes granted monies for a subsequent phase could be rethought in light of the designated priority areas.

The "Right to Art and Culture" strategy brought about pronounced changes having to do with the roles and responsibilities associated with CKU's programmes. Prior to 2013, programmes were developed, to some extent funded, and largely managed by the Danish embassies in the Danish government's designated "programme countries", the role of CKU at the time being related to quality assurance. Following the introduction of the new strategy, development, funding and oversight of the culture and development programmes became the responsibility of CKU. Advantages of this approach are seen as including a streamlining of activities with an eye to achieving greater impact. Under the new dispensation, CKU came to emphasise sustainable projects with the potential to be scaled up, including through regional synergies involving South/South cooperation. The embassies have, however, retained an important role, as Louise Friis Pedersen, CKU's programme manager for West Africa, remarks:

> We still work closely with the embassies. They have to feel the programme document makes sense. We can't just come up with a programme without their requesting that we develop it. So there's still a sense of ownership for them, but without the administrative burdens.
>
> *(interview, Friis Pedersen)*

Although the interest of the West and East African programmes lies in their commitment to moving images, it is important to note that CKU always develops multidisciplinary interventions, typically with three to five distinct elements, each with its own sub-programme. Thus, for example, the "Uganda Youth Cultures Project" focuses on capacity building in five areas seen as relevant to the future of young Ugandans: film, music, dance, theatre and electronic media. CKU conducts team-based research in each selected country and the findings inform the design of the new programme. Each research team includes a national consultant with local know-how. Also, the fact-finding brief includes consultation with national stakeholders, including local government, the aim being to ensure that programmes dovetail with the priorities of local government. Thus, for example, the elements in the "Ugandan Youth Cultures" programme are meant to align with the Government of Uganda's "Peace, Recovery and Development Plan for Northern Uganda" (PRDP), and, further, to contribute to Uganda's pursuit of a "culturally vibrant, cohesive and progressive nation" through its national cultural policy (Royal Danish Embassy 2010: 7). Funding allocated to the programmes varies. In the case of "Ugandan Youth Cultures" 5,600,000 DKK were allocated over a three-year period, 2,543,835 of them for film (Ibid.: 46). Funding for programmes that progress to a second phase, as in the case of Mali, is typically significantly higher. Support for the Mali–Denmark Programme in its second phase was 10,599,000 DKK, with 3,099,000 being earmarked for film (Danida 2012: 29).

Unfortunately, CKU's programmes have now come to an end. The centre-right government led by Lars Løkke Rasmussen since June 2015 closed CKU at the end of 2016, asking embassies, according to Kenyan lawyer Elizabeth Maina, CKU's programme officer in Nairobi, to continue to administer programmes through 2017 (interview, Maina). The elimination of CKU represents a significant loss and is symptomatic of neoliberal priorities, political expediency, and a diminished political appetite for funding not only development work, but also culture. Given the context of CKU's demise, an account of its milieu-building efforts on behalf of moving image cultures in the Global South is especially timely.

Youth and Film Uganda

By all accounts CKU's film programme in Uganda, which targets children and young people aged 13–20, has been especially successful. An important factor in this regard is no doubt the quality and appropriateness of the collaborative partnerships it has generated. The primary Ugandan partner was Maisha (meaning "life" in Swahili), a non-profit organisation established in Kampala in 2004 by the New York-based Indian filmmaker Mira Nair (well known for *Salaam Bombay*, 1988, India; *Mississippi Masala*, 1991, UK/USA; *Monsoon Wedding*, 2001, USA/India; *Vanity Fair*, 2004, USA/UK/India; *The Namesake*, 2006, USA/India; *Amelia*, 2009, USA/Canada and, most recently, *The Reluctant Fundamentalist*, 2012, USA/Pakistan, an adaptation of Pakistani writer Mohsin Hamid's eponymous post-9/11 novel). Guided by the motto "If we don't tell our stories, no one else will", Maisha targets "aspiring and established screenwriters and filmmakers of all ages from Rwanda, Kenya, Tanzania, and Uganda". The Maisha Foundation seeks to "empower artists", to "enrich World Cinema" and to "establish the roots of a self-sustaining film industry in East Africa" (Maisha).

The primary Danish partner was (up until the end of the first phase) the DFI, through its Children and Youth Department, Headed by Charlotte Giese. Giese played a significant role in the design of the programme, having been part of the research team led by then CKU Head of Projects, Vibeke Munk Petersen. Giese brought considerable expertise in the area of filmmaking for children and young people to the project. Equally helpful was Giese's earlier collaboration with the Zanzibar International Film Festival (ZIFF), focusing on film programming for children and youth and capacity building in the area of film production for young people. Denmark's longstanding commitment, supported by policymaking, to young people's cultural right to experience diverse, high quality, age-appropriate films provided a basis for the DFI's involvement with ZIFF. More specifically, Tanzanian filmmaker and Australian academic Martin Mhando (director of the award-winning film *Maangamizi: The Ancient One*, 2001, Tanzania/USA, Maisha Lab mentor, and long-serving Director of ZIFF) saw considerable potential, within a development context, in film's ability to speak to the concerns, needs and aspirations of a sizeable percentage of the East African population. Mhando's vision is supported by demographic data: for example, according to *New Vision*, Uganda's leading daily, Uganda had the youngest population in the world in 2012, with 78 per cent of Ugandans under 30 years of age and 52 per cent under 15 (Bwambale 2012).

The primary partners were charged with subcontracting a certain amount of work. In the case of Maisha, it was a matter of reaching agreements with the Amakula International Film Festival and the Straight Talk Foundation, both in Uganda, and with CPH:DOX/DOX:LAB in Denmark. Maisha hired Denis Pato, through Straight Talk, to coordinate mobile cinema screenings (two Danish, two African and two international films in each year's film programme) and to establish cine-clubs in five selected areas—Gulu, Kampala, Moroto, Mbale and Mbarara (interview, Pato)—as well as to run 5-day film training Labs in Gulu and Kampala, with participants recruited through the cine-clubs (Ibid.). Pato brought an especially appropriate skillset to his role as project manager: a social science degree, a postgraduate diploma in project planning and management, further studies in international relations and diplomacy, and significant experience at Straight Talk, a foundation that pursues social change through a variety of media by engaging young people with health rights. Maisha's agreement with CPH:DOX/DOX:LAB concerned the recruitment of emerging young Ugandan filmmakers to the Copenhagen International Documentary Film Festival's talent development programme, DOX:LAB. Maisha also invited Ugandan filmmaker Frederick Kigozi, an alumnus of the 2010 Maisha Lab, to serve as a mentor for CKU's Youth and Film Uganda filmmaking Labs.

On the Danish side of things, the DFI was charged with subcontracting training tasks to Station Next, a film school established on the grounds of the Zentropa Film Town in Avedøre, Denmark. Devoted to talent development targeting young people aged 13–18 and reaching approximately 6,000 aspiring young filmmakers ever year, Station Next has established an enviable reputation due to its insistence on professional standards and a pedagogy focused on learning by doing (Station Next 2016). Station Next's role in the Youth and Film Uganda programme involved sharing its youth-oriented practice-based film curriculum with the Lab mentors in Uganda, so as jointly to develop an approach appropriate to the Ugandan context. Claus Michaelsen from Station Next was also on site in Uganda to assist with the running of some of the annual film production Labs.

A number of films were produced through Youth and Film Uganda, some of them by young people aged 13–20, others by emerging filmmakers who were recommended to DOX:LAB organisers Patricia Drati and Tine Fischer for participation in CPH:DOX's DOX:LAB. Youth and Film Uganda funded the participation of three Ugandan filmmakers in DOX:LAB's "twinning" of European and non-European directors. In each case the brief given to the directorial "twins" was to develop an idea for a film together in Copenhagen—during the CPH:DOX festival, where the first phase of DOX:LAB unfolds—and to complete it before the next edition of the CPH:DOX festival. Ugandan filmmaker Caroline Kamya had been twinned with Danish Boris Bertram during DOX:LAB 2009–2010. The two filmmakers successfully produced *Chips and Liver Girls* (2010, Denmark/Uganda), about young Ugandan women and the "men who pay for their studies and a modern life in luxury" (CPH:LAB). Interviews with Patricia Drati (2013) and Palestinian filmmaker Mahasen Nasser-Eldin (2012, a member of the same talent development cohort), indicate that Kamya was an especially appreciated participant in the first Lab. The Youth and Film Uganda programme document (Royal Danish Embassy 2010: 14) refers to her participation in DOX:LAB and to the success of her feature film *Imani* (2010, Sweden/Uganda), about the former child soldier Olweny. Kamya's talents and achievements and earlier training with Maisha (Maisha Film Lab 2006) were clearly seen as providing a rationale for links between the Kampala-based organisation and DOX:LAB in Copenhagen. The CKU-funded Ugandan participants in DOX:LAB are as follows: Donald Mugisha (2010–2011), who made *The Kampala Story* (2012, Uganda) with Danish Kasper Bisgaard; Frederick Kigozi, who was paired with Danish Mira Jargil but ended up making *This Is My Family* (2012, Denmark/Uganda) mostly on his own; and Peter Tukei Muhumuza, who co-directed *Walk with Me* (2013, Uganda/Denmark/Sweden) with Danish Johan Oettinger. Of special interest here is Kigozi's *This Is My Family*, given the filmmaker's crucial role as a Lab mentor for the CKU project. Trained in Abu Dhabi, Kigozi had participated in a Maisha Lab in 2010, where he made a poignant short called *Rough Boy*, about "issues of mental illness and the difficulties individual families have dealing with the fallout from it" (interview, Kigozi). This film, which straddles the fiction/non-fiction divide in ways that are entirely consistent with the CPH:DOX and DOX:LAB concept, became the basis for Kigozi's acceptance to DOX:LAB 2011–2012. A fascinating film about polygamy, *This Is My Family* originated in discussions between Jargil and Kigozi, with the former recalling her parents' experiments with an open marriage and the latter expressing critical views about family arrangements involving multiple wives in Uganda. Due to pregnancy, Jargil was unable to travel to Uganda to shoot the film, but Kigozi sees the pair's early sparring as positive and as having substantially shaped the film (interview, Kigozi).

The Labs for young people (aged 13–20) in Gulu and Kampala also produced important work. Two of the films, *The Secret Note* (Youth Lab, 2011, Gulu, Isaac Titus Odokorach) and *Christmas Turkey* (Youth Film, 2011, Kampala, Reagan Washiwala)[2] were accepted to the Chicago International Children's Festival and Pato recalls the effects produced by this recognition in Uganda:

> When we announced in the film club that two of our films were accepted at the Chicago international Children's Festival, it was wildfire in the club. Everyone wanted to make a film and get it accepted at some festival somewhere. And we were very happy about that. We began to receive more scripts, more phone calls from our youth.
>
> *(interview, Pato)*

It is worth underscoring that both films are issues-oriented, focusing on problems on which the children and young people participating in the Labs wished to reflect. In the case of *The Secret Note*, the central issue is misunderstanding and jealousy among school children. *Christmas Turkey* explores dysfunctional parenting, through the eyes of a teenage boy who seeks to counteract the effects of his father's alcoholism. Also, it is important to recall the overarching goals that shaped the various activities of Youth and Film Uganda, including the filmmaking in the Labs. Among other things, the CKU programme aimed to work towards "reunification among youth groups", the bolstering of young people's "self esteem", and "conflict reduction among youth" (Royal Danish Embassy 2010: 12). The context for these goals is the history of violent conflict in Uganda, with much of it targeting young people. Gulu, for example, is close to the Northern town of Atiak, where Joseph Kony's Lord's Resistance Army, having massacred hundreds of civilians on 20 April 1995, forced "youth [. . .] to join the LRA to serve as the next generation of combatants and sexual slaves" (Liu Institute for Global Issues and the Gulu NGO Forum 2007: 2). Pato's reflections on the filmmaking activities in this context suggest that the goal of nurturing positive youth cultures in post-conflict areas was achieved on a modest, yet promising scale:

> When you talk about conflict reduction, we worked in conflict zones, like Gulu, in Northern Uganda, and Moroto. You must know about the rebel activities of Joseph Kony in Northern Uganda. For years they shattered the lives of young people and adults alike and today people still live with post-conflict trauma in these zones. So when this project was taken to Gulu, we hoped we'd target the young people who are suffering from post-conflict trauma and that we'd be able to fit them into this club, so that they could get out of the conflict, away from the traumatic scenes that keep replaying in their minds. I can't boast about this because we did not really access the young people who are suffering from post-conflict trauma on a large scale. But the few that we did manage to access, we have been able, for lack of a better word, to "rehabilitate". We don't address every young person in Uganda, but we have started the process. And that's part of the reason why we need this project to continue. We think it's helping.
>
> *(interview, Pato)*

Pato was keen to see the project, including the approach taken, continue. He did, however, indicate that the project goals would be more readily achievable with enhanced funding. As he saw it, the rhythm of the Labs, which were run on an annual basis, made it difficult to build momentum, to access enough young people, to sustain their commitment to creative expression and problem solving through moving images, and to further develop their emerging skillsets (interview, Pato).

A particularly important outcome of the Youth and Film Uganda project has to do with pedagogy and its role in nurturing self-esteem. Michaelsen (from Station Next 2016), as well as Pato and Kigozi (from Maisha) all agree that one of the most productive aspects of the transnational capacity-building partnership was the forging of a space for a youth-focused pedagogy in Uganda. Michaelsen recalls his first encounter with the Gulu Lab participants (who made *The Secret Note*) and the sense of fear that permeated their interactions with the trainers at first, due to their having been exclusively exposed to disciplinarian schooling. Pato is especially eloquent about the need for alternative, youth-centred pedagogies in Uganda:

> One of the things that has been happening in this country is that young people are downtrodden by their parents and their teachers. Young people are not allowed to express their most honest opinions when they are with adults. Sometimes it is seen as disrespect. A young person cannot argue with an adult, even if she is arguing without necessarily disrespecting the adult. It is seen as a sign of disrespect. So, personally, when I took up this project, that's one of the things that I was so passionate about. It was one of the circles I wanted to break. I wanted to help young people to feel free to air their opinions, to have discussions with adults without necessarily disrespecting them. In many ways this helped us as an organisation to achieve the goal of empowering young people through this project.
>
> *(interview, Pato)*

As Michaelsen sees it, the exchanges between Danes and Ugandans, including the young people themselves, about student-centred as compared with more authoritarian pedagogies, led to an approach that "was really the best of both worlds" (interview, Michaelsen). His view is clearly shared by his Ugandan peers, who also describe the collaborative efforts as especially productive in the area of pedagogy, and as having helped to develop young Ugandans' self-esteem, as specified by the film programme's overall goals.

Transnational capacity building in Kenya, Mali and Burkina Faso

CKU's work with film in Uganda provides a regional context for the most recent East African programme, the "Kenya Culture and Development Programme (2014–2017)", with CKU's country report on Kenya referring to the "great potential" for "synergies" with "CKU's culture and development programmes in Tanzania and Uganda" (CKU 2014: 4) and to the possibility of exchanges with "Maisha Film Lab in Uganda [and] ZIFF in Tanzania" (CKU 2014: 24). With reference to the "Right to Art and Culture" strategy, the Kenyan programme adopts two strategic foci: "empowering people through active participation in art and cultural activities" and "enhancing economic growth through creative industries". Two other goals in the strategy—"ensuring freedom of expression for artists and cultural actors" and "strengthening peace and reconciliation in post-conflict areas through art and cultural activities"—are identified, not as strategic foci, but as "cross-cutting areas" (CKU 2014: 5). The emphasis in the film-related part of the programme is on audience building for independent, creative documentary films, and not, as in the case of Uganda, on film production. Yet, inasmuch as the principal film partner is Docubox, a documentary film fund that "supports intimate, character-driven storytelling and encourages new forms of ownership and authorship in East Africa" (Irura 2013), film production and film training are a crucial part of the picture, although not directly funded by CKU. An important goal, in fact, is to encourage interest in making the sorts of films that Docubox funds, and to do this through audience building. Docubox's audience building, through screenings of films by Africans and about Africa, takes place in Nairobi—at Shalom House and more recently through activist photojournalist Boniface Mwangi's organisation PAWA254—but also in counties outside the capital, such as Nakuruu and Machakos. Judy Kibinge, one of East Africa's most accomplished filmmakers, founded Docubox in 2012, with support from the Ford Foundation. Especially noteworthy films by Kibinge include the fiction feature *Something Necessary* (2013, Germany/Kenya), evoking post-election violence in Kenya in 2007/2008 and its implications, and the documentary *Scarred: Anatomy of a Massacre* (2015, Kenya), which is about the until recently largely unacknowledged massacre of Somalis in Wajir, in Northeastern Kenya, in 1984 (Figure 40.1).

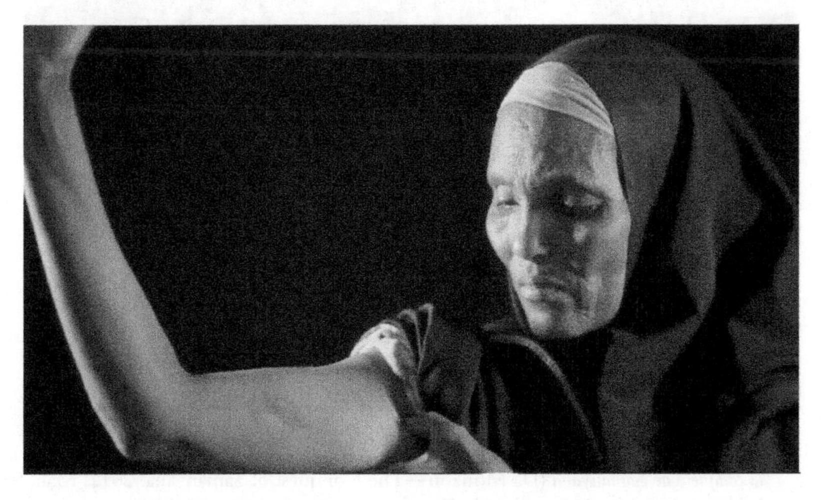

Figure 40.1 A survivor of the 1984 Wagalla massacre displays her scars: *Scarred: Anatomy of a Massacre* (2015, Kenya, Judy Kibinge).

Designed with specific challenges and opportunities in Mali in mind, CKU's "Mali–Denmark: Cultural Co-Operation Programme" pursues poverty reduction through culture and adds further elements to the story of North/South capacity building in film. A key figure in this case is the Danish filmmaker Per Fly, well known for the trilogy consisting of *Bænken* (*The Bench*, 2000, Denmark/Sweden), *Arven* (*The Inheritance*, 2003, Denmark/Sweden/Norway/UK), and *Drabet* (*Manslaughter*, 2005, Denmark/Sweden/Norway/UK): Fly's friendship with the Danish ambassador to Mali, visits to the country, encounter with the work of the CNCM (Le centre national de cinématographie du Mali, established in 1979, under the Ministry of Culture), and strong desire to enable Malian filmmakers to undertake post-production work on their films in Mali itself were all important factors during the early stages of the programme's formulation (interview, Anne Juul). The CKU-funded activities are based on collaboration between the CNCM, the Danish Film Institute's Film Archive, and the production companies Zentropa and Creative Alliance (the latter being an initiative from 2013, launched by leading Danish filmmakers, including Per Fly). A primary objective of the Mali–Denmark programme was to establish a fully-fledged post-production facility at the CNCM and this has been achieved. Motivating the creation of such a facility was Fly's realisation that post-production for Sidy Diabaté's *Da Monzon, la conquête de Samanyana* (Da Monzon—The Conquest of Samanyana, 2011, Mali) could not be completed in Mali and that this had serious implications for authorial control (Figure 40.2). Early collaboration between the CNCM and Zentropa thus concentrated on the post-production for this film, with the director travelling to Copenhagen in order to be part of the process. Further capacity-building efforts in the area of post-production have taken the form of workshop-style training at the CNCM in Bamako, Mali. Also, four trainees were selected for a mentorship programme in Denmark, where they worked intensively with top-tier Danish professionals specialising in colour grading, sound, visual effects, and post-production coordination (CKU 2015: 38). During the first phase of the Mali–Denmark programme, distribution and audience building were also a priority. A number of mobile cinemas were secured, with the aim of complementing fixed cinemas in Bamako and Ségou and of taking films such as *Da Monzon* to audiences outside the capital. Working with the CNCM, the DFI's film archive developed

Figure 40.2 Da Monzon asserts his right to the throne, in the wake of his father's death: *Da Monzon, la conquête de Samanyana* (Da Monzon—The Conquest of Samanyana, 2011, Mali, Sidy Diabaté). ©Centre National de la Cinématographie du Mali (CNCM)

yet another element in the collaborative programme: a project to digitalise selected celluloid films and thereby to contribute to the preservation of Mali's film heritage. Moussa Ouane, the CNCM's director, Assane Kouyaté and Sidi Bécaye Traoré, both also from the CNCM, selected works from their collection of some 1700 cans of film and these were subsequently digitalised by Jacob Trock and his colleagues at the archive in Glostrup, Denmark. The Malians were fully included in the process, which was seen as the basis for knowledge exchange between the DFI archive and the CNCM. Overall, the archive's intervention was a significant one, for Trock estimates that about seventy-five cans of film were saved from inevitable destruction by hot and dusty conditions in Bamako (interview, Trock).

In addition to clear successes, the Mali–Denmark programme has also brought disappointments. Security issues related to the presence of al-Qa'ida in the Lands of Islamic Maghreb (AQIM) and al-Murabitoun have been a factor, as have communication difficulties arising from the instability of the Internet in Mali. Post-production on Cheick Oumar Sissoko's *Rapt à Bamako* (Rapt in Bamako, 2014, Mali), an action film exploring difficulties thwarting multi-party democracy in Africa, was originally to have been completed in the fully professionalised facilities at the CNCM, but was finally moved to Morocco. This departure from an original intention is seen by some of the Danish partners as symptomatic of a number of organisational problems. These, they claim, must be resolved if they are to continue to invest time in what, for them, has always been a passion-driven undertaking rather than a fully remunerated job (interview, Juul). The programme has also produced unexpected benefits, however. Thus, for example, film production manager Anne Juul and archivist Jacob Trock both describe the program's fostering of new types of relationships and exchanges among film practitioners in Denmark—between the archive and production companies, for example—as positive, even energizing. Juul also refers to friendships with remarkable people and to rich encounters with Malian culture, including the country's musical traditions (interview, Juul).

Development cooperation between Denmark and Burkina Faso began as early as 1973, and included provision for the support of film culture in 1989. More specifically, DANICOM, then a division of the Danish Broadcasting Corporation, assisted with film marketing, AV-engineering, and press relations in connection with FESPACO (The Panafrican Film and Television Festival of Ouagadougou) from 1989–1999 (CKU 2011: 4). More recently, the "Culture and Development Programme for Burkina Faso (2011–2013)" has sought to bring a variety of resources to three areas: animation, film and music. The film component was based on a partnership between Gaston Kaboré's IMAGINE, an independent training site established in 2003 by the filmmaker and his wife Edith Ouédraogo, and the continuing education arm of the National Film School of Denmark, which is overseen by Tina Sørensen. Capacity building in animation has been pursued through a partnership between Association Burkinabé du Cinéma d'Animation (ABCA) in Ouagadougou, Burkina Faso, and the Animation Workshop in Viborg, Denmark. The national broadcaster Radio Télévision du Burkina (RTB) also made an initial commitment to the project (which it did not honour) in connection with plans for an animated TV series, *Afrogames* (interview, Friis Pedersen).

In Burkina Faso, there were essentially two dimensions to capacity building in the area of film: improvement of the conditions for training at IMAGINE through the purchase of equipment and workshops (on cinematography, sound, editing and script to screen processes), all conducted at IMAGINE in Ouagadougou. The programme included an element of mobility, Kaboré having been invited to Denmark (for the purposes of selecting an appropriate Danish partner) and Daouda Zallé to the National Film School of Denmark. Implementation of the programme has not always been smooth. Most problems appear to have been related to diverging conceptions of pedagogy, to cultural differences regarding hierarchy/authority and equality in professional interactions, and to the absence, in some cases, of a shared language (interview, Sørensen).

The animation project is generally seen as having been especially successful. More specifically, it is seen as having aligned well with aspirations, embedded in Burkina Faso's national poverty reduction strategy (Stratégie de Croissance Accélérée et de Développement Durable 2011–2015 (SCADD)), to enhance culture's contributions to economic growth and job creation. Resources were invested in training twenty animators in 2D techniques in Ouagadougou. Eight of these trainees then spent six months at the Animation Workshop in Viborg, where they developed a pilot for an envisaged TV series, *Afrogames*, in which children play "unusual games".[3] The concept for *Afrogames* emphasises young people's ability to resolve problems, some of them related to inherited wisdom regarding practices such as female genital mutilation. The site featuring information about the series describes ABCA as a group consisting of "many ethnicities and backgrounds—animators, filmmakers, painters, singers and students". These animators, we are told, "grew up watching American, Japanese, and European series" and are now "ready to share" their own stories with the "world" (Afrogames-Burkina Animated 2016). Resources for further developing the series have been sought through crowd funding, with Serge Pitroipa from ABCA appealing to the African diaspora to mobilise in support of what is essentially a "Pan-African project". In addition to the *Afrogames* pilot, CKU's animation programme has allowed for the production of a documentary about the prospects for animation in Burkina Faso (*Cinéma d'animation—une nouvelle ère pour le Burkina* [Animation—a new era for Burkina, 2014, France/Burkina Faso, ABCA]), and two animated shorts (*Pawit Raogo et la vieille menteuse* [*Pawit Raogo and the old Liar,* 2015, France/Burkina Faso, ABCA] and *Imagine et donne vie* [Imagine and give life, 2014, France/Burkina Faso, ABCA]). The ABCA collective participated fully in these films' production and they thus served as a platform for broader capacity building in Burkina Faso. CKU project manager Louise Friis Pedersen identifies advocacy work on behalf of animators in Burkina Faso as yet another significant result of the collaboration between ABCA and the Animation Workshop. A lawyer, funded by CKU, was recruited to assist ABCA in seeking amendments to Burkina Faso's legal framework for cinema and the audiovisual sector, the point being to ensure that animation is specifically mentioned and appropriately considered (interview, Friis Pedersen).

The North/South partnerships funded through CKU in the context of a rights-based development strategy that fully recognises the transformative power of culture have been largely successful. There is considerable evidence to suggest that the partnerships have been constructive, mutually respectful and genuine, in part because stakeholders have been fully included in the design of the programmes. The human rights framework, far from functioning as an imperial or neocolonial imposition, establishes strategic priorities that leave considerable room for the articulation, by the practitioners themselves, of a wide variety of aspirations arising from the specificities of quite different sites. What is more, CKU's "management" of the programmes has been anything but bureaucratic, reflecting, rather, a genuine understanding of the practitioners' perspectives. Recalling her time as CKU Head of Projects, Munk Petersen points to the long-term effects of various programmes:

> The collaboration produces much more than you pay for. It all continues long after the funding stops, and people end up collaborating in all sorts of ways. A lot of really solid friendships have emerged and I think that's really exciting.
>
> *(interview, Munk Petersen)*

World Cinema, it would seem, can only be well served by the sort of transnational milieu-building efforts that CKU has supported, and that are now, sadly, being discontinued.

Notes

1 The work described in this chapter was fully supported by a grant from the Research Grants Council of the Hong Kong Special Administrative Region, China (RGC Ref. No. 340612/CB 1384, Lingnan University, 2013–2016).
2 The two best-known Lab films can be seen here: www.youtube.com/watch?v=H2BnEXi3mgQ; www.youtube.com/watch?v=Fu4ZkMtcSmE, viewed 28 March 2016.
3 For the Afrogames pilot, see www.youtube.com/watch?v=fh9u1n0k22o, viewed 28 March 2016.

References

Afrogames-Burkina Animated (2016) 28 March, www.indiegogo.com/projects/afrogames-burkina-animated#/.

Andrew, D. (2004) "An Atlas of World Cinema", *Framework: The Journal of Cinema and Media Studies* 45 (2): 9–23.

Bondebjerg, I. (2016) "Regional and Global Dimensions of Danish Film Culture and Film Policy", in Hjort, M. and Lindqvist, U. (eds) *A Companion to Nordic Cinema*, Malden, MA: John Wiley & Sons, 19–39.

Bwambale, T. (2012) "Uganda Has the Youngest Population in the World", *New Vision*, www.newvision.co.ug/new_vision/news/1311368/uganda-population-world.

CKU (2011) "DANFASO—Culture and Development Programme for Burkina Faso 2011–2013", Copenhagen.

—— (2013) "Mid-Term Review: CKU Culture and Development Programme in Mali", Copenhagen.

—— (2014) "Kenya Culture and Development Programme October 2014 to October 2017", Copenhagen.

CPH:LAB (2016) cphlab.dk/?previousteams=caroline-kamya-boris-bertram.

Danida (2012) "Mali–Denmark: Cultural Co-Operation Programme 2012–2016", Copenhagen.

—— (2013) "The Right to Art and Culture—Strategic Framework for Culture and Development", Copenhagen.

—— (2015) "Mid-term Review—CKU Culture and Development Programme in Mali", Copenhagen, 13 July.

Danish Government (2012) "The Right to a Better Life—Strategy for Denmark's Development Cooperation", Copenhagen.

Douzinas, C. (2000) *The End of Human Rights*, Portland, OR: Hart Publishing.

Grøn, N. (2016) "Developing a Bhutanese Film Sector in the Intersection between Gross National Happiness and Danish Guidance", in Hjort, M. and Lindqvist, U. (eds) *A Companion to Nordic Cinema*, Malden, MA: John Wiley & Sons, 41–59.

Hjort, M. (2005) *Small Nation, Global Cinema*, Minneapolis, MN: University of Minnesota Press.

—— (2010a) *Lone Scherfig's "Italian for Beginners"*, Washington, Seattle and Copenhagen: University of Washington Press and Museum Tusculanum.

—— (2010b) "On the Plurality of Cinematic Transnationalism", in Ďurovičová, N. and Newman, K. (eds) *World Cinemas, Transnational Perspectives*, New York: Routledge, 12–33.

—— (2013) "Art and Networks: The National Film School of Denmark's "Middle East Project", in Hjort, M. (ed.) *The Education of the Filmmaker in Africa, the Middle East, and the Americas*, New York: Palgrave, 125–152.

—— (2016) "Crossing Borders: Going Transnational with 'Danish' Film Training, Capacity Building, and Talent Development", in Hjort, M. and Lindqvist, U. (eds) *A Companion to Nordic Cinema*, Malden, MA: John Wiley & Sons, 148–171.

Hjort, M. and Petrie, D. (eds) (2007) "Introduction", in *The Cinema of Small Nations*, Edinburgh: Edinburgh University Press, pp. 1–23.

Hopgood, S. (2013) *The Endtimes of Human Rights*, Ithaca, NY: Cornell University Press.

Ignatieff, M. (2001) *Human Rights as Politics and Idolatry*, Princeton, NJ: Princeton University Press.

Irura, E. (2013) "Docubox Announce New East African Film Fund and Launch Call for Applications", *Film Kenya*, 7 August, http://filmkenya.co.ke.

Liu Institute for Global Issues and the Gulu NGO Forum (2007) "Remembering the Atiak Massacre April 20th 1995", Justice and Reconciliation Project (JRP), Guli, Uganda.
Maisha (2016) http://maishafilmlab.org.
Ministry of Foreign Affairs (2103) "External Grant Committee Meeting 8 May 2013", File No.: 104. DAN.4-59.J.
Moyn, S. (2010) *The Last Utopia*, Cambridge, MA: Harvard University Press.
Nagib, L. (2006) "Towards a Positive Definition of World Cinema", in Dennison, S. and Lim, S. H. (eds) *Remapping World Cinema: Identity, Culture and Politics in Film*, London: Wallflower Press, 30–37.
Novrup Redvall, E. (2010) "Teaching Screenwriting in a Time of Storytelling Blindness: The Meeting of the Auteur and the Screenwriting Tradition in Danish Film-Making", *Journal of Screenwriting* 1 (1): 57–79.
Philipsen, H. (2004) *Dansk films nye bølge, afsæt og aftryk fra Den Danske Filmskole* (The New Wave of Danish Film—Influences and Imprints from the National Film School of Denmark), PhD dissertation, Odense: University of Southern Denmark.
Royal Danish Embassy (2010) "Uganda Youth Cultures Project 2010–2013", Kampala.
Station Next (2016) www.station-next.dk/side.asp?side=7&id=81&ver=uk.

INDEX

Compiled by Esther Santamaría-Iglesias